Advertising and Integrated Brand Promotion

Seventh Edition

Thomas Clayton O'Guinn
Professor of Marketing
Research Fellow,
Center for Brand and Product Management
University of Wisconsin—Madison

Chris T. Allen
Arthur Beerman Professor of Marketing
University of Cincinnati

Richard J. Semenik
Professor Emeritus of Marketing
Montana State University

Angeline Close Scheinbaum
Assistant Professor
University of Texas at Austin
Texas Advertising and Public Relations

CENGAGE
Learning·

Australia • Brazil • Mexico • Singapore • United Kingdom • United States

Advertising and Integrated Brand Promotion, Seventh Edition

Thomas Clayton O'Guinn, Chris T. Allen, Richard J. Semenik, Angeline Close Scheinbaum

Vice President, General Manager, Social Science & Qualitative Business: Erin Joyner

Product Director: Mike Schenk

Sr. Product Manager: Mike Roche

Associate Content Developer: Josh Wells

Sr. Product Assistant: Megan Fischer

Sr. Marketing Manager: Robin LeFevre

Sr. Content Project Manager: Martha Conway

Sr. Media Developer: John Rich

Manufacturing Planner: Ron Montgomery

Content Digitization Project Manager: Nikkita Bankston

Production Service: PreMediaGlobal

Sr. Art Director: Stacy Jenkins Shirley

Cover and Internal Designer: Joe Devine, Red Hangar Design

Sr. Rights Acquisitions Specialist: Deanna Ettinger

Text and Image Permissions Research: PreMediaGlobal

Cover Images: TV: © bluehand/Shutterstock.com; Old Paper Scroll: © MIGUEL GARCIA SAAVEDRA/Shutterstock.com; Brick Wall: © My Life Graphic/Shutterstock.com; Shampoo Bottle: © Denis Komarov/Shutterstock.com; Gold Frame: © Iakov Filimonov/Shutterstock.com; iPad: © Radu Bercan/Shutterstock.com; Hands with bottle: © Dr. Cloud/Shutterstock.com; Daisy lady: © Aleksie/Shutterstock.com; 1900's lady: © Michaela Stejskalova/Shutterstock.com; 1940's lady: © Malyugin/Shutterstock.com; Books: © iStockphoto.com/kyoshino

Library of Congress Control Number: 2013953892

Student Edition:

ISBN 13: 978-1-285-75844-2

ISBN 10: 1-285-75844-7

Student Edition with CourseMate:

ISBN 13: 978-1-285-18781-5

ISBN 10: 1-285-18781-4

Cengage Learning
200 First Stamford Place, 4th Floor
Stamford, CT 06902
USA

Cengage Learning is a leading provider of customized learning solutions with office locations around the globe, including Singapore, the United Kingdom, Australia, Mexico, Brazil, and Japan. Locate your local office at: **www.cengage.com/global**.

Cengage Learning products are represented in Canada by Nelson Education, Ltd.

To learn more about Cengage Learning Solutions, visit **www.cengage.com**.

Purchase any of our products at your local college store or at our preferred online store **www.cengagebrain.com**.

Printed in the United States of America
1 2 3 4 5 6 7 18 17 16 15 14

Thomas Clayton O'Guinn is Professor of Marketing at the University of Wisconsin–Madison. He is also Research Fellow in the Center for Brand and Product Management, also at UW–Madison. Before joining the University of Wisconsin–Madison faculty, he was on the faculty of the University of Illinois at Urbana-Champaign. He has also taught at UCLA and Duke. He is currently visiting Georgetown University. Tom has published widely. His research is about brands and the sociology of consumption. Tom has served on many editorial and advisory boards, and his research has won several awards. He has assisted several major marketers with their advertising and marketing. Professor O'Guinn's Ph.D. is from the University of Texas at Austin.

Chris T. Allen is the Arthur Beerman Professor of Marketing at the University of Cincinnati. He has also held faculty positions at Northwestern University and the University of Massachusetts at Amherst. His research has investigated the influence of affect and emotion in decision making and persuasive communication. Other published work has examined consumption issues in diverse domains such as determinants of household spending, motives for blood donation, fostering energy conservation, and the effects of news reporting on consumers' attitudes. It has appeared in numerous journals and compilations, including *JCR, JMR, JM, JPP&M, JBR, Journalism Quarterly, Journal of Advertising, Harvard Business Review, Advances in Nonprofit Marketing,* and *Handbook of Consumer Psychology*. Chris has served on the editorial review boards of *JCR, JCP, JM,* and *JA,* and has been a frequent reviewer for programs such as the Ferber Award, and the AMA/Howard, ACR/Sheth, and MSI dissertation competitions. He has also served as program administrator for P&G's Marketing Innovation Research Fund—a funding source for dissertation research. He received his Ph.D. in Marketing and Consumer Psychology from Ohio State.

Richard J. Semenik is Professor Emeritus of Marketing and former Dean of the College of Business at Montana State University–Bozeman, as well as founder and Executive Director of the College's Center for Entrepreneurship for the New West. Before coming to Montana State, Rich served as head of the Marketing Department at the Eccles School of Business at the University of Utah and Associate Dean for Research. He also has cofounded two companies. He has given numerous speeches and seminars across the United States, as well as in Ireland, Italy, the Netherlands, Finland, Mexico, Germany, France, Belgium, and Scotland. He also has been a visiting research scholar at the Vrije Universiteit in Amsterdam, the Netherlands, and a visiting scholar at Anahuac Universidad in Mexico City, Mexico. His research has appeared in the *Journal of Advertising, Journal of Consumer Research,* and *Journal of International Advertising.* He has consulted with major corporations, advertising agencies, and early stage start-up companies. He received his undergraduate degree from the University of Michigan, an MBA from Michigan State University, and a Ph.D. from the Ohio State University.

© THOMAS O'GUINN

Angeline Close Scheinbaum At the University of Georgia, Angeline studied advertising (ABJ 2000) and mass communication (MMC 2001) at the Grady College of Journalism & Mass Communication, and marketing at the Terry College of Business (Ph.D. 2006). Angeline is Assistant Professor at the University of Texas at Austin in Advertising and Public Relations. Professor Close researches sponsorship and *event marketing*—namely how consumers' experiences at sponsored events influence attitudes and consumer behavior. Her research explains how events inform and persuade adolescents, consumers' engagement with events, drivers of effective event sponsorships, how entertainment impacts affect toward events/ purchase intention toward sponsors, the role of sponsor–event congruity, and why consumers may resist events or marketing efforts. Publications are in the *Journal of Advertising, Journal of the Academy of Marketing Science, Journal of Advertising Research, Journal of Business Research, Advances in Consumer Research, International Journal of Sports Marketing and Sponsorship,* and *Sport Marketing Quarterly*. Professor Close edited *Consumer Behavior Knowledge for Effective Sports and Event Marketing* (2011) and *Online Consumer Behavior: Theory and Research in Social Media, Advertising, and E-Tail* (2012). She is currently teaching Integrated Communication Management and Psychology of Advertising. She has taught MBA Market Opportunity Analysis, Advertising Management, IMC, Professional Sales, Marketing Management, Marketing Research, and Marketing Strategy. Service to the academy includes serving as President of the Consumer Behavior SIG of the American Marketing Association (2006–current) and Director of Doctoral Student and Junior Faculty Initiatives for the Academy of Marketing Science. She serves on the editorial review boards for *Journal of the Academy of Marketing Science and Sport Marketing Quarterly*.

PREFACE

Some brands flourish, some brands face huge challenges, and some brands disappear altogether. Some brand managers are very smart, and some are very lucky and not so smart. The same is true of advertising executives. In this book, we write about how companies read the market environment, evolve their brands effectively, and nurture brand equity and loyalty. And we have done the same thing with this edition of *Advertising and Integrated Brand Promotion*. We added a new coauthor, Angeline Close Scheinbaum, from the University of Texas at Austin, who is a widely recognized expert in social and digital media. We have established a highly interactive online component to the book to give users access to contemporary issues throughout a term. We have evolved our brand along with the evolving advertising and promotion environment.

We've read the current environment and made extensive changes to the treatment of advertising and integrated brand promotion processes. Throughout the first six editions of the book, we sought and received extensive feedback from faculty, students, and practitioners. As we began to prepare this seventh edition of *Advertising and Integrated Brand Promotion,* the feedback was particularly informative and meaningful. You wanted a shorter book with more direct discussion. You wanted extensive coverage of social networking and digital media applications in both advertising and promotion. You wanted us to keep the highly visual presentation of material so prominent in prior editions. And, you wanted us to retain the issue-focused, contemporary topics from prior editions. We have addressed all of your desires and requests. This new edition is now reduced to about 400 pages from over 700. The book is full of social networking and digital media content both in the main discussions and in the new special "Insights Online" that provide access to current applications. The book is shorter, more direct, more focused. It is still very honest.

Despite all the changes and the tighter focus, there is one point we want to make emphatically: *Advertising and Integrated Brand Promotion,* seventh edition, remains the most current and forward-thinking book on the market. Since the launch of the first edition in 1998, we have alerted students to leading-edge issues and challenges facing the advertising and promotion industries. We were the first to devote an entire chapter to the Internet as an advertising medium (1998), the first to alert students to the "dot-com" agency incursion on traditional advertising structure (2000), the first to raise the issue of consumers seeking and seizing control of their personal communications environment (2003), and the first to highlight blogs and DVRs and the role they played in disseminating (or blocking) information about brands (2006). Also, we were the first to alert students to the emergence and growing potential of the early social networking sites, back then MySpace and YouTube, that began showing up on the Web (2009). This seventh edition follows the legacy of the prior editions of the book by highlighting the most contemporary and significant changes being experienced in the advertising and promotion industries—particularly the application of social networking and digital media in the advertising and promotion process.

There is a deep and lasting commitment among the authors to seek out both the best traditional and the newest contemporary thinking about advertising and integrated brand promotion from a wide array of both academic and trade publications. You will see this commitment manifest in the breadth, depth, and currency of the references in each chapter. Within this context, let's consider the "personality" features of this new edition. We are confident you will find the content and perspective of this new edition a worthy addition to students' classroom experience.

WHY WE WRITE THIS BOOK

When we introduced the first edition of *Advertising and Integrated Brand Promotion,* we summed up our attitude and passion about advertising in this way:

> *Advertising is a lot of things. It's democratic pop culture, capitalist tool, oppressor, liberator, art, and theater, all rolled into one. It's free speech, it's creative flow, it's information, and it helps businesses get things sold. Above all, it's fun.*

We still feel the same way. Advertising and promotion are fun, and this book reflects it. Advertising and promotion are also important businesses, and this edition carries forward a perspective that clearly conveys that message as well. Like other aspects of business, advertising and integrated brand promotion are the result of hard work and careful planning. Creating good advertising is an enormous challenge. We understand that and give homage and great respect to the creative process. We understand advertising and promotion in its business, marketing, and creative context. But we also felt, and still feel, that other books on the market do not emphasize enough a focus on the *brand* in the advertising and promotional effort. Brands are the reasons advertising exists. While most books of this type have IMC (Integrated Marketing Communication) in the title, we choose to emphasize the brand in the title and throughout the topics in the book.

This book is written by four people with lots of experience in both academic and professional settings. We have collectively been consultants for many firms and their agencies. Thus, this book is grounded in real-world experience. It is not, however, a book that seeks to sell you a "show-and-tell coffee-table book" version of the advertising and promotion industries. Rather, we highlight the challenges facing advertisers and offer complete treatment of the tools they use to meet those challenges.

As much as we respected our academic and practitioner colleagues the first six times around, we respect them even more now. This book is completely real-world, but the real world is also explained in terms of some really smart academic scholarship. This book copies no one yet pays homage to many. More than anything, this book seeks to be honest, thoughtful, and imaginative. It acknowledges the complexity of human communication and consumer behavior.

Students like this book—they tell us so over and over. You liked the last six editions, and you'll like this one even more. We've spent considerable time reviewing student and instructor likes and dislikes of other advertising textbooks, in addition to examining their reactions to our own book. With this feedback, we've devoted pages and pictures, ideas, and intelligence to creating a place for student and teacher to meet and discuss one of the most important and intrinsically interesting phenomena of contemporary times: advertising and promotion in the service of brands.

Relevant, Intelligent Organization

We offer an organization we adamantly believe is superior. The organizational structure of this book is unique and highly valued by users. Rather than have a section with one or two chapters followed by a section with nine or ten chapters, we offer a patterned and well-paced five-part organization. Instructors and students alike find this approach relevant, intelligent, and easy to follow. The organization of the text is so popular because it lays out the advertising and IBP process the same way it unfolds in practice and application:

Part 1: Advertising and Integrated Brand Promotion in Business and Society. Part 1 recognizes that students really need to understand just what advertising and IBP are all about and have a good perspective on how the process works. This section contains the core fundamentals (more about this in a minute). It describes the entire landscape of advertising and promotion, and provides a look at the structure of the industry and a historical perspective on the evolution of the process. But we have infused this part of the book with extensive coverage of the challenges and opportunities being presented by social networks and the mobile devices (smartphones, tablets, mobile marketing communications) that are changing the landscape for advertising and promotion. This part concludes with the key social, ethical, and regulatory issues facing practitioners and consumers.

Part 2: Analyzing the Environment for Advertising and Integrated Brand Promotion. Part 2 provides all the essential perspectives needed to understand how to carry out effective advertising and IBP. Key strategic concepts related to the overall process, including consumer behavior analysis, market segmentation, brand differentiation, and brand positioning, are considered. Then, this section proceeds to a discussion of the types of research advertising and promotion planners rely on to develop effective advertising and IBP. Additionally, there is special emphasis on "consuming in the real world" and how advertising and IBP need to adapt to consumer lifestyles and consumer adoption of new technologies to facilitate those lifestyles.

Whether you are teaching or studying advertising and promotion in a business school curriculum or an advertising/journalism curriculum, the first two parts of the book provide the background and perspective that show how advertising and IBP have become the powerful business and societal forces they are in the 21st century.

Part 3: The Creative Process. Part 3 is all about creativity: creativity itself, as a managerial issue, and as a part of art direction, copywriting, and message strategy. Most adopters in advertising and communication programs use this section and put particular focus on Chapter 10, in which the tensions between the creative and management processes are highlighted. Some business school adopters (particularly those on 6- and 10-week modules or classes) skip some of the creative chapters in Part 3. We believe everyone will find Chapter 11, which offers a highly integrated discussion of the overall creative effort, a useful and realistic perspective on the process.

Part 4: Placing the Message in Conventional and "New" Media.

Part 4 focuses on the use and application of all media—including social, mobile, and digital media—to reach target audiences. These chapters are key to understanding many of the execution aspects of good advertising and integrated brand promotion strategies. It is in this section that you will learn not just about the traditional mass media, which have struggled in the new digital environment but also about the array of new media options and consumers' new-found power in managing their information environments through these options. Of particular note is the recognition of the opportunities now offered by mobile devices as another way to reach consumers.

Part 5: Integrated Brand Promotion.

Part 5 covers the many tools of integrated brand promotion. We bundled these four chapters together, since our business school adopters often use them. We think they are good for everyone. Here you will find the best coverage of sales promotion, event sponsorship, product placement, direct marketing, personal selling, branded entertainment, influencer marketing, public relations, and corporate advertising. Nearly twenty percent of the book's pages are devoted to IBP tools beyond advertising.

Compelling Fundamentals

We fully expect our book to continue to set the standard for coverage of new topics and issues. It is loaded with features, insights, and commonsense advertising perspectives about the ever-changing nature of the advertising and promotion industry, and we continue to incorporate coverage of new issues in *every* chapter.

That said, we feel a truly distinguishing strength of this book is that we do not abandon complete and high-level treatment of the fundamentals of advertising and promotion. You simply *cannot* appreciate the role of the new media or new technologies without a solid understanding of the fundamentals. If you doubt our commitment to the fundamentals, take a good look at Chapters 2 through 8. This is where we, once again, part company with other books on the market. *Advertising and Integrated Brand Promotion,* seventh edition, is the only book on the market that ensures the deep economic roots of advertising and promotion are fully understood (e.g., the economic effects of advertising, primary vs. selective demand). Also, we take the time to be certain that not just the business but also the social context of advertising is clear. Check out just how completely the foundational aspects are covered.

Also, notice that we don't wait until the end of the book to bring the legal, ethical, and social issues

(Chapter 4) into mainstream thinking about advertising and IBP. While most books put these issues as one of the last chapters—as if they are an afterthought—we feel strongly that they are mainstream to the development of high quality and responsible advertising and promotional efforts.

Extensive Social and Digital Media Coverage

In-depth consideration of new media vehicles is provided throughout Part 1 but is truly highlighted in Part 4 of the book, "Placing the Message in Conventional and 'New' Media." Chapter 14 is all about advertising and marketing in the social and digital media era, and it reviews many technical considerations for working with this—now not-so-new, but still challenging and evolving—method for reaching and affecting consumers. Chapter 15 highlights all the new ways advertising and promotion can provide an experiential encounter with the brand. But these sections are not the only place new media coverage is prominent. Chapters 1 and 2 highlight how consumers use new social media options as a way to control their information flow, and Chapter 5 considers the effects of new media on consumer decision making.

Student Engagement and Learning

You will find that this book provides a clear and sophisticated examination of advertising fundamentals and contemporary issues in lively, concise language. We don't beat around the bush, we don't avoid controversies, and we're not shy about challenging conventions. In addition, the book features a stylish internal design (worthy of an advertising book!) and hundreds of illustrations. Reading this book is an engaging experience.

The markers of our commitment to student learning are easily identified throughout the book. Every chapter begins with a statement of the *learning objectives* for that chapter. (For a quick appreciation of the coverage provided by this book, take a pass through it and read the learning objectives on the first page of each chapter.) Chapters are organized to deliver content that responds to each learning objective, and the *Chapter Summaries* are written to reflect what the chapter has offered with respect to each learning objective. After the chapter summaries, students will find *Key Terms* from the chapter which appear in bold type throughout the chapter. Full definitions of these terms are provided at the end of the book.

We also believe that students must be challenged to go beyond their reading to think about the issues raised in the book. We provide online access to *Questions* for each chapter that demand thoughtful analysis rather than mere regurgitation, and additional exercises will help students put their learning to use in ways that will help them take more away from the course than just textbook learning. Complete use of this text and its ancillary materials will yield a dramatic and engaging learning experience for students of all ages who are studying advertising for the first time.

A CLOSER LOOK AT SOME SEVENTH EDITION FEATURES

In Every Chapter:

① Learning Objectives and a Built-In Integrated Learning System. The text and test bank are organized around the learning objectives that appear at the beginning of each chapter, to provide you and your students with an easy-to-use, integrated learning system. A numbered icon like the one shown here identifies each chapter objective and appears next to its related material throughout the chapter. This integrated learning system can provide you with a structure for creating lesson plans as well as tests.

The integrated system also gives structure to students as they prepare for tests. The icons identify all the material in the text that fulfills each objective. Students can easily check their grasp of each objective by reading the text sections and reviewing the corresponding summary sections. They can also return to appropriate text sections for further review if they have difficulty with end-of-chapter questions.

Concise Chapter Summaries. Each chapter ends with a summary that distills the main points of the chapter. Chapter summaries are organized around the learning objectives so that students can use them as a quick check on their achievement of learning goals.

Key Terms. Each chapter ends with a listing of the key terms found in the chapter. Key terms also appear in boldface in the text. Students can prepare for exams by scanning these lists to be sure they can define or explain each term.

The Online Component. One of the frustrations that we have had as authors was the inability to provide current examples and to convey the most dynamic examples of advertising, which include video and audio, in a print medium. Now technology allows us to achieve this, and we have partnered with Cengage Learning and *Ad Age* to provide students with access to current issues in advertising as well as examples of effective advertising through the content of *Ad Age on Campus*. We have selected exciting content from *Ad Age* and related it to the concepts in each chapter. We have also created assessments to provide assurances to both students and instructors that they comprehend the material. As well, rather than illustrate our printed book with examples from print media, we have selected contemporary advertisements from television and interactive online advertising to provide examples and applications of concepts.

For every chapter we have selected two or three articles from *Ad Age* that highlight interesting, unusual, or just plain entertaining information as it relates to the chapter. The articles are not diversions unrelated to the text, nor are they rambling, page-consuming, burdensome tomes. Rather, they provide concise, highly relevant examples that can be fully integrated as gradable assignments. The articles are for teaching, learning, and reinforcing chapter content. Three different types of articles are available for assignment: *Ethics, Globalization,* and *Social Media.* After each selection we have included a synopsis about how the article relates to the chapter content and have provided some assessment questions that will demonstrate a student's understanding of the concepts. Let's take a look at each.

Ethics: It is important that business decisions be guided by ethical practices. Advertising and IBP practices are particularly prone to questions by lay people relating to ethics. Because of the importance of ethics, proper business practice, and its appeal to students' interests, special ethics articles appear throughout this edition online. Students will gain insights into ethical business practices that will be useful not only in their advertising course but in future business courses and their careers.

Globalization: The globalization articles provide an insightful, real-world look at the numerous challenges advertisers face internationally. Many issues are discussed in these timely boxes, including the development of more standardized advertising across cultures with satellite-based television programming, how U.S.-based media companies such as MTV and Disney/ABC are pursuing the vast potential in global media, obstacles to advertising in emerging markets, and cross-cultural global research.

Social Media: While we integrate social media issues and applications within the main chapter content, there are so many facets to this emerging phenomenon that featuring social media examples in box treatments seemed useful and informative for students. These social media articles highlight both the nature of the phenomenon and applications by firms; for example, Facebook, Twitter, YouTube, and other social media and networking sites.

In addition to the specific content that has been selected to complement the concepts in each chapter, students will also have access to the *Ad Age on Campus* premium website where they can research a wealth of content.

Ad Age on Campus. Students will have access to a wealth of resources through the *Ad Age on Campus* page of adage.com through the access code provided with every new copy of this book, as well as other delivery options that will be discussed later in this Preface. This website provides access to a variety of resources including:

Daily News AdAge.com is the premier industry source of breaking news in the marketing, advertising, and media world, and includes trend stories, features, and analysis on the most important matters of the day.

Commentary Leading executives contribute every day to AdAge.com blogs and viewpoint columns, giving students critical insight into what the thought leaders are saying and advocating for the future of marketing.

The Work Each week, Ad Age publishes the best work of the week, as selected by the editors of Creativity, the Ad Age Group's source for advertising professionals in creative departments. Students have a window into the ideas, trends, and breakthrough work that has the industry sitting up and taking notice.

Research *Ad Age on Campus* subscribers have access to a select group of white papers published by the Ad Age Insights division, including demographic studies of female consumers, "Rise of the Real Mom" and "The Reality of the Working Woman," as well as a deep dive into "Building Brands Online" and a look at digital adopters, "Shiny New Things."

DataCenter Students also have access to AdAge.com's premium content in the DataCenter, the industry's source of key information about the industry's most important companies. Comprehensive and thorough reports rank by spending, revenue, and income the 100 leading national advertisers; the top global marketers; 100 leading media companies; interactive ventures of top media and agency companies; and Creativity's awards winners list—the definitive online tally of the best agencies, brands, creatives, production companies, and directors, according to a weighted tabulation of the major advertising awards shows.

Additional Online Material and Critical Thinking Questions

Online critical thinking questions for each chapter are designed to challenge students' thinking and to go beyond the "read, memorize, and regurgitate" learning process.

Below is a sampling of the types of critical thinking questions found in *Advertising and Integrated Brand Promotion,* seventh edition. As consumers exercise ever greater individual control over when and how they receive information, how are advertisers adapting their messages? What is the role, if any, for traditional media options in this new environment? Will mobile marketing efforts, including directing advertising to smartphones, be accepted by consumers?

End-of-Part Activities

Each part has a project-based activity which provides practical experience working in groups. Your students can expand their advertising knowledge with challenging, project-based group activities at the end of each part. Students work together in teams to complete work that emphasizes many of today's well-known, actual companies.

MindTap and CengageNOW

For *Advertising and Integrated Brand Promotion,* seventh edition, we offer two exciting alternatives for users depending on how the course is to be taught, in either a hybrid print and online version or versions that provide a completely integrated online version delivery through a platform called MindTap. MindTap is a fully online, highly personalized learning experience built upon authoritative Cengage Learning content. By combining readings, multimedia, activities, and assessments into a singular Learning Path, MindTap guides students through their course with ease and engagement. Instructors personalize the Learning Path by customizing Cengage Learning resources and adding their own content via apps that integrate into the MindTap framework seamlessly with Learning Management Systems. For instructors that want to incorporate the online component of *Advertising and Integrated Brand Promotion* into a traditional Learning Management System, the online content can be accessed via CengageNOW which provides instructors ways to manage assignments, quizzes and tests throughout the semester.

A FULL ARRAY OF TEACHING/ LEARNING SUPPLEMENTARY MATERIALS

Supplements:

Advertising Age: The Principles of Advertising and Marketing Communication at Work (ISBN 9781111528751) by Esther Thorson and Margaret Duffy, both of the University of Missouri–Columbia.

David Ogilvy, named one of the "100 most influential advertising people of the century" by *Advertising Age,* said this: "It takes a big idea to attract the attention of consumers and get them to buy your product. Unless your advertising contains a big idea, it will pass like a ship in the night." *Advertising Age* itself exemplifies a big idea. It's a journal that for 80 years has chronicled the day-to-day triumphs and heartbreaks of this dynamic profession. Its talented editors and reporters create compelling, informative stories that aren't only important—they're sharp, literate, and fun to read. Taking a cue from *Advertising Age,* this book seeks to showcase the lessons and the fun of the business for students.

Instructor's Manual. The instructor's manual has been thoroughly revised to update all previous content, including comprehensive lecture outlines that provide suggestions for using other ancillary products associated with the text and suggested answers for all exercises found within the text. The Instructor's Manual is available on the Instructor's Resource CD-ROM.

PowerPoint®. This edition's PowerPoint® presentation is of the highest quality possible. The PowerPoint® presentation is available on the Instructor's Resource CD-ROM.

Test Bank. This comprehensive test bank is organized around the main text's learning objectives. Each question is labeled according to the learning objective that is covered, the difficulty level of the question, and A-heads. Each question is also tagged to interdisciplinary learning outcomes, marketing disciplinary learning outcomes, and Bloom's taxonomy. Grouping the questions according to type allows for maximum flexibility in creating tests that are customized to individual classroom needs and preferences. The test bank includes true/false, multiple-choice, scenario application, and essay questions. There are approximately 1,800 questions. All questions have been carefully reviewed for clarity and accuracy. The test bank Word files are available on the Instructor's Resource CD-ROM.

Cognero Testing Software. The Cognero Testing system is a full-featured, online assessment system that allows you to manage content, create and assign tests, deliver tests through a secure online test center, and have complete reporting and data dissemination at your fingertips. The following are some of the features of the Cognero Testing System:

- Access from anywhere
  Web-based software that runs in a Web browser. No installs are required to start using Cognero. Works in Windows, Mac, and Linux browsers.

- Desktop-like interface
  Looks and feels like a desktop application. Uses the latest Web functionality to imitate desktop usability features like drag-and-drop and wizards.

- Full-featured test generator
  Author and manage your assessment content as well as build tests using the only online test generator that

supports all of the major functionality of its desktop competitors. Cognero is complete with a full-featured word processor, multilanguage support, Math-ML compliant equation editor, algorithmic content support, native support for 15 question types (true/false, modified true/false, yes/no, multiple choice, multiple response, numeric response, completion, matching, objective short answer, subjective short answer, multi-mode, ordering, opinion scale/Likert, essay, and custom), unlimited metadata, ability to print professional paper tests with multiple styles and versions, and more.

- Class Management and Assignments
  Manage your students, classes, and assignments with the ease of simple drag-and-drop. You can build or import rosters, have students self-register for a class, and move students easily from class to class. Once your roster is set, simply drag a test to a class to schedule and put your students to work.

- Secure Online Testing
  Cognero has an integrated secure online testing center for your students. Along with delivering traditional tests, your students can receive immediate feedback on each question and/or receive a detailed end-of-assignment report to help them know exactly how they are doing.

- Complete Reporting System
  What is the use of assessment without being able to disseminate the data derived from it? Cognero allows you to analyze how your students are performing on a real-time basis and from multiple approaches to allow for immediate intervention. You can also quickly analyze your questions and perform a gap analysis of student testing.

- Content Management System
  Cognero has a unique set of tools to allow for the creation of products (groups of question sets and tests) for distribution to other users. This system includes workflow management for the shared authoring environment, the ability to authorize specific users to access your content, and the ability to edit content and push changes through to subscribers. There are also a number of design features to make high volume authoring within Cognero very efficient. All content created in this system has built-in digital rights management, meaning that your content is protected against unauthorized use.

Product Support Site (http://www.cengagebrain. com). The product support site features "Instructor Resources" that include the instructor's manual, test bank, PowerPoint®, and videos. For students, we include the following for each chapter: learning objectives, crossword puzzles using key terms, and interactive quizzes.

ACKNOWLEDGMENTS

The most pleasant task in writing a textbook is expressing gratitude to people and institutions that have helped the authors. We appreciate the support and encouragement we received from many individuals, including the following:

- Thank you also to Senior Product Manager Mike Roche, Senior Content Project Manager Martha Conway, and Content Developers Julie Klooster, Josh Wells, and Joanne Dauksewicz, and Media Developer John Rich at Cengage Learning for their dedicated efforts on this project.

- David Moore, Vice President/Executive Producer at Leo Burnett, who gave us invaluable insights on the broadcast production process and helped us secure key materials for the text.

- Matt Smith of Arnold Finnegan & Martin, for providing us with the Watermark ad and sketches in Chapter 11.

- Connie M. Johnson, for years and years of great and loving observations about the human condition. Connie is connected to the universe in some very special way.

- Patrick Gavin Quinlan, for years of great advice and best friendship.

- Marilyn A. Boland, for her love, creativity, smart suggestions, great questions, support, and wonderful images.

- David Bryan Teets, University of Illinois, for help with the TV-commercial-director-becomes-movie-director lists and references. Dave knows film.

- Professor John Murphy II, Joe C. Thompson Centennial Professor in Advertising at the University of Texas at Austin, who has given us great feedback and continued support. John went well beyond the call with effort and creativity with the author interview film. John also keeps our feet on the ground. Thanks, John.

- Steve Hall, who supports, critiques, and gives his all to his students at the University of Illinois. Steve is a creative and gifted teacher, whose continued feedback helps us write better books for real students. Like John Murphy, Steve goes well beyond the call and helped the team produce some really cool video projects. Steve, thanks.

- Rance Crain, Allison Arden, and Ann Marie Kerwin of *Ad Age* for their help in bringing a rich set of content to students.

We are also grateful to the following individuals from the business/advertising community:

Dick Antoine
President of the National Academy of Human Resources and the President of AO Consulting

Nate Carney
Bridge Worldwide

Jack Cassidy
Cincinnati Bell

Lauren Dickson
Saatchi & Saatchi

Patricia Dimichele
Procter & Gamble

Dixon Douglas
GMR Marketing

Denise Garcia
Conill Advertising Inc.

Mike Gold
Flying Horse Communications— Bozeman, Montana

Jacques Hagopian
Procter & Gamble

Lisa Hillenbrand
Procter & Gamble

Karen Klei
Procter & Gamble

Dave Knox
Rockfish Interactive

Fred Krupp
Environmental Defense

Greg Lechner
Luxottica Retail

Liv Lewis
DeVries-pr

Marsha Lindsay
Lindsay, Stone & Briggs

Dave Linne
ConAgra

Brian Lipman
ConAgra

Mike Loyson
Procter & Gamble

James Moorhead
Procter & Gamble

Emily Morrison
GMR Marketing

Emily Neidhardt
Grey

Jim Neupert
Isthmus Partners

Bill Ogle
Motorola

Mason Page
imc^2

Kavya Peerbhoy
StrawberryFrog

Jackie Reau
Game Day Communications

Kathy Selker
Northlich

Jim Stengel
The Jim Stengel Company

John Stichweh
Bridge Worldwide

Meghan Sturges
Saatchi & Saatchi

Candace Thomas
Jack Morton Worldwide

Mauricio Troncoso
Procter & Gamble

Ted Woehrle
Newell Rubbermaid

We are particularly indebted to our reviewers—past and present—and the following individuals whose thoughtful comments, suggestions, and specific feedback shaped the content of *Advertising and Integrated Brand Promotion*. Our thanks go to:

Dr. Edward E. Ackerley
University of Arizona

Robert B. Affe
Indiana University

Ron Bernthal
Sullivan County Community College

Jeff W. Bruns
Bacone College

Claudia M. Bridges
California State University, Sacramento

Dr. Janice Bukovac-Phelps
Michigan State University

Trini Callava
Miami Dade College

Joshua Coplen
Santa Monica College

Anne Cunningham
University of Tennessee

John Davies
University of North Florida

Deborah S. David
Fashion Institute of Technology

Dr. De'Arno De'Armond
West Texas A&M University

Federico deGregorio
University of Akron

Raj Devasagayam
Siena College

Jeffrey F. Durgee
Rensselaer Polytechnic Institute

Mary Edrington
Drake University

Brendan P. Ferrara
Savannah Technical College

Dr. Aubrey R. Fowler III
Valdosta State University

Jon Freiden
Florida State University

Cynthia Frisby
University of Missouri–Columbia

Gary E. Golden
Muskingum College

Corliss L. Green
Georgia State University

Cynthia Grether
Delta College

Thomas Groth
University of West Florida

Scott Hamula
Keuka College

Michael Hanley
Ball State University

Joseph P. Helgert, Ph.D.
Grand Valley State University

Wayne Hilinski
Penn State University

David C. Houghton, Ph.D.
Charleston Southern University

E. Lincoln James
Washington State University

Karen James
Louisiana State University–Shreveport

Michelle Jasso
New Mexico State University

Ed Johnson, Ph.D.
Campbell University

Donald Jugenheimer
Southern Illinois University

George Kelley
Erie Community College–City Campus

Patricia Kennedy
University of Nebraska–Lincoln

Robert Kent
University of Delaware

Kirk D. Kern
Bowling Green State University

Marshall R. Kohr, II
Northwestern University

Priscilla LaBarbera
New York University

Barbara Lafferty
University of South Florida

William LaFief
Frostburg State University

Debbie Laverie
Texas Tech

Mary Alice LoCicero
Oakland Community College

Gail Love
California State University, Fullerton

Tina M. Lowrey
University of Texas at San Antonio

Deanna Mader
Marshall University

Mike Marn
University of Nebraska at Kearney

Marty Matthews
University of Washington

John A. McCarty
The College of New Jersey

Norman D. McElvany
Johnston State College

Nancy Mitchell
University of Nebraska–Lincoln

Elizabeth Moore
University of Notre Dame

Deborah Morrison
University of Oregon

Cynthia R. Morton
University of Florida

Darrel Muehling
Washington State University

John H. Murphy, II
University of Texas at Austin

Andrew T. Norman
Iowa State

Marcella M. Norwood
University of Houston

James Pokrywczynski
Marquette University

John Purcell
Castleton State College

William E. Rice
CSU Fresno

Maria del Pilar Rivera
University of Texas at Austin

Ann H. Rodriguez
Texas Tech University

Jim Rose
Bauder College

Dana K. Saewitz
Temple University

Debra Scammon
University of Utah

Allen D. Schaefer
Missouri State University

Carol Schibi
State Fair Community College

Trina Sego
Boise State University

Andrea Semenik
Simon Fraser University

Kim Sheehan
University of Oregon

Daniel A. Sheinin
University of Rhode Island

Alan Shields
Suffolk County Community College

Sloane Signal
University of Nebraska–Lincoln

Jan Slater
Syracuse University

Lewis F. Small
York College of Pennsylvania

Barry Solomon
Florida State University

Melissa St. James
CSU Dominguez Hills

Marla Royne Stafford
University of Memphis

Patricia Stout
University of Texas at Austin

Lynn Walters
Texas A&M

Brian Wansink
Cornell University

Jon P. Wardrip
University of South Carolina

Robert O. Watson
Quinnipiac University

Marc Weinberger
University of Massachusetts–Amherst

Professor Joan R. Weiss
Bucks County Community College

Gary B. Wilcox
University of Texas at Austin

Kurt Wildermuth
University of Missouri–Columbia

Dr. Janice K. Williams
University of Central Oklahoma

Patti Williams
Wharton

Dr. Amy Wojciechowski
West Shore Community College

Doreen (DW) Wood
Rogue Community College

Christine Wright-Isak
Florida Gulf Coast University

Adrienne Zaitz
University of Memphis

Molly Ziske
Michigan State University

Lara Zwarun
UT Arlington

Thank you to the reviewers of the *Advertising and Integrated Brand Promotion,* sixth edition, whose feedback helped shape the seventh edition:

Wendi L. Achey
Northampton Community College

Kelli S. Burns
University of South Florida

John Dinsmore
University of Cincinnati

Brendan P. Ferrara
Savannah Technical College

George J. Gannage Jr.
West Georgia Technical College

Joe R. Hanson
Des Moines Area Community College

Jeff Kallem
Des Moines Area Community College

Jacquie Lamer
Northwest Missouri State University

David H. Lange
Grand Rapids Community College

John H. Murphy, II
University of Texas at Austin

William E. Rice
California State University Fresno

Melissa St. James
CSU Dominguez Hills

Gary B. Wilcox
University of Texas at Austin

Courtney Worsham
University of South Carolina

BRIEF CONTENTS

CONTENTS

PART 2   ANALYZING THE ENVIRONMENT FOR ADVERTISING AND INTEGRATED BRAND PROMOTION 104

PART 3   THE CREATIVE PROCESS   178

© VLADGRIN/Shutterstock.com

PART 4   PLACING THE MESSAGE IN CONVENTIONAL AND "NEW" MEDIA   244

PART 5   INTEGRATED BRAND PROMOTION   302

Advertising and Integrated Brand Promotion

PART 1

Advertising and Integrated Brand Promotion in Business and Society

This first part of the book, "Advertising and Integrated Brand Promotion in Business and Society," sets the tone for our study of advertising. The chapters in this part emphasize that advertising is much more than the old-style mass media messages of the past. Mass media are still, no doubt, a huge part of the advertising effort. But advertising is now much more diverse and dynamic and is part of a process you will learn about called integrated brand promotion (IBP). IBP is the process of using all sorts of different promotional techniques and tools—from television ads to billboards to digital media like iPod broadcasts—that send messages about brands to consumers. Now, the rapid ascent of digital media—particularly social networking sites like Facebook and Twitter—have radically changed the landscape for advertising and IBP. And advertising and IBP communications are not just marketing messages. They are also part of a social communication process that has evolved over time with changes in culture, technology, and business strategies. This is where the "brand" plays a leading role in communications. We all know brands because we hear about them and use them every day—Apple, Nike, Pantene, Starbucks, and literally hundreds of others. We know (and learn) about brands because companies use advertising and IBP to tell us about them. But we also learn about brands by using them and by seeing them being used in society. This first part of the book lays out the broad landscape of the advertising and IBP processes that expose us to brands and what they have to offer.

CHAPTER 1

The World of Advertising and Integrated Brand Promotion introduces and defines advertising and integrated brand promotion and the roles they play within a firm's overall marketing program. We'll get a clear definition of both advertising and IBP and learn that firms communicate to consumers using a broad range of tools that often go far beyond advertising and traditional mass media. Sales promotion, event sponsorship, direct marketing, brand placements in movies, television programs and video games, point-of-purchase displays, the Internet, podcasting, influencer marketing (social networks), personal selling, and public relations—the tools of IBP—are available to help a firm compete effectively, develop customer brand loyalty, and generate greater profits.

CHAPTER 2

The Structure of the Advertising and Promotion Industry: Advertisers, Agencies, Media, and Support Organizations highlights the people in the industry and their activities. This chapter demonstrates that effective advertising requires the participation of a variety of organizations and especially skilled people, not just the companies who make and sell brands. Advertising agencies, research firms, production facilitators, designers, media companies, Web developers, public relations firms, and Internet portals all play a role. This chapter also highlights that the structure of the industry is in flux. New media options, like streaming video, blogs, and social networking sites, and new organizations, like talent agencies, product placement firms, and software companies, are forcing change. This chapter looks at the basic structure of the industry and how it is evolving with the market and with changing consumer preferences for information reception.

CHAPTER 3

The History of Advertising and Brand Promotion puts the processes of advertising and IBP into both a historical and a contemporary context. This chapter identifies the prominent eras of advertising—from the pre-1880s to the present day—and the unique communications emphasis that has distinguished each era. Special recognition is given to the fact that advertising and IBP have evolved and proliferated because of fundamental market and cultural influences related to free enterprise, economic development, and tradition. Change has also occurred as a reflection of contemporary social values and the advent of new technologies. We also address the effect the Great Recession of 2008–2011 in the United States had on advertising spending, processes, and strategies.

CHAPTER 4

Social, Ethical, and Regulatory Aspects of Advertising and Promotion examines the broad societal aspects of advertising and IBP. From a social standpoint, we must understand that advertising and promotion can have positive effects on standard of living, address consumer lifestyle needs, support communications media, and are contemporary art forms. Critics argue that advertising and other promotions waste resources, promote materialism, are offensive and intrusive, perpetuate stereotypes, or can make people do things they don't want to do. Ethical issues focus on truthful communication, invasion of privacy, advertising and promoting to children, and advertising and promoting controversial products. Regulatory aspects highlight that while government organizations play a key role in shaping the way advertising and IBP are carried out, consumer groups and societal values also put pressure on advertising and IBP to change and evolve with cultural values.

CHAPTER 1

The World of Advertising and Integrated Brand Promotion

After reading and thinking about this chapter, you will be able to do the following:

1 Know what advertising and integrated brand promotion (IBP) are and what they can do.

2 Discuss a basic model of communication.

3 Describe the different ways of classifying audiences for advertising and IBP.

4 Understand advertising as a business process.

5 Understand the various types of advertising.

You know what? You're a real challenge for companies. You like to get your information from your friends through social media. You read blogs instead of newspaper advertising. You skip television ads, and you listen to satellite radio stations with no advertising at all. So, how are companies supposed to reach you with their advertising and brand messages? Well, these companies are struggling with that challenge. So, they *are* using traditional mass media advertising, but they are also using newer forms of communication to try to get their brand messages across to you.

You'll still see advertising during your favorite television show or in your favorite magazine—a lot of advertising, in fact. But if you haven't encountered some of the new "smart ads" from companies, you will before too long. If you are a smartphone user, advertising is already working its way into a variety of your apps. If you're a video-game player, your favorite games are already full of ads in the cyberscenery—over $1 billion worth of advertising a year, actually.[1] The next time you go to the grocery store, you just might find an electronic video tablet attached to the shopping cart that asks you to swipe your store loyalty card before you start touring the aisles. That way the store's computers can prepare a shopping list of items you've purchased before for your convenience. When you've finished your grocery shopping and are heading home, your smartphone might alert you to a special on oil changes just as you're approaching a lube shop. Companies are spending nearly $4 billion a year on these new "mobile ad" formats, just to try to reach you in new and different ways with their brand messages.[2] Welcome to the new world of advertising and integrated brand promotion (IBP).

1-1 THE NEW WORLD OF ADVERTISING AND INTEGRATED BRAND PROMOTION

The world of advertising and IBP is going through enormous change. What you will learn in this book and in your class discussions is that companies are trying to keep up with how and where consumers want to receive information about brands.

Mass media are not dead, but they are being supplemented and supported by all sorts of new ways to reach consumers. Consumer preferences and new technologies are reshaping the communication environment. You'll also learn that the lines between information, entertainment, networking, and commercial messages are blurring. As one analyst put it, "The line of demarcation was obliterated years ago, when they started naming ballparks after brands."[3] Companies are turning to branded entertainment, the Internet, influencer marketing (i.e., social networks), and other innovative communication techniques to reach consumers and get their brand messages integrated into consumers lifestyles (like the shopping cart tablet). The vice president of marketing for Audi America described this new process of integrating brands into consumers' lifestyles as "acupuncture marketing" where you go "narrow and deep" with your messages.[4]

Analysts speculate that advertising, IBP, and marketing overall will be more digital, more interactive, and more social. Their reasoning is not hard to understand. Firms have not fully exploited all the opportunities presented by mobile marketing. **Mobile marketing** is communicating with target markets through mobile devices like smartphones or iPad or Surface tablet devices. Digital and interactive techniques can "funnel" consumers to retail sites and online shopping and purchasing. But for now, the "new world of advertising" is still in transition and still has some fundamentals that will not change, no matter what, as the next section describes.

1-1a Old Media/New Digital Media—It's All about the Brand

We need to remain clear about one thing. No matter how much technology changes or how many new media options and opportunities are available for delivering messages—it's still all about the brand! Just because an advertiser offers consumers the opportunity to "follow" them on Twitter or visit the brand's Facebook page, these new communications options do not change the fundamental challenge and opportunity—communicating effectively about the brand and the brand's values (see Insights Online [Exhibit 1.1] for an interesting example). As consumers, we know what we like and want, and advertising—regardless of the method—can help expose us to brands that can meet our needs. And there is a simple truth—a brand that does *not* meet our needs will not succeed—no matter how much advertising there is or whether that advertising is delivered through old traditional media or new digital media and mobile marketing. Another truth is how much consumers emphasize brands in striving to meet their needs. Consumers are irresistibly drawn to brands to fulfill their needs and desires and also for the social symbolism that brands represent. Consider the case of fine jewelry. Jewelry does not blatantly display a brand mark or brand name in the way Nike shoes, an Apple iPad or iPhone, or a Mercedes Benz automobile does. These brands prominently display a brand logo and often the brand name itself—but jewelry does not. But, modern consumers are so brand oriented that now they ask "Is that a new ring? Who are you wearing?"—totally oriented to searching out, wanting to know, and wanting to own conspicuous brands.[5]

Now consider the complex case of Cadillac. In the early 1950s, Cadillac held a stunning 75 percent market share in the luxury car market and was a leading advertiser in the market year after year. But by 2007, that market share had fallen to about 9 percent—an unprecedented loss in the history of the automobile industry or most other industries for that matter. What happened to the Cadillac brand? It wasn't the advertising. A series of product missteps confused the market's perception of the brand: the 1986 Cimarron, for example, used a Chevy chassis and looked cheap, and the 1987 Allante sports car was slow and leaked like a sieve. Formidable competitors like Lexus and Infiniti entered the market with powerful and stylish alternatives that were effectively advertised. Does it seem like social networking the brand on Twitter or Facebook could have changed Cadillac's fate during this period of decline? Not likely—even though there are over 15 million monthly users of Facebook.[6] Reaching a large number of consumers with information about a poor product will not make the product a success. But now, GM has reinvested in the Cadillac brand and committed $4.3 billion to redesign, advertise, and promote the brand to change consumers' perceptions about Cadillac relative to luxury brands from Europe like Mercedes and Audi (see Exhibit 1.2). Also, the company has upped its spending on digital platforms to 25 percent of its marketing spending.[7]

Analysts are adamant about the process of maintaining a contemporary market-driven image and identity for a brand (as Cadillac finally has started to do), and advertising and promotion are essential to the effort. This is particularly true with established brands that become well known to consumers. If the firm does not regularly invest in well-conceived and carefully crafted advertising and IBP programs, a brand can "drift into a vague oblivion."[8]

► **INSIGHTS ONLINE**

1.1 Go online to see the AdAge feature, "Fiat Branding via Social Drive—A Voice-Activated Feature Giving Social Media Updates."

EXHIBIT 1.2 GM is trying to reinvent the Cadillac brand with new body and interior designs and a new "brand story" in advertising in order to compete effectively with luxury European brand autos like Mercedes and Audi.

WHERE PHYSICS AND METAPHYSICS CONVERGE

The SRX V8: physics beautifully applied. The longest wheelbase in its class.* A carefully calculated, low-to-the-ground stance. And available Magnetic Ride Control, the world's fastest-reacting suspension system. The end result is nothing short of magical. A vehicle that delivers dynamic, road-gripping handling and still offers a utility's high-riding visibility. The Nürburgring-refined 4.6L Northstar V8 VVT delivers a balanced

320 hp and 315 lb-ft of torque. Beyond the measurable advantages are immeasurable sensations. The rush of an S-curve, the thrill of a long straightaway, the satisfaction of a well-executed maneuver. Finally, a utility that can seat seven** and excite a whole world. Discover more amazing feats of SRX engineering at cadillac.com/srx_physics. The Cadillac SRX performance utility. Calculated innovation. Exhilaration beyond measure.

SRX

General Motors

LO ①

1-2 WHAT ARE ADVERTISING AND INTEGRATED BRAND PROMOTION?

Now that we've set the new and dynamic context for communication, let's consider the tools companies use: advertising and IBP. We'll start with advertising. You have your own ideas about advertising because you see some advertising every day—even if you try to avoid most of it. You need to know that advertising means different things to different people, though. It's a business, an art form, an institution, and a cultural phenomenon. To the CEO of a multinational corporation, like Pepsi, advertising is an essential marketing tool that helps create brand awareness and brand loyalty. To the owner of a small retail shop, advertising is a way to bring people into the store. To the art director in an advertising agency, advertising is the creative expression of a concept. To a media planner, advertising is the way a firm uses the media to communicate to current and potential customers. To a website manager, it's a way to drive traffic to the URL. To scholars and museum curators, advertising is an important cultural artifact, text, and historical record. Advertising means something different to all these people. In fact, sometimes determining just what is and what is not advertising is a difficult task!

Even though companies believe in and rely heavily on advertising, it is not a process that the average person clearly understands or values. Most people have some significant misperceptions about advertising and what it's supposed to do, what it can do, and what it can't do. Many people think advertising deceives others but rarely themselves. Most think it's a semi-glamorous profession but one in which people are either morally bankrupt con artists or pathological liars. At worst, advertising is seen as hype, unfair capitalistic manipulation, banal commercial noise, mind control, postmodern voodoo, or outright deception. At best, the average person sees advertising as amusing, informative, somewhat annoying, sort of helpful, and occasionally hip.

INSIGHTS ONLINE

1.3 Go online to see the AdAge feature, "Newcastle Brown Ale—Advertising and Outdoor Art."

The truth about advertising lies somewhere between the extremes. Sometimes advertising is hard-hitting and powerful; at other times, it's boring and ineffective. One thing is for sure: advertising is anything but unimportant. Advertising plays a pivotal role in world commerce and in the way we experience and live our lives. It is part of our language and our culture. It is a complex communication process, a dynamic business process, and now a part of the social interaction process (see Insights Online [Exhibit 1.3] for a notable example).

1-2a Advertising Defined

Keeping in mind that different people in different contexts see advertising so differently and that advertising suffers from some pretty complex controversies, we offer this straightforward definition:

> **Advertising** *is a paid, mass-mediated attempt to persuade.*

As direct and simple as this definition seems, it is loaded with distinctions. First, advertising is *paid* communication by a company or organization that wants its information disseminated. In advertising language, the company or organization that pays for advertising is called the **client** or **sponsor**. If a communication is *not paid for*, it's not advertising. For example, a form of public relations promotion called *publicity* is not advertising because it is not paid for. Let's say Will Smith appears on the *Late Show with David Letterman* to promote his newest movie. Is this advertising? No, because the producer or film studio did not pay the *Late Show with David Letterman* for airtime. In this example, the show gets an interesting and popular guest, the guest star gets exposure, and the film gets plugged. Everyone is happy, but no advertising took place—it might be public relations, but it is not advertising. But when the film studio produces and runs ads on television and in newspapers across the country for the newest Will Smith movie, this communication is paid for by the studio, it is placed in media to reach consumers, and therefore is most definitely advertising.

For the same reason, public service announcements (PSAs) are not advertising either. True, they look like ads and sound like ads, but they are not ads. They are not commercial in the way an ad is because they are not paid for like an ad. They are offered as information in the public (noncommercial) interest. When you hear a message on the radio that implores you to "Just Say No" to drugs, this sounds very much like an ad, but it is a PSA. Simply put, PSAs are excluded from the definition of advertising (even though there are lots of them) because they are unpaid communication.

Second, advertising is *mass mediated*. This means it is delivered through a communication medium designed to reach more than one person, typically a large number—or mass—of people. Advertising is widely disseminated through familiar means—television, radio, newspapers, and magazines—and other media such as direct mail, billboards, video games, the Internet, tablets, and smartphones. The mass-mediated nature of advertising creates a communication environment where the message is not delivered in a face-to-face manner. This distinguishes advertising from personal selling as a form of communication.

Third, all advertising includes an *attempt to persuade*. To put it bluntly, ads are communications designed to get someone to do something. Even an advertisement with a stated objective of being purely informational still has persuasion at its core. The ad informs the consumer for some purpose, and that purpose is to get the consumer to like the brand, and because of that liking, to eventually buy the brand. An "ad" can be extremely subtle, like a Sprite bottle and logo appearing in the "Green Eyed World" video series on YouTube. Or, it can be loud and blatant like a Saturday morning infomercial. Consider the PUR water filter ad in Exhibit 1.4. It doesn't carry a lot of explicit product information. But it's interesting, and most of us would say, "Yeah, I like that ad." With that reaction, this ad is persuasive. In the absence of a persuasive intent, a communication might be news, but it would not be advertising.

At this point, we can say that for a communication to be classified as advertising, three essential criteria must be met:

1. The communication must be *paid for.*
2. The communication must be delivered to an audience via *mass media.*
3. The communication must be *attempting persuasion.*

It is important to note here that advertising can be persuasive communication not only about a product or service but also about an idea, a person, or an entire organization. When Colgate and Honda use advertising, this is product advertising and meets all three criteria. When TD Ameritrade, Delta Air Lines, Terminix, or your dentist run advertisements for their services, these advertisements meet all three criteria. And when political candidates run ads on television or in newspapers, these (people) ads meet all three criteria as well (see Insights Online [Exhibit 1.5] for another interesting example).

EXHIBIT 1.4 In order for a communication to be advertising, it has to have a persuasive intent. Even though this PUR water filter ad is not overtly persuasive with a lot of message copy, the fact that it is interesting and designed to create a positive impression on the audience results in persuasive intent.

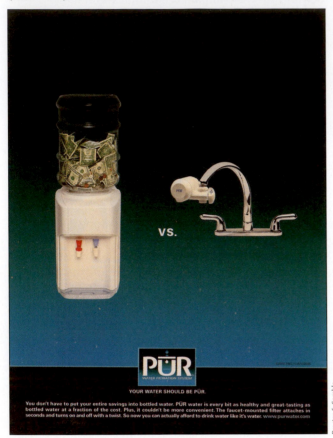

Procter & Gamble

1-2b **Integrated Brand Promotion Defined**

Now that we have defined advertising, let's consider the other important context for the book—the process of integrated brand promotion, or IBP. As we discussed earlier, communication is all about the brand and, as such, promotion is all about the brand as well. To fully understand integrated brand promotion, let's first define IBP and describe all the tools used for IBP. Then we can talk about how it is related to and yet distinct from advertising. First the definition:

> **integrated brand promotion (IBP)** *is the process of using a wide range of promotional tools that work together to create widespread brand exposure.*

Just as the definition of advertising was loaded with meaning, so too is the definition of integrated brand promotion. First, IBP is a process. It has to be. It is complicated and needs to be managed in an integrated

fashion. Second, IBP uses a wide range of promotional tools that have to be evaluated and scheduled. IBP creates exposure for the *brand*.

It can be a branded product or an overall corporate brand, but the IBP process is squarely focused on brand exposure. Here is a list of the most prominent tools marketers use for IBP:

- Advertising in mass media (television, radio, newspapers, magazines, billboards)
- Sales promotions (coupons, premiums, discounts, gift cards, contests, samples, trial offers, rebates, frequent user-affinity programs, trade shows)
- Point-of-purchase (in-store) advertising
- Direct marketing (catalogs, telemarketing, email offers, infomercials)
- Personal selling
- Internet advertising (banners, pop-ups/pop-unders, websites)
- Social networks/blogs
- Podcasting/smartphone messaging
- Event sponsorships
- Branded entertainment (product placement/insertion in television programming, apps, Webcasts, video games, and films), also referred to as "advertainment"
- Outdoor signage
- Billboard, transit, and aerial advertising
- Public relations
- Influencer marketing (peer-to-peer persuasion often through social networks)
- Corporate advertising

Notice that this long list of IBP tools includes various types of advertising but goes well beyond traditional advertising forms. From mass media of advertising to influencer marketing and social networks, the tools of IBP are varied and wide ranging. All of these tools allow a marketer to reach target customers in different ways with different kinds of messages to achieve broad exposure for a brand.

Third, the definition of IBP highlights that all of these tools need to work together. That is, they need to be integrated to create a consistent and compelling impression of the brand. Having mass media advertising send one message and create one image and then have mobile messaging or personal selling deliver another message will confuse consumers about the meaning and relevance of the brand—this is a very bad thing!

Finally, the definition of IBP emphasizes that all of the advertising and promotional effort undertaken by a firm is designed to create widespread exposure for a brand. Unless consumers are reached by these various forms of messages, they will have a difficult time understanding the brand and deciding whether to use it regularly.

1-2c Advertisements, Advertising Campaigns, and Integrated Brand Promotion

Now that we have working definitions of advertising and IBP, we can turn our attention to some other important distinctions and definitions. Let's start with the basics. An **advertisement** refers to a specific message that an organization has created to persuade an audience. An **advertising campaign** is a series of coordinated advertisements that communicate a reasonably cohesive and integrated theme about a brand. The theme may be made up of several claims or points but should advance an essentially singular theme. Successful advertising campaigns can be developed around a single advertisement placed in multiple media, or they can be made up of several different advertisements with a similar look, feel, and message. A good example is represented by the Altoids ads in Exhibits 1.6 and 1.7. Notice the excellent use of similar look and feel in this advertising campaign. Advertising campaigns can run for a few weeks or for many years. The advertising campaign requires a keen sense of the complex environments within which a company must communicate to different audiences.

How does IBP fit in with advertisements and advertising campaigns? As we discussed earlier, IBP is the use of many promotional tools, including advertising, in a coordinated manner to build and then maintain brand awareness, identity, and preference. When marketers combine contests, a website, event sponsorship, and point-of-purchase displays with advertisements and advertising campaigns, they create an IBP. BMW did just that when the firm (re)introduced the Mini Cooper auto to the U.S. market. The IBP campaign used billboards, print ads, an interactive website, and "guerrilla" marketing (a Mini was mounted on top of a Chevy Suburban and driven around New York City). Each part of the campaign elements was coordinated with all the others. (See Insights Online [Exhibit 1.8] for a key example.) Note that the word *coordinated* is

EXHIBITS 1.6 AND 1.7   A well-conceived and well-executed advertising campaign offers consumers a series of messages with a similar look and feel. These two ads from a broader Altoids campaign are excellent examples of images that create a similar look and feel.

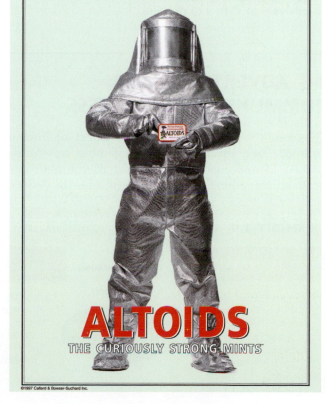

INSIGHTS ONLINE

1.8 Go online to see the AdAge feature, "The Walking Dead Gets an Online Following from Facebook Fans."

central to the IBP effort. Without coordination among these various promotional efforts, there is not an integrated brand promotion. Rather, the consumer will merely encounter a series of individual, unrelated (and therefore confusing) communications about a brand.

1-2d A Focus on Advertising

Integrated brand promotion will be a key concept throughout our discussion of advertising. The fact that this phrase is included in the title of the book signals its importance to the contemporary marketing effort. As consumers encounter a daily blitz of commercial messages, brands and the images they project allow consumers to quickly identify and evaluate the relevance of a brand to their lives and value systems. The marketer who does not use advertising and IBP as a way to build brand identity and meaning for consumers will, frankly, be ignored.

We will develop the concept and describe the execution of IBP throughout the text and demonstrate how advertising is central to the process. The encounters between consumers and advertising, advertisements, and advertising campaigns, specifically, are the focus of our next discussion. Elaboration on the features and application of other IBP tools will be covered extensively in Part 5 of the text.

LO 2

1-3 ADVERTISING AS A COMMUNICATION PROCESS

Communication is a fundamental aspect of human existence, and advertising is one of those communications. To understand advertising at all, you must understand something about communication in general

and about mass communication in particular. To help with gaining this understanding, let's consider a contemporary model of mass communication. We'll apply this basic model of communication as a first step toward understanding advertising.

1-3a A Model of Mass-Mediated Communication

As we said earlier, advertising is mass-mediated communication; it occurs not face-to-face but through a medium (such as radio, magazines, television, on the side of a building, or on your computer or smartphone). Although there are many valuable models of mass communication, a contemporary model of mass-mediated communication is presented in Exhibit 1.9. This model shows mass communication as a process where people, institutions, and messages interact. It has two major components: production (by the sender of a message) and reception (by the receiver of a message). Between production and reception are the mediating (interpretation) processes of accommodation and negotiation. It's not as complex as it sounds. Let's investigate each part of the model.

Moving from left to right in the model, we first see the process of communication production, where the content of a mass communication is created. An advertisement, like other forms of mass communication, is the product of institutions (such as corporations, organizations, advertising agencies, and governments) interacting to produce content (what is created for a print ad, television ad, radio ad, podcast, or on a computer screen at a company's website). The creation of the advertisement is a complex interaction of the company's brand message; the company's expectations about the target audience's desire for information; the company's assumptions about how members of an audience will interpret the words and images in an ad; and the rules and regulations of the medium that transmits the message.

Continuing on to the right, we see that the mediating processes of accommodation and negotiation lie between the production and reception phases.

EXHIBIT 1.9 A model of mass-mediated communication.

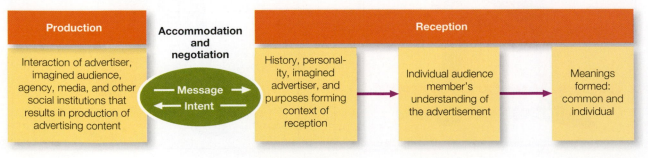

Accommodation and negotiation are the ways in which consumers interpret ads. Individual audience members have some ideas about how the company wants them to interpret the ad (we all know the rules of advertising—somebody is trying to persuade us to buy something or like their brand or idea). And each consumer has needs, agendas, and preferred interpretations based on history, experience, and individual value systems. Given all this, every consumer who sees an ad arrives at an interpretation of the ad that makes sense to them individually, serves their needs, and fits their personal history with a product category and a set of brands. You'll learn more about the wide range of influences on each consumer in Chapter 5—"Advertising, Integrated Brand Promotion, and Consumer Behavior."

What's interesting about the whole progression of consumer receipt and then interpretation of a communication is that it is often wholly *incompatible* with the

No ad contains a single meaning or even the same meaning for each audience members. Ads are interpreted by each audience member according to her or his unique set of experiences, values, and beliefs.

way the company wants consumers to see an ad! In other words, the receivers of the communication must *accommodate* their perceived multiple meanings and personal agendas and then *negotiate* a meaning—that is, an interpretation—of the ad according to their individual life experiences and value systems. That's why we say that communication is inherently a *social* process: What a message means to any given consumer is a function not of an isolated solitary thinker but of an inherently social being responding to what he or she knows about the producers of the message (the companies), other receivers of it (peer groups, for example), and the social world in which the brand and the message about it resides. Now, admittedly, all this interpretation happens very fast and without much contemplation. Still, it happens. The level of conscious interpretation by each receiver might be minimal (mere recognition) or it might be extensive (thoughtful, elaborate processing of an ad), but there is *always* interpretation.

The communication model in Exhibit 1.9 underscores a critical point: No ad contains a single meaning or even the same meaning for each audience members. Ads are interpreted by each audience member according to her or his unique set of experiences, values, and beliefs. An ad for a pair of women's shoes means something different for women than it does for men. An ad that achieved widespread popularity (and controversy) is the ad for Diet Coke shown in Exhibit 1.10, which may be interpreted differently by men and women. For example, does the ad suggest that men drink Diet Coke so that they can be the object of intense daily admiration by a group of female office workers? Or does the ad suggest that Diet Coke is a part of a modern woman's lifestyle, granting her "permission" to freely admire attractive men in the same way women have been eyed by male construction workers (or executives) for years? Each audience member decides what meaning to take away from a communication.

EXHIBIT 1.10 This Coke ad is a good example of how the meaning of an ad can vary for each individual receiver of the ad. How would you interpret the meaning of this ad? Think of someone quite different from yourself. What meaning might they take away from this ad?

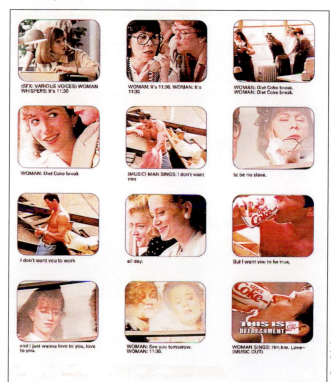

The Coca-Cola Company

LO ③

1-4 THE AUDIENCES FOR ADVERTISING

We've been referring to audiences, so now it's time to define them. In the language of advertising, an **audience** is a group of individuals who receive and interpret messages sent from companies or organizations.

The audience could be made up of household consumers, college students, or business people, for example. Any large group of people can be an audience. A **target audience** is a particular group of consumers singled out by an organization for an advertising or IBP campaign. These target audiences are singled out because the firm has discovered that these specific audience members like the product category and might prefer their particular brand within that product category. Target audiences are always *potential* audiences because a company can never be sure that the message will actually get through to them as intended. By the way, there is nothing sinister about the targeting process. Targeting audiences simply means that a company wants to reach you with a message. Do you feel like something bad happens to you when the Gap targets you with an ad and you see it on TV or a banner on a Web page? Of course not! Somewhere along the line, the word *targeting* and the phrase *target audience* have picked up some negative connotations—ignore them.

Even though companies can identify dozens of different target audiences, five broad audience categories are commonly described: household consumers, members of business organizations, members of a trade channel, professionals, and government officials and employees.

1-4a Audience Categories

Household consumers are the most conspicuous audience in that most mass media advertising is directed at them. McDonald's, Nissan, Miller Brewing, Verizon, and State Farm Insurance have products and services designed for the consumer market, and so their advertising targets household consumers.

The most recent information indicates that there are about 115 million households in the United States and approximately 316 million household consumers who spend trillions of dollars a year on retail goods and services.[9] Under the very broad heading of "consumer advertising," very fine audience distinctions can be made by advertisers. A target audience definition such as men, 25 to 45, in professional occupations, living in metropolitan areas, with incomes greater than $50,000 per year would be the kind of target audience description an advertiser might develop.

Members of business organizations are the focus of advertising for firms that produce business and industrial goods and services, such as office equipment, production machinery, supplies, and software. Although products and services targeted to this audience often require personal selling, advertising is used to create awareness and a favorable

attitude among potential buyers. IBM used advertising during the U.S. Open tennis tournament to reach Chief Marketing Officers within organizations who, IBM strategists believed, were becoming more influential regarding hardware and software decisions within corporations.[10] Not-for-profit businesses such as universities, some research laboratories, philanthropic groups, and cultural organizations also represent an important and separate business audience for advertising. Exhibit 1.11 is an example of an ad directed at members of business organizations. Right Management provides services to corporations with respect to specifying and then managing the firm's labor force and the types of skills employees need to have at all levels. Right Management's advertising is directed at business organizations and is placed in publications like *The Economist, Fortune*, and *Forbes* magazines—ideal media to reach their target audience.

Members of a trade channel include retailers (like Best Buy for consumer electronics), wholesalers

EXHIBIT 1.11   Right Management is a global leader in talent and career management workforce solutions. The firm designs manpower programs that align a company's talent with its business strategy. The firm uses advertising to reach business target audiences that can benefit from its services.

Talent.

On a planet of nearly 7 billion, it's still your most precious resource.

Right Management®
ManpowerGroup

Right Management

(like Castle Wholesalers for construction tools), and distributors (like Sysco Food Services for restaurant supplies). These members of the trade channel are a target audience for producers of both household and business goods and services. So, for example, if Microsoft cannot gain adequate retail and wholesale distribution through trade channels for the Xbox, the brand will not reach target customers. That being the case, it's important to direct advertising at the trade level of the market. Various forms of advertising can be used to develop demand among members of a trade channel. The promotional tool used most often to communicate with this group is personal selling. This is because this target audience represents a relatively small, easily identifiable group that can be reached with personal selling. When advertising is also directed at this target audience, it can serve an extremely useful purpose, as we will see later in the section on advertising as a business process.

Professionals form a special target audience and are defined as doctors, lawyers, accountants, teachers, electricians, or any other professional group that has special training or certification. This audience warrants a separate classification because its members have specialized needs and interests. Advertising directed to professionals typically highlights products and services uniquely designed to serve their more narrowly defined needs. The language and images used in advertising to this target audience often rely on esoteric terminology and unique circumstances that members of professions readily recognize. Advertising to professionals is predominantly carried out through trade publications. **Trade journals**, like *Electrical Contractor*, are magazines published specifically for members of a trade and carry highly technical articles.

Government officials and employees constitute an audience in themselves due to the large dollar volume of buying that federal, state, and local governments do. Government organizations from universities to road maintenance operations buy huge amounts of various types of products. Producers of items such as office furniture, construction materials and equipment, vehicles, fertilizers, computers, and business services all target government organizations with advertising. Advertising to this target audience is dominated by direct mail, catalogs, personal selling, and Web advertising.

1-4b **Audience Geography**

Audiences can also be broken down by geographic location. Because of cultural differences that often accompany geographic location, very few ads can be effective for all consumers worldwide.

Global advertising is advertising that is used worldwide with only minor changes in the visual and message content. Very few ads can use global advertising. These are typically brands that are considered "citizens of the world" and whose manner of use does not vary tremendously by culture. Using a Sony television or taking a trip on Singapore Airlines doesn't change much from culture to culture and geographic location to geographic location. Exhibits 1.12 and 1.13 use nearly identical appeals in two different ads for Rolex watches—another product category where product use across cultures is the same. Note that these two Rolex ads—one for the French market and one for the Italian market—feature the images of tennis players. Tennis attracts an upscale consumer (particularly in Europe) consistent with Rolex's target market. Firms that market brands with global appeal, like Singapore Airlines, IBM, Sony, and Pirelli Tires, try to develop and place advertisements with a common theme and presentation in all markets around the world where the firm's brands are sold. Global placement is effective *only* when a brand and the messages about that brand have a common appeal across diverse cultures (see Insights Online [Exhibit 1.14] for an interesting example).

International advertising occurs when firms prepare and place different advertising in different national markets for the same brand outside their home market. Each international market may require unique advertising due to product adaptations or message appeals tailored specifically for that market. Unilever prepares different versions of ads for its laundry products for nearly every international market because consumers in different cultures approach the laundry task differently. Consumers in the United States use large and powerful washers and dryers and a lot of hot water. Households in Brazil use very little hot water and hang clothes out to dry. Few firms enjoy the luxury of having a brand with truly cross-cultural appeal and global recognition, as is necessary for global advertising as described in the previous section. International advertising differs from global advertising in that different ads for the same brand are tailored for each market.

National advertising reaches all geographic areas of a single nation. National advertising is the term typically used to describe the kind of advertising we see most often in the mass media in the domestic U.S. market. Does international advertising use many different national advertising efforts? Yes, that is exactly the relationship between international advertising and national advertising.

Regional advertising is carried out by producers, wholesalers, distributors, and retailers that concentrate

EXHIBITS 1.12 AND 1.13 Global advertising can be used for brands where there is little difference between cultures in the way the product is used. The only real difference in these two Rolex ads is language (German vs. Italian), while other aspects of the ads— Rolex's appeal to an affluent elite who likely follow tennis—remain the same.

Rolex Watch U.S.A., Inc

Rolex Watch U.S.A., Inc

---

their efforts in a relatively large, but not national, geographic region. Albertson's, a regional grocery chain, has stores in 31 western, northwestern, midwestern, and southern states. Because of the nature of the firm's markets, it places advertising only in regions where it has stores.

Finally, **local advertising** is directed at an audience in a single trading area, either a city or state. Under special circumstances, national companies will share advertising expenses in a market with local dealers to achieve specific advertising objectives. This sharing of advertising expenses between national companies and local merchants is called **cooperative advertising** (or **co-op advertising**). TUMI luggage regularly supports its retailers, with co-op magazine advertising.

LO ④

1-5 ADVERTISING AS A BUSINESS PROCESS

So far we have talked about advertising as a communication process and as a way companies reach diverse audiences with persuasive brand information. But we need to appreciate another dimension: advertising is very much a business process as well as a communication process. For multinational organizations like Unilever and Boeing, as well as for small local retailers, advertising is a basic business tool that is essential to retaining current customers and attracting new customers. We need to understand that advertising functions as a business process in three ways. First, we'll consider the role advertising plays in the overall marketing and brand development programs in firms. Second, we will look at the types of advertising used by firms. Finally, we will take a broader look at advertising by identifying the economic effects of the process.

To truly appreciate advertising as a business process, we have to understand the role advertising plays in a firm's marketing effort. To begin with, realize that every organization *must* make marketing decisions. There simply is no escaping the need to develop brands, price them, distribute them, and advertise and promote them to a target audience. The role of advertising relates to four important aspects of the marketing process: (1) contributing to the marketing mix; (2) developing and managing the brand; (3) achieving effective market segmentation, differentiation, and positioning; and (4) contributing to revenue and profit generation.

1-5a The Role of Advertising in the Marketing Mix

A formal definition of marketing reveals that advertising (as a part of overall promotion) is one of the primary marketing tools available to any organization:

> **Marketing** *is the process of planning and executing the conception, pricing, promotion, and distribution of ideas, goods, and services to create exchanges that satisfy individual and organizational objectives.*[11]

Marketing people assume a wide range of responsibilities in an organization related to conceiving, pricing, promoting, and distributing goods, services, and even ideas. Many of you know that these four areas of responsibility and decision making in marketing are referred to as the **marketing mix**. The word *mix* is used to describe the blend of strategic emphasis on the product versus its price versus its promotion (including advertising) versus its distribution when a brand is marketed to consumers. This blend, or mix, results in the overall marketing program for a brand. Advertising is important, but it is only *one* of the major areas of marketing responsibility *and* it is only one of many different IBP tools relied on in the marketing mix. Under Armour unleashed "an audacious $25 million campaign" with the slogan "The future is ours!" to introduce its non-cleated shoe line. Under Armour sales in that category did not grow the following year—competition from Nike, Adidas, and Reebok proved too formidable. Advertising alone, no matter how "audacious," could not overcome competitors' product features and distribution.[12]

Exhibit 1.15 lists the strategic decision factors typically considered in each area of the marketing mix. You can see that decisions under each of the marketing mix areas can directly affect the advertising message. The important point is that a firm's advertising effort must be consistent with and complement the overall marketing mix strategy being used by a firm.

The Role of Advertising in Brand Management. One of the key issues to understand about the role of advertising is that it plays a critical role in brand development and management. We have been referring to the brand and integrated brand promotion throughout our discussion of the process of advertising so far. All of us have our own understanding of what a brand is. After all, we buy brands every day. A formal definition of a **brand** is a name, term, sign, symbol, or any other feature that identifies one seller's good or service as distinct from those of other sellers.[13] Advertising plays a significant role in brand development and management. A brand is in many ways the most precious business asset owned by a firm. It allows a firm to communicate consistently and efficiently with the market.

Is it really worth investing all that time, effort, and money in building a brand name and image? The answer to that question would be YES! *Business Week* magazine, in conjunction with Interbrand, a marketing analysis and consulting firm, has attached a dollar value to brand names based on a combination of sales, earnings, future sales potential, and intangibles (which includes a brand's market recognition). Often, a brand name is worth much more than the annual sales of the brand. Coca-Cola, the most valuable brand in the world, is estimated to be worth almost $77 billion even though sales of branded Coca-Cola products amount to only about $47 billion a year. The value of other notable brands include Nike at $15 billion and Harley-Davidson at a mere $3 billion.[14]

Brands either benefit or suffer from the advertising effort. Well-conceived and well-executed advertising campaigns create visibility and a positive predisposition for the brand in the minds of consumers. Or, a brand can be put at a serious competitive disadvantage without effective communication provided by advertising. Staples, the office supply retailer, was struggling with an outdated advertising campaign featuring the tagline "Yeah, we've got that." Customers were complaining that items were out of stock and sales staff didn't care. So the company's vice president of marketing, Shira Goodman, determined that shoppers wanted an "easier" shopping experience with well-stocked shelves and helpful staff. Once those marketing mix operational changes were made, Staples introduced the "Staples: That Was Easy" campaign, featuring big red "Easy" buttons that were also available for sale at the stores. Now, with clear, straightforward ads and customers spreading the word (called "viral" marketing) by having their "Easy" push-buttons in offices all across the country, Staples became a runaway leader in office retail.[15]

EXHIBIT 1.15 These are the factors that an organization needs to consider in creating a marketing mix. Advertising messages, media placement, and IBP techniques must be consistent with and complement strategies in all other areas of the marketing mix.

Product	Promotion
Functional features	Amount and type of advertising
Aesthetic design	Number and qualifications of salespeople
Accompanying services	Extent and type of personal selling program
Instructions for use	Sales promotion—coupons, contests, sweepstakes
Warranty	Trade shows
Product differentiation	Public relations activities
Product positioning	Direct mail or telemarketing
	Event sponsorships
	Internet communications/mobile marketing

Price	Distribution
Level:	Number of retail outlets
Top of the line	Location of retail outlets
Competitive, average prices	Types of retail outlets
Low-price policy	Catalog sales
Terms offered:	Other nonstore retail methods—Internet
Cash only	Number and type of wholesalers
Credit:	Inventories—extent and location
Extended	Services provided by distribution:
Restricted	Credit
Interest charges	Delivery
Lease/rental	Installation
	Training

© Cengage Learning

For every organization, advertising affects brand development and management in five important ways.

Information and Persuasion. Target audiences can learn about a brand's features and benefits through advertising and, to a lesser extent, other promotional tools (most other promotional tools, except the Web and personal selling, are not heavy on content). But advertising has the best ability to inform or persuade target audiences about the values a brand has to offer. No other variable in the marketing mix is designed to accomplish this communication. For example, branding is crucially important in the multibillion-dollar cell phone market as Verizon, T-Mobile, and AT&T compete for millions of wireless subscribers. In many ways, marketing and advertising a cellular service brand is much like marketing and advertising brands of bottled water. One cell phone/smartphone works about like another (though iPhone users would not agree!), and there are plenty of alternative monthly programs, just like one brand of bottled water is pretty much the same as the next brand. But advertising, with its ability to use images and emotionally appealing messages, can distinguish a brand from others even when there are few true functional differences.

Introduction of New Brand or Brand Extensions (Variants). Advertising is absolutely critical when organizations introduce a new brand or extensions of existing brands to the market. Consider the case of the new brand Snuggie—that somewhat funny-looking blanket with sleeves. The president of Snuggie used low-budget direct response ads on low-ratings cable programs to introduce the brand. Now, Snuggie is distributed in Lord & Taylor, college book stores, and pet stores.[16] A **brand extension** (also referred to as a **brand variant**) is an adaptation of an existing brand to a new product area. For example, the Snickers Ice Cream Bar is a brand extension of the original Snickers candy bar, and Ivory Shampoo is a brand extension of Ivory Dishwashing Liquid. When brand extensions are brought to market, advertising and IBP play a key role in attracting attention to the brand—so much so that researchers now suggest that "managers should favor the brand extension with a greater allocation of the ad budget.[17] This is often accomplished with advertising working in conjunction with other promotional activities such as sales promotions and point-of-purchase displays. Exhibit 1.16 shows another example of advertising being used to extend a famous brand name into a totally different, though related, product category. Crest, known widely for its toothpaste brand, introduced a line of toothbrushes to extend the brand with a complimentary item.

Building and Maintaining Brand Loyalty among Consumers. Loyalty to a brand is one of the most important assets a firm can have. **Brand loyalty** occurs when a consumer repeatedly purchases the same brand to the exclusion of competitors' brands. This loyalty can result because of habit, because brand names are prominent in the consumer's memory, because of barely conscious associations with brand images, or because consumers have attached some fairly deep meanings to the brands they buy.

EXHIBIT 1.16 Advertising helps companies implement brand extension strategies. Here the famous Crest name is being used as Procter & Gamble extends the Crest brand name to toothbrushes. What value does a widely recognized brand name lend to the brand extension process?

AP Publicity Photo/Crest Procter & Gamble

Even though brand features are the most important influence on building and maintaining brand loyalty, advertising plays a key role in the process as well. Advertising reminds consumers of those brand features—tangible and intangible. Other promotional tools can offer similarly valuable communications that help build and strengthen lasting and positive associations with a brand—such as a frequent-flyer or frequent-buyer program. The importance of brand loyalty cannot be overstated. When a firm creates and maintains positive associations with the brand in the mind of consumers and builds brand loyalty, then the firm goes on to develop what is called brand equity. **Brand equity** is a set of brand assets linked to a brand, its name, and symbol.[18] Even though brand equity occurs over long periods of time, short-term advertising activities are key to long-term success.[19] Recent research has affirmed that integrated communications is a "critical component of brand equity strategy."[20] This advertising fact of life became clear to strategists at food giant Kraft as it devised a strategy to defend its Kraft Miracle Whip brand against a new campaign by competitor Unilever for Imperial Whip. In order to protect Miracle Whip's $229 million in sales and brand equity with consumers, Kraft invested heavily in television advertising just before Unilever lowered prices on the Imperial Whip brand.[21] Similarly, when Microsoft introduced its Windows 8 operating system,

it launched a $1 billion global advertising campaign to retain loyal Windows users.[22]

Creating an Image and Meaning for a Brand. As we discussed in the marketing mix section, advertising can communicate how a brand fulfills needs and desires and therefore plays an important role in attracting customers to brands that appear to be useful and satisfying. But advertising can go further. It can help link a brand's image and meaning to a consumer's social environment and to the larger culture, and in this way, advertising can actually deliver a sense of personal connection for the consumer.

The Schiff ad for prenatal vitamins in Exhibit 1.17 is a clear example of how advertising can create an image and deeper meaning. The message in this ad is not just about the health advantages of using a nutritional supplement during pregnancy. The message mines associations related to love and caring for an unborn or recently born child. Even the slogan for the brand, "Benefits Beyond Your Daily Requirements," plays on

EXHIBIT 1.17 The message in this Schiff vitamin ad creates meaning for the vitamins that goes beyond the daily nutritional role vitamins can play. What are the many meanings in this message being offered to the audience?

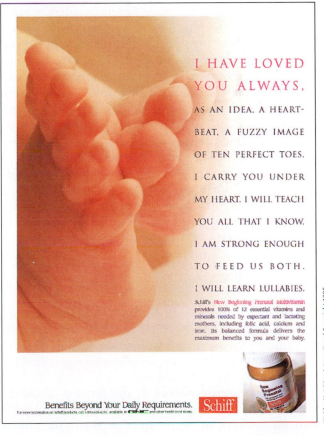

I HAVE LOVED YOU ALWAYS, AS AN IDEA, A HEART-BEAT, A FUZZY IMAGE OF TEN PERFECT TOES. I CARRY YOU UNDER MY HEART. I WILL TEACH YOU ALL THAT I KNOW. I AM STRONG ENOUGH TO FEED US BOTH. I WILL LEARN LULLABIES.

Schiff's New Beginning Prenatal Multivitamin provides 100% of 12 essential vitamins and minerals needed by expectant and lactating mothers, including folic acid, calcium and iron. Its balanced formula delivers the maximum benefits to you and your baby.

Benefits Beyond Your Daily Requirements.   Schiff

Weider Nutrition International Copyright 1995

the notion that a vitamin is more than a vehicle for dosing up on folic acid. Other promotional tools in the IBP process, such as personal selling, sales promotions, event sponsorship, or the Internet, simply cannot achieve such creative power or communicate the symbolic meanings a brand can have to a consumer. We'll look at the creative power of advertising later in the text (Chapter 11).

Building and Maintaining Brand Loyalty within the Trade. It might not seem as if wholesalers, retailers, distributors, and brokers would be brand loyal, but they can indeed favor one brand over others given the proper support from a manufacturer. Advertising and particularly advertising integrated with other brand promotions is an area where support can be given. Marketers can provide the trade with sales training programs, collateral advertising materials (e.g., brochures, banners, posters), point-of-purchase advertising displays, premiums (giveaways like t-shirts or free app downloads), Web traffic–building advertising, and foot traffic–building special events. Exide, the battery company, spent several million dollars a year to be the official battery of NASCAR racing. Mike Dever, Exide's vice president of marketing and product management, explained: "Both our distributors and our distributors' customers, for the most part, are race fans, so it's the place we want to be."[23]

Also, remember that trade buyers (retailers, wholesalers, distributors, brokers) can be key to the success of new brands or brand extensions, as we pointed out earlier in the discussion of the trade market as a target audience. Marketers have little hope of successfully introducing a brand if there is no cooperation in the trade channel among wholesalers and retailers. This is where IBP as a factor in advertising becomes prominent. Trade buyers are generally less responsive to advertising messages than they are to other forms of promotion. Direct support to the trade in terms of displays, contests, increased margins, and personal selling combined with advertising in an IBP program helps ensure the success of a brand. Research also shows that retailer acceptance of a brand extension is key to the success of the new product, and advertising and IBP, in turn, help achieve retailer acceptance.[24]

The Role of Advertising in Market Segmentation, Differentiation, and Positioning. The third role for advertising in marketing is helping the firm implement the important market strategies of market segmentation, differentiation, and positioning.

Market segmentation is the process of breaking down a large, widely varied (*heterogeneous*) market into submarkets, or segments, that are more similar than dissimilar in terms of consumer characteristics. Underlying the strategy of market segmentation are the facts that consumers differ in their wants and that the wants of one person can differ under various circumstances. The market for automobiles can be divided into submarkets for different types of automobiles based on the needs and desires of various groups of buyers: large or small, luxury or economy, sedan or SUV or minivan. In addition to needs or desires, markets are also segmented on characteristics of consumers related to demographics (such as age, marital status, education, gender, and income) or psychographics (attitudes, beliefs, personality, lifestyle, and values). These data are widely available and tend to be related to product preference and use. Advertising's role in the market segmentation process is to develop messages that appeal to the needs and desires of different segments and then to transmit those messages via appropriate media. For example, Bayer has four different versions of its basic aspirin brand. There is regular Bayer for headache relief; Bayer Enteric Safety Coated 81 mg aspirin for people with cholesterol and heart concerns; Women's Bayer, which includes a calcium supplement; and Children's Bayer, which has a lower dose and is chewable. Each of these versions of the Bayer brand of aspirin addresses different needs and characteristics of consumers in the market, and advertising follows through with messages highlighting those differences. Nowhere is the segmentation challenge greater than in the U.S. food market. The number of items in a typical grocery store has exploded to over 38,000 from just 10,000 25 years ago. Segments are more fragmented and consumers are more mindful of exactly what they want, demanding the marketers offer messages about brands that match the segments' interests and desires.[25]

Differentiation is the process of creating a perceived difference, in the mind of the consumer, between a brand and its competition. Notice that this definition emphasizes that brand differentiation is based on *consumer perception*. The perceived differences can be tangible differences, or they may be based on image or style factors. The critical issue in differentiation is that consumers *perceive* a difference between brands. If consumers do not perceive a difference, then whether real differences exist or not does not matter. Further, if a firm's brand is not perceived as distinctive and attractive by consumers, then consumers will have no reason to choose that brand over one from the competition or to pay higher prices for the "better" or "more meaningful" brand. Think about bottled water (Evian), bananas (Chiquita), or meat (Niman Ranch), where marketers have been able to differentiate their brands with excellent advertising and branding strategies.[26]

In order for advertising to help create a difference in the mind of the consumer between a brand and its competitors' brands, the ad may emphasize performance features, or it may create a distinctive image for the brand. The essential task for advertising is to develop a message that is different and unmistakably linked to a company's brand. The ad in Exhibit 1.18 is distinctive and pursues product differentiation in a product category where differentiation is hard to come by. Most consumers would tend not to choose a ceiling fan based on image. But with this ad, Hunter Fan uses an appealing visual to attract attention to the brand and tries to differentiate the brand on image as well as functional performance features.

Positioning is the process of designing a brand so that it can occupy a distinct and valued place in the target consumer's mind relative to other brands. This distinctiveness can be communicated through advertising. Positioning, like differentiation, depends on a perceived image of tangible or intangible features.

EXHIBIT 1.18 An important role for advertising is to help a firm differentiate its brand from the competition with a distinctive message and presentation. This Hunter Fan ad focuses on the functional features of its air purifier line as the basis for differentiation—and does so with a distinctive visual presentation.

The importance of positioning can be understood by recognizing that consumers create a *perceptual space* in their minds for all the brands they might consider purchasing. A perceptual space is how one brand is seen on any number of dimensions—such as quality, taste, price, or social display value—in relation to those same dimensions in other brands.

There are really three positioning strategic decisions to be made. A firm must decide on the **external position** for a brand—that is, the niche the brand will pursue relative to all the competitive brands on the market. Additionally, an **internal position** must be achieved with regard to the other, similar brands the firm itself markets. With the external-positioning decision, a firm tries to create a distinctive *competitive* position based on design features, pricing, distribution, or promotion or advertising strategy. Some brands are positioned at the very top of their competitive product category, such as BMW's 550i, priced around $100,000. Other brands seek a position at the low end of all market offerings, such as the Chevrolet Cruze, with a base price of about $16,000. Finally, **repositioning** occurs when a firm believes that a brand needs to be revived or updated to address changing market or competitive conditions.

Effective external positioning is achieved when the firm carefully segments the market, develops brand features and values that are distinctive from the competition, and follows through with advertising and IBP messages that highlight the distinctions.

Effective internal positioning is accomplished by developing vastly different products *within* the firm's own product line. Ben & Jerry's ice cream, for example, offers plenty of distinctive flavors, as shown in Exhibit 1.19. Ben & Jerry's has a somewhat easier task in meeting this challenge since each of the ice creams they need to internally position has a tangible feature to highlight (flavor, ingredients, etc.) A more challenging approach to internal position is creating advertising messages that appeal to different consumer needs and desires when there are few conspicuously tangible differences. Procter & Gamble (P&G) successfully positions its many laundry detergent brands both internally and externally using a combination of product design and effective advertising. Although some of these brands assume different positions within P&G's line due to substantive differences (a liquid soap versus a powder soap, for example), others with minor differences achieve distinctive positioning through advertising. One P&G brand is advertised as being effective on kids' dirty clothes, whereas another brand is portrayed as effective for preventing colors from running. In this way, advertising helps create a distinctive position, both internally and externally. In contrast to P&G's success, the long and painful decline

EXHIBIT 1.19 Firms with multiple brands in a single product category have to internally position these brands to differentiate them from one another in the minds of consumers. Ben & Jerry's achieves internal product positioning by emphasizing the distinctly different flavor of each of its ice creams.

of Kmart is attributed to the firm's lack of brand identity and positioning relative to competitors Walmart and Target. Analysts suggest that Kmart's singular focus on pricing (which is easy for competitors to copy) rather than using effective advertising to position the brand resulted in a "slow motion train wreck" for the brand.[27]

Finally, repositioning is accomplished by offering consumers new and distinctive features or images of the brand. Repositioning is aided by a variety of advertising and IBP tactics. An advertising message can be altered to appeal to consumer behavior trends. Packaging can be changed to attract attention, or the brand's logo can be updated to provide a more powerful visual representation of the brand. Some analysts refer to the process of repositioning with such visual elements of IBP as "the best way into a consumer's mind is not with verbal nails, but with a visual hammer."[28]

The methods and strategic options available to an organization with respect to market segmentation, product differentiation, and positioning will be fully discussed in Chapter 6. For now, realize that advertising plays an important role in helping an organization put these most basic marketing strategies into operation.

The Role of Advertising in Contributing to Revenue and Profit Generation. There are many who believe that the fundamental purpose of marketing (and the advertising that is used in marketing strategies) can be stated quite simply: to generate revenue. Marketing is the only part of an organization that has revenue generation as its primary purpose. In the words of highly regarded management consultant and scholar Peter Drucker, "Marketing and innovation produce results: all the rest are 'costs.'"[29] The "results" Drucker refers to are revenues. The marketing process is designed to generate sales and therefore revenues for the firm.

Helping create sales as part of the revenue-generating process is where advertising plays a significant role. As we have seen, advertising communicates persuasive information to audiences based on the values created in the marketing mix related to the product, its price, or its distribution. This advertising communication then highlights brand features—performance, price, emotion values, or availability—and then attracts a target market. In this way, advertising makes a direct contribution to the marketing goal of revenue generation. Notice that advertising *contributes* to the process of creating sales and revenue. It cannot be solely responsible for creating sales and revenue—it's not that powerful. Some organizations mistakenly see advertising as a panacea—the salvation for an ambiguous or ineffective overall marketing mix strategy. Advertising alone cannot be held responsible for sales—period. Sales occur when a brand has a well-conceived and complete marketing mix—including good advertising.

The effect of advertising on profits is a bit more involved and complicated. Its effect on profits comes about when advertising gives an organization greater flexibility in the price it *charges* for a product or service. Advertising can help create pricing flexibility by (1) contributing to economies of scale and (2) helping create inelasticity (insensitivity) of demand to price changes. When an organization creates large-scale demand for its brand, the quantity of product produced is increased, and **economies of scale** lead to lower unit production costs. Cost of production decreases because fixed costs (such as rent and equipment costs) are spread over a greater number of units produced.

How does advertising play a role in helping create economies of scale? When Colgate manufactures hundreds of thousands of tubes of its Colgate Total toothpaste and ships them in large quantities to warehouses, the fixed costs of production and shipping per unit are greatly reduced. With lower fixed costs per unit, Colgate can realize greater profits on each tube of toothpaste sold. Advertising contributes to demand stimulation by communicating to the market about the features and availability of a brand. By contributing to demand stimulation, advertising then contributes to the process of creating these economies of scale, which ultimately translates into higher profits per unit for the organization.

Remember the concept of brand loyalty we discussed earlier? Well, brand loyalty and advertising work together to create another important economic effect related to pricing flexibility and profits. When consumers are brand loyal, they are generally less sensitive to price increases for the brand. In economic terms, this is known as **inelasticity of demand**. When consumers are less price sensitive, firms have the flexibility to maintain higher prices and increase profit margins. Advertising contributes directly to brand loyalty, and thus to inelasticity of demand, by persuading and reminding consumers of the satisfactions and values related to a brand and why they want to choose that brand over competitors' brands.

These arguments related to the positive business effects of advertising were recently supported by a large research study. The study found that companies who build strong brands and raise prices are more profitable than companies who cut costs as a way to increase profits—by nearly twice the profit percentage. This research is supported by such real-world examples as Louis Vuitton. The maker of luxury handbags ($1,000 per bag or more) and other luxury items enjoys an operating margin of 45 percent supported by the image created and maintained in advertising for the brand.[30]

1-5b Types of Advertising

So far, we've discussed advertising in a lot of different ways, from its most basic definition through how it can help an organization stimulate demand and generate profits. But to truly understand advertising, we need to go back to some very basic typologies that categorize advertising according to fundamental approaches to communication. Until you understand these aspects of advertising, you really don't understand advertising at all.

Primary versus Selective Demand Stimulation. In **primary demand stimulation**, a company would be trying to create demand for an entire *product category*. Primary demand stimulation is challenging and costly, and research evidence suggests that it is likely to have an impact only for totally new products on the market—not brand extensions or product categories that have been around a long time (known as mature products). An

example of effective primary demand stimulation was the introduction of the VCR to the consumer market in the 1970s. With a product that is totally new to the market, consumers need to be convinced that the product category itself is valuable and that it is, indeed, available for sale. When the VCR was first introduced in the United States, RCA, Panasonic, and Quasar (see Exhibit 1.20) ran primary demand stimulation advertising to explain to household consumers the value and convenience of taping television programs with this new product called a VHS video recorder—something no one had ever done before at home. When the DVR was introduced to the market, consumers already knew the process and value of recording programs at home—the VHS recorder had paved the way decades before—so no primary demand stimulation was needed for the DVR.

EXHIBIT 1.20 When new innovative products are first introduced to the market, a type of advertising called primary demand stimulation is often used. Primary demand stimulation attempts to stimulate demand for an entire product category by educating the consumer about the values and benefits of the product category as a whole rather than the values and benefits of an individual brand. Way back when the VHS video cassette player was introduced to the market, consumers needed to learn about the values of this new device.

For organizations that have tried to stimulate primary demand in mature product categories, typically trade associations, the results have been dismal. The National Fluid Milk Processor Promotion Board has tried for years to use advertising to stimulate primary demand for the entire product category of milk. An example of the campaign is shown in Exhibit 1.21. Even though the "milk mustache" campaign is popular and wins awards, milk consumption has *declined* every year during the time of this campaign.[31] The newest data shows that milk consumption has continued to decline to the present day.[32] This is despite the fact that more than $1.1 billion in advertising have been invested in the campaign. Even if it is argued that the attempts at primary demand stimulation have reduced the overall decline in milk consumption (which can't be determined), this is still not a very impressive result. This should come as no

surprise, though. Research over decades has clearly indicated that attempts at primary demand stimulation in mature product categories (orange juice, beef, pork, and almonds have also been tried) have *never* been successful.[33] The fact is that advertising is not powerful enough to stimulate primary demand. Only broad influences on society, like demographics, cultural values, or technology, can affect primary demand for a product category. In the case of milk, declining birth rates and cultural preferences for (perceived) lower calorie drinks are postulated to explain the decline in milk consumption—advertising is no match for large-scale societal influences such as these.[34]

Although some corporations have tried primary demand stimulation, the true power of advertising is realized when it functions to stimulate demand for a particular company's brand—which is what has been described throughout this chapter. This is known as selective demand stimulation. The purpose of **selective demand stimulation** advertising is to point out a brand's unique benefits compared to the competition. This is the proper role for advertising.

Direct versus Delayed Response Advertising.

Another important type of advertising involves how quickly we want consumers to respond. **Direct response advertising** asks consumers to act immediately. All those ads you see that suggest you "call this toll-free number" or "mail your $19.95 before midnight tonight" or "click here to order NOW" are examples of direct response advertising. In most cases, direct response advertising is used for products that consumers are familiar with, that do not require inspection at the point of purchase, and that are relatively low cost. However, the proliferation of toll-free numbers and websites that provide detailed information and direct online ordering, and the widespread use of credit cards, have been a boon to direct response for higher priced products as well.

Delayed response advertising relies on imagery and message themes that emphasize the benefits and satisfying characteristics of a brand. Rather than trying to stimulate an immediate action from an audience, delayed response advertising attempts to develop awareness and preference for a brand over time. In general, delayed response advertising attempts to create brand awareness, reinforce the benefits of using a brand (i.e., brand loyalty), develop a general liking for the brand, and create an image for a brand. When a consumer enters the purchase process, the information from delayed response advertising comes into play. Most advertisements we see on television and in magazines are of the delayed response type. Exhibit 1.22, an ad for a hypoallergenic detergent, provides an example of this common form of

EXHIBIT 1.21   Advertising that attempts to stimulate primary demand is often tried by industry associations such as the National Fluid Milk Processor Promotion Board. Trouble is, it doesn't work. Primary demand stimulation has been shown to be ineffective in mature product categories, such as milk, but rather is appropriate for products totally new to the market, like PDAs or MP3 players were.

EXHIBIT 1.22 Delayed response advertising attempts to reinforce the benefits of using a brand and to create a general liking for the brand. This ad for ALL detergent is an example of delayed response advertising. It builds an image and preference for a brand rather than asking consumers to take immediate action.

advertising. In this ad, the message has as much to do with being a good parent (an image and delayed response–type message) as with the actual performance features of the brand.

Corporate versus Brand Advertising. **Corporate advertising** is not designed to promote a specific brand but is meant to create a favorable attitude toward a company as a whole. Prominent users of corporate advertising include Apple, BP, and General Electric ("Imagination at Work"). As an example, Philips, the Dutch electronics and medical device conglomerate, turned to corporate advertising to unify the image of its brand name across a wide range of superior technologies.[35] **Brand advertising**, as we have seen throughout this chapter, communicates the specific features, values, and benefits of a particular brand offered for sale by a particular organization. By contrast, the firms that have long-established corporate campaigns have designed them to generate favorable public opinion toward the corporation as a whole. This type of

advertising can also have an effect on the shareholders of a firm. When shareholders see good corporate advertising, it instills confidence and, ultimately, long-term commitment to the firm and its stock. We'll consider this type of advertising in great detail in Chapter 18.

Another form of corporate advertising is carried out by members of a trade channel, mostly retailers. When corporate advertising takes place in a trade channel, it is referred to as **institutional advertising**. Retailers such as Nordstrom, The Home Depot, and Walmart advertise to persuade consumers to shop at their stores. Although these retailers may occasionally feature a particular manufacturer's brand in the advertising (Nordstrom often features Clinique cosmetics, for example), the main purpose of the advertising is to get the audience to shop at their store.

1-5c The Economic Effects of Advertising

Our discussion of advertising as a business process so far has focused strictly on the use of advertising by individual business organizations. But you cannot *truly* understand advertising unless you know something about how advertising has effects across the entire economic system of a country—the macro effects. (This isn't the most fun you'll have reading this book, but it is a very important topic.)

Advertising's Effect on Gross Domestic Product. **Gross domestic product (GDP)** is the measure of the total value of goods and services produced within an economic system. Earlier, we discussed advertising's role in the marketing mix. Recall that as advertising contributes to marketing mix strategy, it can contribute to sales along with the right product, the right price, and the right distribution. Because of this role, advertising is related to GDP in that it can contribute to levels of overall consumer demand when it helps introduce new products, such as DVRs, smartphones, or alternative energy sources. As demand for these new products grows, the resultant consumer spending fuels retail sales, housing starts, and corporate investment in finished goods and capital equipment. Consequently, GDP is affected by sales of products in new, innovative product categories.[36]

Advertising's Effect on Competition. Advertising is alleged to stimulate competition and therefore motivate firms to strive for better products, better production methods, and other competitive advantages that ultimately benefit the economy as a whole. Additionally, when advertising serves as a way to enter new markets, competition across the economic system is fostered.

For example, Exhibit 1.23 shows an ad in which plastics manufacturers present themselves as competitors to manufacturers of other packaging materials.

Advertising is not universally hailed as a stimulant to competition. Critics point out that the amount of advertising dollars needed to compete effectively in many industries is often prohibitive. As such, advertising can act as a barrier to entry into an industry; that is, a firm may have the capability to compete in an industry in every way *except* that the advertising dollars needed to compete are so great that the firm cannot afford to get into the business. In this way, advertising is argued to decrease the overall amount of competition in an economy.

Advertising's Effect on Prices. One of the widely debated effects of advertising has to do with its effect on the prices consumers pay for products and services. Firms like GM and Procter & Gamble spend billions of dollars on advertising products and services, so it goes to reason that these products and services would

EXHIBIT 1.23   Advertising can affect the competitive environment in an economy. This ad by a plastics manufacturer's council is fostering competition with the manufacturers of other packaging materials.

cost much less if firms did no advertising. Right? Wrong!

First, across all industries, advertising costs incurred by firms range from about 2 percent of sales in the automobile and certain retail industries up to 20 percent of sales in luxury products businesses like perfume and toiletries. One important fact to realize is there is no consistent and predictable relationship between advertising spending and sales—it all depends on the product category, competition, size of market, and complexity of the message. In 2011, Ford Motor Company spent about $2.1 billion in advertising to generate about $132 billion in sales or about 1.6 percent of sales; American Express spent exactly the same amount on advertising as Ford, $2.1 billion, but generated only about $29 billion in sales, making ad spending about 7.3 percent of sales; and Walmart spent $1.9 billion on advertising (seems like a big number, right) but generated a whopping $464 billion in sales, making ad spending a puny four-tenths of 1 percent of sales![37] Different products and different market conditions demand that firms spend different amounts of money on advertising. These same conditions make it difficult to identify a predictable relationship between advertising and sales.

It is true that the cost of advertising is built into product costs, which may be ultimately passed on to consumers. But this effect on price must be judged against a couple of cost savings that *lower* the price consumers pay. First, there is the reduced time and effort a consumer has to spend in searching for a product or service. Second, economies of scale, discussed earlier, have a direct impact on the cost of goods produced and then on prices. Recall that economies of scale serve to lower the cost of production by spreading fixed costs over a large number of units produced. This lower cost can be passed on to consumers in terms of lower prices, as firms search for competitive advantage with lower prices. Nowhere is this effect more dramatic than the price and performance of personal computers. In the early 1980s, an Apple IIe computer that ran at about 1 MHz and had 64 KB of total memory cost more than $3,000. Today, a Dell computer that has multiple times more power, speed, and memory costs about $600.

Advertising's Effect on Value.   *Value* is the password for successful marketing. **Value**, in modern marketing and advertising, refers to a perception by consumers that a brand provides satisfaction beyond the cost incurred to obtain that brand. The value perspective of the modern consumer is based on wanting every purchase to be a "good deal." Value can be added to the consumption experience by advertising. Consider the effect of branding on bottled water. Advertising helps create enough value in the minds of consumers that they (we) will *pay* for water that comes free out of the tap.

Advertising also affects a consumer's perception of value by contributing to the symbolic value and the social meaning of a brand. **Symbolic value** refers to what a product or service means to consumers in a nonliteral way. For example, branded clothing such as Lululemon, Michael Kohrs, Puma, or The North Face can symbolize self-concept for some consumers. Exhibit 1.24 shows an ad that seeks to create symbolic value for Ray-Ban sunglasses. The symbolism of an attractive, seemingly confident, well-dressed young man cast Ray-Ban sunglasses in a positive symbolic light (no pun intended). In reality, all branded products rely to some extent on symbolic value; otherwise they would not be brands but just unmarked commodities (like potatoes).

Social meaning refers to what a product or service means in a societal context. For example, social class is marked by any number of products, such as cars, beverages, and clothes that are used and displayed to signify class membership. Often, the brand's connection to social class values addresses a need within consumers to move up in class.

Researchers from various disciplines have long argued that objects (brands included) are never just objects. They take on meaning from culture, society, and consumers.[38] It is important to remember that these meanings often become just as much a part of the brand as the physical features. Because advertising is an essential way in which the image of a brand is developed, it contributes directly to consumers' perception of the value of the brand. The more value consumers see in a brand, the more they are willing to pay to acquire the brand. If the image of a Gucci watch, a Nissan coupe, or a Four Seasons hotel is valued by consumers, then consumers will pay a premium to acquire that value (see Insights Online [Exhibit 1.25] for a related example).

EXHIBIT 1.24 Advertising contributes to the symbolic value that brands have for consumers. What is it about this ad for Ray-Ban sunglasses that contributes to the symbolic value of this brand?

Courtesy of Advertising Archives

LO ⑤

1-6 FROM ADVERTISING TO INTEGRATED MARKETING COMMUNICATIONS TO INTEGRATED BRAND PROMOTION

As we discussed at the beginning of your introduction to the world of advertising and IBP, it is important to recognize that advertising is only one of many promotional tools available to impress and persuade consumers. There is another distinction that is important for you to recognize as you embark on learning about advertising and IBP.

Beginning in about 1990, the concept of mixing various promotional tools was referred to as **integrated marketing communications (IMC)**. But as the discussions throughout this chapter have highlighted, the reality of promotional strategies in the 21st century demands that the emphasis on *communication* give way to an emphasis on the *brand*. Organizations of all types are not interested in merely communicating with potential and existing customers through advertising and promotion. They want to build brand awareness, identity, and preference through advertising and promotion.

Recall from the definition earlier in the chapter that IBP is the use of various communication tools, including advertising, in a coordinated manner to build and maintain brand awareness, identity, and preference. The distinction between IBP and IMC is pretty obvious. IMC emphasizes the communication effort per se and the need for coordinated and synergistic messages. IBP retains the emphasis on coordination and synergy of communication but goes beyond the parameters of

IMC. In IBP, the emphasis is on the brand and not just the communication. With a focus on building brand awareness, identity, and ultimately preference, the IBP perspective recognizes that coordinated promotional messages need to have brand-building effects in addition to the communication effects.

SUMMARY

 Know what advertising and integrated brand promotion (IBP) are and what they can do.

Since advertising has become so pervasive, it would be reasonable to expect that you might have your own working definition for this critical term. But an informed perspective on advertising goes beyond what is obvious and can be seen on a daily basis. Advertising is distinctive and recognizable as a form of communication by its three essential elements: its paid sponsorship, its use of mass media, and its intent to persuade. An advertisement is a specific message that a company has placed to persuade an audience. An advertising campaign is a series of ads and other promotional efforts with a common theme also placed to persuade an audience over a specified period of time. Integrated brand promotion (IBP) is the use of many promotional tools, including advertising, in a coordinated manner to build and maintain brand awareness, identity, and preference.

 Discuss a basic model of communication.

Advertising cannot be effective unless some form of communication takes place between the company and the audience. But advertising is about mass communication. There are many models that might be used to help explain how advertising works or does not work as a communication platform. The model introduced in this chapter features basic considerations such as the message-production process versus the message-reception process, and this model says that consumers create their own meanings when they interpret advertisements.

 Describe the different ways of classifying audiences for advertising and IBP.

Although it is possible to provide a simple and clear definition of what advertising is, it is also true that advertising takes many forms and serves different purposes from one application to another. One way to appreciate the complexity and diversity of advertising is to classify it by audience category or by geographic focus. For example, advertising might be directed at households or government officials. Using another perspective, it can be global or local in its focus.

 Understand advertising as a business process.

Many different types of organizations use advertising to achieve their business purposes. For major multinational corporations, such as Procter & Gamble, and for smaller, more localized

businesses, such as the San Diego Zoo, advertising is one part of a critical business process known as marketing. Advertising is one element of the marketing mix; the other key elements are the firm's products, their prices, and the distribution network. Advertising must work in conjunction with these other marketing mix elements if the organization's marketing objectives are to be achieved. It is important to recognize that of all the roles played by advertising in the marketing process, none is more important than contributing to building brand awareness and brand equity. Similarly, firms have turned to more diverse methods of communication beyond advertising that we have referred to as integrated brand promotion. That is, firms are using communication tools such as public relations, sponsorship, direct marketing, and sales promotion along with advertising to achieve communication goals.

 Understand the various types of advertising.

There are six fundamental types of advertising described in contrasting pairs:

a. Primary versus selective demand stimulation. Primary demand stimulation is the attempt to stimulate demand for an entire product category—milk, toothpaste, automobiles, computers. Selective demand stimulation is the attempt to stimulate demand for a brand within a product category—Dairygold Milk, Crest toothpaste, Nissan Altima automobile, Dell computer. While primary demand has been attempted in various industries (the milk industry being the most prominent example), advertising is not powerful enough to stimulate demand for a product category—only broad influences like demographics, cultural values, or technology can stimulate primary demand. Selective demand is what advertising does and can be very effective at doing. It is the type of advertising that firms spend billions of dollars a year on to build brand awareness and preference.

b. Direct versus delayed response advertising. Direct response advertising asks consumers to act immediately upon receipt of the advertising message—call this toll-free number, click through to order now, and so on. Delayed response advertising develops awareness, preference, and an image for a brand that takes much longer to affect consumer choice.

c. Corporate versus brand advertising. Corporate advertising features an entire corporation rather than any brand marketed by that corporation. GM can run corporate advertising to increase recognition of the firm itself. Or, GM can run brand advertising for Chevrolet or Buick or GM trucks.

KEY TERMS

mobile marketing	national advertising	repositioning
advertising	regional advertising	economies of scale
client, or sponsor	local advertising	inelasticity of demand
integrated brand promotion (IBP)	cooperative advertising, or co-op	primary demand stimulation
advertisement	advertising	selective demand stimulation
advertising campaign	marketing	direct response advertising
audience	marketing mix	delayed response advertising
target audience	brand	corporate advertising
household consumers	brand extension (variant)	brand advertising
members of business organizations	brand loyalty	institutional advertising
members of a trade channel	brand equity	gross domestic product (GDP)
professionals	market segmentation	value
trade journals	differentiation	symbolic value
government officials and employees	positioning	social meaning
global advertising	external position	integrated marketing
international advertising	internal position	communications (IMC)

ENDNOTES

1. Jake Gaskill, "In-Game Advertising Spending to Hit $1 Billion in 2014," *G4TV*, May 26, 2009, http://g4tv.com/thefeed/blog/post/695860/in-game-advertising-spending-to-hit-1-billion-in-2014.html.

2. "Social Media Facts," U.S. Net Mobile Ad Revenue, *Advertising Age*, September 17, 2012, Special Insert.

3. Question of the Week, Ad Infinitum, *BusinessWeek*, November 20, 2006, 18.

4. Jean Halliday, "Audi Taps Ad Whiz to Direct Branding," *Advertising Age*, May 8, 2006, 4, 88.

5. Cotten Timberlake, "Is That a New Ring? Who Are You Wearing?" *Bloomberg News*, December 10, 2012, www.bloomberg.com, accessed December 15, 2012.

6. 2011 Facebook User Demographics and Statistics, iStrategylabs Report, posted January 3, 2011, at iStrategylabs.com.

7. Michael Learmonth, "In Bid to Go Global, Cadillac Shifts Advertising Dollars to Digital," *Adage.com*, October 25, 2012.

8. Lee Peterson, "As Your Brand Ages, Don't Drift into a Vague Oblivion," *Advertising Age*, October 15, 2012, 28.

9. U.S. Census Bureau FactFinder, "Population of the United States 2011," http://factfinder2.census.gov, accessed online November 24, 2012.

10. Natalie Zmuda, "IBM Uses U.S. Open to Debut TV Ads Targeting CMOs," AdAge.com, August 27, 2012, accessed November 28, 2012.

11. This definition of marketing was approved in 1995 by the American Marketing Association (http://www.marketingpower.com) and remains the official definition offered by the organization.

12. Jeremy Mullman, "Under Armour Can't Live Up to Own Hype," *Advertising Age*, November 2, 2009, 3, 51.

13. Peter D. Bennett, *Dictionary of Marketing Terms*, 2nd ed. (Chicago: American Marketing Association, 1995), 4.

14. Data drawn from "Best Global Brands 2012," Interbrand, www.Interbrand.com, accessed November 24, 2012.

15. Michael Myser, "Marketing Made Easy," *Business 2.0*, June 2006, 43–45.

16. Jack Neff, "Snuggie," *Advertising Age*, November 16, 2009, 25.

17. Douglas W. Vorhies, "Brand Extension Helps Parent Gain Influence," *Marketing News*, January 20, 2003, 25. This concept was verified in academic research as well. See Franziska Volckner and Henrik Sattler, "Drivers of Brand Extension Success," *Journal of Marketing*, vol. 70 (April 2006), 18–34.

18. David A. Aaker, *Managing Brand Equity* (New York: The Free Press, 1991), 15.

19. Kevin L. Keller, "Conceptualizing, Measuring, and Managing Customer-Based Brand Equity," *Journal of Marketing*, vol. 57 (January 1993), 4.

20. Streedhar Madhavaram, Vishag Badrinarayanan, and Robert E. McDonald, "Integrated Marketing Communication (IMC) and Brand Identity as Critical Components of Brand Equity Strategy," *Journal of Advertising*, vol. 34, no. 4 (Winter 2005), 69–80.

21. Stephanie Thompson, "Kraft Counters Unilever Launch," *Advertising Age*, August 25, 2003, 4.

22. Beth Snyder Bulik, "Microsoft Spends $1B on Operating-System Launch, but Are Ads Windows-Washing?" *Advertising Age*, October 23, 2012, 10.

23. Beth Snyder Bulik, "The Company You Keep," *Sales & Marketing Management*, November 2003, 14.

24. Franziska Volckner and Henrik Sattler, "Drivers of Brand Extension Success," *Journal of Marketing*, vol. 70 (April 2006), 18–34.

25. E.J. Schultz, "How We Eat," *Advertising Age*, November 12, 2012, 30–33.

26. Paul Kaihla, "Sexing Up a Piece of Meat," *Business 2.0*, April 2006, 72–76.

27. E.J. Schultz, "How Kmart Lost the Attention of Discount Shoppers," *Advertising Age*, March 19, 2012, 8.

28. Laura Ries, "Repositioning 'Positioning': The Best Way into a Consumer's Mind Is Not with Verbal Nails, but with a Visual Hammer," *Advertising Age*, March 12, 2012, 12–13.

29. Peter F. Drucker, *People and Performance: The Best of Peter Drucker* (New York: HarperCollins, 1997), 90.

30. The research study is reported in Robert G. Docters, Michael R. Reopel, Jeanne-Mey Sun, and Stephen M. Tanney, *Winning the Profit Game: Smarter Pricing, Smarter Branding* (New York: McGraw-Hill, 2004); information on Louis Vuitton was taken from Carol Matlack et al., "The Vuitton Machine," *BusinessWeek*, March 22, 2004, 98–102.

31. "Got Results?" *Marketing News*, March 2, 1998, 1; current data obtained from ProCon.org, http://milk.procon.org/viewresource.asp?resourceID=660#Introduction, accessed November 25, 2012.

32. Ian Berry and Kelsey Gee, "The U.S. Milk Business Is in 'Crisis,'" *Wall Street Journal*, December 11, 2012, B1.

33. For excellent summaries of decades of research on the topic of primary demand stimulation, see Mark S. Abion and Paul W. Farris, *The Advertising Controversy: Evidence of the Economic Effects of Advertising* (Boston: Auburn House, 1981); and J. C. Luik and M. S. Waterson, *Advertising and Markets* (Oxfordshire, England: NTC Publications, 1996).

34. Ian Berry and Kelsey Gee, "The U.S. Milk Business Is in 'Crisis,'" *Wall Street Journal*, December 11, 2012, B1.

35. Kerry Capell, "How Philips Got Brand Buzz," *BusinessWeek.com*, July 31, 2006, http://yahoo.businessweek.com, accessed August 1, 2006.

36. There are several highly sophisticated historical treatments of how advertising is related to demand and overall GDP. See, for example, Neil H. Borden, *The Economic Effects of Advertising* (Chicago: Richard D. Irwin, 1942), 187–189; and John Kenneth Galbraith, *The New Industrial State* (Boston: Houghton Mifflin, 1967), 203–207.

37. "100 Leading National Advertisers," *Advertising Age*, June 28, 2012, 4–14.

38. For a historical perspective on culture, consumers, and the meaning of goods, see Ernest Ditcher, *Handbook of Consumer Motivations* (New York: McGraw-Hill, 1964), 6. For a contemporary view, see David Glen Mick and Claus Buhl, "A Meaning-Based Model of Advertising Experiences," *Journal of Consumer Research*, vol. 19 (December 1992), 312–338.

CHAPTER 2

The Structure of the Advertising and Promotion Industry: Advertisers, Agencies, Media, and Support Organizations

After reading and thinking about this chapter, you will be able to do the following:

① Discuss important trends transforming the advertising and promotion industry.

② Describe the advertising and promotion industry's size, structure, and participants.

③ Discuss the role played by advertising and promotion agencies, the services provided by these agencies, and how the agencies are compensated.

④ Identify key external facilitators who assist in planning and executing advertising and integrated brand promotion campaigns.

⑤ Discuss the role played by media organizations in executing effective advertising and integrated brand promotion campaigns.

2-1 THE ADVERTISING INDUSTRY IN CONSTANT TRANSITION

There have always been power struggles in the advertising and promotion industry: brand versus brand, one agency against another agency, agency versus media company, big advertiser with lots of money versus big retailer with lots of money. But those old-style power struggles were child's play compared with the 21st-century power struggle going on now. Estimates put the number of ads the average consumer encounters in a single day at somewhere between 1,000 and 5,000![1] Guess what? Consumers are tired of the barrage of ads and are looking for ways to avoid most of them. So, the big power struggle now is about how the advertising industry can successfully adapt to the new technologies that consumers are willing and, in many cases, eager to use as they seek more control over their information environment. Stated more directly, how

can the ad industry overcome the fact that none of us is really eager to have a 30-second television ad interrupt a television program we are really enjoying? Or have our magazines be 30 percent advertising, which disrupts the flow of our reading and enjoyment? The solution, in part, seems to be that advertisers will continue in the "digital divide." That is, dividing their total advertising spending more into digital media—Web advertising, social media, and mobile marketing—and continue to move away from traditional mass media like television, newspapers, magazines, and radio.

The reason for the digital divide is that consumers, who as we saw in Chapter 1 are the primary target of most advertising and promotion, are discovering digital technologies and media options that give them more control over the communications they see and hear. From Facebook to Twitter to millions of individual blogs and specialty websites, consumers are seeking out information environments, digital information access, where *they* control their exposure to information rather than an advertiser or media company being in control. The effects are widespread. Advertising in traditional media plunged by nearly 15 percent back in 2009 with 77 percent of advertisers surveyed saying they shifted more than 70 percent of their savings from traditional media to digital alternatives—social network media and online advertising.[2] That digital switch seems to have been sustained since today about 21 percent of media spending by advertisers in the United States is directed to Internet media including display ads, paid search, podcasts, social media ads, and mobile marketing. Analysts expect that percentage to rise to 36 percent of media spending by 2016.[3]

We are all living the new technology reality—but how did it used to work? The old system worked like this: An advertiser, like Nike or Hewlett-Packard, would work with an advertising agency, like Leo Burnett or Omnicom, and think of really creative television, radio, newspaper, magazine, or billboard ads. Then, the advertiser and its agency would work with a media company, like NBC television or Hearst newspapers, and buy time or space to place the ad so that you, as the consumer, would see it when you watched television or read your morning newspaper. Don't get us wrong, this still happens—a lot. Major media like television, radio, and magazines still rake in about $300 billion worldwide in a year, and individual media companies like Hearst Corp. generate several billion dollars annually in revenue.[4] But much has changed about the way advertisers, agencies, and media companies are trying to reach control-seeking consumers. And some very smart people think that we are truly heading into a totally new age with the industry on the cusp of even more dramatic changes.[5] As Michael Mendenhall, chief marketing officer at Hewlett-Packard, put it, "Marketers want to move from interruptive to engagement. They can do that more effectively in the digital space."[6] By that, Mendenhall means that digital media allow interaction between consumer and advertiser where traditional media have not and cannot.

Let's explore what's going on in the structure of the industry in some greater detail. First, from the consumer side. With the large number of digital media options available for news, information, and entertainment, "media fragmentation" is a boon to consumers and a huge headache for advertisers and their advertising agencies. The new "control seeking" generation of consumers is behaving very differently from the cable-TV generation that preceded it. Today's consumers are insisting on the convenience and appeal (and control) of their PC, smartphone, iPad, and DVR. There is some large degree of irony in the control that consumers are starting to exert, however. Even though the traditional

structure of the advertising and media industry may be changed forever, the *goal* of that old traditional structure has not changed—the brand still needs to be highlighted with persuasive communications. In fact, the change in consumer orientation will make product branding even *more* important as consumers choose what persuasive messages they want to be exposed to and where they want to see them.

Change in the advertising industry is nothing new, as the following section highlights. But the pace of change and the complexity of the change are more challenging than any the industry has ever faced. We'll spend our time in this chapter considering the structure in the industry and all the "players" that are creating and being affected by change. This chapter also highlights how the industry and its structure is changing now and has changed over time. While we consider the change and its effects, we need to keep in mind that the fundamental *process* of advertising and the role it plays in organizations remains steadfastly the same: persuasive communications directed at target audiences—no matter what is happening with technology, economic conditions, society, or business philosophies. The underlying role and purpose of advertising and promotion has not changed and will not change.

The section that follows highlights trends affecting change. Then, we will turn our attention to understanding how advertising and other promotional tools are managed in the communications industry. Along the way, we'll consider all the different participants in the process, particularly the advertisers and their advertising and promotion agencies.

LO ❶

2-2 TRENDS AFFECTING THE ADVERTISING AND PROMOTION INDUSTRY

The following are trends affecting the advertising and promotion industry. Many have to do with new technologies and how their application has changed the structure and the very nature of the way communications occur. Others have to do with consumer culture and what sort of communication makes sense to the modern consumer. But in the end, what is important is the critical need to focus on the brand, its image, and a persuasive, integrated presentation of that brand to the target market.

To understand the change that is affecting the advertising and promotion industry and the use of promotional tools, let's consider five broad trends in the marketplace.

2-2a Consumer Control: From Social Media to Blogs to DVRs

Yep, top of the list. As we have highlighted so far, consumer control is at the top of the list of trends affecting the advertising and promotion industry. As featured at the outset of the chapter, consumers are now in greater control of the information they receive about product categories and the brands within those categories. Collectively, individuals' sharing and creating content through blogs, social media, wikis, and video sites like YouTube are referred to as Web 2.0—the second generation of Web-based use and services that emphasize online collaboration and sharing among users; Web 3.0 is just around the corner, where computers and tablets will understand and interpret information from the Web as quickly and correctly as humans can.

The simplest and most obvious example of Web 2.0 is when consumers log on to the Internet and visit sites *they* choose to visit for either information or shopping. But it gets a lot more complicated from there. **Social media,** those highly accessible Web-based media that allow the sharing of information between individuals and between individuals and groups (like Facebook and Yelp), have emerged as the most significant form of consumer control over information creation and communication. You will examine the breadth and intensity of use of social media in Chapter 14—"Media Planning: Advertising and IBP in Digital and Social Media," but for now it is important to have a perspective on the digital side of advertising and communications. Facebook has about 1 billion users worldwide sharing 100 billion connections collectively.[7] Twitter has more than 50 million users who post 8 billion tweets a year.[8] Honda launched a Facebook page in August of 2009 and three months later had 2 million friends on the site (see Exhibit 2.1) and currently has over 3 million "likes."[9] While firms are not *exactly* sure of the value and impact of engaging consumers through social media sites like Facebook, no firm wants to be absent from the social media scene. As such, firms are already spending nearly $2.2 billion on social media, and that number is expected to rise to nearly $5 billion by 2016.[10]

EXHIBIT 2.1   Firms of all types are trying to use social media effectively to engage and communicate with consumers. When Honda launched its Facebook page, the firm immediately had 2 million "friends" on the site and now has nearly 3 million "likes." Do you think having a social media presence affects consumers' attitudes toward a brand positively?

Another way consumers control their information is through blogs. **Blogs,** websites frequented by individuals with common interests where they can post facts, opinions, and personal experiences, have emerged as sophisticated (although typically not very objective) sources of product and brand information. Once criticized as the "ephemeral scribble" of 13-year-old girls and the babble of techno-geeks, blogs are gaining greater recognition and organization with two-thirds of U.S. Internet users reading blogs on a regular basis. Web-based service firms like Blogdrive and Blogger are making blogs easier to create, use, and make accessible to the masses. Advertisers should pay attention not only to the popularity of social media sites and blogs but also to the power of their communications. Research has shown that such "word of mouth" communication between consumers results in longer lasting impressions and greater new customer acquisition effects than traditional marketing efforts.[11]

As discussed earlier, another dramatic example of consumer control is the growth in use of digital video recorders (DVRs) like TiVo. Analysts expect that the use of DVRs could ultimately reduce ad viewership by as much as 30 percent. That translates into taking $100 billion out of U.S. advertising industry revenue. Currently, DVR usage stands at about 8 percent of all television viewing.[12]

Obviously, advertisers and their agencies are trying to adapt to the concept that consumers are gaining greater control over the information they choose to receive. How will they adapt? Creativity is one answer. The more entertaining and informative an ad is, the more likely consumers will want to actually watch the ad. Another technique, less creative but certainly effective, is to run advertising messages along the bottom of the programming. You know the ones we're talking about—those annoying, jumpy little messages in the lower right- or lower left-hand corner of your screen. This way, even the ad-skipping DVR users have to see messages since they are embedded in the broadcast.

2-2b Media Proliferation, Consolidation, and "Multiplatform" Media Organizations

At another level of the industry, the media level, proliferation and consolidation have been taking place simultaneously. The proliferation of cable television channels, direct marketing technology, Web options, and alternative new media (mobile marketing, for example) have caused a visible proliferation of media options. Diversity of media options and the advertising dollars they can attract has always been a driving force for many media companies

(see Insights Online [Exhibit 2.2] for an interesting example).

Media companies of all types tend to pursue more and more "properties" if they are allowed to legally, thus creating what are now referred to as "multiplatform" media organizations.[13] The ultimate multiplatform may be Walt Disney Co., which owns the ABC broadcasting network and the ESPN cable network group, plus multiple other cable stations, 15 radio stations, a couple of dozen websites, eight podcasting operations, video on demand, books, and magazines—you name it, Disney uses it to reach audiences and generates $40 billion in worldwide revenue.[14]

Not to be outdone, the Web has its own media conglomerates. InterActiveCorp (IAC) has amassed a media empire of Internet sites that are as diverse as they are successful. IAC is an Internet conglomerate with a grab bag of online offerings, including search engine Ask.com, online dating service Match.com, and various Internet start-ups and smaller properties. Together, these sites generate about $2 billion in worldwide revenue. Other Internet merchants like Google are even bigger at about $37 billion in worldwide revenue and even more diversified with all sorts of search (Chrome), entertainment (YouTube), and service sites (like Blogger mentioned earlier). One commercial service offered by Google is DoubleClick, which provides advertisers and agencies services designed to simplify complex online campaigns using a proprietary digital ad management platform (see Exhibit 2.3).

The point is that media companies, in an effort to effectively "cover all the bases" in reaching audiences, have been wheeling and dealing during the last decade to engage consumers in as many ways as possible, from traditional media—broadcast television, newspapers, radio, and magazines—to cable and satellite broadcast and all forms of Internet-based and mobile communication.

2-2c Media Clutter and Fragmentation Means More IBP

Even though the media and agency levels of the industry may be consolidating into fewer and fewer large firms, this does not mean that there are fewer media options. Quite the contrary is true. There are *more* ways to try to reach consumers than ever before. In 1994,

EXHIBIT 2.3 Media proliferation and fragmentation, caused mostly by new technologies, has given rise to specialized media organizations. Double Click, now part of the Google organization, specializes in digital marketing and advertising solutions as well as tracking services.

Miller Lite chairs by game day. The chairs were a tie-in with a national advertising campaign that began during the regular season before the Super Bowl.

Given the backlash against advertising that clutter can cause, advertisers and their agencies are rethinking the way they try to communicate with consumers. Fundamentally, there is a greater focus on integrating more tools within the overall promotional effort in an attempt to reach more consumers in more different ways. This approach by advertisers is wreaking havoc on traditional media expenditures. Starting several years ago, Johnson & Johnson began shifting $250 million in spending from traditional media—television, magazines, newspapers—to "digital media," including the Internet and blogs.[15]

Advertisers are shifting spending out of traditional media and are looking to the full complement of promotional opportunities in sales promotions (like the Miller chairs), event sponsorships, new media options, and public relations as means to support and enhance the primary advertising effort for brands. In fact, some advertisers are enlisting the help of Hollywood talent agencies in an effort to get their brands featured in television programs and films. The payoff for strategic placement in a film or television show can be huge. Getting Coca-Cola cups placed on the desk in front of the judges on *American Idol* is estimated to be worth up to $20 million in traditional media advertising.[16] This strategy of placing brands with television shows, movies, and video games is covered in Chapter 16 when we consider branded entertainment (advertainment) in detail.

the consumer had access to about 27 television channels. Today, the average U.S. household has access to more than 100 channels. In 1995, it took three well-placed TV spots to reach 80 percent of women television viewers! Today, it takes multiple times more spots across a variety of media to achieve the same effect. From television ads to virtual billboards to banner ads on the Internet to podcasts of advertising messages, new and increased media options have resulted in so much clutter that the probability of any one advertisement breaking through and making a real difference continues to diminish. Advertisers are developing a lack of faith in advertising alone, so promotion options such as online communication, brand placement in film and television, point-of-purchase displays, and sponsorships are more attractive to advertisers. For example, advertisers on the Super Bowl, notorious for its clutter and outrageous ad prices (about $2.5 million to $3 million for a 30-second spot), have turned instead to promotional tie-ins to enhance the effect of the advertising. To combat the clutter and expense at one Super Bowl, Miller Brewing distributed thousands of inflatable

2-2d **Crowdsourcing**

Crowdsourcing (and the related concept of user-generated content) is a fairly simple concept. **Crowdsourcing** involves the online distribution of certain tasks to groups (crowds) of experts, enthusiasts, or even consumers.[17] Dell launched the "Idea Storm" website to solicit computing ideas from the public. Starbucks' "MyStarbucksIdea" asks Starbucks customers to recommend new products and services for Starbucks' outlets. The idea behind crowdsourcing is to get consumers more involved with and committed to a brand in a way that passive, intrusive advertising simply cannot. Consumers help "build the brand" with recommendations for features or even advertising campaign images. They also can communicate about the brand to audiences in ways that seem natural and credible—something corporate-launched advertising struggles with. Consider the elaborate crowdsourcing effort conceived by Visa International. As part of Visa's promotional effort at the 2012 London Olympic Games, the firm's ad agencies came up with the idea of "Cheer" as

EXHIBIT 2.4 Visa uses multiple campaign themes. Visa used a crowdsourcing strategy during the 2012 London Olympics to cheer on the athletes. Crowdsourcing is the process of gathering feedback from consumers—through social media sites—and incorporating that feedback into a firm's marketing strategy.

navigation devices (known as PNDs or GPS systems) can also accommodate messages in the wireless world. But when advertisers send messages to these sorts of mobile devices, it flies directly in the face of consumers' desire for information control. The process of mobile marketing and mobile media is relatively simple. Since all these mobile devices have wireless capability, advertisers can negotiate ways of including brand messages that will show up on the devices. The obvious opportunity is to send ads directly to the devices—likely to meet with harsh reaction from consumers. But other, more subtle opportunities exist. Advertisers could sponsor content and apps on e-readers. Another would be embedding brand visuals in the rich multimedia content that tablets are capable of receiving.[19] But analysts offer the perhaps obvious caution to advertisers: "But it's not, 'What's the available media I can buy?' It's thinking about how consumers are behaving and what role do devices play in the way they behave."[20] So far, consumers don't seem too put off. AdMob, the firm that serves up graphical banner and text link ads for mobile devices, is seeing *billions* of ad requests a month! Advertisers are eager to jump on board. Spending on mobile marketing is expected to grow to more than $20 billion annually by 2016—second only to spending on display advertising (Web ads) and search marketing in the interactive marketing category.[21]

For decades to come, these trends and the changes they bring about will force advertisers to think differently about advertising and IBP. Similarly, advertising agencies will need to think about the way they serve their clients and the way communications are delivered to audiences. As you have read, big spenders such as Procter & Gamble, Starbucks, Miller Brewing, and Visa are already demanding new and innovative programs to enhance the impact of their advertising and promotional dollars. The goal of creating persuasive communication remains intact—attract attention and develop preference for a brand—and so the dynamics of the communications environment just discussed all directly impact that overall goal.

a central campaign theme (see Exhibit 2.4). As part of the "online cheer" effort, fans were asked to upload a text, photo, or video cheer they created for the athletes. Visa's Facebook page served as the global hub for the collection of consumer-submitted cheers and athletes' responses, as well as behind-the-scenes videos of the athletes' stories and training. Fans could also submit "one-click cheers" online or via mobile on social media including YouTube or through partner sites such as Yahoo! and Sports Illustrated.[18]

2-2e **Mobile Marketing/Mobile Media**

Of the trends affecting the advertising and promotion industry, mobile media may turn out to be the biggest—or at least the most relevant. It all depends on consumer reaction. Technology has resulted in significant opportunity for advertisers to reach consumers with messages directed to consumers' mobile devices—primarily smartphones and tablets like Apple's iPad and Microsoft's Surface—but personal

LO 2

2-3 **THE SCOPE AND STRUCTURE OF THE ADVERTISING AND PROMOTION INDUSTRY**

To fully appreciate the structure of the advertising and promotion industry, let's first consider the absolute size. The advertising industry is huge: nearly $400 billion is spent annually in the United States alone on various categories of advertising, with nearly $600 billion spent worldwide. Spending on other forms of IBP is no less impressive. Spending on all forms of IBP worldwide, including advertising, exceeds a trillion dollars a year.[22]

Another perspective on the scope of advertising and promotion is the amount spent on advertising by individual firms. Exhibit 2.5 shows spending for 2011 and 2010 among the top 20 U.S. advertisers. Hundreds of millions of dollars a year and, in the case of the largest spenders, billions of dollars a year is truly a huge amount of money to spend on advertising. But we have to realize that the $3.05 billion spent by General Motors on advertising was only about 2.6 percent of GM's sales. Similarly, Procter & Gamble spent about $4.9 billion, but this amount represented only about 6 percent of its sales. So even though the absolute dollars seem huge, the relative spending is often much more modest. Also note that among the top 20 spenders in Exhibit 2.5, six showed a *decrease* in ad spending.

2-3a Structure of the Advertising and Promotion Industry

Beyond the scope of spending, the *structure* of the industry is really the key issue. When we understand the structure of the advertising and promotion industry, we know *who* does *what, in what order,* during the process. The industry is actually a collection of a wide range of talented people, all of whom have special expertise and perform a wide variety of tasks in planning, preparing, and placing of advertising. Exhibit 2.6 shows the structure of the advertising and promotion industry by showing who the different participants are in the process.

Exhibit 2.6 demonstrates that *advertisers* (such as Kellogg) can employ the services of *agencies* (such as Grey Group) that may (or may not) contract for specialized services with various *external facilitators* (such as Simmons Market Research Bureau), which results in advertising and promotion being directed with the help of various *media organizations* (such as the TBS cable network and Google) to one or more *target audiences* (like you!).

Note the dashed line on the left side of Exhibit 2.6. This line indicates that advertisers do not always need to employ the services of agencies. Nor do advertisers or agencies always seek the services of external facilitators. Some advertisers deal directly with media organizations and Internet portals for placement of their advertisements or implementation of their promotions. This happens either when an advertiser has an internal advertising/promotions department that prepares all the materials for the process, or when media organizations (especially radio, television, and newspapers) provide technical assistance in the preparation of materials. The new interactive and mobile media formats also provide advertisers the opportunity to work directly with entertainment programming firms, such as Walt Disney, Sony, and LiveNation, to provide integrated programming that features brand placements in films and television programs or at entertainment events. And, as you will see, many of the new media agencies provide the creative and technical assistance advertisers need to implement campaigns through new media (However, see Insights Online [Exhibit 2.7] for another perspective on social media).

Each level in the structure of the industry is complex. So let's take a look at each level, with particular emphasis on the nature and activities of agencies. When you need to devise advertising or a fully integrated brand promotion,

EXHIBIT 2.5 The 20 Largest Advertisers in the United States in 2011 (U.S. dollars in millions)

Marketer	Total U.S. Ad Spending		
	2011	2010	% Change
Procter & Gamble	$4,971.5	$4,710.1	5.6%
General Motors	3,055.7	2,746.3	11.3
Verizon Communications	2,523.0	2,451.0	2.9
Comcast Corp.	2,465.4	2,156.2	14.3
AT&T	2,359.0	2,989.0	−21.1
JP Morgan Chase & Co.	2,351.8	1,923.0	22.3
Ford Motor Co.	2,141.3	1,914.9	11.8
American Express Co.	2,125.3	2,259.8	−6.0
L'Oreal	2,124.6	1,978.8	7.4
Walt Disney Co.	2,112.2	1,931.7	9.3
Pfizer	2,071.7	2,146.4	−3.5
Time Warner	2,050.9	2,044.3	0.3
Johnson & Johnson	1,939.6	2,026.5	−4.3
Walmart Stores	1,890.9	2,055.3	−8.0
Fiat (Chrysler Group)	1,770.9	1,164.0	52.1
Toyota Motor Co.	1,727.6	1,721.7	0.3
Bank of America Corp.	1,704.6	1,552.6	9.8
Sears Holding Co.	1,688.2	1,806.2	−6.5
Target Corp.	1,616.0	1,508.0	7.2
Macy's	1,507.0	1,417.0	6.4

Adapted from *Advertising Age*, Data Center (adage.com/datacenter "100 Leading National Advertisers."

EXHIBIT 2.6 The structure of the advertising and promotion industry and participants in the process.

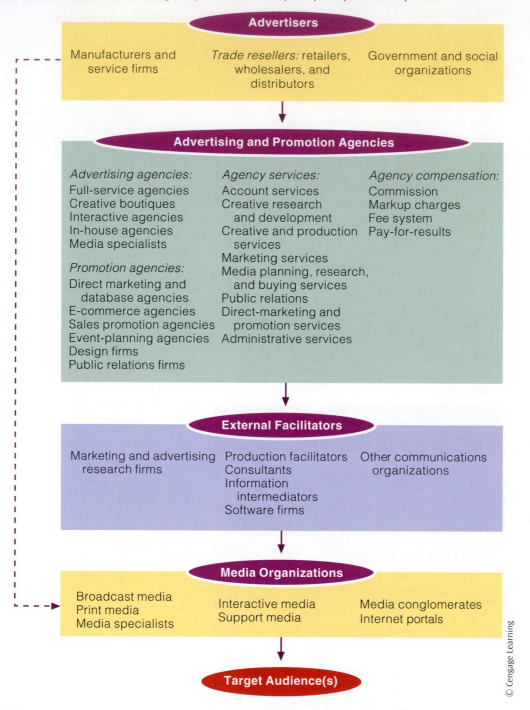

© Cengage Learning

INSIGHTS ONLINE

2.7 Go online to see the AdAge feature, "Twitter as a Platform for Consumer Complaints."

no source will be more valuable than the advertising or promotion agency with which you work. Advertising and promotion agencies provide the essential creative firepower to the process and represent a critical link in the structure.

2-3b **Advertisers**

First in the structure of advertising are the advertisers themselves. From your local pet store to multinational corporations, organizations of all types and sizes seek to benefit from the effects of advertising. **Advertisers** are business, not-for-profit, and government organizations that use advertising and other promotional techniques to communicate with target markets and to stimulate awareness and demand for their brands. Advertisers are also referred to as **clients** by their advertising and promotion agency partners. Different types of advertisers use advertising and promotion somewhat differently, depending on the type of product or service they market. The following categories describe the different types of advertisers and the role advertising plays for them.

Manufacturers and Service Firms. Large national manufacturers of consumer products and services are the most prominent users of advertising and promotion, often spending billions of dollars annually. Procter & Gamble, General Foods, Verizon, and Anheuser-Busch InBev all have national or global markets for their products and services. The use of advertising, particularly mass media advertising, by these firms is essential to creating awareness and preference for their brands. But advertising is useful not to just national or multinational firms; regional and local producers of household goods and services also rely heavily on advertising. For example, regional dairy companies sell milk, cheese, and other dairy products in regions usually comprising a few states. These firms often use ads placed in newspapers and regional editions of magazines. Further, couponing and sampling are ways to communicate with target markets using the tools of IBP that are well suited to regional application. Some breweries and wineries also serve only regional markets. Local producers of products are relatively rare, but local service organizations are common. Medical facilities, hair salons, restaurants, auto dealers, and arts organizations are examples of local service providers that use advertising to create awareness and stimulate demand. What car dealer in America has not advertised a holiday event or used a remote local radio broadcast to attract attention!

Trade Resellers. The term **trade reseller** is simply a general description for all organizations in the marketing channel of distribution that buy products to resell to customers. As Exhibit 2.6 shows, resellers can be retailers, wholesalers, or distributors. These resellers deal with both household consumers and business buyers at all geographic market levels.

Retailers that sell in national or global markets are the most visible reseller advertisers and promotion users. Walmart, The Gap, and McDonald's are examples of national and global retail companies that use various forms of IBP to communicate with customers. Regional retail chains, typically grocery chains such as Albertson's or department stores such as Dillard's serve multistate markets and use advertising suited to their regional customers. At the local level, small retail shops of all sorts rely on newspaper, radio, television, and

billboard advertising and special promotional events to reach a relatively small geographic area. The ad for a motorcycle shop in Exhibit 2.8 is designed to reach a local market extending no more than a couple hundred miles from the shop's location. This ad was placed in newspapers and local magazines.

Wholesalers and distributors, such as Ideal Supply, Inc. (a company that supplies contractors with blasting

EXHIBIT 2.8 Advertising and promotion are not reserved for just big companies with national or global markets like Microsoft or Kellogg's. Organizations that serve local and regional markets, like Rocky Mountain Choppers, can make effective use of adverting and promotion as well, as this magazine ad demonstrates.

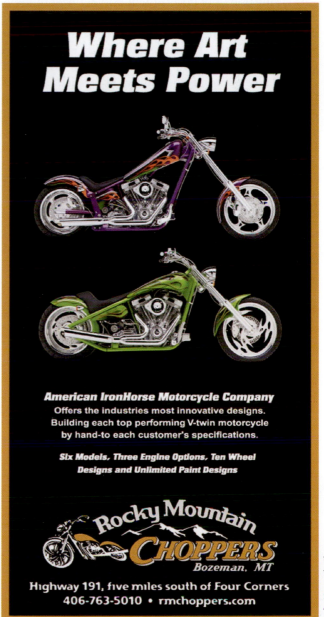

and surveying equipment), are a completely different breed of reseller. Technically, these types of companies deal only with business customers, since their position in the distribution channel dictates that they sell products either to producers (who buy goods to produce other goods) or to retailers (who resell goods to household consumers). Wholesalers and distributors have little need for mass media advertising over media such as television and radio. Rather, they use trade publications, directory advertising such as the Yellow Pages and trade directories, direct mail, personal selling, and their Internet websites as their main advertising media.

Federal, State, and Local Governments. At first, you might think it is odd to include governments as advertising users, but government bodies invest millions of dollars in advertising annually. The U.S. government often ranks as one of the 100 largest spenders on advertising in the United States, with expenditures typically in the range of $1 billion annually.[23] And that's just on advertising. If you add in other IBP expenses like brochures, recruiting fairs, and the personal selling expense of recruiting offices, the U.S. government easily spends more than $2 billion annually. The federal government's spending on advertising and promotion is concentrated in two areas: armed forces recruiting and social issues. As an example, the U.S. government regularly uses broad-based advertising campaigns for military recruiting.[24] The U.S. Army's "Army Strong" campaign uses television, magazine, newspapers, and interactive games ("America's Army") hosted at the army recruiting website (http://www.goarmy.com).

Social and Not-for-Profit Organizations. Advertising by social organizations at the national, state, and local level is common. The Nature Conservancy, United Way, American Red Cross, and art organizations use advertising to raise awareness of their organizations, seek donations, and attempt to shape behavior (deter drug use or encourage breast self-examinations, for example). Organizations such as these use both the mass media and direct mail to promote their causes and services. Exhibit 2.9 shows an ad for the American Red Cross urging people take a personal approach to emergency preparedness. Organizations like the Red Cross serve large and diverse segments of people, so using advertising is an effective way to reach these segments with important messages. But also note in Exhibit 2.9 that the Red Cross is not just relaying a message, the organization is also prominently featuring its logo as a way to promote the Red Cross brand.

Aside from big national organizations like the Red Cross, every state has its own unique statewide organizations, such as Citizens against Hunger, a state arts council, a tourism office, an economic development office, or a historical society. Social organizations in local communities represent a variety of special interests, from computer clubs to fraternal organizations to neighborhood child care organizations. The advertising used by social organizations has the same fundamental purpose as the advertising carried out by major multinational corporations: to stimulate demand and disseminate information. While big multinationals might use national or even global advertising, local organizations rely on advertising through local media

EXHIBIT 2.9 Government, social, and not-for-profit organizations can use advertising as effectively as corporations. Here the American Red Cross is using advertising to communicate to families the importance of having a "family disaster plan" in case of a fire or other catastrophe. Note how the American Red Cross is highlighting its logo in this ad as a way of developing "brand" recognition—just like corporations do!

American Red Cross

and local events and promotions to reach local audiences.

Do all these advertisers sound familiar? They should. Remember from Chapter 1 that we discussed these types of advertisers as distinct "audiences." We need to realize that firms can be targets for advertising as well as advertisers themselves.

2-3c The Role of the Advertiser in IBP

Very few of the advertisers just discussed have the employees or the financial resources to strategically plan and then totally prepare effective advertising and IBP programs. This is where advertising and promotion agencies play such an important role in the structure of the advertising industry. But there is an important role played by the advertiser *before* the services of an agency are enlisted. Advertisers of all sizes and types, as just discussed, have to be prepared for their interaction with an agency in order for the agency to do *its* job effectively. That is, it is the advertiser's role to:

- Fully understand and describe the value that the firm's brand(s) provides to users.
- Fully understand and describe the brand's position in the market relative to competitive brands.
- Describe the firm's objectives for the brand in the near term and long term (e.g., brand extensions, international market launches).
- Identify the target market(s) that are most likely to respond favorably to the brand.
- Identify and manage the supply chain/distribution system that will most effectively reach the target markets.
- Be committed to using advertising and other promotional tools as part of the organization's overall marketing strategy to grow the brand.

Once an advertiser has done its job with respect to the six factors above, then and *only* then is it time to enlist the services of an agency to help effectively and creatively develop the market for the brand. This is not to say that an agency will not work with an advertiser to help better define and refine these factors. Rather, it is a mistake for an advertiser to enter a relationship with an agency (of any type) without first doing its homework and being prepared for a productive partnership.

> *The advertising used by social organizations has the same fundamental purpose as the advertising carried out by major multinational corporations: to stimulate demand and disseminate information.*

2-3d Advertising and Promotion Agencies

Advertisers are fortunate to have a full complement of agencies that specialize in literally every detail of advertising and promotion. Let's take a closer look at the types of agencies advertisers can rely on to help create their advertising and IBP campaigns.

Advertising Agencies. Most advertisers choose to enlist the services of an advertising agency. An **advertising agency** is an organization of professionals who provide creative and business services to clients in planning, preparing, and placing advertisements. The reason so many firms rely on advertising agencies is that agencies house a collection of professionals with very specialized talent, experience, and expertise that simply cannot be matched by in-house talent.

Most big cities and even small towns in the United States have advertising agencies. Advertising agencies often are global businesses as well. As discussed in the section on trends affecting the advertising industry, megamergers between agencies have been occurring for several years. Exhibit 2.10 shows the world's 10 largest advertising organizations and their worldwide gross income. Worldwide revenue for U.S.-based advertising and marketing communications agencies reached $33.2 billion in 2011.[25]

It should be noted that one of the biggest events in the history of advertising agencies began to evolve on July 27, 2013. On that date, the world's second largest agency, Omnicom, and the world's third largest agency, Publicis, announced a merger that would create the largest advertising agency in the world. Combined, the two agencies would have revenues exceeding $22 billion and over 130,000 employees.[26] The new firm will be known as Publicis Omnicom. While a merger like this certainly has to do with economies of scale and the goal of pursuing increased efficiency, the investor presentation by the agencies cited the "explosion of big data, analytics and insights" as the strategic rationale for the megamerger.[27] This means that the vast amounts of data being generated by tracking Web traffic and social media interactions is motivating companies to combine resources so that they themselves can be "big enough" to handle the data that is available in developing and then tracking campaigns for clients. As of the announcement

EXHIBIT 2.10 The world's top 10 advertising organizations (ranked by worldwide gross revenue, U.S. dollars in millions).

Rank		Agency	Headquarters	Worldwide Revenue			U.S. Revenue			Revenue Outside the U.S.		
2011	2010			2011	2010	% CHG	2011	2010	% CHG	2011	2010	% CHG
1	1	WPP	Dublin	$16,053	$14,416	11.4	$5,046	$4,786	5.4	$11,008	$9,630	14.3
2	2	Omnicom Group	New York	13,873	12,543	10.6	7,049	6,683	5.5	6,824	5,859	16.5
3	3	Publicis Groupe	Paris	8,086	7,175	12.7	3,783	3,451	9.6	4,303	3,724	15.5
4	4	Interpublic Group of Cos.	New York	7,015	6,507	7.8	3,888	3,710	4.8	3,127	2,797	11.8
5	5	Dentsu Inc.	Tokyo	4,067	3,600	13.0	316	232	36.3	3,750	3,368	11.4
6	6	Havas	Puteaux, France	2,291	2,069	10.7	724	676	7.2	1,567	1,393	12.5
7	7	Hakuhodo DY Holdings	Tokyo	1,934	1,674	15.5	NA	NA	NA	1,934	1,674	15.5
8	8	Aegis Group	London	1,821	1,455	25.1	252	198	27.3	1,569	1,257	24.8
9	10	MDC Partners	New York	943	689	36.9	758	574	32.1	185	115	60.8
10	11	Alliance Data Systems Corp.'s Epsilon	Plano, Texas	847	613	38.1	782	550	42.2	66	64	2.6

Adapted from "The World's 50 Largest Agency Companies," *Advertising Age*, adage.com/datacenter, accessed December 15, 2012.

date, the merger still had multiple regulatory hurdles to navigate before getting final approval.

The types of agency professionals who help advertisers in the planning, preparation, and placement of advertising and other promotional activities include the following:

Account planners	Creative directors
Marketing specialists	Sales promotion and event planners
Account executives	Copywriters
Media buyers	Direct marketing specialists
Art directors	Radio and television producers
Graphic designers	Web developers
Lead account planners	Researchers
Chief executive officers (CEOs)	Interactive media planners
Chief financial officers (CFOs)	Artists
Chief technology officers (CTOs)	Social media experts
Chief marketing officers (CMO)	Public relations specialists

© Cengage Learning

As this list suggests, some advertising agencies can provide advertisers with a host of services, from campaign planning through creative concepts to interactive campaigns to measuring effectiveness. Also note from this list that an agency is indeed a business. Agencies have CEOs, CFOs, and CTOs just like any other business. Salaries in the positions listed above range from about several million a year for a big agency CEO (Barry Diller made $10 million in salary and stock options at InterActiveCorp in 2011!) to about $100,000 a year for an experienced media planner and over $200,000 for production directors.[28] Of course, those salaries change depending on whether you're in a big urban market or a small regional or local market.

Several different types of agencies are available to the advertiser. Be aware that there are all sorts of agencies with varying degrees of expertise and services. It is up to the advertiser to dig deep into an agency's background and determine which agency or set of multiple agencies will fulfill the advertiser's needs. A short description of the major different types of agencies follows.

Full-Service Agencies. A **full-service agency** typically includes an array of advertising professionals to meet all the promotional needs of clients. Often, such an agency will also offer a client global contacts and services. Omnicom Group and Dentsu are examples. Full-service agencies are not necessarily large organizations employing hundreds or even thousands of people. Smaller shops can be full service with just a few dozen employees and

serve big clients. Crispin Porter+Bogusky is a highly creative shop in Miami—not New York or Los Angeles—and has produced full-service, highly creative campaigns for VW, Burger King, and Mini USA.

Creative Boutiques. A **creative boutique** typically emphasizes creative concept development, copywriting, and artistic services to clients. An advertiser can employ this alternative for the strict purpose of infusing greater creativity into the message theme or individual advertisement. Advertisers find that boutique agencies can bring deep expertise in trying to reach special target segments. One such agency distinguishes itself by focusing on brands with U.S. manufacturing operations and another boutique specializes in older consumers.[29] Creative boutiques are idea factories. Some large global agencies such as McCann-Erickson Worldwide and Leo Burnett have set up creative-only project shops that mimic the services provided by creative boutiques, with mixed results. The truth is that as the advertising industry continues to evolve, the creative boutiques may become a casualty of expansion–contraction–expansion by the big global multiservice agencies. Be assured, there are still some great independent creative boutiques around, like Fusion Idea Lab (http://www.fusionidealab.com), which has provided the creative firepower for ads like the Bud Light series and Target stores.

The creative boutique's greatest advantage, niche expertise, may be its greatest liability as well. As firms search for IBP programs and make a commitment to IBP campaigns, the creative boutique may be an extra expense and step that advertisers simply don't feel they can afford. But, as you will learn in Chapter 9 on creativity and advertising, the creative effort is so valuable to effective brand building that creativity often rises to prominence in the process, and creative boutiques are well positioned to deliver that value.

Digital/Interactive Agencies. These agencies help advertisers prepare communications for new media such as the Internet, mobile marketing, and interactive television. **Digital/interactive agencies** focus on ways to use Web-based solutions for direct marketing and target market communications. Interactive agencies do work for BMW, Oracle, Nintendo, and the U.S. Army. Today, even a midsize full-service agency will offer digital and interactive services to clients. This being the case, many firms have consolidated all their IBP needs, including interactive media, with their main full-service agency. In fact, top digital agencies like Digitas and Organic are owned by large full-service agencies Publicis and Omnicom. That doesn't mean there are not hundreds of highly creative smaller shops like B-Reel and H-Res that produce leading-edge digital campaigns. Digital and interactive agencies have also taken over a wide range

INSIGHTS ONLINE

2.11 Go online to see the AdAge feature, "Google Uses Their Digital Platform to Help People Share Their New Year's Resolutions to an International Audience."

of e-commerce activities that formerly required specialized agency services. 24/7 real media used to specialize in e-commerce solutions and now provides a full range of services through digital/interactive programs and consulting (see Insights Online [Exhibit 2.11] for an interesting example).

An **in-house agency** is often referred to as the advertising department in a firm and takes responsibility for the planning and preparation of advertising materials. This option has the advantage of greater coordination and control in all phases of the advertising and promotion process. Some prominent advertisers who have done most of their work in-house are Benetton, Calvin Klein, and Revlon. There are some advantages of preparing advertising and IBP internally. The advertiser's own personnel have control over and knowledge of marketing activities, such as product development and distribution tactics that can provide unique insights into target markets. Another advantage is that the firm can essentially keep all commissions that an external agency would have earned. Even though the advantages of doing advertising work in-house are attractive, there are two severe limitations. First, there may be a lack of objectivity, thereby constraining the execution of all phases of the advertising process. Second, it is highly unlikely that an in-house agency could ever match the breadth and depth of talent available in an external agency.

Media Specialists. Although not technically agencies, **media specialists** are organizations that specialize in buying media time and space and offer media strategy consulting to advertising agencies and advertisers. The task of strategic coordination of media and promotional efforts has become more complex because of the proliferation of media options and extensive use of promotional tools beyond advertising. One additional advantage of using media specialists is that since they buy media in large quantities, they often acquire media time at a much lower cost than an agency or advertiser could. Also, media specialists often have time and space in inventory and can offer last-minute placement to advertisers. Media-buying services have been a part of the advertising industry structure for many years. In recent years, however, media planning has been added to the task of simply buying media space. At one point, Unilever, the Dutch consumer products conglomerate, decided to turn over its $575 million media-buying and planning tasks to a specialized agency, MindShare. Firms are finding that a media firm that buys the space can also provide keen insights into the media strategy as well.[30]

Promotion Agencies. Although advertisers often rely on an advertising agency as a steering organization for their promotional efforts, many specialized agencies often enter the process and are referred to as **promotion agencies.** This is because advertising agencies, even full-service agencies, will concentrate more on the advertising and often provide only a few key ancillary services for other promotional efforts. This is particularly true in the current era, in which new media are offering so many different ways to communicate to target markets. Promotion agencies can handle everything from sampling to event promotions to retail promotional tie-ins. But we also have to remember that consolidation is also a trend among agencies, so many full-service agencies do, in fact, provide specialized promotion services. Descriptions of different types of promotional agencies and their services follow.

Direct Marketing and Database Agencies. These agencies (sometimes also called **direct response agencies**) provide a variety of direct marketing services. **Direct marketing agencies** and **database agencies** maintain and manage large databases of mailing lists as one of their services. These firms can design direct marketing campaigns that use either (1) mail or telemarketing or (2) direct response campaigns using all forms of media. These agencies help advertisers construct databases of target customers, merge databases, develop promotional materials, and then execute the campaign. In many cases, these agencies maintain **fulfillment centers,** which ensure that customers receive the product ordered through direct mail.

Many of these agencies are set up to provide creative and production services to clients. These firms will design and help execute direct response advertising campaigns using traditional media such as radio, television, magazines, and newspapers. Also, some firms can prepare **infomercials** for clients: 5- to 60-minute information programs that promote a brand and offer direct purchase to viewers.

Sales Promotion Agencies. These specialists design and then operate contests, sweepstakes, special displays, or coupon campaigns for advertisers. It is important to recognize that these agencies can specialize in **consumer sales promotions** and will focus on price-off deals, coupons, sampling, rebates, and premiums. Other firms specialize in **trade-market sales promotions** designed to help advertisers use promotions aimed at wholesalers, retailers, vendors, and trade resellers. These agencies are experts in designing incentive programs, trade shows, sales force contests, in-store merchandising, and point-of-purchase materials.

Event-Planning Agencies. Event sponsorship can also be targeted to household consumers or the trade market. **Event-planning agencies** and organizers are experts in finding locations, securing dates, and putting together a team of people to pull off a promotional event: audio/visual people, caterers, security experts, entertainers, celebrity participants, or whoever is necessary to make the event come about successfully. The event-planning organization will also often take over the task of advertising the event and making sure the press provides coverage (publicity) of the event. When an advertiser sponsors an entire event, such as a PGA golf tournament, managers will work closely with the event-planning agencies. If an advertiser is just one of several sponsors of an event, such as a NASCAR race, then it has less control over planning and execution.

Design Firms. Designers and graphics specialists do not get nearly enough credit in the advertising and promotion process. If you take a job in advertising or promotion, your designer will be one of your first and most important partners. Even though designers are rarely involved in strategy planning, they are intimately involved in the execution of the advertising or IBP effort. In the most basic sense, **designers** help a firm create the visual impression of a firms advertising materials—particularly print, in-store display, or Web graphics. Designers are also enlisted to create a firm's **logo**—the graphic mark that identifies a company—and other visual representations that promote an identity for a firm. This mark will appear on everything from advertising to packaging to the company stationery, business cards, and signage (think Nike swoosh). But beyond the logo, graphic designers will also design most of the materials used in supportive communications such as the package design, coupons, in-store displays, brochures, outdoor banners for events, newsletters, and direct mail pieces. One of the largest consumer package goods firms in the world, Procter & Gamble, long ago made a large commitment to design across all aspects of its marketing and promotion, claiming that design was critical to "winning customers in the store with packaging and displays [being] major factors in the outcome (referring to consumer brand choice)."[31] Similarly, Pepsi created the position of Chief Design Officer to "build a design culture" in the organization spanning everything from packaging to visuals in the firms digital media advertising and promotion.[32]

Public Relations Firms. Public relations firms manage an organization's relationships with the media, the local community, competitors, industry associations, and government organizations. The tools of public relations include press releases, feature stories, lobbying, spokespersons, and company newsletters. Most advertisers do not like to handle their own public relations tasks for two reasons. First, public relations require highly specialized skills and talent not normally found within the company ranks. Second, managers are too close to public relations problems and may not be capable of handling a situation, particularly a negative situation, with measured public responses. For these reasons, advertisers,

and even advertising agencies, turn to outside public relations firms. In keeping with the movement to incorporate the Internet across all forms of promotion, there are even organizations that will handle putting all of a firm's news releases online. One such firm is PR Newswire (http://www.prnewswire.com).

In a search for more and distinctive visibility for their brands, advertisers have been turning to public relations firms and film companies to achieve a wide range of film and television placements. One film-making venture that began by sprinkling films with brands and brand images ultimately grew into a company that shot ads for brands such as Revlon and Activision.[33]

2-3e **Agency Services**

Advertising and promotion agencies offer a wide range of services. The advertiser may need a large, global, full-service advertising agency to plan, prepare, and execute its advertising and IBP campaigns. On the other hand, a creative boutique or digital/interactive agency may offer the right combination of specialized services. Similarly, a large promotion firm might be needed to manage events and retail promotions while a design firm is enlisted for design work, but nothing else. The most important issue, however, is for the advertiser and the agency to negotiate and reach an agreement on the services being provided before any agency is hired. Exhibit 2.12 shows one typical version of the organizational structure of a full-service advertising agency that also provides a significant number of IBP services.

But a word of caution needs to be issued here. Many agencies, large and small, have been flattened—literally and figuratively. In response to downturns in consumer spending and corporate revenues, advertisers have cut advertising and promotion budgets over the last five to seven years. In turn, many agencies have seen large, lucrative accounts shrink or disappear completely. BBDO Worldwide, a large and prestige global firm with 287 offices in 79 countries, had to completely shut down its Detroit, Michigan, office in the United States. During a short, two-year period, the Detroit agency went from more than 700 employees to zero. The reason? The agency could not negotiate a new contract with the office's single client, Chrysler, which at the time was on the verge of bankruptcy.[34] Although shuttering an entire office is a dramatic example of agencies' responses to economic downturns, other radical changes have occurred as well. Many big agencies have consolidated all forms of production under one manager. Where there used to be print production, film/video production, radio production, and retail advertising, now there is just "production." Other structural changes have occurred as well. Omnicom group's TBWA has created a new position: Chief Compensation Officer. Executives in the firm stated the creation of the new position was in reaction to

EXHIBIT 2.12 This is a typical structure for a full-service advertising agency. Note that this structure includes significant IBP services as well as strict advertising services and functions. Be aware that many agencies, in response to the changing technological environment, have added more digital and interactive services to their structure.

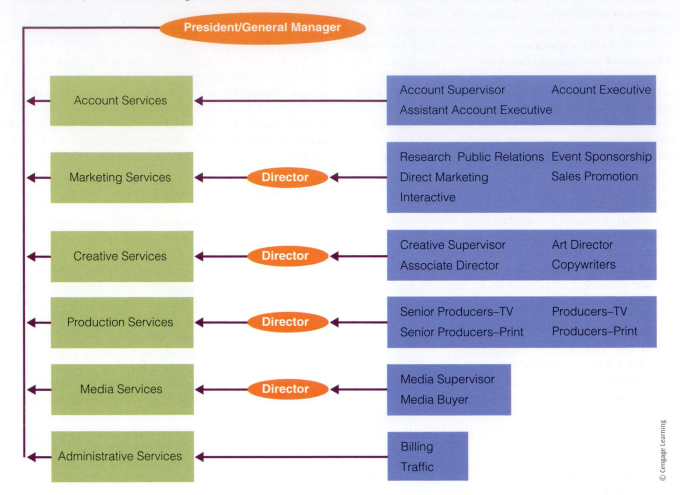

© Cengage Learning

the fact that financial discussions between clients and agencies had deteriorated to the point where neither side was satisfied.[35]

The word of caution above is prelude to the discussion that follows. Although the services discussed are still relevant and the organizational structure presented here is still generally representative, any one agency structure and menu of services many be quite different than the one shown. The types of services commonly offered by advertising and promotion agencies are discussed in the following sections.

Account Services. These services are offered by managers who have titles such as account executive, account supervisor, or account manager and who work with clients to determine how the brand can benefit most from advertising and IBP. **Account services** entail identifying the benefits a brand offers, its target audiences, and the best competitive positioning, and then developing a complete plan. In some cases, account services in an agency can provide basic marketing and consumer behavior research, but in general the client

should bring this information to the table as noted earlier in the chapter. Knowing the target segment, the brand's values, and the positioning strategy are really the responsibility of the advertiser (more on this in Chapters 5 and 6).

Account services managers also work with the client in translating cultural and consumer values into advertising and promotional messages through the creative services in the agency. Finally, they work with media services (both internal and external) to develop an effective media strategy for determining the best vehicles for reaching the targeted audiences. (See Insights Online [Exhibit 2.13] for a notable example) One of the primary tasks in account services is to keep the various agency teams' creativity, production, and media efforts on schedule and within budget.

INSIGHTS ONLINE

2.13 Go online to see the AdAge feature, "Robitify Me Helps Consumers Have a Better Online Experience."

Marketing Research Services. Research conducted by an agency for a client usually consists of the agency locating studies (conducted by commercial research organizations) that have bearing on a client's market or advertising and IBP objectives. The research group will help the client interpret the research and communicate these interpretations to the creative and media people. If existing studies are not sufficient, research may be conducted by the agency itself. As mentioned in the account services discussion, some agencies can assemble consumers from the target audience to evaluate different versions of proposed advertising and determine whether messages are being communicated effectively. These are usually done in a focus group format—something you will learn about in Chapter 7, "Advertising Research."

Many agencies have established the position of account planner to coordinate the research effort. An **account planner**'s stature in the organization is on par with that of an account executive. The account planner is assigned to clients to ensure that research input is included at each stage of development of campaign materials. Some agency leaders, like Jay Chiat of Chiat/Day, think that account planning has been the best new business tool ever invented.[36] Others are a bit more measured in their assessment. Jon Steel, director of account planning at Goody, Silverstein and Partners, described account planning this way: "[Account] planning, when used properly, is the best *old* business tool ever invented."[37] Either way, agencies understand that research, signaled by the appointment of an account planner, is key to successful promotional campaigns.

Creative and Production Services. The **creative services** group in an agency comes up with the concepts that express the value of a company's brand in interesting and memorable ways. In simple terms, the creative services group develops the message that will be delivered through advertising, sales promotion, direct marketing, social networks, mobile marketing, event sponsorship, or public relations.

Clients will push their agencies hard to come up with interesting and expressive ways to represent the brand. Geoffrey Frost, vice president of consumer communications for Motorola's Personal Communications Sector, expressed his company's approach to demanding creative excellence by saying, "What we've challenged the agencies to do was to help us to figure out how to position Motorola as the company that has really figured out the future."[38] That statement beautifully captures the kind of creative services advertisers seek from their agencies. The creative group in an agency will typically include a creative director, art director, illustrators or designers, and copywriters. In specialized promotion agencies,

EXHIBIT 2.14 Advertising agencies, from large global agencies to smaller regional shops, provide a wide range of services for their clients. The greatest contribution an agency makes to the process is, perhaps, its creative prowess. Here, FJCandN, a regional agency, once implored advertisers to "aim higher" with their advertising effort. A nice bit of creativity by an agency to tout its services to potential clients.

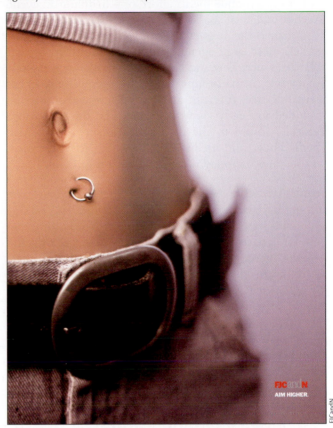

event planners, contest experts, and interactive media specialists will join the core group. Exhibit 2.14 shows how a small advertising agency, FJCandN, promoted its own creative services with a wonderfully creative ad. This ad was placed in magazines serving the regional market where the agency provided services.

Production services include producers (and sometimes directors) who take creative ideas and turn them into advertisements, direct mail pieces, and other IBP materials. Producers generally manage and oversee the endless details of the production of the finished advertisement or other promotion effort. Advertising agencies maintain the largest and most sophisticated creative and production staffs.

Media Planning and Buying Services. This service was discussed earlier as a specialized agency effort through which advertisers can contract for media buying and planning. Advertising agencies themselves provide **media planning and buying services** similar to those of the specialized agencies. The central challenge is to determine how a client's message can most effectively and efficiently reach the target audience. Media planners and buyers examine an enormous number of options to put together an effective media plan within the client's budget. But media planning and buying is much more than simply buying ad space, timing a coupon distribution, launching a mobile media effort, or scheduling an event. A wide range of media strategies can be implemented to enhance the impact of the message. As mentioned earlier, most large agencies, such as Omnicom Group, TBWA/Chiat/Day, and Fallon, set up their own digital/ interactive media groups years ago in response to client demands that Internet and mobile media option be included in nearly every IBP plan. The three positions typically found in the media area are media planner, media buyer, and media researcher. This is where most of the client's money is spent; it's very important.

Administrative Services. Like other businesses, agencies have to manage their business affairs. Agencies have personnel departments, accounting and billing departments, and sales staffs that go out and sell the agency to clients. Most important to clients is the traffic department, which has the responsibility of monitoring projects to be sure that deadlines are met. Traffic managers make sure the creative group and media services are coordinated so that deadlines for getting promotional materials to printers, Web designers, retailers, and media organizations are met. The job requires tremendous organizational skills and is critical to delivering the other services to clients.

2-3f Agency Compensation

The way agencies get paid is somewhat different from the way other professional organizations are compensated. While accountants, doctors, lawyers, and consultants often work on a fee basis, advertising agencies have historically based compensation on a commission or markup system. Promotion agencies occasionally work on a commission basis but more often work on a fee or contract basis. The atmosphere surrounding agency compensation has been tense for several years. Clients are demanding more services at lower cost. Clients are including "procurement officers" in planning meetings with agencies, and in response, agencies are bringing their own financial executives (thus the Chief Compensation Officer of TBWA discussed earlier). Agencies are starting to push back on clients who are demanding a fee structure for services that are lower than the cost to produce the services. Such was the case when agency JWT pulled out of a pitch for shipping giant UPS's $200 million account because agency management determined that the demanded fee structure was simply unprofitable.[39]

We will examine the four most prevalent agency compensation methods: commissions, markup charges, fee systems, and now prevalent pay-for-results plans. Realize that all aspects of client–agency compensation are up for negotiation, however.

Commissions. The traditional method of agency compensation is the **commission system,** which is based on the amount of money the advertiser spends on media. Under this method, 15 percent of the total amount billed by a media organization is retained by the advertising or promotion agency as compensation for all costs in creating advertising/promotion for the advertiser. The only variation is that the rate typically changes to 16 percent for outdoor media. Exhibit 2.15 shows a simple example of how the commission system works.

During the past 20 years, and particularly in the past five years with the change in consumer media use, the wisdom of the commission system has been questioned by both advertisers and agencies themselves. About half of all advertisers compensate their agencies using a commission system based on media cost. But only about 14 percent of advertisers responding to a recent survey still use the traditional 15 percent commission. More advertisers are using other percentage levels of commission, often negotiated levels, as the basis for agency compensation. But even the use of media-based commissions is under fire. Jim Stengel, global marketing officer for Procter & Gamble, laid the foundation for change several years ago when he told American Association of Advertising Agencies (AAAA) members at a media conference that the media-based model dependent on the 30-second TV spot is "broken" and that the industry needs to understand the complexity of media use by contemporary consumers.[40] This message indirectly calls into question the whole issue of basing compensation on media billings at all.

Markup Charges. Another method of agency compensation is to add a percentage **markup charge** (sometimes referred to as cost-plus) to a variety of services the agency purchases from outside suppliers. In many cases, an agency will turn to outside contractors for art, illustration, photography, printing, research, and production. The agency then, in agreement with the client, adds a markup charge to these services. The reason markup charges became prevalent in

EXHIBIT 2.15 Calculation of agency compensation using a traditional commission-based compensation system.

Agency bills client	$1,000,000	for television airtime
—		
Agency pays television media	$ 850,000	for television airtime
=		
Agency earns	$ 150,000	15% commission

© Cengage Learning

the industry is that many promotion agencies began providing services that did not use traditional media. Since the traditional commission method was based on media charges, there was no way for these agencies to receive payment for their work. This being the case, the markup system was developed. A typical markup on outside services is 17.65 to 20 percent.

Fee Systems.   A **fee system** is much like that used by consultants or attorneys, whereby the advertiser and the agency agree on an hourly rate for different services provided. The hourly rate can be based on average salaries within departments or on some agreed-on hourly rate across all services. This is the most common basis for promotion agency compensation.

Another version of the fee system is a fixed fee, or contract, set for a project between the client and the agency. It is imperative that the agency and the advertiser agree on precisely what services will be provided, by what departments in the agency, over what specified period of time. In addition, the parties must agree on which supplies, materials, travel costs, and other expenses will be reimbursed beyond the fixed fee. Fixed-fee systems have the potential for causing serious rifts in the client–agency relationship because out-of-scope work can easily spiral out of control when so many variables are at play, as the earlier example of JWT pulling out of the UPS pitch illustrated.

Agencies have generally been opposed to the fee system approach. They argue that creative impact cannot be measured in "work hours" but rather must be measured in "the value of the materials the agency is creating for the client."[41] Analysts agree. They refer to the fee system as "very flawed" and believe that the proper compensation model is performance based as described in the next section.[42]

Pay-for-Results.   Many advertisers and agencies alike have been working on compensation programs called **pay-for-results** or incentive-based compensation that base the agency's fee on the achievement of agreed-on results. Historically, agencies would not (rightly so) agree to be evaluated on results because results were often narrowly defined as "sales." The key effects on sales are related to factors outside the agency's control such as brand features, pricing strategy, and distribution programs (i.e., the overall marketing mix, not just advertising or IBP). An agency may agree to be compensated based on achievement of sales levels, but more often (and more appropriately), communications objectives such as awareness, brand identification, or brand feature knowledge among target audiences will serve as the main results criteria.

As if this long list of agencies and intricate compensation schemes weren't complicated enough, let's complicate things a bit more and consider a fairly long list of external facilitators and what their agencies rely on to create and execute promotional campaigns.

2-3g **External Facilitators**

Even though agencies offer clients many services and are adding more, advertisers often need to rely on specialized external facilitators in planning, preparing, and executing promotional campaigns. **External facilitators** are organizations or individuals that provide specialized services to advertisers and agencies. The most important of these external facilitators are discussed in the following sections.

Marketing and Advertising Research Firms.   Many firms rely on outside assistance during the planning phase of advertising. Research firms such as Burke and Simmons can perform original research for advertisers using focus groups, surveys, or experiments to assist in understanding the potential market or consumer perceptions of a product or services. Other research firms, such as SRI International, routinely collect data (from grocery store scanners, for example) and have these data available for a fee.

Advertisers and their agencies also seek measures of promotional program effectiveness after a campaign has run. After an advertisement or promotion has been running for some reasonable amount of time, firms such as Starch INRA Hooper will run recognition tests on print advertisements. Other firms such as Burke offer day-after recall tests of broadcast advertisements. Some firms specialize in message testing to determine whether consumers find advertising messages appealing and understandable.

Consultants.   A variety of **consultants** specialize in areas related to the promotional process. Advertisers can seek out marketing consultants for assistance in the planning stage regarding market segment behaviors and macro-economic and cultural trends. Creative and communications consultants provide insight on issues related to message strategy and message themes. Consultants in event planning and sponsorships offer their expertise to both advertisers and agencies. Public relations consultants often work with top management. Media experts can help an advertiser determine the proper media mix and efficient media placement.

Three new types of consultants have emerged in recent years. One is a database consultant, who works with both advertisers and agencies. Organizations of this type help firms identify and then manage databases that allow for the development of integrated marketing communications programs. Diverse databases from research sources discussed earlier can be merged or cross-referenced in developing effective communications programs. Database consultants are particularly useful in planning couponing or direct mail (email) campaigns. Another new type of consultant specializes in website development and management. These consultants typically have the creative skills to develop websites and corporate home pages and the technical skills to advise advertisers on managing the technical aspects of the user interface. The third type of consultant works with a firm to integrate information across a wide variety of customer contacts (including social media activities) and to organize all this information to achieve customer relationship management (CRM). In recent years, traditional management consultants—such as IBM, Accenture, and McKinsey—have started to work with agencies on structure and business strategy. These sorts of consultants can also advise on image strategy, market research procedure, and process and account planning. But the combination of traditional consulting and advertising has not always produced compelling results, and the typical role of consultants—focusing on marketing, creative, or technical issues—is the more likely role for consultants in the future.

Production Facilitators. External **production facilitators** offer essential services both during and after the production process. Production is the area where advertisers and their agencies rely most heavily on external facilitators. All forms of media advertising require special expertise that even the largest full-service agency, much less an advertiser, typically does not retain on staff. In broadcast production, directors, production managers, songwriters, camera operators, audio and lighting technicians, and performers are all essential to preparing a professional, high-quality radio or television ad. Production houses can provide the physical facilities, including sets, stages, equipment, and crews, needed for broadcast production. Similarly, in preparing print advertising, brochures, and direct mail pieces, graphic artists, photographers, models, directors, and producers may be hired from outside the advertising agency or firm to provide the specialized skills and facilities needed in preparing advertisements. In-store promotions and trade show booths are other areas where designing and producing materials requires the skills of a specialty organization.

Just as there are digital agencies, there are also digital production houses that assist both agencies and advertisers with the development of video and animation for both online and traditional media applications. These digital production houses are the ones that come up with the digital special effects that can make both online and broadcast production ads much more interesting (think of the exploding Nissan Sentra television ad). One such production company, B-Reel, has entered the mainstream of production and helps advertisers incorporate digital technology across many different media applications.[43]

The specific activities performed by external facilitators and the techniques employed by the personnel in these firms will be covered in greater detail in Part 3 of the text. For now, it is sufficient to recognize the role these firms play in the advertising and promotions industry.

Software Firms. An interesting and complex new category of facilitator in advertising and promotion is that of software firms. The technology in the industry, particularly new media technology, has expanded so rapidly that a variety of software firms facilitate the process. Some of these firms are well established and well known, such as Microsoft and Oracle. SAP (see Exhibit 2.16) is another company that can help advertisers. Database management software can assist advertisers in making strategic decisions. Databases offer the opportunity to gatherer and analyze data related to Web surfing behavior, broadband streaming audio and video, and managing relationships with trade partners. These firms offer the kind of expertise that is so esoteric that even the most advanced full-service or digital agency would have to seek their assistance.

LO ⑤

2-3h **Media Organizations**

The next level in the industry structure, shown separately in Exhibit 2.17, comprises the media available to advertisers. The media available for placing advertising,

EXHIBIT 2.16 Software firms like SAP provide advertisers with key assistance in the areas of audience analysis and broadband communications. With specialized software, advertisers can gather and analyze online customer data and a variety of advertising- and promotion-related strategic databases.

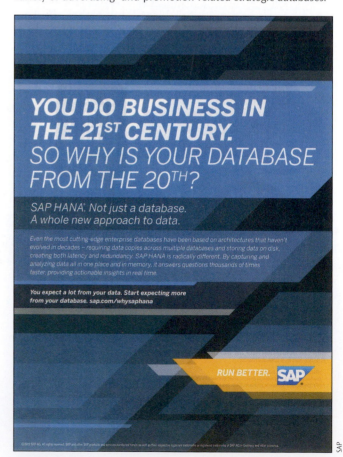

such as broadcast and print media, are well known to most of us simply because we're exposed to them daily. In addition, the Internet has created media organizations through which advertisers can direct and distribute their advertising and promotional messages.

Advertisers and their agencies turn to media organizations that own and manage the media access to consumers. In traditional media, major television networks such as NBC and Fox, as well as national magazines such as *Maxim* and *People,* provide

EXHIBIT 2.17 Advertisers have an array of media organizations available to them. Notice that the choices range from traditional print and broadcast media to interactive media to media conglomerates.

Broadcast

Television
Major network
Independent station
Cable
Broadband

Radio
Network
Local

Satellite

Interactive Media

Online Computer Services

Home-Shopping Broadcasts

Interactive Broadcast Entertainment Programming

CD-ROMs

Internet

Smartphones

e-readers

Media Conglomerates

Multiple Media Combinations
Time Warner
Liberty Media
Comcast
Walt Disney Co.
Clear Channel
Hearst Corp.

Print

Magazines
By geographic coverage
By content

Direct Mail
Brochures
Catalogs
Videos

Newspapers
National
Statewide
Local

Specialty
Handbills
Programs

Banners

Support Media

Outdoor
Billboards
Transit
Posters

Directories
Yellow Pages
Electronic directories

Premiums
Keychains
Calendars
Logo clothing
Pens

Point-of-Purchase Displays

Film and Program Brand Placement

Event Sponsorship

advertisers with time and space for their messages at considerable cost.

Other media options are more useful for reaching narrowly defined target audiences. Specialty programming on cable television, tightly focused direct mail pieces, and a well-designed Internet or mobile marketing campaign may be better ways to reach a specific audience. One of the new media options, broadband, offers advertisers the chance to target very specific audiences. Broadband allows Internet users to basically customize their programming by calling on only specific broadcasts from various providers. Advertisers can target different types of audiences using broadband for interactive broadcasts. Organizations like Starband (see Exhibit 2.18) provide high-speed satellite Internet service to consumers that is available nationwide. These broadband

Internet options are great for consumers who want dramatically faster download speeds than dial-up.

Note the inclusion of media conglomerates in the list shown in Exhibit 2.17. This category is included because organizations such as Viacom and Comcast own and operate companies in broadcast, print, and interactive media. Viacom brings you cable networks such as Nickelodeon, VH1, and TV Land. Time Warner and its sister company Time Warner Cable is one of the world's largest media conglomerates and provides broadcasting, cable, music, film, print publishing, and a dominant Internet presence.

The support media organizations listed here include all those places that advertisers want to put their messages other than mainstream traditional or interactive media. Often referred to as out-of-home media, these support media organizations include transit companies (bus and taxi boards), billboard organizations, specialized directory companies, and sports and performance arenas for sponsorships, display materials, and premium items. (See Insights Online [Exhibit 2.19] for an interesting example.)

2-3i Target Audiences

The structure of the advertising and promotion industry and the flow of communication would obviously be incomplete without an audience: no audience, no communication. One interesting thing about the audiences for promotional communications is that, with the exception of household consumers, they are also the *advertisers* who use advertising and IBP communications. We are all familiar with the type of advertising directed at us in our role as consumers: toothpaste, window cleaner, sport-utility vehicles, soft drinks, insurance, and so on.

But business and government audiences are key to the success of a large number of firms that sell only to business and government buyers. While many of these firms rely heavily on personal selling, many also use a variety of advertising and IBP tools. Accenture Consulting uses high-profile television and magazine advertising and sponsors events. Many business and trade sellers regularly need public relations, and most use direct mail to communicate with potential customers as a prelude to a personal selling call.

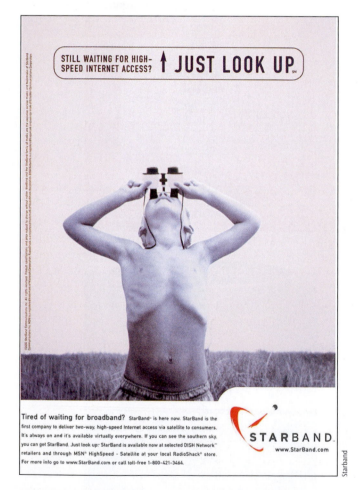

EXHIBIT 2.18 Broadband offers advertisers the ability to send audio and video through the Internet in a way that lets Web users maximize their viewing and listening experiences. Starband is a satellite Internet provider to consumers that facilitates this broadband experience.

SUMMARY

Discuss important trends transforming the advertising and promotion industry.

Recent years have proven to be a period of dramatic change for the advertising and promotion industry. The trend affecting advertisers, agencies, and the media the most is that consumers are now in greater control of the information they receive about brands. Collectively, individuals are gravitating toward sharing and creating information through websites, blogs, social media, wikis, and video sites like YouTube. The simplest example is when consumers log on to the Internet and visit sites they choose to visit for either information or shopping. Social media have emerged as the most significant form of consumer control over information creation and communication most recently. Facebook has approximately 1 billion users worldwide sharing content with each other every week. Twitter has more than 50 million users who post billions of tweets a year. As consumers search for more control over their information flow, advertisers, agencies and media organizations are struggling to adapt to consumer desires.

Next, the proliferation of media from cable television to satellite radio to the Internet has created new advertising options, and giant media conglomerates are expected to control a majority of these television, radio, and Internet properties. Media proliferation has, in turn, led to increasing media clutter and fragmentation, reducing the effectiveness of advertisements; as a result, advertisers are using more IBP tools like sales promotions, event sponsorships, and public relations to supplement and enhance the primary advertising effort. Crowdsourcing is the next big trend affecting the industry. The idea behind crowdsourcing is to get consumers more involved with and committed to a brand in a way that passive, intrusive advertising simply cannot. Consumers help "build the brand" with recommendations for features, advertising, or events. They also can communicate about the brand to audiences in ways that seems natural and credible—something corporate-launched advertising struggles with. Finally, mobile marketing/mobile media may turn out to be the biggest trend that affects the industry. Technology has resulted in significant opportunity for advertisers to reach consumers with messages directed to consumers' mobile devices—primarily smartphones, tablets like Apple's iPad, and e-readers like Amazon's Kindle—but personal navigation devices (PNDs) can also accommodate messages in the wireless world.

Describe the advertising and promotion industry's size, structure, and participants.

Many different types of organizations make up the industry. To truly appreciate what advertising is all about, one must understand who does what and in what order in the creation and delivery of an advertising or IBP campaign. The process begins with an organization that has a message it wishes to communicate to a target audience. This is the advertiser. Next, advertising

and promotion agencies are typically hired to launch and manage a campaign, but other external facilitators are often brought in to perform specialized functions, such as assisting in the production of promotional materials or managing databases for efficient direct marketing campaigns. New to the industry in recent years are digital/interactive agencies, which specialize in mobile marketing and social media campaigns. External facilitators also include consultants with whom advertisers and their agencies may confer regarding advertising and IBP strategy decisions. All advertising and promotional campaigns must use some type of media to reach target markets. Advertisers and their agencies must therefore also work with companies that have media time or space.

Discuss the role played by advertising and promotion agencies, the services provided by these agencies, and how the agencies are compensated.

Advertising and promotion agencies come in many varieties and offer diverse services to clients with respect to planning, preparing, and executing advertising and IBP campaigns. These services include market research and marketing planning, the actual creation and production of ad materials, the buying of media time or space for placement of the ads, and traffic management to keep production on schedule. Some advertising agencies appeal to clients by offering a full array of services under one roof; others, such as creative boutiques, develop a particular expertise and win clients with their specialized skills. Promotion agencies specialize in one or more of the other forms of promotion beyond advertising. New media agencies are proliferating to serve the Internet and other new media needs of advertisers. Compensation schemes in the industry vary. The four most prevalent ways to compensate an agency for services rendered are commissions, markups, fee systems, and the new pay-for-results programs.

Identify key external facilitators who assist in planning and executing advertising and integrated brand promotion campaigns.

Marketing and advertising research firms assist advertisers and their agencies in understanding the market environment. Consultants of all sorts from marketing strategy through event planning and retail display are another form of external facilitators. Perhaps the most widely used facilitators are in the area of production of promotional materials. In advertising, a wide range of outside facilitators is used in the production of both broadcast and print advertising. In promotions, designers and planners are called on to assist in creation and execution of promotional mix tools. Software firms fill a new role in the structure of the industry. These firms provide expertise in tracking and analyzing consumer usage of new media technology.

Discuss the role played by media organizations in executing effective advertising and integrated brand promotion campaigns.

Media organizations are the essential link in delivering advertising and IBP communications to target audiences. There are traditional media organizations such as television, radio, newspaper, and magazines. Interactive media options include not only the Internet and wireless access to consumers through smartphones and iPads but also through broadband video streaming. Media conglomerates such as AT&T, Time Warner, and News Corp. control several different aspects of the communications system, from cable broadcast to Internet communications and emerging high-speed broadband communications technologies.

KEY TERMS

social media
blog
crowdsourcing
advertiser
client
trade reseller
advertising agency
full-service agency
creative boutique
digital/interactive agency
in-house agency
media specialist

promotion agency
direct response agency
direct marketing agency
database agency
fulfillment center
infomercial
consumer sales promotion
trade-market sales promotion
event-planning agency
designer
logo
public relations firm

account services
account planner
creative services
production services
media planning and buying services
commission system
markup charge
fee system
pay-for-results
external facilitator
consultant
production facilitator

ENDNOTES

1. Matthew Creamer, "Caught in the Clutter Crossfire: Your Brand," *Advertising Age*, April 2, 2007, 1, 35.

2. "Ad Spending Heads into Tepid Recovery," *Advertising Age*, Annual 2010, December 28, 2009, 8; Brian Steinberg, "Marketers Say TV Spending Will Drop. Nets Stay Bullish. Let the Deals Begin," *Advertising Age*, February 8, 2010, 3.

3. "100 Leading National Advertisers 2012," U.S. Spending Totals, *Advertising Age*, June 25, 2012, 22. Also see Matthew Creamer, "Marketing's Five-Year Plan," *Advertising Age*, October 12, 2012, 20.

4. "100 Leading National Advertisers 2012," U.S. Spending Totals, *Advertising Age*, June 25, 2012, 22. Hearst annual media revenue was $3.9 billion in 2011, www.adage.com/datacenter, "100 Leading Media Companies."

5. Bob Garfield, "The Chaos Scenario 2.0: The Post Advertising Age," *Advertising Age*, March 26, 2007, 1, 12–14. "Media 2015: The Future of Media," *The Futures Company*, Special Report 2010.

6. Tim Bradshaw, "Adverts Mark a Seismic Shift to Digital," FT.com (*Financial Times*), June 29, 2009, www.ft.com/cms.

7. Data drawn from Checkfacebook at www.checkfacebook.com and Anson Alexander, "Facebook User Statistics 2012," www.ansonalex.com /infographics, both accessed on December 12, 2012.

8. "Social Media Facts 2012," *Advertising Age*, Special Insert, September 17, 2012

9. Jean Halliday, "Honda Feels the Love on Facebook," *Advertising Age*, October 26, 2009, 53. Current Honda "likes" data available at www .Facebook.com/Honda, accessed December 21, 2012.

10. Shar VanBoskirk, "US Interactive Marketing Forecast, 2011 to 2016," Forrester Research, Inc., August 24, 2011, 3.

11. Michael Trusov, Randolph E. Bucklin, and Koen Pauwels, "Effects of Word-of-Mouth versus Traditional Marketing: Findings from an Internet Social Networking Site," *Journal of Marketing*, vol. 73 (September 2009), 90–102.

12. Pat McDonough, "As TV Screens Grow, So Does DVR Usage," NielsonWire, February 29, 2012, http://www.nielsen.com/us/en /newswire/2012/as-tv-screens-grow-so-does-u-s-dvr-usage.html, accessed December 23, 2012.

13. Nat Ives, "Special Report: More Than Magazines," *Advertising Age*, March 12, 2007, s1–s6.

14. "Media Family Trees 2012," Advertising Age Data Center, www.adage .com/datacenter/mediatrees2012, accessed December 23, 2012.

15. Jack Neff, "J&J Jolts 'Old Media' with $250M Spend Shift," *Advertising Age*, March 19, 2007, 1, 29.

16. Betsy Streisand, "Why Great American Brands Are Doing Lunch," *Business 2.0*, September 2003, 146–150.

17. Garrik Schmitt, "Can Creativity Be Crowdsourced?" *Advertising Age*, Digital Next, http://ad.age.com/digitalnext, accessed April 16, 2009.

18. Beth Snyder Bulik, "Visa's 'Social-by-Design' Effort Makes Its Debut on Global Stage with London Games Being Heralded as First Social Media Olympics," adage.com, May 28, 2012, www.adage.com, accessed December 23, 2012.

19. Rita Chang, "Mobile Marketing Beyond the Mobile Phone," *Advertising Age*, November 30, 2009, 10.

20. Ibid.

21. Mobile ad spending data from "US Mobile Ad Spending Jumps to $4 Billion," *eMarketer*, December 18, 2012, www.emarketer.com, accessed

December 21, 2012; data on display and search marketing from Shar Van-Boskirk, "US Interactive Marketing Forecast, 2011–2016," Forrester Research, Inc., August 24, 2011, 3.

22. "100 Leading National Advertisers 2012," *Advertising Age*, June 25, 2012, 11.

23. The 2011 ranking for the U.S. Government ad spending was 56th in the United States at $738 million annual spending, "100 Leading National Advertisers," *Advertising Age*, June 25, 2012, 16.

24. Bob Garfield, "Army Ad Strong—If You Totally Forget We're at War," *Advertising Age*, November 13, 2006, 57.

25. Bradley Johnson, "Agency Report 2012," *Advertising Age*, April 30, 2012, 11.

26. Diane Bartz and Foo Yun Chee, "Experts Predict Long Antitrust Road for Omnicom, Publicis," Reuters, July 29, 2013, http://articles.chicagotribune.com, accessed August 4, 2013.

27. Kate Kaye and Abbey Klaassen, "How Publicis-Omnicom Could Make Enormous Scale Equal Data Expertise," *Advertising Age*, July 30, 2013, http://adage.com, accessed August 4, 2013.

28. Shareen Pathak, "Looking for New Hires? Be Prepared to Pay Up," *Advertising Age*, April 30, 2012, 9.

29. Matthew Creamer, "Adland's New Era of Specialization," *Advertising Age*, April 30, 2012, 4.

30. Richard Linnett, "Unilever Win Affirms MindShare Strategy," *Advertising Age*, December 4, 2000, 4.

31. Jack Neff, "P&G Boosts Design's Role in Marketing," *Advertising Age*, February 9, 2004, 1, 52.

32. Natalie Zumda "Pepsi Creates Chief Design Officer Role," adage.com, accessed June 8, 2012

33. Burt Helm, "Hollywood's Ad Auteur," *Bloomberg Businessweek*, January 18, 2010, 50–51.

34. Jean Halliday, "Detroit Industry Faces Future Without BBDO," *Advertising Age*, November 16, 2009, 3, 46.

35. Rupal Parekh, "TBWA's Answer to Client Squeeze: Anoint a Chief Compensation Officer," *Advertising Age*, February 8, 2010, 1, 21.

36. Jon Steel, *Truth, Lies & Advertising: The Art of Account Planning* (New York: John Wiley & Sons, 1998), 42.

37. Ibid, 43.

38. Tobi Elkin, "Motorola Tenders Brand Challenge," *Advertising Age*, August 14, 2000, 14

39. Rupal Parekh, "Fed-Up Shops Pitch a Fit at Procurement," *Advertising Age*, October 26, 2009, 1, 55.

40. Jeff Neff and Lisa Sanders, "It's Broken," *Advertising Age*, February 16, 2004, 1, 30.

41. Lisa Sanders and Alice Z. Cuneo, "Fed-Up Agencies Quit Punching the Clock," *Advertising Age*, January 27, 2007.

42. Matthew Creamer, "Marketing's Five-Year Plan," *Advertising Age*, October 8, 2012, 22.

43. Ann-Christine Diaz, "Production Company of the Year: B-Reel," *Advertising Age*, February 20, 2012, 10.

CHAPTER 3
The History of Advertising and Brand Promotion

After reading and thinking about this chapter, you will be able to do the following:

1 Tell the story of advertising's birth.

2 Discuss several significant eras in the evolution of advertising in the United States, and relate important changes in advertising practice to fundamental changes in society and culture. How did successful advertising leverage the social and cultural forces of their day? What are the basic advertising strategies that came from these historical moments and still exist today?

3 Tell the story of greater consumer access to information and connectivity to one another, branded entertainment, and how it works.

4 Identify forces that will continue to affect the evolution of advertising and integrated brand promotion. Put history to work today.

Some of the best advertising of all time has something in common: it leverages existing anxiety; it seeks to resolve cultural contradictions; it seeks to calm the individual consumer, and reinforces a marketer-friendly vision of society. Today, the same basic dynamics persist, only the specifics differ. Knowing the past makes you much better in the present.

First, understand that ads are part of their times. Great advertising uses the contemporary culture to its advantage. To really understand advertising and do well in the advertising business, you must understand that successful advertisements convey a particular version of (clearly self-serving and sometimes pointedly paranoid) contemporary culture and society. If you are in the advertising business, you are in the culture and society business. If you don't get that, you ought to work somewhere else.

We can usually best see the workings of culture at a distance. This is why there are such valuable lessons to be found in advertising's history. Most of us are too close to our own contemporary culture to see culture's consequences as easily as we can when separated by time. The idea is to get good at doing that: understanding your culture in the moment, in

the present. The really great ones have that ability. But to learn how to do that, most of us need lessons from the past. So when the sands of culture and society shift beneath consumers' feet, opportunities for advertisers present themselves, if one can see them. History helps one to see them.

This chapter is about advertising history—not just some disconnected names and dates—but practical lessons learned in the past that can be applied today. Throughout the decades, advertisers have tried many different strategies and approaches, and you can learn from their successes and failures. Most (but not all) ad strategies used today were invented decades ago—only the specifics have changed, sometimes not even those. Studying advertising history will allow you to know when a given advertising technique is really something new, and when and (most importantly) why it worked. You can see how particular advertising strategies leveraged the social forces of their day—and how you can leverage the ones of your day. History is very practical. Hint: When you are interviewing for a job in the business, explain how an advertiser's current ad campaigns works (or doesn't). That usually impresses them.

3-1 THE RISE OF ADVERTISING

Advertising is sometimes said to have had its origins in ancient times. Well, that is not really the case, at least not in any meaningful sense. Advertising is a product of modern times and modern media.

Before we get into a brief history of advertising in the Western world, let's first consider some of the major factors that gave rise to advertising in the first place. Advertising came into being as a result of at least four major factors:

1. The rise of capitalism
2. The Industrial Revolution
3. The Emergence of Modern Branding
4. The rise of modern mass media

3-1a The Rise of Capitalism

The tenets of capitalism warrant that organizations compete for resources, called *capital,* in a free-market environment. Part of the competition for resources involves stimulating demand for the organization's goods or services. When an individual organization successfully stimulates demand, it attracts capital to the organization in the form of money (or other goods) as payment. One of the tools used to stimulate demand is advertising. So, as the Western world turned to capitalism as the foundation of economic systems, the foundation was laid for advertising to become a prominent part of the business environment.

3-1b The Industrial Revolution

The **Industrial Revolution** was an economic force that yielded the need for advertising. Beginning about 1750 in England, the revolution spread to North America and progressed slowly until the early 1800s, when the War of 1812 in the United States boosted domestic production. The emergence of the principle of interchangeable parts and the perfection of the sewing machine, both in 1850, coupled with the American Civil War a decade later, set the scene for widespread industrialization. The Industrial Revolution took Western societies away from household self-sufficiency as a method of fulfilling material needs to dependency on a marketplace as a way of life. The Industrial Revolution was a basic force behind the rapid increase in mass-produced goods that required stimulation of demand—something that

advertising can sometimes be good at. By providing a need for advertising, the Industrial Revolution was a basic influence in its emergence and growth in Western economies.

Part of the Industrial Revolution was a revolution in transportation, dramatically symbolized by the east–west connection of the United States in 1869 by the railroad. This connection represented the beginnings of the distribution network needed to move the mass quantities of goods for which advertising would help stimulate demand. In the 1840s, the **principle of limited liability**, which restricts an investor's risk in a business venture to only his or her shares in a corporation rather than all personal assets, gained acceptance and resulted in the accumulation of large amounts of capital to finance the Industrial Revolution. Finally, rapid population growth and urbanization began taking place in the 1800s. From 1830 to 1860, the population of the United States nearly tripled, from 12.8 million to 31.4 million. During the same period, the number of cities with more than 20,000 inhabitants grew to 43. Historically, there is a strong relationship between per capita outlays for advertising and an increase in the size of cities.[1] Modernity gave rise to both urbanism and advertising. Overall, the growth and concentration of population provided the marketplaces that were essential to the widespread use of advertising. As the potential grew for goods to be produced, delivered, and introduced to large numbers of people residing in concentrated areas, the stage was set for advertising to emerge and flourish.

3-1c The Emergence of Modern Branding

Modern capitalism required **branding**. Manufacturers had to develop brand names so that consumers could focus their attention on a clearly identified item. Manufacturers began branding previously unmarked commodities, such as work clothes and package goods. In the late 1800s, Ivory (1882), Coca-Cola (1886), Budweiser (1891), and Maxwell House (1892) were among the first branded consumer products to show up on shopkeepers' shelves.

Once a product had a brand mark and name that consumers could identify, marketers gained power. Brands command a higher price than a commodity (think Ivory vs. soap). Branding required advertising. It's no accident of history that modern branding and modern advertising agencies appeared at exactly the

Brands command a higher price than a commodity (think Ivory vs. soap).

same time in the late 19th century. Brand demand also gives marketers added power over retailers: if consumers demand Charmin, the retailer better stock Charmin.[2]

3-1d The Rise of Modern Mass Media

Advertising is also tied to the rise of mass communication. With the invention of the telegraph in 1844, a communication revolution was set in motion. The telegraph not only allowed nations to benefit from the inherent efficiencies of rapid communication, but also did a great deal to engender a sense of national identity. People began to know and care about people and things going on thousands of miles away. This changed not only commerce, but society as well.[3] Also, during this period, many new magazines designed for larger and less socially privileged audiences made magazines a viable mass advertising medium.[4] Through advertising in these mass-circulation magazines, national brands could be projected into national consciousness. National magazines made national advertising possible; national advertising made national brands possible. Without the rise of mass media, there would be no national brands, and no advertising.

It is critical to realize that for the most part, mass media are supported by advertising. Television networks, radio stations, newspapers, magazines, and websites produce shows, articles, films, programs, and Web content not for the ultimate goal of entertaining or informing, but to make a healthy profit from selling brands through advertising and branded entertainment. Media vehicles sell audiences to make money (see Insights Online [Exhibit 3.1] for an interesting example).

> ### INSIGHTS ONLINE
>
> **3.1** Go online to see the AdAge feature, "Flu App Allows You to See Who to Avoid Because They Have Flu Symptoms."

LO ②

3-2 THE ERAS OF ADVERTISING

So far, our discussion of the evolution of advertising has identified the fundamental social and economic influences that fostered advertising's rise. Now we'll turn our focus to the evolution of advertising in practice. A few important periods can be identified and considered. In each are valuable lessons on how advertising really works.

3-2a The Preindustrialization Era (Pre-1800)

In the 17th century, printed advertisements appeared in newsbooks (the precursor to the newspaper).[5] The messages were informational in nature and appeared on the last pages of the tabloid. In America, the first newspaper advertisement is said to have appeared in 1704 in the *Boston News Letter*. Two notices were printed under the heading "Advertising" and offered rewards for the return of merchandise stolen from an apparel shop and a wharf.[6]

Advertising grew in popularity during the 18th century in both Britain and the American colonies. The *Pennsylvania Gazette* printed advertisements and was the first newspaper to separate ads with blank lines, which made the ads both easier to read and more prominent.[7] As far as we know, it was also the first newspaper to use illustrations in advertisements. But advertising changed little during the next 70 years. Even though the early 1800s saw the advent of the penny newspaper, which resulted in widespread distribution of the news media, advertisements in penny newspapers were dominated by simple announcements by skilled laborers. As one historian notes, "Advertising was closer to the classified notices in newspapers than to product promotions in our media today."[8] Advertising was about to change dramatically, however.

3-2b The Era of Industrialization (1800 to 1875)

In practice, users of advertising in the mid- to late 1800s were trying to cultivate markets for growing production in the context of an increasing urban population. A middle class, spawned by the rise of regular wages from factory jobs, was beginning to emerge. This newly developing population with the economic means to consume was concentrated in cities.

By 1850, circulation of the **dailies**, as newspapers were then called, was estimated at 1 million copies per day. The first advertising agent—thought to be Volney Palmer, who opened shop in Philadelphia—basically worked for the newspapers by soliciting orders for advertising and collecting payment from advertisers.[9] This new opportunity to reach consumers was embraced readily by merchants, and newspaper advertising volume soared.[10]

With the expansion of newspaper circulation fostered by the railroads and growing urban centers, a new era of opportunity emerged for advertising. Further, there were virtually no laws or regulations to restrict advertisers from saying or doing anything they cared to. Advertisers

EXHIBIT 3.2 The expansion of newspapers fostered widespread use of advertising. Unfortunately, some of this advertising helped give advertising a bad name. Ads like this one promised cures for just about everything, and we mean everything. At that time there were no laws to prevent advertisers from saying anything they wanted. So, the next time someone asks who needs regulation, remind them of what advertisers did before the government stepped in.

Bull's Sarsaparilla Newspaper

could outright lie, deceive, and otherwise cheat with little or no threat of being punished by government. Many advertisers took advantage of the situation and advertising was commonly considered an embarrassment (or worse) by many segments of society. At one point, firms even risked their credit ratings if they used advertising—banks considered the practice a sign of financial weakness. Advertising for patent medicines reinforced this tawdry reputation. These advertisements promised a cure for everything from rheumatism and arthritis to cancer. They were also one of the very first large categories of consumer packaged goods advertised on a mass scale. Exhibit 3.2 shows a typical ad of this period. It is for Bull's Sarsaparilla and if you will look closely at the ad's copy, you will be glad to read that Bull's will cure liver problems, kidney problems, syphilis, and that "faint gnawing feeling at the pit of the stomach." Whew, what a relief; I thought I was really sick

3-2c The "P. T. Barnum Era" (1875 to 1918)

Shortly after the Civil War in the United States, modern advertising began. This is advertising that we would recognize as advertising. Even though advertising existed during the era of industrialization, it wasn't until America was well on its way to being an urban, industrialized nation that advertising became a vital and integral part of the social landscape. From about 1875 to 1918, advertising ushered in what has come to be known as **consumer culture**, or a way of life centered on consumption. True, consumer culture was advancing prior to this period, but during this age it took hold, and the rise of modern advertising had a lot to do with it. Advertising became a full-fledged industry in this period. It was the time of advertising legends: Albert Lasker, head of Lord and Thomas in Chicago, possibly the most influential agency of its day; Francis W. Ayer, founder of N. W. Ayer; John E. Powers, the most important copywriter of the period; Earnest Elmo Calkins, champion of advertising design; Claude Hopkins, influential in promoting ads as "dramatic salesmanship"; and John E. Kennedy, creator of "reason why" advertising.[11] These were the founders, the visionaries, and the artists who played principal roles in the establishment of the advertising business. One interesting side note is that several of the founders of this industry had fathers who shared the very same occupation: minister. This very modern industry was founded in no small part by the sons of preachers. More that a coincidence, these young men would have been exposed to public speaking and the passionate selling of ideas, as well as to the need of 19th-century clergy to adapt to modernity: city life, science, progress, and public consumption. Sons of preachers were the ideal apostles of advertising and consumer culture.

By 1900, total sales of patent medicines in the United States had reached $75 million—an early demonstration of the power of advertising.[12] In this period the first advertising agencies were founded and the practice of branding became the norm. Advertising was motivated by the need to sell the vastly increased supply of goods brought on by mass production and by the demands of an increasingly urban population seeking social identity through (among other things) branded products. In earlier times, when shoppers went to the general store and bought soap sliced from a large, locally produced cake, advertising had no real place. But with advertising's ability to create meaningful differences between near-identical soaps, advertising suddenly became critical. Advertising made unmarked commodities into social symbols and identity markers, and it allowed marketers to charge far more money for them. Consumers were quite willing to pay more money for brands (e.g., Ivory) than for unmarked commodities (generic soap wrapped in plain paper), even if they were otherwise identical. This is the power of brands; the power of advertising—helping bestow desired meanings on things for sale.

Advertising was completely unregulated in the United States until 1906. In that year, Congress passed the **Pure Food and Drug Act,** which required manufacturers to list the active ingredients of their products on their labels. You could still put some pretty amazing things in products; you just had to now tell the consumer. The direct effect of this federal act on advertising was minimal; advertisers could continue to say just about anything—and usually did. Many advertisements still took on the style of a "snake oil" sales pitch. The tone and spirit of advertising of this period owed more to P. T. Barnum—"There's a sucker born every minute"—than to any other influence. Of course, Barnum was the famous showman and circus entrepreneur (Barnum and Bailey Circus) of his day. So, it's no surprise that ads of this period were bold, carnivalesque, garish, and often full of dense copy that hurled incredible claims at prototype modern consumers.

Several things are notable about these ads: more copy (words) than in today's ads; very little color, very little photography, and plenty of exaggeration and even some lies (yes, lies). During this period there was variation and steady evolution, but this is what ads were generally like up until around World War I.

Consider the world in which these ads existed. It was a period of rapid urbanization, massive immigration, labor unrest, and significant concerns about the abuses of capitalism. Some of capitalism's excesses and abuses, in the form of deceptive and misleading advertising, were the targets of early reformers. It was also the age of the suffrage movement, the progressive movement, silent motion pictures, and mass culture. The world changed rapidly in this period, and it was no doubt disruptive and unsettling to many—but advertising was there to offer solutions to the stresses of modern life, no matter how real, imagined, or ad-created. Advertisers had something to solve just about any problem. Remember, social and cultural change opens up opportunities for advertisers. Further, had World War I not occurred, and attention diverted, it is very possible that there would have been more meaningful and earlier regulation of advertising. Just before World War I there was a real and growing movement to significantly limit and regulate advertising, but that didn't happen. Exhibit 3.3 shows an ad that tries to use patriotism for the war effort by either joining the Armed Forces, or buying war bonds. Compare that message to the Armed Forces advertisements today. Are today's ads highlighting the purchase or war bonds or just appealing to patriotism to boost enlistment? Is the aspect of patriotism in the form of financially supporting the Armed Forces addressed via other advocacy groups?

3-2d The 1920s (1918 to 1929)

In many ways, the Roaring Twenties really began a couple of years early. After World War I, advertising found respectability, fame, and even glamour. Working in an advertising agency was the most modern of all professions; it was, short of being in the movies, one of the most fashionable. According to popular perception, it was where the young, smart, and sophisticated worked and played. During the 1920s, advertising was also a place of very few restrictions. The prewar movement to reform and regulate advertising was pretty much dissipated by the distractions of the war and advertising's role in the war effort. During World War I the advertising industry learned a valuable lesson: Donating time and personnel to the common good is not only good civics (make your own judgment on war) but also smart business. Exhibit 3.3 is a World War I–era example. Look at the ad closely; it entreats the reader to be patriotic and buy war bonds, a long-forgotten way of actually financing a war. Its images are of soldiers fighting for a mythic female embodiment

EXHIBIT 3.3 The ad shown here illustrates cooperation between the American advertising industry and the U.S. government. As a result of its efforts in World War I, advertising became an often-used instrument of government policy and action. Sadly, Madison Avenue and war know each other well.

Swim Ink 2, LLC/Corbis

of country with Stars and Stripes. As a result of World War I, advertising became an often-used instrument of government policy and action.

The 1920s were generally prosperous times. Most (but not nearly all) enjoyed a significantly improved standard of living. It was an age in which public pleasure was a lesser sin than in the Victorian era. Most importantly, a great social experiment in the joys of consumption was underway. Victorian repression and modesty gave way to a somewhat more open sexuality, and to pleasure in general, and a love affair with modernity. Advertising was made for this burgeoning hedonism; advertising gave people permission to enjoy, and to enjoy now. The 1920s and advertising were made for each other. Ads of the era exhorted consumers to have a good time and instructed them how to do it. Consumption and advertising were becoming respectable.

During these relatively good economic times, advertising instructed consumers how to be thoroughly modern and how to avoid the pitfalls or side effects of this new age. An important advertising logic is that good times always come with side effects, and then a product to remedy the side effect. Consumers learned of halitosis from Listerine advertising and about body odor from Lifebuoy advertising. Look at the ad in Exhibit 3.4, a Lifebuoy ad from 1926. See the expression on the face of the man on the right—body odor alert. The other guy is not going to get a raise; he may get fired—for body odor.

Not too surprisingly, there just happened to be a product with a cure for just about any social anxiety and personal failing one could imagine, many of which had supposedly been brought on as side effects of modernity. This was perfect for the growth and entrenchment of advertising as an institution: Modern times bring on many wonderful new things, but the new way of life has side effects that, in turn, have to be remedied by even more modern goods and services, and on and on. For example, modern canned food replaced fresh fruit and vegetables, thus "weakening the gums," causing dental problems—which could be cured by a modern toothbrush. But, the new toothbrush would require a new toothpaste—which then needed every better ingredients and additives. Thus, an endless consumption chain was created: Needs lead to products; new needs are created by the unintended side effects of modern times and new products; even newer products solve even newer needs, and on and on. This **chain of needs** is essential to a capitalist economy, which must continue to expand in order to survive. This makes a necessity of advertising.

Other ads from the 1920s emphasized other modernity themes, such as the division between public workspace, the male domain of the office, and the

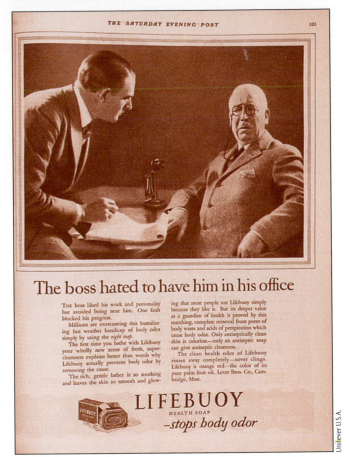

private, "feminine" space of the home. Thus, two separate consumption domains were created, with women placed in charge of the latter—the one advertisers really cared about. Advertisers soon figured out that women were responsible for as much as 90 percent of household purchases. While 1920s men were out in the jungle of the work world, women made most purchase decisions. So, from this time forward, women became advertising's primary target.

Another very important aspect of advertising in the 1920s, and beyond, was the role that science and technology began to play. Science and technology were in many ways the new religion of the modern era. The modern way was the scientific way. So one saw ads appealing to the popularity of science in virtually all product categories of advertising during this period. Ads stressed the latest scientific offerings. The style of 1920s ads was more visual than in the past. Twenties ads showed slices of life, or carefully constructed "snapshots" of social life with the brand. In these ads, the relative position, background, and dress of the people using or needing the advertised product were carefully crafted, as they are today. These visual lessons were generally about how to fit in with the "smart" crowd, how to be urbane and modern by using the newest conveniences, and how not to fall victim to the perils and pressure of the new fast-paced modern world. The social context of product use became critical. This is when and where "slice-of-life" advertising came from. It remains one of advertising's most popular and successful message forms. Reasons for its power are its inherently social nature, and its ability to place brands in a carefully constructed social setting or moment in which ongoing social tensions and cultural contradictions can be resolved by merely purchasing the advertised brand.

Sometime during the 1920s or just before, advertising began regularly constructing relationships between people and branded products by depicting the social settings and circumstances into which people and things fit, and what that fit yielded in terms of the consumer's life satisfaction. Consider Exhibit 3.5. Here is a major advertiser trying to sell plumbing. The ad doesn't say a word about the plumbing, its physical qualities, its price, or anything else. But look at the attention paid to the social setting into which plumbing fixtures were to fit. Is the ad really about plumbing? Yes, in a very important way it is. It's the 1920s, being a modern parent was very important. To be modern means to have a bathroom where there are few porous services, for example, tile replacing wood. The bathroom has to look almost as clean as an operating theater. Why? Well, in 1918 the great influenza epidemic killed millions of Americans, many of them children. Germ theory was new. People were being told that germs killed. Modern, scientific parents would be the first to protect their families from these things called germs. A baby is being weighed. Why did the advertising include this? Infant mortality was dropping rapidly due to the adoption of these very same sanitary practices, but was still a major concern. So, you should have this kind of bathroom with Standard Plumbing . . . and your new baby will have a better chance of reaching its second birthday. To this day the best way to know that your baby is doing well or "thriving" is to measure his weight. The father is in a suit: a modern professional man. The mother is in the style of the new modern 1920s woman. The ad is perfect and probably sold a lot of Standard Plumbing. The ad works because it demonstrates plumbing in a social context that works for both advertiser and consumer: it soothes anxieties, and resolves tensions and contradictions. It is very effective advertising.

The J. Walter Thompson advertising agency was the dominant agency of the period. Stanley Resor, Helen Resor, and James Webb Young brought this agency to a leadership position through intelligent management, vision, and great advertising. Helen Resor

EXHIBIT 3.5 This is one of the best ads ever. Look at it: it is selling plumbing and never says a word about plumbing. It doesn't have to. The slice-of-life technique is used to perfection here. People in the 1920s knew why the baby was being weighed and why the modern bath looked so uncluttered and almost sterile.

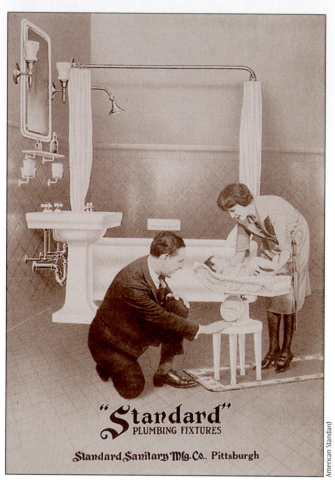

was the first prominent female advertising executive and was instrumental in J. Walter Thompson's success. Still, the most famous ad person of the era was a very interesting man named Bruce Barton. He was not only the leader of BBDO but also a best-selling author, most notably of a 1924 book called *The Man Nobody Knows.*[13] The book was about Jesus and portrayed him as the archetypal ad man. This blending of Christian and capitalist principles was apparently very attractive to a people struggling to reconcile traditional religious thought, which preached against excess, and the new consumer culture, which embraced it. This was a best-selling book, indicating the popularity of reconciling things people feel conflicted about—cultural contradictions. Remember, brands (including books) that can resolve (even wishfully or partially) cultural contradictions and soothe social disruptions will often be effective.

3-2e **The Depression (1929 to 1941)**

By 1932, a quarter of American workers were unemployed. But matters were worse than this suggests, for three-quarters of those who had jobs were working part-time—either working short hours, or faced with chronic and repeated layoffs. . . . Perhaps half the working population at one time or another knew what it was like to lose a job. Millions actually went hungry, not once, but again and again. Millions knew what it was like to eat bread and water for supper, sometimes for days at a stretch. A million people were drifting around the country begging, among them thousands of children, including numbers of girls disguised as boys. People lived in shanty towns on the fields at edges of cities, their foods sometimes weeds plucked from the roadside.[14]

If you weren't there, you have no idea how bad it was. We don't, but your grandparents or great-grandparents did. The Great Depression was brutal, crushing, and mean. It killed people; it broke lives. Those who lived through it and kept their dignity are to be deeply admired. Many of this greatest generation went on to fight in World War II. They gave of themselves for the common good; they may have been the last truly unselfish generation of Americans. The way people thought about work, money, and consumption would change forever after World War II. The change would be profitable for the advertising industry; whether or not it was good for society and its citizens is another question.

The **Great Depression** forever changed the way people thought about a great many things: their government, business, money, spending, saving, credit, and, not coincidentally, advertising. Just as sure as advertising was glamorous in the 1920s, it was suspect in the 1930s. Advertising was part of big business, and big business, big greed, and big lust had gotten America into the great economic depression beginning in 1929—or so the simple story goes. The public now saw advertising as something more suspect, something that had tempted and seduced people into the excesses for which they were being punished. The advertising industry's collective response only made things worse.

Advertisers responded to the depression by adopting a tough, no-frills advertising style. The stylish ads of the 1920s gave way to harsher, more cluttered, inappropriately sexual, and often egregiously unethical advertising. As one historian said, "The new hard-boiled advertising mystique brought a proliferation of 'ugly,' attention-grabbing, picture-dominated copy in the style of the tabloid newspaper."[15] Clients wanted their money's worth, and agencies responded by cramming every bit of copy and image they could into their ads, or using obviously inappropriate sex appeals. Advertisers played on the anxieties and vulnerabilities of troubled people. In the short run, these ads may have worked more often than not because they leveraged the social disruptions and cultural contradictions of the times. But, their long-term effect was not positive. This type of advertising made the relationship between the public and the institution of advertising worse. It hurt advertising's public image; the public was getting wise to the opportunistic techniques and resented them, even when they worked. Regrettably, doing exactly the same thing is still an industry impulse in bad economic times today. The themes in advertisements traded on the anxieties of the day; losing one's job meant being a bad provider, spouse, or parent, unable to give the family what it needed, or when nothing else came to mind: sex. The ad in Exhibit 3.6 is stylish, and done in the pin-up girl style. Cigarettes, late-night booty-call, and satin sheets: we get it.

Another notable event during these early years was the emergence of radio as a significant advertising

EXHIBIT 3.6 Look closely at this 1935 ad. It is done by famed pin-up artist George Petty (1894 to 1975) for Old Gold Cigarettes. It is so 30s. Sex appeal, cigarettes, and a late-night "tele-phoney." Times like this call for an Old Gold. Predictably tawdry and a bit of a stretch in terms of the brand's promise: 1930s advertising at its best.

Tortured by a Tele-phoney?
. . . light an Old Gold

Old Gold
CIGARETTES
THE TREASURE OF THEM ALL

ONLY FINE OLD TOBACCO *can give that natural aroma and fragrance*

When a pointless phoner ruins your beauty-sleep by calling late, talking long, and saying nothing . . . don't hang up. Light a smooth Old Gold. Its genial fragrance will make the dumb-cluck sound witty.

AT TRYING TIMES. . . . TRY A *Smooth* OLD GOLD

Thomas O'Guinn

medium. During the 1930s, the number of radio stations rose from a handful to 814 by the end of the decade, and the number of radio sets in use more than quadrupled to 51 million, slightly more than one radio set per household. Radio was in its heyday as a news and entertainment medium, and it would remain so until the 1950s when television emerged. An important aspect of radio was its ability to create a sense of community in which people thousands of miles apart listened to and became involved with their favorite radio soap opera, so named in reference to the soap sponsors of these shows. Radio's contribution to advertising history should not be underestimated. It not only ushered in the idea of broadcasting, but it also socialized consumers to depend on a connection to distant characters, programs, brands, and the idea that there were other people "out there" who shared this connection—a mass audience. Voices of radio friends from afar made good company particularly during hard times.

The advertising industry, like the rest of the country, suffered during this period. Agencies cut salaries and forced staff to work four-day weeks without being paid for the mandatory extra day off. Clients demanded frequent review of work, and agencies were compelled to provide more and more free services to keep accounts. Advertising would emerge from this depression, just as the economy itself did, during World War II. However, the advertising industry would never again reach its pre-Depression cultural status. The U.S. Congress passed real advertising reform in this period. In 1938, the Wheeler–Lea Amendments to the Federal Trade Commission Act declared "deceptive acts of commerce" to be against the law; this was interpreted to include advertising. This changed the entire game: Now individual advertisers could be held liable for deceptive practices. Between 1938 and 1940, the FTC issued 18 injunctions against advertisers, including "forcing Fleischmann's Yeast to stop claiming that it cured crooked teeth, bad skin, constipation and halitosis."[16] Believe it or not, eating yeast was successfully promoted by Fleishman's as a healthy practice. Government agencies soon used their new powers against a few large national advertisers, including Lifebuoy and Lux soaps. Advertisers would have to be at least a little more careful.

3-2f World War II and the 1950s (1942 to 1960)

In the 1950s,

Almost one-half of all women married while they were still teenagers. Two out of three white women in college dropped out before they graduated. In 1955, 41 percent of women "thought the ideal number of children was four."[17]

Many people mark the end of the Great Depression with the start of America's involvement in World War II in December 1941. During the war, advertising often made direct reference to the war effort, linking the advertised brand with patriotism, and further helping to rehabilitate the tarnished image of advertising. During the war advertisers sold war bonds and encouraged conservation. Of all companies, Coca-Cola probably both contributed and benefited the most from their amazingly successful efforts to get Coca-Cola to the front lines.[18] Their World War II–period ads are classics; they create a social world in which Coca-Cola is expected, natural, and always welcoming. If what you know of World War II came just from Coca-Cola ads, you would think World War II was a pleasant stroll across the globe in smart uniforms. Examine the ad in Exhibit 3.7. The liberation of Paris is made all the more meaningful with Coke. Apparently, "Have a Coke" means "We're allies—we wish you well."

In addition, women joined the workforce in what were nontraditional roles, as seen in the so-called Rosie

EXHIBIT 3.7 Study this ad. In it you will see an illustration by the artist Louis Bouche (1886 to 1969) in which the newly liberated Paris is cast through the prism of one of the world's very first global brands: Coca-Cola. Think about how the ad uses the moment (1945) to sell Coke.

the Riveter ads. The ad in Exhibit 3.8 for the Penn Railroad is a good example of this style. Again, a smart advertiser leverages a social change.

Following World War II, the economy continued (with a few notable starts and stops) to improve, and the consumption spree was on again. The first shopping malls were built in the suburbs to follow affluent populations and to create a more "feminine" (and white) shopping environment. It is during this period that consumer culture became the new normal, a permanent central feature of society. Historian Liz Cohen terms it "a consumer's republic."

This time, however, public sentiment toward advertising itself was different from what it had been in the 1920s, following World War I. Public attitudes toward advertising were more negative, more skeptical, and the public largely assumed that it was very powerful. But, why, advertisers had been so patriotic during the war?

The reason is fairly simple. After World War II, there was widespread belief that America's successful propaganda experts at the War Department simply moved over to Madison Avenue and started manipulating consumer minds. At the same time, there was great concern about the rise of communism and its use of "mind control" in the Cold War. Perhaps it was only natural to believe that advertising was involved in the same type of pursuit. The United States was filled with suspicion related to McCarthyism, the bomb, repressed sexual thoughts (witness a resurgence of Freudian thought), and creatures from atomic science gone bad: *The Fifty-Foot Woman* (Exhibit 3.9), *Pods, Blob, The Un-Dead,* and *Body-Snatchers,* to name a few. One of the common themes of these films was that it was hard to know who was "one of them" and who was "one of us." This was often said to be allegory to not knowing who was a communist working to subvert American ideals while looking, acting, and sounding just like "us." People were building bomb shelters in their backyards, wondering whether listening to rock 'n' roll would make their daughters less virtuous.

EXHIBIT 3.8 During the war, advertisers encouraged women to work outside the home, as this ad for Penn Railroad illustrates. The advertisers served the interests of government and promoted itself. Only a couple of years later advertisers would tell a very different story to women.

EXHIBIT 3.9 Irradiated '50s women were part of the 1950s culture of titillation and great ambivalence to modern science. This was the culture; and ads were the culture—no wonder 1950s ads were so thoroughly weird.

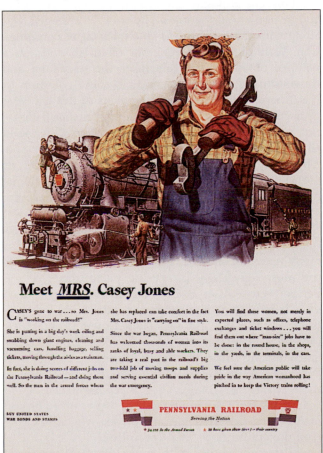

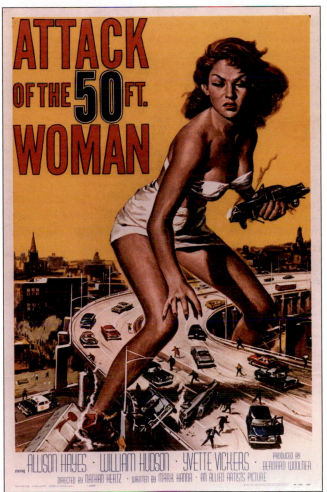

The 1950s were about fear, and advertisers again leveraged the accompanying disruption. Fearful people might be coaxed into anything that made them feel more secure. But at the same time, that fear of being manipulated by "modern science" and "mind control" made them very wary of advertising. Like other times, advertisers would turn these anxieties, contradictions, and social disruptions into advertising strategies.

In this environment of mass fear, stories began circulating in the 1950s that advertising agencies were doing motivation research and using the "psychological sell," which served only to fuel an underlying suspicion of advertising. It was also during this period that Americans began to fear they were being seduced by **subliminal advertising** (subconscious advertising) to buy all sorts of things they didn't really want or need. There had to be a reason that homes and garages were filling up with so much stuff; it must be all that powerful advertising—what a great excuse. In fact, a best-selling 1957 book, *The Hidden Persuaders,* offered the answer: Slick advertising worked on the subconscious.[19] This very popular book made a lot of sense to 1950s consumers, and suspicions about slick advertising's power persist to this day.

The most incredible story of the period involved a man named James Vicary. According to historian Stuart Rogers, in 1957, Vicary convinced the advertising world, and most of the U.S. population, that he had successfully demonstrated a technique to get consumers to do exactly what advertisers wanted. He claimed to have placed subliminal messages in a motion picture, brought in audiences, and recorded the results. He claimed that the embedded messages of "Eat Popcorn" and "Drink Coca-Cola" had increased sales of popcorn by 57.5 percent and Coca-Cola by 18.1 percent. He held press conferences and took retainer fees from advertising agencies. According to later research, he then skipped town, just ahead of reporters who had figured out that none of his claims had ever happened. He completely disappeared, leaving no bank accounts and no forwarding address. He left town with about $4.5 million (around $28 million in today's dollars) in advertising agency and client money.[20] The bigger problem is that a lot of people, including members of Congress, still believe in the hype Vicary was selling and that advertisers can actually do such things—and easily.

The 1950s were also about sex, and sex in a very paradoxical and conflicting way. On the one hand, the 1950s were about conformity, chastity, the nuclear family, and very strict gender roles and sexual norms. On the other, this was the time of neo-Freudian pop psychology and pre-sex-plotation films dripping with sexual innuendo and titillation. Sexual desire is everywhere in 1950s popular culture, but so is the countervailing message: chastity for women; a tempered "boys-will-be-boys" for young men. Double standards for adult sexual behavior were common—men couldn't help themselves—woman had to. In fact, it

was during the latter part of this period that ad consultant Ernest Dichter actually advised one of the big three U.S. carmakers to remember: think of the family car (station wagon; big sedan) as a man's wife; the sports car his "mistress." Now, there is one large cultural contradiction to exploit—and they did. This was not advertising's finest hour.

What's more, the kids of the 1950s would be advertised to with a singular focus and force never seen before, becoming, as a result, the first TV-kid market, and then the first "teen" ad targets. Because of their sheer numbers, they would ultimately constitute an unstoppable youth culture, one that everyone else had to deal with and try to please—the baby boomers. They would, over their parents' objections, buy rock 'n' roll records in numbers large enough to revolutionize the music industry. Now they buy SUVs, mutual funds, and $15,000 bicycles, and will retire with you in the wake (and debt) of their consumption.

And then there was TV. Nothing like it had happened before. Its rise from pre–World War II science experiment to 90 percent penetration in U.S. households occurred during this period. At first, advertisers didn't know what to do with it and produced two- and three-minute commercials, typically demonstrations. Of course, they soon began to learn TV's look and language.

This era also saw growth in the U.S. economy and in household incomes. The suburbs emerged, and along with them there was an explosion of consumption. Technological change was relentless and was a national obsession. The television, the telephone, and the automatic washer and dryer became common to the American lifestyle. Advertisements of this era were characterized by scenes of modern life, social promises, and reliance on science and technology. Chemicals, all kind of chemicals, were good, and good for you. The ad in Exhibit 3.10 is real. That's right: "DDT IS GOOD FOR ME." This ad ran in 1947. Yes, a chemical that has been banned in the United States since the 1970s was sold as being "good for you."

Essentially, 1950s advertising projected a confused, often harsh, while at other times sappy, presence. It is rarely remembered as advertising's golden age. Two of the most significant advertising personalities of the period were Rosser Reeves of the Ted Bates agency, who is best remembered for his ultra-hard-sell style (see Exhibit 3.11), and consultant Ernest Dichter, best remembered for his motivational research, which focused on the subconscious and symbolic elements of consumer desire. *Mad Men* watchers, do you recognize these characters? Exhibit 3.11 is representative of the advertising from this contradictory and jumbled period in American advertising. Can you see why advertising (and the culture) needed a revolution?

Fifties ads show mythic nuclear families, well-behaved children, our "buddy" the atom, an uneasy

EXHIBIT 3.10 Yes, DDT is "a benefactor of all humanity." You just thought it was just another banned toxic chemical. Study the ad, it was not uncommon then, nor now, for industrial products or practices (think the "fracking" industry today) to be advertised in this style: a multipictured case for the many benefits.

An ad for Penn Salt Chemicals boasts "DDT is good for me!" and "The great expectations held for DDT have been realized."

Penn Salt

EXHIBIT 3.11 This is an ad from the famous Rosser Reeves at the Ted Bates agency. His style dominated the 1950s: harsh, abrasive, repetitive, and diagrammatic. He believed that selling the brand had virtually nothing to do with art or winning creative awards. His style of advertising is what the creative revolution revolted against.

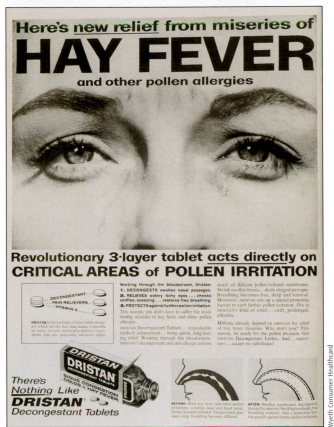

Wyeth Consumer Healthcard

3-2g Peace, Love, and the Creative Revolution (1960 to 1972)

faith in science, and rigid (but about to break loose) gender roles, while the rumblings of the sexual revolution of the 1960s were just audible. In a few short years, the atom would no longer be our friend (as it is in Exhibit 3.12); we would question science; youth would rebel and become a hugely important market; women and African Americans would demand inclusion and fairness; and bullet bras would be replaced with no bras. Oral birth control's introduction in 1960 would change the culture's view of appropriate sexual behavior, or at least consequences. A period of great social change would occur, which is usually a very good time for advertisers: new needs, new liberties, new anxieties, new goods and services, and new brands. Again, social disruption and cultural contradictions in need of resolution; it is in this space that many great brands and great advertising emerged.

As you probably know, there was a cultural revolution in the 1960s. It affected just about everything—including advertising. Ads started to take on the themes, the language, and the look of the 1960s. But as an institution, advertising during the 1960s was actually slow to respond to the massive social revolution going on all around it. While the world was struggling with civil rights, the Vietnam War, the sexual revolution, and the youth revolution, advertising was, for the most part, still portraying women and other minorities in subservient roles (Exhibit 3.13). As writer Thomas Frank has pointed out, advertising leveraged the trappings and the revolutionary impulse of the decade to sell things, yet it remained a fairly conservative capitalist institution. Advertising agencies stayed one of the whitest industries in America. Gays and lesbians, as far as advertising was concerned, didn't exist. And in ads, much of the sexual revolution wasn't exactly liberating for everyone.

EXHIBIT 3.12 Check out the atomic symbol next to this early computer from IBM. That would be very odd to see today, but it made perfect sense in the atomic 1950s.

EXHIBIT 3.13 Something special in the air. This ad from American Airlines shows that not everyone got the memo on the revolution. What is this ad about? We're pretty sure it's not about more legroom in coach. Hello.

The thing really revolutionary about 1960s advertising was the creativity. This creative revolution was characterized by the "creatives" (art directors and copywriters) having a bigger say in the management of their agencies, and the look and feel of the ads. The emphasis in advertising turned "from ancillary services to the creative product; from science and research to art, inspiration, and intuition."[21] At first, the look of this revolutionary advertising was clean and minimalist, with simple copy and a sense of self-effacing humor. Later (around 1968 or so), it became something more. In the late 1960s, advertising had finally changed in meaningful ways. For one, it became fairly self-aware. Advertising admitted being advertising (and even poked fun at itself). Ads during the late 1960s and into the early 1970s conveyed the sentiment, "ok, here's an ad, you know it's an ad—and so do we." That was something new. Advertising began to trade on insider status (we're all in on it)—making fun of the straight and now silly ads of the 1950s and by playing to a sense of irony. This insider ironic orientation made advertising occasionally hip. The 1960s was when advertising began to understand that it was all about hip, cool, youth, and rebellion. From that point on, defining and chasing

cool was a prime advertising directive. But as typically the case, the 1960s cultural revolution soon became ad copy. Everything became rebellion; even an unhip brand like Dodge tried to cash in with the "Dodge Rebellion."[22] Once advertising learned that it could successfully attach itself to youth, hipness, and revolution, it never went back. Even hip anti-advertising sentiment could be used to help sell stuff through advertising. That is ironic.

The creative revolution, and the look it produced, is most often associated with four famous advertising agencies: Leo Burnett in Chicago, Ogilvy & Mather in New York (a little less so), Doyle Dane Bernbach in New York (the most), and Wells Rich and Green in New York (deserving of more credit than they get). They were led in this revolution by agency heads Leo Burnett, David Ogilvy, Bill Bernbach, and Mary Wells. The Volkswagen and Braniff ads pictured in Exhibits 3.14 and 3.15 are 1960s ads prepared by Bernback and Wells, respectively. Recognize anyone in *Mad Men?* A great deal of the story line and characters come from here.

Of course, not all 1960s ads were revolutionary. Plenty of ads in the 1960s still reflected traditional values and relied on relatively worn-out executions.

EXHIBIT 3.14 Doyle Dane Bernbach made VW in the United States a reality. They did it by self-effacing and very cool advertising. Study this ad; it is from the most famous U.S. campaign of all time.

EXHIBIT 3.15 Mary Wells was one of the giants of the creative revolution. Here, she sells Braniff Airlines (no longer with us) through the space bikini motif. This is very 1960s.

Pepsi may have taken better advantage of the disruptions of the 1960s than any other advertiser. As late as the mid-1950s, Coke had an enormous lead over Pepsi. Up until the 1960s, Pepsi kept trying to sell Pepsi as a product based on taste. It was only when they switched from trying to sell the product (a cola) to selling the consumers who drank it, "those who think young," that they began to eat up Coke's lead. As noted by Thomas Frank and others, it was Pepsi's new strategy to "name and claim the youth revolution as their own." There was a growing generation gap/war; Pepsi leveraged that beautifully. Coke is for old un-hip people; Pepsi is for us cool kids (Exhibit 3.16), traded on youth and the idea of youth. Within a few short years, Pepsi had pulled almost even with Coke, erasing a 3 to 1 lead coming out of World War II. Again, they did it by leveraging the contractions, anxieties, and social dislocations of the day—cultural marketing and advertising at work.

A final point that needs to be made about the era from 1960 to 1972 is that this was a period when advertising as an institution became generally aware of its own role in consumer culture. While advertising played a role in encouraging consumption, it had become a symbol of consumption itself. Musicians (think Bob Dylan,

The Who, The Rolling Stones), artists (think Warhol, Lichtenstein), film makers, poets, and authors are all very aware that advertising, consuming, youth, revolution, sex, satisfaction, and identity were all jumbled up together. The paradox of advertising/marketing/consuming had gone public. The love/hate relationship was now being celebrated in art (Warhol, Lichtenstein) and in movies and in songs. Advertisers learned that people (particularly youth) play out their revolutionary impulse *through* consumption—even when it's an anti-consumption revolution, you've got to have the right look, the right clothes, the right revolutionary garb. In a very significant way, advertising learned how to forever dodge the harshest criticism of the very thing that advanced capitalism: Hide in plain sight. Paradox is good business.

Perhaps it's a bit too cynical, but Thomas Frank tells revolutionaries or us that since the 1960s nothing has been really new—just another branded faux-revolution. True?

Every few years, it seems, the cycles of the 60s repeat themselves on a smaller scale, with new rebel youth cultures bubbling their way to a happy replenishing of the various culture industries' depleted arsenal of cool. New generations obsolete the old, new celebrities render old ones ridiculous, and on and on in an ever-ascending spiral of hip upon hip. As ad-man Merle Steir wrote back in 1967, "Youth has won. Youth must always win. The new naturally replaces the old." And we will have new generations of youth rebellion as certainly as we will have generations of mufflers or toothpaste or footwear.[23]

EXHIBIT 3.16 Pepsi "created" a generation and traded on the discovery of the vast youth market. Pepsi claimed youth as its own. http:\\www.pepsiworld.com

EXHIBIT 3.17 Claiming authenticity is tried and true branding, particularly when it is at the center of cultural conversations and social disruption. It was during the 1960s and 1970s. Is it now?

3-2h The 1970s (1973 to 1980)

Mr. Blutarski, fat, drunk, and stupid is no way to go through life.

—Dean Vernon Wormer (John Vernon) in
National Lampoon's *Animal House*, 1978

Dean Wormer's advice to John Belushi's character in *Animal House* captured essential aspects of the 1970s, a time of excess and self-induced numbness. It was the end of the cultural revolution.

The reelection of Richard Nixon in 1972 marked the real start of the 1970s. The 1970s was the age of polyester, disco, blow, and driving 55. But more than anything else, it was America's age of self-doubt. America had just suffered through its first lost war, the memory of four student protesters shot and killed by the National Guard at Kent State University in the spring of 1970 was still vivid, Mideast nations appeared to be dictating the energy policy of the United States, and the Americans were, as President Jimmy Carter suggested late in this period, in a national malaise. In this environment, advertising retreated a bit

from the creative revolution. The ads of this period took sexual sell a bit further, seemed a little less artistic, were a little more racially integrated, and used a bit more hard-sell.

The major social shifts of the decade were the second-wave of American feminism, the self-doubt of Western democracies, and a significant mass identity/authenticity question "Who am I; What is real?" (See how the Coca-Cola company smartly answered the question, Exhibit 3.17.) "What can I believe in?" Part of this was the rise of the self-help-therapy industry; the philosophy and advice that seemed to sell the best was "it's ok to be selfish." "Me" became the biggest word in the 1970s; what a great environment for advertising. All of society was telling people that it was not only OK to be selfish, but it was the right thing to do. Selfishness was said to be natural and good. A refrain similar to "Hey babe, I can't be good to you if I'm not good to me?" became a 1970s standard riff. Of course, being good to ones' self often meant self-indulgence, self-gifting, and buying stuff—always good for advertising. It's funny how that worked out.

Still, all periods have countercurrents: the 1970s saw added regulation for the protection of special audiences. First, there was growing concern over what effect $200 million a year in advertising had on children. A group of women in Boston formed **Action for Children's Television**, which lobbied the government to limit the amount and content of advertising directed at children. Established regulatory bodies, in particular the **Federal Trade Commission (FTC)** and the industry's **National Advertising Review Board**, demanded higher standards of honesty and disclosure from the advertising industry. A clever end-run around this was the advent of what were essentially program-length commercials (PLCs), particularly in children's television. Product/show blends for toys like Strawberry Shortcake made regulation more difficult: If it's a show about a product, then it's not really an ad (and can't be regulated as an ad)—or is it? This drove regulators crazy, but program-length commercials were here to stay, at least in the United States.[24] They were generally treated by regulators as shows (with some degree of First Amendment protection) and opened the door for countless imitators. So in a real sense, what is now being called the "new" branded entertainment had its start in the 1970s.

Several firms were subjected to legislative mandates and fines because their advertising was judged to be misleading. Most notable among these firms were Warner-Lambert (for advertising that Listerine mouthwash could cure and prevent colds), Campbell's (for putting marbles in the bottom of a soup bowl to bolster its look), and Anacin (for advertising that its aspirin could help relieve tension).

During the 1970s, advertising agency hiring and promotion practices with respect to minorities were formally challenged in the courts. The industry remained very white. In what is to this day an odd segregation, "specialty" agencies emerged for serving various ethnic groups. Two important agencies owned and managed by African Americans thrived: Thomas J. Burrell founded Burrell Advertising, and Byron Lewis founded Uniworld. Burrell is perhaps best known for ads that rely on the principle of "positive realism." Positive realism is "people working productively; people engaging in family life . . . people being well-rounded . . . and thoughtful; people caring about other people; good neighbors, good parents . . . people with dreams and aspirations; people with ambition." Burrell once said "in 30 seconds you can build a brand and break a stereotype." He also believed that "whites are easier to reach through black advertising than vice versa."[25] "The idea was that we don't have to be the same as white people to be equal to white people; that

we should celebrate our differences while not shying away from demanding our rights."[26]

One of Burrell's ads is shown in Exhibit 3.18. (Go to http://www.littleafrica.com/resources/advertising.htm for a current list of major African-American advertising agencies and resources.) Another very important person was John H. Johnson, founder of *Ebony* magazine, and in many ways the man who made the black American experience in publishing, marketing, and advertising possible. He opened up enormous opportunities for black entrepreneurs, advertisers, and artists. His funeral was attended by a former U.S. president, U.S. senators, celebrities, and a lot of people who simply adored him. He was very important in advertising and beyond.

The 1970s also signaled a period of growth in communications technology. Consumers began to surround themselves with devices related to communication. The VCR, cable television, and the laser disc

EXHIBIT 3.18 Although a bad economy and a national malaise caused a retreat to the tried-and-true styles of decades before, a bright spot of 1970s advertising was the portrayal of people of color. Thomas Burrell created ads that portrayed African Americans with "positive realism."

EXHIBIT 3.19 This Burger King ad was appropriate for the period and also foreshadowed the coming trend of customization.

Crispin Porter + Bogusky

3-2i The Designer Era (1980 to 1992)

Greed, for a lack of a better word, is good.

—Gordon Gekko (Michael Douglas) in
Wall Street, 1987

"In 1980, the average American had twice as much real income as his parents had had at the end of WWII."[27] The political, social, business, and advertising landscape changed in 1980 with the election of Ronald Reagan. The country made a right, and conservative politics were the order of the day. There was, of course, some backlash and many countercurrents, but the conservatives were in the mainstream. Greed was good, stuff was good, and advertising was good. American, Britain, and the West generally experienced a profound political and consumption shift. In the fall of 1989, the Berlin Wall fell and those in the East were now free to buy. Mass-market capitalism and consumerism experienced some glory days.

In the 1980s we witnessed the label moving from inside the shirt to the outside. Although it had started in the 1970s, the 1980s saw the explosion of designer goods: everything became about public consumption status and their markers. Not surprisingly, many ads from the designer era are particularly social-class conscious and values conscious. They openly promote consumption, but in a conservative way, wrapped up in "traditional American values." The quintessential 1980s ad may be the 1984 television ad for President Ronald Reagan's reelection campaign, "Morning in America." The storyboard for this ad is shown in Exhibit 3.20. This ad is soft in texture, but it is a firm reaffirmation of family and country—and capitalism. Other advertisers quickly followed with ads that looked similar to "Morning in America." The 1980s were also about designer labels, social-class consciousness, and having stuff.

Television advertising of the 1980s period was influenced by the rapid-cut editing style of MTV: rapid cuts with a very self-conscious character.

The advertising of the 1980s had a few other changes. One was the growth and creative impact of British agencies, particularly Saatchi and Saatchi. One of the things Saatchi and Saatchi realized earlier than most was that politics, culture, and products all resonate together. The Saatchi and Saatchi ads of this period were often sophisticated and politically non-neutral. In the United Kingdom, they more openly blended politics and advertising. They worked, and began to be copied (at least the sensibility) in other places, including the United States. Exhibit 3.21 is pretty typical of 1980s North American ads. Please look at its visual composition and the relatively few number of words (copy). Eighties ads were visually a bit "in your face."

player were all developed during the 1970s. Cable TV claimed 20 million subscribers by the end of the decade. Similarly, cable programming grew in quality, with viewing options such as ESPN, CNN, TBS, and Nickelodeon. As cable subscribers and their viewing options increased, advertisers learned how to reach more specific audiences through the diversity of programming on cable systems.

There was, as always, a youth undercurrent of revolution (with a small "r") in the 1970s. This one was more cynical and ambivalent about consumption and advertising than the one a decade earlier. Their anti-consumption thesis was set to music by hundreds of British punk and American alternative bands. Although notably more ironic and cynical than their 1960s counterparts, it was still about finding authenticity, identity, and meaning in a sea of consumption and ads. The ad in Exhibit 3.19 is pretty typical of the period. As you can see from this ad, there was more inclusion by the 1970s. It was not, however, even across categories. You can also see a pretty typical 1970s visual style, a bit crowded, somewhat reminiscent of the 1930s. The headline "Have it Your Way" was one of Burger King's most famous. It noted BK's willingness to customize your burger, a rare thing at the time.

EXHIBIT 3.20 An ad that embodied the tone and style of 1980s advertising was Ronald Reagan's 1984 reelection campaign ad "Morning in America." The ad is soft in texture but firm in its affirmation of the conservative values of family and country.

EXHIBIT 3.21 Look over the ad below. Tight visual focus, edgy for its day, and few words, all are pretty typical of the 1980s print ad style.

3-2j The E-Revolution Begins (1993 to 2000)

Some say that Internet advertising became truly viable around 1993. One can argue with the exact date, but somewhere near the mid-1990s is the point where it became clear that Internet adverting and other e-brand promotions were not only here to stay, but were going to change the entire advertising landscape. From that date until the dot-com meltdown in 2000, advertising was struggling with all sorts of new possibilities and challenges. Ads in traditional media were getting edgier while e-ads were still trying to define themselves: find their best form.

There were scary moments for those heavily vested in traditional advertising. In May 1994, Edwin L. Artzt, then chairman and CEO of Procter & Gamble, the then $40 billion-a-year marketer of consumer packaged goods, dropped a bomb on the advertising industry. During an address to participants at the American Association of Advertising Agencies (4As) annual conference, he warned that agencies must confront a "new media" future that won't be driven by traditional advertising. Although at that time P&G was spending about $1 billion a year on television advertising, Artzt

told the 4As audience, "From where we stand today, we can't be sure that ad-supported TV programming will have a future in the world being created—a world of video-on-demand, pay-per-view, and subscription TV. These are designed to carry no advertising at all."[28] This was not good news to those who preferred business as usual. Then, just when the industry had almost recovered from Artzt's dire proclamation, William T. Esrey, chairman and CEO of Sprint, gave it another jolt a year later at the same annual conference. Esrey's point was somewhat different but equally challenging to the industry. He said that clients are "going to hold ad agencies more closely accountable for results than ever before. That's not just because we're going to be more demanding in getting value for our advertising dollars. It's also because we know the technology is there to measure advertising impact more precisely than you have done in the past."[29] Esrey's point: new **interactive media** will allow direct measurement of ad exposure and impact, quickly revealing those ads that perform well and those that do not. Secondly, the agency will be held accountable for results. The saga continues. Still unsure of what could be delivered and what could be counted, in August 1998, Procter & Gamble hosted an Internet "summit," due to "what is widely perceived as the poky pace of efforts to eliminate the difficulties confronted by marketers using online media to pitch products."[30] Some of these problems were technological: incompatible standards, limited bandwidth, and disappointing measurement of both audience and return on investment. Others were the result of naïveté. Advertisers such as P&G want to know what they were getting and what it costs when they place an Internet ad. Does anyone notice these ads, or do people click right past them? What would "exposure" in this environment really mean? Is "exposure" really even a meaningful term in the new media ad world? How do you use these new media to build brands? At the end of this summit, P&G reaffirmed its commitment to the Internet.

But history again showed that measurement of bang for buck (return on investment, ROI) in advertising (Internet or not) is very elusive. Although better than TV, the Internet was fundamentally unable to yield precise measurements of return on investment in advertisement, too many variables, too much noise in the system, too many delayed effects, and too many uncertainties about who is really online. But advertisers still became more demanding in terms of "results." This has been largely the case throughout advertising's history. Ad agencies are now operating with fewer staff and smaller margins than before. Clients are more tightfisted these days and at least try to demand accountability. Things have certainly changed, particularly in print advertising, but not all old media are sick, much less dead.

Another change has come in the form of a significant challenge on New York's claim as the center of the advertising universe. In the United States, the center moved west, with the ascendancy of agencies in California, Minnesota, Oregon, and Washington, not to mention international hot spots such as London and Singapore. In the 1990s these agencies tended to be more creatively oriented and less interested in numbers-oriented research than those in New York. Other hot or nearly hot ad-shop markets include Minneapolis, Austin, Atlanta, Houston, and Dallas. Outside the United States, London emerged as the key player, with Singapore and Seoul as close seconds.

In terms of style and cultural connections, the 1990s was (like most eras) a mixed bag. But one clear trend was what some have referred to as an abundance of irony and soft cynicism. In the 1990s, self-parody of advertising was the inside joke, except everyone was "inside." Winks and nods to the media-savvy audience were pretty common. Ads said in a sense, "This is an ad . . . you know it, we know it, but we are still going to try to sell you something." This was said to be a product of the Generation-X mind-set. This

EXHIBIT 3.22 This ad leverages the well-known mom–teenager language problem. The visual style is a cool, pen-drawn look.

Susan Van Etten

was slacker cynicism: laid-back cool; no ladder climbing; just hanging out; having heard it all before. These words from 1999s Fight Club say it well:

> Advertising has us chasing cars and clothes, working jobs we hate so we can buy **** we don't need. We're the middle children of history, man. No purpose or place. We have no Great War. No Great Depression. Our Great War's a spiritual war . . . our Great Depression is our lives. We've all been raised on television to believe that one day we'd all be millionaires and movie gods and rock stars. But we won't. And we're slowly learning that fact. And we're, very p *** ed off.

The Fight Club, Nirvana, et al. spirit was the touchstone of cutting-edge 1990s ads. Advertising was fast, and it was self-consciously hip. Exhibit 3.22 is a good example of this period's print style. For a newer version of what is now cutting-edge, check out the Insights Online feature described in Exhibit 3.23.

INSIGHTS ONLINE

3.23 Go online to see the AdAge feature, "Diesel Runs a Contest Asking Consumers to Unplug from Social Media Posting for Three Days."

─────── **LO** ───────

3-3 CONSUMER ACCESS, CONNECTIONS, BRANDED ENTERTAINMENT, AND THE GREAT RECESSION (2000 TO PRESENT)

As you may be aware, the dot-com bubble burst in 2000. Lots of Internet companies that burned cash like kindling never turned a profit and died. Part of the problem was the lack of a good Web advertising revenue model. Pop-ups and easy-to-avoid Internet ads had not generated enough advertising revenue. Online buying continued to grow, but online advertising couldn't catch up until companies became more sophisticated at using new media to generate sales. The corner seems to have been turned around 2002. Phase II of the e-ad-revolution (tied to Web 2.0) has been much more successful. One major difference between Web 2.0 and what came before is the basic consumer-advertising/brand promotion model—it is now much more about pull than push. Before Web 2.0, the model was still: find consumers through mass exposure, and push ads (and brands) at them. In Web 2.0 it is: get consumers to seek you out, or bump into you on the Web, and then pull them to you. Of course, consumers still have to somehow hear about your brand in the first place, but that's where the integration of media comes in: one medium makes you aware, another pulls you, and another engages you (more in Chapter 15).

Although there are many social and cultural trends that could be leveraged, one thing is undeniable in this latest period: consumers have much easier access to information and each other than before. Consumers can now communicate with each other, actually talk back to the marketer with one voice or millions, and even make their own ads and distribute them on social media such as YouTube. The advertising industry has pretty much accepted the fact that consumers can now do many of the very same things that only big studios, agencies, and distributors could do a decade ago. Consumers now "co-create" brand messages and brands in a meaningful way. Consumers' reactions (particularly young people) are fused with agency "professional" creatives to make ads that are one step from homemade, or in some cases completely homemade. Doritos actually had consumers make Super Bowl ads. This is typically called **consumer-generated content (CGC).** Because of this the industry bible, *Advertising Age,* has declared this era the "post-advertising age." Although that's a bit much, things really have changed a lot in the last few years, and greater consumer connectivity and information access is a big part of it.

EXHIBIT 3.24 "Drink up, Rock Out"—really? Is this ad as simpleminded as it seems? Are we missing some greater meaning, or is it just Rock Out=Pepsi? OK. Could you do better? We think you could.

Pepsi Cola Company

Think about this period. What do you think are the major cultural contradictions, social disruptions, and identity issues of this period? How have these been leveraged by smart advertisers? How have anxieties about security since 9/11 been used? How about the election of the first black U.S. President? What of growing Chinese power? What about the recent right-wing populism of the United States? What of the contradictions of the Great Recession? What about the rapidly growing gulf between the very rich in the United States and everyone else, the disappearance of U.S. middle class? What about shrinking populations in countries like Italy? What about a tough job market for college graduates . . . having to live with your parents until you are 30, but wanting (and almost expecting) the cool housing seen on TV? How about a small gray cube instead of the corner office? See any reason to be nervous, anxious, conflicted, hopeful, independent/dependent, or resigned/determined?

Well, these all make for great leverage in advertising campaigns. Do you see any of these conditions being leveraged in this recent ad (Exhibit 3.24), or do you just see pretty traditional product-based pitches, or maybe just cool images that get attention? Check them out. For yet another example, see Insights Online (Exhibit 3.25).

► **INSIGHTS ONLINE**

3.25 Go online to see the AdAge feature, "Oscar Meyer Provides Bacon for Virtual Bartering in an Online Video."

The Great Recession of December 2007 to June 2009—had its impact on the advertising industry. Many advertisers cut their ad budgets during this period. Many used the economy as a reason to invest more in branded entertainment and nontraditional advertising and brand promotion. These changes have now been institutionalized. For example, media companies such as Nielsen now keep comprehensive data on product placements. Guerrilla marketing, Brand Hi-Jacks, and the building of brands like Red Bull and Pabst's Blue Ribbon through nontraditional means are now fairly commonplace. See Insights Online [Exhibit 3.26] for a notable example.

And don't forget about business-to-business promotion on the Web, known as e-business. **E-business** is another form of e-advertising and promotion in which companies selling to business customers (rather than to household consumers) rely on the Internet to send messages and close sales (we'll cover this in detail in Chapter 16).

Because of advances in technology, firms like Procter & Gamble continue to invest heavily in newer means of connecting with consumers and potential consumers. Reaching target customers, P&G has developed and maintains dozens of websites for the company's approximately 300 brands to serve and interact with customers.[31] P&G also has gone beyond just product-oriented sites and has launched "relationship building" sites like Beinggirl, a teen community site. With such a site, the firm can gather data, test new product ideas, and experiment with interactivity. For example, if a website visitor wants to know what nail polish will match the lipstick she just saw in a commercial, she can get an immediate answer (see Exhibit 3.27). Thus, target audiences do not have to be broadly defined by age or geographic groups—individual households can be targeted through direct interaction with audience members. Consumers come to the advertiser looking for things, rather than the advertisers merely shouting at millions hoping something sticks here and there. Also note that P&G can reach a global audience through Beinggirl.com without the cost and time-consuming effort of placing traditional media ads in dozens of markets. Furthermore, the consumer comes willingly to the advertiser, not the other way around as in the case of the more intrusive traditional media that seek consumers out, whether they like it or not. Social networking sites such as Facebook have made brand communities and personal identity projects the stuff of e-commerce.

INSIGHTS ONLINE

3.26 Go online to see the AdAge feature, "IBM Sponsors the Tennis Major, the U.S. Open, and Adds a Data Wall for the Tennis Fans at the Event."

EXHIBIT 3.27 This is a website P&G believes builds brand community. Do you think it does? Do you find the ethics of it a bit troubling, or not? Is it clear to everyone that one very real intent here is to sell tampons?

Beinggirl

See Insights Online (Exhibit 3.28) for another interesting example about targeting online communities.

INSIGHTS ONLINE

3.28 Go online to see the AdAge feature, "Rovio and Angry Birds Expand to a New Game with the Birds' Archrival."

3-4 BRANDED ENTERTAINMENT

Branded entertainment is the blending of advertising and integrated brand promotion with entertainment, primarily film, music, and television programming. A subset of branded entertainment is *product placement,* the significant placement of brands within films or television programs. When Tom Cruise wore Ray Bans in the film *Top Gun,* when James Bond switched to the BMW Z8 from his beloved Aston Martin (by the way, he has switched back), and when the cast of *Friends* drank Pepsi, audiences took notice. Well, branded entertainment takes product placement a quantum leap forward. With branded entertainment, a brand is not only a bit player, it also is the star of the program. An early participant in branded entertainment and still a leader in using the technique is BMW. BMW launched the BMW Web film series in 2001 and

EXHIBIT 3.29 Look at the brands on the stage. Is this better than a traditional ad, or does it just get lost in the background?

AP Images/PRNewsFoto/DR. PEPPER

has featured the work of well-known directors, including Wong Kar-Wai, Ang Lee, John Frankenheimer, Guy Ritchie, and Alejandro González Iñárritu. Other sites featuring entertainment by featuring the brand include Lipton Tea (http://www.lipton.com) and the U.S. Army at its Web-based computer game (http://www.goarmy.com). There are many advantages to branded entertainment—among them, not running into the consumer's well-trained resistance mechanisms to ads and not having to go through all the ad regulations. In an ad BMW has to use a disclaimer ("closed track, professional driver") when it shows its cars tearing around, but in movies, like *The Italian Job*, no such disclaimer is required. Also, movies have been seen by the courts as artistic speech, not as the less protected "commercial speech." Branded entertainment, therefore, gets more First Amendment protection than ordinary advertising does. This is an important distinction, since regulation and legal fights surrounding ads represent a large cost of doing business. This merger of advertising with music, film, television, and other telecom arenas (such as cell phones) is often referred to as Madison & Vine, a nod to New York's Madison Avenue, the traditional home of the advertising industry, and the famous Hollywood intersection of Hollywood and Vine. We will talk more about this later. Suffice it to say for now, branded entertainment has opened up enormous real possibilities for what has become a much cluttered and a bit beat-up traditional

advertising industry. See Exhibit 3.29, which illustrates branded advertising at a concert. How many brands do you count on stage? Do you think this type of promotion moves brands, or just underwrites concerts? The truth is, no one is really sure. Most experts make two comments: (1) if one advertiser doesn't do it, another will, and (2) it seems to boost sales a bit, for a bit, that's it. We think most throw in for the show because they are afraid not too, and typically it isn't all that expensive.

As you can imagine, advertisers love the exposure that branded entertainment can provide. And entertainment venues are more fully protected (as artistic expression) by the First Amendment provisions for free speech in the United States and therefore skirt much of the regulation imposed on traditional advertising. But not all consumers are wildly enthusiastic about the blurring line between advertising and entertainment. But in just exactly what real world is it that there are no real brands visible and being used? Personally, we don't think today's consumers find it particularly distracting, particularly if it's done well. (See Insights Online [Exhibit 3.30] for an interesting example.)

LO 4

3-5 THE VALUE OF HISTORY

As intriguing as mobile apps and other new technology is, and as exciting as new communications options like Web films may be, we shouldn't jump to the conclusion that everything about advertising will change. So far, it hasn't fundamentally changed. Advertising remains a paid attempt to persuade. As a business process, advertising will still be one of the primary marketing mix tools that contribute to revenues and profits by stimulating demand and nurturing brand loyalty. Even though the executives believe there is a whole new world of communication and have developed dozens of websites to take advantage of this new world, these firms still spend most of their money on traditional advertising through traditional media. It is also safe to argue that consumers will still

be highly involved in some product decisions and not so involved in others, so that some messages will be particularly relevant and others will be completely irrelevant to forming and maintaining beliefs and feelings about brands. To this date, technology (particularly e-commerce and m-commerce, or mobile commerce) has changed the way people shop, gather information, attend events, and purchase. And although the advance in online advertising continues, net TV revenues are still attractive. Where else are you going to get such an enormous audience with sight and sound? Don't confuse technology with persuasion.

In this chapter, we offered a historical perspective on advertising. As a lot of smart people know, history is very practical. You don't have to make the same mistakes over and over. Avoid *Groundhog Day* reality. Learn what works and doesn't work from the past. But don't get so focused on the past that you lose sight of the present and future.

SUMMARY

1 Tell the story of advertising's birth.

Although some might contend that the practice of advertising began thousands of years ago, it is more meaningful to connect advertising as we know it today with the emergence of modernity and capitalism. The explosion in production capacity that marked the Industrial Revolution gave demand-stimulation tools added importance. Mass moves of consumers to cities and modern times helped create, along with advertising, consumer culture.

2 Discuss several significant eras in the evolution of advertising in the United States, and relate important changes in advertising practice to fundamental changes in society and culture. How did successful advertising leverage the social and cultural forces of their day?

Before the Industrial Revolution, advertising's presence in the United States was barely noticeable. With an explosion in economic growth around the turn of the century, modern advertising was born: The "P. T. Barnum era" and the 1920s established advertising as a major force in the U.S. economic system, but was harsh, unregulated, and often unethical. It was carnivalesque. Advertising's heyday may have been the 1920s. In this period advertising was stylish, ands many of the techniques used today were invented. With the Great Depression and World War II, cynicism toward and distrust of advertising began to grow. This concern led to refinements in practice and more careful regulation of advertising in the 1960s and 1970s. The 1960s saw advertisers truly refine their skills in terms of resolving seemingly contradictory things:

advertising could now sell a revolution against un-hip consumption. Consumption was once again in vogue during the designer era of the 1980s. The new communication technologies that emerged in the 1990s gave rise to greater consumer connectivity (with each other) and access to relevant consumer information. From then until the current period, we have seen advertisers adjust to new media, the greatest economic upheaval since the Great Depression, and the merging of advertising with other entertainment and communication technologies. In all of this change, the constant is that advertiser rely on familiar strategies to react to a changing culture and society.

3 Tell the story of greater consumer access to information and connectivity to one another, branded entertainment, and how it works.

Integrated, *interactive*, and *wireless* have become the advertising buzzwords of the early 21st century. These words represent notable developments that are reshaping consumer behavior, marketing, and advertising practice.

4 Identify forces that will continue to affect the evolution of advertising and integrated brand promotion. Put history to work today.

Knowing the story of branded entertainment will be helpful because advertising will always be a paid attempt to persuade. Consumers will continue to be affected by social and cultural change and provide opportunities for advertisers. Understanding history can help them understand what works and avoid making the same mistakes again.

KEY TERMS

Industrial Revolution	chain of needs	interactive media
principle of limited liability	Great Depression	consumer-generated content (CGC)
branding	subliminal advertising	e-business
dailies	Action for Children's Television	branded entertainment
consumer culture	Federal Trade Commission (FTC)	
Pure Food and Drug Act	National Advertising Review Board	

ENDNOTES

1. Julian Simon, *Issues in the Economics of Advertising* (Urbana: University of Illinois Press, 1970), 41–51.

2. Vincent P. Norris, "Advertising History—According to the Textbooks," *Journal of Advertising*, vol. 9, no. 3 (1980), 3–12.

3. James W. Carey, *Communication as Culture: Essays on Media and Society* (Winchester, MA: Unwin Hyman, 1989).

4. Christopher P. Wilson, "The Rhetoric of Consumption: Mass-Market Magazines and the Demise of the Gentle Reader, 1880–1920," in Richard Weightman Fox and T. J. Jackson Lears (Eds.), *The Culture of Consumption: Critical Essays in American History, 1880–1980* (New York: Pantheon, 1983), 39–65.

5. Frank Presbrey, *The History and Development of Advertising* (Garden City, NY: Doubleday, Doran & Co., 1929), 7.

6. Ibid., 11.

7. Ibid., 40.

8. James P. Wood, *The Story of Advertising* (New York: Ronald, 1958), 45–46.

9. Daniel Pope, *The Making of Modern Advertising and Its Creators* (New York: William Morrow, 1984), 14.

10. Cited in Stephen Fox, *The Mirror Makers: A History of American Advertising and Its Creators* (New York: William Morrow, 1984), 14.

11. Ibid., 14.

12. Presbrey, *The History and Development of Advertising*, 16.

13. Bruce Barton, *The Man Nobody Knows* (New York: Bobbs-Merrill, 1924).

14. James Lincoln Collier, *The Rise of Selfishness in America* (New York: Oxford University Press, 1991), 162.

15. Ibid., 303–304.

16. Fox, *The Mirror Makers*, 168.

17. Wini Breines, *Young, White and Miserable: Growing Up Female in the Fifties* (Boston: Beacon, 1992).

18. Mark Pendergrast, *For God, Country & Coca-Cola: The Definitive History of the Great American Soft Drink and the Company That Makes It* (New York: Basic Books, 2003).

19. Vance Packard, *The Hidden Persuaders* (New York: D. McKay, 1957). With respect to the effects of "subliminal advertising," researchers have shown that although subliminal *communication* is possible, subliminal *persuasion*, in the typical real-world environment, remains all but impossible. As it was discussed, as mind control, in the 1950s, it remains a joke. See Timothy E. Moore, "Subliminal Advertising: What You See Is What You Get," *Journal of Marketing*, vol. 46 (Spring 1982), 38–47.

20. Stuart Rogers, "How a Publicity Blitz Created the Myth of Subliminal Advertising," *Public Relations Quarterly* (Winter 1992–1993), 12–17.

21. Fox, *The Mirror Makers*, 218.

22. Thomas Frank, *The Conquest of Cool: Business Culture, Counterculture, and the Rise of Hip Consumerism* (Chicago: University of Chicago Press, 1997).

23. Ibid., 235.

24. Tom Engelhardt, "The Shortcake Strategy," in Todd Gitlin (Ed.), *Watching Television* (New York: Pantheon, 1986), 68–110.

25. http://www.ciadvertising.org/studies/student/99_fall/theory/cal/aainadvertising/folder/burrell.html

26. http://blackmbamagazine.net/articles/docs/2005-2_an%20advertising%20legend%20leads%20with%20passion%20purpose%20and%20power.pdf

27. Collier, *The Rise of Selfishness in America*, 230.

28. This quote and information from this section can be found in Steve Yahn, "Advertising's Grave New World," *Advertising Age*, May 16, 1994, 53.

29. Kevin Goodman, "Sprint Chief Lectures Agencies on Future," *The Wall Street Journal*, April 28, 1995, B6.

30. Stuart Elliot, "Procter & Gamble Calls Internet Marketing Executives to Cincinnati for a Summit Meeting," *The New York Times*, August 19, 1998, D3, http://www.nytimes.com, accessed February 20, 1999.

31. Beth Snyder Bulik, "Procter & Gamble's Great Web Experiment," *Business 2.0*, November 28, 2000, 48–54.

Social, Ethical, and Regulatory Aspects of Advertising and Promotion

After reading and thinking about this chapter, you will be able to do the following:

1 Identify the benefits and problems of advertising and promotion in a capitalistic society and debate a variety of issues concerning their effects on society's well-being.

2 Explain how ethical considerations affect the development and implementation of advertising and IBP campaigns.

3 Discuss the role of government agencies and consumers in the regulation of advertising and promotion.

4 Explain the meaning and importance of self-regulation for firms that develop and use advertising and promotion.

5 Discuss the regulation of the full range of techniques used in the IBP process.

In this chapter, we consider a wide range of social, ethical, and legal issues related to advertising and the many tools of integrated brand promotion, and will do so in an analytical fashion. What is socially responsible or irresponsible, ethically acceptable, politically correct, or legal? As technology, cultural trends, and consumer behavior change, the answers to these questions are constantly changing as well. As a society changes, so does its perspectives and values. Like anything else with social roots and implications, advertising and promotion will affect and be affected by these changes.

We will start with advertising—the promotional tool that tends to get the most scrutiny because of its global presence—and then we will move on to other promotional tools in IBP.

LO 1

4-1 THE SOCIAL ASPECTS OF ADVERTISING

The social aspects of advertising are often volatile. For those who feel that advertising is intrusive, crass,

and manipulative, the social aspects usually provide the most fuel for heated debate.

We can consider the social aspects of advertising in several broad areas that highlight both the positive and negative social aspects of advertising. On the positive side, we'll consider advertising's effect on consumers' knowledge, standard of living, and feelings of happiness and well-being, and its potential positive effects on media. On the negative side, we'll examine a variety of social criticisms of advertising, ranging from the charge that advertising wastes resources and promotes materialism to the argument that advertising perpetuates stereotypes.

Our approach is to offer the pros and cons on several issues about which critics and advertisers commonly argue. Be forewarned—these are matters of opinion, with no clear right and wrong answers. You will have to draw your own conclusions. But above all, be analytical and thoughtful. These are important issues and without understanding and contemplating these issues, you really haven't studied advertising and promotion at all.

4-1a **Advertising Educates Consumers**

Does advertising provide valuable information to consumers, or does it seek only to confuse or entice them? Here's what the experts on both sides have to say.

Pro: Advertising Informs. Supporters of advertising argue that advertising educates consumers, equipping them with the information they need to make informed purchase decisions. By regularly assessing information and advertising claims, consumers become more educated regarding the features, benefits, functions, and value of products. Further, consumers can become more aware of their own tendencies toward being persuaded by certain types of product information. Historically, the very positive position has been offered that advertising is "clearly an immensely powerful instrument for the elimination of ignorance."[1] (See Insights Online [Exhibit 4.1] for an interesting example.) Now, that might be a *little* bit overstated, but according to this argument, better-educated consumers enhance their lifestyles and economic power through astute marketplace decision making—can't argue with that!

A related argument is that advertising *reduces product search time*—that is, the amount of time an individual spends to search for desired products and services is reduced because of advertising, access to the Web, and mobile messages from advertisers. The large amount of information readily available through advertising and websites allows consumers to easily assess information about the potential value of brands without spending time and effort traveling from retail store to retail store trying to evaluate each one. The information contained in an advertisement "reduces drastically the cost of search."[2]

Another aspect of informing the public has to do with the role advertising can play in communicating about important social issues. Miller Brewing devotes millions of dollars a year to promoting responsible drinking with both print and television advertisements like the one shown in Exhibit 4.2.

Con: Advertising Is Superficial and Intrusive. Critics argue that advertising does not provide good product information at all and that it is so pervasive and intrusive to daily life that it is impossible to escape. The basic criticism of advertising with respect to it being superficial focuses on the argument that many ads don't carry enough actual product information. What it does carry is said to be hollow ad-speak. Ads are rhetorical; there is no pure "information." All information in an ad is biased, limited, and inherently deceptive. Continuing on, critics of advertising believe that ads should contain information on brands that relates strictly to functional features and performance results—things that can be measured and tested brand by brand. Critics

would argue that between the two ads that appear in Exhibits 4.3 and 4.4, only the Suzuki ad on the left carries "real" and "informative" product information because the message contains functional feature information.

Advertisers argue in response that, in many instances, consumers are interested in more than a physical, tangible product with performance features and purely functional value. The functional features of a brand may be secondary in importance to consumers in both the information search and the choice process. Emotional and lifestyle factors play an important role in consumers' choices. The Honda ad in Exhibit 4.4 is just such a lifestyle ad. This ad has only one short line of message copy: "There are minivans, then there's the Odyssey." The ad is more about the lifestyle the Honda Odyssey minivan can facilitate. The advertisers' position with respect to this ad and similar lifestyle ads is to say that critics often dismiss as unimportant or ignore the totality of brand benefits that consumers seek, including emotional, hedonic (pleasure-seeking), or aesthetic aspects. The relevant information being used by a buyer may focus on criteria that are nonutilitarian or nonfunctional in nature—but not irrelevant. Although the Suzuki ad in Exhibit 4.3 carries the type of information critics would prefer, advertisers would argue that the

INSIGHTS ONLINE

4.1 Go online to see the AdAge feature, "Google Maps Move on to Oceans."

EXHIBIT 4.2 Advertising can be used to inform the public about important social issues. Miller Brewing spends millions of dollars a year promoting responsible drinking behavior.

EXHIBITS 4.3 AND 4.4 Critics of advertising complain that ads often carry little, if any, product information and would prefer that all advertising be rich in "information" like the Suzuki ad in Exhibit 4.3. Do you think the Honda ad in Exhibit 4.4 is devoid of "information"?

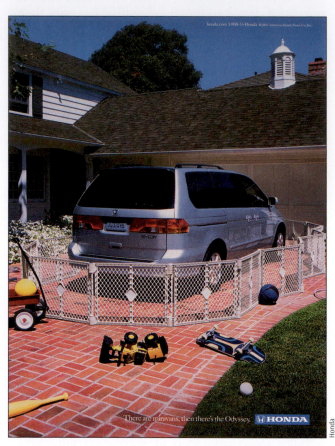

information in the Honda ad in Exhibit 4.4 provides information that is just as relevant to consumers—emotional/lifestyle information.

With respect to the intrusive aspect of advertising, the argument is that advertising has become so widespread (in some critics' view, ubiquitous) that consumers are starting to revolt. In a Planetfeedback .com survey where respondents expressed their annoyance with pop-up ads, the study found that more than 95 percent of consumers considered themselves "angry" or "furious" over email spam and website pop-up ads.[3] Similarly, consumers are getting increasingly concerned and frustrated with brands working their way into entertainment and information programming. The so-called commerce-content crossover—brand placement (like the Coca-Cola cups that sit on the desk in front of *American Idol* judges) and paid bloggers who write about brands but don't reveal their affiliation with companies—was rated as allowing advertising to become too pervasive by 72 percent of consumers surveyed.[4] Despite widespread consumer aggravation, it would seem that advertisers really aren't paying much attention. On the one hand, consumers seem to be saying loud and clear that advertising

is getting just too widespread and intruding on their lives and lifestyles. On the other hand, big advertisers like American Express are pushing to become more "relevant" to consumers than a mere 30-second advertising spot and to make their brands part of consumer lifestyles. So much so that the chief marketing officer at American Express said in a keynote speech to a large advertising audience, "We need to adapt to the new landscape by thinking not in day-parts [referring to television advertising schedules] but to mindparts."[5] We'll let you decide what you think of that one.

But the advertising industry should really be paying attention to consumers' aggravation with the clutter and intrusiveness of advertising for one very important reason—clutter and intrusiveness reduce the effectiveness of advertising. According to one expert, "The ability of the average consumer to even remember advertising 24 hours later is at the lowest level in the history of our business."[6] Is the industry likely to work to reduce clutter? Probably not. Another industry expert suggests that "New media have more potential to deliver even more saturation, clutter, and intrusiveness than traditional media, in which case the new media will only worsen marketing resistance."[7]

4-1b Advertising Improves the Standard of Living

Whether advertising raises or lowers the general standard of living is hotly debated. Opinions vary widely on this issue and go right to the heart of whether advertising is a good use or a waste of energy and resources. (See Insights Online [Exhibit 4.5] for an example of an advertising message that appeals to a healthier lifestyle.)

Pro: The Economic Effects of Advertising Lower the Cost of Products. Four aspects of the nature of advertising, supporters argue, help lower the cost of products:

- Due to the economies of scale (it costs less to produce products in large quantities), partly created by advertising's contribution to stimulating demand, products cost less than if there were no advertising at all. As broad-based demand stimulation results in lower production and administrative costs per unit produced, lower prices are passed on to consumers.

- Consumers have a greater variety of choice in products and services because advertising increases the probability of success that new products will succeed. The more products that succeed, the fewer losses firms incur from failed product introductions. In the end, this should make products cost less.

- The pressures of competition and the desire to have fresh, marketable brands motivate firms to produce improved products and brands and introduce lower-priced brands.

- The speed and reach of the advertising process aids in the diffusion of innovations. This means that new discoveries can be delivered to a large percentage of the marketplace very quickly. Innovations succeed when advertising communicates their benefits to the customer.

All four of these factors can contribute positively to the standard of living and quality of life in a society. Advertising may be instrumental in bringing about these effects because it serves an important role in demand stimulation and keeping customers informed.

Con: Advertising Wastes Resources and Raises the Standard of Living Only for Some. In response to the positive economic effects of advertising, one of the traditional, long standing criticisms of advertising is that it represents an inefficient, wasteful process that does little more than "shuffling of existing total demand," rather than contributing to the expansion of total demand.[8] Advertising thus brings about economic stagnation and a lower standard of living, not a higher standard of living. Similarly, critics argue that brand differences are trivial and that the proliferation of brands does not offer a greater variety of choice but rather a meaningless waste of resources and confusion and frustration for the consumer. Finally, they argue that advertising is a tool of capitalism that only helps widen the gap between rich and poor, creating strife between social classes.

INSIGHTS ONLINE

4.5 Go online to see the AdAge feature, "Special K Offers Cracker Crisps as a Healthier Alternative to Chips."

4-1c Advertising Affects Happiness and General Well-Being

Critics and supporters of advertising differ significantly in their views about how advertising affects consumers' happiness and general well-being. As you will see, this is a complex issue with multiple pros and cons. (See Insights Online [Exhibit 4.6] for a more positive perspective.)

Con: Advertising Creates Needs. A common cry among critics is that advertising creates needs and makes people buy things they don't really need or even want. The argument is that consumers are relatively easy to seduce into wanting the next shiny bauble offered by marketers. Critics would say, for example, that a quick examination of any issue of *Seventeen* magazine reveals a magazine intent on teaching the young women of the world to covet slim bodies and a glamorous complexion. Recently, consumers have become active with regard to the issue of advertising effects on women. An ad run by a luxury fitness chain sparked outrage when the firm ran an ad featuring "waif-like women languishing around a mansion in sexually suggestive positions" without a single treadmill or work-out machine in site.[9] Similarly, cosmetics giants like Estée Lauder and Revlon typically spend from 15 to 30 cents from every dollar of sales to promote their brands as the ultimate solution for those in search of the ideal complexion.

Pro: Advertising Addresses a Wide Variety of Basic Human Needs. A useful and informative place to start in discussing whether advertising can create needs or not is to consider the basic nature of human needs. Abraham Maslow, a pioneer in the study of human motivation (and

INSIGHTS ONLINE

4.6 Go online to see the AdAge feature, "The Peace Button Is a Button You Push on Your Computer or Mobile Device That Lets You Show Your Support of Peace Day; It Is Done by Agency Euro RSCG London."

someone you probably read about in your psychology or management class), conceived that human behavior progresses through the following hierarchy of need states[10]:

- *Physiological needs:* Biological needs that require the satisfaction of hunger, thirst, and basic bodily functions.

- *Safety needs:* The need to provide shelter and protection for the body and to maintain a comfortable existence.

- *Love and belonging needs:* The need for affiliation and affection. A person will strive for both the giving and receiving of love.

- *Esteem needs:* The need for recognition, status, and prestige. In addition to the respect of others, there is a need and desire for self-respect.

- *Self-actualization needs:* This is the highest of all the need states and is achieved by only a small percentage of people, according to Maslow. The individual strives for maximum fulfillment of individual capabilities.

It must be clearly understood that Maslow was describing *basic* human needs and motivations, not consumer needs and motivations. But in the context of an affluent society, individuals can and do turn to goods and services to satisfy needs. Many products are said to directly address the requirements of one or more of these need states. Food and health care products, for example, relate to physiological needs. Home security systems and smoke detectors help address safety needs. Many personal care products, such as the skin care brand highlighted in Exhibit 4.7, can promote feelings of self-esteem, confidence, glamour, and romance. In this ad, Garnier features a beautiful young woman as a way to communicate the brand's purpose of providing skin nurturing benefits which contribute to feelings of confidence and self-esteem.

In the pursuit of esteem, many consumers buy products they perceive to have status and prestige: expensive jewelry, clothing, automobiles, and homes are examples. Although it may be difficult to buy self-actualization (the highest level of Maslow's hierarchy), educational pursuits and high-intensity leisure activities (e.g., extreme sports and the gear it takes to pursue them) can certainly foster feelings of pride and accomplishment that contribute to self-actualization. Supporters maintain that advertising may be directed at many different forms of need fulfillment, but it is in no way powerful enough to *create* basic human needs. That is, the need exists as a human motivation and advertised products offer a means to pursue that

motivation. (See Insights Online [Exhibit 4.8] for an interesting example.)

Con: Advertising Promotes Materialism. It is also claimed that individuals' wants and aspirations may be distorted by advertising. The long-standing argument is that in societies characterized by heavy advertising, there is a tendency for conformity and status-seeking behavior, both of which are considered materialistic and superficial.[11] Material goods are placed ahead of spiritual and intellectual pursuits. Advertising, which portrays brands as symbols of status, success, and happiness, contributes to the materialism and superficiality in a society. It creates wants and aspirations that are artificial and self-centered. This, in turn, results in an overemphasis on the production of private goods, to

INSIGHTS ONLINE

4.8 Go online to see the AdAge feature, "Twitter Cake Serves as Techno-Art."

the detriment of public goods (such as highways, parks, schools, social services, and infrastructure).[12]

Pro: Advertising Only Reflects Society's Priorities.
Although advertising is undeniably in the business of promoting the good life, defenders of advertising argue that it did not create the American emphasis on materialism. For example, in the United States, major holidays such as Christmas (gifts), Thanksgiving (food), and Easter (candy and clothing) have become festivals of consumption. This is the American way. Historian and social observer Stephen Fox concludes his treatise on the history of American advertising as follows:

> One may build a compelling case that American culture is—beyond redemption—money-mad, hedonistic, superficial, rushing heedlessly down a railroad track called Progress. Tocqueville and other observers of the young republic described America in these terms in the early 1800s, decades before the development of national advertising. To blame advertising now for these most basic tendencies in American history is to miss the point. . . . The people who have created modern advertising are not hidden persuaders pushing our buttons in the service of some malevolent purpose. They are just producing an especially visible manifestation, good and bad, of the American way of life.[13]

Although we clearly live in the age of consumption, goods and possessions have been used by all cultures throughout history to mark special events, to play significant roles in rituals, and to serve as vessels of special meaning long before there was modern advertising. Still, have we taken it too far? Is excess what we do best in consumer cultures?

4-1d Advertising: Demeaning and Deceitful, or Liberating and Artful?

Without a doubt, advertisers are always on the lookout for creative and novel ways to grab and hold the attention of their audience. In addition, an advertiser has a very specific profile of the target customer in mind (more about this in Chapter 6) when an ad is being created. Both of these fundamental propositions about how ads get developed can spark controversy.

Con: Advertising Perpetuates Stereotypes.
Advertisers often portray people in advertisements that look like members of their target audience with the hope that people who see the ad will be more prone to relate to the ad and attend to its message. Critics charge that this practice yields a very negative effect—it perpetuates stereotypes. The portrayal of women, the elderly, and ethnic minorities are of particular concern. It is argued

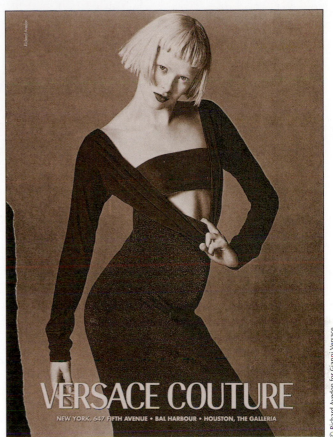

© Richard Avedon for Gianni Versace

that women are still predominantly cast as homemakers or objects of desire. Critics would argue that the model in the Versace ad in Exhibit 4.9 stereotypes women as frivolous and objects of desire rather than portraying women in the diverse, responsible roles they hold in society from top management positions to deftly heading households. The elderly are often shown as helpless or ill, even though many active seniors enjoy a rich lifestyle. Critics contend that advertisers' propensity to feature African American or Latin athletes in ads is simply a more contemporary form of stereotyping.

Pro: Advertisers Are Showing Much More Sensitivity.
Advocates of advertising counter with the argument that the stereotyping described above has become less prevalent and becoming part of the past. Advertisements from prior generations do show a vivid stereotyping problem. But in today's setting, the Dove ad in Exhibit 4.10 shows that women can be featured as strong and feminine in contemporary advertising. Dove launched its "Campaign for Real Beauty" with a series of ads featuring real women (not models) whose appearances do not conform to the stereotypical and relatively narrow norms of beauty. The ads asked viewers to judge the women's looks

EXHIBIT 4.10   Advertisers today realize the diverse reality of consumers' lives. This Dove ad is a beautiful example of advertisers' efforts to represent diversity.

©Unilever USA, Inc. and Edelman

(*Oversized? Outstanding? or Wrinkled? Wonderful?*) and invited them to cast their votes and join in a discussion of beauty issues at www.campaignforrealbeauty .com. In addition, advertisers ranging from financial services, to retirement communities, to cruise lines now show seniors in fulfilling, active lifestyles—hardly a demeaning portrayal of that demographic group. Advertisers are realizing that a diverse world requires diversity in the social reality that ads represent and help construct. However, many remain dissatisfied with the pace of change.

Con: Advertising Is Often Offensive. A long-standing criticism of advertising is that it is often offensive and the appeals are in poor taste. We certainly saw some of that in Chapter from advertising eras gone by. Moreover, some would say that the trend in American advertising is to be rude, crude, and sometimes lewd, as advertisers struggle to grab the attention of consumers who have learned to tune out the avalanche of advertising messages they are confronted with each day. GoDaddy made its mark in a highly competitive market with just such a lewd and crude ad campaign featuring Danica Patrick the race car driver. Of course, taste is just that, a personal and inherently subjective evaluation. What is offensive to one person is merely satiric to another. What should we call an ad prepared for the Australian market that shows the owner of an older Honda Accord admiring a newer model? In an ad campaign prepared for the Australian market, a Honda owner's admiration of a newer Honda

model spurs the old version to lock its doors, rev its motor, and drive off a cliff—with the owner still inside. Critics decry the ad as trivializing suicide—an acute problem among young people, who are also the target market for this ad.[14]

But not all advertising deemed offensive has to be as extreme as these examples. Many times, advertisers get caught in a firestorm of controversy because certain, and sometimes relatively small, segments of the population are offended. The history of advertising is loaded with examples. A highly popular ad seen as controversial by some was the "People Taking Diet Coke Break" ad (this ad was featured in Chapter 1). In this television spot, a group of female office workers is shown eyeing a construction worker as he takes off his T-shirt and enjoys a Diet Coke. Coca-Cola was criticized for using reverse sexism in this ad. Although Coca-Cola may have ventured into a delicate area, consider the following advertisers, who were caught completely by surprise when their ads were deemed offensive:

- In a public service spot developed by Aetna Life & Casualty insurance for a measles vaccine, a wicked witch with green skin and a wart was cause for a challenge to the firm's ad from a witches' rights group.

- A Nynex spot was criticized by animal-rights activists because it showed a rabbit colored with blue dye.

- A commercial for Black Flag bug spray had to be altered after a war veterans' group objected to the playing of "Taps" over dead bugs.

In the end, we have to consider whether advertising is offensive or whether society is merely pushing the limits of what is appropriate for freedom of speech and expression. The now infamous "wardrobe malfunction" that plagued Janet Jackson during a Super Bowl halftime show and incidents like shock radio DJs' profanity are drawing attention not only from fed-up consumers but also from the U.S. Senate as well, which several years ago approved a tenfold increase in fines for television and radio stations that violate rules on airing profanity and sexually explicit materials.[15] And even though government may move to provide a legal remedy to deter offensive broadcasts—whether advertising messages or programming—the fact is that what is acceptable and what is offensive changes over time in a culture.

Pro: Advertising Is a Source of Fulfillment and Liberation. On the other end of the spectrum, some argue that the consumption that advertising glorifies is actually quite good for society. Most people sincerely appreciate modern conveniences that liberate us from the more foul facets of everyday life, such as body odor, close contact with dirty diapers, and washing clothes by hand. Some observers remind us that when the Berlin Wall came down, those in East Germany did not immediately run to libraries and churches—they ran to department stores and shops. Before the modern consumer age, the consumption of many goods was restricted by social class. Modern advertising has helped bring us a "democratization" of goods. Observers argue that there is a liberating quality to advertising and consumption that should be appreciated and encouraged.

Con: Advertisers Deceive via Subliminal Stimulation. There is much controversy, and almost a complete lack of understanding that persists about the issue of subliminal (below the threshold of consciousness) communication and advertising.[16] Since there is so much confusion surrounding the issue of subliminal advertising, let us clarify: No one ever sold anything by putting images of breasts in ice cubes or the word sex in the background of an ad. Furthermore, no one at an advertising agency, except the very bored or the very eager to retire, has time to sit around dreaming up such things. We realize it makes for a great story, but hiding pictures in other pictures doesn't work to get anyone to buy anything. Although there is some evidence for some types of unconscious ad *processing*, these effects are very short-lived and found only in laboratories. The Svengali-type hocus-pocus that has become advertising mythology simply does not exist.[17] If the rumors are true that some advertisers are actually trying to use subliminal messages in their ads, the best research on the topic would conclude that they're wasting their money.[18]

Pro: Advertising Is Democratic Art. Some argue that one of the best aspects of advertising is its artistic nature. The pop art movement of the late 1950s and 1960s, particularly in London and New York, was characterized by a fascination with commercial culture. Some of this art critiqued consumer culture and simultaneously celebrated it. Above all, Andy Warhol, himself a commercial illustrator, demonstrated that art was for the people and that the most accessible art was advertising. Art was not restricted to museum walls; it was on Campbell's soup cans, LifeSavers candy rolls, and Brillo pads. Advertising is anti-elitist, pro-democratic, widely accessible art. Warhol said this about America, democracy, and Coke:

> What's great about this country is that America started the tradition where the richest consumers buy essentially the same things as the poorest. You can be watching TV and see Coca-Cola, and you can know that the President drinks Coke, Liz Taylor drinks Coke, and just think, you can drink Coke, too. A Coke is a Coke and no amount of money can get you a better Coke than the one the bum on the corner is drinking. All the Cokes are the same and all the Cokes are good. Liz Taylor knows it, the President knows it, the bum knows it, and you know it.[19]

4-1e Advertising Has a Powerful Effect on the Mass Media

One final issue that advertisers and their critics debate is the matter of advertising's influence on the mass media. Here again, we find a very wide range of viewpoints.

Pro: Advertising Fosters a Diverse and Affordable Mass Media. Advertising fans argue that advertising is the best thing that can happen to an informed democracy. Magazines, newspapers, television, radio stations, and websites are supported by advertising expenditures. In 2011, mass media advertising expenditures in the United States exceeded $102 billion.[20] Much of this spending went to support television, radio, magazines, and newspapers. If you include online advertising's support of websites, the number approaches $200 billion. With this sort of monetary support of the media, citizens have access to a variety of information and entertainment sources at low cost. Network television and radio broadcasts would not be free commodities, and newspapers and magazines would likely cost two to four times more in the absence of advertising support. Websites would be by monthly subscription. Now, as advertisers urgently try to access consumers through social media sites like Twitter and Facebook, social media are finding support from advertisers as well.

Another argument in support of advertising is that it provides invaluable exposure to issues. When noncommercial organizations (like social service organizations) use advertising, members of society receive information on important social and political issues. A dramatic example of the noncommercial use of advertising was a multimedia campaign launched by the U.S. government, working in conjunction with the Partnership for a Drug-Free America, to remind the American public of the ruinous power of drugs such as heroin.[21] During five years the campaign spending

EXHIBIT 4.11 This ad both appeals to our fascination with celebrities and shocks the viewer with the realization that drug use can be fatal. The Partnership for a Drug-Free America hones this message further at its website to communicate that drug use is anything but glamorous.

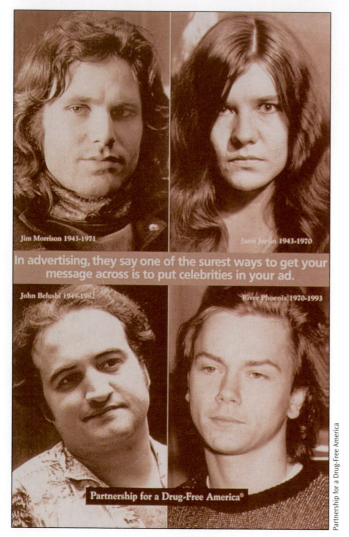

Jim Morrison 1943–1971   Janis Joplin 1943–1970

In advertising, they say one of the surest ways to get your message across is to put celebrities in your ad.

John Belushi 1949–1982   River Phoenix 1970–1993

Partnership for a Drug-Free America®

Partnership for a Drug-Free America

approached $1 billion. A stockpile of nearly 400 ads was available for use in this comprehensive campaign. Some, like the one shown in Exhibit 4.11, involved powerful messages about the ultimate consequence of drug abuse. Consumers are highly attentive to news about celebrities and ads featuring four widely known and talented celebrities who were lost to drug use was a powerful message indeed.

Con: Advertising Affects Programming. Critics argue that advertisers who place ads in media have an unhealthy effect on shaping the content of information contained in the media. And there are some pretty dramatic examples. The CEO of a firm headed for prosecution was accused of hiring a public relations firm to turn out a series of newspaper articles sympathetic

to the CEO's firm.[22] Similarly, there have been several instances of "stealth sponsorship" of newspaper opinion editorials where the journalists were being paid by corporations who were receiving favorable treatment in the editorials.[23]

Another charge leveled at advertisers is that they purchase airtime only on programs that draw large audiences. Critics argue that these mass market programs lower the quality of television because cultural and educational programs, which draw smaller and more selective markets, are dropped in favor of mass market programs. Watch a few episodes of *Survivor* or *Bridezilla* and it's hard to argue against the proposition that shallow content is indeed winning out over culture and education.

In addition, television programmers have a difficult time attracting advertisers to shows that may be valuable, yet address controversial social issues. Programs that deal with abortion, sexual abuse, or AIDS may have trouble drawing advertisers who fear the consequences of any association with controversial issues given the predictable public reaction that would come from the religious right.

LO ❷

4-2 THE ETHICAL ASPECTS OF ADVERTISING

Many of the ethical aspects of advertising border on and interact with both the social and legal considerations of the advertising process. **Ethics** are moral standards and principles against which behavior is judged. Honesty, integrity, fairness, and sensitivity are all included in a broad definition of ethics. Much of what is judged as ethical or unethical comes down to personal judgment. We will discuss the ethical aspects of advertising in three areas: truth in advertising, advertising to children, and advertising controversial products.

4-2a Truth in Advertising

Although truth in advertising is a key legal issue, it has ethical dimensions as well. The most fundamental ethical issue has to do with **deception**—making false or misleading statements in an advertisement. The difficulty regarding this issue, of course, is in determining just what is deceptive. A manufacturer who claims a laundry product can remove grass stains is exposed to legal sanctions if the product cannot perform the task. Another manufacturer who claims to have "The Best Laundry Detergent in the World," however, is perfectly within its rights to employ superlatives. The use of absolute superlatives such as "Number One" or

"Best in the World" is called **puffery** and is considered completely legal. The courts have long held that superlatives are understood by consumers as simply the exaggerated commercial language of advertising and are interpreted by consumers as such.

We also need to be aware that various promotional tools are often challenged as being deceptive. The "small print" that accompanies many contests or sweepstakes is often challenged by consumers. Similarly, the appeal of a "free" gift for listening to a pitch on a resort time share often draws a harsh reaction from consumers. Consumer watchdog groups argue that a variety of advertising and promotional practices are deceptive. One such group, Public Citizen's Commercial Alert, has argued for years that television networks are deceiving consumers by not disclosing that they are taking money for highlighting brands within shows and films. The organizations states that, "Product placements are inherently deceptive, because many people do not realize that they are, in fact, advertisements."[24]

Another area of debate regarding truth in advertising relates to emotional appeals. It is fundamentally impossible to legislate against emotional appeals such as those made about the beauty- or prestige-enhancing qualities of a brand, because these claims are unquantifiable. Since these types of appeals are legal, the ethics of such appeals fall into a gray area. Beauty and prestige, it is argued, are in the eye of the beholder, and such appeals are neither illegal nor unethical.

As you can see, there is nothing clear cut about the issue of ethics in advertising. Showing beautiful, slim, successful people in an ad is completely legal and puts a brand in a favorable setting—do you think that is unethical? If a newspaper or magazine features a brand in an editorial—do you think that is unethical? What about when Tom Cruise says he wants a Red Stripe beer in the movie *Top Gun?* Do you think that is unethical? The challenge is to develop your own ethical standards and values against which you will judge yourself and the actions of any organization for which you may work.

4-2b Advertising to Children

Children are viewed as vulnerable consumers and the desire to restrict advertising aimed at children is based on a wide range of concerns, not the least of which is that at one time it was estimated that children between 2 and 11 years old see around 25,600 ads in a year.[25] (See Insights Online [Exhibit 4.12] for an example of advertising to children using social media.) One concern about this heavy volume of advertising directed at children is that advertising promotes superficiality and creates values founded in material goods and consumption. Another is that children are inexperienced

consumers and easy prey for the sophisticated persuasions of advertisers, and as such, advertising influences children's demands for everything from toys to snack foods. These demands, in turn, create an environment of child–parent conflict. Parents find themselves having to say no over and over again to children whose desires are piqued by effective advertising. Add to that, the historical view held by child psychologists who contend that advertising advocates violence, is responsible for child obesity, creates a breakdown in early learning skills, and results in a destruction of parental authority.[26]

There is also concern that many television programs, videos, and films aimed at children constitute program-length commercials. This movement began in 1990 when critics argued that 70 programs airing at the time were based on commercial products such as He-Man, the Smurfs, and the Muppets.[27] Today's "commercial" stars include Shrek and SpongeBob SquarePants. There have been several attempts by special-interest groups to strictly regulate this type of programming aimed at children, but, to date, the Federal Communications Commission permits such programming to continue.

There have been movements to restrict the amount of advertising children might see. One of the earliest restrictions was due to the efforts of the special-interest group Action for Children's Television that helped get the Children's Television Act passed in 1990. This regulation restricts advertising on children's programming to 10.5 minutes per hour on weekends and 12 minutes per hour on weekdays.[28] In 2006, the Council of Better Business Bureaus and 10 large food marketers—like McDonald's, Kraft, Pepsi, and General Mills—signed the Children's Food and Beverage Advertising Initiative. Now 16 companies have joined the initiative. The initiative is a voluntary commitment by firms to address the issue of obesity among children. A key element of the agreement is that food and beverage marketers will devote half of their advertising dollars to ads promoting healthier eating alternatives for children.[29]

You should be aware, however, that there is another side of the advertising to children ethical debate. There is the fairly well-supported argument that children grow up in a system where consumption is a part of everyday life. As such, they learn the rules of "commerce" early and understand full well that people are trying to sell them "stuff." Research has found that at a fairly young age children understand what advertising is, gain a healthy skepticism for advertising, and clearly recognize its intent.[30]

4-2c Advertising Controversial Products

Some people question the wisdom of allowing the advertising of controversial products and services, such as tobacco, alcoholic beverages, gambling and lotteries, and firearms. Critics charge that tobacco and alcoholic beverage firms are targeting adolescents with advertising and with making dangerous and addictive products appealing.[31] This is, indeed, a complex issue. Many medical journals have published survey research that claims that advertising "caused" cigarette and alcohol consumption—particularly among teenagers.[32] The controversy over alcohol has moved to the forefront as recent looser restrictions by networks have caused a huge spike in spending and ad placement on television by alcoholic beverage marketers.[33]

It is essential to note, however, that these recent studies completely contradict research conducted since the 1950s carried out by marketing, communications, psychology, and economics researchers—including assessments of all the available research by the Federal Trade Commission.[34] These early studies (as well as several Gallup polls during the 1990s) found that family, friends, and peers—not advertising—are the primary influence on the use of tobacco and alcohol products. Studies published in the late 1990s and early 2000s have reaffirmed the findings of this earlier research.[35] Although children at a very early age can, indeed, recognize tobacco advertising characters like "Joe Camel," they also recognize as easily the Energizer Bunny (batteries), the Jolly Green Giant (canned vegetables), and Snoopy (life insurance)—all characters associated with adult products. Kids are also aware that cigarettes cause disease and know that they are intended as an adult product. Research in Europe offers the same conclusion: "Every study on the subject [of advertising effects on the use of tobacco and alcohol] finds that children are more influenced by parents and playmates than by the mass media."[36]

Why doesn't advertising cause people to smoke and drink? The simple answer is that advertising just isn't that powerful. The more detailed answer is that advertising cannot create primary demand in mature product categories. **Primary demand** is demand for an entire product category (recall the discussion from Chapter 1). With mature products—like milk, automobiles, toothpaste, cigarettes, and alcohol—advertising isn't powerful enough to have that effect. Research across several decades has demonstrated repeatedly that advertising does not create primary demand for tobacco or alcohol or any other mature product category.[37] Advertising is only

> ### *Advertising is only capable of stimulating demand for a brand within a product category.*

capable of stimulating demand for a *brand within* a product category. Product category demand is the result of social and cultural trends, economic conditions, technological change, and other broad influences on consumers' needs and lifestyles.

No one has ever said that smoking or drinking is good for you. (Except for maybe that glass of wine with dinner.) That's not what we're saying here, either. The point is that these behaviors emerge in a complex social context, and the vast weight of research evidence throughout 50 years asserts that advertising is not a significant causal influence on initiation behavior (e.g., smoking, drinking). Rather, advertising plays its most important role in consumers' choice of brands (e.g., Camel, Coors) after consumers have decided to use a product category (e.g., cigarettes, beer).

Gambling and state-run lotteries represent another controversial product area with respect to advertising. What is the purpose of this advertising? Is it meant to inform gamblers and lottery players of the choices of games and places to play? This would be selective (i.e., brand) demand stimulation. Or is such advertising designed to stimulate demand for engaging in wagering behavior? This would be primary demand stimulation. What about compulsive gamblers? What is the state's obligation to protect "vulnerable" citizens by restricting the placement or content of lottery advertising?

When the term "vulnerable" is used, questions as to the basis for the claim of vulnerability can become complex and emotionally charged. Those on one side of the issue argue that gamblers as an audience are among the "information poor." That is, they are not prone to seeking out information from a wide range of sources. Those on the other side find such claims of "information poverty" demeaning, patronizing, and paternalistic. And a new era of gambling emerged when online gambling became widespread and proved to be a fast and easy way for people to lose their life savings. Stories of out-of-control online gambling were widespread.

The issue of advertising controversial products can indeed be complex. One would not normally put food in the "controversial products" category. But, as people began suing companies claiming that their advertising caused them to eat unhealthy food and made them fat—well, suddenly there is a controversy. McDonald's and other food companies had to defend themselves against lawsuits from people who have claimed food providers "made them fat." The food industry has countered with the proposition that kids are fat because of unconcerned parents, underfunded school systems that have dropped physical activity programs, and sedentary entertainment, like home video games.[38]

This issue is troublesome enough that the U.S. government had to pass legislation barring people from suing food companies for their obesity. In March 2004, the U.S. House of Representatives overwhelmingly approved legislation nicknamed the "Cheeseburger Bill" that would block lawsuits blaming the food industry for making people fat. During the debate on the bill, one of the bill's sponsors said it was about "common sense and personal responsibility."[39] Many marketers are worried about the intense focus on this global health problem. The chief creative officer of Coca-Cola Co. put it this way: "Our Achilles heel is the discussion about obesity. It dilutes our marketing and works against us. It's a huge, huge issue."[40] And, as you read earlier, advertisers have entered into a voluntary agreement to devote 50 percent of their ad dollars to promoting healthy food alternatives to children as a way to show good faith with respect to the advertising and obesity issue.

Although we can group these ethical issues of advertising into some reasonable categories—truth in advertising, advertising to children, and advertising controversial products—it is not as easy to make definitive statements about the status of ethics in advertising. Ethics will always be a matter of personal values and personal interpretation. (See Insights Online [Exhibit 4.13] for an interesting example.) And as long as there are unethical people in the world, there will be ethics problems in advertising just like in every other phase of business and life.

INSIGHTS ONLINE

4.13 Go online to see the AdAge feature, "Food Is Part of Consumer Ritual at Thanksgiving, and Now Celebrities at Your Thanksgiving Dinner Photo?"

LO ③

4-3 THE REGULATORY ASPECTS OF ADVERTISING

The term *regulation* immediately brings to mind government scrutiny and control of the advertising process. Indeed, various government bodies do regulate advertising. But consumers themselves and several different industry organizations exert as much regulatory power over advertising as government agencies. Three primary groups—consumers, industry organizations, and government bodies—regulate advertising in the truest sense: Together they shape and restrict the process. The government relies on legal restrictions, while consumers and industry groups use less-formal controls. Like the other topics in this chapter, regulation of advertising can be controversial, and opinions about what does and doesn't need to be regulated can be highly variable.

4-3a Areas of Advertising Regulation

There are three basic areas of advertising regulation: deception and unfairness in advertising, competitive issues, and advertising to children. Each area is a focal point for regulatory action.

Deception and Unfairness. Agreement is widespread that deception in advertising is unacceptable—period. The problem, of course, is that it is as difficult to determine what is deceptive from a regulatory standpoint as it is from an ethical standpoint. The Federal Trade Commission's (FTC's) policy statement on deception is the authoritative source when it comes to defining deceptive advertising. It specifies the following three elements as essential in declaring an ad deceptive[41]:

1. There must be a representation, omission, or practice that is likely to mislead the consumer.

2. This representation, omission, or practice must be judged from the perspective of a consumer acting reasonably in the circumstance.

3. The representation, omission, or practice must be a "material" one. The basic question is whether the act or the practice is likely to affect the consumer's conduct or decision with regard to the product or service. If so, the practice is material and therefore consumer harm is likely because consumers are likely to have chosen differently if not for the deception.

If this definition of deception sounds like carefully worded legal jargon, that's because it is. It is also a definition that can lead to diverse interpretations when it is actually applied to advertisements in real life. One critical point about the FTC's approach to deception is that both implied claims and *missing* information can be bases for deeming an ad deceptive. Obviously, the FTC expects any explicit claim made in an ad to be truthful, but it also is on the lookout for ads that deceive through allusion and innuendo or ads that deceive by not telling the whole story.

Although the FTC and the courts have been reasonably specific about what constitutes deception, the definition of unfairness in advertising has been left relatively vague. In 1994, Congress ended a long-running dispute in the courts and in the advertising industry by approving legislation that defines **unfair advertising** as "acts or practices that cause or are likely to cause substantial injury to consumers, which is not reasonably avoidable by consumers themselves, and not outweighed by the countervailing benefits to consumers or competition."[42] This definition obligates the FTC to assess both the benefits and costs of advertising, and rules out reckless acts on the part of consumers, before a judgment can be rendered that an advertiser has been unfair.

Competitive Issues. Because the large dollar amounts spent on advertising may foster inequities that literally can destroy competition, several advertising practices relating to maintaining fair competition are regulated. Among these practices are cooperative advertising, comparison advertising, and the use of monopoly power.

Vertical cooperative advertising is an advertising technique whereby a manufacturer and dealer (either a wholesaler or retailer) share the expense of advertising. This technique is commonly used in regional or local markets where a manufacturer wants a brand to benefit from a special promotion run by local dealers (recall the co-op advertising example in Chapter 1). There is nothing illegal, per se, about this practice and it is used regularly.

The competitive threat inherent in the process, however, is that dealers (especially since the advent of first department store chains and now mega retailers like Walmart, Target, and Home Depot) can be given bogus cooperative advertising allowances from manufacturers. These allowances require little or no effort or expenditure on the part of the dealer/retailer and thus represent hidden price concessions. As such, they are a form of unfair competition and are deemed illegal. If an advertising allowance is granted to a dealer, that dealer must demonstrate that the funds are applied specifically to advertising.

Next, the potential exists for firms to engage in unfair competition if they use comparison ads inappropriately. **Comparison advertisements** are those in which an advertiser makes a comparison between the firm's brand and competitors' brands. The comparison may or may not explicitly identify the competition. Again, comparison ads are completely legal, are used frequently by all sorts of organizations, and are typically an effective technique.[43] The ad in Exhibit 4.14 is an example of straightforward and completely legal comparison advertising. SC Johnson, the maker of Ziploc storage bags, is comparing claiming that the Ziploc freezer bag with an extra inner layer can prevent freezer "burn" better than a standard freezer bag. But, such campaigns can get quite aggressive—the long-running and entertaining Apple vs. PC ads is an example and could have attracted regulatory scrutiny.[44]

If an advertisement is carried out in such a way that the comparison is not fair, then there is an unfair competitive effect. Further, the FTC may require a firm using comparison to substantiate claims made in an advertisement and prove that the claims do not tend to deceive. A slightly different remedy is the use of a disclaimer to help consumers understand comparative product claims. That's what Duracell had to do when it claimed its "Coppertop" battery lasted longer than Energizer's heavy duty battery. Although the

EXHIBIT 4.14 The advertising industry provides guidelines to advertisers to ensure that comparison ads offer fair comparisons. This Ziploc ad meets all the fair comparison criteria perfectly.

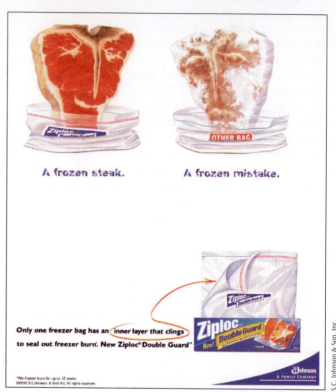

A frozen steak.   A frozen mistake.

Only one freezer bag has an *inner layer that clings* to seal out freezer burn. New Ziploc® Double Guard™

claim was technically true, the Coppertop is an alkaline battery and was not being compared to Energizer's alkaline battery—deemed an unfair comparison. Gillette, makers of Duracell, agreed to include a disclaimer in subsequent ads and then finally pulled the campaign altogether.[45]

Finally, some firms are so powerful in their use of advertising that **monopoly power** by virtue of their advertising spending can become a problem. This issue normally arises in the context of mergers and acquisitions. As an example, the FTC carefully investigated the acquisition of AdMob by Google based on the concern that the merging of the two companies would diminish competition in the mobile-advertising marketing.[46]

Advertising to Children. As we discussed in the area of ethics earlier in the chapter, critics argue that continually bombarding children with persuasive stimuli can alter their motivation and behavior. Even though government organizations, such as the FTC, have been active in trying to regulate advertising directed at children, industry and consumer groups have been just as successful in securing restrictions. Recall that the consumer group known as Action for Children's Television was actively involved in getting Congress to approve the Children's Television Act (1990). This act limits the amount of commercial airtime during children's programs to 10.5 minutes on weekends and 12 minutes on weekdays. One area of regulation where the FTC has recently reduced its efforts is the attempt to restrict the advertising of food products to children. Despite pressure from consumer organizations[47] who claim food advertising contributes to the problem of obesity in children, the FTC has stated that "the commission does not support legislation restricting food advertising to children."

The Council of Better Business Bureaus established a Children's Advertising Review Unit and has issued a set of guidelines for advertising directed at children. These guidelines emphasize that advertisers should be sensitive to the level of knowledge and sophistication of children as decision makers. The guidelines also urge advertisers to make a constructive contribution to the social development of children by emphasizing positive social standards in advertising, such as friendship, kindness, honesty, and generosity.

The Internet era has spawned an additional FTC regulation aimed at protecting children and limits the collection of information from preteen children. The Children's Online Privacy Protection Act (COPPA) regulates websites directed at children under 13. Any such site that gathers information must obtain parent or guardian consent before doing so. But, pre-teens are pretty creative, so often they find ways to circumvent the protection. Watchdog groups have asked that the regulation be strengthened because of the lack of means to strictly enforce regulation.[48]

4-3b Regulatory Agents

Earlier in this section, we noted that consumer and industry groups as well as government agencies all participate in the regulation of advertising. We will now discuss examples of each of these agents along with the kind of influence they exert. Given the multiple participants, this turns out to be a highly complex activity that we can only overview in this discussion. Note that the discussion here focuses on regulatory activities in the United States, but advertising regulation can vary dramatically from country to country.

Government Regulation. Governments have a powerful tool available for regulating advertising: the threat of legal action. In the United States, several different government agencies have been given the power and responsibility to regulate the advertising process. Exhibit 4.15 identifies the seven agencies that have legal mandates concerning advertising and their areas of regulatory responsibility. The newest, the Consumer Finance Protection Bureau (CFPB), was established as part of the Dodd–Frank Wall Street

Reform and Consumer Protection Act of 2010, in part, as a result of the financial crisis in 2009 caused by lack of banking regulations. Its authority includes the regulation of home loan and credit card practices as well as a regulatory system for financial services advertising.

Several other agencies have minor powers in the regulation of advertising, such as the Civil Aeronautics Board (advertising by air carriers), the Patent Office (trademark infringement), and the Library of Congress (copyright protection). The agencies listed in Exhibit 4.15 are the most directly involved in advertising regulation. Most active among these agencies is the Federal Trade Commission. The FTC has been granted legal power through legislative mandates and also has developed programs for regulating advertising.

The FTC Legislative Mandates. The Federal Trade Commission was created by the Federal Trade Commission Act in 1914. The original purpose of the agency was to prohibit unfair methods of competition. In 1916, the FTC concluded that false advertising was one way in which a firm could take unfair advantage of another, and advertising was established as a primary concern of the agency.

It was not until 1938 that the effects of deceptive advertising on consumers became a key issue for the FTC. The Wheeler-Lea Amendment (1938) broadened the FTC's powers to include regulation of advertising that was misleading to the public (regardless of the effect on competition). Through this amendment, the agency could order a firm to stop its deceptive practices.

Several other acts provide the FTC with legal powers over advertising. The Robinson–Patman Act (1936) prohibits firms from providing phantom cooperative-advertising allowances as a way to court important dealers. Consumer protection legislation, which seeks to increase the ability of consumers to make more-informed product comparisons, includes the Fair Packaging and Labeling Act (1966), the Truth in Lending Act (1969), and the Fair Credit Reporting Act (1970). The FTC Improvement Act (1975) expanded the authority of the commission by giving it the power to issue trade regulation rules.

Recent legislation has expanded the FTC's role in monitoring and regulating product labeling and advertising. The 1990 Nutrition Labeling and Education Act (NLEA) requires uniformity in the nutrition labeling of food products and establishes strict rules for claims about the nutritional attributes of food products. The standard "Nutrition Facts" label required by the NLEA now appears on everything from breakfast cereals to barbecue sauce.

EXHIBIT 4.15 Primary government agencies regulating advertising.

Government Agency	Areas of Advertising Regulation
Federal Trade Commission (FTC)	Most widely empowered agency in government. Controls unfair methods of competition, regulates deceptive advertising, and has various programs for controlling the advertising process.
Federal Communications Commission (FCC)	Prohibits obscenity, fraud, and lotteries on radio and television. Ultimate power lies in the ability to deny or revoke broadcast licenses.
Food and Drug Administration (FDA)	Regulates the advertising of food, drug, cosmetic, and medical products. Can require special labeling for hazardous products such as household cleaners. Prohibits false labeling and packaging.
Securities and Exchange Commission (SEC)	Regulates the advertising of securities and the disclosure of information in annual reports.
U.S. Postal Service (USPS)	Responsible for regulating direct mail advertising and prohibiting lotteries, fraud, and misrepresentation. It can also regulate and impose fines for materials deemed to be obscene.
Bureau of Alcohol, Tobacco, Firearms, and Explosives (ATF)	Most direct influence has been on regulation of advertising for alcoholic beverages. This agency was responsible for putting warning labels on alcoholic beverage advertising and banning active athletes as celebrities in beer ads. It has the power to determine what constitutes misleading advertising in these product areas.
Consumer Finance Protection Agency (CFPA)	As proposed, the agency would have broad oversight over nearly every consumer financial product, including credit cards, debit cards, mortgages, money transfers and payday loans. It would make sure that the disclosure for financial products are clearly presented to consumers, and would protect against abuse and fraud. The CFPA would also be charged with ensuring that traditionally underserved consumers have access to the credit system and other financial services.

© Cengage Learning

Of course, the Internet has spawned all sorts of scrutiny by the FTC. One area of particular scrutiny regarding children is privacy, which led to the Children's Online Privacy Act (COPPA) of 1998 in which the FTC states explicitly that:

> It is unlawful for an operator of a website or online service directed to children, or any operator that has actual knowledge that it is collecting personal information from a child, to collect personal information from a child in a manner that violates the regulations prescribed under subsection (b).[49]

Subsection (b) mandates that full disclosure of the website's information gathering (if any) must plainly appear on the website.

The FTC's Regulatory Programs and Remedies. The application of legislation has evolved as the FTC exercises its powers and expands its role as a regulatory agency. This evolution of the FTC has spawned several regulatory programs and remedies to help enforce legislative mandates in specific situations.

The **advertising substantiation program** of the FTC was initiated in 1971 with the intention of ensuring that advertisers make supporting evidence for their claims available to consumers. The program was strengthened in 1972 when the commission forwarded the notion of "reasonable basis" for the substantiation of advertising. This extension suggests not only that

advertisers should substantiate their claims, but also that the substantiation should provide a reasonable basis for believing the claims are true.[50] Simply put, before a company runs an ad, it must have documented evidence that supports the claim it wants to make in that ad. The kind of evidence required depends on the kind of claim being made. For example, health and safety claims will require competent and reliable scientific evidence that has been examined and validated by experts in the field (go to www.ftc.gov for additional guidance). Most recently, the FTC has had to issue guidelines with respect to "green" claims being made by companies. The FTC is requiring firms to provide more concrete substantiation regarding products' "sustainability" and "environmental impact" than firms are currently providing.[51]

The consent order and the cease-and-desist order are the most basic remedies used by the FTC in dealing with deceptive or unfair advertising. In a **consent order,** an advertiser accused of running deceptive or unfair advertising agrees to stop running the advertisements in question, without admitting guilt. For advertisers who do not comply voluntarily, the FTC can issue a **cease-and-desist order,** which generally requires that the advertising in question be stopped within 30 days so that a hearing can be held to determine whether the advertising is deceptive or unfair. For products that have a direct effect on consumers' health or safety (e.g., foods and nutraceuticals), the FTC can issue an immediate cease-and-desist order.

Affirmative disclosure is another remedy available to the FTC. An advertisement that fails to disclose important material facts about a product can be deemed deceptive, and the FTC may require **affirmative disclosure,** whereby the important material absent from prior ads must be included in subsequent advertisements. The absence of important material information may cause consumers to make false assumptions about products in comparison to the competition.

The most extensive remedy for advertising determined to be misleading is **corrective advertising**.[52] In cases where evidence suggests that consumers have developed incorrect beliefs about a brand based on deceptive or unfair advertising, the firm may be required to run corrective ads in an attempt to dispel those faulty beliefs. The goal of corrective advertising is to rectify erroneous beliefs created by deceptive advertising, but it hasn't always worked as intended. During its long history, the corrective advertising remedy has been required of ads ranging from Warner Lambert's Listerine mouthwash ads in the 1970s claiming that it could "cure and prevent colds" (which it couldn't) to more recent ad campaigns for pain relievers.

Another area of FTC regulation and remedy involves **celebrity endorsements, testimonials, and bloggers.** The FTC has specific rules for advertisements that use an expert or celebrity as a spokesperson for a product and guidelines for bloggers who feature brands in their blogs. In the case of experts (those whose experience or training allows a superior judgment of products), the endorser's actual qualifications must justify his or her status as an expert. Like a doctor recommending a cold remedy or surgical procedure. In the case of "average consumer" endorsements, the ad must reveal whether the results being portrayed are "typical" of brand use. In the case of celebrities (such as Jamie Lee Curtis as the spokesperson for Activia), FTC guidelines state that the celebrity must be an actual user of the product, or the ad is considered deceptive. Finally, the FTC has recently issued guidelines, which specify that bloggers who feature brands in their blogs and who receive cash or in-kind payments (e.g., free products) must disclose this material relationship with the firm.[53]

These regulatory programs and remedies provide the FTC a great deal of control over the advertising process. Numerous ads have been interpreted as questionable under the guidelines of these programs, and advertisements have had to be altered. It is also likely that advertisers and their agencies, which are keenly aware of the ramifications of violating FTC precepts, have developed ads with these constraints in mind.

State Regulation. State governments do not have extensive policing powers over the promotional activities of firms. Since the vast majority of companies are involved in interstate marketing of goods and services, any violation of fair practice or existing regulation is a federal government issue. There is typically one state government organization, the attorney general's office, which is responsible for investigating questionable promotional practices.

Since the 1980s, the National Association of Attorneys General, whose members include the attorneys general from all 50 states, has been active as a group in monitoring advertising and sharing its findings. Overall, however, states will rely on the vigilance of the federal agencies discussed earlier to monitor promotional practices and then act against firms with questionable activities.

— LO **4** —

Industry Self-Regulation. The promotion industry has come far in terms of self-control and restraint. Some of this improvement is due to tougher government regulation, and some to industry self-regulation. **Self-regulation** is the promotion industry's attempt to police itself. Supporters say it is a shining example of how unnecessary government intervention is, whereas critics point to it as a joke, an elaborate shell game. According to the critics, meaningful self-regulation occurs only when the threat of government action is imminent. How you see this controversy is largely dependent on your own personal experience and level of cynicism.

Several industry and trade associations and public service organizations have voluntarily established guidelines for promotion within their industries. The reasoning is that self-regulation is good for the promotion community as a whole and creates credibility for, and therefore enhances, the effectiveness of promotion itself. Exhibit 4.16 lists some of the organizations that have taken on the task of regulating and monitoring promotional activities, including Internet advertising, and the year when each established a code of standards.

The purpose of self-regulation by these organizations is to evaluate the content and quality of promotional activities specific to their industries. The effectiveness of such organizations depends on the cooperation of members and the policing mechanisms used. Each organization exerts an influence on the nature of promotion in its industry. Some are particularly noteworthy in their activities and warrant further discussion.

But industry self-regulation is not just the result of efforts by industry organizations. Firms themselves often voluntarily regulate their behavior. The Walt Disney Company, in an attempt to respond to consumers' concerns about child obesity, decided to carefully monitor

EXHIBIT 4.16 Selected business organizations and industry associations with advertising self-regulation programs.

Organization	Code Established
Advertising Associations	
American Advertising Federation	1965
American Association of Advertising Agencies	1924
Association of National Advertisers	1972
Business/Professional Advertising Association	1975
Special Industry Groups	
Council of Better Business Bureaus	1912
Household furniture	1978
Automobiles and trucks	1978
Carpet and rugs	1978
Home improvement	1975
Charitable solicitations	1974
Children's Advertising Review Unit	1974
National Advertising Division/National Advertising Review Board	1971
Media Associations	
American Business Press	1910
Direct Mail Marketing Association	1960
Direct Selling Association	1970
National Association of Broadcasters	
Radio	1937
Television	1952
Outdoor Advertising Association of America	1950
Selected Trade Associations	
American Wine Association	1949
Wine Institute	1949
Distilled Spirits Association	1934
United States Brewers Association	1955
Pharmaceutical Manufacturers Association	1958
Proprietary Association	1934
Bank Marketing Association	1976
Motion Picture Association of America	1930
National Swimming Pool Institute	1970
Toy Manufacturers Association	1962

© Cengage Learning

all products advertised on the firm's child-focused television channels to insure that all ads complied with strict new nutritional standards.[54]

The National Advertising Review Board. One important self-regulation organization is the **National Advertising Review Board (NARB).** The NARB is the operations arm of the Advertising Self-Regulatory Council (ASRC) which establishes the policies and procedures for advertising industry self-regulation, including the National Advertising Division (NAD), Children's Advertising Review Unit (CARU), National Advertising Review Board (NARB), Electronic Retailing Self-Regulation Program (ERSP), and Online Interest-Based Advertising Accountability Program (Accountability Program). Complaints received from consumers, competitors, or local branches of the Better Business Bureau (BBB) are forwarded to the NAD. Most such complaints come from competitors. After a full review of the complaint, the issue may be forwarded to the NARB and evaluated by a panel. The general procedure for dealing with complaints (although variations exist) is detailed in Exhibit 4.17. Note in particular that the NARB process starts with a recommendation from the NAD that an advertising or promotional campaign complaint be fully evaluated. Some examples of the types of complaints received and processed include:

- Hardee's sued rival Jack in the Box to stop TV ads that it says suggest that Hardee's uses cow anus to make Angus beef burgers.

- The Sugar Association sued Johnson & Johnson over a marketing campaign related to J&J's artificial sweetener Splenda, accusing the company of misleading buyers into believing that Splenda is a natural product.

- Procter & Gamble sued McLane Company, Salado Sales, and Consumer Value Products, charging that the companies are selling products in packages that copy P&G's packaging for Bounty, Charmin, and Vicks NyQuil and DayQuil.[55]

The NAD maintains a permanent professional staff that works to resolve complaints with the advertiser and its agency before the issue gets to the NARB. If no resolution is achieved, the complaint is appealed to the NARB, which appoints a panel made up of three advertiser representatives, one agency representative, and one public representative. This panel then holds hearings regarding the advertising in question. The advertiser is allowed to present its case. If no agreement can be reached by

EXHIBIT 4.17   The NAD and NARB regulatory process.

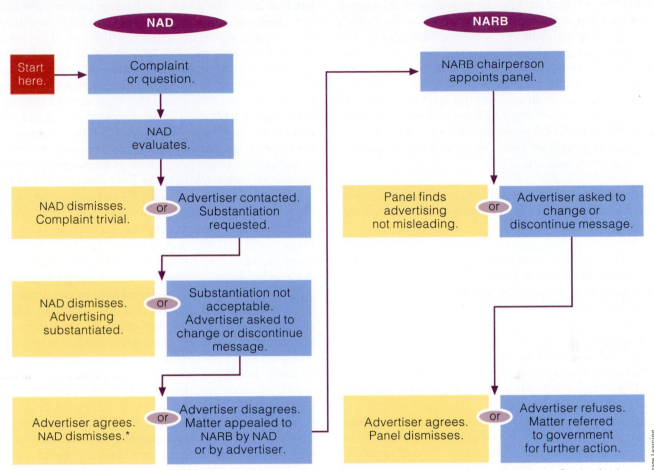

*If the complaint originated outside the system, the outside complainant can appeal at this point to the NARB chairperson for a panel adjudication. Granting of such an appeal is at the chairperson's discretion.

© Cengage Learning

the panel either to dismiss the case or to persuade the advertiser to change the advertising, then the NARB initiates two actions. First, the NARB publicly identifies the advertiser, the complaint against the advertiser, and the panel's findings. Second, the case is forwarded to an appropriate government regulatory agency (usually the FTC).

The NAD and the NARB are not empowered to impose penalties on advertisers, but the threat of going before the board acts as a deterrent to deceptive and questionable advertising practices. Further, the regulatory process of the NAD and the NARB is probably less costly and time-consuming for all parties involved than if every complaint were handled by a government agency.

State and Local Better Business Bureaus. Aside from the national BBB, there are more than 140 separate local bureaus. Each local organization is supported by membership dues paid by area businesses. The three divisions of a local BBB—merchandise, financial, and

solicitations—investigate the advertising and selling practices of firms in their areas. A local BBB has the power to forward a complaint to the NAD for evaluation.

Beyond its regulatory activities, the BBB tries to avert problems associated with advertising by counseling new businesses and providing information to advertisers and agencies regarding legislation, potential problem areas, and industry standards.

Advertising Agencies and Associations. It makes sense that advertising agencies and their industry associations would engage in self-regulation. An individual agency is legally responsible for the advertising it produces and is subject to reprisal for deceptive claims. The agency is in a difficult position in that it must monitor not only the activities of its own people, but also the information that clients provide to the agency. Should a client direct an agency to use a product appeal that turns out to be untruthful, the agency is still responsible.

The American Association of Advertising Agencies (4As) has no legal or binding power over its agency members, but it can apply pressure when its board feels that industry standards are not being upheld. The 4As also publishes guidelines for its members regarding various aspects of advertising messages. One of the most widely recognized industry standards is the 4As' Creative Code. The code outlines the responsibilities and social impact advertising can have and promotes high ethical standards of honesty and decency. You can view the 4As standards of practice, including the creative code, at www.aaaa.org.

Media Organizations. Individual media organizations evaluate the advertising they receive for broadcast and publication. The National Association of Broadcasters (NAB) has a policing arm known as the Code Authority, which implements and interprets separate radio and television codes. These codes deal with truth, fairness, and good taste in broadcast advertising.

Newspapers have historically been rigorous in their screening of advertising. Many newspapers have internal departments to screen and censor ads believed to be in violation of the newspaper's advertising standards. Although the magazine industry does not have a formal code, many individual publications have very high standards.

Direct mail may have a poor image among many consumers, but its industry association, the Direct Marketing Association (DMA), is active in promoting ethical behavior and standards among its members. It has published guidelines for ethical business practices. In 1971, the association established the Mail Preference Service, which allows consumers to have their names removed from most direct mail lists.

A review of all aspects of industry self-regulation suggests not only that a variety of programs and organizations are designed to monitor advertising, but also that many of these programs are effective. Those whose livelihoods depend on advertising are just as interested as consumers and legislators in maintaining high standards. If advertising is perceived by consumers as an unethical and untrustworthy business activity, the economic vitality of many organizations will be compromised. Self-regulation can help prevent such a circumstance and is in the best interest of all the organizations discussed here.

Internet Self-Regulation. Because there are few federal guidelines established for advertising and promotion on the Internet (with the exception of anti-spam legislation and COPPA), the industry itself has been the main governing body. The most significant organization is the Digital Advertising Alliance (DAA) which was launched around the Self-Regulatory Principles

for Online Behavioral Advertising which was formulated in 2009. The DAA is a leading industry association applying consumer-friendly standards to online behavioral advertising across the Internet. The DAA operates as a true industry self-regulatory body in that it cannot mandate punishment for what it perceives as a violation of codes of good practice. As an example of its impact however, the organization recently challenged a KIA advertising campaign which did not include the AdChoices icon (an icon that is linked to information on how a consumer's browsing history is being used to target ads and offers users the option to opt out of such tracking). The only power of the DAA was to issue a "decision" that KIA did not comply with the industry's guidelines.[56]

Another organization, The Center for Digital Democracy (CDD) was founded in 2001 and focuses on research, public education, and advocacy designed to protect consumers in the digital age. Internationally, the United Kingdom has the Internet Watch Foundation and Canada has Canadian Association of Internet Providers offering self-regulation guidelines. You will see later in this chapter that several special interest groups are questioning the ethics of some Internet promotional practices. And there are those who are skeptical that the industry can regulate itself.

Consumers as Regulatory Agents. Consumers themselves are motivated to act as regulatory agents based on a variety of interests, including product safety, reasonable choice, the right to information, and privacy. Advertising tends to be a focus of consumer regulatory activities because of its conspicuousness. Consumerism and consumer organizations have provided the primary vehicles for consumer regulatory efforts.

Consumerism, the actions of individual consumers or groups of consumers designed to exert power in the marketplace, is by no means a recent phenomenon. The earliest consumerism efforts can be traced to 17th-century England. In the United States, there have been recurring consumer movements throughout the 20th century. *Adbusters* magazine and its website is a recent example. The organization claims to be "a not-for-profit, reader-supported, 120,000-circulation magazine concerned about the erosion of our physical and cultural environments by commercial forces."[57]

In general, these consumer movements have focused on the same issue: Consumers want a greater voice in the whole process of product development, distribution, and information dissemination. Consumers commonly try to create pressure on firms by withholding patronage through boycotts. Some boycotts have been effective. Firms as powerful as Procter & Gamble, Kimberly-Clark, and General Mills all have historically responded to threats of boycotts by pulling advertising consumers found offensive. In a recent incident, Huggies had to pull an ad that showed dads so consumed by sports on TV that they neglected to tend to diapers on their babies. Fathers across the United States took offense and argued that they are fully involved in their babies' well-being.[58] When conservative talk show host Rush Limbaugh used aggressive and derogatory remarks in describing a student who was lobbying for health care coverage, seven advertisers, under pressure from consumers, immediately canceled their advertising on the radio show.[59]

Consumer Organizations. The other major consumer effort to bring about regulation is through established consumer organizations. The following are the most prominent consumer organizations and their prime activities:

- *Consumer Federation of America (CFA).* This organization, founded in 1968, now includes more than 300 national, state, and local consumer groups and labor unions as affiliate members. The goals of the CFA are to encourage the creation of consumer organizations, provide services to consumer groups, and act as a voice for consumers at the state and federal legislative level (www.consumerfed.org).

- *Consumers Union.* This nonprofit consumer organization is best known for its publication of *Consumer Reports.* Established in 1936, Consumers Union describes itself as "an expert, independent, nonprofit organization whose mission is to work for a fair, just, and safe marketplace for all consumers and to empower consumers to protect themselves."[60]

This organization supports itself through the sale of publications and accepts no funding, including advertising revenues, from any commercial organization and now claims to have the most subscribers to its website of any organization of its type (www.consumersunion.org).

These two consumer organizations are the most active, widely known, and potent of the consumer groups, but there are hundreds of such groups organized by geographic location or product category. Consumers have proven that when faced with an organized effort, corporations can and will change their practices. In one of the most publicized events in the history of marketing, consumers applied pressure to Coca-Cola and, in part, were responsible for forcing the firm to remarket the original formula of Coca-Cola after the firm had removed it from the market and had introduced "New" Coke. If consumers are able to exert such a powerful and nearly immediate influence on a firm such as Coca-Cola, one wonders what other changes they could affect in the market.

4-4 THE REGULATION OF OTHER PROMOTIONAL TOOLS

As firms broaden the scope of the promotional effort beyond advertising, the regulatory constraints placed on other IBP tools become relevant. We will consider the current and emerging regulatory environment for direct marketing, e-commerce, sales promotion, and public relations.

4-4a Regulatory Issues in Direct Marketing and the Internet

The most pressing regulatory issue facing direct marketing and e-commerce is database development and the privacy debate that accompanies the practice. The crux of the privacy issue has to do with the developing ability of firms to merge off-line databases with the online Web search and shopping behavior of consumers often referred to as behavioral ads.

Privacy. Privacy in direct marketing and on the Internet focuses on a wide range with behavioral targeting issues made possible by technology. **Behavioral targeting** is the process of database development facilitated by online tracking markers that advertisers place on a Web surfer's devices in order to track that person's online behavior. The current environment is annoying and feels like a huge invasion of privacy. As one analyst put it "online privacy is a big oxymoron."[61] Here's the problem. Big online content providers, like Facebook, Google, and Apple, don't charge users a fee for access to a variety of data and information services. As such, they have to generate revenue somehow from these services, so they sell your online behavior patterns to advertisers. The director of an Internet think tank put it this way, "Free on the Internet almost always means in exchange for your data."[62] Social media companies like Facebook want to change that. Facebook would like to create the equivalent of a digital "calling card" that could identify people just about wherever they go on the Web. That way, Facebook can sell your profile to advertisers who can, in turn, target you with advertising while you surf. Another iteration of this privacy invasion is the now widespread capability to track consumers' physical whereabouts by virtue of GPS devices embedded in smartphones. Consider this real possibility: you stop in front of a Gap clothing store and your smartphone alerts you to a message from the Gap announcing the sale items inside the store. Big social network and Internet providers are fighting privacy laws that prevent mobile tracking. If they don't sell your data, then they would have to start charging a use fee for all the apps you paid a small fee for and now use for free.

However, there is some hope for improved privacy. Twitter has recently agreed to adopt a "do-not-track" policy option which is a privacy initiative being heavily promoted by the FTC, privacy advocates, and even Mozilla (the developer of the Firefox Web browser). In addition, Google said it is considering implementing the do-not-track option on its Chrome browser.[63]

Spam. Few of us would argue with the allegation that **spam,** unsolicited commercial messages sent through the email system, is the scourge of the Internet. A particularly insidious version of spam is **phishing** where spammers try to entice Web users to enter personal information on a fake website that is forged to look like it is from a bank, the IRS, or other organization that will get the email user's attention. To put the problem into perspective, it is estimated that about 7.7 *trillion* spam messages are sent every year.[64] Spam can be so bad it has actually shut down a company's entire operations. To cope with the onslaught, individuals and companies are turning to spam filtering software to stem the flow and take back control of their email systems. The FTC convened a brainstorming session to determine what, if anything, could be done legally. Then in October of 2003, the U.S. Senate voted unanimously 97–0 to implement the CAN SPAM Act. The Senate followed in November of 2003 with its support, voting 392–5 in favor of the legislation. The act does not outlaw all unsolicited email, but rather targets fraudulent, deceptive, and pornographic messages, which is estimated to make up about two-thirds of all commercial unsolicited email.[65] There have been several prosecutions under the CAN SPAM Act and violators are actually spending time in jail.

Contests, Sweepstakes, Coupons. Even though privacy and spam are huge direct marketing and e-commerce issues, they are not the only ones. The next biggest legal issue has to do with sweepstakes, contests, and coupons. (See Insights Online [Exhibit 4.18] for an interesting example of a social media contest.) Because of the success and widespread use of sweepstakes in direct marketing (such as the Publishers Clearing House sweepstakes), Congress has imposed limits on such promotions. The existing limits on direct mail sweepstakes include the requirements that the phrases "No purchase is necessary to win"

INSIGHTS ONLINE

4.18 Go online to see the AdAge feature, "Trident Brazil's Social Media Game Allows Consumers to Interact with Virtual Licks."

and "A purchase will not improve an individual's chance of winning" must be repeated three times in letters to consumers and again on the entry form. In addition, penalties can be imposed on marketers who do not promptly remove consumers' names from mailing lists at the consumer's request.

Coupons distributed through direct mail, newspapers, magazines, or the Internet require legal protection for the *marketer* more than anything else. Fraud abounds in the area of couponing, aggravated by the fact that approximately 90 percent of the U.S. population still uses coupons and redeems billions of dollars worth of coupons a year. Phony coupons can easily be reproduced and redeemed well after the firm's planned promotional campaign. Starbucks ended up with a promotional nightmare by not enacting safeguards for a "Free Iced Beverage" coupon that it intended for a small email distribution. Instead, the coupons were forwarded in huge numbers, and consumers all across the United States tried to redeem them. Because of the unexpected nationwide demand, Starbucks had to cancel the offer before the coupons' expiration date, frustrating many customers.[66] Safeguards like stating strict limitations on redemption, geographic limitations, or encrypted bar codes that can be scanned to detect fraud are all ways to reduce problems with contests, sweepstakes, and coupons.

Telemarketing. Another legal issue in direct marketing that has hit the headlines in recent years has to do with telemarketing practices. The first restriction on telemarketing was the Telephone Consumer Fraud and Abuse Prevention Act of 1994 (later strengthened by the FTC in 1995), which requires telemarketers to state their name, the purpose of the call, and the company they work for. The act prohibits telemarketers from calling before 8 a.m. and after 9 p.m., and they cannot call the same customer more than once every three months. Regulations have been strengthened recently to bar the use of automatic dialing machines, which make so-called "robocalls" that contain recorded messages, and they must keep a list of consumers who do not want to be called.[67]

The original telemarketing law was benign compared to recent legislation aimed at telemarketers. At the center of new regulation restricting telemarketing is the Do Not Call Law, which allows consumers to sign up for a Do Not Call Registry (see Exhibit 4.19) (www.donotcall.gov). The Federal Trade Commission, the Federal Communications Commission, and states started to enforce the registry on October 1, 2003. The program exempts political and charitable fund-raisers as well as pollsters. Currently, more than 70 percent of all U.S. households have registered with the registry to restrict telemarketing calls to their phones.

EXHIBIT 4.19 The Federal Trade Commission, the Federal Communications Commission and state governments started to enforce the Do Not Call Registry on October 1, 2003. Registering your phone number(s) with the registry blocks a wide variety of telemarketers from calling you with a sales pitch.

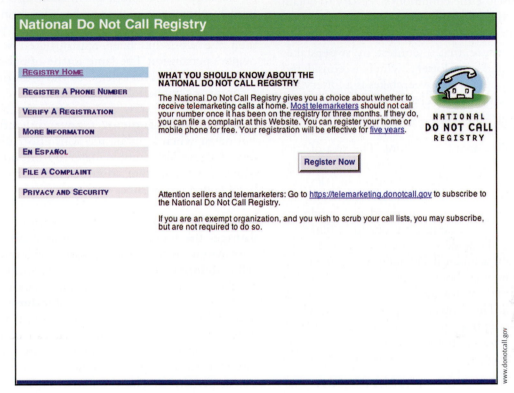

There are organizations with rights to continue telemarketing efforts, so even if you have registered with the Do Not Call Registry, you can still get calls from[68]:

- Charities, politicians, pollsters, and market researchers
- Companies you do business with
- Companies that have sold you something or delivered something to you within the previous 18 months
- Businesses *you've* contacted in the past three months
- Companies that obtain your permission to call you

4-4b Regulatory Issues in Sales Promotion

Regulatory issues in sales promotion focus on three areas: premium offers, trade allowances, and contests and sweepstakes.

Premium Offers. With respect to **premiums** (an item offered for "free" or at a greatly reduced price with the purchase of another item), the main area of regulation has do with requiring marketers to state the fair retail value of the item offered as a premium.

Trade Allowances. In the area of trade allowances, marketers need to be familiar with the guidelines set forth in the original Robinson-Patman Act of 1936. Even though this is an old piece of legislation, it still applies to contemporary trade promotion practices. The Robinson-Patman Act requires marketers to offer similar customers (particularly wholesalers and retailers) similar prices on similar merchandise and quantities. This means that a marketer cannot use special allowances as a way to discount the price to highly attractive customers. This issue was raised earlier in the context of vertical cooperative advertising. Remember that vertical cooperative advertising is perfectly legal if used properly. Honda provided its dealers with $250 million of advertising money to place ads that featured certain Honda vehicles and the dealers' locations.[69]

Contests and Sweepstakes. In the area of sweepstakes and contests, the issues discussed in the previous section under direct marketing and e-commerce also apply, but there are other issues as well. The FTC has specified four violations of regulations that marketers must avoid in carrying out sweepstakes and contests:

- Misrepresentations about the value (e.g., stating an inflated retail price) of the prizes being offered

- Failure to provide complete disclosure about the conditions necessary to win (are there behaviors required on the part of the contestant?)

- Failure to disclose the conditions necessary to obtain a prize (are there behaviors required of the contestant after the contestant is designated a "winner"?)

- Failure to ensure that a contest or sweepstakes is not classified as a lottery, which is considered gambling—a contest or sweepstakes is a lottery if a prize is offered based on chance and the contestant has to give up something of value in order to play

Product/Brand Placement (Insertion). The area of sales promotion receiving attention most recently in the regulatory arena is brand/product placement in television programs and films. As discussed earlier, consumer groups feel that unless television networks and film producers reveal that brands are placed into a program or film for a fee, consumers could be deceived into believing that the product use is natural and real. The industry counterclaim is, "There is a paranoia about our business that shouldn't be there. We don't control the storyline, or the brands that are included. The writers and producers do." There are, of course, exceptions to this industry claim. Coca-Cola originally paid a reported $20 million during the first season of *American Idol* to have those Coke cups in front of the judges.

4-4c **Regulatory Issues in Public Relations**

Public relations is not bound by the same sorts of laws as other elements of the promotional mix. Because public relations activities deal with public press and public figures, much of the regulation relates to these issues. The public relations activities of a firm may place it on either side of legal issues with respect to privacy, copyright infringement, or defamation through slander and libel.

Privacy. The privacy problems facing a public relations firm center on the issue of appropriation. **Appropriation** is the use of pictures or images owned by someone else without permission. If a firm uses a model's photo or a photographer's work in an advertisement or company brochure without permission, then the work has been appropriated without the owner's permission. The same is true of public relations materials prepared for release to the press or as part of a company's public relations kit.

Copyright Infringement. Copyright infringement can occur when a public relations effort uses written, recorded, or photographic material from others' works. Much as with appropriation, written permission must be obtained to use such works.

Defamation. When a communication occurs that damages the reputation of an individual because the information in the communication was untrue, this is called **defamation** (you may have heard it referred to as "defamation of character"). Defamation can occur either through slander or libel. **Slander** is oral defamation and in the context of promotion would occur during television or radio broadcast of an event involving a company and its employees. **Libel** is defamation that occurs in print and would relate to magazine, newspaper, direct mail, or Internet reports.

The public relations practitioner's job is to protect clients from slanderous or libelous reports about a company's activities. Inflammatory TV "investigative" news programs are often sued for slander and are challenged to prove the allegations they make about a company and personnel working for a company. The issues revolve around whether negative comments can be fully substantiated. Erroneous reports in major magazines and newspapers about a firm can result in a defamation lawsuit as well. Less frequently, public relations experts need to defend a client accused of making defamatory remarks.

SUMMARY

 Identify the benefits and problems of advertising and promotion in a capitalistic society and debate a variety of issues concerning their effects on society's well-being.

Advertisers have always been followed by proponents and critics. Proponents of advertising argue that it offers benefits for individual consumers and society at large. At the societal level, proponents claim, advertising helps promote a higher standard of living by allowing marketers to reap the rewards of product improvements and innovation. Advertising also "pays for" mass media in many countries and provides consumers with a constant flow of information not only about products and services, but also about political and social issues. Throughout the years critics have leveled many charges at advertising and advertising practitioners. Advertising expenditures in the multibillions are condemned as wasteful, offensive, and a source of frustration for many in society who see the lavish lifestyle portrayed in advertising, knowing they will never be able to afford such a lifestyle. Critics also contend that advertisements rarely furnish useful information but instead perpetuate superficial stereotypes of many cultural subgroups. For many years, some critics have been concerned that advertisers are controlling us against our will with subliminal advertising messages. Most recently, issues of privacy have been debated as new technologies offer the possibility of "behavioral targeting" based on consumers' Web search behavior or even tracking consumers' physical whereabouts by virtue of GPS-equipped smartphones.

 Explain how ethical considerations affect the development and implementation of advertising and IBP campaigns.

Ethical considerations are a concern when creating advertising and promotion. Deception in advertising and promotion is never acceptable or defendable. The ethical considerations get more complex especially when advertising is targeted to children or involves controversial products such as firearms, gambling, alcohol, or cigarettes. Although ethical standards are a matter for personal reflection, it certainly is the case that unethical people can create unethical advertising. But there are also many safeguards against such behavior, including the corporate and personal integrity of advertisers.

 Discuss the role of government agencies and consumers in the regulation of advertising and promotion.

Governments typically are involved in the regulation of advertising and promotion. It is important to recognize that advertising and promotion regulations can vary dramatically from one country to the next. A variety of government organizations have jurisdiction over advertising and promotional practices. In the United States, the Federal Trade Commission (FTC) is particularly empowered and has been especially active in trying to deter deception and unfairness in advertising. The FTC was established in 1914, and since then a variety of legislation has been passed to clarify its powers. The FTC has also developed regulatory remedies that have expanded its involvement in advertising regulation, such as the advertising substantiation program. State governments in the United States have limited powers due to the interstate nature of most advertising and promotion, thereby making any legal issues federal in nature.

 Explain the meaning and importance of self-regulation for firms that develop and use advertising and promotion.

Some of the most important controls on advertising and promotion are voluntary; that is, they are a matter of self-regulation by advertising and marketing professionals. For example, the American Association of Advertising Agencies has issued guidelines for promoting fairness and accuracy when using comparative advertisements. Many other organizations, such as the Better Business Bureau, the National Association of Broadcasters, and the Direct Marketing Association, participate in the process to help ensure fairness and assess consumer complaints about advertising and promotion.

 Discuss the regulation of the full range of techniques used in the IBP process.

The regulation of other tools in the IBP process focuses on direct marketing, e-commerce, sales promotions, and public relations. In direct marketing and e-commerce, the primary concern has to do with consumer privacy. New legislation, like the Do Not Call Registry, the CAN SPAM Act, and revised regulation on blogging and testimonials, is restricting the ways in which companies can contact consumers with a sales offer or portray their brands in use. The legislation is a reaction to new technologies that have enabled firms to match consumers' online behavior with off-line personal information. Another aspect of e-commerce has to do with contests and sweepstakes and the potential for such games to actually be gambling opportunities. In sales promotions, premium offers, trade allowances, and off-line contests and sweepstakes are subject to regulation. Firms are required to state the fair value of "free" premiums, trade allowances must follow the guidelines of fair competition, and contests and sweepstakes must follow strict rules specified by the FTC. The regulation of public relations efforts has to do with privacy, copyright infringement, and defamation. Firms must be aware of the strict legal parameters of these factors.

KEY TERMS

ethics
deception
puffery
primary demand
unfair advertising
vertical cooperative advertising
comparison advertisements
monopoly power
advertising substantiation program

consent order
cease-and-desist order
affirmative disclosure
corrective advertising
celebrity endorsements, testimonials, and bloggers
self-regulation
National Advertising Review Board (NARB)

consumerism
behavioral targeting
spam
phishing
premiums
appropriation
defamation
slander
libel

ENDNOTES

1. George J. Stigler, "The Economics of Information," *Journal of Political Economy* (June 1961), 213–220.

2. Ibid., 220.

3. Jack Neff, "Spam Research Reveals Disgust with Pop-Up Ads," *Advertising Age*, August 23, 2003, 1, 21.

4. Ibid., 1, 21.

5. Hank Kim, "Just Risk It," *Advertising Age*, February 9, 2004, 1, 51.

6. Matthew Creamer, "Caught in the Clutter Crossfire: Your Brand," *Advertising Age*, April 2, 2007, 1, 35.

7. Ibid., 35.

8. Richard Caves, *American Industry: Structure, Conduct, Performance* (Upper Saddle River, NJ: Prentice Hall, 1964), 102.

9. Piper Weiss, "Outrage over Gym's Skinny Model Campaign. Members Want More Muscle," *Healthy Living*, January 5, 2012, www.shine.yahoo.com/healthy-living, accessed January 7, 2012.

10. A. H. Maslow, *Motivation and Personality* (New York: Harper & Row, 1970).

11. Vance Packard, *The Status Seekers* (New York: David McKay, 1959).

12. This argument was first offered by authors George Katona, *The Mass Consumption Society* (New York: McGraw-Hill, 1964), 54–61, and John Kenneth Galbraith, *The Affluent Society* (Boston: Houghton Mifflin, 1958).

13. Stephen Fox, *The Mirror Makers: A History of American Advertising and Its Creators* (New York: William Morrow, 1984), 330.

14. Normandy Madden, "Honda Pulls Suicide Car Ad from Australian TV Market," *Advertising Age*, September 22, 2003, 3.

15. Jeremy Pelofsky, "U.S. Senate Backs Ten Fold Hike in Indecency Fines," *Reuters News Service*, May 18, 2006, www.reuters.com, accessed May 19, 2006.

16. Don E. Schultz, "Subliminal Ad Notions Still Resonate Today," *Marketing News*, March 15, 2007, 5, 9.

17. Murphy, Monahan, and Zajonc, "Additivity of Nonconscious Affect: Combined Effects of Priming and Exposure," *Journal of Personality and Social Psychology*, vol. 69 (1995), 589–602.

18. Timothy E. Moore, "Subliminal Advertising: What You See Is What You Get," *Journal of Marketing*, vol. 46 (Spring 1982), 38–47, and Timothy E. Moore, "The Case Against Subliminal Manipulation," *Psychology and Marketing*, vol. 5, no. 4 (Winter 1988), 297–317.

19. Andy Warhol, *The Philosophy of Andy Warhol: From A to B and Back Again* (New York: Harcourt Brace Jovanovich, 1975), 101.

20. "100 Leading National Advertisers," *Advertising Age*, June 25, 2012, 22.

21. B. G. Gregg, "Tax Funds Bankroll New Anti-Drug Ads," *Cincinnati Enquirer*, July 10, 1998, A1, A17.

22. Jay Reeves, "Scrushy Said to Pay for Positive Stories," *Associated Press*, January 19, 2006, www.news.yahoo.com, accessed January 20, 2006.

23. Eamon Javers, "This Opinion Brought to You By . . . " *BusinessWeek*, January 30, 2006, 35.

24. This quote is taken from the Commercial Alert website and is part of the organization's discussion of the deceptive nature of product placement within television shows, videos, video games, and a process they refer to as "adversongs," http://www.commercialalert.org/issues/culture/product-placement, accessed January 6, 2013.

25. "Children Not Seeing More Food Ads on Television," *Federal Trade Commission Report*, www.ftc.gov, released June 1, 2007.

26. Richard Linnett, "Psychologists Protest Kids' Ads," *Advertising Age*, September 11, 2000, 4.

27. Patrick J. Sheridan, "FCC Sets Children's Ad Limits," *1990 Information Access Company*, vol. 119, no. 20 (1990), 33.

28. Laura Bird, "NBC Special Is One Long Prime-Time Ad," *The Wall Street Journal*, January 21, 1994, B1, B4.

29. Current guidelines regarding this initiative can be found at http://www.bbb.org/us/about-the-initiative/

30. J. Goldstein, "Children and Advertising—The Research," *Commercial Communications*, July 1998, 4–7; Tina Mangelburg and Terry Bristol, "Socialization and Adolescent's Skepticism toward Advertising," *Journal of Advertising*, vol. 27, no. 3 (Fall 1998), 11–21.

31. While there are a large number of articles alleging this practice by the tobacco industry, a representative piece during the height of the argument is: Kathleen Deveny, "Joe Camel Ads Reach Children, Research Finds," *The Wall Street Journal*, December 11, 1991, B1, B6.

32. As an example of this type of research see, Joseph R. DiFranza et al., "RJR Nabisco's Cartoon Camel Promotes Camel Cigarettes to Children," *Journal of the American Medical Association*, vol. 266, no. 22 (1991), 3168–3153.

33. E. J. Schultz, "Liquor Advertising Pours into TV," *Advertising Age*, May 14, 2012, 1, 41.

34. For a summary of more than 60 articles dating back to the 1960s that address the issue of alcohol and cigarette advertising and the lack of a relationship between advertising and cigarette and alcohol industry demand, see Mark Frankena et al., "Alcohol, Consumption, and Abuse," *Bureau of Economics, Federal Trade Commission*, March 5, 1985. For a similar listing of research articles where the same conclusions were drawn during congressional hearings on the topic, see "Advertising of Tobacco Products," Hearings before the Subcommittee on Health and the Environment, Committee on Energy and Commerce, House of Representatives, 99th Congress, July 18 and August 1, 1986, No. 99–167. The findings of these early articles were recently reaffirmed: Michael L. Capella, Charles R. Taylor, and Cynthia Webster, "The Effect of Cigarette Advertising Bans on Consumption: A Meta-Analysis," *Journal of Advertising*, vol. 37, no. 2 (Summer 2008), 7–18.

35. For examples of the more recent studies that reaffirm peers and family rather than advertising as the basis for smoking initiation, see Charles R. Taylor and P. Greg Bonner, "Comment on 'American Media and the Smoking-Related Behaviors of Asian Adolescents,'" *Journal of Advertising Research* (December 2003), 419–430; Bruce Simons Morton, "Peer and Parent Influences on Smoking and Drinking Among Early Adolescents," *Journal of Health Education and behavior* (February 2000); and Karen H. Smith and Mary Ann Stutz, "Factors that Influence Adolescents to Smoke," *Journal of Consumer Affairs*, vol. 33, no. 2 (Winter 1999), 321–357.

36. With regard to cartoon characters see, for example, Lucy L. Henke, "Young Children's Perceptions of Cigarette Brand Advertising: Awareness, Affect and Target Market Identification," *Journal of Advertising*, vol. 24, no. 4 (Winter 1995), 13–27, and Richard Mizerski, "The Relationship between Cartoon Trade Character Recognition and Attitude toward the Product Category," *Journal of Marketing*, vol. 59 (October 1995), 58–70. The evidence in Europe is provided by Jeffrey Goldstein, "Children and Advertising—the Research," *Commercial Communications*, July 1998, 4–8.

37. For research on this topic across several decades, see Richard Schmalensee, *The Economics of Advertising* (Amsterdam and London: North-Holland, 1972); Mark S. Albion and Paul W. Farris, *The Advertising Controversy* (Boston: Auburn House, 1981); Michael J. Waterson, "Advertising and Tobacco Consumption: An Analysis of the Two Major Aspects of the Debate," *International Journal of Advertising*, 9 (1990), 59–72; Michael L. Capella, Charles R. Taylor, and Cynthia Webster, "The Effect of Cigarette Advertising Bans on Consumption: A Meta-Analysis," *Journal of Advertising*, vol. 37, no. 2 (Summer 2008), 7–18.

38. Mercedes M. Cardona, "Marketers Bite Back as Fat Fight Flares Up," *Advertising Age*, March 1, 2004, 3, 35.

39. Rep. Ric Keller (R–Florida), quoted in Joanne Kenen, "U.S. House Backs Ban on Obesity Lawsuits," *Reuters*, Reuters.com, published March 10, 2004; accessed March 14, 2004.

40. Stephanie Thompson and Kate MacArthur, "Obesity Fear Frenzy Grips Food Industry," *Advertising Age*, April 23, 2007, 1, 46.

41. The definition of deception and the FTC criteria can be found at http://www.ftc.gov/bcp/policystmt/ad-decept.htm

42. Christy Fisher, "How Congress Broke Unfair Ad Impasse," *Advertising Age*, August 22, 1994, 34. For additional discussion of the FTC's definition of unfairness, see Ivan Preston, "Unfairness Developments in FTC Advertising Cases," *Journal of Public Policy and Marketing*, vol. 14, no. 2 (1995), 318–321.

43. Paul W. Miniard, Michael J. Barone, Randall L. Rose, and Kenneth C. Manning, "A Further Assessment of Indirect Comparative Advertising Claims of Superiority over All Competitors," *Journal of Advertising*, vol. 35, no. 4 (Winter 2006), 53–64.

44. Emily Bryson York, "Nasty Comparative Campaigns," *Advertising Age*, December 14, 2009, 28.

45. Daniel Golden and Suzanne Vranica, "Duracell's Duck Will Carry Disclaimer," *The Wall Street Journal*, February 7, 2002, B2.

46. Ville Heiskanen, "Google's AdMob Deal Criticized," *BusinessWeek*, www.businessweek.com, accessed December 28, 2009.

47. E. J. Schultz, "FTC's Attempt to Limit Food Marketing to Kids Peters Out," *Advertising Age*, May 7, 2012, 3, 103.

48. Anthony D. Miyazaki, Andrea J. S. Stanaland, and May O. Lwin, "Self-Regulatory Safeguards and the Online Privacy of Preteen Children," *Journal of Advertising*, vol. 38, no. 4 (Winter 2009), 80.

49. The full text and specifications of the Children's Online Privacy Act can be found at www.ftc.gov/ogc/coppa1.htm.

50. For a discussion of the origins and intent of the FTC's advertising substantiation program and its extension to require reasonable basis, see Debra L. Scammon and Richard J. Semenik, "The FTC's 'Reasonable Basis' for Substantiation of Advertising: Expanded Standards and Implications," *Journal of Advertising*, vol. 12, no. 1(1983), 4–11.

51. Jack Neff, "FTC Issues Final Version of Green Guides," www.adage.com, posted October 1, 2012; accessed October 15, 2012.

52. The history and intent of the corrective advertising concept and several of its applications are provided by Debra L. Scammon and Richard J. Semenik, "Corrective Advertising: Evolution of the Legal Theory and Application of the Remedy," *Journal of Advertising*, vol. 11, no. 1 (1982), 10–20.

53. "FTC Publishes Final Guides Governing Endorsements, Bloggers, Testimonials," Press Release, Federal Trade Commission, October 5, 2009, www.ftc.gov.

54. Brooks Barnes, "Promoting Nutrition, Disney to Restrict Junk-Food Ads," *The New York Times*, www.nytimes.com, posted June 5, 2012; accessed June 5, 2012.

55. Gary Gentile, "Jack in the Box Ads Called Misleading," *Associated Press*, May 25, 2007, biz.yahoo.com, accessed May 26, 2007; Sophie Walker, "J&J Sued Over Splenda Ad Campaign," *Reuters News Service*, January 31, 2005, story.news.yahoo.com, accessed February 1, 2005; and Bizjournals.com, "P&G Sues Companies Over Product Packaging," December 22, 2005, biz.yahoo.com/bizj, accessed December 22, 2005.

56. Cotton Delo, "Industry Group Calls Out Kia for not Disclosing Behavioral Ads," *Advertising Age*, October 1, 2012, 6.

57. Statement of the organizations purpose taken from the Adbusters website, www.adbusters.org.

58. Jack Neff, "Huggies Pulls Ads after Dads Insulted," www.adage.com, posted March 8, 2012; accessed March 15, 2012.

59. Brian Stelter, "Limbaugh Advertisers Flee Show amid Storm," *The New York Times*, March 5, 2012, www.nytimes.com, accessed March 5, 2012.

60. This statement of purpose was taken from the Consumers Union website at www.consumersunion.org, accessed January 7, 2013.

61. Javier E. David, "Why Online Privacy is a Big Oxymoron," *CNBC*, January 7, 2013, www.finance.yahoo.com, accessed January 7, 2013, 1.

62. Ibid., 1.

63. Gerry Shih, "Twitter Agrees to Adopt Do-Not-Track Privacy Option," *Reuters*, May 18, 2012, www.reuters.com, accessed May 18, 2012.

64. Sara Radicati, "Email Statistics Report, 2012–2016," *The Radicati Group, Inc.*, April 2012, 3; Huffpost Tech, "SMS Fraud: 95M Span Text Messages Sent per Day, Up 300% in 12 Months," www.huffingtonpost.co.uk, posted May 28, 2012; accessed January 8, 2013.

65. "Senate Approves Antispam Bill," *Reuters News*, reported on the Internet on October 22, 2003, at news.reuters.com.

66. Melissa Allison, "Starbucks Coupon Gets Out of Hand," *Seattle Times*, August 31, 2006, available at archives.seattletimes.nwsource.com/web.

67. "New Rules," *Marketing News Special Report*, November 30, 2009, 8.

68. Lorraine Woellert, "The Do-Not-Call Law Won't Stop the Calls," *BusinessWeek*, September 29, 2003, 89.

69. "Honda to Shower Its Dealers with up to $250 million for Ads," *Advertising Age Briefings*, October 8, 2012, 5.

PART 2

Analyzing the Environment for Advertising and Integrated Brand Promotion

Successful advertising and integrated brand promotion rely on a clear understanding of how and why consumers make their purchase decisions. Successful advertising and brand communication are rooted in sound marketing strategies and careful research about a brand's market environment. This understanding of consumer and the market, strategy, and research are brought together in an advertising and IBP plan. The chapters in Part 2, "Analyzing the Environment for Advertising and Integrated Brand Promotion," discuss the many important ways to assess the environment in the development of an advertising and IBP plan. Consumer behavior (Chapter 5) must be understood, segments must be analyzed, positioning the brand needs to be determined (Chapter 6), and research must be carried out in a systematic and analytical manner (Chapter 7). This part concludes with a complete chapter that lays out the process of planning advertising and integrated brand promotion, including the unique challenges of planning for international markets (Chapter 8).

CHAPTER 5

Advertising, Integrated Brand Promotion, and Consumer behavior is the most contemporary and insightful treatment of advertising and consumer behavior you will find anywhere. The chapter is divided into parts, each representing a valuable way of looking at consumer behavior, branding, and advertising. The first treats consumer behavior as a psychological and decision-making exercise. It is a "between-the-ears" approach. It deals with information processing, decision processes, and how advertisers try to game or manipulate them for their best results. The second section is more "between-the-peers;" that is, it is more sociological and cultural in its approach.[1] It examines what happens outside of individual consumer's heads, out there in the real world, where social forces and culture matter. This section includes a discussion of ads as "social text" and how they transmit sociocultural meaning and in doing so help create meaningful brands. Pay particular attention to the discussion of "cultural branding," a particularly effective way to understand how consumers relate to brand messages. You will also find innovative perspectives on income inequality, rebellion, and authenticity and how these factors can affect consumer behavior, and how advertisers use them to their advantage.

CHAPTER 6

Market Segmentation, Positioning, and the Value Proposition is a bedrock analysis to effective advertising and IBP planning. This chapter details how these three fundamental marketing planning efforts are developed by an organization. With a combination of audience, market and competitive information product and service brands are developed to provide benefits that are both valued by target customers and different from those of the competition. The process for segmenting business markets is also addressed. Finally, this is all put back into the context of how advertising is then used to communicate with value to consumers.

CHAPTER 7

Advertising Research is organized into three main parts that discuss the key types of research conducted by advertisers and their agency partners in planning an advertising and IBP effort. These three parts are developmental advertising and IBP research, copy research, and results research. The methods used to track the effectiveness of ads during and after a launch are highlighted. Finally, account planning's role is also covered in this chapter, which has evolved over time to include new participants and planning techniques.

CHAPTER 8

Planning Advertising and Integrated Brand Promotion explains how formal advertising plans are developed. The chapter begins by putting the advertising and IBP planning process into the context of the overall marketing planning process. Early in the chapter is a discussion of planning for advertising and IBP in international markets. Overcoming cultural barriers to communication is considered with particular emphasis on avoiding ethnocentrism and self-reference criteria in the planning process. The inputs to the advertising and IBP plan are laid out in detail, and the process of setting advertising objectives—both communications and sales objectives—is described. The methods for setting budgets are presented, including the widely adopted and preferred objective-and-task approach. A detailed discussion of implementing the objective and task budgeting approach is also provided. Finally, the important issue of the agency's role in planning advertising and IBP in coordination with the advertiser is described.

CHAPTER 5

Advertising, Integrated Brand Promotion, and Consumer Behavior

After reading and thinking about this chapter, you will be able to do the following:

1 Describe the four basic stages of consumer decision making.

2 Explain how consumers adapt their decision-making processes as a function of involvement and experience.

3 Discuss the role of memory and emotion in how advertising may influence consumer behavior.

4 Discuss the role of culture on consumer behavior and in creating good advertising.

5 Discuss the role of social class, taste, and cultural capital in consumer behavior and advertising.

6 Discuss the role of family, identity, gender, and community on consumer behavior and advertising.

7 Describe and then discuss cultural branding. Give an example.

8 Discuss how effective advertising uses sociocultural meaning in order to sell things.

Consumer behavior is defined as all things related to how humans operate as consumers. In other words, if it has anything to do with consuming, it's consumer behavior. It is far better for advertisers to understand consumer behavior than not, although we readily admit some companies do very well with only a very thin understanding of how their customers choose their brands. Due to simply being the first, the biggest, or the luckiest, many companies do just fine. This is especially true in the case of so-called low involvement goods, such as **consumer packaged goods (CPG)**—think trash bags, papers towels, laundry detergent, canned soup. Can you imagine a new company having enough money to launch a new brand that would successfully unseat Tide or Crest? It's possible, but not very likely. CPG consumer

behavior, like most low involvement examples, is mostly about memory and habit. Throw enough money at a brand name, and you can get people to remember it. This may even lead to habit, with consumers buying the same brand time after time without thinking or even noticing. This type of consumer behavior is actually not all that complicated, at least at the applied level. To tell you the truth, it's actually not all that difficult to do, or all that interesting either. But, it is profitable. This tells you that you should not assume enormous sophistication by all advertisers. Perhaps surprising to those that have never worked with or for advertisers, it is nonetheless true. But, when you can either transform CPG or other low involvement brands from simple memory-based ones (**mindshare brands**) into more culturally and socially meaningful ones through advertising, or when you are dealing with more high involvement categories such as automobiles or clothing, then the advertising and the related consumer behavior is a lot more interesting and fun. In any case, all advertisers could significantly improve their odds and profits by better understanding their consumers, even the old, big, too-big-to-fail, and lucky ones.

This chapter summarizes the concepts and frameworks we believe are most helpful in trying to understand consumer behavior as it most closely relates to advertising and integrated brand promotion. We explain consumer behavior from two different perspectives, one psychological and the other sociocultural. The psychological is what happens in consumers' heads. It portrays consumers as systematic (but not always rational) information seekers (or at least recipients), processors, and decision makers. The psychological perspective can be useful for either high involvement or low involvement goods. But typically, this perspective is most relevant when discussing low-cost, low involvement goods. This type of brand advertising is often called "mindshare" marketing. The term refers to the fact that this kind of brand advertising is hugely dependent on how easily the brand name, and maybe some very small set of attributes, is retrieved from memory. Easily remembered brands are said to have a high mindshare. Frankly, this is not the most exciting type of advertising, but it is where a lot of money is spent and made.

The second perspective views consumers as social beings who operate in their societies and cultures and thus behave largely as a function of social circumstance and cultural forces. To us, this is where the action is. This is where advertising and brand management can create truly sustainable great brands, not just memory or habit by repeating a brand name 10 million times due to enormous ad budgets. This second type of brand advertising is often referred to as "cultural branding," because it leverages social and cultural forces. It is typically used for more expensive and higher involvement categories, although some truly great low-cost brands such as Coca-Cola are brilliant users of cultural marketing. Although differing in assumptions and focus, both of these perspectives offer something valuable to the task of creating effective advertising and brand promotion.

5-1 PERSPECTIVE ONE: THE CONSUMER AS DECISION MAKER

One way to view consumer behavior is as a fairly predictable sequential process culminating with the individual's reaping a set of benefits from a product or service that satisfies that person's perceived needs. In this basic view, we can think of individuals as purposeful decision makers who either weigh and balance alternatives,

or resort, typically in times of complexity and too much information, to simple decision rules of thumb (heuristics) to make decisions.

(See Insights Online [Exhibit 5.1] to learn how Target helps customers make decisions about buying gifts.) Often, but not always, this process occurs in a straightforward sequence:

1. Need recognition
2. Information search and alternative evaluation
3. Purchase
4. Postpurchase use and evaluation

5-1a The Consumer Decision-Making Process

A brief discussion of what typically happens at each stage will give us a foundation for understanding consumers from a psychological perspective, and it can also illuminate opportunities for developing effective advertising.

Need Recognition. From the psychological perspective, the consumption process begins when people perceive a need. A **need state** arises when one's desired state of affairs differs from one's actual state of affairs. Need states are accompanied by a mental discomfort or anxiety that motivates action; the severity of this discomfort can be widely variable depending on the genesis of the need. For example, the need state that arises when one runs out of toothpaste would involve very mild discomfort for most people, whereas the need state that accompanies the breakdown of one's automobile on a dark and deserted highway in North Dakota or Alberta in mid-February can approach true desperation.

One way advertising works is to point to and thereby activate needs that will motivate consumers to buy a product or service. For instance, in the fall, advertisers from product categories as diverse as autos, snowblowers, and footwear roll out predictions for another severe winter and encourage consumers to prepare themselves before it's too late. Every change of season brings new needs, large and small, and advertisers are always at the ready. Or, you see the ad in Exhibit 5.2 and think about your last few business trips—you now are the proud owner of a new need: in-flight screen privacy and a new solution, 3M Privacy Film.

EXHIBIT 5.2 This ad helps you recognize that you need better computer privacy, and 3M has something that will satisfy that need.

privacy. even in the middle seat.

If you get stuck in the middle seat, you're not out of luck.

Whether it's your laptop, mobile device or desktop LCD, there's a 3M Privacy Solution to protect all your confidential information wherever you might be sitting. With 3M™ Privacy Filters and 3M™ Mobile Privacy Film, you see your screen clearly when looking at it straight on. But to anyone seated to the left or the right of you, the screen will look completely black, blocking out any chance of annoying snooping. So while it still might not be your favorite choice, the next time you find yourself stuck in the middle, rest assured you can keep your information private with 3M Privacy Solutions.

1.800.553.9215 / 3Mprivacyfilter.com

© 3M 2009   9168SA052909

3M

© 3M 2009

A variety of needs can be fulfilled through consumption, and it is reasonable to suggest that consumers' needs are often sufficiently recognized and motivating to many consumers. Products and services should provide benefits that fulfill consumers' needs; hence, one of the advertiser's primary jobs is to make the connection between the two for the consumer. Whatever the consumer perceives as a need is a need. Marketers are sometimes said to turn wants into needs, but in reality if the consumer thinks of it as a need, then it's a need. Advertising can sometimes help this along, but in the world of advertising, everything is a need.

Information Search and Alternative Evaluation.

Given that a consumer has recognized a need, it is often not obvious what would be the best way to satisfy that need. For example, if you have a fear of being trapped in a blizzard in Alberta, a condo on Miami Beach may be a better solution than a jeep or new snow tires. But maybe that's not practical, so you need a great all-wheel drive vehicle.

Need recognition simply sets in motion a process that may involve extensive information search and careful evaluation of alternatives prior to purchase. During this search and evaluation, there are numerous

opportunities for the advertiser to influence the final purchase decision. (See Insights Online [Exhibit 5.3] for an interesting example.)

Once a need has been recognized, information for the decision is acquired through an internal or external search. The consumer's first option for information is to draw on personal experience and prior knowledge. This **internal search** for information may be all that is required. When a consumer has considerable prior experience with the products in question, thoughts and feelings about the alternatives may be well established and determine choice.

An internal search can also tap into information that has accumulated in one's memory as a result of repeated advertising exposures, such as "Tide's In, Dirt's Out," or stored judgments, for example, "Apple computers are best." Advertisers want the result of internal search to result in their brand being in the **"evoked set,"** that is, the set of brands (usually two to five) that come to mind when a category is mentioned. I say "laundry detergent," and you say "Tide, All, and Wisk." Here, the evoked set consists of three brands, all stored internally, found through internal search, and probably the product of lots of advertising, use, and habit. The evoked set is usually highly related to the **consideration set,** the set of the brands the consumer will consider for purchase. If your brand is the first mentioned, you have achieved something even better: **"top of mind."** Top-of-mind awareness is a pretty good predictor of fairly inexpensive and low-risk CPG purchases. Affecting people's beliefs about a brand before their actual use of it, or merely establishing the existence of the brand in the consumer's consciousness, is a critical function of advertising and other integrated brand promotion. As noted in Chapter 1, the purpose of delayed response advertising is to generate recognition of and a favorable predisposition toward a brand so that when consumers enter into search mode, that brand will be one they immediately consider as a possible solution to their needs. If the consumer has not used a brand previously and has no recollection that it even exists, then that brand probably will not be the brand of choice. Good retailing (such as point-of-purchase displays) can help, but prior awareness is a very good thing, and something advertising can actually do.

It is certainly possible that an internal search will not turn up enough information to yield a decision. The consumer then proceeds with an **external search.** An external search typically involves visiting retail stores or looking online to examine the alternatives, seeking input from friends and relatives about their experiences with the products in question, or perusing professional product evaluations furnished in various publications such as *Consumer Reports.* In addition, when consumers are in an active information-gathering mode, they may be receptive to detailed, informative advertisements delivered through any of the print media, or they may deploy a shopping agent or a search engine to scour the Internet for the best deal or for opinions of other users. These days, online customer reviews are critical in this regard.

During an internal or external search, consumers are not merely gathering information for no purpose. They have some need that is propelling the process, and their goal is to make a decision that yields benefits for them. The consumer searches for and is simultaneously forming thoughts and opinions about possible alternatives. This is the alternative-evaluation component of the decision process, and it is another key phase for the advertiser to target.

Alternative evaluation will be structured by the consumer's consideration set and evaluative criteria. The consideration set is the subset of brands from a particular product category that becomes the focal point of the consumer's evaluation. Most product categories contain too many brands for all to be carefully considered, so the consumer finds some way to focus the search and evaluation. For example, for autos, consumers may consider only cars priced less than $25,000, or only cars that have all-wheel drive, or only foreign-made cars, or only cars sold at dealerships within a 20-mile radius of their work or home. A critical function of advertising is to make consumers aware of the brand and keep them aware so that the brand has a chance to be part of the consideration set.

As the search-and-evaluation process proceeds, consumers form evaluations based on the characteristics or attributes of those brands in their consideration set. These product attributes or performance characteristics are referred to as **evaluative criteria.** Evaluative criteria differ from one product category to the next and can include many factors, such as price, texture, warranty terms, service support, color, scent, or carb content.

It is critical for advertisers to have as complete an understanding as possible of the evaluative criteria that consumers use to make their buying decisions. They should also know how consumers rate their brand in comparison with others from the consideration set. Understanding consumers' evaluative criteria furnishes a powerful starting point for any advertising campaign (see Insights Online [Exhibit 5.4] for more on this).

Purchase. At this third stage, purchase occurs. The consumer has made a decision, and a sale is made. Great, right? Well, to a point. As nice as it is to make a sale, things are far from over at the point of sale. In fact, it would be a big mistake to view purchase as the culmination of the decision-making process.

No matter what the product or service category, the consumer is likely to buy from it again in the future. So, what happens after the sale is very important to advertisers. Advertisers want trial; they then want **conversion** (repeat purchase). They want brand loyalty. Some want to create **brand ambassadors,** users who will become apostles for the brand, spreading the brand gospel. At the same time, competitors will be working to convince consumers to give their brand a try.

Postpurchase Use and Evaluation. The goal for marketers and advertisers must not be simply to generate a sale; it must be to create satisfied and, ultimately, loyal customers. The data to support this position are quite astounding. Research shows that about 65 percent of the average company's business comes from its present, satisfied customers, and that 91 percent of dissatisfied customers will never buy again from the company that disappointed them.[2] Thus, consumers' evaluations of products in use become a major determinant of which brands will be in the consideration set the next time around.

Customer satisfaction derives from a favorable postpurchase experience. It may develop after a single use, but more likely it will require sustained use. Advertising can play an important role in inducing customer satisfaction by creating appropriate expectations for a brand's performance, or by helping the consumer who has already bought the advertised brand to feel good about doing so.

Advertising plays an important role in alleviating the **cognitive dissonance** that can occur after a purchase. Cognitive dissonance is the anxiety or regret that lingers after a difficult decision, sometimes called "buyer's remorse." Often, rejected alternatives have attractive features that lead people to second-guess their own decisions. If the goal is to generate satisfied customers, this dissonance must be resolved in a way that leads consumers to conclude that they did make the right decision after all. Purchasing high-cost items or choosing from categories that include many desirable and comparable brands can yield high levels of cognitive dissonance.

When dissonance is expected, it makes good sense for the advertiser to reassure buyers with detailed information about its brands. Postpurchase reinforcement programs might involve direct mail, email, or other types of personalized contacts with the customer. This post-purchase period represents a great opportunity for the advertiser to have the undivided attention of the consumer and to provide information and advice about product use that will increase customer satisfaction. Without satisfied customers, it is very difficult to have a successful business. Nowadays, consumers often go to the Internet to find other purchasers of the product to tell them they did the right thing. Want to reduce your anxiety that you bought the right car? Go to a chat group or brand community for that brand, and the members will almost always tell you that you were really smart buying what you did. Some advertisers provide this type of postpurchase information to make you a satisfied customer.

LO 2
5-1b Four Modes of Consumer Decision Making

As you may be thinking, consumers aren't always deliberate and systematic; sometimes they are hasty, impulsive, or even irrational. Do they always go through these four stages in a slow and deliberate manner? No, not always. The search time that people put into their purchases can vary dramatically for different types of products. Would you give the purchase of a tube of toothpaste the same amount of effort as the purchase of a new backpack? Probably not, unless you've been chastised by your dentist recently: Buy a tartar control toothpaste. Why is that T-shirt you bought at Pitchfork more important to you than the brand of orange juice you had for breakfast this morning? Does buying a Valentine's gift from Victoria's Secret create different feelings than buying a pack of gum? When you view a TV ad for car batteries, do you carefully memorize the information being presented so that you can draw on it the next time you're evaluating the brands in your consideration set, or will you wait to seek out that information when you really need it—like when your car won't start and the guy in the wrecker says your battery is dead?

Some purchase decisions are just more engaging than others. In the following sections we will elaborate on the view of consumer as decision maker by explaining four decision-making modes that help advertisers appreciate the richness and complexity of consumer behavior. These four modes are determined by a consumer's involvement and prior experiences with the product or service in question.

Sources of Involvement. To accommodate the complexity of consumption decisions, those who study consumer behavior typically talk about the involvement level of any particular decision. **Involvement** is the degree of perceived relevance and personal importance

accompanying the choice of a certain product or service within a particular context: How much it matters to you. Many things affect an individual's level of involvement with a consumption decision. People can develop interests and avocations in many different areas, such as cooking, photography, pet ownership, and exercise and fitness. Such ongoing personal interests can enhance involvement levels in a variety of product categories. Also, any time a great deal of risk is associated with a purchase—perhaps as a result of the high price of the item, or because the consumer will have to live with the decision for a long period of time—one should also expect elevated involvement. So, cars are usually high involvement, and things like gum are typically low involvement. There are exceptions, but most CPG (e.g., laundry detergent, paper towels) are low involvement. Sometimes, advertisers try to make an otherwise low involvement choice into a high involvement one. These are often some of the most ridiculous and lampooned ads out there: "What if I use the wrong paper towel and my husband is upset?" People who make ads like this must think we are idiots.

Consumers can, of course, sometimes derive important symbolic meaning from products and brands. Ownership or use of some products can help people reinforce some aspect of their self-image or make a statement to other people who are important to them. If a purchase carries great symbolic and real consequences—such as choosing the right gift for a special someone on Valentine's Day—it will be highly involving. If a brand expresses your preferred identity to the world, then it is probably high involvement. Think about clothing. Think about cars. Think about smartphones.

Higher involvement may be a function of a **consumer–brand relationship.** By relationship, we do not mean that the consumer sees the brand as their best friend, their father, or anything like that. It just means that the consumer has come to have some sort of emotional attachment to the brand, or even the category. Maybe the consumer is a cyclist, and the entire category is meaningful, but their first nice road bike was a Trek brand. They now have a consumer–brand relationship that brings with it high involvement. Brand relationships are formed by all sorts of things, including serendipity. But if you can get consumers to develop strong brand relationships, you have pushed the brand into the high involvement side of things, and you are generally much better off.

Involvement levels vary not only among product categories for any given individual, but also among individuals for any given product category. For example, some pet owners will feed their pets only the expensive canned products that look and smell like people food. IAMS, whose ad is featured in Exhibit 5.5, understands this and made a special premium dog food for

EXHIBIT 5.5 People who think of their pets as humans take their selection of pet food very seriously. IAMS offers serious pet food for the serious dog owner. www.iams.com

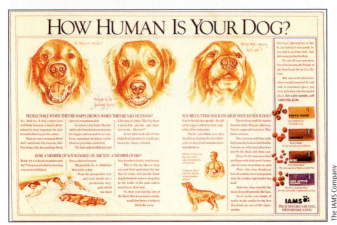

EXHIBIT 5.7 High involvement and low experience typically yield extended problem solving. Buying an engagement ring is a perfect example of this scenario. This ad offers lots of advice for the extended problem solver. De Beers is more than happy to be helpful here. wwwadiamondisforever.com

consumers who think of their pets as close-to-human. Many other pet owners, however, are perfectly happy with feeding Rover from a 50-pound, economy-size bag of dry dog food.

Now we will use the ideas of involvement and prior experience to help conceive four different types or modes of consumer decision making. These four modes are shown in Exhibit 5.6. Any specific consumption decision is based on a high or low level of prior experience with the product or service in question and a high or low level of involvement. This yields the four modes of decision making: (1) extended problem solving, (2) limited problem solving, (3) habit or variety seeking, and (4) brand loyalty. Each is described in the following sections.

Extended Problem Solving. When consumers are inexperienced in a particular consumption setting, yet find the setting highly involving, they are likely to engage in **extended problem solving.** In this mode, consumers go through a deliberate decision-making process that begins with explicit need recognition, proceeds with careful internal and external search, continues through alternative evaluation and purchase, and ends with a lengthy postpurchase evaluation.

Examples of extended problem solving come with decisions such as choosing a home or a diamond ring, as suggested by Exhibit 5.7. These products are typically expensive and can carry a considerable amount of

risk in terms of making an uneducated decision. Buying one's first new automobile and choosing a college are two other consumption settings that may require extended problem solving. Extended problem solving is the exception, not the rule.

Limited Problem Solving. In this decision-making mode, experience and involvement are both low. **Limited problem solving** is a more common mode of decision making. In this mode, a consumer is less systematic in his or her decision making. The consumer has a new problem to solve, but it is not a problem that is interesting or engaging, so the information search is limited to simply trying the first brand encountered. For example, let's say a young couple has just brought home a new baby, and suddenly they perceive a very real need for disposable diapers. At the hospital they received complimentary trial packs of several products, including Pampers disposables. They try the Pampers, find them an acceptable solution to their messy new problem, and take the discount coupon that came with the sample to their local grocery, where they buy several packages. In the limited-problem-solving mode, we often see consumers simply seeking adequate solutions to mundane problems. It is also a mode in which just trying a brand or two may be the most efficient way of collecting information about one's options. Of course, smart marketers realize that trial offers can be a preferred means of collecting information, and they facilitate trial

EXHIBIT 5.6 Four modes of consumer decision making.

	High Involvement	Low Involvement
Low Experience	Extended problem solving	Limited problem solving
High Experience	Brand loyalty	Habit or variety seeking

of their brands through free samples, inexpensive "trial sizes," or discount coupons. It is in this mode that much of CPG advertising and brand promotion occurs. Here, consumer memory is a huge factor.

Habit or Variety Seeking. Habit and variety seeking occur in settings where a decision isn't involving and a consumer repurchases from the category over and over again. In terms of sheer numbers, habitual purchases are probably the most common decision-making mode. Consumers find a brand of laundry detergent that suits their needs, they run out of the product, and they buy it again. The cycle repeats itself many times per year in an almost mindless fashion. Getting in the habit of buying only one brand can be a way to simplify life and minimize the time invested in "nuisance" purchases. When a consumer perceives little difference among the various competitive brands, it is easier to buy the same brand repeatedly. A lot of consumption decisions are boring but necessary. Habits help us minimize the inconvenience.

In some product categories where a buying habit would be expected, an interesting phenomenon called variety seeking may be observed instead. Remember, **habit** refers to buying a single brand repeatedly as a solution to a simple consumption problem. It is not the same as brand loyalty. This can be very boring, and some consumers fight the boredom through variety seeking; this of course happens in many life domains. **Variety seeking** refers to the tendency of consumers to switch their selection among various brands in a given category in a seemingly random pattern. This is not to say that a consumer will buy just any brand; he or she probably has two to five brands that all provide similar levels of satisfaction to a particular consumption problem. However, from one purchase occasion to the next, the individual will switch brands from within this set, just for the sake of variety.

Variety seeking is most likely to occur in frequently purchased categories where sensory experience, such as taste or smell, accompanies product use. In such categories, no amount of ad spending can overcome the consumer's basic desire for fresh sensory experience.[3] Satiation occurs after repeated use and leaves the consumer looking for a change of pace. Product categories such as soft drinks and alcoholic beverages, snack foods, breakfast cereals, and fast food are prone to variety seeking, so marketers in these categories must constantly be introducing new possibilities to consumers to feed their craving for variety. One day you open your lunch and your old, faithful bologna and cheese on white bread just doesn't cut it anymore—especially if a marketer has presented you with a fresh new choice (see Exhibit 5.8). It may not be all that exciting, but Thomas is offering you more choice.

EXHIBIT 5.8 Bored with sliced bread? Thomas offers you a chance for a little variety.

Brand Loyalty. The final decision-making mode is typified by high involvement and rich prior experience. In this mode, **brand loyalty** becomes a major consideration in the purchase decision. Consumers demonstrate brand loyalty when they repeatedly purchase a single brand as their choice to fulfill a specific need and have some degree of emotional connection to the brand. In one sense, brand-loyal purchasers may look as if they have developed a simple buying habit; however, it is important to distinguish brand loyalty from simple habit. Brand loyalty is based on an emotional connection toward the brand and a conscious commitment to find this brand each time the consumer purchases from this category. Conversely, habits are merely consumption simplifiers that are not based on the power of an emotional relationship, however minor, with the brand. Habits can be disrupted through a skillful combination of advertising and sales promotions. Spending advertising dollars to persuade truly brand-loyal consumers to try an alternative can be a great waste of resources.

Brands such as Starbucks, Apple, Gerber, Oakley, Coke, Heineken, IKEA, and Harley-Davidson have inspired very loyal consumers. Brand loyalty is something that any marketer aspires to have, but in a world filled with more-savvy consumers and endless product (and advertising) proliferation, it is becoming harder and harder to attain. Brand loyalty may emerge because the consumer perceives that one brand simply outperforms all others in providing some critical benefit. For example, the harried business executive may have grown loyal to FedEx's overnight delivery service as a result of repeated satisfactory experiences with FedEx—and as a result of FedEx's advertising that has repeatedly posed the question, "Why fool around with anyone else?"

Perhaps even more important, brand loyalty can be due to the emotional benefits that accompany certain brands. One of the strongest indicators for brand loyalty has to be the tendency on the part of some loyal consumers to tattoo their bodies with the insignia of their favorite brand. Although statistics are pretty new on this sort of thing, it is claimed that the worldwide leader in brand-name tattoos is Harley-Davidson. So, you are going to put something on your body for a lifetime—a brand name. What accounts for Harley's fervent following? Is Harley's brand loyalty simply a function of performing better than its many competitors? Or, does a Harley rider derive some deep emotional benefit from taking that big bike out on the open road and leaving civilization far behind? Is part of the Harley loyalty due to membership in a brand community and buying into the mythology of the slightly outlaw nature of the Harley mystique? Harley's ads often try to leverage these feelings and connections.

Recent research has shown that when consumers have an emotional connection to a brand, they actually distort information in a positive way to favor that brand and distort information in a negative way to diminish competing brands. This is called **predecisional distortion** and has been shown at the brain level to be very important in brand selection.[4] This suggests that one way to create true brand loyalty is through emotional advertising, ads that link a certain emotion with the brand. We will talk more about this in Chapter 11. Many companies are now using the Internet to create dialogue and manage relations with their customers; more on this in Chapter 14.

--- LO ③ ---

5-1c Advertising, Consumer Behavior, and Memory

Memory is of obvious importance to advertisers. It is thus helpful to understand just a few basics of human memory.

Semantic (Word) Memory. Semantic memory is very important where advertising is concerned. This is the kind of memory through which names, words, and concepts are stored and retrieved from our minds. It is the type of memory that drives a great deal of low involvement or mindshare brands. CPG are the most common users of semantic memory–based advertising, for example, laundry detergent, canned foods, and paper goods. It is a relatively well-understood form of human memory and is very easily used by advertisers.

The more easily you can retrieve something from semantic memory, the more accessible it is. Greater **accessibility** is a good thing for advertised brand names for at least two reasons. The first is obvious; you are more likely to buy a low involvement good for a brand you remember than one you don't. The second reason is a bit more complicated, but suffice it to say that the more easily (or more quickly) one retrieves something from memory, the more frequent or popular one believes it to be. So, if I ask for the name of a laundry detergent and you quickly say Tide, odds are that you also will overestimate Tide's market share and believe it to be a more popular brand than it actually is. This is called the **accessibility bonus**.[5] So, easily recalled brands are a very good thing. That is why advertisers for so-called mindshare brands spend so much money getting you to remember them. Anything that can be done to promote better recall is important in advertising. More on how to do this in Chapter 11.

Episodic Memory. Episodic memory is just like it sounds: memories of episodes. It is your memory of events, what you did last night, your friend's party, and so on. It could also be a consumption experience like driving a certain car or eating a brand of ice cream. It could also be an ad, most likely a video ad from TV, computer, or smartphone. Episodic memory is not as well understood as semantic memory. It is also true that episodic memory is much more fluid and less fixed than we had thought. We no longer think of this type of memory as a mental video recorder that makes a perfect record of everything we experience. Instead, we now view it as a system driven as much by motivation and how we choose to remember as anything. The fact that these memories are so easily altered makes opportunities for advertisers to shape them in ways that benefit the brand. We will talk more about how this is done in Chapter 11.

Emotion. We have come to appreciate that emotion is incredibly important in consumer behavior. Researchers have shown that if a brand is associated with a positive emotion or feeling, the subsequent information about the brand is actually distorted in favor of the emotion-linked brand and against others. By this, we mean that consumers actually change the nature of incoming information to favor this emotional brand connection. It then affects subsequent consumer decisions in favor of the emotion-linked brand. This power clearly favors the use of emotional branding techniques, brand relationship building, including advertising. We will get more into this in Chapter 11.

Information Overload and Simplification. As you know, there is a lot of advertising in our lives. In fact, there is, particularly with the ease of computer information search now, an enormous amount of information. Two things are almost always true in this context: (1) consumers will say the more information, the better and (2) that is not always true. Consumers appear to have a strong desire to have as much information as possible; they have always been told that good consumer decisions are based on having the most information. But it turns out to those who study consumer decision making that there is such a thing as information overload. Consumers simply get too much information and confront too many choices to be able to comprehensively and effectively apply all the information to the choice task. What they do then is to use a decision heuristic, or way of simplifying the task. Common ones include buying the most popular brand, the least expensive, the most expensive, the one you have heard the most about, or the one you bought last. Advertisers know this problem, but in the escalating war of advertising, saying less is hard to do, even when saying less is really saying more.

Clutter and Attention. **Advertising clutter** derives from the context in which ads are processed. Even if a person wanted to, it would be impossible to process and integrate every advertising message that he or she is exposed to each day. Pick up today's newspaper and start reviewing every ad you come across. Will you have time today to read them all? The clutter problem is further magnified by competitive brands making very similar performance claims.[6] Was it Advil, Anacin, Aveda, Aleve, Avia, Aflexa, Aveya, Actonel, Motrin, Nuprin, or Tylenol Gelcaps that promised you 12 hours of relief from your headache? (Can you select the brands from this list that aren't headache remedies?) The simple fact is that each of us is exposed to hundreds, maybe thousands, of ads each day, and no one has the time or inclination to sort through them all. Some industry experts and researchers believe that the simple mass of advertising, the enormous number of ads, is now working very hard against the institution of advertising itself. Ironic as it is, advertising might be the death of advertising.

Exhibit 5.9 is an excellent illustration of clutter: the outer blue circle is the total amount of measured U.S. advertising in a recent year. The smaller and light magenta circle represents all automotive advertising (the largest category in the United States) that same year. The smaller beige circle represents estimated spending of a large automobile company, and the tiny red dot is the amount spent on one of its leading brands. When you do the math, only about one out of every 2,000 ads was for this typically advertised brand. So, what

EXHIBIT 5.9 An ad in a sea of ads. So just how much can advertising really do?

© Cengage Learning

chance do you think that ad had to actually affect consumer behavior in a sea of other ads? This is a very big question facing the industry right now.

Advertisers employ a variety of tactics to break through the clutter. Popular music, celebrity spokespersons, sexy models, rapid scene changes, and anything that is novel are devices for combating selective attention. (See Insights Online [Exhibit 5.10] for a notable example.) Remember, as we discussed in Chapter 4, advertisers constantly walk that fine line between novel and obnoxious in their never-ending battle for the attention of the consumer. They really don't want to insult you or anyone else; they just want to be noticed. Of course, they often step over the annoyance line.

The battle for consumers' attention poses another dilemma for advertisers. Without attention, there is little chance that an advertiser's message will have its desired impact; however, the provocative, attention-attracting devices used to engage consumers often become the focal point of consumers' ad processing. They remember seeing an ad featuring 27 Elvis Presley impersonators, but they can't recall what brand was being advertised or what claims were being made about the brand. If advertisers must entertain consumers to win their attention, they must also be careful that the brand and message don't get lost in the shuffle.

▶ INSIGHTS ONLINE

5.10 Go online to see the AdAge feature, "Google Introduces a New Media-Viewing Platform."

5-2 PERSPECTIVE TWO: THE CONSUMER AS SOCIAL BEING

In this section we present a second perspective on consumer behavior, branding, and advertising, a perspective based on social and cultural factors. It should be considered another part of the larger story of how advertising works. Remember, we are still talking about the same consumers discussed in the preceding section; we are just viewing their behavior from a different vantage point. Ad professionals have long been believers in culturally and socially based advertising and branding.

Consumers are more than information processors, and ads are more than socially isolated attempts at **attitude** manipulation with this approach, **meaning** is the focus, and consumer behavior is meaningfully social. The social meaning–based approach centers on knowing how to connect with human beings around their lives and consumption practices with advertising and other brand promotion. That's why advertising agencies commonly hire people who know about material culture (anthropology), demography and social forces (sociology), the history of brands and consumption practices (history), communication, text (literature), and art. More valuable than anything else is for ad professionals to have a strong understanding of their culture: cultural and social knowledge is the stuff of which great advertising is made. So if you want to make great advertising, pay attention to culture and society.

The social meaning-based approach centers on knowing how to connect with human beings around their lives and consumption practices with advertising and other brand promotion.

LO 4

5-2a Consuming in the Real World

Let's consider some major components of consumers' real lives:

Culture. If you are in the ad business, you are in the culture business.

Culture is what a people do, or "the total life ways of a people, the social legacy the individual acquires from his (her) group."[7] It is the way we eat, groom, celebrate, travel, play, get together, communicate, and otherwise express feelings. It is the way things are done. Cultures may be large and national, or they may be regional or local, or not geographic at all: *urban hipster culture, teen tech-nerd, Junior League,* and so on. It's usually easier to see and note culture when it's more distant and unfamiliar. For most people, this is when they travel. For example, if you've traveled beyond your own country, you have no doubt noticed that people in other national cultures do things differently. Further, members of a culture often find the ways they do things to be perfectly natural and normal. Culture is also said to be nearly invisible to those who are immersed in it. If everyone around us behaves in a similar fashion, we do not easily think about the existence of some large and powerful force acting on us all. But it's there; this constant background force is the force of culture, and it's powerful. To really see the culture that is all around you, to really see what you take as ordinary, or to see it like you were a visitor to a strange land is what the sociocultural perspective offers.

Culture surrounds the creation, transmission, reception, and interpretation of ads and brands, just as it touches every aspect of consumption. Culture is about as "real world" as it gets. How do you as an advertiser create or leverage cultural forces to sell something? That's the idea. Why do we have the particular rituals we perform on certain days? Are there market opportunities in those rituals? Or, who makes up the rules of gift giving? If you are Tiffany, Hallmark, De Beers, General Mills, or Unilever you have a very good reason to understand why people do things a certain way (e.g., buy things for one holiday but not for another, or eat certain things for breakfast in a certain way, or wash clothes, or clean and decorate themselves with soaps and beauty products).

Rituals are "often-repeated formalized behaviors involving symbols."[8] Cultures participate in rituals; consumers participate in rituals. Rituals are core elements of culture. Cultures affirm, express, and maintain themselves through rituals. They are a way in which individuals are made part of the culture, and a method by which the culture constantly renews and perpetuates itself. For example, ritual-laden holidays such as Thanksgiving, Christmas, Hanukah, and the Fourth of July help perpetuate aspects of American culture through their repeated reenactment (tradition). Globally, there are a myriad of very important cultural rituals, all involving consumption (e.g., feasts and gift giving). This is true around the world, and rituals help intertwine culture and consumption practices in a very real way. For example, Jell-O may have attained the prominence of an "official" American holiday food because of its regular usage as part of the Thanksgiving dinner ritual.[9] In the American South, it is common to eat black-eyed peas on New Year's Day to ensure good luck. In one sense it is "just done," but in another it is just done because it is a ritual embedded in a culture. If you are a consumer packaged goods manufacturer, understanding these types of ritual is not a trivial concern at all. Exhibit 5.11 shows that Kraft is very aware of the role of consumption rituals. The ad is there to make sure you don't forget it.

Rituals also occur every day in millions of other contexts. For example, when someone buys a new car or a new home, they do all sorts of "unnecessary" things to make it theirs. They clean the carpets even if they were just cleaned, they trim trees that don't need trimming, they hang things from the mirror of the used car they just bought, they change oil that was just changed—all to make the new possession theirs and remove any trace of the former owner. These behaviors are not only important to anthropologists, they are also important to those making and trying to sell products such as paint, rug shampoos, household disinfectants, lawn and garden equipment, auto accessories, and on and on.

Rituals don't have to be the biggest events of the year. There are everyday rituals, such as the way we eat, clean ourselves, and groom. Think about all the habitual things you do from the time you get up in the morning until you crawl into bed at night. These things are done in a certain way; they are not random.[10] Members of a common culture tend to do them one way, and members of other cultures do them other ways. Again, if you've ever visited another country, you have no doubt noticed significant differences.

Daily rituals seem inconsequential because they are habitual and routine, and thus "invisible." If, however, someone tried to get you to significantly alter the way you do these things, he or she would quickly learn just how important and resistant to change these rituals are. If a product or service cannot be incorporated into an already-existing ritual, it is very difficult and expensive for advertisers to effect a change. If, on the other hand, an advertiser can successfully incorporate the consumption of its good or service into an existing ritual, then success is much more likely. Imagine how important rituals are to the global beauty industry. Cleaning and beauty practices are highly ritualized. So are breakfast habits (see Insights Online [Exhibit 5.12] for an interesting example).

EXHIBIT 5.11 This ad promotes Kraft products as an integral part of family rituals and traditions. www.kraftfoods.com

KRAFT is a registered trademark. Used with permission of Kraft Foods

—————— LO ⑤ ——————

Stratification. **Stratification** refers to systematic inequalities in things such as wealth, income, education, power, and status. For example, some members of society exist within a wealthier group (stratum), others within a less affluent stratum. Race and gender are also unequally distributed across income; for example, men generally have higher incomes than women. Thus a cross section, or slice, of American society would reveal many different levels (or strata) of the population along these different dimensions. Some combination of these inequalities is what we think of when we say "social class." Social class is hard to pin down in some contemporary societies, easier in others. In America, a very large number of folks with a huge range in income, wealth, and education call themselves "middle class."

In North America, and much of the world, social class was most strongly determined by income: higher-income Americans were generally seen as being in a higher social class, and lower-income Americans were considered to be in a lower class. But that is an imperfect relationship. For example, successful plumbers often had higher incomes than some types of lawyers (the United States has lots of lawyers), but their occupation was (to some) less prestigious, and thus their social class

INSIGHTS ONLINE

5.12 Go online to see the AdAge feature, "Taco Bell Seeks to Change Consumers' Breakfast Ritual."

designation was lower. So, the prestige of one's occupation also entered into what we called "social class." Education also has something to do with social class, but a person with a little college experience and a lot of inherited wealth would probably rank higher than an insurance agent with an MBA. Bill Gates left Harvard without a degree, and he has pretty high social standing, not to mention wealth. Thus income, education, and occupation are three important variables for indicating social class but are still individually, or even collectively, inadequate at capturing its full meaning.

Important to marketers is the belief that members of the same social strata tend to live in similar ways, have similar views and philosophies, and, most critically, tend to consume in somewhat similar ways. You could supposedly tell "social class" from what people consume and how they consume; at least, that's what lots of marketers and advertisers believed. Social class and stratification was supposed to be reflected in a consumer's taste and thus their consumption. The traditional view was that advertisers cared about social class and stratification because consumers used their choices to reflect their class. But this assumption has been challenged lately. Some believe that traditional social class—consumption taste hierarchies have collapsed, or at least become much less stable. What do you think—can you tell someone's social standing by how they consume? Are tastes related to social stratification a thing of the past? Are social class markers still around? We see this situation as fluid but believe that class, social status, and taste indicators are still with us and still matter to consumers, and, therefore, to advertisers.

What do you think? Put it to the test: Go to a mall, walk around, and check people out. Do you think you could guess their income, education, occupation, and whether they live downtown or in the 'burbs from the way they look, what they are wearing, and which stores they shop in? Most advertisers think you can, and that's why stratification matters.

We are also living in a time of great and **increasing income inequality.** In the United States, for example, the wealthy are pulling away from the rest at a very sharp clip. There has been no or very little real income growth for most Americans lately. Upward mobility in the United States is nowhere near what it once was. England, a country of considerable class consciousness, now has more upward mobility than the United States. This, some fear, will become the new normal, an economy and a society of lowered expectations and possibilities, but with the wealthy doing very well, and better and better. If this is the case, how will it affect consumption and advertising? Will luxury brands flourish for the upper 1 or 2 percent, and the rest seek greater and greater value? Look at the ad in Exhibit 5.13; here is a very expensive watch being sold to the wealthy. It even defends and makes a virtue of inherited wealth.

EXHIBIT 5.13 Inherited wealth in the form of a very expensive watch either is completely tone-deaf to the current economic and sociopolitical climate or is providing needed justification to the very fortunate to drop tens of thousands of dollars on a wristwatch.

How will this increasing income inequality affect the various ways advertising attempts to link social status to brands? Brands tend to suffer when their prices and profit margins decline. If they go too low, they become commodities, sold on price. When that happens, advertising tends to be a smaller player, because the only meaning you are trying to convey is related to everyday low prices and value. That means more retail and less national advertising. It means Sunday newspaper ad bundles, coupons, and retail promotions. None of that is very good for national or creative advertising.

Taste. This brings us to taste. **Taste** refers to a generalized set or orientation to consumer aesthetic preferences. If social class affects consumption through tastes, it also affects media preferences (e.g., *RV Life* versus *Wine Spectator*). We think of tennis more than bowling as belonging to the upper classes, chess more than checkers, and brie more than Velveeta. Ordering wine instead of beer has social significance, as does wearing Tommy Hilfiger rather than Lee jeans or driving a Volvo rather than a Chevy. We believe social stratification and taste are intertwined while acknowledging that consumption preferences and strata are a little less dependable than in the past. Some smart advertisers have successfully leveraged the "democatization" of taste. Target has done it better than anyone else so far, but will they be able to keep that strategy if another major recession comes? Look at the ad in Exhibit 5.14 from Target. See how they make a store with prices as low, or almost as low, as Walmart's into something stylish.

Another important concept is *cultural capital,* the value that cultures place on certain consumption practices and objects. For example, a certain consumption practice, say snowboarding, has a certain capital or value (like money) for some segment of the population. If you own a snowboard (a certain amount of cultural capital) and can actually use it (more cultural capital) and look good while using it (even more capital), then this activity is like cultural currency or cultural money in the bank. A pair of Tory Burch boots has cultural capital, as do Lululemon yoga wear, Land Rover SUVs, and Kendra Scott earrings. By ownership, the consumer

gets a little cultural capital, points if you will, in the culture. Capital is by definition worth something. It gets you things you want. A Porsche has a certain cultural capital among some groups, as does wearing khakis, drinking PBR, ordering the right pinot noir, knowing how to hail a cab, flying first class, or knowing about the latest band or cool thing on YouTube. This capital may exist within a hipster culture, or a 40-something wine-snob culture, or a redneck culture—it's still cultural capital. In all of these cultures certain consumer practices are favored or valued. Advertisers try to figure out which ones are valued more and why, and how to make their product sought after because it has higher cultural capital and can be sold at a higher price. Does an iPhone have more cultural capital than a Samsung? To whom? To what cultural group? To what market segment? Having good "taste" helps you know which things have high cultural capital. Ads try to emphasize the cultural capital, style, and taste to be found in the product, and then transferred to the consumer. How does the D&B ad in Exhibit 5.15 do this? What is the extent and nature of D&B's cultural capital? Who thinks this brand is cool, why?

The interaction of social stratification and cultural capital becomes apparent when a person moves

EXHIBIT 5.14 Target leveraged once-collapsing style and taste hierarchies better than anyone. Will they stay on this strategy, or go Walmart on us? Which would be better? Why?

Photo courtesy of Target Stores, Minneapolis

EXHIBIT 5.15 This ad points to the cultural capital of Dooney and Bourke. See how meaning is moved from the surrounding culture, captured in the ad by the setting, and then moved to the shoes, and finally transferred to the consumer.

DOONEY & BOURKE

® Dooney & Bourke

from one stratum into another. Consider the following example: Bob and Jill move into a more expensive neighborhood. Both grew up in lower-middle-class surroundings and moved into high-paying jobs after graduate school. They have now moved into a fairly upscale neighborhood, composed mostly of "older money." On one of the first warm Sundays, Bob goes out to his driveway and begins to do something he has done all his life: change the oil in his car. One of Bob's neighbors comes over and chats, and ever so subtly suggests to Bob that people in this neighborhood have "someone else" do "that sort of thing." Bob gets the message: It's not cool to change your oil in your own driveway. This is not how the new neighbors behave. It doesn't matter whether you like to do it or not; it is simply not done. To Bob, paying someone else to do this simple job seems wasteful and uppity. He's a bit offended and a little embarrassed. But, over time, he decides that it's better to go along with the other people in the neighborhood. Over time, Bob begins to see the error of his ways and changes his attitudes and his behavior.

This is an example of the effect of stratification and (negative) cultural capital on consumer behavior. Bob will no longer be a good target for Fram, Purolator, AutoZone, or any other product or service used to change oil at home. On the other hand, Bob is now a perfect candidate for quick-oil-change businesses such as Jiffy Lube.

---------------- LO ⑥ ----------------

Family. The consumer behavior of families is also of great interest to advertisers. Advertisers want not only to discern the needs of different kinds of families but also to discover how decisions are made within families. The first is possible, the latter much more difficult. For a while, consumer researchers tried to determine who in the traditional nuclear family (i.e., mom, dad, and the kids) made various purchasing decisions. This was largely an exercise in futility. Due to errors in reporting and conflicting perceptions between partners, it became clear that the family purchasing process is anything but clear. Even though some types of purchases are handled by one family member, many decisions are actually diffuse nondecisions, arrived at through what consumer researcher C. W. Park aptly calls a "muddling-through" process.[11] These "decisions" just get made, and no one is really sure who made them, or even when. For an advertiser to influence such a diffuse and vague process is indeed a challenge. The consumer behavior of the family is a complex and often subtle type of social negotiation. One person handles this, one takes care of that. Sometimes specific purchases fall along gender lines, but sometimes they don't. Even though they

may not be the buyer in many instances, children can play important roles as initiators, influencers, and users in many categories, such as cereals, clothing, vacation destinations, fast-food restaurants, and technology (like computers). Still, some advertisers capitalize on the flexibility of this social system by suggesting in their ads who *should* take charge of a given consumption task, and then arming that person with the appearance of expertise so that whoever wants the job can take it and defend his or her purchases.

Advertisers often focus on the major or gross differences in types of families, because different families have different needs, buy different things, and are reached by different media. Family roles often change when both parents (or a single parent) are employed outside the home. For instance, a teenage son or daughter may be given the role of initiator and buyer, while the parent or parents serve merely as influences. There are a lot of single parents and quite a few second and even third marriages. The point is that *family* is a very open concept. Due to the civil rights issue of our day, gay marriage is now possible in several states, and public opinion has changed dramatically in a relatively short time. Families are not defined as much by marriage as in the past. Plenty of cohabitating but not married families exist and are just as legitimate as any other—certainly from the secular view of a company trying to sell them branded goods and services. In addition to the "traditional" nuclear family and the single-parent household, there is the extended family (nuclear family plus grandparents, cousins, and others), including single parents and same-sex households with and without children.

Advertisers are often interested in knowing things such as the age of the youngest child, the size of the family, and the family income. The age of the youngest child living at home tells an advertiser where the family is in terms of its needs and obligations (i.e., toys, investment instruments for college savings, clothing, and vacations). When the youngest child leaves home, the consumption patterns of a family change. Advertisers like to track the age of the youngest child living at home and use it as a planning criterion. This is called a **life-stage** variable and is used frequently in advertising and promotion planning.

Identity is a sociological concept; it matters a great deal to advertisers. There is no sense of identity outside the social context. All humans think of themselves relative to others. Our very idea of self is meaningless in the absence of others. Across the life-course, there are several times when identity is particularly in play. The most obvious and painful is adolescence. One reason that teenagers are such a great market segment is that their identity is in constant flux, and to express identity they constantly consume things: clothing, music, electronics, sports and recreational goods and services, jewelry, and so on. With each identity they try on, they spend money on branded goods.[12] Later in life, identity is also challenged occasionally: birth of first child, retirement, last child goes to college, and so on. At these pressure points, consumption changes, and advertisers are there to help consumers work out their identity issues. It is also worth saying that when consumers are identity-challenged, good ethics are really important. You can do harm.

Race and Ethnicity. Race and ethnicity provide other ways to think about important social groups. Answering the question of how race and ethnicity figure into consumer behavior is very difficult. Our discomfort stems from having, on the one hand, the desire to say, "Race doesn't matter, we're all the same," and on the other hand not wanting (or not being able) to deny the significance of race and ethnicity in terms of reaching ethnic cultures and influencing a wide variety of behaviors, including consumer behavior. The truth is we are less and less sure what *race* is and what it means. Obviously, a person's pigmentation, in and of itself, has almost nothing to do with preferences for one type of product over another. But because race and ethnicity have mattered in culture, they do still matter in consumer behavior. By the middle of the 21st century, white Americans will probably be close to minority status in U.S. population. Do you believe this demographic reality will be important to advertisers and marketers?

There probably isn't an area in consumer behavior where research is more inadequate. This is probably because everyone is terrified to discuss it and because many of the findings we do have are suspect. What is attributed to race is often due to another factor that is itself associated with race. For example, you will sometimes hear advertisers say something to the effect that African Americans and Latinos are more brand loyal than their Anglo counterparts. Data on the frequency of brand switching is offered, and lo and behold, it does appear that white people switch brands more often. But why? Some ethnic minorities live in areas where there are fewer retail choices. When we statistically remove the effect of income disparities between white people and people of color, we see that the brand-switching effect often disappears. This suggests that brand loyalty is not a function of race but of disposable income and shopping options. For example, does anyone really think certain ethnicities just love living in food deserts? What might appear as super-loyalty to fast-food chains is just a lack of real choice.

But race does affect one's social identity to varying degrees. One is not blind to one's own ethnicity. African Americans, Latinos, and other ethnic groups have culturally related consumption preferences. Certain brands become associated with racial or ethnic groups. It is not enough, however, for advertisers to say one group is different from another, or that they prefer one brand to another simply because they are members of a racial or ethnic category. If advertisers really want a good, long-term relationship with their customers, they must acquire, through good consumer research, a deeper understanding of who their customers are and how this identity is affected by culture, felt ethnicity, and race. In short, advertisers must ask why groups of consumers are different, or prefer different brands, and not settle for an easy answer. It wasn't until the mid- to late 1980s that most American corporations made a concerted effort to court African-American consumers or even to recognize their existence (see Insights Online [Exhibit 5.16] for more discussion).[13]

Politics. At first, it might seem odd to mention politics in the same breath as consumer behavior. It shouldn't. There are many places in the world where religious–ethnic–political strife is abundant and this strife is then played out in consumption contexts. This is done for many reasons, including a company's labor history (e.g., Coors, Walmart), its connection to a colonial power (think old British brands in Ireland and India), its perceived working-class status (Pabst Blue Ribbon), or its degree of greenness. Are soda companies like Coca-Cola making us obese and giving us diabetes? Are they the tobacco companies of this period? How about Chic-Filet's founder's antigay statement? In many parts of the world, consumption and branding have a long political history, so brand–political associations are commonplace. That is happening more now in the United States as well. Think about the Great Recession and the recent rise of populism in the United States. How could brands leverage this social disruption? How about "green" politics? In Exhibit 5.17 the politics of labor are leveraged.

Gender. Obviously, gender matters in consumption. But are men and women really that different in any meaningful way in their consumption behavior, beyond the obvious? Again, to the extent that gender informs a "culture of gender," the answer is yes. As long as men and women are the products of differential socialization, then they will continue to be different in some significant ways. There is, however, no definitive list of gender differences in consumption, because the expression of gender, just like anything else social, depends on the situation and the social circumstances. In the 1920s, advertisers openly referred to women as less logical, more emotional, and the cultural stewards of beauty.[14] (Some critics complain that the same soft, irrational, emotional feminine persona is still invoked in advertising.) Advertising helps construct a social reality

EXHIBIT 5.17 Having a social conscience can be good advertising and smart branding. It's also the right thing to do.

© Thomas C. O'Guinn

in which gender is a predominant feature. Obviously, gender's impact on consumer behavior is not limited to heterosexual men and women. LGBT consumers comprise significant markets. Of late, company after company has begun to see this as a nonissue. Again, these are markets that desire to be acknowledged and served, but not stereotyped and patronized. Study Exhibit 5.18 for how Volvo very matter-of-factly represents its customers.

In the late 1970s, advertisers discovered "working women." In the 1980s, marketers discovered African-American consumers, about the same time they discovered Hispanic consumers. Later they discovered Asian Americans, and just lately they discovered LGBT consumers. Of course, these people weren't missing. They were there all along.

Community. **Community** is a powerful and traditional sociological concept. Its meaning extends well beyond the idea of a specific geographic place. Communities can be imagined or even virtual; they do not

have to be face-to-face. Community members believe that they belong to a group of people who are similar to them in some important way and different from those not in the community. Members of communities often share rituals and traditions and feel some sort of responsibility to one another and the community.

Advertisers are becoming increasingly aware of the power of community, particularly as it relates to social media. Products have social meanings, and community is the quintessential social domain, so consumption is inseparable from the notion of where we live (actually or virtually) and with whom we feel a kinship or a sense of belonging. Communities often exert a great deal of power. A community may be your neighborhood, or it may be people like you with whom you feel a kinship, such as members of social clubs, other consumers who collect the same things you do, or people who have, use, or admire the same brands you do.

Brand communities are groups of consumers who feel a commonality and a shared purpose attached to a consumer good or service.[15] When owners of Timberland, Apple, Mountain Dew, or Coca-Cola experience a sense of connectedness by virtue of their common ownership or usage, a brand community exists. When two perfect strangers stand in a parking lot and act like old friends simply because they both own Volvos, a type of community is revealed. Most of these communities exist online, and some reveal a certain level of brand fanaticism. Other times, these communities reveal an important and more "mainstream" connection between owners, users, or admirers of brands that, with the rise of the Internet, has made these communities important to marketers. Brands matter socially, so brands matter. Social media make brand communities very important.

LO ⑦

5-2b **Cultural Branding and Advertising**

Cultural branding is a type of branding that leverages sociocultural forces to create and maintain great brands. It is often dependent on advertising. Cultural branding has been championed by Harvard Business School professor Doug Holt and a few others.[16] Interestingly, people in the real world were using this approach, maybe without knowing it in certain terms, for the last 100 years or so. But sometimes it takes a Harvard professor to give it a good name and endorse it.

The basic idea is to find some rift or stress in the seams of society and culture and then use this to offer a solution in the form of a branded good. A classic example would be the introduction of the Marlboro Man in 1955. Think about the 1950s: conformity,

EXHIBIT 5.18 Recognition is good business.

WHETHER YOU'RE STARTING A FAMILY

OR CREATING ONE AS YOU GO.

VOLVO
for life

Volvo Cars of North American, LLC

paranoia, displaced women back at home, baby boom, a tightly constrained sense of gender roles and domesticity, the birth of the suburbs, and men who had literally helped save the world, now back home to 9-to-5 jobs (maybe), and conformist society. At the very same time, a couple of reports on the dangers of smoking confirmed a link between cigarettes and lung cancer. But almost 50 percent of American male adults smoked, and smoking had been linked to the risk-taking persona of masculinity in North American culture. But even "real" men didn't want to get lung cancer. So the idea was that if you added a filter to cigarettes, maybe you could take out some of the bad stuff that might give you cancer (it doesn't). But, the only filtered cigarettes, and there were very few, were women's cigarettes. Marlboro had a filter but was a woman's cigarette, one with a filter prior to 1955. Exhibit 5.19 shows a pre-1955 Marlboro ad. Check it out. Study how Marlboro was positioned. Then think about the ad in Exhibit 5.20 and consider the reasons and method behind the dramatic change.

EXHIBIT 5.19 When filters were only for women.

EXHIBIT 5.20 There are only real men in Marlboro country.

Philip Morris approached the Leo Burnett ad agency in Chicago with the problem. The cultural contradiction: real men want to smoke a safer cigarette (filtered), but only women smoke filtered cigarettes; I can't be man if I smoke a girly filtered cigarette.

Enter the Marlboro Man. Invoking a major American mythic character, the cowboy, Leo Burnett resolved the contradiction for many. If the Marlboro Man can smoke filtered cigarettes, then you can too. Also, think about Marlboro country. What is missing? Marlboro country has no women. There is no woman in Marlboro country to tell you to take out the trash or vacuum the floor. When you light up a Marlboro, you don't have to worry about being a sissy. You are in Marlboro Country, and you, sir, are a real man. This campaign has run for about 60 years. Some ad campaigns don't last 60 days. Further Marlboro is one of the most valuable (and deadly) brands in the world.

Other examples are Pepsi's leveraging of the 1960s youth revolution, Mountain Dew's use of California skateboard culture, and Virginia Slims' use of the second wave of American feminism and a desire for thinness to sell cigarettes to "liberated" modern women.

Rebellion and Advertising. Scholars have noted that consumers sometimes use their consumption choices to stake out a position in a "revolution" of sorts.

Author Thomas Frank traces this to the 1960s cultural revolution (discussed in Chapter 3) and sees it as an opportunity, particularly for youth markets, to provide the costumes and consumable accessories for these "revolutionaries." More generally, it must be remembered that anytime there is a significant social movement, a time of rapid change, opportunities galore are opened up to the advertiser. When the earth moves under our feet, we feel off balance and in need of reassurance, and advertised products often promise that reassurance.

Some of these were mentioned in Chapter 3: how Pepsi used the youth revolution to tear into Coca-Cola's huge market share lead in the 1960s, how Virginia Slims used the feminist revolution of the 1970s to let women feel more rebellious (and liberated) by smoking Virginia Slims, or Apple giving those who chose not to see themselves as corporate a "computer for the rest of us." These were advertising's home runs—brands turned into cultural icons—by leveraging rifts or disruptions in the social sphere.

Authenticity. Among the attributes advertising can give to a brand, authenticity (in the eyes of others) is one of the very most powerful. If an advertiser can convince consumers that their brand is the "real," the authentic choice of those in the know, the original, then it is often seen as the best. This is a simple but very powerful brand statement. Sometimes companies just claim to be real so long that it eventually becomes true—sometimes. More on this in Chapter 11.

Now isn't this more interesting than mindshare advertising?

LO ⑧

5-2c **How Ads Transmit Meaning**

Start work in an ad agency and the first thing they teach you is the difference between a product and a brand. That is because it is advertising's job to turn one into another.[17]

—Martin Davidson

Advertising can be thought of as a text. It is "read" and interpreted by consumers. You can think of it as being like other texts: books, movies, posters, paintings, and so on. It is a creative product. In order to "get" ads, you have to know something of the cultural code, or they would make no sense. In order to really understand a movie, to really get it, you have to know something about the culture that created it. Sometimes when you see a foreign film (even in your native tongue), you just don't quite get all the jokes and references, because

you don't possess the cultural knowledge necessary to really effectively "read" the text. Ads try to turn already meaningful things into things with a very special meaning, a crafted meaning with the purpose of selling. Of course, consumers are free to accept, reject, or adjust that meaning to suit their taste. The advertisers say the thing they are selling is cool. The consumer might say, "No, it isn't," or "Yeah, it is," or "Well, yeah, but not in the way they think," or "Maybe for you, but not me." Even though advertisers try very hard to project just the right meaning, it is ultimately consumers who determine the meaning of ads and brands. Likewise, consumers determine what is or is not cool, what has cultural value (capital) to them, and how much. But advertisers are a big part of the conversation.

Yes, ads turn products into brands, and sometimes successful ones. They do this, in large part, by trying to wrap material objects or marketed services with a certain meaning—a meaning that comes from culture. The link between culture and advertising is key. Anthropologist Grant McCracken has offered the model in Exhibit 5.21 to explain how advertising (along with other cultural agents) functions in the transmission of meaning.[18] To understand advertising as a mechanism of cultural meaning transfer is to understand a great deal about advertising. In fact, one could legitimately say that advertisers are really in the meaning-transfer business. You take meaning that exists in the culture and massage it, shape it, and try to transfer it on to your brand.

Think about McCracken's model as you examine the ad for Ugg in Exhibit 5.22. The product—in this

EXHIBIT 5.21 The movement of meaning: how fashion and advertising move meaning to sell things.

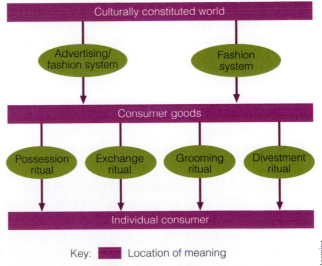

Key: ▮ Location of meaning

⬭ Instrument of meaning transfer

© Cengage Learning

EXHIBIT 5.22 Think about the social setting carefully constructed in this ad and how it gives the advertised brand meaning.

course, is the type of social setting in which potential customers might find, or desire to find, themselves. According to McCracken's model, meaning has moved from the world to the product (shoes) by virtue of its sharing space within the frame of the advertisement. When advertisers put things within the frame of an ad, they want the reader of the ad to put them together seamlessly, to take them together as part of each other. When a consumer purchases or otherwise incorporates that good or service into his or her own life, the meaning is then transferred to the individual consumer. Meaning is thus moved from the world to the product (via advertising) to the individual. When the individual uses the product, that person conveys to others the meaning he or she and the advertisement have now given it. Their use incorporates various rituals that facilitate the movement of meaning from good to consumer. The rituals aren't central to this discussion, but they would be the kinds of things discussed above in the section on rituals. For example, one of the first things you probably do when you buy a home from someone is to make it more "yours" by vacuuming, scrubbing, and painting it, even if you are completely happy with the paint and are convinced it is clean. You put your stuff on the walls partly to make it yours (possession rituals).

Ads also become part of consumers' everyday landscape, language, and reality. Characters, lines, and references all become part of conversations, thoughts, and—coming full circle—the culture. Children, co-workers, family members, and talk-show hosts all pick up phrases, ideas, slogans, and agenda from ads and then replay them, adapt them, and recirculate them just like things from movies, books, and other texts. Ads, in many ways, don't exist just within the sociocultural context; they *are* the sociocultural context of our time. If you want to do well in the real ad world, it's a very good idea to understand that getting the contemporary culture and knowing how to move it into ads and attach it to brands is how you make great advertising. It is how advertising works.

case, shoes—exists "out there" in the culturally constituted world (the real social world), but it needs advertising to link it to certain social scenes, certain slices of life. The advertiser places the advertised product and the slice of social life in an ad to get the two to rub off on each other, to intermingle, to become part of the same social scene. In other words, the product is given social meaning by being placed within an ad that represents an idealized context. This slice of life, of

SUMMARY

① Describe the four basic stages of consumer decision making.

Advertisers need a keen understanding of their consumers as a basis for developing effective advertising. This understanding begins with a view of consumers as systematic decision makers who follow a fairly predictable process in making their choices among products and brands. The process begins when consumers perceive a need, and it proceeds with a search for information that will help in making an informed choice. The search-and-evaluation stage is followed by purchase. Postpurchase

use and evaluation then become critical as the stage in which customer satisfaction is ultimately determined.

② Explain how consumers adapt their decision-making processes as a function of involvement and experience.

Some purchases are more important to people than others, and this fact adds complexity to any analysis of consumer behavior. To accommodate this complexity, advertisers often think about the level of involvement that attends any given purchase.

Involvement and prior experience with a product or service category can lead to four diverse modes of consumer decision making. These modes are extended problem solving, limited problem solving, habit or variety seeking, and brand loyalty.

 Discuss the role of memory and emotion in how advertising may influence consumer behavior.

Advertisements are developed to influence the way people think about products and brands. More specifically, advertising is designed to affect consumers' beliefs and brand attitudes. Advertisers use multiattribute attitude models to help them ascertain the beliefs and attitudes of target consumers. However, consumers have perceptual defenses that allow them to ignore or distort most of the commercial messages to which they are exposed. When consumers are not motivated to thoughtfully process an advertiser's message, it may be in that advertiser's best interest to feature one or more peripheral cues as part of the message.

 Discuss the role of culture on consumer behavior and in creating good advertising.

Advertisers who overlook the influence of culture are bound to struggle in their attempt to communicate with the target audience. For example, rituals are patterns of behavior shared by individuals from a common culture. Violating cultural values and rituals is a sure way to squander advertising dollars. Advertising and integrated brand promotion help turn products into brands. They do this by wrapping brands with cultural meaning. Brands with high cultural capital are worth more. Brands are cocreated by consumers and advertisers.

 Discuss the role of social class, taste, and cultural capital in consumer behavior and advertising.

Consumer behavior is an activity that each of us undertakes before a broad audience of other consumers. Advertising helps the transfer of meaning. Gender, ethnicity, and race are important influences on consumption. Who consumers are—their identity—is changeable; consumers can change aspects of who they are rapidly and frequently through what they buy and use. Celebrities are particularly important in this regard.

 Discuss the role of family, identity, gender, and community on consumer behavior and advertising.

All four of these sociological factors influence how consumers see themselves and other. It affects what they buy.

 Describe and then discuss cultural branding. Give an example.

Cultural branding is a type of branding that leverages sociocultural forces to create and maintain great brands. The basic idea is to find some rift or stress in society and culture and then use this to offer a solution in the form of a branded good. An example would be the introduction of the Marlboro Man in 1955.

 Discuss how effective advertising uses sociocultural meaning in order to sell things.

Advertising transfers a desired meaning to the brand by placing them within a carefully constructed social world represented in an ad, or "slice of life." Advertisers paint a picture of the ideal social world, with all the meanings they want to impart to their brand. Then the brand is carefully placed in that picture, and the two (the constructed social world and the brand) rub off on each other, becoming a part of each other. Meaning is thus transferred from the carefully constructed social world within the ad to the brand.

KEY TERMS

consumer behavior	customer satisfaction	attitude
consumer package goods (CPG)	cognitive dissonance	advertising clutter
mindshare brands	involvement	meaning
need state	consumer–brand relationship	culture
internal search	extended problem solving	rituals
evoked set	limited problem solving	stratification
consideration set	habit	increasing income inequality
top of mind	variety seeking	taste
external search	brand loyalty	life-stage
evaluative criteria	predecisional distortion	identity
conversion	accessibility	community
brand ambassadors	accessibility bonus	brand communities

ENDNOTES

1. John Sherry made this very clever and poetic "between the peers, be-tween the ears distinction" during remarks made at the Marketing Science Institute Conference: Engaging Communities for the Company and the Brand, Boston University, October 2007.

2. Terry G. Vavra, *Aftermarketing: How to Keep Customers for Life through Relationship Marketing* (Homewood, IL: Business One Irwin, 1992), 13.

3. Shirley Leung, "Fast-Food Firms Budgets Don't Buy Consumer Loyalty," *The Wall Street Journal*, July 24, 2003, B4.

4. Gordon Marshall (Ed.), *The Concise Oxford Dictionary of Sociology* (New York: Oxford University Press, 1994), 104–105.

5. Baba Shiv and Antoine Bechara, "Revisiting the Customer Value Propo-sition," in Barbara Loken, Rohini Ahluwalia, and Michael J. Houston (Eds.), *Brands and Brand Management: Contemporary Research Perspectives* (New York and London: Routledge, 2010), 189–206.

6. Clutter creates a variety of problems that compromise the effectiveness of advertising. For instance, research has shown that clutter interferes with basic memory functions, inhibiting a person's ability to keep straight which brands are making what claims. For more details, see Anand Kumar and Shanker Krishnan, "Memory Interference in Advertising: A Replication and Extension," *Journal of Consumer Research,* vol. 30 (March 2004), 602–612.

7. Gordon Marshall (Ed.), *The Concise Oxford Dictionary of Sociology* (New York: Oxford University Press, 1994), 104–105.

8. Ibid., 452.

9. Melanie Wallendorf and Eric J. Arnould, "We Gather Together: Con-sumption Rituals of Thanksgiving Day," *Journal of Consumer Research,* vol. 18, no. 1 (June 1991), 13–31.

10. For a review, see Cele C. Otnes and Tina M. Lowrey (Eds.), *Contem-porary Consumption Rituals: A Research Anthology* (Mahwah, NJ: Lawrence Erlbaum, 2004).

11. C. Whan Park, "Joint Decisions in Home Purchasing: A Muddling-Through Process," *Journal of Consumer Research,* vol. 9 (September 1982), 151–162.

12. Richard Elliot and Andrea Davies, "Symbolic Brands and Authenticity of Identity Performance," in Jonathan E. Schroeder and Miriam Salzer-Morling (Eds.), *Brand Culture* (London: Routledge, 2006), 155–170.

13. Jannette L. Dates, "Advertising," in Jannette L. Dates and William Barlow (Eds.), *Split Image: African Americans in Mass Media* (Washington, D.C.: Howard University Press, 1990), 421–454.

14. Roland Marchand, *Advertising: The American Dream* (Berkeley: Univer-sity of California Press, 1984), 25.

15. Albert Muniz Jr. and Thomas O'Guinn, "Brand Community," *Journal of Consumer Research,* vol. 27 (2001), 412–432.

16. Douglas B. Holt, *How Brands Become Icons* (Cambridge, MA: Harvard Business School Press, 2004).

17. Martin Davidson, "Objects of Desire: How Advertising Works," in Martin Davidson (Ed.), *The Consumerist Manifesto: Advertising in Postmodern Times* (London: Routledge, 1992), 23–60.

18. Grant McCracken, "Culture and Consumption: A Theoretical Account of the Structure and Movement of the Cultural Meaning of Consumer Goods," *Journal of Consumer Research,* vol. 13 (June 1986), 71–84.

CHAPTER 6

Market Segmentation, Positioning, and the Value Proposition

After reading and thinking about this chapter, you will be able to do the following:

(1) Explain the process known as STP marketing.

(2) Describe different bases that marketers use to identify segments.

(3) Discuss the criteria used to target a segment.

(4) Identify the essential elements of an effective positioning strategy.

(5) Review the necessary ingredients for creating a brand's value proposition.

LO 1

6-1 STP MARKETING AND ADVERTISING

Very few marketers advertise to everyone. It is way too expensive and wasteful. Not everyone wants what you are selling. So, advertisers usually have to **segment** their market—that is, cut it into pieces and focus on the piece or pieces (segments) that make the most sense. They then have to **target** (focus advertising and IBC for delivery upon) that segment or segments with advertising and integrated brand promotion. Then they have to **position** their brand for that segment(s). **Positioning** means to attempt to give a brand a certain meaning relative to its competitors. Doing the three together is called the **STP marketing** approach. Markets are segmented; segments of markets (groups of potential customers) are targeted, and brands are positioned. While some of this work is done primarily by the marketer, increasingly advertising and IBP professionals are asked to collaborate on this task. Ultimately, it will come down to the advertising and IBP pros to create the messages that help give the brand the meaning the advertiser desires.

In most product categories one finds that different consumers are looking for different things, and the only way for a company to take advantage of the sales potential represented by different customer segments is to develop and market a different brand for each segment. An example of this is cosmetics juggernaut Estée Lauder.[1] Lauder has more than a dozen cosmetic brands, each developed for a different target segment. For example, there is the original Estée Lauder brand, for women with conservative values and upscale tastes. Then there is Clinique, a no-nonsense brand that represents functional grooming for Middle America. Bobbi Brown is for the working mom who skillfully manages a career and her family and manages to look good in the process, just like the real Bobbi Brown.[2] M.A.C. is a brand for those who want to make a bolder statement: Its spokespersons have been RuPaul, a 6-foot-7-inch drag queen; Boy George; Missy Elliot; Linda Evangelista; and a host of others. Prescriptives is marketed to a hip, urban, multiethnic target segment, and Origins, with its earthy packaging and natural ingredients, celebrates the connection between Mother Nature and human nature. These are just some of the cosmetics brands that Estée Lauder has marketed to appeal to diverse target segments. Check out the company's current brand lineup at www.elcompanies.com. The website actually demonstrates how Estée Lauder segments the market with 25 brands in 60 countries.

Very few marketers advertise to everyone. It is way too expensive and wasteful. Not everyone wants what you are selling.

rule, but you will run across it. In fact, it is not uncommon to find that heavy users in a category account for the majority of a product's sales and thus become the preferred or primary target segment.[3]

For instance, Coffee-mate executives launched a program to get to know their customers better by returning calls to those who had left a complaint or suggestion using the toll-free number printed on the product packaging.[4] As a result they met Paula Baumgartner, a 44-year-old who consumes four jars of Coffee-mate's mocha-flavored creamer every week. (Yes, that's more than 200 jars a year!) Now, that's a heavy user. Conventional marketing thought holds that it is in Coffee-mate's best interest to get to know heavy users like Paula in great depth and make them a focal point of the company's marketing strategy. (See Insights Online [Exhibit 6.2] for an example of how Miller Lite promotes itself as the beer good friends drink when they get together.)

Even though standard wisdom, the heavy-user-focused segmentation plan has some potential downsides. For one, devoted users may need no encouragement at all to keep consuming. In addition, a heavy-user focus takes attention and resources away from those who do need encouragement to purchase the marketer's brand. Perhaps most important, heavy users may differ significantly from average or infrequent users in terms of their motivations to consume, their approach to the brand, or their image of the brand. They may be **brand-freaks**, consumers who are so committed to the brand that their consumer behavior toward it borders on the pathological. However, even the brand freaks are still considered valuable due to their knowledge of the brand and their presumed social influence, which can be used to create branding and advertising.

LO ❷

6-2 SEGMENTING MARKETS

The first step in STP marketing involves breaking down large broader markets into more manageable submarkets or customer segments. This activity is known as market segmentation. It can be accomplished in many ways, but keep in mind that advertisers need to identify a segment with common characteristics that will lead the members of that segment to respond distinctively to a marketing program. For a segment to be really useful, advertisers also must be able to reach that segment with information about the brand. Typically this means that advertisers must be able to identify the media the segment uses so they can best get messages to the segment. In this section we will show how consumer markets are commonly segmented.

Markets can be segmented on the basis of many things, but usage patterns and commitment levels, demographic and geographic information, psychographics and lifestyles, or benefits sought are very common. In the real world, segmentation evolves in such a way that multiple variables are actually used to identify and describe the chosen segment(s). (See Insights Online [Exhibit 6.1] for an example of how Toyota re-identified the market for its Scion.

6-2a Usage and Commitment Level

One of the most common ways to segment markets is by consumers' brand commitment or usage levels. With respect to usage, it is important to recognize that for most products and services, some users will purchase much more, and more frequently, than others. These consumers are called **heavy users**, **committed users**, or **lead users**. Sometimes, by convention, they are defined as the top quintile, or 20 percent of users by volume. This is not a hard-and-fast

6-2b Switchers and Variety Seekers

These consumers often buy what is on sale or choose brands that offer discount coupons or other price incentives. Whether they are pursued through price incentives, high-profile advertising campaigns, or both, **switchers** turn out to be a costly target segment. Much can be spent in getting their business merely to have it disappear just as quickly as it was won.

6-2c Emergent Consumers

These consumers offer the organization an important business opportunity. In most product categories there is a gradual but constant influx of first-time

INSIGHTS ONLINE

6.2 Go online to see the AdAge feature, "See the Spots: 'Miller Time' Ads from DraftFCB Break Tonight."

buyers. The reasons for this influx vary by product category and include purchase triggers such as puberty, college graduation, marriage, a new baby, divorce, a new job, a big raise, or retirement. Immigration can also be a source of numerous new customers in many product categories. Generation X attracted the attention of marketers and advertisers because it was a large group of emergent adult consumers. But inevitably, Generation X lost its emergent status and was replaced by a new age cohort—Generation Y—who took their turn as advertisers' darlings.[5]

Emergent consumers are motivated by many different factors, but they share one notable characteristic: Their brand preferences are still under development. Targeting emergents with messages that fit their age or social circumstances may produce modest effects in the short run, but it eventually may yield a brand loyalty that pays handsome rewards for the discerning organization. Developing advertising campaigns to win with first-time users is often referred to as **point-of-entry marketing**. As a case in point, the marketers of Folgers launch campaigns to appeal specifically to the next generation of coffee drinkers. These of course would be young people just learning the coffee habit. Attracted by coffee titans like Starbucks and Dunkin' Donuts, many people get to know coffee in their teens. But when it's time to start brewing coffee at home, Folgers sees its big chance to get in your cupboard.

To illustrate, the Folgers brand team launched an advertising initiative to attract just-graduated 20-somethings. When young adults move into the "real world" and take that first job with a new apartment in a strange city, they are primed to develop the coffee habit. Folgers aspires to be the brand of choice for these targets as they potentially commit to a morning brew-it-yourself coffee ritual. We all know that mornings are tough, so Folgers just wants to make them tolerable. But how does Folgers, your grandparents' brand, make a connection with a new generation of coffee drinkers? Tried and true slogans ("The best part of waking up is Folgers in your cup") and 30-second TV spots just won't do.

Working with its ad agency Saatchi & Saatchi, the Folgers brand team found another way. It started with the premise that mornings are hard, filled with emails and bosses making demands and those annoying "morning people" (who for some bizarre reason seem to love sunrises). Folgers exists to help a person tolerate mornings, and especially to tolerate those morning people. A short film, titled something like "Happy Mornings: The Revenge of the Yellow People," was produced to show Folgers as your first line of defense when the fanatical Yellow People try to invade your space first thing in the morning (that's them coming out of the sunrise and across the lake in Exhibit 6.3). The film was also designed to steer traffic to a website (per Exhibit 6.4) where other tools (boss-tracker, auto emails, wake-up calls, screensaver) for making mornings go better were available. The campaign also included print ads code-named "Dreamscapes," reflecting that frightful moment just before dawn when the creepy Yellow People are planning their attack.

The provocative aspect of the Yellow People film is that zero dollars were spent on media. That's right, zero dollars. Rather, the spot was submitted to three websites (Adcritic, BestadsonTV.com, and Boards) where 20-somethings had their way with it. Chatter quickly spread across the blogosphere, website hits increased, and the film was soon posted on YouTube (receiving 4 out of 5 stars and more than 300,000 viewings).

6-2d Demographics

Demographic segmentation is widely used in selecting target segments and includes basic descriptors such as age, gender, race, marital status, income, education, and occupation (see the array of possibilities at www.factfinder.census.gov). Demographic information has special value in market segmentation because if an advertiser knows the demographic characteristics of the target segment, choosing media to efficiently reach that segment is much easier.

EXHIBIT 6.3 The Yellow People glow like a sunrise and they want you!

EXHIBIT 6.4 Your best defense when the Yellow People show up unannounced.

© Procter & Gamble. Used by permission

Demographic information has two specific applications. First, demographics are commonly used to describe or profile segments that have been identified with some other variable. If an organization had first segmented its market in terms of product usage rates, the next step would be to describe or profile its heavy users in terms of demographic characteristics such as age or income. In fact, one of the most common approaches for identifying target segments is to combine information about usage patterns with demographics.

Mobil Oil Corporation used such an approach in segmenting the market for gasoline buyers and identified five basic segments: Road Warriors, True Blues, Generation F3, Homebodies, and Price Shoppers.[6] Extensive research on more than 2,000 motorists revealed considerable insight about these five segments. At one extreme, Road Warriors spent at least $1,200 per year at gas stations; they bought premium gasoline and snacks and beverages and sometimes opted for a car wash. Road Warriors were generally more affluent, middle-aged males who drive 25,000 to 50,000 miles per year. (Note how Mobil combined information about usage patterns with demographics to provide a detailed picture of the segment.) In contrast, Price Shoppers spent no more than $700 annually at gas stations, were generally less affluent, rarely buy premium, and showed no loyalty to particular brands or stations. In terms of relative segment sizes, there were about 25 percent more Price Shoppers on the highways than Road Warriors. If you were the marketing vice president at Mobil, which of these two segments would you target? Think about it for a few pages—we'll get back to you.

Second, demographic categories are used frequently as the starting point in market segmentation. Since families commonly plan vacations together, demographics will also be a major consideration for targeting by the tourism industry, where families with young children are often the marketer's primary focus. For instance, the Bahamian government launched a program to attract families to their island paradise. But instead of reaching out to mom and dad, Bahamian officials made their appeal to kids by targeting the 2- to-11-year-old viewing audience of Nickelodeon's cable television channel.[7]

Another demographic group that is receiving renewed attention from advertisers is the "woopies," or well-off older people. In the United States, consumers over 50 years old control two-thirds of the country's wealth. The median net worth of households headed by persons 55 to 64 is 15 times larger than the net worth for households headed by a person under age 35. Put in simple terms, for most people age 20, $100 is a lot of money. For woopies, $100 is change back from the purchase of a $10,000 home theater system. Marketers such as Ford, Sony, Target, Anheuser-Busch, Walt Disney, and Virgin Entertainment Group have all reconsidered their product offerings with woopies in mind.[8] By 2025, the number of people over 50 will grow by 80 percent to become a third of the U.S. population. Growth in the woopie segment will also be dramatic in other countries, such as Japan and the nations of Western Europe. Still, like any other age segment, older consumers are a diverse group, and the temptation to stereotype must be resisted. Some marketers advocate partitioning older consumers into groups aged 50–64, 65–74, 75–84, and 85 or older as a means of reflecting important differences in needs. That's a good start, but again, age alone will not tell the whole story.

6-2e Geographic Location

Geographic segmentation needs little explanation other than to emphasize how useful geography is in segmenting markets. Geographic segmentation may be conducted within a country by region (e.g., the Pacific Northwest versus New England in the United States), by state or province, by city, or even by neighborhood. Climate and topographical features yield dramatic differences in consumption by region for products such as snow tires and surfboards, but geography can also correlate with other differences that are not so obvious. Eating and food preparation habits, entertainment preferences, recreational activities, and other aspects of lifestyle have been shown to vary along geographic lines.

In recent years skillful marketers have merged information on where people live with the U.S. Census Bureau's demographic data to produce a form of market segmentation known as geodemographic segmentation. **Geodemographic segmentation** identifies neighborhoods (by zip codes) around the country that share common demographic characteristics. One such system, known as PRIZM (potential rating index by zip marketing), identifies 62 market segments that encompass all the zip codes in the United States. Each of these segments has similar lifestyle characteristics and can be found throughout the country.

For example, the American Dreams segment is found in many metropolitan neighborhoods and comprises upwardly mobile ethnic minorities, many of whom were foreign-born. This segment's brand preferences are different from those of people belonging to the Rural Industrial segment, who are young families with one or both parents working at low-wage jobs in small-town America. Systems such as PRIZM are very popular because of the depth of segment description they provide, along with their ability to precisely identify where the segment can be found (for more details, Google Claritas PRIZM).

6-2f Psychographics and Lifestyle

Psychographics is a term that advertisers created in the mid-1960s to refer to a form of research that emphasizes the understanding of consumers' activities, interests, and opinions (AIOs). Many advertising agencies were using demographic variables for segmentation purposes, but they wanted insights into consumers' motivations, which demographic variables did not provide. Psychographics were created as a tool to supplement the use of demographic data. Because a focus on consumers' activities, interests, and opinions often produces insights into differences in the lifestyles of various segments, this approach usually results in **lifestyle segmentation**. Knowing details about the lifestyle of a target segment can be valuable for creating advertising messages that ring true to the consumer. (See Insights Online [Exhibit 6.5] for an interesting example of how Samsung appealed to sports enthusiasts.)

Lifestyle or psychographic segmentation can be customized with a focus on the issues germane to a single product category, or it may be pursued so that the resulting segments have general applicability to many different product or service categories. An illustration of the former is research conducted for Pillsbury to segment the eating habits of American households.[9] This "What's Cookin'" study involved consumer interviews with more than 3,000 people and identified five segments of the population, based on their shared eating styles:

- *Chase & Grabbits*, at 26 percent of the population, are heavy users of all forms of fast food. These are people who can make a meal out of microwave popcorn; as long as the popcorn keeps hunger

at bay and is convenient, this segment is happy with its meal.

- *Functional Feeders*, at 18 percent of the population, are a bit older than the Chase & Grabbits but no less convenience-oriented. Since they are more likely to have families, their preferences for convenient foods involve frozen products that are quickly prepared at home. They constantly seek faster ways to prepare the traditional foods they grew up with.

- *Down-Home Stokers*, at 21 percent of the population, involve blue-collar households with modest incomes. They are very loyal to their regional diets, such as meat and potatoes in the Midwest and clam chowder in New England. Fried chicken, biscuits and gravy, and bacon and eggs make this segment the champion of cholesterol.

- *Careful Cooks*, at 20 percent of the population, are more prevalent on the West Coast. They have replaced most of the red meat in their diet with pastas, fish, skinless chicken, and mounds of fresh fruit and vegetables. They believe they are knowledgeable about nutritional issues and are willing to experiment with foods that offer healthful options.

- *Happy Cookers* are the remaining 15 percent of the population but are a shrinking segment. These cooks are family-oriented and take substantial satisfaction from preparing a complete homemade meal for the family. Young mothers in this segment are aware of nutritional issues but will bend the rules with homemade meat dishes, casseroles, pies, cakes, and cookies.

Even these abbreviated descriptions of Pillsbury's five psychographic segments should make it clear that very different marketing and advertising programs are called for to appeal to each group.

6-2g Benefits Sought

Another segmentation approach developed by advertising researchers is **benefit segmentation**. In benefit segmentation, target segments are delineated by the various benefit packages that different consumers want from competing products and brands. For instance, different people want different benefits from their automobiles. Some consumers want efficient and reliable transportation; others want speed, excitement, and glamour; and still others want luxury, comfort, and

EXHIBIT 6.6 This is benefit segmentation.

© Aveda Corp

prestige. One product could not possibly serve such diverse benefit segments. Exhibit 6.6 shows the benefit of Aveda. Do you want straight hair?

6-2h Segmenting Business-to-Business Markets

Thus far, our discussion of segmentation options has focused on ways to segment **consumer markets**. Consumer markets are the markets for products and services purchased by individuals or households to satisfy their specific needs. Consumer marketing is often compared and contrasted with business-to-business marketing. **Business markets** are the institutional buyers who purchase items to be used in other products and services or to be resold to other businesses or households. Although advertising is more prevalent in consumer markets, products and services such as smartphones, overnight delivery, Web hosting, consulting services, and a wide array of business machines and computer-support services are commonly promoted to business customers around the world. Hence, segmentation strategies are also valuable for business-to-business marketers.

Business markets can be segmented using several of the options already discussed. For example, business customers differ in their usage rates and geographic locations, so these variables may be productive bases for segmenting business markets. In addition, one of the most common approaches uses the North American Industry Classification System (NAICS) prepared by the U.S. Census Bureau. NAICS information is helpful for identifying categories of businesses and then pinpointing the precise locations of these organizations.

Some of the more sophisticated segmentation methods used by firms that market to individual consumers do not translate well to business markets.[10] For instance, rarely would there be a place for psychographic or lifestyle segmentation in the business-to-business setting. In business markets, advertisers fall back on simpler strategies that are easier to work with from the perspective of the sales force. Segmentation by a potential customer's stage in the purchase process is one such strategy. It turns out that first-time prospects, novices, and sophisticates want very different packages of benefits from their vendors, and thus they should be targeted separately in advertising and sales programs.

6-3 PRIORITIZING SEGMENTS

Whether it is done through usage patterns, demographic characteristics, geographic location, benefit packages, or any combination of options, segmenting markets typically yields a mix of segments that vary in their attractiveness to the advertiser. In pursuing STP marketing, the advertiser must get beyond this potentially confusing mixture of segments to a selected subset that will become the target for its marketing and advertising programs. Recall the example of Mobil Oil Corporation and the segments of gasoline buyers it identified via usage patterns and demographic descriptors. What criteria should Mobil use to help decide between Road Warriors and Price Shoppers as possible targets?

Perhaps the most fundamental criterion in segment selection revolves around what the members of the segment want versus the organization's ability to provide it. Every organization has distinctive strengths and weaknesses that must be acknowledged when choosing its target segment. The organization may be particularly strong in some aspect of manufacturing, like Gillette, which has particular expertise in mass production of intricate plastic and metal products. Or perhaps its strength lies in well-trained and loyal service personnel, like those at FedEx, who can effectively implement new service programs initiated for customers, such as next-day delivery "absolutely, positively by 10:30 a.m."

To serve a target segment, an organization may have to commit substantial resources to acquire or develop the capabilities to provide what that segment wants. If the price tag for these new capabilities is too high, the organization must find another segment.

Another major consideration in segment selection entails the size and growth potential of the segment. Segment size is a function of the number of people, households, or institutions in the segment, plus their willingness to spend in the product category. When assessing size, advertisers must keep in mind that the number of people in a segment of heavy users may be relatively small, but the extraordinary usage rates of these consumers can more than make up for their small numbers. In addition, it is not enough to simply assess a segment's size as of today. Segments are dynamic, and it is common to find marketers most interested in devoting resources to segments projected for dramatic growth. As we have already seen, the purchasing power and growth projections for people age 50 and older have made this a segment that many companies are targeting.

A second consideration is the forecasted return on investment (ROI) for the segment. While this is difficult to calculate precisely, good estimates can be made. With better and better marketing analytics, this will be more and more possible.

A third selection criterion is the **competitive field**—companies that compete for the segment's business. Advertisers must first look at the competitive field and then decide whether it has a particular expertise, or perhaps just a bigger budget, that would allow it to serve the segment more effectively. This is often discussed in terms of who "owns" a certain segment of the market. Oftentimes marketers are afraid or unwilling to go against a competitor who is already mining a very good segment. But a lot of good opportunities are missed as well. These are largely judgment calls, and that is why those making them get "the big bucks."

The smaller-is-better segmentation principle has become so popular in choosing segments that it is now referred to as **niche marketing**. A market niche is a relatively small group of consumers who have a unique set of needs and who typically are willing to pay a premium price to the firm that specializes in meeting those needs.[11] The small size of a market niche often means it would not be profitable for more than one organization to serve it. Thus, when a firm identifies and develops products for market niches, the threat of competitors developing imitative products to attack the niche is reduced. Exhibit 6.7 is an example of an ad directed toward a very small niche, those who prefer imported Russian tubes for their high-end tube stereo amplifiers.

EXHIBIT 6.7 Niche marketers are usually able to charge a premium price for their distinctive products. If you decide to go with Svetlana the next time you are buying amplifier tubes, expect to pay a little extra.

Niche marketing will continue to grow in popularity as the mass media splinter into a more and more complex and narrowly defined array of specialized vehicles. Specialized cable programming—such as the Health & Fitness Channel, the History Channel, or the 24-hour Golf Channel—attracts small and very distinctive groups of consumers, providing advertisers with an efficient way to communicate with market niches.[12] In addition, perhaps the ideal application of the Internet as a marketing tool is in identifying and accessing market niches.

Now let's return to the question faced by Mobil Oil Corporation. Who should it target—Road Warriors or Price Shoppers? Hopefully you will see this as a straightforward decision. Road Warriors are a more attractive segment in terms of both segment size and growth potential. Although there are more Price Shoppers in terms of sheer numbers, Road Warriors spend more at the gas station, making them the larger segment from the standpoint of revenue generation. Road Warriors are also more prone to buy those little extras,

EXHIBIT 6.8 When a major competitor like BP imitates our strategy, it's a pretty good sign that we got it right. Unfortunately, this may also mean that it's time for us to look for a new strategy to gain another advantage vis-à-vis our competitive field. This is that part of marketing and advertising that makes this field both terribly interesting and terribly frustrating. Just when we get it right, it can be time to start over.

© Chris Allen

such as a sandwich and a coffee, which could be extremely profitable sources of new business. It's just hard (impossible?) to win in gasoline retailing by competing on price.

Mobil selected Road Warriors as its target segment and developed a positioning strategy it referred to as "Friendly Serve." Gas prices went up at Mobil stations, but Mobil also committed new resources to improving all aspects of the gas-purchasing experience. Cleaner restrooms and better lighting alone yielded sales gains between 2 and 5 percent. Next, more attendants were hired to run between the pump and the snack bar to get Road Warriors in and out quickly—complete with their sandwich and beverage. Early results indicated that helpful attendants boosted station sales by another 15 to 20 percent. How can we really say that Mobil made the right choice in targeting Road Warriors? Just look at their competition (e.g., Exhibit 6.8). As suggested by BP's *Wild Bean Café,* coffee is king with the Road Warrior.

6-4 TARGETING

Now that a company has decided on which segment or segments to focus, next comes the question of how to target them. Although this is a media–planning question and will be covered in Chapter 12, targeting cannot be completely separated from segmenting or positioning. For now, let us say this: the main idea of targeting is to efficiently deliver the branding effort to the chosen segments. Frankly, efficiency is much

more a goal than a reality for most advertisers. Also, to the extent that the media matter in terms of fit with the brands sought after meaning (positioning), then efficiency is often sacrificed for clarity of brand meaning. Further, due to social media, the entire targeting playbook has had to be rewritten. Chapter 14 takes this problem head-on.

—— LO ④ ——

6-4a Positioning/ Repositioning

For most professionals, positioning or repositioning is where the fun is. It is where the advertiser and IBP pros work on crafting the meaning of the desired brand. Of course, consumers are going to have something to say about that. For a minute, think about the relative positions of the Apple iPhone and the Samsung Galaxy. How does their brand meaning differ? Go online and look at some of their ads and other IBP material and see if you can explain the difference in positioning. Try it. (See Insights Online [Exhibit 6.9] for yet another interesting example.)

At the heart of any good positioning method is the quest of the brand's meaning relative to other brands. In the case of a new brand: What is the landscape of branding meaning? In the case of repositioning or significantly changing the meaning of an existing brand, the basic same question applies: What should our brand mean relative to other brands? Once this is determined, the advertising and integrated branded communication are deployed in order to project that positioning (relative meaning) to consumers.

6-4b The Bahr–InterBrand Positioning Opportunity Method

The best positioning model we have seen comes from Anne Bahr at InterBrand. InterBrand is the world's largest and most successful brand consultancy. Their longtime former CEO Ann Bahr offers the model in Exhibit 6.10.[13] It has four factors represented

6.9 Go online to see the AdAge feature, "Pepsi's Tropicana Has a New Juice 'Trop50' That Repositions as Less Sugar with Its First Designer Collaboration."

EXHIBIT 6.10 This model shows that a brand's best opportunity for success involves the overlapping of four important factors: current relevance to the consumer, credibility or consumer belief in the brand, differentiation or a recognition of uniqueness, and "stretch" or the potential for consumer relevance over time.

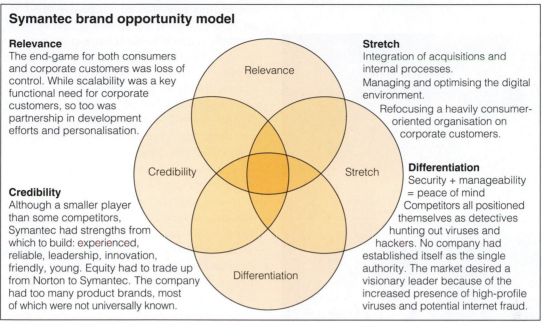

Symantec brand opportunity model

Relevance
The end-game for both consumers and corporate customers was loss of control. While scalability was a key functional need for corporate customers, so too was partnership in development efforts and personalisation.

Stretch
Integration of acquisitions and internal processes.
Managing and optimising the digital environment.
Refocusing a heavily consumer-oriented organisation on corporate customers.

Credibility
Although a smaller player than some competitors, Symantec had strengths from which to build: experienced, reliable, leadership, innovation, friendly, young. Equity had to trade up from Norton to Symantec. The company had too many product brands, most of which were not universally known.

Differentiation
Security + manageability = peace of mind
Competitors all positioned themselves as detectives hunting out viruses and hackers. No company had established itself as the single authority. The market desired a visionary leader because of the increased presence of high-profile viruses and potential internet fraud.

Source: Simmons Clifton, et al., "Brand Positioning and Brand Creation," in *Brands and Branding*, (2004), London: The Economist/Bloomberg, 88.

by overlapping circles. The point at which these four meet is considered the best opportunity, the brand's best position. They are:

- **Relevance:** Where is the strong consumer connection? What is the revealed need(s) of consumers?
- **Differentiation:** Can the brand stand out as significantly different than others?
- **Credibility:** Will consumers believe it?
- **Stretch:** Will the brand's meaning have continued relevance in changing times? Will it foster brand extensions?

To derive a brand's best positioning, you should find the place where the answer to all four questions is "yes." Then you know that your positioning is good and sustainable. Consider these four dimensions in this classic positioning of Apple in Exhibit 6.11. It was part of the very famous "Think Different" campaign (1997–2002). It was the product of close collaboration between Apple and an LA ad agency.

6-4c **Essentials for Effective Positioning Strategies**

Any sound **positioning strategy** includes several essential elements. Effective positioning strategies are based on meaningful commitments of organizational resources to produce substantive value for the target segment. They also are consistent internally and over time, and they feature simple and distinctive themes. Each of these essential elements is described below.

Deliver on the Promise. For a positioning strategy to be effective and remain effective over time, the organization must be committed to creating substantive value for the customer. Take the example of Mobil Oil Corporation and its target segment, the Road Warriors. Road Warriors are willing to pay a little more for gas if it comes with extras such as prompt service or fresh coffee. So Mobil must create an ad campaign that depicts its employees as the brightest, friendliest, most helpful people you'd ever want to meet. The company asks its ad agency to come up with a catchy jingle that will remind people about the great services they can expect at a Mobil station. It spends millions of dollars running these ads over and over and wins the enduring loyalty of the Road Warriors. Right? Well, maybe, and maybe not. Certainly, a new ad campaign will have to be created to make Road Warriors aware of the new Mobil, but it all falls apart if they drive in with great expectations and the company's people do not live up to them.

EXHIBIT 6.11 Look at this ad and think about the four dimensions of how it serves to position the brand. Walk through it: how does this ad position Apple as relevant; how does it differentiate Apple from its competitors, how does it achieve credibility for Apple, and how did it allow Apple to stretch the brand way beyond computers?

Think different.

Effective positioning begins with substance. In the case of Mobil's "Friendly Serve" strategy, this means keeping restrooms attractive and clean, adding better lighting to all areas of the station, and upgrading the quality of the snacks and beverages available in each station's convenience store. It also means hiring more attendants and training and motivating them to anticipate and fulfill the needs of the harried Road Warrior. Effecting meaningful change in service levels at thousands of stations nationwide is an expensive and time-consuming process, but without some substantive change, there can be no hope of retaining the Road Warrior's lucrative business.

There's Magic in Consistency. A positioning strategy also must be consistent internally and consistent over time. Regarding internal consistency, everything must work in combination to reinforce a distinct perception in the consumer's eyes about what a brand stands for. If we have chosen to position our airline as the one that will be known for on-time reliability,

then we certainly would invest in things like extensive preventive maintenance and state-of-the-art baggage-handling facilities. There would be no need for exclusive airport lounges as part of this strategy, nor would any special emphasis need to be placed on in-flight food and beverage services. If our target segment wants reliable transportation, then this should be our obsession. This particular obsession has made Southwest Airlines a very formidable competitor, even against much larger airlines, yielding 37 consecutive years of profitability in a most challenging industry.[14] Doesn't it strike you as ironic that the only airline that can claim that kind of performance record is also one where Bags Fly Free?

A strategy also needs consistency over time. Consumers have perceptual defenses that allow them to screen or ignore most of the ad messages they are exposed to. Breaking through the clutter and establishing what a brand stands for is a tremendous challenge, but it is a challenge made easier by consistent positioning. If year in and year out an advertiser communicates the same basic themes, then the message may get through and shape the way consumers perceive the brand. An example of a consistent approach is the long-running "Good Neighbor" ads of State Farm Insurance. Even though the specific copy changes, the thematic core of the campaign does not change. Exhibit 6.12 shows an exemplar from this long-running campaign, including the "We Live Where You Live" extension to their "Good Neighbor" premise.

Make It Different Simply. Simplicity and distinctiveness are essential to the advertising task. No matter how much substance has been built into a product, it will fail in the marketplace if the consumer doesn't perceive what the product can do. In a world of harried consumers who can be expected to ignore, distort, or forget most of the ads they are exposed to, complicated, imitative messages simply have no chance of getting through. The basic premise of a positioning strategy must be simple and distinctive if it is to be communicated effectively to the target segment.

The value of simplicity and distinctiveness in positioning strategy is nicely illustrated in Jack Daniel's long-running campaign, with ads all around the world like the one in Exhibit 6.13. Jack Daniels began distilling whiskey in 1866 and would not be rushed. Patience was his secret ingredient for producing a smooth sippin' whiskey. It will be good and ready, when it's good and ready. Throughout the decades and around the world, Jack Daniel's advertising turned "can't be rushed" and made "the old-fashioned way" into an art form. The simplicity, consistency, and distinctiveness of their positioning strategy helped make Jack Daniel's a powerhouse global brand from Lynchburg, Tennessee.

EXHIBIT 6.12 Consistency is a definite virtue in choosing and executing a positioning strategy. State Farm's "Good Neighbor" theme has been a hallmark of its advertising for many years. Does State Farm's site (www.statefarm.com) produce substantive value for its target segment? How? What simple and distinctive themes can you find? Why are these elements essential to State Farm's positioning strategy?

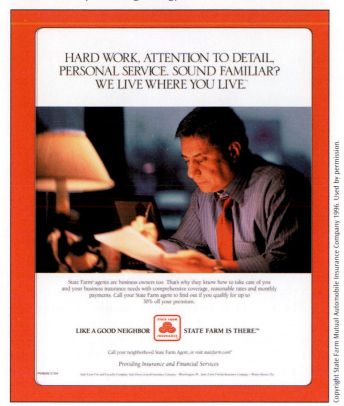

EXHIBIT 6.13 You don't need to be able to read Japanese to get the point here, in part because this ad follows the same style as other Jack Daniel's ads around the world. If you want a smooth sippin' whiskey, it can't be rushed. And in the back hills of Tennessee, no one is rushing anything.

LO ⑤

6-5 WORKING WITH A VALUE PROPOSITION AND A BRAND PLATFORM

Brand positioning is often summarized as a value proposition, a brand promise, or a brand platform. Really, they are three ways of saying (almost) the same thing. In this chapter we have presented several important concepts for understanding how marketers develop strategies for their brands that then have major implications for the integrated advertising campaigns that are executed to build and maintain those brands. One needs to assess customer segments and target markets along with the competitive field to make decisions about various kinds of positioning themes that might be appropriate in guiding the creation of a campaign.

Yes, it can get complicated. Furthermore, as time passes, new people from both the client and agency side will be brought in to work on the brand team. It can be easy for them to lose sight of what the brand used to stand for in the eyes of the target segment. Of course, if the people who create the advertising for a brand get confused about the brand's desired identity, then the consumer is bound to get confused as well. This is a recipe for disaster. Thus, we need a way to capture and keep a record of what our brand is supposed to stand for in the eyes of the target segment. Although there are many ways to capture one's strategy on paper, we recommend doing just that by articulating the brand's value proposition. If we are crystal clear on what value we believe our brand offers to consumers, and everyone on the brand team shares that clarity, the foundation is in place for creating effective advertising and integrated brand promotion.

A **value proposition** is a natural extension of concepts that are already familiar; it simply consolidates

6.14 Go online to see the AdAge feature, "McDonald's Value Position and Value Promotions Help Sales Remain Steady."

the emphasis on customer benefits that has been featured in this chapter. It is a simple sentence or two that clearly says just what value the brand will be to the customer. Here is a value propositions for McDonald's.[15] The **brand promise** is another name for this idea. It is instead expressed in terms of what it is that the brand promises the customer. (See Insights Online [Exhibit 6.14] for more information about McDonald's brand promise.)

McDonald's Value Propositions

- *Functional benefits:* Good-tasting hamburgers, fries, and drinks served fast; extras such as playgrounds, prizes, premiums, and games.

- *Emotional benefits:* Kids—fun via excitement at birthday parties; relationship with Ronald McDonald and other characters; a feeling of special family times. Adults—warmth via time spent enjoying a meal with the kids; admiration of McDonald's social involvement such as McDonald's Charities and Ronald McDonald Houses.

Another way of summarizing or "putting it *all together*" is known as the **brand platform.** Here is what Anne Bahr at InterBrand says:

The Brand Platform: *a core idea that frames an ambition or aspiration for the brand that will be relevant to target audiences over time.*[16]

6-5a Now, Making It Happen

Before moving on it may be helpful to pull together the concepts presented in this chapter using a practical model. The strategic planning triangle proposed by advertising researchers Esther Thorson and Jeri Moore is perfect for this purpose.[17] As reflected in Exhibit 6.15, the apexes of the planning triangle entail the segment(s) selected as targets for the campaign, the brand's value proposition, and the array of persuasion tools that will be deployed to achieve campaign goals.

As we have seen in this chapter, the starting point of STP marketing is identifying who the customers or prospects are and what they want. Hence, Thorson and Moore place identification and specification of the target segment as the paramount apex in their model. Building a consensus between the client and the agency about which segments will be targeted is essential to the campaign's effectiveness. Compelling advertising

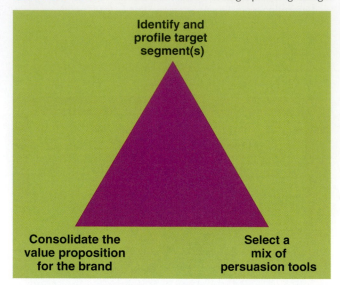

EXHIBIT 6.15 Thorson and Moore's strategic planning triangle.

Identify and profile target segment(s)

Consolidate the value proposition for the brand

Select a mix of persuasion tools

Source: Based on Esther Thorson and Jeri Moore, *Integrated Communication: Synergy of Persuasive Voices* (Mahwah, NJ: Erlbaum, 1996).

begins with insights about one's target segment that are both personal and precise.

The second important apex in the planning triangle entails specification of the brand's value proposition. A brand's value proposition is a statement of the functional, emotional, and/or self-expressive benefits delivered by the brand. In formulating the value proposition one should consider both what a brand has stood for or communicated to consumers in the past and what new types of value or additional benefits one wants to claim for the brand going forward. For mature, successful brands, reaffirming the existing value proposition may be the primary objective for any campaign. When launching a new brand, there is an opportunity to start from scratch in establishing the value proposition.

The final apex of the planning triangle considers the various persuasion tools that may be deployed as part of the campaign. A description of these tools is yet to come. Chapters 12 and 13 emphasize traditional mass media tools, Chapter 14 looks at the dynamic digital options, Chapter 15 considers support media and sales promotions, Chapter 16 examines the exciting new arena of branded entertainment, Chapter 17 provides a comprehensive look at direct marketing, and Chapter 18 fills out the tool kit by discussing the public relations function. The mix of tools used will depend on campaign goals. The point here is simply to reinforce our mantra that advertising and integrated brand promotion always entails finding the right mix to do the job: Knowing the target segment and the value proposition are essential to doing the job right.

SUMMARY

  Explain the process known as STP marketing.

The term *STP marketing* refers to the process of segmenting, targeting, and positioning. Marketers pursue this set of activities in formulating marketing strategies for their brands. STP marketing also provides a strong foundation for the development of advertising campaigns. While no single approach can guarantee success in marketing and advertising, STP marketing should always be considered when consumers in a category have heterogeneous wants and needs.

  Describe different bases that marketers use to identify segments.

In market segmentation, the goal is to break down a heterogeneous market into more manageable subgroups or segments. Many different bases can be used for this purpose. Markets can be segmented on the basis of usage patterns and commitment levels, demographics, geography, psychographics, lifestyles, benefits sought, SIC codes, or stages in the purchase process. Different bases are typically applied for segmenting consumer versus business-to-business markets.

  Discuss the criteria to target a segment.

In pursuing STP marketing, an organization must get beyond the stage of segment identification and settle on one or more segments as a target for its marketing and advertising efforts. Several criteria are useful in establishing the organization's target segment. First, the organization must decide whether it has the proper skills to serve the segment in question. The size of the segment and its growth potential must also be taken into consideration. Another key criterion involves the intensity of the competition the firm is likely to face in the segment. Often, small segments known as market niches can be quite attractive because they will not be hotly contested by numerous competitors.

  Identify the essential elements of an effective positioning strategy.

The *P* in *STP marketing* refers to the positioning strategy that must be developed as a guide for all marketing and advertising activities that will be undertaken in pursuit of the target segment. Effective positioning strategies should be linked to the substantive benefits offered by the brand. They are also consistent internally and over time, and they feature simple and distinctive themes. Benefit positioning, user positioning, and competitive positioning are options that should be considered when formulating a positioning strategy.

  Review the necessary ingredients for creating a brand's value proposition.

Many complex considerations underlie marketing and advertising strategies, so some device is called for to summarize the essence of one's strategy. We advance the idea of the value proposition as a useful device for this purpose. A value proposition is a statement of the various benefits (functional, emotional, and self-expressive) offered by a brand which create value for the customer. These benefits as a set justify the price of the product or service. Clarity in expression of the value proposition is critical for development of advertising that sells.

KEY TERMS

segment	switchers, or variety seekers	consumer markets
target	emergent consumers	business markets
position	point-of-entry marketing	competitive field
positioning	demographic segmentation	niche marketing
STP marketing	geodemographic segmentation	positioning strategy
heavy users, committed users, lead users	psychographics	value proposition
brand freaks	lifestyle segmentation	brand promise
	benefit segmentation	brand platform

ENDNOTES

1. Nina Munk, "Why Women Find Lauder Mesmerizing," *Fortune,* May 25, 1998, 96–106; Netra Shetty, "Marketing Research of Estee Lauder Companies," *managementparadise.com,* April 6, 2011; and Philip Kotler and Kevin Lane Keller, *Marketing Management,* 14th ed. (Upper Saddle River, NJ: Pearson Prentice Hall, 2012), 208.

2. Athena Schindelheim, "Bobbi Brown: How I Did It," *Inc. Magazine,* 2007, 110–112.

3. Don E. Schultz, "Pareto Pared," *Marketing News,* November 15, 2009, 24; Steve Hughes, "Small Segments, Big Payoff," *Advertising Age,* January 15, 2007, 17.

4. Deborah Ball, "Toll-Free Tips: Nestle Hotlines Yield Big Ideas," *The Wall Street Journal,* September 3, 2004, A7.

5. Bonnie Tsui, "Generation Next," *Advertising Age,* January 15, 2001, 14, 16.

6. Allanna Sullivan, "Mobil Bets Drivers Pick Cappuccino over Low Prices," *The Wall Street Journal,* January 30, 1995, B1; and Scott Horsley, "Gas Stations Profit from More Than Just Gas," *NPR,* June 5, 2007.

7. Sally Beatty, "Nickelodeon Sets $30 Million Ad Deal with the Bahamas," *The Wall Street Journal,* March 14, 2001, B6.

8. Kelly Greene, "Marketing Surprise: Older Consumers Buy Stuff, Too," *The Wall Street Journal,* April 6, 2004, A1, A12.

9. Rebecca Piirto, *Beyond Mind Games: The Marketing Power of Psychographics* (Ithaca, NY: American Demographics Books, 1991), 222–223.

10. Thomas S. Robertson and Howard Barich, "A Successful Approach to Segmenting Industrial Markets," *Planning Forum* (November/December 1992), 5–11.

11. Philip Kotler and Kevin Lane Keller, *Marketing Management,* 14th ed. (Upper Saddle River, NJ: Pearson Prentice Hall, 2012), 280.

12. Timothy Aeppel, "For Parker Hannifin, Cable Is Best," *The Wall Street Journal,* August 7, 2003, B3.

13. Anne Bahr Thompson, "Brand Positioning and Brand Creation," in *Brands and Branding* (London: The Economist in Association with Profile Books, 2003), 79–95.

14. Dan Reed, "Continental, Southwest Airlines Land Profits," *usatoday.com,* January 21, 2010.

15. This definition is adapted from David Aaker, *Building Strong Brands* (New York: Free Press, 1996), ch. 3.

16. Anne Bahr Thompson, "Brand Positioning and Brand Creation," in *Brands and Branding* (2003), 79–95.

17. Esther Thorson and Jeri Moore, *Integrated Communication: Synergy of Persuasive Voices* (Mahwah, NJ: Erlbaum, 1996).

CHAPTER 7
Advertising Research

After reading and thinking about this chapter, you will be able to do the following:

1 Explain the purposes served by and the methods used in developmental advertising research.

2 Identify sources of secondary data that can aid the IBP planning effort.

3 Discuss the purposes served by and the methods used in copy research.

4 Discuss the basic research methods used after ads are in the marketplace.

Advertising and brand promotion research is any research that aids in the development, execution, or evaluation of advertising and promotion. Good research can move you closer to producing effective advertising and brand promotion (see Insights Online [Exhibit 7.1] for an interesting case in point).

Although some advertising agencies have had research specialists or even formal research departments for more than 100 years, their real growth occurred in the mid-20th century, with the 1950s being their heyday. During this period, agencies adopted research departments for three basic reasons:

1. The popularity of, naiveté toward, and overconfidence in "social science" during this time legitimized anything called science or research, particularly psychological methods.
2. Other agencies had research departments.
3. There was a real need to better understand how ads work; there still is.

During the 1950s, advertising research entrenched itself in the industry. The popular adoration of science was at its height; the books, the plays, the movies, and the ads of this period were full of the glory of "modern science." Modern science was going to cure or fix everything from hunger to racism. The human mind would be no problem for modern psychology, and by extension, modern marketers. The hubris of this time is, of course, laughable now. But, it made advertising agencies very susceptible to feeling that they could not afford to get behind in the modern consumer psychology race to better manipulation through scientific advertising research.

There was also an economic boom in consumption at the same time; agencies could afford research departments—and indulge in the hope of "scientific advertising." Due in large part to popular belief in the success of propaganda and psychological warfare in World War II, there was a ready-made acceptance of the "science of persuasion." There was a widely held belief that sophisticated mind-control techniques used in the war effort were now being turned into Madison Avenue mind control via sophisticated advertising. A belief in hidden mass persuasion was

INSIGHTS ONLINE

7.1 Go online to see the AdAge feature, "Purina Dog Food's Research Shows Dogs Also Can Benefit from Probiotics."

a cornerstone of Cold War ideology, and Madison Avenue's institutional sales pitch.

Amazingly overconfident social psychologists of the 1950s and 1960s actually thought they were going to eliminate racism, win the Cold War, and take on the relatively easy task of getting people to buy things they neither wanted nor needed. Of course, it didn't work out like that: the ridiculous propaganda of the 1950s hardly ended the Cold War, and even though advertising accelerated consumer culture, individual marketers found out just how difficult it really was to get those pesky consumers to buy their brands. The psychologists' considerable conceit yielded few significant real-world results and eventually led to a backlash.

Thankfully, things changed. First, the creative revolution of the 1960s temporarily sent the psychologists back to manipulating college sophomores for extra credit; the 1970s saw them return, but a lot fewer of them, and this time with less attitude and somewhat better theories. By the early 1980s, advertising agencies again began to openly voice their distrust for their research methods, those established in the very odd 1950s America. These voices of dissent began in London, moved to the U.S. West Coast, and eventually appeared just about everywhere. As we said before, in the past 20 years, several advertising agencies have come to believe that stand-alone research departments are a luxury that they can no longer afford, given the increased demands for accountability, profit, and relevance. But least we throw the proverbial baby out with the bathwater, at least two things are being seen as replacements, when there are replacements: (1) the account planning system, in which research is a more integral part of planning advertising and promotion strategy and execution, and (2) much greater research outsourcing, that is, going outside the agency for specific advertising research when and only when the need arises. Qualitative, naturalistic, ethnographic, and sociocultural methods have been favored by practitioners for at least two decades now.

A lot of things are called advertising and brand promotion research. Not all of them, or even most of them, are performed on the actual ads or promotions themselves. Most of this research is really done in preparation for making the ads and promotions. A lot is done on the client or brand side. To make the discussion easier, we will divide the ad and integrated brand promotion (IBP) research world into three parts: (1) developmental advertising and promotion research (before ads are made), (2) copy research (as the ads are being finished or are finished), and (3) results-oriented research (after the ads are actually in the marketplace).

7-1 STAGE ONE: DEVELOPMENTAL ADVERTISING AND IBP RESEARCH

Developmental advertising and promotion research is used to generate opportunities and messages. It helps creatives (the people who dream up and actually make the ads) and the account team figure out the target audience's identity, what they perceive themselves as needing in a given good or service, and their usage expectations, history, and context, among other things. Developmental research can provide critical information which can be used by creatives in actually producing ads and promotions. It is conducted early in the process so that there is still an opportunity to influence the way the ads, branded entertainment, or other IBPs turn out. Because of this, many consider it the most valuable kind of research. It occurs when you can still do something about it, before you have spent a ton of money and made some really bad mistakes. It is sometimes called **consumer insights.**

7-1a   Design Thinking

Design thinking is a newer way of looking at the integration of research and product development. It is finding its way into advertising and brand promotion as well. The idea is to get marketers and advertisers to think like designers. Designers use a type of thought process that emphasizes getting rid of any preconceived notions of what a good or service is currently and replaces it with a process in which designers partner with users/potential users to actually create from scratch what the good or service should actually look like. Why should a wallet look like existing wallets? Why should a computer look like existing computers? Design thinking emphasizes data acquired from close work with consumers that reveals what they really need and want in a good or service, not what some engineer screwed together, or what they told you in a focus group. It then uses an ongoing process of prototyping, use, feedback, prototyping again (and again and again sometimes), and then communicating what the brand really does (or could do) for real consumers. The hotbeds of design thinking are Stanford, Silicon Valley, MIT, Chicago, and University of Toronto. Companies such as Apple, Intuit, P&G, Target, and The Coca-Cola Company are champions of the movement. Design thinking can help advertisers figure out what the brand really means (or could mean) to consumers, or potential ones, and allows them to better create and shape brand meaning (see Insights Online [Exhibit 7.2] for a notable example).

7-1b Concept Testing

A **concept test** seeks feedback designed to screen the quality of a new idea, using consumers as the judge and jury. Concept testing may be used to screen new ideas for specific advertisements or to assess new product concepts. Before a new product is launched, the advertiser should have a deep understanding of how the product fits current needs and how much consumers are willing to pay for the new product. Concept tests of many kinds are commonly included to get quick feedback on new product or advertising ideas. Lately, design thinking has been replacing the simpler and more limited concept test at the more innovative firms.

7-1c Audience Profiling

Perhaps the most important service provided by developmental advertising research is the profiling of target audiences for the creatives. Creatives need to know as much as they can about the people to whom their ads will speak. This research is done in many ways. One way is through lifestyle research. **Lifestyle research**, also known as **AIO** (activities, interests, and opinions) research, uses survey data from consumers who have answered questions about themselves. From the answers to a wide variety of such questions, advertisers can get a pretty good profile of the consumers they are most interested in talking to. Because the data also contain other product usage questions, advertisers can account for a consumption lifestyle as well. For example, it may turn out that the target for a brand of roach killer consists of male consumers, age 35 to 45, living in larger cities, who are more afraid of "unseen dirt" than most people and who think of themselves as extremely organized and bothered by messes. They also love watching *Cops*. Profiles like this present the creative staff with a finer-grained picture of the target audience and their needs, wants, and motivations. Of course, the answers to these questions are only as

valuable as the questions are valid. In-depth interviews with individual consumers provide an excellent source of information to supplement the findings from AIO research, and vice versa.

7-1d Focus Groups

A **focus group** is a discussion session with (typically) 6 to 10 target customers who have been brought together to come up with new insights about the good or service. With a professional moderator guiding the discussion, the consumers are first asked some general questions; then, as the session progresses, the questioning becomes more focused and moves to detailed issues about the brand in question. Advertisers tend to like focus groups because they can understand them and observe the data being collected. Although focus groups provide an opportunity for in-depth discussion with consumers, they are not without limitations. Even multiple focus groups represent a very small sample of the target audience and are prone to all sorts of errors caused by group dynamics and pleasing the researcher. But remember that generalization is not the goal. The real goal is to get or test a new idea and gain depth of understanding. More than once in a while, what ends up being actual ad copy comes from the mouths of focus group members.

It takes skill to lead a focus group effectively. If the group does not have a well-trained and experienced moderator, some individuals will completely dominate the others. Focus group members also feel empowered and privileged; they have been made experts by their selection, and they will sometimes give the moderator all sorts of strange answers that may be more a function of trying to impress other group members than having anything to do with the product in question. Like most things, focus groups are good at what they do, but people feel compelled to push them in ways they were never meant to go. Again, focus groups are for understanding and insight, not scientific generalizations. Their overall trustworthiness as a method is in the low to mid-range.

7-1e Projective Techniques

Projective techniques are designed to allow consumers to "project" their thoughts, but mostly feelings (conscious or unconscious), onto a "blank" or neutral "surface," like an inkblot or benign painting or scene. It's like seeing zoo animals in clouds, or faces in ice cubes. Projective techniques share a history with Freudian psychology and depend on notions of unconscious or even repressed thoughts. Projective techniques often consist of offering consumers fragments of pictures or words and asking them to complete the fragment. The most common projective techniques are association tests, dialogue balloons, story construction, and sentence or picture completion.

Dialogue balloons offer consumers the chance to fill in the dialogue of cartoon like stories. The story usually has to do with a product use situation. The idea is that the consumers will "project" appropriate thoughts into the balloons. Supposedly, their true feelings will emerge.

Story construction is another projective technique. It asks consumers to tell a story about people depicted in a scene or picture. Respondents might be asked to tell a story about the personalities of the people in the scene, what they are doing, what they were doing just before this scene, what type of car they drive, and what type of house they live in. Again, the idea is to use a less direct method to less obtrusively bring to the surface some unconscious mapping of the brand and its associations.

The **Zaltman Metaphor Elicitation Technique (ZMET)** is also projective in nature. This technique claims to draw out people's buried thoughts and feelings about products and brands by encouraging participants to think in terms of metaphors. A metaphor simply involves defining one thing in terms of another. ZMET draws metaphors from consumers by asking them to spend time thinking about how they would visually represent their experiences with a particular product or service. Participants are asked to make a collection of photographs and pictures from magazines that reflect their experience. For example, in research conducted for DuPont, which supplies raw material for many pantyhose marketers, one person's picture of spilled ice cream reflected her deep disappointment when she spots a run in her hose. In-depth interviews with several dozen of these metaphor-collecting consumers can often reveal new insights about consumers' consumption motives, which then may be useful in the creation of products and ad campaigns to appeal to those motives. Metaphors are believed by many to be one of the most powerful and useful organizing and expressive structures of the human mind and, if they can be tapped successfully, can provide advertisers with very useful information. The ZMET is now widely used by marketers and advertisers. It

EXHIBIT 7.3 The ZMET has been a very successful way of getting consumers to reveal their thoughts and feelings by using our ability to think visually and use metaphors.

Susan Van Etten

was notably used by P&G in the launch of Febreze. Examine Exhibit 7.3; images like these are used in the ZMET to get at consumers' connections, particularly their unconscious ones.

7-1f Method: Fieldwork/ Long Interviews

Two methods of obtaining information about day-to-day consumer behavior is through fieldwork and long interviews.

Fieldwork. **Fieldwork** is conducted outside the agency (i.e., in the "field"), usually in the home or site of consumption. Its purpose is to learn from the experiences of the consumer and from direct observation. Consumers live real lives, and their behavior as consumers is intertwined throughout these real lives. Their consumption practices are **embedded**; that is, they are tightly connected to their social context. More and more, researchers are attempting to capture more of the real embedded experiences of consumers. This research philosophy and related methods are very popular today. Campaigns such as the award-winning and successful "Got Milk?" campaign (see Exhibit 7.4) used fieldwork to get at the real consumption opportunity for milk—a mouth full of cookies and an empty milk carton. This helped form, and then drive, the strategy and creative execution.

Consumers began to remember to be sure to have milk at home, to ask themselves when at the grocery store, "Got milk?" Other advertisers and their agencies make video recordings or have consumers themselves shoot home movies to get at the real usage opportunities

EXHIBIT 7.4 This campaign was largely inspired by qualitative research. Researchers actually went out into the field and found that there was nothing worse than having a cookie/brownie/etc. but no milk.

Cookies aren't the only things that can be dipped with milk.

Nothing keeps me going during a night out, like the refreshing sensation of milk. It tastes great and keeps my body limber and my bones strong – necessities for the twists and twirls of the tango!

got milk?

VALERIE TOWNES, WINNER OF THE ESSENCE "ISLA MILK MUSTACHE DIVA" CONTEST © 2001 AMERICA'S DAIRY FARMERS AND MILK PROCESSORS

AP Topic Gallery

and consumption practices of real consumers in real settings. Advertising researchers can make better messages if they understand the lives of their target audience, and understand it in its actual usage context. Field research uses observation and in-depth study of individuals or small groups of consumers in their own social environment. The advertising industry has long appreciated the value of qualitative data and is currently moving to even more strongly embrace extended types of fieldwork.

Long Interview. The **long interview** is another method of gaining data about the real lives of consumers and the way they think about the brand, the category, and how its consumption fits (or doesn't) into their lives. Long interviews are not just long (meaning more than 15 minutes, usually more like an hour); they are, when conducted by trained researchers, structured in such a way as to best get at important connections. The role of listening in this method cannot be overstated. This is a very popular research method.

INSIGHTS ONLINE

7.5 Go online to see the AdAge feature, "Online 'Captcha' Codes Are Based on Research in Branding That Exposure Can Enhance Recognition."

LO ②

7-2 SOURCES OF SECONDARY DATA

7-2a Mining the Web

It probably goes without saying for today's Web-savvy student that the Internet can be an advertiser's best friend when looking for secondary data of almost any kind. The Internet has revolutionized developmental research, particularly for smaller agencies and advertisers. Common search engines allow the searching of enormous amounts of data previously available only to the wealthiest agencies. Human search costs have been slashed. Of particular value are Web-based interest groups, or online communities. Social media data from companies like Facebook are great resources. Without ever leaving your office, you can see the spread of market ideas through online social network data. As search engines get more and more sophisticated, anyone can find just about anything. But then there are also all the advances in spyware and tracking software: software designed to let companies know where you go on their site, what you do when you are there, where else you go, with whom you share this information, and presumably with what result.

Some researchers mine the Web as if they were doing fieldwork, just online. Professor Robert Kozinets of York University in Toronto coined the term *netnography: net*work eth*nography* (field research). In netnography, the researcher not only observes and collects data from the Web but also actively seeks answers from online informants, much the same way a field researcher would do in an actual face-to-face physical setting. They have enormous cost advantages as well as assessing groups defined by shared interests as opposed to shared physical space. Online surveys of key groups are also employed. These are similar to the kinds of surveys one gets in the mail, or on the phone, but are conducted online. Although researchers are getting better at online sampling, issues of generalizability and representativeness are still present. They are, however, gaining popularity as a way of getting critical information from targeted brand users. Some researchers download and systematically analyze brand-talk (conversations about their brands, and competitors) by systematically searching and sampling online chatter and analyzing words that co–occur; like *Samsung* and *cool*. Over time this can provide a very good source of unobtrusively gathered brand information that can be used to develop new ads and other brand messaging (see Insights Online [Exhibit 7.5] for an interesting perspective).

7-2b Internal Company Sources

Some of the most valuable data are available within a firm itself and are, therefore, referred to as "internal company sources." Commonly available information within a company includes strategic marketing plans, research reports, customer service records, warranty registration cards, letters from customers, customer complaints, and various sales data (broken down by region, by customer type, or by product line). All of these provide a wealth of information relating to the proficiency of the company's advertising programs and, more generally, changing consumer tastes and preferences. Sometimes really great data are right there under the client's or agency's nose.

7-2c Government Sources

Various government organizations generate data on factors of interest to advertising planners; information on population and housing trends, transportation, consumer spending, and recreational activities in the United States is available through government documents. Go to www.lib.umich.edu/govdocs/federal .html for a couple hundred or so pages of great links to data from federal, state, and international government sources. The Census of Population and Housing is conducted every 10 years in years ending in 0. The data (actually tables, not the data itself, unfortunately) are released at various times during the following handful of years after the census. The Census Bureau has a great website with access to numerous tables and papers (www.census.gov/).

A great source of data in the United States is the American Community Survey (ACS), which the Census Bureau actually hopes will replace many aspects of the census. It came online in 2003. The ACS is a new approach for collecting accurate, timely information. It is designed as an ongoing survey that will replace the so-called long form in the 2010 census. The ACS provides estimates of demographic, housing, social, and economic characteristics every year for states, cities, counties, metropolitan areas, and population groups of 65,000 people or more (www.factfinder.census.gov/ home/en/acsdata.html). Demographic changes are key to so many advertising and branding opportunities. Think of how many ads you see for retirement services and planning; do you think the enormous number of aging baby boomers has something to do with that? It's no accident that *Advertising Age*'s parent company, Crain Communications, bought the magazine *American Demographics* and offers it bundled with the bible of the advertising industry. Demographics are important, more so when combined with psychographics and lifestyle analysis, as we will explore.

There is also the Current Population Survey, a national survey conducted monthly since 1940 by the Bureau of the Census for the Bureau of Labor Statistics. It provides information on unemployment, occupation, income, and sources of income, as well as a rotating set of topics such as health, work schedules, school enrollment, fertility, households, immigration, and language (www.census.gov/cps). Population trends rapidly change. Who could believe, given all the immigration occurring in North America and Europe and many other parts of the world, that rapidly changing populations don't affect consumer taste, needs, and preferences? For European surveys, check out Eurobarometer, ec.europa.eu/public_opinion.

You might also check out the International Social Survey Programme at www.issp.org. Here you get valuable data on feelings of consumers from 30 or so nations on, for example, environmental issues (quite a find for companies trying to market "green products"). Another great site is the National Archives and Records Administration, www.nara.gov. This site has an incredible array of information about Americans and American culture—all available, for no charge, from any computer. The array of consumer data available from government sources is a wonderful resource in advertising and planning for businesses of all sizes. These publications/sites are reasonably current. Print versions are available at public libraries. This means that even a small-business owner can access large amounts of information for advertising planning purposes at little or no cost. Again, the Internet has changed the world and the practice of advertising and promotion. Small marketers and their agencies can now obtain data that would have simply either been unavailable or cost too much just a few years ago.

7-2d Commercial Sources

This used to be the only game in town, but not after the Internet. There are still lots of commercial research suppliers, but it is getting harder to sell things you can get for free online. Because information has become such a critical resource in marketing and advertising decision making, commercial data services have emerged to provide data of various types and to package existing data. So, while traditional advertising agencies are more and more getting out or downsizing the research business, innovative companies (some of them start-ups) see an opportunity opening up here, particularly for those who can collect, package, or repackage online data. Some firms specialize in data-gathering efforts at the household or neighborhood level. Prizm is a good example. Prizm's owner, Neilsen (who also brings you television ratings and Web ratings), collects data at the ZIP code level on consumption. This way, a marketer can see a pretty interesting profile of who is most likely to consume a given good or service, and also *where*. This is based on the assumption that most consumers within a given ZIP code are more alike than different in their consumption habits. However, this assumption is not accepted universally. Sometimes there are significant variations in consumer practices within a given geographic area. More often than not, people living in close proximity to one another are more like each other (in consumption practices) than people living in different geographic areas. This simple reality is what makes geographic clustering research methods work at all.

Information from commercial data vendors is reasonably comprehensive and is normally gathered using reasonably sound methods. Information from these sources costs more than information from government sources but is specifically designed to be of benefit to advertisers and marketers. Many offer consumer surveys (one-shot attempts: one person answers the survey one time) and consumer panels (surveys in which the same members stay on the panel and are asked questions numerous times over months or years). Data from the Pew Center, a widely respected public opinion survey center, is also very valuable. It is particularly good at tracking general consumer attitudes.

Professional Publications. Another secondary data source is professional publications. Professional publications are periodicals in which marketing and advertising professionals report significant information related to industry trends or new research findings. Examples include the *Progressive Grocer* and *Beverage*. These should not be overlooked.

—————— LO ③ ——————
7-3 STAGE TWO: COPY RESEARCH

The second major type of advertising and promotion research is known as copy research, or *evaluative research*. It is an old term created when ads were mostly words. Now, it means research on the actual ads or promotional texts themselves, finished or unfinished. Copy research is used to judge or *evaluate* ads and promotions. This research usually occurs right before or after the ad is finalized.

This brings us to motives and expectations of the agency and the client: Why are certain tests done? Well, we do things because of history and habit; we know these don't make perfect sense. Just what is it that advertising professionals want out of their copy research? The answer depends on whom you ask.

Generally speaking, the account team (AKA "suits") wants some assurance that the ad does essentially what it's supposed to do, or at least is defensible in terms of copy test scores. Many times, the team simply wants whatever the client wants. The client typically wants to see some numbers, generally meaning **normative test scores**—scores relative to the average for a category of ads. The client wants to see how well a particular ad scored against average commercials of its type that were tested previously. From a practical standpoint, having a good normative copy test score (above the average for the category) lowers the probability of getting fired. You can point to the score and say it "tested well" and assert that you (and/or your agency) should not be fired. There is a lot of cover in these scores, perhaps in reality their greatest value.

How about the people who actually make the ads, the creatives? What do they want out of this? Well, generally they hate copy testing and wish it would go away. They are generally uninterested in normative tests. The creatives who actually produced the ad typically believe there is no such thing as the average commercial, and they are quite sure that if there are average commercials, theirs are not among them. Besides benefiting the sales of the advertised product or service, the creatives wouldn't mind another striking ad on their reel or in their book, another Addy or Clio on their wall. But copy research scores are unlikely to predict awards, which are the official currency of creatives. So, creatives don't tend to be fans of copy tests. Creatives want awards. Copy tests often stand in the way and seem meaningless.

Copy tests generate a type of report card, and some people, particularly on the creative side of advertising, resent getting report cards from people in suits. Creatives also argue that these numbers are often misleading and misapplied. Further, they argue that ads are artistic endeavors, not kitchen appliances to be rated by *Consumer Reports*. Advertising, they say, is art, not science. Again, they have a point. Because of these problems, and the often conflicting career agenda of creatives (awards, career as a filmmaker or writer) and account managers (keep your job, sell more stuff, maybe get to move to the brand side), copy research is often the center of agency tensions. Other than corner offices, copy tests have probably been at the center of more agency fights than just about anything.

Whenever people begin looking at the numbers, there is a danger that trivial differences can be made monumental. Other times, the mandatory measure is simply inappropriate. Still other times, creatives wishing to keep their jobs simply want to give the client what he or she wants, as suggested in Exhibit 7.6. If simple recall is what the client wants, then increasing the frequency of brand mentions might be the answer. It may

EXHIBIT 7.6 Creative pumps up DAR numbers.

Bob, a creative at a large agency, has learned from experience how to deal with lower-than-average day-after recall (DAR) scores. As he explains it, there are two basic strategies: (1) Do things that you know will pump up the DAR. For example, if you want high DARs, never simply super (superimpose) the brand name or tag at the end of the ad. Always voice it over as well, whether it fits or not. You can also work in a couple of additional mentions in dialogue; they may stand out like a sore thumb and make consumers think, "Man, is that a stupid commercial," because people don't talk that way. But it will raise your DARs. (2) Tell them (the account executive or brand manager and other suits) that this is not the kind of product situation that demands high DARs. In fact, high DARs would actually hurt them in the long run due to quick wear out and annoyance. Tell them, "You're too sophisticated for that ham-handed kind of treatment. It would never work with our customers." You can use the second strategy only occasionally, but it usually works. It's amazing.

© Cengage Learning

Sometimes advertisers just want to know if audience members "get" the ad. Do they generally understand it, get the joke, see the connection, or get the main point? The reasoning behind this assessment is so obvious it hurts. It makes sense; it can be easily defended— even to copy-research-hating creatives. Brand managers understand this criterion; so do account executives. Do you get the ad in Exhibit 7.7?

not make for a better commercial, but it may make for a better score and, presumably, a happy client in the short run. A lot of games are played with copy tests.

Despite the problems and politics involved, copy-testing research is *probably* a good idea, at least some of the time. Properly conceived, correctly conducted, and appropriately applied, copy research can yield important data that management can then use to determine the suitability of an ad. Knowing when it is appropriate and when it is not, and sticking to your guns, is, quite simply, very hard in the advertising and IBP world— too many careers and too much money are on the line. The following section will help you understand which test to use, and when to test at all.

7-3a Evaluative Criteria and Methods

There are a few common ways ads are judged. Again, these "tests" are usually done right as the ad is being finished, or is finished. They are, more than anything else, traditional. Some make a great deal of sense and are very useful for brand advertising and integrated promotion; others are horribly overused and misapplied. Below we go through and discuss the major evaluative criteria and the major methods of assessing ads and promotions on these criteria. Of the three types of research, this is probably the least useful in actual industry practice. It is, however, alive (if not well) because of tradition.

Communication Tests. A **communication test** simply seeks to discover whether a message is communicating something close to what the advertiser desired.

Communication tests are usually done in a group setting, with data coming from a combination of pencil-and-paper questionnaires and group discussion. Members of the target audience are shown the ad, or some preliminary or rough version of it. They typically see it several times. Then a discussion is held. One reason communication tests are performed is to prevent a major disaster, to prevent communicating something completely wrong, something the creators of the ad are too close to see but that is entirely obvious to consumers. This could be an unintended double entendre, an inadvertent sexual allusion, or anything else "off the wall." With more transnational or global advertising, it could be an unexpected interpretation of the imagery that emerges as that ad is moved from country to country around the world. Remember, if the consumer sees things, it doesn't matter whether they're intended or not—to the consumer, they're there. However, advertisers should balance this against the fact that communication test members feel privileged and special, and thus they may try too hard to see things, and see things that no one else sees. This is another instance where well-trained and experienced researchers must be counted on to draw a proper conclusion from the testing. These tests are either conducted in-house (at the advertising agency itself) or outsourced to a commercial testing service.

What Do They Remember? It is assumed that if the consumer was exposed to the ad, something of that ad remains in the consumer's mind: cognitive residue, pieces of the ads mixed with the consumer's own thoughts and reactions. It might be a memory

EXHIBIT 7.7 Do you get the message? Does the main message come across? Is the right image projected?

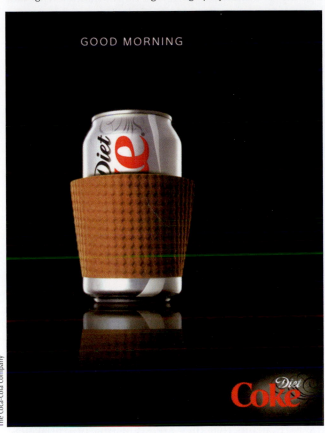

GOOD MORNING

Diet Coke

of the headline, the brand name, the joke in a TV spot, a stray piece of copy, a vague memory trace of an executional element in the ad, or just about anything. So for decades advertisers have tried to score this cognitive residue, or the things left in consumers' minds from the ads. If "remembering stuff" from the ad matters, this makes sense at some basic level, yet we have known for at least 30 to 40 years that most memory measures of ads (not brands) don't tend to predict actual sales very well at all. Why is this? Well, for one thing, consumers may remember all sorts of things in ads, and not care for the advertised brand at all. Or they remember things that are completely irrelevant to the advertiser's intended message, or some of their thoughts actually interfere with associating the advertiser's brand name with the ad itself. Humorous ads are great example of this. The consumer remembers what is funny, but not the brand name—or worse yet, remembers the competitor's brand name. Now some companies are insisting on recall measures for branded entertainment.

It is also the case that these tests are premised on an increasingly out-of-fashion view of human memory. Not so very long ago, psychologists thought that whatever a human experienced made its way into memory pretty much like streaming video or an unedited movie of one's life. It is becoming clear that motivation is much more important in what is remembered than previously recognized. So the focus of lots of advertising research was on the accurate and faithful retrieval of an ad, or at least important pieces of the ad, as if it existed unaltered in memory. Lately, though, a new way of thinking about human memory has emerged. Inspired from research into false memories in child abuse cases, psychologists now believe memory to be fluid and highly subject to motivation: remembering things as we care to remember them, even things that never happened. Memory appears to be much more of an interpretive act than previously thought. Advertising researcher Kathryn Braun-LaTour has shown that one can actually be fairly easily made to remember brands that don't exist and consumption experiences that never happened.[1] This work tells us that to rely so strongly on memory as a measure of advertising effectiveness is a very bad idea. There are certainly times when such measures are appropriate, like memory of a brand name or a key attribute, but nowhere near as much as they are used. There will be more on this in Chapter 9.

7-3b Common Methods for Assessing Cognitive Impact

Thought Listings. It is commonly assumed that advertising and promotions generate some thoughts during and following exposure. Copy research that tries to identify specific thoughts that were generated by an ad is referred to as **thought listing**, or **cognitive response analysis.** These are tests of knowledge, cognitive impact, and to a lesser degree feelings and emotions. Thought-listing tests are either conducted in-house or obtained from a commercial-testing service. They are most often used with television ads, although they can be applied to all ads. Here the researcher is interested in the thoughts that an ad or promotion generates in the mind of the audience. Typically, cognitive responses are collected by having individuals watch the commercial in groups and, as soon as it is over, asking them to write down all the thoughts that were in their minds while watching the commercial. They are then asked about these thoughts and asked to explain or amplify them. The hope is that this will capture what the potential audience members made of the ad and how they responded, or "talked back to it in their head."

These verbatim responses can then be analyzed in a number of ways. Usually, simple percentages or box scores of word counts are used. The ratio of favorable to unfavorable thoughts may be the primary interest of the researcher. Alternatively, the number of times the person made a self-relevant connection—that is, "That would be good for me" or "That looks like something I'd like"—could be tallied and compared for different ad executions. The idea itself is appealing: capturing people's stream of thoughts about an ad at the time of exposure. But in its actual practice problems arise. These thoughts are in reality more retrospective than online; in other words, people are usually asked to write these down seconds to minutes after their thoughts actually occurred. They are also highly self-edited—some of your thoughts are not very likely to be shared. These thoughts are obtained in artificial environments and mental states typically unlike those in which real people are actually exposed to ads in real environments, such as sitting in their living room, talking, half-listening to the TV, and so on. But the researchers asked; you have to tell them something. Still, even with all these problems, there is something of value in these thoughts. The trick, of course, is to know what is valuable and what is just "noise." A lot has to do with how well matched the ad and the procedure are. Some ads, for example, are designed in such a way that the last thing the advertiser really wants is a lot of deep thought (more on this in Chapter 10). For other ads (those where certain conclusions and judgments are the desired goal), it can be a good test.

Recall Tests. These are one of the most commonly employed tests in advertising, and the most controversial. They are used to get at the cognitive residue of ads. The basic idea is that if the ad is to work, it has to be remembered. Following on this premise is the further assumption that the ads best remembered are the ones most likely to work. Thus, the objective of these tests is to see just how much, if anything, the viewer of an ad remembers of the message. Recall is used most in testing television advertising. In television **recall tests,** the big companies are Ipsos-ASI and Burke. In print, the major recall testing services are Gallup & Robinson and Mapes and Ross. In print, however, **recognition** is generally the industry standard. Recognition simply means that the audience members indicate that they have seen an ad before (i.e., recognize it), whereas recall requires more actual memory (recalling from memory) of an ad. Recall is more common for television, recognition for print. Cyber ads or social media sites, or branded video, tend to use both recall and recognition tests.

In television, the basic recall procedure is to recruit a group of individuals from the target market who will be watching a certain channel during a certain time on a test date. They are asked to participate ahead of time and are simply told to watch the show. A day after exposure, the testing company calls the individuals on the phone and determines, of those who actually saw the ad, how much they can recall. The day-after-recall (DAR) procedure generally starts with questions such as, "Do you remember seeing a commercial for any laundry detergents? If not, do you remember seeing a commercial for Tide?" If the respondent remembers, he or she is asked what the commercial said about the product: "What did the commercial show? What did the commercial look like?" The interview is recorded and transcribed. The verbatim interview is coded into various categories representing levels of recall, typically reported as a percentage. *Unaided recall* is when the respondent demonstrates that he or she saw the commercial and remembered the brand name without having the brand name mentioned. If the person had to be asked about a Tide commercial, it would be scored as *aided recall*. Industry leader Burke reports two specific measures: *claim-recall* (percent who claim seeing the ad), and *related-recall* (percent who accurately recall specific elements of the ad).[2] Ipsos-ASI uses a similar procedure but with one major difference. Like Burke, Ipsos-ASI recruits a sample but tells the participants that they are evaluating potential new television shows. What they are really evaluating are the ads. The shows are mailed to the sample audience members' home and they are given instructions. A day after viewing, the company contacts the viewers and asks them questions about the shows and the ads. From their responses, various measures are gathered, including recall. The advantage is the deception. If audience members think they are evaluating the shows, the researchers may get a more realistic assessment of the ads. It is not the same as a truly natural exposure environment, but it's probably an improvement over asking directly about the ad only. (See Insights Online [Exhibit 7.8] for some noteworthy results gleaned from Sports Illustrated research.)

Recognition Tests. **Recognition tests** are the standard memory test for print ads and promotions. Rather than asking you if you recall something, they ask if you *recognize* an ad, or something in an ad. This type of testing attempts to get a little more

INSIGHTS ONLINE

7.8 Go online to see the AdAge feature, "Sports Illustrated Research Shows Greater Recall for iPad Ads than Print Ads."

EXHIBIT 7.9 Recognition testing uses the ad itself to test whether consumers remember it and can associate it with its brand and message. This unusual, comically fanciful image would likely make this ad easy to recognize. But imagine this ad with the Altoids brand name blacked out. If consumers recognize the ad, will they also remember the Altoids brand name? Novel imagery sometimes actually distracts readers, enticing them to overlook brand names. Visit the Altoids site (www.altoids.com) and evaluate how it reinforces or dilutes recognition in the minds of consumers. Are the interactive features useful or distracting? Does the site achieve "cool," or is it too over-the-top to reinforce brand recognition?

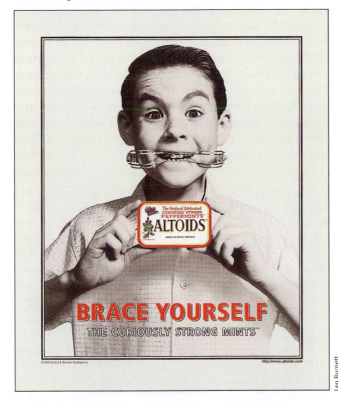

than evidence of exposure residue. Recognition tests ask magazine readers (and sometimes television viewers) whether they remember having seen particular advertisements and whether they can name the company sponsoring the ad. For print advertising, the actual advertisement is shown to respondents, and for television advertising, a script with accompanying photos is shown. For instance, a recognition test might ask, "Do you remember seeing [the ad in Exhibit 7.7]?" This is a much easier task than recall in that respondents are cued by the very stimulus they are supposed to remember, and they aren't asked to do anything more than say yes or no.

Companies such as **Starch Readership Services** that do this kind of research follow some general procedures. Subscribers to a relevant magazine are contacted and asked if an interview can be set up in their home. The readers must have at least glanced at the issue to qualify. Then each target ad is shown, and the readers are asked if they remember seeing the ad (if they *noted* it), if they read or saw enough of the ad to notice the brand name (if they *associated* it), if they *read any* part of the ad copy, or if they claim to have read at least 50 percent of the copy *(read most)*. This testing is usually conducted just a few days after the current issue becomes available. The *noted, associated,* and *read most* scores are calculated (see Exhibit 7.9). With print ads, Starch is the major supplier of recognition (they also term them "readership") tests.

Bruzzone Research Company provides recognition scores for TV ads. Essentially, a sample of television viewers is selected. A photoboard (a board with still frames from the actual ad) of the TV commercial is sent out to a sample of viewers, but the brand name is obscured (both in picture and copy). Then recognition questions such as "Do you remember seeing this commercial on TV?" are asked. The respondent is asked to identify the brand and answer some attitude items. A recognition score is then presented to the client, along with attitude data. This method has advantages in that it is fairly inexpensive (and may be becoming less so through use of the Internet), and, due to its manner of blocking brand names, may provide a more valid measure of recognition (see Exhibit 7.10).

Recognition scores have been collected for a long time, which allows advertisers to compare

EXHIBIT 7.10 This company lets consumers test ads online.

their current ads with similar ones done last week, last month, or 50 years ago. This is a big attraction of recognition scores. The biggest problem with this test is that of a yea-saying bias. In other words, many people say they recognize an ad that in fact they haven't seen. After a few days, do you really think you could correctly remember which of the three ads in Exhibits 7.11 through 7.13 you really saw, if you saw the ads under natural viewing conditions? Still, on a relative basis, these tests may tell which ads are way better or way worse than others.

Now here's the rub: Considerable research indicates there is little relation between recall or recognition scores and actual sales.[3] But doesn't it make sense that the best ads are the ads best remembered? Well, the evidence for that is simply not there. This seeming contradiction has perplexed scholars and practitioners for a long time. And as ads become more and more visual, recall of words and claims is more and more irrelevant except, usually, for simple brand names. The fact is that, as measured, the level of recall for an ad seems to have relatively little (if anything) to do with sales. This may be due to highly inflated and artificial recall scores. It may also be that ads that were never designed to elicit recall are being tested as if they were. By doing this, by applying this test so widely and so indiscriminately, it makes the test itself look bad. We believe that when, but only when, recall or recognition is the desired result are these tests appropriate and worthwhile.

A recall measurement does make sense when simple memory goals are the aim of the commercial. For example, saying "Kibbles and Bits" 80 times or so in 30 seconds indicates an ad aimed at one simple goal: Remember "Kibbles and Bits." That's all. For an ad like that, recall is the perfect measure. But as advertising moves to fewer words and more pictures, recognition tests, good recognition tests, may become much more valuable than recall. And for most ads or branded entertainment that operate at a far more sophisticated and advanced level than either recall or recognition, these measures are very likely insufficient.

EXHIBITS 7.11 THROUGH 7.13 All of these ads, so strikingly similar, do little to (1) differentiate the product, (2) make it memorable for the consumer, or (3) promote the brand, although presumably GM and Ford had intended to do all three with these ads. Compare and contrast the new Cadillac models (www.cadillac.com) with the Ford luxury models (www.lincoln.com). Has either company broken any new ground in its approach to advertising these vehicles? Do you think in a few days you could distinguish between these models or remember the message of these websites?

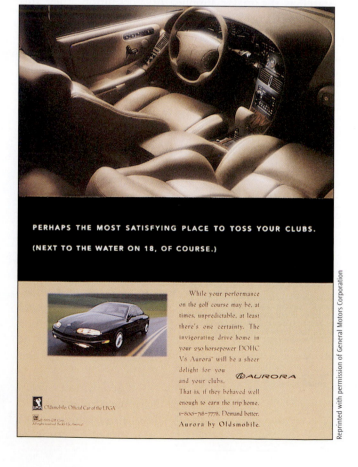

Implicit Memory Measures. What we have been discussing up to this point are explicit memory measures, measures and procedures that require the research subject to recall the actual exposure. As a contrast, **implicit memory measures** do not refer back to the ad or exposure but try to get at memory by using tasks like word fragments: say, part of a brand name, like S R N T for Sprint. Subjects are asked to complete the brand name (that is scored) along with other recollections. The idea is that this is a much more sensitive, less demanding (artificial), and perhaps a more meaningful measure of advertising. It is being used occasionally in actual practice, but its intensive procedure and instrumentation make it more of an academic pursuit than an applied one. Professor Julie Irwin at the University of Texas at Austin has produced some very promising research in this area showing that implicit attitude measures can be very meaningful indicators of closely held attitudes rather than those reported to researchers.

Knowledge. Knowledge is a big step up from cognitive residue. To have knowledge about a brand that could have come only from an ad is a much more meaningful measure of advertising effectiveness. This knowledge may take several forms. It could be a brand claim or a belief about the brand. For example, the advertisers may believe that Brand X cleans twice as well as Brand Y. If Brand X's advertising and promotion has been stressing this very fact, then we may generally assume that the consumer has learned something from the promotion and advertising, and that brand knowledge has been created. But with the explosion in available information for consumers, it's really getting hard to figure out just where some piece of knowledge came from.

Attitude Change. Attitudes suggest where a brand stands in the consumer's mind. Attitudes can be influenced both by what people know and by what people feel about a brand. In this sense, attitude or preference is a summary evaluation that ties together the influences of many different factors.

Common sense tells us that attitudes would be worthwhile in assessing ads. Did the ads change the consumers' attitudes in the right direction? Although the usefulness of the attitude concept itself has come under fire, attitude studies are still used, though more often at the results stage. One of the big problems is getting advertisers to run true scientific experiments with tight controls. They just don't seem to see the value in it, or the relevance of it. There just isn't much of this done other than on college campuses by professors assuming that stimulus material are the same as real ads. Industry rarely uses experiments.

One cannot assume that a favorable attitude toward the ad will always lead to a favorable and meaningful attitude toward the brand. We can all think of ads we love for brands we don't. Further, attitude research is in decline generally. It turns out that attitudes are not very strong predictors of actual behavior, subject to all kinds of social desirability bias and other measurement problems. Still, in the right circumstance, when the correct attitude dimensions are defined, assessing summary evaluations makes sense. In practice, however, attitude research is all too rarely useful. There will more on this when we discuss specific methods and message strategies in Chapter 9.

Attitude Studies. The typical industry **attitude study** measures consumer attitudes after exposure to an ad. The studies may also be administered by survey, including Internet surveys. Essentially, people from the target market are recruited, and their attitudes toward the advertised brand as well as toward competitors' brands are noted. Ideally, there would be pre- and post-exposure attitude measurement so that one could see the change related to seeing the ad in question. Unfortunately, industry practice and thinner agency profit margins have created a situation in which only post-exposure measures are now typically taken. True pre–post tests are becoming rare.

To the extent that attitudes reflect something meaningful and something important, these tests may be very useful. Their validity is typically premised on a single ad exposure (sometimes two) in an unnatural viewing environment. Many advertisers believe that commercials don't register their impact until after three or four exposures in a real environment; others believe the number is much higher. Still, a significant swing in attitude scores with a single exposure suggests that something is going on and that some of this effect might be expected when the ad reaches real consumers in the comfort of their homes. The hard cold bottom line is that attitude studies have not been very predictive of actual behavior under the best of conditions—conditions that almost never exist in commercial advertising research.

Feelings and Emotions. Advertisers have always had a special interest in feelings and emotions. Ever since the "atmospheric" ads of the 1920s, there has been the belief that feelings may be more important than thoughts as a reaction to ads. Recent research by business professor Michel Pham and others[4] has shown that feelings have three distinct properties that make them very powerful in reactions to advertisements and the advertised goods and services: (1) Consumers monitor and access feelings very quickly—consumers

EXHIBIT 7.14 Words and rational arguments are not what makes this ad work.

YOUR LEFT HAND IS THE SENSIBLE ONE. YOUR RIGHT HAND IS THE CRAZY ONE. YOUR LEFT HAND DOES WHAT IT SHOULD. YOUR RIGHT HAND DOES WHAT IT PLEASES. YOUR LEFT HAND WILL SUPPORT YOU. YOUR RIGHT HAND WILL SURPRISE YOU. WOMEN OF THE WORLD, RAISE YOUR RIGHT HAND.

often know how they feel before they know what they think; (2) there is much more agreement in how consumers feel about ads and brands than in what they think about them; and (3) feelings are very good predictors of thoughts. This research adds a great deal of support to the argument that, in many ways, feelings are more important than thoughts when it comes to advertising. It also appears that ads that use feelings produce stronger and more lasting effects than those that try to persuade by thought alone. For example, the way a consumer feels about imagery in the ad in Exhibit 7.14 may be far more important than what they say they think about them.

Resonance Tests. In a **resonance test,** the goal is to determine to what extent the message resonates or rings true with target audience members. The question becomes: Does this ad match consumers' own experiences? Does it produce an affinity reaction? Do consumers who view it say, "Yeah, that's right; I feel just like that"? (Exhibit 7.15) Do consumers read the ad and make it their own? The method is pretty much the same as a communication test. Consumers see an ad in a group several times and then discuss it. It can be conducted in-house by agency planners and researchers or "sent out" to a research supplier. How do you feel about this ad? How does it make you feel?

Frame-by-Frame Tests. **Frame-by-frame tests** are usually employed for ads where the emotional component is seen as key, although they may also be used to obtain thought listing as well. These tests typically work by getting consumers to turn dials (like/dislike) while viewing television commercials in a theater setting. The data from these dials are

then collected, averaged, and later superimposed over the commercial for the researchers in the form of a line graph. The height of the line reflects the level of interest in the ad. The high points in the line represent periods of higher interest in the ad, and the dips show where the audience had less interest in that particular point of the ad. Whereas some research companies do ask consumers what they were thinking or feeling at certain points along the trace, and sometimes these responses are diagnostic, others do not. In those cases (such as the one shown in Exhibit 7.16), what the trace line really does then is measure the levels of interest at each specific moment in the execution—it does not explain whether or why consumers' reactions were positive or negative. The downside of frame-by-frame tests is that they involve somewhat higher costs than other methods, and there are some

EXHIBIT 7.15 Some ads are judged by their resonance, or how true they ring. www.wisk.com

Wisk tablets remove dirt like it never happened.

If only they could do the same for your daughter's new tattoo.

Introducing Wisk® Dual Action Tablets with blue stain-fighting enzymes. So powerful, it's as if dirt never happened at all.

©2001 Lever Brothers Company

EXHIBIT 7.16 Here consumers' interest levels are measured while they watch the ad in real time.

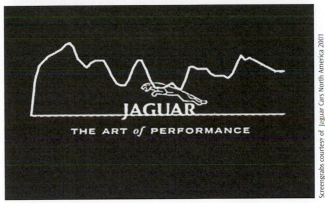

Screengrabs courtesy of Jaguar Cars North America 2001

point most of the work involves magnetic resonance imaging (MRI). The idea is to see which parts "light up" during exposure to various stimuli, or during certain tasks, and to understand what is happening when they light up. (Exhibit 7.17 shows MRI testing.) But at least at this point, understanding of actual process—beyond isolating the activity in certain parts of the brain known to be involved in certain types of processing—has been promising. Practical applications to advertising appear at the level of a better basic understanding of the human mind, which is valuable in and of itself. Actual common use in copy research seems distant. The brightest hope is in the area of understanding emotional advertising. Stanford professor Baba Shiv and others have presented some very exciting findings on how emotion unconsciously affects decision making.

Eye Tracking. Eye-tracking systems have been developed to monitor eye movements across print ads. With one such system, respondents wear a goggle-like device that records (on a computer system) pupil dilations, eye movements, and length of time each sector of an advertisement is viewed.

Behavioral Intent. This is essentially what consumers say they intend to do. If, after exposure to Brand X's advertising, consumers' stated intent to purchase Brand X goes up, there is some reason to believe that

validity concerns in that you are asking consumers to do something they do not normally do while watching television. On the other hand, the method has some fans. It is sexy; it impresses clients.

There is a lot of current interest in developing better measures of the feelings and emotions generated by advertising. This has included better paper-and-pencil measures as well as dial-turning devices. Assessment of feelings evoked by ads is becoming a much more important goal of the advertising industry.

Physiological Changes. Every few years there is renewed interest in the technology of **physiological assessment** of advertising. Most recently, advances in brain imaging have raised hopes of understanding how the human mind actually processes advertisements. At this

EXHIBIT 7.17 These are examples of MRIs. The tool is now being used for basic research on advertising. Its real-world application is unlikely.

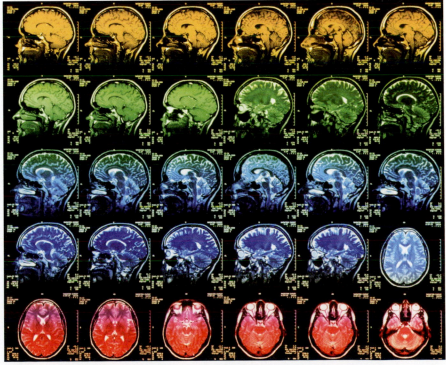

© Thomas C. O'Guinn

the tested advertising had something to do with it. Of course, we all know the problem with intended behavior: It's a poor substitute for actual behavior. Think about it: You really intended to call your mom, put the check in the mail, "I'll call you," and all those other things we say and maybe mean at the time. But it just didn't work out that way. The same thing is true when these are the criteria for testing consumer response to advertising. On a relative basis (say, percentage who intend to buy Pepsi versus percentage who intend to buy Coke, or at least who tell some researcher that), these measures can be meaningful and helpful, particularly if the changes are really large. Beyond that, don't take them to the bank.

7-4 STAGE THREE: RESULTS

At this stage, the ads are already out in the world, and the advertisers are trying to assess whether or not they are working.

7-4a Method: Tracking Studies

Tracking studies are one of the most commonly used advertising and promotion research methods. Basically, they "track" the apparent effect of advertising and branded entertainment over time. They typically assess attitude change, knowledge, behavioral intent, and self-reported behavior. They assess the performance of advertisements before, during, or after the launch of an advertising campaign or branded entertainment. This type of advertising research is almost always conducted as a survey. Members of the target market are surveyed on a fairly regular basis to detect any changes. Any change in awareness, belief, or attitude is usually attributed (rightly or wrongly) to the advertising effort. Even though the participants are susceptible to other influences (e.g., news stories about the brand or category), these are fairly valuable tests because they do occur over time and provide ongoing assessment rather than the one-time, one-shot approach of so many other methods. The method has been extended to even things like advertising within gaming, which presents new ethical issues given that most gamers are young. Their weakness resides largely in the meaningfulness of the specific measures. Sometimes attitudes shift a bit but translate into no noticeable increase in sales and no return on investment (ROI).

7-4b Method: Direct Response

Direct response advertisements in print, the Internet, and broadcast media offer the audience the opportunity to place an inquiry or respond directly through a website, reply card, or toll-free phone number. These ads produce **inquiry/direct response measures.** These measures are quite straightforward in the sense that advertisements that generate a high number of inquiries or direct responses, compared to historical benchmarks, are deemed effective. Additional analyses may compare the number of inquiries or responses to the number of sales generated. For example, some print ads will use different 800 numbers for different versions of the ad so that the agency can compute which ad is generating more inquiries. These measures are not relevant for all types of advertising, however. Ads designed to have long-term image building or brand identity effects should not be judged using such short-term response measures. Internet response measures will be discussed in more detail in Chapter 14. With the Internet, various measures of drill-down, click-through, and actual purchase are employed. Again, there will be more on this in Chapter 14.

7-4c Method: Estimating Sales Derived from Advertising

Other advertisers really want to see evidence that the new ads will actually get people to do something: generally, to buy their product. It is, to some, the gold standard. But for reasons explained earlier, there are so many things that can affect sales that the use of actual sales as a measure of advertising effectiveness is considered inherently flawed, but not flawed enough not to be used. Here is a place where advertising and promotion are really different. In the case of the more easily and precisely tracked effects of promotions, some IBPs, and some sales data collected via the Internet, sales are the gold standard. That's because you can better isolate the effect of the promotion. In the case of media advertising, statistical models are employed to try to isolate the effect of advertising on sales. Work by Dominique Hanssens, a marketing professor at the University of California at Los Angeles, has demonstrated that in some industries very sophisticated and fairly time-intensive mathematical modeling can isolate advertising effects over time, but these powerful models are underemployed by industry and require more time, data, and expertise than many companies have at their disposal.[5] Results generally indicate that advertising has its greatest impact on sales early in the product life cycle, or when a new version or model or other innovation is made. After that, advertising loses steam. Sometimes a host of other variables that might also affect sales, from the weather (say you represent a theme park) to competing advertising, are factored into these mathematical models.

Another downside is that these models are constructed long after the fact, long after the ad campaign to be assessed has been in place and sales data have come in. But if the model is strong enough, it will be applicable to many situations. Behavioral data are sometimes derived from test markets, situations where the advertising is tested in a few select geographic areas before its wider application. Although expensive, these tests can be telling. Ideally, measures of actual behavior would come from tightly controlled field experiments. Unfortunately, meaningfully controlled field experiments are incredibly difficult and expensive and thus very rare in real advertising and IBP practice. The area of greatest hope for those who believe real behavior is the best test of advertising effectiveness is the use of the Internet for experiments, although that is still in its early stages; there have been some very promising and successful results (particularly in consumer electronics and software). Several on-line advertisers, along with the search engine providers, are running field experiments continuously.

We believe that advertising is more art than science; it wraps culture around goods and services in order to give brands meaning. Many current research methods are simply at odds with that reality. Others, particularly the more culturally and socially based methods, are much better in this respect.

7-4d Method: All-in-One Single-Source Data

With the advent of universal product codes (UPCs) on product packages and the proliferation of cable television, research firms are now able to engage in *single-source research* to document the behavior of individuals—or, more typically, households—in a respondent pool by tracking their behavior from the television set to the checkout counter. **Single-source data** provide information from individual households about brand purchases, coupon use, television advertising exposure by combining grocery store scanner data with TV-viewing data from monitoring devices attached to the households' televisions, and increasingly search data from internet tracking software. See Exhibit 7.18; it is a tool (DoNotTrackMe) that claims to allow you to stop advertisers from tracking you, and reports who has been trying. With these different types of data combined, a better assessment can be made of the real impact of advertising and promotion on consumers'

EXHIBIT 7.18 Web tracking is controversial. DoNotTrackMe is anti-tracking software that claims to stop advertisers from tracking you, and the cool part, shows you who has been trying. If you go to work in the ad business you might be a tracker. Do you want to be tracked? Advertisers claim it allows them to better serve you. What do you think?

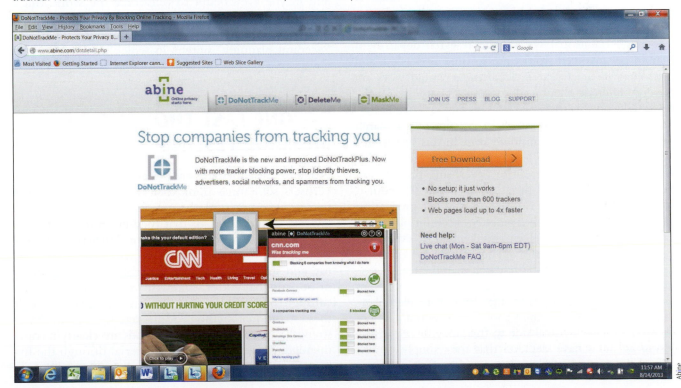

actual purchases. This is not an inexpensive method of assessment, and it still remains difficult (if not impossible) to know exactly what specific aspects of advertising had what effects on consumers. The best-known supplier of this type of testing is **IRI BehaviorScan.**

7-5 ACCOUNT PLANNING VERSUS ADVERTISING RESEARCH

Jon Steel, director of account planning and vice chairman of Goodby, Silverstein and Partners—its clients include Anheuser-Busch, the California Milk Processors Board ("Got Milk?"), Nike, Porsche, and Hewlett-Packard—has called account planning "the biggest thing to hit American advertising since Doyle Dane Bernbach's Volkswagen campaign."[6] That is stretching it a bit, but account planning is a big story in the industry. What is it? Well, good question. (See Exhibit 7.19.)

You will hear a lot about **account planning.** It's quite the term, and has been for a decade or so. It is defined in contrast to traditional advertising research. We've mentioned this before, but it probably deserves repeating. It differs mostly in three ways. First, in terms of organization, agencies that use this system typically assign an "account planner" to work cooperatively with the account executive on a given client's business. Rather than depending on a separate research department's occasional involvement, the agency assigns the planner to a single client (just like an advertising executive) to stay with the projects on a continuous basis—even though, in this organizational scheme, there is typically an account planning department. In the more traditional system, the research department would get involved from time to time as needed, and members of the research department would work on several different clients' advertising. (There are several variations on this theme.)

Second, this organizational structure puts research in a different, more prominent role. In this system, researchers (or "planners") seem to be more actively involved throughout the entire advertising process and seem to have a bigger impact on it as well. (Of course, some of the difference is more agency self-promotion than reality.) Agencies that practice "account planning" tend to do more developmental and less evaluative research. Third, "planning agencies" tend to do more qualitative and naturalistic research than their more traditional counterparts. But these differences, too, seem fairly exaggerated—even though Jay Chiat called planning "the best new business tool ever invented."[7] There is another, more cynical side to this story: Many advertising agencies have decided that they simply cannot afford the cost of a full-time research staff. It's cheaper

EXHIBIT 7.19 Much ado is made about the account planner versus traditional advertising research.

and maybe even better to outsource the work. But a quieter and more devious way of downsizing (or eliminating these expensive departments) is to go to the "account planning" system, in which a researcher will always be a part of the team.

7-6 ONE LAST THOUGHT ON MESSAGE TESTING

None of these methods are perfect, not even close. Advertisers sometimes think that consumers watch new television commercials the way they watch new, eagerly awaited feature films, or that they listen to radio spots like they listen to a symphony, or read magazine ads like a Steinbeck novel. We watch TV while we work, talk, eat, and study; we use it as a night light, background noise, and babysitter. Likewise, we typically thumb through magazines very, very quickly. Even though these traditional methods of message testing have their strengths, more naturalistic methods are clearly recommended. We get promotional material through the Internet, often while trying to do something else. Still, it would be a mistake to throw the baby out with the bathwater; good and appropriate behavioral science can sometimes produce better advertising.

7-7 WHAT WE NEED

Advertising and IBP research could do with some change. The way we think about ads and advertising is certainly changing. The move to a visual advertising style has also put into question the appropriateness of a set of tests that focus on the acceptance of message claims, as well as verbatim remembrance of words (copy). Also, the Internet has significantly challenged and changed the whole concept of audience, response, and associated measures. It's a brave new world (see Insights Online [Exhibit 7.20] for more discussion).

The account planning way of thinking merges the research and the brand management business. Good research can play an important role in this; it can be very helpful or an enormous hindrance, as advertisers are realizing more and more. Top-down delivered marketing is not considered realistic by many in the industry. With this new realization comes new terms.

One is the idea of account planning as a substitute for the traditional research efforts of an agency. There has been a very recent but very significant turn in thinking about research and its role in advertising, promotion, and brand management.

As you can see, advertising and promotion research is used to judge advertising, but who judges advertising research, and how? First of all, not enough people, in our opinion, question and judge advertising research. Research is not magic or truth, and it should never be confused with such. Research can be a wonderful tool when applied correctly, but it is routinely poorly matched to the real-world situation. We believe that advertising is more art than science; it wraps culture around goods and services in order to give brands meaning. Many current research methods are simply at odds with that reality. Others, particularly the more culturally and socially based methods, are much better in this respect.

INSIGHTS ONLINE

7.20 Go online to see the AdAge feature, "Ten Statistics That Will Make You Change the Way You See Video."

SUMMARY

 Explain the purposes served by and methods used in developmental advertising research.

Advertising and promotion research can serve many purposes in the development of a campaign. There is no better way to generate fresh ideas for a campaign than to listen carefully to the customer. Qualitative research involving customers is essential for fostering fresh thinking about a brand. Audience definition and profiling are fundamental to effective campaign planning and rely on advertising research. In the developmental phase, advertisers use diverse methods for gathering information. Focus groups, projective techniques, the ZMET, and fieldwork are trusted research methods that directly involve consumers and aid in idea generation and concept testing.

 Identify sources of secondary data that can aid the IBP planning effort.

Because information is such a critical resource in the decision-making process, several sources of data are widely used. Internal company sources such as strategic marketing plans, research reports, customer service records, and sales data provide a wealth of information on consumer tastes and preferences. Government sources generate a wide range of census and labor statistics, providing key data on trends in population, consumer spending, employment, and immigration. Commercial data sources provide advertisers with a wealth of information on

household consumers. Professional publications share insider information on industry trends and new research. Finally, the Internet is a revolutionary research tool that delivers rich data at virtually no cost. In particular, advertisers can obtain sophisticated research data at thousands of consumer- and brand-based online community sites.

 Discuss the purposes served by and methods used in copy research.

Copy research (evaluative research) aims to judge the effectiveness of actual ads. Advertisers and clients try to determine if audiences "get" the joke of an ad or retain key knowledge concerning the brand. Tracking changes in audience attitudes, feelings and emotions, behavior, and physiological response is important in gauging the overall success of an ad, and various methods are employed before and after the launch of a campaign to assess the impact on audiences. Communication tests, recall testing, pilot testing, and the thought-listing technique are a few of the methods that try to measure the persuasiveness of a message. Some agencies, attempting to bypass the high cost and inconclusive results of research, substitute account planning for traditional advertising and promotion research. Advocates of this trend believe an account planning system merges the best in research and brand management.

Discuss the basic research methods used after ads are in the marketplace.

Once an ad campaign has reached the marketplace, agencies and firms turn to results-oriented research to try to determine whether the ad has succeeded—whether, quite simply, the ad prompted consumers to buy the product or service. One of the most commonly employed methods of results-oriented research is the use of tracking studies to measure the apparent affect of advertising over time. Another long-standing method is the use of reply cards or toll-free numbers, which can track the direct responses of consumers to a particular campaign. Technology is also producing new results-oriented techniques. The development of universal product codes, combined with television monitoring devices, allows advertisers in some instances to track household consumption patterns from the television to the checkout lane. Researchers are also evaluating sophisticated models to more accurately track estimated sales from advertising, what has been a painstaking and expensive endeavor.

KEY TERMS

consumer insights
concept test
lifestyle (AIO) research
focus group
projective techniques
dialogue balloons
story construction
Zaltman Metaphor Elicitation
    Technique (ZMET)
fieldwork
embedded

long interview
normative test scores
communication test
thought listing (cognitive response
    analysis)
recall tests
recognition
recognition tests
Starch Readership Services
implicit memory measures
attitude study

resonance test
frame-by-frame test
physiological assessment
eye-tracking system
tracking studies
direct response
inquiry/direct response measures
single-source data
IRI BehaviorScan
account planning

ENDNOTES

1. Kathryn A. Braun, "Postexperience Advertising Effects on Consumer Memory," *Journal of Consumer Research*, vol. 25 (March 1999), 319–334.

2. Terence A. Shimp, *Advertising, Promotion and Supplemental Aspects of Integrated Marketing Communications* (Cincinnati, OH: South-Western, 2002).

3. Rajeev Batra, John G. Meyers, and David A. Aaker, *Advertising Management*, 5th ed. (Upper Saddle River, NJ: Prentice Hall, 1996), 469.

4. Michel Tuan Pham, Joel B. Cohen, John W. Pracejus, and G. David Hughes, "Affect Monitoring and the Primacy of Feelings in Judgment," *Journal of Consumer Research*, vol. 28 (September 2001), 167–188.

5. D. M. Hanssens, P. Leeflang, and D. R. Wittink, "Market Response Models and Marketing Practice," *Applied Stochastic Models in Business and Industry*, July–October 2005.

6. Jon Steel, *Truth, Lies & Advertising: The Art of Account Planning* (New York: John Wiley & Sons, 1998), jacket.

7. Ibid., p. 42.

CHAPTER 8

Planning Advertising and Integrated Brand Promotion

After reading and thinking about this chapter, you will be able to do the following:

1 Describe the basic components of an advertising plan.

2 Compare and contrast two fundamental approaches for setting advertising objectives.

3 Explain various methods for setting advertising budgets.

4 Discuss the role of the agency in formulating an advertising plan.

There is great complexity involved in executing a comprehensive advertising and integrated brand promotion (IBP) effort. You don't go out and spend millions of dollars promoting a brand that is vital to the success of a firm without giving the entire endeavor considerable forethought. Such an endeavor will call for a plan. As you will see in this chapter, the marketing team and its agencies follow a detailed process of building an advertising effort based on several key features of the advertising plan. An advertising plan is the culmination of the planning effort needed to deliver effective advertising and IBP.

8-1 THE ADVERTISING PLAN AND MARKETING CONTEXT

An ad plan should be a direct extension of a firm's marketing plan. As suggested in the closing section of Chapter 6, one device that can be used to explicitly connect the marketing plan with the advertising plan is the statement of a brand's value proposition. A statement of what the brand is supposed to stand for in the eyes of the target segment derives from the firm's marketing strategy and will guide all ad-planning activities. The advertising plan, including all IBPs, is a subset of the larger marketing plan. The IBP component must be built into the plan in a seamless and synergistic way. Everything has to work together, whether the plan is for a global advertiser like Apple or for a business with far fewer resources. At Apple, Steve Jobs said, there is no substitute for good teamwork between agency and client in the development of compelling marketing and advertising plans.

An **advertising plan** specifies the thinking, tasks, and timetable needed to conceive and implement an effective advertising effort. We particularly like Apple examples because they always illustrate the wide array of options that can be deployed in creating interest and communicating the value proposition for brands like iPad or iPhone. Jobs and his agency choreograph public relations activities, promotions and events, cooperative advertising, broadcast advertising, product placements, billboard advertising, digital media, and more as part of their launches. Advertising planners should review all the options before selecting an integrated set to communicate with the target audience.

For a variety of reasons that will become increasingly clear to you, it is critical to think beyond traditional broadcast media and digital media

EXHIBIT 8.1 The advertising plan.

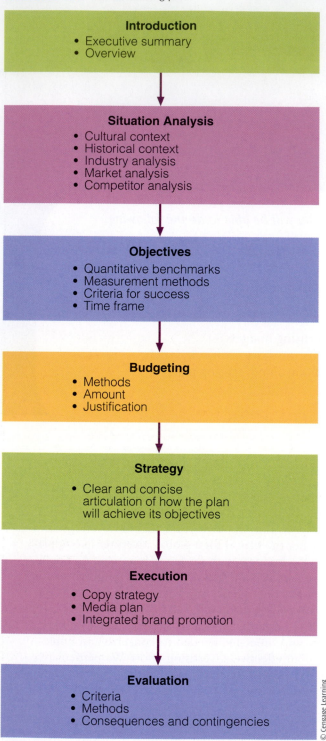

© Cengage Learning

planning is to consider literally everything as media. When you adopt the philosophy that *everything* is media, it's much easier to surround the consumer with a message and make a deep connection on behalf of the brand.

Exhibit 8.1 shows the components of an advertising plan. It should be noted that there is a great deal of variation in advertising plans from advertiser to advertiser. Our discussion of the advertising plan will focus on the seven major components shown in Exhibit 8.1: the introduction, situation analysis, objectives, budgeting, strategy, execution, and evaluation. Each component is discussed in the following sections.

8-2 INTRODUCTION

The introduction of an advertising plan consists of an executive summary and an overview. An executive summary, typically two paragraphs to a page in length, is offered to state the most important aspects of the plan. This is the take-away part of the plan. That is, it is what the reader should remember from the plan. It is the essence of the plan.

As with many documents, an overview is also customary. An overview ranges in length from a paragraph to a few pages. It sets out what is to be covered, and it structures the context. All plans are different, and some require more setup than others. Don't underestimate the benefit of a good introduction. It's where you can make or lose a lot of points with your boss or client.

8-3 SITUATION ANALYSIS

When someone asks you to explain a decision you've made, you may say something like, "Well, here's the situation. . . ." In what follows, you try to distill the situation down to the most important points and how they are connected in order to explain why you made a decision. An ad plan **situation analysis** is no different. It is where the client and agency lay out the most important factors that define the market and consumer situation, and then explain the importance of each factor.

A lengthy list of potential factors (e.g., demographic, technology, social and cultural, economic, and political/regulatory) can define a situation analysis. Some books offer long but incomplete lists. We prefer to play it straight with you: There is no complete or perfect list of situational factors. The idea is not to be exhaustive or encyclopedic when writing a plan, but

when considering the best way to break through the clutter of the modern marketplace and get a message out to your customer. Miami's Crispin Porter + Bogusky (CP+B) is another agency that has built its reputation on finding novel ways to register clients' messages with consumers. As you will learn in Chapter 9, one of CP+B's principles for success in campaign

to be smart in choosing the few important factors that really describe the situation, and then explain how the factors relate to the advertising task at hand. Market segmentation and consumer research provide the organization (remember Chapters 6 and 7) with insights that can be used for a situation analysis, but ultimately you have to decide which of the many factors are really the most critical to address in your advertising. This is the essence of smart management.

Let's say you represent the credit card company American Express. How would you define the firm's current advertising situation? What are the most critical factors? What image has prior advertising established for the card? Would you consider the changing view of prestige cards to be critical? What about the problem of hanging on to an exclusive image while trying to increase your customer base by having your cards accepted at discount stores? Does the proliferation of gold and platinum cards by other banks rate as critical? Do the diverse interest rates offered by bank cards seem important to the situation? What about changing social attitudes regarding the responsible use of credit cards? What about the current high level of consumer debt? You get the picture—this is complicated.

Just think about how credit card marketing is influenced by the economic conditions of the day and the cultural beliefs about the proper way to display status. In the 1980s, it was acceptable for advertisers to tout the self-indulgent side of plastic (e.g., MasterCard's slogan "MasterCard, I'm bored"). Today, charge and credit card ads often point out just how prudent it is to use your card for the right reasons (and get cash back at the end of the year). Now, instead of just suggesting you use your plastic to hop off to the islands when you feel the first stirrings of a bout with boredom, credit card companies often detail functional benefits for their cards with a specific market segment in mind. A similar, highly complex situation is now facing the health care industry. Firms like United Health Care (featured in Exhibit 8.2) must consider the impact of a host of situational factors in planning advertising and IBP: implementation of the Affordable Health Act, long-term care insurance coverage, the swelling ranks of seniors due to maturing baby boomers, changes in FDA drug approval processes, and new regulations on direct-to-consumer advertising in the health care field.

Basic demographic trends are often the single most important situational factor in advertising plans. Whether it's baby boomers or Generation X, Y, or Z, who or where the people are is usually where the sales are. As the population age distribution varies with time, new markets are created and destroyed. The baby boom generation of post–World War II disproportionately dictates consumer offerings and demand simply

EXHIBIT 8.2 Firms like United Health Care conduct a careful situation analysis when they plan advertising. What do the photo and copy in this ad tell you about how United Health Care has assessed the contemporary market situation for offering health care coverage to consumers?

because of its size. As the boomers age, companies that offer the things needed by tens of millions of aging boomers will have to devise new appeals (consider Exhibit 8.2 again). Think of the consumers of this generation needing long-term health care, geriatric products, and things to amuse themselves in retirement. Will they have the disposable income necessary to have the bountiful lifestyle many of them have had during their working years? After all, they aren't the greatest savers. And what of today's 20-somethings? When do you tend to model your parents (if ever)? When do you look to put space between yourself and your parents? Knowing which generation(s) to target is critical in your situation analysis (see Insights Online [Exhibit 8.3] for an interesting example).

INSIGHTS ONLINE

8.3 Go online to see the AdAge feature, "Old Spice Rebrands from Your Grandpa's Smelly Cologne to Younger Generations with Humor in Advertising."

8-3a **Cultural Context**

International advertising is advertising that reaches across national and cultural boundaries. Adopting an international perspective is often difficult for marketers and represents a major challenge in developing ad plans. The reason is that experience gained throughout a career and a lifetime creates a cultural "comfort zone." That is, one's own cultural values, experiences, and knowledge serve as a subconscious guide for decision making and behavior. Another name for this subconscious guide is "bias," unfortunately.

Managers must overcome two related biases to be successful in international markets. **Ethnocentrism** is the tendency to view and value things from the perspective of one's own culture. Additionally, **self-reference criterion (SRC)** is the unconscious reference to one's own cultural values, experiences, and knowledge as a basis for decisions. These two closely related biases are primary obstacles to success when conducting marketing and advertising planning that demand a cross-cultural perspective (see Insights Online [Exhibit 8.4] for a notable case in point).

A decision maker's SRC and ethnocentrism can inhibit his or her ability to sense important cultural distinctions between markets. This in turn can blind advertisers to their own culture's "fingerprints" on the ads they've created. Sometimes these are offensive or, at a minimum, markers of "outsider" influence. Even the savviest of marketers can overlook cultural nuances in the development of their advertising plans.

Toyota's launch of the Prado Land Cruiser in China provides a nice example of the challenges a firm must overcome in developing advertising to reach across national (and cultural) boundaries. Now keep in mind, this is Toyota, from just across the East China Sea in Toyota City, Japan, not some newcomer to the Asian continent. To launch its big SUV in China, Toyota's ad agency Saatchi & Saatchi (also highly experienced in international advertising) created a print campaign showing a Prado driving past two large stone lions, which were saluting and bowing to the Prado. This seems to make sense because the stone lion is a traditional sign of power in the Chinese culture. As one Saatchi

> When firms take the time to carefully research international markets, they can adapt their brands and avoid the serious pitfalls of ethnocentrism and self-reference criteria.

executive put it, "These ads were intended to reflect Prado's imposing presence when driving in the city: You cannot but respect the Prado."[1]

But Chinese consumers saw it differently. For starters, Chinese words often have multiple meanings, and Prado can be translated into Chinese as **badao**, which means "rule by force" or "overbearing." In addition, the use of the stone lions prompted scathing commentary on the Internet about a contentious time in China's relationship with Japan. Some thought the stone lions in the Prado ad resembled those that flank the Marco Polo Bridge in China, a site near Beijing that marked the opening battle of Japan's invasion of China in 1937.[2] These of course are not the kind of reactions that an advertiser is looking for when launching a new product. The automaker quickly pulled 30 magazine and newspaper ads and issued a formal apology, illustrating that no one, not even highly experienced global marketers and agencies, is immune to the subtle but powerful influences of culture.

It is the unanticipated or underappreciated elements that will get you into trouble every time, and many global marketers now subscribe to the theory that, to get the message right, you must get face time with consumers in any geographic market you are targeting. In doing so, several firms have cleverly and successfully adapted their brands to big foreign markets like India and China. PepsiCo learned that Indians might find the firm's Frito-Lay chips somewhat bland, so reformulated the product as a spicier snack called Kurkure. Similarly, Kraft altered the Oreo cookie for the Chinese market by using less sugar and adding green tea as a flavoring.[3] When firms take the time to carefully research international markets, they can adapt their brands and avoid the serious pitfalls of ethnocentrism and self-reference criteria.

8-3b **Historical Context**

No situation is entirely new, but all situations are unique. Just how a firm arrived at the current situation is very important. Before trying to design Apple's iPad campaign, the agency should learn a lot about the history of all the principal players, the industry, the brand, the corporate culture, critical moments in the company's past, its big mistakes, and big successes. Long relationships between client and agency, as between Apple and TWBA Chiat/Day, will obviously help with this, but most are not so fortunate.

> ## INSIGHTS ONLINE
> **8.4** Go online to see the AdAge feature, "'Viva Young' Taco Bell Super Bowl Ad Spot Plays on the Inauthenticity of Taco Bell's Mexican Cuisine with a Bad Cover of Fun.'s 'We are Young' Song."

All new decisions are situated in a firm's history, and an agency should be diligent in studying that history. For example, would an agency pitch new business to Green Giant without knowing something of the brand's history and the rationale behind the Green Giant character? The history of the Green Giant dates back decades. The fact is that no matter what advertising decisions are made in the present, the past has a significant impact.

Apart from history's intrinsic value, sometimes the real business goal is to convince the client that the agency knows the client's business, its major concerns, and its corporate culture. A brief history of the company and the brand are included in ad plans to demonstrate the thoroughness of the agency's research, the depth of its knowledge, and the scope of its concern.

8-3c Industry Analysis

An **industry analysis** is just that; it focuses on developments and trends within an entire industry and on any other factors that may make a difference in how an advertiser proceeds with an advertising plan. An industry analysis should enumerate and discuss the most important aspects of a given industry, including the supply side of the supply–demand equation. Most market analyses focus almost exclusively on a demand side analysis—how much market share can we get and how many units can we sell. But, when great advertising overstimulates demand that can't be matched by supply, one can end up with lots of unhappy customers—and good-bye brand position.

No industry faces more dramatic trends and swings in consumers' tastes than the food business. In recent years, the low-carb, low-calorie healthy meal craze has challenged industry giants—from Nestlé to Hershey Foods to H.J. Heinz Co. to McDonald's—to come up with new products and reposition old ones to satisfy consumers' growing concerns about sugar, white flour, fat—you name it. At one point, food industry research indicated that 30 million Americans described themselves as being on a low-carb diet, and another 100 million were expected to join them in a matter of just months. It was time for food marketers to reposition and reformulate.[4] It is hard to imagine the marketing and advertising plans of any food maker not giving some consideration to the carb issue as part of an analysis of their industry. As suggested by Exhibit 8.5, no one is immune. Here, pizza purveyor UNO Chicago Grill launches a new line of low-carb entries including ultra-low-carb grilled salmon to try to respond to changing industry conditions.

EXHIBIT 8.5 Pizzeria UNO Chicago Grill built its business around the classic Chicago-style deep-dish pizza. But, when the United States went crazy with carb counting, the firm had to offer entrees that were responsive to consumer eating trends.

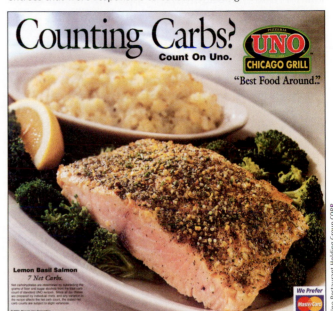

8-3d Market Analysis

A **market analysis** complements the industry analysis, emphasizing the demand side of the equation. In a market analysis, an advertiser examines the factors that drive and determine the overall market for a product or service category within which the advertiser offers a brand (or brands). First, the advertiser needs to decide just exactly what the market is for a product category. Often, the market for a given good or service is (over-) simply defined as current users. The idea here is that consumers figure out for themselves whether the product category fits their needs or not and thus define the market for themselves, and for the advertiser. This approach has some wisdom to it. It's simple, easy to defend, and very conservative. Few executives get fired for choosing this market definition. However, it completely ignores those consumers who might otherwise be entering the market category through lifestyle, demographic, technological, cultural, or attitudinal changes.

A wise market analysis commonly begins by stating just who the current users are, how many of them there are, and (hopefully) why they are the current users of the product category. Consumers' motivations for using one product or service category but not another may very well provide the advertiser with the means toward understanding whether a significant expansion of the entire market may or may not occur (recall the low-carb craze in the United States). If there are forces signaling that demand for a product category may grow (also consider United Health Care's opportunity with aging baby boomers), then the firm's slice of that market has a chance to grow as well. The advertiser's job in a market analysis is to find out the most important market factors and how they may affect overall market demand.

8-3e Competitor Analysis

Once the industry and market are studied and analyzed, attention turns to **competitor analysis**. Here an advertiser determines just exactly who the competitors are to the firm's brand(s), discussing their strengths, weaknesses, tendencies, and any threats they pose. When planning the launch of one of its new smartphones, Motorola faced a formidable obstacle—Apple's iPhone. Fortunately for Motorola, they didn't have to go it alone versus Steve Jobs and company. The Motorola phone would run Google software and be supported on Verizon's nationwide network.[5] In addition, Verizon brought significant resources to the table for a bold launch of the Droid, taking aim at the iPhone.[6] With stark, futuristic, and robotic overtones (think Terminator), there was no way one could mistake a Droid ad for an iPhone ad; and with its tagline of "In a world of doesn't, Droid does," Motorola and Verizon definitely meant to suggest that their phone will outperform the iPhone. Good news for all players in this category—with surging primary demand for smartphones generally, it appeared there was plenty of opportunity for both the cool/pretty and the dark/daring phones to continue to grow their sales revenues well into the future.

When archrivals go head-to-head trying to win customers' loyalty, it is common to see their advertisements feature a competitive positioning strategy, as discussed in Chapter 6. Another excellent illustration is featured in Exhibit 8.6. Here we see a regional telecom provider (Cincinnati Bell) taking on its rival, Time Warner. In conjunction with its partner, DirecTV, Cincinnati Bell is seeking to win over Time Warner's core customer, the cable subscriber. There is nothing subtle in the approach here. And it's pretty hard to argue with the premise that "Cable bills bite."

8-4 OBJECTIVES

Advertising objectives lay the framework for the subsequent tasks in an advertising plan and take many different forms. Objectives identify the goals of the advertiser in concrete terms. The advertiser, more often than not, has more than one objective for an ad campaign. An advertiser's objective may be:

(1) to increase consumer awareness of and curiosity about its brand,

(2) to change consumers' beliefs or attitudes about its brand,

EXHIBIT 8.6 Cincinnati Bell takes direct aim at the market share of a key competitor with a compelling visual element that works perfectly with the headline—"Cable bills bite." The value proposition for Cincinnati Bell's offering is based on a bundle of services for one low monthly fee.

(3) to influence the purchase intent of customers and potential customers,

(4) to stimulate trial use of the brand,

(5) to convert one-time brand users into repeat purchasers,

(6) to switch consumers from a competing brand to its brand, or

(7) to increase sales (the lamest of all statements of objective).

Let's consider each of these objectives separately. Creating or maintaining brand awareness is a fundamental advertising objective. **Brand awareness** is an indicator of consumer knowledge about the existence of the brand and how easily that knowledge can be retrieved from memory. For example, a market researcher might ask a consumer to name five insurance companies. **Top-of-the-mind awareness** is represented by the brand listed first. Ease of retrieval from memory is important because for many goods or services, ease of retrieval is predictive of market share.

This proved to be the case for Aflac (American Family Life Assurance Co.), the insurance company that uses a determined duck quacking *aaa-flack* in its ad campaign as a means to building brand awareness.

If you've seen this ad, we suspect that you'll never forget that duck. If you haven't seen it, you might be thinking that a duck as your primary spokesperson sounds pretty dopey. Maybe yes, maybe no, but that duck helped Aflac become a major player in the U.S. insurance market. Similarly, the Geico Gecko was so effective in winning attention for Geico Corporation that the chief marketing officer of rival Allstate Insurance has said, "I'd like to squash it."[7]

Social media offer tremendous opportunities for brand strategists to engage consumers and create tremendous brand awareness. Before Super Bowl XLVII, Coca-Cola huddled with its interactive agency, its primary agency, its media agency, and PR shop and used film from Super Bowl XLVI to plot how they would respond, in real time, to big plays during the current Super Bowl. Coke was creating an ad for the Super Bowl called "Mirage" which featured (potentially) showgirls, cowboys, or badlanders racing through the desert for a bottle of Coke. Viewers of the Super Bowl would be encouraged to vote for their favorite team

EXHIBIT 8.7 Kellogg's is targeting a very specific consumer group with its NutriGrain cereal bars. Given the list of features of the brand that Kellogg's highlights in this ad—whole grains, wholesome fiber, made with real fruit, no high fructose corn syrup—what objectives do you think Kellogg's is pursuing with this ad?

and sabotage competitors through social media voting, all of which would ultimately determine which Coke ad would run post-game.[8]

Creating, changing, or reinforcing attitudes is another important function of advertising, and thus makes for a common advertising objective. As we saw in Chapter 5, one way to go about changing people's attitudes is to give them information designed to alter their beliefs. There are many ways to approach this task. One way is exemplified by the Kellogg's ad in Exhibit 8.7. Here we see an information-dense approach where a number of appealing features are offered to shape beliefs regarding the NutriGrain cereal bar. Kellogg's offers the health conscious new mom a cereal snack that has whole grains, wholesome fiber, made with real fruit, no high fructose corn syrup— just the stuff to keep a busy mom healthy and alert for her baby. For the consumer willing to digest (no pun intended) this detailed set of appeals, the features are likely to prove quite compelling. Conversely, one can let a picture tell the entire story, as in Exhibit 8.8. Here the approach depends on the visual imagery and the consumer's willingness to interpret the loudspeaker heads depicted in the ad. Not a problem for anyone

EXHIBIT 8.8 The approach taken by Sony plugs into any air traveler's nightmare scenario: being seated directly in front of a screaming baby with the incessantly reprimanding mom on a flight to Paris.

who has traveled coach class. The obvious serenity of the handsome young man wearing the Sony Noise-Canceling Headphones speaks for itself. One thus infers something about Sony without any text. Whether through direct, logical arguments or thought-provoking visual imagery, advertisements are frequently designed to deliver their objective of belief formation and attitude change.

Purchase intent is another popular criterion in setting objectives. Purchase intent is determined by asking consumers whether they intend to buy a product or service in the near future. The appeal of influencing purchase intent is that intent is closer to actual behavior, and thus closer to the desired sale, than attitudes are. Even though this makes sense, it does presuppose that consumers can express their intentions with a reasonably high degree of reliability. Sometimes they can, sometimes they cannot. Purchase intent, however, is fairly reliable as an indicator of relative intention to buy, and it is, therefore, a worthwhile advertising objective. Simply stated, using advertising and IBP to effect purchase intent is a matter of elevating the brand's esteem in the minds of consumers so that *next time* they make a purchase, the firm's brand is just that much closer to being the one chosen.

Trial usage reflects actual behavior and is commonly used as an advertising objective. Many times, the best that we can ask of advertising is to encourage the consumer to try our brand. At that point, the product or service must live up to the expectations created by our advertising. In the case of new products, stimulating trial usage is critically important. In the marketing realm, the angels sing when the initial purchase rate of a new product or service is high. Of course, trial usage is facilitated by a variety of IBP tools—coupons, rebates, free samples, and premium offers (buy one item and get another item attached for free).

The **repeat purchase,** or conversion, objective is aimed at the percentage of consumers who try a new product and then purchase it a second time. A second purchase is reason for great rejoicing. The odds of long-term product success go way up when this percentage is high. In-package coupons and rebates on the initial purchases are IBP tools ideally suited to this objective.

Brand switching is the most competitively aggressive objective. In some product categories, switching is commonplace, even the norm—as in garbage bags or paper towels. In others, it is rare—as in toothpaste. When setting a brand-switching objective, the advertiser must neither expect too much nor rejoice too much over a temporary gain. Persuading consumers to switch brands can be a long and expensive task.

Finally, increasing sales as an objective hardly warrants mentioning. The only reason we included it in this list of objectives is that it often shows up in advertising plans. Yes, the advertiser likes to hear that you are going to "increase sales" with advertising and IBP dollars. But, is there a more lame statement of objective? There are two mortal problems with this statement of objective. First, advertising and IBP alone cannot increase sales. Only the right product, strategically priced, with proper distribution, and then effective advertising and promotion has the potential to increase sales. Second, to state that the objective is "to increase sales" is completely devoid of any strategic process or purpose. So, if you are ever on a team proposing objectives for advertising and IBP, don't ever say the objective is to increase sales. That's a marketing plan objective, not an advertising plan objective (see Insights Online [Exhibit 8.9] for a helpful example).

— LO ❷ —

8-4a **Communications versus Sales Objectives**

To follow up on the prior discussion of sales as an advertising plan objective, let's take the discussion one giant step further and distinguish between communication and sales as objectives. As just discussed, analysts argue that as a single variable in a firm's overall marketing mix, it is not reasonable to set strict sales expectations for advertising when other variables in the mix might undermine the advertising effort or be responsible for sales in the first place. In fact, some advertising analysts argue that communications objectives are the *only* legitimate objectives for advertising. This perspective has its underpinnings in the proposition that advertising is but one variable in the marketing mix and cannot be held solely responsible for sales. Rather, advertising should be held responsible for creating awareness of a brand, communicating information about product features or availability, or developing a favorable attitude that can lead to consumer preference for a brand. All of these outcomes are long term and based on communications impact.

There are some major benefits to maintaining a strict communications perspective in setting advertising objectives. First, by viewing advertising as primarily a communications effort, marketers can consider a broader range of advertising strategies. Second, they can gain a greater appreciation for the complexity of the overall communications process. Designing an integrated communications program with sales as the sole objective neglects aspects of message design, media choice, public relations, or sales force deployment that should be effectively integrated across all phases of a firm's communication efforts. Using advertising messages to support the efforts of the sales force and/or drive people to your website is an example of integrating diverse communication tools to build synergy that then may ultimately produce a sale.

Yet there is always a voice somewhere in the organization forcibly offering the perspective that there is only one rule: *Advertising must sell.*[9] Nowhere is the tension between communication and sales objectives better exemplified than in the annual debate about what advertisers really get for the tremendous sums of money they spend on Super Bowl ads. Every year, great fanfare accompanies the ads that appear during the Super Bowl, and numerous polls are taken after the game to assess the year's most memorable ads. But more often than not, these polls turn out to be nothing more than popularity contests, with the usual suspects—like Budweiser, Doritos, Go-Daddy, and those brash E-Trade babies—having all the fun.[10] But the question remains—Does likability translate to sales? If a Super Bowl ad introducing Sheryl Crow as the new spokesperson for a Revlon hair coloring product doesn't affect women's purchase intentions, can it be worth the millions of dollars it takes to produce and air it? And for that matter, who really believes that Sheryl Crow colors her hair herself out of a box?

Although there is a natural tension between those who advocate sales objectives and those who push communications objectives, nothing precludes a marketer from using both types when developing an overall plan for a brand. Indeed, combining marketing plan sales objectives such as market share and household penetration with advertising plan communications objectives such as awareness and attitude change can be an excellent means of motivating and evaluating the planning effort. Unilever, the big Dutch consumer goods conglomerate, seeks to strike just the right balance between communications and sales objectives with the strategy their Chief Marketing Officer (CMO) calls "magic along with logic." Unilever had a history of winning creative advertising awards (Cannes) but watching market share shrink. The CMO rebalanced the creative communications and sales emphasis and started producing sales growth in the 7 percent range—near the top of the firm's competitive set.[11]

Objectives that enable a firm to make intelligent decisions about resource allocation must be stated in an advertising plan in terms specific to the organization. Articulating such well-stated objectives is easier when advertising planners do the following:

1. **Establish a quantitative benchmark.** Objectives for advertising are measurable only in the context of quantifiable variables. Advertising planners should

begin with quantified measures of the current status of market share, awareness, attitude, or other factors that advertising is expected to influence. The measurement of effectiveness in quantitative terms requires a knowledge of the level of variables of interest before an advertising effort, and also afterward. For example, a statement of objectives in quantified terms might be, "Increase the market share of heavy users of the product category using our brand from 22 to 25 percent." In this case, a quantifiable and measurable market share objective is specified.

2. **Specify measurement methods and criteria for success.** It is important that the factors being measured be directly related to the objectives being pursued. It is of little use to try to increase the awareness of a brand with advertising and then judge the effects based on changes in sales. If changes in sales are expected, then measure sales. If increased awareness is the goal, then change in consumer awareness is the legitimate measure of success. This may seem obvious, but in a classic study of advertising objectives, it was found that claims of success for advertising were unrelated to the original statements of objective in 69 percent of the cases.[12] In this research, firms cited increases in sales as proof of success of advertising when the original objectives were related to factors such as awareness, conviction to a brand, or product-use information. But maybe that just says when sales do go up, we forget about everything else.

3. **Specify a time frame.** Objectives for advertising should include a statement of the period of time allowed for the desired results to occur. In some cases, as with direct-response advertising, the time frame may be related to a seasonal selling opportunity like the Christmas holiday period. For communications-based objectives, the measurement of results may not be undertaken until the end of an entire multi-week campaign. The point is that the time period for accomplishment of an objective and the related measurement period must be stated in advance in the ad plan.

These criteria for setting objectives help ensure that the planning process is organized and well directed. By relying on quantitative benchmarks, an advertiser has guidelines for making future decisions. Linking measurement criteria to objectives provides a basis for the equitable evaluation of the success or failure of advertising. Finally, the specification of a time frame for judging results keeps the planning process moving forward. As in all things, however, moderation is a good thing. A single-minded obsession with watching the numbers can be dangerous in that it minimizes or entirely misses the importance of qualitative and intuitive factors.

LO ❸

8-5 BUDGETING

One of the most agonizing tasks is budgeting the funds for an advertising and IBP effort. Normally, the responsibility for the budget lies with the firm itself. Within a firm, budget recommendations come up through the ranks; for example, from a brand manager to a category manager and ultimately to the executive in charge of marketing. The sequence then reverses itself for the allocation and spending of funds. In a small firm, such as an independent retailer, the sequence just described may include only one individual who plays all the roles. In large firms, one might think that the CMO would be responsible for allocating funds. But recently, CMOs have begun focusing their attention on the bigger picture and pushing the budgetary authority and responsibility down the organization to the vice president of communications or brand strategy levels.[13]

In some cases, a firm will rely on its advertising agency to make recommendations regarding the size of the advertising budget. When this is done, it is typically the account executive at the agency in charge of the brand who will analyze the firm's objectives and its creative and media needs and then make a recommendation to the company. The account exec's budget planning will likely include working closely with the brand and product-group managers to determine an appropriate spending level. (See Insights Online [Exhibit 8.10] for an interesting example of how the U.S. Defense industry handled recent budget constraints.)

To be as judicious and accountable as possible in spending money on advertising and IBP, marketers rely on various methods for setting an advertising budget. To appreciate the benefits (and failings) of these methods, we will consider each of them in turn.

8-5a Percentage of Sales

A **percentage-of-sales approach** to budgeting calculates the budget based on a percentage of the prior year's sales or the projected year's sales. This technique is easy to understand and implement. The budget decision makers merely specify that a particular percentage of either last year's sales or the current year's estimated sales will be allocated to the advertising process. It is common to spend between 2 and 12 percent of sales on advertising and IBP depending on the product category. Remember from Chapter 2 that Walmart's billion-dollar-plus budget was less than 1 percent of sales, while a firm like L'Oreal might spend 12 percent of sales.

Even though simplicity is certainly an advantage in decision making, the percentage-of-sales approach is fraught with problems. First, when a firm's sales are decreasing, the advertising budget will automatically decline. Periods of decreasing sales may be precisely the time when a firm needs to increase spending on advertising; if a percentage-of-sales budgeting method is being used, this won't happen. Second, this budgeting method can easily result in overspending on advertising. Once funds have been earmarked, the tendency is to find ways to spend the budgeted amount. Third, and the most serious drawback from a strategic standpoint, is that the percentage-of-sales approach does not relate advertising and IBP dollars to objectives in any way. Basing spending on past or future sales is devoid of analytical evaluation and implicitly presumes a direct cause-and-effect relationship between advertising and sales. But here, we have sales "causing" advertising. That's backward!

A variation on the percentage-of-sales approach is to base current spending on "historical spending levels"—whatever that is. The only reason we raise this perspective here is that when managers are asked how they allocate their advertising budgets, nearly 70 percent have responded to surveys with the answer "based on historical levels."[14] We suspect they are referring to percentage-of-sales or an even less defendable "whatever we can get" approach to spending, but we want to alert you to the prospect of hearing language like this in budget discussions.

8-5b Share of Market/Share of Voice

With this method, a firm monitors the amount spent by various significant competitors on advertising and allocates an amount equal to the amount of money spent by competitors or an amount proportional to (or slightly greater than) the firm's market share relative to the competition.[15] This will provide the advertiser with a **share of voice**, or an advertising presence in the market, that is equal to or greater than the competitors' share of advertising voice. Exhibit 8.11 shows the share of market and share of voice for automakers in the United States.

This method is often used for advertising-budget allocations when a new product is introduced. Conventional wisdom suggests that some multiple of the desired first-year market share, often 2.5 to 4 times, should be spent in terms of share-of-voice advertising expenditures. For example, if an advertiser wants a 2 percent first-year share, it would need to spend up to 8 percent of the total dollar amount spent in the

EXHIBIT 8.11 Share of market versus share of voice for major car manufacturers in 2002 (in U.S. dollars).

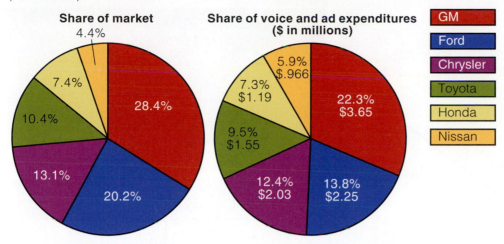

Source: Market share information taken from *Market Share Report*, 2004 and *Los Angeles Times*, January 4, 2003, p. C1. Share of voice-ad expenditures calculated from 100 Leading Nation Advertisers, *Advertising Age*, Special Report, June 23, 2003 and Domestic Advertising Spending by Company, *Advertising Age*, 2002.

industry (for an 8 percent share of voice). The logic is that a new product will need a significant share of voice to gain notice among a group of existing, well-established brands.[16]

Although the share-of-voice approach is sound in its emphasis on competitors' activities, there are important challenges to consider with this approach. First, it may be difficult to gain access to precise information on competitors' spending. Second, there is no reason to believe that competitors are spending their money wisely. Third, the flaw in logic with this method is the assumption that every advertising/IBP effort is of the same quality and will have the same effect from a creative-execution standpoint. Such an assumption is especially shaky when one tries to compare expenditure levels across today's diverse advertising forms. Take Dove's experience with Super Bowl advertising versus its short film placed on YouTube. The film, *Dove Evolution*, generated the biggest traffic spike ever at CampaignForRealBeauty.com, three times more than Dove's Super Bowl ad.[17] The YouTube video aired for $0, versus $2 million or so for the Super Bowl ad. No doubt that *Dove Evolution* was a huge contributor to Dove's share-of-voice at the time, but predicting the effects of innovative executions such as this one will always challenge conventional models.

8-5c **Response Models**

Using response models to aid the budgeting process has been a widespread practice among larger firms for many years.[18] The belief is that greater objectivity can be maintained with such models. Although this may or may not be the case, response models do provide useful information on what a given company's advertising response function looks like. An **advertising response function** is a mathematical relationship that associates dollars spent on advertising and sales generated. To the extent that past advertising predicts future sales, this method is valuable. Using marginal analysis, an advertiser would continue spending on advertising as long as its marginal spending was exceeded by marginal sales. Margin analysis answers the advertiser's question, "How much more will sales increase if we spend an additional dollar on advertising?" As the rate of return on advertising expenditures declines, the wisdom of additional spending is challenged.

Theoretically, this method leads to a point where an optimal advertising expenditure results in an optimal sales level and, in turn, an optimal profit. The relationship between sales, profit, and advertising spending is shown in the marginal analysis graph in Exhibit 8.12. Data on sales, prior advertising expenditures, and consumer awareness are typical of the numerical input to such quantitative models.

Unfortunately, the advertising-to-sales relationship assumes simple causality, and we know that that assumption isn't true. Many other factors, in addition to advertising, affect sales directly. Still, some feel that the use of response models is a better budgeting method than guessing or applying the percentage-of-sales or other budgeting methods discussed thus far.

8-5d **Objective and Task**

The methods for establishing an advertising budget just discussed all suffer from the same fundamental deficiency: a lack of specification of how expenditures are related to advertising objectives. The only method of budget setting that focuses on the relationship between spending and advertising/IBP objectives is the **objective-and-task approach.** This method begins with the stated objectives for a campaign. Goals related to production costs, target audience reach, message effects, behavioral effects, media placement, duration of the effort, and the like are specified. Then, the budget is formulated by identifying the specific tasks necessary to achieve different aspects of the objectives.

EXHIBIT 8.12 Sales, profit, and advertising curves used in marginal analysis.

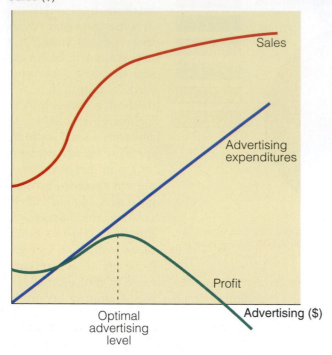

Source: David A. Aaker, Rajeev Batra, and John G. Meyers, *Advertising Management*, 4th ed. (Englewood Cliffs, N.J.: Prentice-Hall, 1992), 469. Reprinted by permission of the authors.

EXHIBIT 8.13 Steps in implementing the objective-and-task budgeting approach.

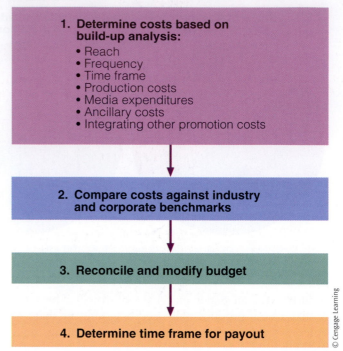

There is a lot to recommend this procedure for budgeting. A firm identifies any and all tasks it believes are related to achieving its objectives. Should the total dollar figure for the necessary tasks be beyond the firm's financial capability, reconciliation must be found. But even if reconciliation and a subsequent reduction of the budget result, the firm has at least identified what *should* have been budgeted to pursue its objectives.

The objective-and-task approach is the most logical and defensible method for calculating and then allocating an advertising and IBP budget. It is the only budgeting method that specifically relates spending to the objectives being pursued. It is widely used among major advertisers. For these reasons, we will consider the specific procedures for implementing the objective-and-task budgeting method.

8-5e Implementing the Objective-and-Task Budgeting Method

Proper implementation of the objective-and-task approach requires a data-based, systematic procedure. Because the approach ties spending levels to specific advertising goals, the process depends on proper execution of the objective-setting process described earlier. Once a firm and its agency are satisfied with the specificity and direction of stated objectives, a series

of well-defined steps can be taken to implement the objective-and-task method. These steps are shown in Exhibit 8.13 and summarized in the following sections.

Determine Costs Based on Build-up Analysis. Having identified specific objectives, an advertiser can now begin determining what tasks are necessary for the accomplishment of those objectives. In using a **build-up analysis**—building up the expenditure levels for tasks—the following factors must be considered in terms of costs:

- *Reach.* The geographic and demographic exposure the advertising is to achieve.

- *Frequency.* The number of exposures required to accomplish desired objectives.

- *Time frame.* Estimate when communications will occur and during what period of time.

- *Production costs.* The decision maker can rely on creative personnel and producers to estimate the costs associated with the planned execution of advertisements.

- *Media expenditures.* Given the preceding factors, the advertiser can now define the appropriate media, media mix, and frequency of insertions that will directly address objectives set earlier. Further, differences in geographic allocation, with special attention to regional or local media strategies, and digital and mobile strategies are considered at this point. The complete discussion of strategic allocation of funds across and between different media will be covered in Chapters 12 through 14.

- *Ancillary costs.* There will be a variety of related costs not directly accounted for in the preceding factors. Prominent among these are costs associated with advertising to the trade and specialized research unique to the campaign.

- *Integrating other promotional costs.* In this era of advertising and IBP, sometimes it is the novel promotion that delivers the best bang for the buck. New and improved forms of brand promotion, like the one illustrated in Exhibit 8.14, must also be considered as part of the planning and budgeting process.

Compare Costs against Industry and Corporate Benchmarks.
After compiling all the costs through a build-up analysis, an advertiser will want to make a quick reality check. This is accomplished by checking the percentage of sales that the estimated set of costs represents relative to industry standards for percentage of sales allocated to advertising. If most competitors are spending 4 to 6 percent of gross sales on advertising, how does the current budget compare to this percentage? Another recommended technique is to identify the share of industry advertising that the firm's budget represents. Another relevant reference point is to compare the current budget with prior budgets. If the total dollar amount is extraordinarily high or low compared to previous years, this variance should be justified based on the objectives being pursued. The use of percentage of sales on both an industry and internal corporate basis provides a reference point only. The percentage-of-sales figures are not used for decision making per se (as discussed earlier), but rather as a benchmark to judge whether a budgeted amount is so unusual as to need reevaluation.

Reconcile and Modify the Budget.
There is always a fear that the proposed budget will not meet with approval. It may not be viewed as consistent with corporate policy related to advertising expense, or it may be considered beyond the financial capabilities of the organization. Modifications to a proposed budget are common, but having to make radical cuts in proposed spending is disruptive. The objective-and-task approach is designed to identify what a firm will need to spend in order to achieve the desired impact. To have the budget level compromised after such planning can result in an impotent advertising effort because necessary tasks cannot be funded.

Every precaution should be taken against having to radically modify a budget. Planners should be totally aware of corporate policy and financial circumstances *during* the objective-setting and subsequent task-planning phases. This will help reduce the extent of budget modification.

Determine a Time Frame for Payout.
It is important that budget decision makers recognize when the budget will be available for funding the tasks associated with the proposed effort. Travel expenses, production expenses, and media time and space are tied to specific calendar dates. For example, media time and space are often acquired and paid for far in advance of the completion of finished advertisements. Knowing when and how much money is needed improves the odds of the plan being carried out smoothly.

If these procedures are followed for the objective-and-task approach, an advertiser will have a defendable budget with which to pursue key objectives. One point to be made, however, is that the budget should not be viewed as the final word in funding an advertising effort. The dynamic nature of the market and rapid developments in media require flexibility in budget execution. This can mean changes in expenditure levels; it can also mean changes in payout allocation.

EXHIBIT 8.14 What could be better on a warm summer day than a stroll down Chicago's Navy Pier? Smart marketers like Best Buy want to be part of your day, and thus they bring their high-tech playground right to where the action is. The idea here is to build deeper relationships with potential customers by contributing to their good times in a special venue. Converts, sporting events, fairs, and carnivals are all great places to show off your brand.

Like any other business activity, a marketer must take on an advertising effort with clearly specified intentions for what is to be accomplished. Intentions and expectations for advertising are embodied in the process of setting objectives. Armed with information from market planning and an assessment of the type of advertising needed to support marketing plans, advertising objectives can be set. These objectives should be in place before steps are taken to determine a budget for the advertising effort and before the creative work begins. Again, this is not always the order of things, even though it should be. These objectives will also affect the plans for media placement.

8-6 STRATEGY

Returning now to the other major components of the advertising plan (revisiting Exhibit 8.1 is a good idea at this point), next up is strategy. Strategy represents the mechanism by which something is to be done. It is an expression of the means to an end. All of the other factors are supposed to result in a strategy. Strategy is what you do, given the situation and objectives. There are numerous possibilities for advertising strategies. For example, if you are trying to get more top-of-the-mind awareness for your brand of chewing gum, a simple strategy would be to employ a high-frequency, name-repetition campaign (Double your pleasure with Doublemint, Doublemint, Doublemint gum). Exhibit 8.15 presents an ad from Danskin's campaign designed to address a more ambitious objective; that is, broadening the appeal of the brand beyond dance accessories and repositioning the brand to the much larger fitness-wear market. Danskin's advertising strategy thus features unique "fitness" celebrities as implicit endorsers of the brand.

More sophisticated goals call for more sophisticated strategies. You are limited only by your resources: financial, organizational, and creative. Ultimately, strategy formulation is a creative endeavor. It is best learned through the study of what others have done in similar situations and through a thorough analysis of the focal consumer. To assist in strategy formulation, a growing number of ad agencies have created a position called the account planner. This person's job is to synthesize all relevant consumer research and draw inferences from it that will help define a coherent advertising strategy. You will learn a great deal more about the connection between ad objectives and creative strategy options in Chapter 10.

EXHIBIT 8.15 This ad provides an excellent example of repositioning strategy. The slogan says is all: "Danskin—Not Just for Dancing."

She picked up her toys.
She picked up her cat.
She picked up her clothes.

Danskin is the proud sponsor of the
National Association for Girls & Women in Sport 1993 Wade Trophy

Please call 1-800-288-6749 for more information. Danskin fitness wear is available at Sports Authority, SportMart, Academy and other fine stores nationwide. Made from Lycra® spandex and Supplex® nylon. Lycra and Supplex are registered trademarks of Dupont. ©1994 Danskin, Inc.

Danskin, Inc.

Now she picks up her husband.

Carla Dunlap Kaan
Bodybuilder
World Professional Champion
Former Ms Olympia
Member Team Danskin

DANSKIN
Not Just for Dancing.

Danskin, Inc.

8-7 **EXECUTION**

The actual "doing" is the execution of the plan. It is the making and placing of ads across all media. To quote a famous bit of advertising copy from a tire manufacturer, this is where "the rubber meets the road." There are two elements to the execution of an advertising plan: determining the copy strategy and devising a media plan.

8-7a **Copy Strategy**

A copy strategy consists of copy objectives and methods, or tactics. The objectives state what the advertiser intends to accomplish in headlines, subheads, and text, while the methods describe how the objectives will be achieved. Chapter 11 will deal extensively with these executional issues.

8-7b **Media Plan**

The media plan specifies exactly where ads will be placed and what strategy is behind their placement. In an integrated communications environment, this is much more complicated than it might first appear. Back when there were just three broadcast television networks, there were already more than a million different combinations of placements that could be made. With the explosion of media and promotion options today, the permutations are almost infinite.

It is at this point—devising a media plan—where all the money is spent, and so much could be saved. This is where the profitability of many agencies is really determined. Media placement strategy can make a huge difference in profits or losses and is considered in depth in Part 4 of the text. In addition, the dynamic influence on media planning of devices like iPad, Kindle, Droid, iPhone, HP Slate, and many more is another point of emphasis in Part 4. Mobile marketing programs developed specifically for the likes of iPad promise to cut media spend with precisely targeted messages delivered at precisely the right time.[19]

8-7c **Integrated Brand Promotion**

Many different forms of brand promotion may accompany the advertising effort in launching or maintaining a brand; these should be spelled out as part of the overall plan. There should be a complete integration of all communication tools in working up the plan. For example, in the launch of its Venus shaving system for women, Gillette had the usual multimillion-dollar budget allocation for traditional mass media. But along with its aggressive advertising effort, several other promotional tools were deployed.[20] At the Gillette Venus website, women could sign up for an online sweepstakes to win vacations in Hawaii, New York City, and Tuscany, and provide friends' email addresses to increase their own chances of winning. Gillette also put a pair of 18-wheelers on the road to spread the word about Venus at beaches, concerts, college campuses, and store openings. So the launch of Venus integrated tools that ran the gamut from TV ads to the Web to Interstate 95. You'll learn much more about a variety of IBP tools in Part 5.

8-8 **EVALUATION**

Last but not least in an ad plan is the evaluation component. This is where an advertiser determines how the agency will be graded: what criteria will be applied and how long the agency will have to achieve the agreed-on objectives. It's critically important for the advertiser and agency to align around evaluation criteria up front. John Wanamaker's classic line still captures the challenge associated with evaluation; he said, "I know half my advertising is wasted, I just don't know which half." In a world where the pressures on companies to deliver short-term profitability continue to intensify, advertising agencies find themselves under increasing pressure to show quantifiable outcomes from all advertising and IBP activities.

8-9 **THE ROLE OF THE AGENCY IN PLANNING ADVERTISING AND IBP**

Now that we have covered key aspects of the advertising planning process, one other issue should be considered. Because most marketers rely heavily on the expertise of an advertising agency, understanding the role an agency plays in the advertising planning process is important. Various agencies will approach their craft with different points of emphasis. Even though not everyone does it the same way, it is still important to ask: What contribution to the planning effort can and should an advertiser expect from its agency? (See Insights Online [Exhibit 8.16] for an interesting example.)

The discussion of advertising planning to this point has emphasized that the marketer is responsible for the marketing-planning inputs as a type of self-assessment that identifies the firm's basis for offering value to customers. This assessment should also clearly identify, in the external environment, the opportunities and threats that can be addressed with advertising. A firm should bring to the planning effort a well-articulated

> **INSIGHTS ONLINE**
>
> **8.16** Go online to see the AdAge feature, "In an Innovative Media Execution by Ad Agency Dentsu Tokyo, an Augmented Reality Smartphone App Changes Newspaper Stories to a Child-Friendly Format."

statement of a brand's value proposition and the marketing mix elements designed to gain and sustain competitive advantage. However, when client and agency are working in harmony, the agency may take an active role in helping the client formulate the marketing plan. Indeed, when things are going right, it can be hard to say exactly where the client's work ended and the agency's work began. This is the essence of teamwork, and as Steve Jobs noted about working with Apple's long-time partner, TBWA/Chiat/Day: "Creating great advertising, like creating great products, is a team effort." The agency's crucial role is to translate the current market and marketing status of a firm and its advertising objectives into advertising strategy and, ultimately, finished advertisements and IBP materials. Here, message strategies and tactics for the advertising effort and for the efficient and effective placement of ads in media need to be hammered out. At this point, the firm (as a good client) should turn to its agency for the expertise and talent needed for planning and executing at the stage where design and creative execution bring marketing strategies to life.

In the final analysis, it's really no mystery what agencies and clients want from each other. Marketers/clients know they need help in two key areas. The first involves integration. Clients have trouble keeping up with the dynamic media environment and expect their agency to be an expert on a wide array of options for getting the message out to the target consumer. So they need the various divisions and departments in an agency to be working as a team, coming up with communication solutions that build synergy between and among multiple channels. Simply stated, they want *integrated* brand promotion. Second, clients know they need new ideas and fresh approaches to break through the ever-increasing clutter in today's marketplace. Here again, the agency will be expected to ride to the rescue. Even though creativity can be an elusive aim, nonetheless, clients expect it. In fact, a survey that posed the simple question, "What do clients want?" discovered the top four priorities to be creativity (92.7 percent), data and analytics (92.0 percent), efficient business processes (91.4 percent), and effective money managers (89.4 percent).[21]

In addition, an agency should never be shocked to learn that clients expect results from their investment in advertising. The relationship will unravel quickly if an agency is not sensitive to this issue. The best way for agencies to stay on top of this key issue is to spend lots of time and attention on the client's business during the ad planning process so that everyone is clear on the goals for a campaign and the metrics that will be used in judging success or failure (as discussed earlier in communications versus sales as objectives). Most clients are reasonable people. They don't expect magic. They can live with an occasional failure. But if a campaign didn't work, the client will want to understand why, and will certainly expect better results the next time around.

Agencies also have a set of things that they want from every client. Here again the list starts with the need for collaboration and mutual respect. The agency wants to be treated as a partner, not a vendor. The agency also needs the time and resources so that it can do its best work. But of course, there is never enough time and the budget is never large enough. There are two things clients must do to help everyone cope with resource issues. First, get the agency involved early in the planning process so that the agency is well informed about dates and deadlines. Second, the agency needs honest, upfront assessments regarding budget. Everyone is used to a world where one must do more with less. But it kills a relationship to find out at the last minute, "Oh no, we never had the funding for something like that."

Finally, because agencies know that clients are going to be results oriented, they are looking for clients that will set them up for success. Agencies love clients who can articulate clearly the outcomes they seek. Agencies love clients that provide constructive and timely feedback. Agencies love clients who respect and value their expertise and are ready to step aside and let the agency do its thing when the time is right. When you have that kind of trust in your expertise, you also have a partner (see Insights Online [Exhibit 8.17] for an excellent example).

INSIGHTS ONLINE

8.17 Go online to see the AdAge feature, "Ad Agency DDB Honors Australia and Works with McDonald's to Change Name to 'Macca's' in Australia."

SUMMARY

1 **Describe the basic components of an advertising plan.**

An advertising plan is motivated by the marketing planning process and provides the direction that ensures proper implementation of an advertising campaign. An advertising plan incorporates decisions about the segments to be targeted, communications and/or sales objectives with respect to these segments, and salient message appeals. The plan should also specify the dollars budgeted for the campaign, the various communication tools that will be employed to deliver the messages, and the measures that will be relied on to assess the campaign's effectiveness.

Compare and contrast two fundamental approaches for setting advertising objectives.

Setting appropriate objectives is a crucial step in developing any advertising plan. These objectives are typically stated in terms of either communications or sales goals. Both types of goals have their proponents, and the appropriate types of objectives to emphasize will vary with the situation. Communications objectives feature goals such as building brand awareness or reinforcing consumers' beliefs about a brand's key benefits. Sales objectives are just that: They hold advertising directly responsible for increasing sales of a brand.

 Explain various methods for setting advertising budgets.

Perhaps the most challenging aspect of any advertising campaign is arriving at a proper budget allocation. Companies and their advertising agencies work with several different methods to arrive at an advertising budget. A percentage-of-sales approach is a simple but naive way to deal with this issue. In the share-of-voice approach, the activities of key competitors are factored into the budget-setting process. A variety of quantitative models may also be used for budget determination. The objective-and-task approach is difficult to implement, but with practice it is likely to yield the best value for a client's advertising dollars.

④ **Discuss the role of the agency in formulating an advertising plan.**

An advertising plan will be a powerful tool when firms partner with their advertising agencies in its development. The firm can lead this process by doing its homework with respect to marketing strategy development and objective setting. The agency can then play a key role in managing the preparation and placement phases of campaign execution.

KEY TERMS

advertising plan
situation analysis
ethnocentrism
self-reference criterion (SRC)
industry analysis
market analysis

competitor analysis
brand awareness
top-of-the-mind awareness
purchase intent
trial usage
repeat purchase

brand switching
percentage-of-sales approach
share of voice
advertising response function
objective-and-task approach
build-up analysis

ENDNOTES

1. Norihiko Shirouzu, "In Chinese Market, Toyota's Strategy Is Made in USA," *The Wall Street Journal,* May 26, 2006, A1, A8.

2. Laurel Wentz, "China's Ad World: A New Crisis Every Day," *Advertising Age,* December 11, 2006, 6.

3. Schumpeter, "The Emerging-World Consumer Is King," *The Economist,* January 5, 2013, 53.

4. Stephanie Thompson, "Low-Carb Craze Blitzes Food Biz," *Advertising Age,* January 5, 2004, 1, 22.

5. Niraj Sheth and Yukari Kane, "Phone Makers Scramble to Stand Out," *online.wsj.com,* October 28, 2009.

6. Rita Chang, "With $100M Saturation Campaign, Droid Will Be Impossible to Avoid," *Advertising Age,* November 9, 2009, 3, 34.

7. Suzanne Vranica, "How a Gecko Shook Up Insurance Ads," *The Wall Street Journal,* January 2, 2007, B1.

8. Natalie Zmuda, "Behind the Scenes of Coca-Cola's Super Bowl and 2013 Ad Plans," *Advertising Age,* February 4, 2013, www.adage.com; accessed February 6, 2013.

9. Sergio Zyman, *The End of Advertising as We Know It* (Hoboken, NJ: Wiley, 2002).

10. "Top 10 Best-Liked, Most-Recalled TV Spots of 2009," adage.com, January 11, 2010.

11. Jack Neff, "How Unilever Found the Balance between Creativity and Sales," *Advertising Age,* September 10, 2012, 58.

12. Stewart Henderson Britt, "Are So-Called Successful Advertising Campaigns Really Successful?" *Journal of Advertising Research,* vol. 9 (1969), 5–15.

13. Brian Steinberg, "Meet the Marketing Execs Who Dole Out the Money," *Advertising Age,* September 9, 2012, www.adage.com; accessed September 10, 2012.

14. Jack Neff, "Marketers Don't Practice ROI They Preach," *Advertising Age,* March 12, 2012, 1, 19.

15. The classic treatment of this method was first offered by James O. Peckham, "Can We Relate Advertising Dollars to Market-Share Objectives?" in Malcolm A. McGiven (Ed.), *How Much to Spend for Advertising* (New York: Association of National Advertisers, 1969), 24.

16. James C. Shroer, "Ad Spending: Growing Market Share," *Harvard Business Review* (January–February 1990), 44–50.

17. Jack Neff, "A Real Beauty: Dove's Viral Makes a Big Splash for No Cash," *Advertising Age,* October 10, 2006, 1, 45.

18. James E. Lynch and Graham J. Hooley, "Increasing Sophistication in Advertising Budget Setting," *Journal of Advertising Research,* vol. 19 (February–March 1990), 72.

19. Niraj Chokshi, "Apple's iPad Advertising Aspirations," *theatlantic.com /business,* March 29, 2010.

20. Betsy Spethmann, "Venus Rising," *Promo Magazine,* April 2001, 52–61.

21. Julie Liesse, "What Clients Want," *Advertising Age,* July 12, 2012, C4–C5.

PART 3

The Creative Process

This section of the text marks an important transition in our study of advertising and integrated brand promotion (IBP). The topics to this point have laid out the essential process and planning issues that make advertising and IBP powerful business communication tools. Now we need to take the plunge into the actual preparation of advertising and IBP materials.

Creativity is the soul of advertising and IBP. Without the creative execution, no one will pay any attention. It's the one thing that communication cannot get by without. Yet most advertising and promotion books treat it as either a bunch of creative "rules" or dry lectures about the value of various fonts. We take a different approach. We first consider the idea of creativity itself: What is it, what distinguishes it, what is its beauty, when is it a beast? What makes creative people creative? We then present the creative/managerial interface, which doesn't always go smoothly but is a real and valuable part of the creative process. We discuss honestly what many textbooks don't mention at all: the problem of the competing reward systems of brand managers, account executives, and creatives. We then offer a chapter like no other—Creative Message Strategy—in which we detail message strategies and their strategic pluses and minuses. We then offer the best basic chapter on copywriting, art direction, and production available. These chapters have been developed and refined with constant input from industry professionals. If you read them carefully, you will know a lot about the process and execution of the creative effort.

CHAPTER 9

Managing Creativity in Advertising and IBP A famous dancer once said, "If I could describe dancing, I wouldn't have to do it." Well, we feel the same way about creativity in advertising—it really is impossible to describe fully. But in Chapter 9, "Managing Creativity in Advertising and IBP," we do our best to give you insights into the creative process by giving examples of how the creative process is worked out in an advertising context—how the "creatives" work with the "strategists." Here, special attention is paid to working through the tension that inevitably arises in the creative/management interface. Beyond strategy and management, though, we also try to provide insight into this wonderfully slippery thing called creativity. We do this by drawing on many sources and on the examples of some of the most creative minds of the past century, from physics to painting. Although creativity is creativity, we move from the general discussion to the particular context of advertising creativity and its unique opportunities and problems. Creativity is the soul of advertising, and this chapter tries to reveal the magic of advertising that comes from the creativity.

CHAPTER 10

Creative Message Strategy is a chapter like no other anywhere. We take key and primary message objectives and the multiple matching strategies of each and explore them in detail—including the newest strategic objective of tying a brand's appeal to social and cultural movements (think "green"). We give you a lot of specific real-world examples and walk you through each one. We discuss the advantages and disadvantages of each and tell you when they should be used and when they should not.

CHAPTER 11

Executing the Creative Chapters 9 and 10 establish the process and context for the creative effort. Chapter 11 follows through on that context and describes the actual effort involved in bringing the "creative" to life through copywriting, art direction, and production. Executing the creative begins with the "creative brief": the details relating to how the creative effort can be manifest in the presentation of a brand to the target audiences. The entire creative team—copywriter, art director, account planner, and media planner—works together with the creative brief to build ads for any and all media including digital media. Copywriting explores the development of copy, including guidelines for writing effective copy and common mistakes in copywriting. A full discussion of print, broadcast, and digital/interactive copy formats is considered. A typical copy approval process used by advertisers and agencies is also presented. In this chapter you will first learn about creating effective print advertisements destined for magazines, newspapers, and direct-marketing promotions and then move on to the exciting and complex process of creating broadcast advertising. The emphasis in this chapter is on the creative team and how creative concepts are brought to life. Once again, art direction and production for application in digital/interactive media, including mobile marketing applications, are considered.

CHAPTER 9

Managing Creativity in Advertising and IBP

After reading and thinking about this chapter, you will be able to do the following:

1 Describe the core characteristics of great creative minds.

2 Contrast the role of an agency's creative department with that of business managers/account executives and explain the tensions between them.

3 Assess the role of teams in managing tensions and promoting creativity in advertising and IBP applications.

4 Examine yourself and your own passion for creativity.

9-1 WHY DOES ADVERTISING THRIVE ON CREATIVITY?

Why do humans need oxygen? The question makes about as much sense.

So what is it about creativity that makes it such a big deal in the advertising business? Why do successful marketing firms like Procter & Gamble send their employees on expensive junkets to the Cannes Lions International Advertising Festival to make connections with the best creative minds in the ad business? Why is creativity the secret sauce that determines the winners and losers?

Let's start with clutter. Clutter is the enemy of effective advertising. Great creative can defeat clutter. Everyone hates ad clutter. But, to try to overcome clutter, advertisers generate more ads, which just increases the clutter. Yes, clutter begets clutter in a process that no one seems to be able to shut off.[1] If you want your message heard and seen, you'll need a way to stand out from the crowd, and that will require good, perhaps even great creativity. Research shows that a primary benefit of award-winning, creative ads is that they break through the clutter

and get remembered.[2] But creativity in advertising is a lot more than getting attention; it makes the ads or other branding efforts make sense to consumers, it sets the agenda, and gives meaning to the brand. And since brands are packages of popular meaning,[3] then there is no sustainable branding without message creativity.

Another way of saying it is that great brands make meaningful, often emotional, connections with consumers. You can advertise your tires through a lot of mundane details, or you can engage consumers emotionally, as in Exhibit 9.1. Brands make emotional connections when they engage consumers through sensory experiences and emotional episodes.[4] Advertising and IBP in their many forms help create these experiences, but great creative execution brings it all to life. For instance, Apple's iPod wasn't the first MP3 player. Creative Technology Ltd. had a good one on the market almost two years before Apple.[5] But the iPod was the first MP3 player to be brought to the market with great advertising—advertising that made iPod synonymous with hip and cool; advertising that made the brand relevant in social context. Think of elegant creative genius of the iPod silhouettes.

EXHIBIT 9.1 Don't overthink it—it's an emotional appeal.

GRAFFIA
L'ASFALTO

YOKOHAMA
Specie Tecnologiche

Advertising Agency: IDUE

EXHIBIT 9.2 How does this ad use creativity to define the brand and give it meaning?

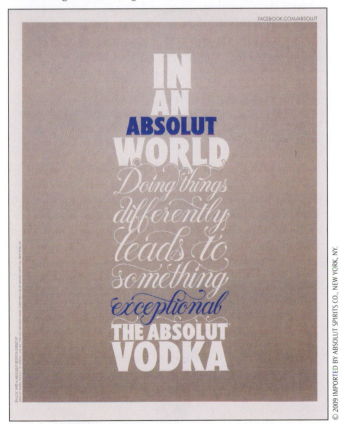

FACEBOOK.COM/ABSOLUT

IN AN ABSOLUT WORLD
Doing things differently leads to something exceptional
THE ABSOLUT VODKA

© 2009 IMPORTED BY ABSOLUT SPIRITS CO., NEW YORK, NY.

They were everywhere and we couldn't stop watching them. They showed us what we needed to do if we too wanted to become cool. The creatives for Absolut (Exhibit 9.2) turned a rather low–class liquor into a hip new thing. Look at the ad in Exhibit 9.2; why was this campaign both creative and successful? What makes it creative?

9-2 CREATIVITY ACROSS DOMAINS

The creative mind plays with the objects it loves.

—C. G. Jung[6]

Before examining how the creative function plays out in the world of advertising and IBP, let's consider creativity as it manifests in other domains. Creativity, in its essence, is the same no matter what the domain. People who create, create, whether they write novels, take photographs, ponder the particle physics that drives the universe, craft poetry, write songs, play a musical instrument, dance, make films, design buildings, paint, or make ads. Great ads can be truly great creative accomplishments.

Creativity is the ability to consider and hold together seemingly inconsistent elements and forces, making a new connection. This ability to step outside of everyday logic, to free oneself of thinking in terms of "the way things are" or "the way things have to be," apparently allows creative people to put things together in a way that, once we see it, makes sense, is interesting, and is thus, creative. To see love and hate as the same entity, to see "round squares," or to imagine time bending like molten steel is to have this ability. Ideas born of creativity reveal their own logic, and then we all say, "Oh, I see."

Creativity is usually seen as a gift—a special way of seeing the world. Throughout the ages, creative people have been seen as special, revered, and reviled. They have served as powerful political instruments (for good and evil), and they have been ostracized, imprisoned, and killed for their art. Creativity has been associated with various forms of madness:

> *Madness, provided it comes as the gift of heaven, is the channel by which we receive the greatest blessings… [T]he men of old who gave their names saw no disgrace or reproach in madness; otherwise they would not have connected it with the name of the noblest of all arts, the art of discerning the future, and called by our ancestors, madness is a nobler thing than sober sense… [M]adness comes from God, whereas sober sense is merely human.*

—Socrates[7]

Creativity reflects early childhood experiences, social circumstances, and cognitive styles. In one of the best books ever written on creativity, *Creating Minds,* Howard Gardner examines the lives and works of seven of the greatest creative minds of the 20th century: Sigmund Freud, Albert Einstein, Pablo Picasso, Igor Stravinsky, T. S. Eliot, Martha Graham, and Mahatma Gandhi.[8]

His work reveals fascinating similarities among great creators. All seven of these individuals, from physicist to modern dancer, were self-confident, alert, unconventional, hardworking, and committed obsessively to their work. Social life or hobbies are almost immaterial, representing at most a fringe on the creator's work time.[9]

Apparently, total commitment to one's craft is the rule. Although this commitment sounds positive, there is also a darker reflection:

> *The self confidence merges with egotism, egocentrism, and narcissism: highly absorbed, not only wholly involved in his or her own projects, but likely to pursue them at costs of other individuals.*[10]

Let's be clear: One should not stand between a great creator and his or her work. It's not safe. Or maybe the creator will just ignore you. Not coincidentally, these great creative minds had troubled personal lives and simply did not have time for ordinary people (such as their families). According to Gardner, they were generally not very good to those around them. This was true even of Gandhi.

All seven of these great creative geniuses were also great self-promoters. Well-recognized creative people are not typically shy about seeking exposure for their work. Apparently, fame in the creative realm rarely comes to the self-effacing and timid.

All seven of these great creators were, very significantly, childlike in a critical way. All of them had the ability to see things as a child does. Einstein spent much of his career revolutionizing physics by pursuing in no small way an idea he produced as a child: What would it be like to move along a strand of pure light? Picasso commented that it ultimately was his ability to paint like a child (along with amazingly superior technical skills) that explained much of his greatness. Freud's obsession with and interpretation of his childhood dreams had a significant role in what is one of his most significant works, *The Interpretation of Dreams.*[11] T. S. Eliot's poetry demonstrated imaginative abilities that typically disappear past childhood. The same is true of Martha Graham's modern dance. Even Gandhi's particular form of social action was formulated with a very simple and childlike logic at its base. These artists and creative thinkers never lost the ability to see the ordinary as extraordinary, to not have their particular form of imagination beaten out of them by the process of "growing up."

Of course, the problem with this childlike thinking is that these individuals also behaved as children

> *So the trick is, how do you get creatives to want to pursue cool ads that also sell?*

throughout most of their lives. Their social behavior was often selfish. They expected those around them to be willing to sacrifice at the altar of their gift. Gardner put it this way: "The carnage around a great creator is not a pretty sight, and this destructiveness occurs whether the individual is engaged in solitary pursuit or ostensibly working for the betterment of humankind."[12] They can, however, be extraordinarily charming when it suits their ambitions. They could be monsters at home, and darlings when performing.

Apparently, creative minds also desire marginality.[13] They love being outsiders. This marginality seems to have been absolutely necessary to these people and provided them with some requisite energy.

Emotional stability did not mark these creative lives either. All but Gandhi had a major mental breakdown at some point in their lives, and Gandhi suffered from at least two periods of severe depression. Extreme creativity, just as the popular myth suggests, seems to come at some psychological price.

9-2a Creative Genius in the Advertising Business

Although not as influential as the Gandhis or the Freuds, it is common to see individuals from the ad business praised for remarkable careers of creative genius. One example is Lee Clow, the main creative force with TBWA/Chiat/Day. You know his work. The Energizer Bunny, billboards for Nike, "Dogs Rule" for Pedigree, and the "1984" spot that launched Apple's Mac are from his portfolio. So are the ads featured in Exhibits 9.3 and 9.4. Think about the Taco Bell ad in Exhibit 9.3. Why did this ad work

EXHIBIT 9.3 Chihuahuas want Taco Bell.

EXHIBIT 9.4 The ad that changed the music business forever.

AP Topic Gallery/Apple Computers

so well? What is it about a Spanish-speaking Chihuahua that defines the brand and moves the sales needle? Why is it creative? Ask the same questions about the iPod silhouette ads: Why did they work, why did they sell, how did they define the brand, what is creative about them? Explain, *por favor*. (See Insights Online [Exhibit 9.5] for another interesting example.)

Lee Clow is one of the great creative maestros of the modern advertising business. *Ad Age* referred to him simply as "The Dude Who Thought Different."[14] But those who have worked at his side say his real gift is as the synthesizer. Sorting through a wall full of creative ideas in the form of rough sketches, Lee is the guy who knows how to pick a winner. The one simplest marketing idea that is most likely to resonate with consumers, as in "Impossible is Nothing" for Adidas or "Shift" for Nissan. Some say he is fervent about great creativity; others say he is prone to fits of temper and can be mean to those who don't see things his way.[15] Now doesn't that sound a lot like the other great creators discussed earlier? (See Insights Online [Exhibit 9.6] for another great example.)

INSIGHTS ONLINE

9.5 Go online to see the AdAge feature, "Google Uses Creativity to Launch Google Play with a Tutorial from Cookie Monster."

INSIGHTS ONLINE

9.6 Go online to see the AdAge feature, "Priceline Creative Strategy Returns with 'The Negotiator' William Shatner."

9-2b Creativity in the Business World

The difficulty of determining who is creative and who is not or what is creative and what is not in the artistic world is paralleled in the business world. Certainly, no matter how this trait is defined, creativity is viewed in the business world as a positive quality for employees. It has been said that creative individuals assume almost mythical status in the corporate world. Everybody needs them, but no one is sure who or what they are. Furthermore, business types often expect that working with creative people will not be easy. Often, they are right.

9-2c Can You Become Creative?

This is an important question. The popular answer in a democratic and optimistic society would be to say, "Yes, sure; you too can be a Picasso." But in the end, the genius of a Picasso or an Einstein is a very high standard, one that most of us will not be able to achieve. And given some of the costs associated with intense creativity, maybe we don't want to be that anyway. But this question really depends on what one means by *creativity*. Is a person creative because he or she can produce a creative result? Or is a person creative because of the way he or she thinks? Our personal view is that some people are just more creative than others but that you can unleash what abilities you do have. Further, who gets to determine what is creative and what is not? To us, creativity is a form of intelligence—maybe the best form of intelligence. Computers can do amazing math; only humans can be creative. So don't let someone tell you that you aren't smart because you can't do calculus. Tell them that you are creative, and that's far more valuable. If they bug you too much, just tell them to go calculate something while you create something.

9-2d Notes of Caution

In concluding our discussion about the traits of extraordinarily creative people, a couple of notes of caution are in order. First, it should be understood that just because you are in a "creative" job, it doesn't follow that you are actually creative. Second, just because you are on the account or business side (a.k.a., "a suit") doesn't mean you are uninspired as in Exhibit 9.7. Sometimes even the client (gasp!) can have a good idea. Tension and conflict (e.g., suits versus the creatives) are regular occurrences in producing great advertising. It's normal. One needs to anticipate and manage this conflict in positive ways to get good outcomes. We take up the issues involved in this challenge now.

EXHIBIT 9.7 Artist David Ross's Swimming Suits, a view of corporate individuality and creative that is often shared by art directors and copywriters.

Doing Business: The Art of David Ross, knowledge. 10/andrew and McMeel. A Universal Press Syndicate Co. 4520 Main St., Kansas City, MO 64111. Library of Congress #96-83993 TCRN:0-8362-2178-8

LO ②

9-3 AGENCIES, CLIENTS, AND THE CREATIVE PROCESS

As an employee in an agency creative department, you will spend most of your time with your feet up on a desk working on an ad. Across the desk, also with her feet up, will be your partner—in my case, an art director. And she will want to talk about movies.

In fact, if the truth be known, you will spend fully one-fourth of your career with your feet up talking about movies. The ad is due in two days. The media space has been bought and paid for. The pressure's building. And your muse is sleeping off a drunk behind a dumpster somewhere. Your pen lies useless. So you talk movies.

That's when the traffic person comes by. Traffic people stay on top of a job as it moves through the agency; which means they also stay on top of you. They'll come by to remind you of the horrid things that happen to snail-assed creative people who don't come through with the goods on time…

So you try to get your pen moving. And you begin to work; and working in this business means staring at your partner's shoes.

That's what I've been doing from 9 to 5 for almost 20 years. Staring at the bottom of the disgusting tennis shoes on the feet of my partner, parked on the desk across from my disgusting tennis shoes. This is the sum and substance of life at an agency.

—Luke Sullivan, copywriter and author[16]

Lots of time is spent trying to get an idea, or the right idea. You turn things over and over in your head, trying to see the light. You try to find that one way of seeing it that makes it all fall into place. Or it just comes to you, real easy, just like that. Magic. Every creative pursuit involves this sort of thing. However, advertising and IBP, like all creative pursuits, are unique in some respects. Ad people come into an office and try to solve a problem, always under time pressure, given to them by some businessperson. Often the problem is poorly defined, or there are competing agendas. They work for people who seem not to be creative at all, and who seem to be doing their best not to let them be creative. They are housed in the "creative department," which makes it seem as if it's some sort of warehouse where the executives keep all the creativity so that they can find it when they need it and so that it won't get away. This implies that one can pick some up, like getting extra batteries at Target.

9-3a Oil and Water: Conflicts and Tensions in the Creative/Management Interface

Here are some thoughts on management and creativity by two advertising greats:

The majority of businessmen are incapable of original thinking, because they are unable to escape from the tyranny of reason. Their imaginations are blocked.

—William Bernbach[17]

If you're not a bad boy, if you're not a big pain in the ass, then you are in some mush in this business.

—George Lois[18]

As you can see, this topic rarely yields tepid, diplomatic comments. Advertising is produced through a social process. As a social process, however, it's marked by the struggles for control and power that occur within departments, between departments, and between the agency and its clients on a daily basis.[19]

Most research concerning the contentious environment in advertising agencies places the creative department in a central position within these conflicts. One explanation hinges on reactions to the uncertain nature of the product of the creative department. What do they do? From the outside it sometimes appears that they are having a lot of fun and just screwing around while everyone else has to wear a suit to the office and try to sell more stuff for the client. This creates tension between the creative department and the account services department.

In addition, these two departments do not always share the same ultimate goals for advertisements. In short, as Exhibit 9.8 points out, creatives work for awards; account executives work to please the client. They are not always the same. Individuals in the creative department see an ad as a vehicle to communicate a personal creative ideology that will further their careers. The account manager or account executive, serving as liaison between client and agency, sees the goal of the communication as achieving some predetermined objective in the marketplace, like growing market share for the client's brand.

Another source of conflict is attributed to differing perspectives due to differing background knowledge of members of creative groups versus account services teams. Account managers must be generalists with broad knowledge of the agency and all its functions, whereas creatives are specialists who must possess great expertise in a single area. Creatives, above all, must be tuned in to contemporary culture. Not all account managers, or brand managers, are.

Regardless of its role as a participant in conflict, the creative department is recognized as an essential part of any agency's success. It is a key quality for potential clients when they select advertising agencies. Creativity has been found to be crucial to a positive client–advertiser relationship.

However, many clients don't recognize their role in killing the very same breakthrough ideas that they claim to be looking for.[20] Anyone who has worked in the creative department of an advertising agency for any length of time has a full quiver of client stories—like the one about the client who wanted to produce a single 30-second spot for his ice cream novelty company. The creative team went to work and brought in a single spot that everyone agreed delivered the strategy perfectly, set up further possible spots in the same campaign, and, in the words of the copywriter, was just damn funny. It was the kind of commercial that you actually look forward to seeing on television. During the storyboard presentation, the client laughed in all the right places and admitted the spot was on strategy. He then decided to move his money to a national coupon drop, no ads.

It's easy and sometimes fun to blame clients for all of the anxieties and frustrations of the creatives, especially if you've worked in a creative department. You can criticize the clients all you want and, since they aren't in the office next to you, they can't hear you. But, despite the obvious stake that creative departments have in generating superior advertising, it should be mentioned that no creative ever put $10 million of his or her own money behind a campaign.

Indeed, you can't always blame the client. Sometimes the conflicts and problems that preclude wonderful

EXHIBIT 9.8 Team One Advertising has an interesting spin on what motivates agency creatives; here, it parodies Maslow's hierarchy to make its point.

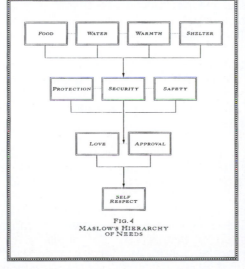
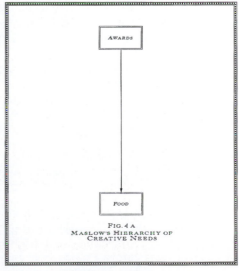

creative work occur within the walls of the advertising agency itself. To say there can be conflict between the creative department and other departments within an agency is a bit like saying there will be conflict when Jerry Springer walks into a TV studio. In advertising, the conflict often centers on the creative department versus account services. So why doesn't everybody pull together and love each other within an agency?

When a client is unhappy, it fires the agency. Billings and revenue drop. Budgets are cut and pink slips fly. It's no wonder that conflict occurs. When someone is looking out for his or her job, it's tough not to get involved in struggles over control of the creative product. **Account executives (AEs)** are the liaison between the agency and the client. For AEs to rise in their career, they must excel in the care and feeding of clients. It's a job of negotiation, gentle prodding, and ambassadorship. For creatives to rise, their work must challenge. It must arrest attention. It must provoke. At times, it must shock. It must do all

the things a wonderful piece of art must do. Yet, as we indicated earlier, this is all the stuff that makes for nervous clients. And that is an account executive's nightmare. As suggested in Exhibit 9.9, it is little wonder that it can be so hard to find AEs with just the right disposition.

This nightmare situation for the AEs produces the kind of ads that win awards for the creatives. People who win awards are recognized: Their work gets published in *The One Show* and *Communication Arts* and appears on the Clios. They are in demand, and they are wined and dined by rival agencies. They become famous and, yes, rich by advertising standards.

So the trick is, how do you get creatives to want to pursue cool ads that also sell? The ideal AE finds a way to keep both clients and creatives happy—not an easy thing, but in the end an essential thing. As ad agencies have downsized in recent years because of the economic slump, one of the first positions to be cut has been the AE. Given the critical role of AEs in bridging the gap

EXHIBIT 9.9 How to identify a good AE.

For some 25 years, I was an advertising agency "AE," eventually rising through the crabgrass to become a founder, president, chairman, and now chairman emeritus of Borders, Perrin and Norrander, Inc.

During all those years, I pondered the eternal question: Why do some advertising agencies consistently turn out a superior creative product while others merely perpetuate mediocrity? Is the answer simply to hire great writers and art directors? Well, certainly that has a lot to do with it, but I would suggest that there is another vital component in the equation for creative success.

Outstanding creative work in an ad agency requires a ferocious commitment from all staffers, but especially from the account service person. The job title is irrelevant—account executive, account manager, account supervisor—but the job function is critical, particularly when it comes to client approvals. Yes, I am speaking of the oft-maligned AE, the "suit" who so frequently is the bane of the Creative Department.

So how in the wide world does one identify this rare species, this unusual human being who is sensitive to the creative process and defends the agency recommendations with conviction and vigor? As you might expect, it is not easy. But there are some signals, some semihypothetical tests that can be used as diagnostic tools:

To begin with, look for unflappability, a splendid trait to possess in the heat of battle. In Australia last year, I heard a chap tell about arriving home to "find a bit of a problem" under his bed. An eight-foot python had slithered in and coiled around the man's small dog. Hearing its cries, he yanked the snake out from under the mattress, pried it loose from the mutt, tossed it out the door, and "dispatched it with a garden hoe." Was he particularly frightened or distressed? Not at all. "I've seen bigger snakes," he said, helping himself to another Foster's Lager. Now, that's the kind of disposition that wears well in account service land.

Wes Perrin, "How to Identify a Good AE," *Communication Arts Advertising Annual 1988* (Palo Alto, CA: Coyne and Blanchard, Inc., 1988), 210.

between clients and creatives, cutting them out seems like a path that can only lead to more friction between agencies and clients. That's a path where nobody wins.[21]

The difficulty of assessing the effectiveness of an advertisement can also create antagonism between the creative department and the research department.[22] One authority states that the tumultuous social environment between creative departments and ad testers represents the "historical conflict between art and science . . . these polarities have been argued philosophically as the conflict between Idealism and Materialism or Rationalism and Empiricism."[23] In the world of advertising, people in research departments are put in the unenviable position of judging the creatives. So, again, "science" judges art. Creatives don't like this, particularly when it's bad science or not science at all. Of course, researchers are sometimes creative themselves, and they don't typically enjoy being an additional constraint on those in the creative department.

So is there any way around all the tension and conflict inherent in the very people-intensive business of creating advertising and IBP? As detailed in Exhibit 9.10,

EXHIBIT 9.10 Assuring poor creativity.

One of the advantages of being a practitioner-turned-educator is the opportunity to interact with a large number of agencies. Much like Switzerland, an academic is viewed as a neutral in current affairs and not subject to the suspicions of a potential competitor.

The result of my neutral status has been the opportunity to watch different agencies produce both great and poor work. And, as a former associate creative director, I'd like to share the trends I've seen in the development of bad creative. The revelation: Bad work is more a matter of structure than talent. Here are 12 pieces of advice if you want to institutionalize bad creative work in your agency:

1. Treat your target audience like a statistic.

Substituting numbers for getting a feel for living, breathing people is a great way to make bad work inevitable. It allows you to use your gut instinct about "women 55 to 64" rather than the instinct that evolves from really understanding a group of folks. The beauty with staying on the statistical level is that you get to claim you did your homework when the creative turns out dreadful. After all, there were 47 pages of stats on the target.

2. Make your strategy a hodgepodge.

Good ads have one dominant message, just one. Most strategies that result in lousy work have lots more than one. They are political junkyards that defy a creative wunderkind to produce anything but mediocrity. So make everybody happy with the strategy and then tell your creatives to find a way to make it all work. You'll get bad work, for sure.

3. Have no philosophy.

William Bernbach believed in a certain kind of work. His people emulated his philosophy and produced a consistent kind of advertising that built a great agency. Now, to be controversial, I'll say the exact same thing about Rosser Reeves. Both men knew what they wanted, got it, and prospered.

The agency leaders who do hard sell one day, then new wave the next, create only confusion. More important, the work does not flow from a consistent vision of advertising and a code of behavior to achieve that advertising. Instead, there is the wild embrace of the latest fashion or the currently faddish bromide making the rounds at conventions. So beware of those who have a philosophy and really are true to it. They are historically at odds with lousy work.

4. Analyze your creative as you do a research report.

The cold, analytical mind does a wonderful job destroying uncomfortable, unexpected work. Demand that every detail be present in every piece of creative and say it is a matter of thoroughness. The creative work that survives your ice storm will be timid and compromised and will make no one proud.

5. Make the creative process professional.

"Creative types collect a paycheck every two weeks. They'd better produce and do it now. This is, after all, a business." The corporate performance approach is a highly recommended way of developing drab print and TV. Treating the unashamedly artistic process of making ads as if it were an offshoot of the local oil filter assembly plant promises to destroy risk taking and morale. Your work will become every bit as distinctive as a gray suit. More important, it will be on schedule. And both are fine qualities in business and we are a business, aren't we?

Continued

6. Say one thing and do another.

Every bad agency says all the right things about risk taking, loving great creative, and admiring strong creative people. It is mandatory to talk a good game and then do all the things that destroy great work. This will help keep spirits low and turnover high in the creatives who are actually talented. And then you'll feel better when they leave after a few months because you really do like strong creative people—if they just weren't so damn defensive.

7. Give your client a candy store.

To prove how hard you work, insist on showing numerous half-thought-out ideas to your client. The approved campaign will have lots of problems nobody thought about and that will make the final work a mess.

Campaigns with strong ideas are rare birds, and they need a great deal of thinking to make sure they're right. So insist on numerous campaigns and guarantee yourself a series of sparrows rather than a pair of eagles.

8. Mix and match your campaigns.

Bring three campaigns to your client, and then mix them up. Take a little bit of one and stick it on another. Even better, do it internally. It's like mixing blue, red, and green. All are fine colors, but red lacks the coolness of blue. Can't we add a little? The result of the mix will be a thick muddy clump. Just like so many commercials currently on the air.

9. Fix it in production.

Now that your procedure has created a half-baked campaign that is being mixed up with another, tell the creative to make it work by excellent production values. Then you can fire the incompetent hack when the jingle with 11 sales points is dull.

10. Blame the creative for bad creative.

After all, you told them what they should do. ("Make it totally unexpected, but use the company president and the old jingle.") The fault lies in the fact that you just can't find good talent anymore. Never mind that some creative departments have low turnover and pay smaller salaries than you do.

11. Let your people imitate.

"Chiat/Day won awards and sales for the Apple *1984* commercial, so let's do something like that for our stereo store account." This approach works wonders because your imitation appears lacking the original surprise that came from a totally expected piece of work. You can even avoid the controversy that surrounded Chiat/Day when half the industry said the ad was rotten. Your imitation can blend right in with all the other imitations and, even better, will have no strategic rationale for your bizarre execution.

12. Believe posttesting when you get a good score.

That way you can be slaughtered by your client when your sensitive, different commercial gets a score 20 points below norm. The nice things you said about posttesting when you got an excellent score with your "singing mop" commercial cannot be taken back. If you want to do good work, clients must somehow be made to use research as a tool. If you want to do bad creative, go ahead, and believe that posttesting rewards excellent work.

Naturally, a lot of bad creative results from egomania, laziness, incompetence, and client intractability—but a lot less than most believe. I have found that bad work usually comes from structures that make talented people ineffective and that demand hard work, human dedication, and tremendous financial investment to produce work that can be topped by your average high school senior.

John Sweeney, a former associate creative director at Foot, Cone & Belding, Chicago, teaches advertising at the University of North Carolina—Chapel Hill.

the insights of John Sweeney—a true expert on advertising creativity—make it clear what *not* to do if creativity is the goal. Professor Sweeney also gives us the hint we need about what we should do. He notes that bad work is more a matter of structure than talent. So given a pool of talented people, we have to provide some structure that allows them to produce their best work. Creative types, AEs, marketing managers, and ad researchers have to find a way to make beautiful music together. Here's how they can.

LO ❸

9-4 MAKING BEAUTIFUL MUSIC TOGETHER: COORDINATION, COLLABORATION, AND CREATIVITY

Metaphors help us understand (see Insights Online [Exhibit 9.11] for a notable example). Let's use a metaphor to appreciate the challenge of executing sophisticated advertising and IBP campaigns. Executing an IBP campaign is very much like the performance of a symphony orchestra. To produce glorious music, many individuals must make their unique contributions to the performance, but it sounds right only if the maestro brings it all together at the critical moment. Make it a point to attend a symphony and get there early so that you can hear each individual musician warming up with his or her instrument. Reflect on the many years of dedicated practice that this individual put in to master that instrument. Reflect on the many hours of practice that this individual put in to learn his or her specific part for tonight's performance. As you sit there listening to the warm-up, notice how the random collection of sounds becomes increasingly painful to the ears. With each musician doing his or her own thing, the sound is a collection of hoots and clangs that grows louder as the performance approaches. Mercifully, the maestro finally steps to the podium to quell the cacophony. All is quiet for a moment. The musicians focus on their sheet music for reassurance, even though by now they could play their individual parts in their sleep. Finally, the maestro calls the orchestra into action. As a group, as a collective, as a team, with each person executing a specific assignment as defined by the composer, under the direction of the maestro, they make beautiful music together.

So it goes in the world of advertising. Preparing and executing breakthrough IBP campaigns is a people-intensive business. Many different kinds of expertise will be needed to pull it off, and this means many different people must be enlisted to play a variety of roles. But some order must be imposed on the collection of players. Frequently, a maestro will need to step in to give the various players a common theme or direction for their work. Lee Clow of TBWA Worldwide quite naturally received a conductor's baton as a gift. About the role of maestro he has said: "I was a pretty good soloist when I joined the orchestra, but

I think I'm a much better conductor than I was a soloist. If we can make beautiful music together, that makes me happy . . . . And different people end up getting to do the solos and get the standing ovations."[24] Lee Clow gets it. . (See Insights Online [Exhibit 9.12] for another great example.)

Coordination and collaboration will be required for executing any kind of advertising, which means simply that advertising is a team sport. Moreover, the creative essence of the campaign can be aided and elevated by skillful use of teams. Teams can generate a synergy that allows them to rise above the talents of their individual members on many kinds of tasks. (Yes, the whole can be greater than the sum of the individual parts.) So even without an Igor Stravinsky, Pablo Picasso, or Martha Graham in our midst, a group of diverse and motivated people can be expected to not only generate big ideas but also put them into action.

Great advertising and great teamwork go hand in hand, which of course means that we don't just want to hope for a good team, we need to make it happen. Great teamwork can't be left to chance. It must be planned for and facilitated if it is to occur with regularity. So next we will introduce several concepts and insights about teams to make you better at teamwork. In addition, you will come to appreciate how important teams can be in producing that one elusive thing that everyone wants: *creativity*.

9-4a What We Know about Teams

No doubt you have taken a class where part of your grade was determined by teamwork. Get used to it. More and more instructors in all sorts of classes are incorporating teamwork as part of their courses because they know that interpersonal skills are highly valued in the real world of work. In fact, an impressive body of research indicates that teams have become essential to the effectiveness of modern organizations. In their book *The Wisdom of Teams*, consultants Jon Katzenbach and Douglas Smith review many valuable insights about the importance of teams. Here we summarize several of their key conclusions.[25]

Teams Rule! There can be little doubt that in a variety of organizations, teams have become the primary means for getting things done. The growing number of performance challenges faced by most businesses—as a result of factors such as more demanding customers, technological changes, government regulation, and intensifying competition—demand speed and quality in work products that are simply beyond the scope of what an individual can offer. Roger Martin, dean of the Rotman School of Management at University of Toronto, asserts that the complexity of today's business problems can only be solved through collaboration.[26] In most instances, teams are the only valid option for getting things done. This is certainly the case for advertising.

It's All about Performance. Research shows that teams are effective in organizations where the leadership makes it perfectly clear that teams will be held accountable for performance. Teams are expected to produce results that satisfy the client and yield financial gains for the organization.

Synergy through Teams. Modern organizations require many kinds of expertise to get the work done. The only reliable way to mix people with different expertise to generate solutions where the whole is greater than the sum of the parts is through team discipline. Research shows that blending expertise from diverse disciplines often produces the most innovative solutions to many different types of business problems.[27] The "blending" must be done through teams.

The Demise of Individualism? Rugged individualism is the American way. Always look out for number one! Are we suggesting that a growing reliance on teams in the workplace must mean a devaluation of the individual and a greater emphasis on conforming to what the group thinks? Not at all. Left unchecked, of course, an "always look out for number one" mentality can destroy teams. But teams are not incompatible with individual excellence. Effective teams find ways to let each individual bring his or her unique contributions to the forefront. When an individual does not have his or her own contribution to make, then one can question that person's value to the team. As the old saying goes, "If you and I think alike, then one of us is unnecessary."

Teams Promote Personal Growth. An added benefit of teamwork is that it promotes learning for each individual team member. In a team, people learn about their own work styles and observe the work styles of others. This learning makes them more effective team players in their next assignment. Once team principles take hold in an organization, momentum builds.

Leadership in Teams. A critical element in the equation for successful teams is leadership. Leaders do many things for their teams to help them succeed.[28] Teams ultimately must reach a goal to justify their standing, and here is where the leader's job starts. The leader's first job is to help the team build consensus about the goals they hope to achieve and the approach they will take to reach those goals. Without a clear sense of purpose, the team is doomed. Once goals and purpose are agreed upon, the leader plays a role in ensuring that the work of the team is consistent with the strategy or plan. This is a particularly important role in the context of creating IBP campaigns.

Finally, team leaders must help do the real work of the team. Here, the team leader must be careful to contribute ideas without dominating the team. There are also two key things that team leaders should never do: *They should not blame or allow specific individuals to fail, and they should never excuse away shortfalls in team performance.*[29] Mutual accountability must be emphasized over individual performance.

Direct Applications to the Account Team. Think of an agency's **account team** as a bicycle wheel, with the team leader as the hub of a wheel. Spokes of the wheel then reach out to the diverse disciplinary expertise needed in today's world of advertising and IBP. The spokes will represent team members from direct marketing, public relations, broadcast media, graphic design, interactive, creative, accounting, and so on. The hub connects the spokes and ensures that all of them work in tandem to make the wheel roll smoothly. To illustrate the multilayered nature of the team approach to IBP, each account team member can also be thought of as a hub in his or her very own wheel. For example, the direct marketing member on the account team is the team leader for her own set of specialists charged with preparing direct marketing materials. Through this type of multilevel "hub-and-spokes" design, the coordination and collaboration essential for effective IBP campaigns can be achieved (see Insights Online [Exhibit 9.13] for a notable case in point).

Fostering Collaboration through the Creative Brief. The **creative brief** is a little document with a huge role in promoting good teamwork and fostering the creative process. It sets up the goal for any advertising effort in a way that gets everyone moving in the same direction but should never force or mandate a particular solution. It provides basic guidelines with plenty of room for the creatives to be creative. Preparation of the creative brief is a joint activity involving the client lead and the AE. When the creative brief is done right, a whole bunch of potential conflicts are prevented. An efficient template for the creative brief is featured in Exhibit 9.14.

EXHIBIT 9.14 Template for a creative brief.

CLIENT: **DATE:**   **JOB NO.:**
Prepared by:

WHAT IS THE PRODUCT OR SERVICE?
Simple description or name of product or service.

WHO/WHAT IS THE COMPETITION?
Provide a snapshot of the brand situation, including current position in the category, brand challenges, competitive threats, and future goals.

WHO ARE WE TALKING TO?
Clear definition of who the target is both demographically and psychographically. Be as specific as possible in defining the target so that the creative can connect target and brand in the most compelling way.

WHAT CONSUMER NEED OR PROBLEM DO WE ADDRESS?
Describe the unmet consumer need that this product or service fills or how this product addresses a need in a way that's unique.

WHAT DOES THE CONSUMER CURRENTLY THINK ABOUT US?
Uncover target insights to get at attitudes and behaviors related to broader context as well as specific category and brand. Determine whether insights currently exist or whether new research needs to be conducted.

WHAT ONE THING DO WE WANT THEM TO BELIEVE?
Be as single-minded as possible. Write in benefit (functional, emotional, or self-expressive) language. Should differentiate us… no other brand in the category can or is currently saying it.

WHAT CAN WE TELL THEM THAT WILL MAKE THEM BELIEVE THIS?
Not a laundry list of available support but the few things that clearly support the "one thing we want them to believe."

WHAT IS THE TONALITY OF THE ADVERTISING?
A few adjectives or phrase that captures the tonality and personality of the advertising.

Of particular note:
Write it in the consumer's language; not business-speak.

Make every word count; be simple and concise.

Make as evocative as possible. Think of the brief as the first "ad." The brief should make creatives jump up and down in their excitement to start executing it!

© Cengage Learning

Teams Liberate Decision Making. With the right combination of expertise assembled on the account team, a carefully crafted creative brief, and a leader that has the team working well as a unit, what appears to be casual or spur-of-the-moment decision making can turn out to be breakthrough decision making. This is one of the huge benefits of good teamwork. As they say at Crispin Porter + Bogusky (CP+B), a good idea can come from anywhere. Teams composed of members who trust one another are liberated to be more creative because no one is worried about having their best ideas stolen. No one is worried about trying to look good for the boss. It's the team that counts. This type of "safe" team environment allows everyone to contribute and lets the whole be greater than the sum of the parts.

9-4b When Sparks Fly: Igniting Creativity through Teams

Whether account teams, subspecialist teams, creative teams, or hybrid teams involving persons from both the client and agency side, all will play critical roles in preparing and executing integrated advertising campaigns. Moreover, impressive evidence shows that when managed in a proactive way, teams come up with better ideas, that is, ideas that are both creative and useful in the process of building brands.[30] One can get pretty serious about the subject of managing creativity, and good teamwork may be serious stuff. But it doesn't have to be complicated, and it certainly will get rowdy at times. The key elements are building teams with the right expertise and diversity of thought, pushing individuals in those teams to challenge and build on each others' ideas, and creating just the right amount of tension to get the sparks flying.

Cognitive Styles. According to the stereotype, business types favor left-brain thinking and advertising types (especially the creatives) favor right-brain thinking. Business types like to talk about testing and data and return on investment, whereas advertising types like to talk about movies and the Cannes Film Festival.[31] Although such stereotypes misrepresent individual differences, the old left-brain/right-brain metaphor serves to remind us that people approach problem solving with different styles. That is, people prefer to think about things in their own style.

The unique preferences of each person for thinking about and solving a problem are a reflection of **cognitive style**. For instance, some people prefer logical and analytical thinking; others prefer intuitive and nonlinear thinking. Numerous categorization schemes have been developed for classifying people based on their cognitive styles. Psychologist Carl Jung was an

early pioneer among cognitive stylists. He proposed essential differences among individuals along three dimensions of cognitive style: sensing versus intuiting, thinking versus feeling, and extraverted versus introverted. The important point for teams and creativity is that the more homogeneous a team is in terms of cognitive styles, the more limited will be the range of their solutions to a problem. Simply stated, diversity of thought nourishes creativity.

Creative Abrasion. Teamwork is not a picnic in the park. That's why it's called team**work.** Moreover, when teams bring together people with diverse cognitive styles, and they truly get engaged in the task, there will be friction. Friction can be both good and bad.[32] On the one hand, we can have **creative abrasion**, which is the clash of ideas, and from which new ideas and breakthrough solutions can evolve. That's obviously the good thing. On the other hand, we can have **interpersonal abrasion**, which is the clash of people, from which communication shuts down and new ideas get slaughtered. That's obviously the bad thing. So, as we pointed out earlier, teams must have leadership that creates a safe environment allowing creative abrasion to flourish while always looking to defuse interpersonal abrasion. It's a fine line, but getting it right means the difference between creativity and chaos.

Using Brainstorming and Alien Visitors. Many of us have sat in a conference room and shot the breeze for an hour and when it was all over decided we just wasted another hour. Groups can waste a lot of time if not proactively managed, and one of the key means for getting groups or teams to generate novel solutions is through the use of a process called brainstorming. **Brainstorming** is an organized approach to idea generation in groups. There is a right way and a wrong way to brainstorm. Follow the rules laid out in Exhibit 9.15, and you can call it brainstorming. Otherwise, you're just shooting the breeze and most likely wasting time.

Adding more diversity to the group is always a way to foster creative abrasion; moreover, well-established teams can get stale and stuck in a rut. To ramp up the creative abrasion may require a visit from an alien. If you can get one from Pluto or Mars that's fine, but more likely this alien will just be a person or persons from outside the normal network. They can be from elsewhere in your organization, or from outside the organization entirely. Perhaps the team will need to take a field trip together to visit some aliens. Teams that insulate themselves from outside influences run the risk over time of losing their spark.[33] Tranquility and sameness can be enemies of creativity.

EXHIBIT 9.15 Don't waste time; do it right!

Eight Rules for Brilliant Brainstorming

#1—Build off each other. One proven path to creativity entails building on existing ideas; don't just generate ideas, build on each others'.

#2—Fear drives out creativity. If people believe they will be teased, demoted, or otherwise humiliated in the group, no need to even consider brainstorming. It won't work.

#3—Prime individuals before and after. Encourage individuals to learn about the problem before and after the group session; teams always benefit when individuals apply their unique expertise.

#4—Make it happen. Great organizations develop a brainstorming culture where everyone knows the rules and honors them; to achieve such a culture, it is essential that ideas developed in brainstorm sessions lead to actions. We can't just talk big ideas; we must also put them to work.

#5—It's a skill. Leading a productive brainstorming session is not a job for amateurs; facilitating a brainstorming session is a skill that takes months or years to master. Don't pretend to brainstorm without a skilled facilitator.

#6—Embrace creative abrasion. If your team has been formed appropriately, it will contain people with conflicting cognitive styles. Celebrate that diversity, welcome everybody into the group, and then let the sparks fly!

#7—Listen and learn. Good brainstorming sessions foster learning among people who have diverse expertise and divergent cognitive styles. Trust builds and suspicion fades.

#8—Follow the rules, or you're not brainstorming (and pretending just wastes everybody's time).

Based on Robert I. Sutton, "The Truth about Brainstorming," *Inside BusinessWeek*, September 25, 2006, 17–21.

9-4c Final Thoughts on Teams and Creativity

Creativity in the preparation of an IBP campaign can be fostered by the trust and open communication that are hallmarks of effective teams. But it is also true that the creativity required for breakthrough campaigns will evolve as personal work products generated by individuals laboring on their own. Both personal and team creativity are critical in the preparation of advertising ad campaigns. The daunting task of facilitating both often falls in the lap of an agency's creative director.

The position of creative director in any ad agency is very special because, much like the maestro of the symphony orchestra, the creative director must encourage personal excellence but at the same time demand team accountability. We interviewed veteran creative directors to get more insights about the challenge of channeling the creative energies of their teams. All acknowledge that creativity has an intensely personal element, often motivated by the desire to satisfy one's own ego or sense of self. But despite this personal element, team unity has to be a priority.

In orchestrating creative teams, these are some good principles to follow:

- Take great care in assigning individuals to a team in the first place. Be sensitive to their existing workloads and the proper mix of expertise required to do the job for the client.

- Get to know the cognitive style of each individual. Listen carefully. Because creativity can be an intensely personal matter, one has to know when it is best to leave people alone, versus when one needs to support them in working through the inevitable rejection.

- Make teams responsible to the client. Individuals and teams are empowered when they have sole responsibility for performance outcomes.

- Beware of adversarial and competitive relationships between individuals and between teams. They can quickly lead to mistrust that destroys camaraderie and synergy.

- In situations where the same set of individuals will work on multiple teams over time, rotate team assignments to foster fresh thinking, or bring in some aliens!

Here we see once again that the fundamentals of effective teams—communication, trust, complementary expertise, and leadership—produce the desired performance outcome. There's simply no alternative. Advertising is a team sport.

LO 4

9-5 HAVE *YOU* DECIDED TO BECOME MORE CREATIVE?

A great way to summarize the factors that foster creativity is via the **3Ps creativity framework**.[34] People is the first P, and as we emphasized at the beginning of this chapter, the field of advertising has always embraced the concept of great creative minds, as in a Lee Clow, an Alex Bogusky, or a Bill Bernbach. But we also know that the Process used in developing creative work and the Place or environment wherein the work is done are also big factors in generating creative outcomes. (See Insights Online [Exhibit 9.16] for an interesting example.) As one agency leader put it: "We sell ideas, and if your employees are unhappy, you are not going to get a lot of good ideas."[35] All that makes sense, but now, as promised, it's time to circle back to YOU.

Most of us are not going to model our lives after creative geniuses like Pablo Picasso or Martha Graham. Even though it's great to have role models to inspire us, we don't think it's realistic to aspire to be the next Gandhi or Einstein. But we all can take stock of our own special skills and abilities and should candidly assess our own strengths and weaknesses. For example, referring to some of the terminology used earlier in this chapter, we all can complete assessments that reveal our own cognitive styles and then compare ourselves to others. And if you want to calibrate your level of creativity, just search the Internet for "creativity tests" or "creativity

assessments" and a host of options will present themselves. It is a good thing to get to know your own self and start thinking about your unique skills and abilities. In addition, if you have any interest in a career in advertising, it would be a good thing to decide right now that you are going to make yourself more creative. Although we all may start in different places, it is a worthy goal to aspire to become more creative. Yale psychologist Robert Sternberg, who has devoted his professional career to the study of intelligence and creativity, advises his students as follows:

> To make yourself more creative, decide now to:
> Redefine problems to see them differently from other people;
> Be the first to analyze and critique your own ideas, since we all have good ones and bad ones;
> Be prepared for opposition whenever you have a really creative idea;
> Recognize that it is impossible to be creative without adequate knowledge;
> Recognize that too much knowledge can stifle creativity;
> Find the standard, safe solution and then decide when you want to take a risk by defying it;
> Keep growing and experiencing, and challenging your own comfort zone;
> Believe in yourself, especially when surrounded by doubters;
> Learn to cherish ambiguity, because from it comes the new ideas.
> Remember that research has shown that people are most likely to be creative when doing something they love.[36]

It's good advice.

INSIGHTS ONLINE

9.16 Go online to see the AdAge feature, "Subaru Decides to Become More Creative with a 'Dog Chat Facebook App' Where You Can Chat with Dogs."

SUMMARY

 Describe the core characteristics of great creative minds.

A look at the shared sensibilities of great creative minds provides a constructive starting point for assessing the role of creativity in the production of great advertising. What Picasso had in common with Gandhi, Freud, Eliot, Stravinsky, Graham, and Einstein—including a strikingly exuberant self-confidence, (childlike) alertness, unconventionality, and an obsessive commitment to the work—both charms and alarms us. Self-confidence, at some point, becomes crass self-promotion; an unconstrained childlike ability to see the world as forever new devolves, somewhere along the line, into childish self-indulgence. Without creativity,

there can be no advertising. How we recognize and define creativity in advertising rests on our understanding of the achievements of acknowledged creative geniuses from the worlds of art, literature, music, science, and politics.

2 Contrast the role of an agency's creative department with that of business managers/account executives and explain the tensions between them.

What it takes to get the right idea (a lot of hard work), and the ease with which a client may dismiss that idea, underlies the contentiousness between an agency's creative staff and its

AEs and clients. Creatives provoke. Managers restrain. Ads that win awards for creative excellence don't necessarily fulfill a client's business goals. All organizations deal with the competing agendas of one department versus another, but in advertising agencies, this competition plays out at an amplified level. The difficulty of assessing the effectiveness of any form of advertisement only adds to the problem. Advertising researchers are put in the unenviable position of judging the creatives, pitting "science" against "art." None of these tensions changes the fact that creativity is essential to the vitality of brands. Creativity makes a brand, and it is creativity that reinvents established brands in new and desired ways.

 Assess the role of teams in managing tensions and promoting creativity in advertising and IBP applications.

There are many sources of conflict and tension in the business of creating great advertising. It's the nature of the beast. One way that many organizations attempt to address this challenging issue is through systematic utilization of teams. Teams, when effectively managed, will produce outputs that are greater than the sum of their individual parts. Teams need to be managed proactively to promote creative abrasion but limit interpersonal abrasion if they are to produce "beautiful music together." Guidance from a maestro (like a Lee Clow or an Alex Bogusky) will be required. Another important tool to get teams headed in the right direction and to preempt many forms of conflict in the advertising arena is the creative brief. It's a little document with a very big function.

 Examine yourself and your own passion for creativity.

Self-assessment is an important part of learning and growing, and now is the perfect time to be thinking about yourself and your passion for creativity. If advertising is a profession that interests you, then improving your own creative abilities should be a lifelong quest. Now is the time to decide to become more creative.

KEY TERMS

creativity
account executive (AE)
account team

creative brief
cognitive style
creative abrasion

interpersonal abrasion
brainstorming
3P's creativity framework

ENDNOTES

1. Matthew Creamer, "Caught in the Clutter Crossfire: Your Brand," *Advertising Age,* April 2, 2007, 1, 35

2. Brian Till and Daniel Baack, "Recall and Persuasion: Does Creative Advertising Matter?" *Journal of Advertising,* Fall 2005, 47–57; Daniel Baack, Rick Wilson, and Brian Till, "Creativity and Memory Effects," *Journal of Advertising,* Winter 2008, 85–94.

3. Thomas C. O'Guinn and Albert Muniz, Jr., "The Social Brand: Towards a Sociological Model of Brands," in Barbara Loken, Rohini Ahluwalia, and Michael J. Houston (Eds.), *Brands and Brand Management: Contemporary Research Perspectives* (New York and London: Routledge, 2010), 133–159.

4. Marc Gobe, *Emotional Branding: The New Paradigm for Connecting Brands to People* (New York: Allworth, 2011).

5. Ibid.

6. Cris Prystay, "When Being First Doesn't Make You No. 1," *The Wall Street Journal,* August 12, 2004, B1, B2.

7. Carl G. Jung, cited in Astrid Fitzgerald, *An Artist's Book of Inspiration: A Collection of Thoughts on Art, Artists, and Creativity* (New York: Lindisfarne, 1996), 58.

8. Socrates, quoted in Plato, *Phaedrus and the Seventh and Eighth Letters,* Walter Hamilton, trans (Middlesex, England: Penguin, 1970), 46–47; cited in Kay Redfield Jamison, *Touched with Fire: Manic-Depressive Illness and the Artistic Temperament* (New York: Free Press, 1993), 51.

9. Howard Gardner, *Creating Minds: An Anatomy of Creativity Seen through the Lives of Freud, Einstein, Picasso, Stravinsky, Eliot, Graham, and Gandhi* (New York: Basic Books, 1993).

10. Ibid., 364.

11. Ibid., 145; Sigmund Freud, *The Interpretation of Dreams,* in A. A. Brill (Ed.), *The Basic Writings of Sigmund Freud* (New York: Modern Library, 1900/1938).

12. Gardner, *Creating Minds,* 369.

13. Ibid.

14. Alice Cuneo, "The Dude Who Thought Different," *Advertising Age,* July 31, 2006, 1, 25.

15. Ibid.

16. Luke Sullivan, "Staring at Your Partner's Shoes," in *Hey Whipple, Squeeze This: A Guide to Creating Great Ads* (New York: Wiley, 1998), 20–22.

17. William Bernbach, quoted in Thomas Frank, *The Conquest of Cool: Business Culture, Consumer Culture, and the Rise of Hip Consumerism* (Chicago, IL: University of Chicago Press, 1997).

18. George Lois, quoted in Randall Rothenberg, *Where the Suckers Moon* (New York: Knopf, 1994), 135–172.

19. Christy Ashley and Jason Oliver, "Creative Leaders," *Journal of Advertising,* Spring 2010, 115–130.

20. Sheila Sasser and Scott Koslow, "Desperately Seeking Advertising Creativity," *Journal of Advertising*, Winter 2008, 5–19.

21. Jeremy Mullman, "Think Twice before Axing Account Management," *Advertising Age*, April 26, 2010, 8.

22. A. J. Kover and S. M. Goldberg, "The Games Copywriters Play: Conflict, Quasi-Control, a New Proposal," *Journal of Advertising Research*, vol. 25, no. 4 (1995), 52–62.

23. R. L. Vaughn, "Point of View. Creatives versus Researchers—Must They Be Adversaries?" *Journal of Advertising Research*, vol. 22, no. 6 (1983), 45–48.

24. Cuneo, "The Dude Who Thought Different."

25. Jon R. Katzenbach and Douglas K. Smith, *The Wisdom of Teams: Creating the High-Performance Organization* (Boston, MA: Harvard Business School Press, 1993).

26. Roger Martin, *The Opposable Mind* (Boston, MA: Harvard Business School Press, 2009).

27. Dorothy Leonard and Susaan Straus, "Putting Your Company's Whole Brain to Work," *Harvard Business Review*, July–August 1997, 111–121.

28. Katzenbach Smith, *The Wisdom of Teams,* Ch. 7.

29. Ibid., 144.

30. Jacob Goldenberg, Amnon Levav, David Mazursky, and Sorin Solomon, *Cracking the Ad Code* (Cambridge, UK: Cambridge University Press, 2009).

31. Dale Buss, "Bridging the Great Divide in Marketing Thinking," *Advertising Age*, March 26, 2007, 18, 19.

32. Dorothy Leonard and Walter Swap, *When Sparks Fly: Igniting Creativity in Groups* (Boston, MA: Harvard Business School Press, 1999).

33. Ibid.

34. Sasser and Koslow, "Desperately Seeking Advertising Creativity."

35. Brooke Capps, "Playtime, Events, Perks Go Long Way in Team Building," *Advertising Age*, January 15, 2007, 30.

36. Robert J. Sternberg, "Creativity as a Decision," *American Psychologist*, May 2002, 376; and Robert J. Sternberg, "Identifying and Developing Creative Giftedness," *Roeper Review*, vol. 23, no. 2 (2000), 60–65.

CHAPTER 10
Creative Message Strategy

After reading and thinking about this chapter, you will be able to do the following:

1. Identify 10 objectives of creative message strategy.

2. Identify methods for achieving each creative message objective.

3. Discuss the strategic implications of various methods used to execute each message strategy objective.

10-1 MESSAGE STRATEGY

Now: actually creating messages. The first thing we need is an objective: What do you want to accomplish with your advertising and other brand messaging? How are you going to use advertising and brand promotion to achieve marketing goals? How are you going to use advertising and integrated brand promotion (IBP) to give the brand meaning?

The message strategy defines the goals of the advertiser. This chapter offers 10 essential message objectives and then discusses and illustrates the methods most often used to achieve them. It covers the most important message strategies. Exhibit 10.1 summarizes the 10 message objectives presented here. Also, you must understand that you will certainly see ads that are not pure cases and ads that are combinations of strategies.

When you see an ad you should ask: What is this ad trying to do, and how is it trying to accomplish that?

— LO 1 —
10-2 ESSENTIAL MESSAGE OBJECTIVES AND STRATEGIES

The 10 message objectives are presented from simplest to most sophisticated, from pure and relatively mundane "mindshare" advertising to very sophisticated social and cultural branding through advertising and

IMC. For each one we will tell you about the logic behind the strategy, the basic mechanisms involved, how it works, how success or failure is typically determined, and a strategic summary of those methods.

10-2a Objective #1: Promote Brand Recall

This is the simplest type of advertising, and we mean simple. Since modern advertising's earliest days, getting consumers to remember the advertised brand's name has been a goal. The very obvious idea behind this objective is that if consumers remember the brand name, and can easily recall it, they are more likely to buy it. They may not buy it but, all else being equal, remembering the advertisers name raises the odds that they will. It's a pretty simple and straightforward idea.

Although human memory is a very complex topic, the relationship between repetition and recall has been pretty well understood for a long time. We know that repetition generally increases the odds of recall. So, by repeating a brand name over and over, the odds of recalling that brand name go up—again, pretty simple.

But advertisers typically don't just want consumers to remember their name; they want their name to be the *first* brand consumers remember, or what advertisers call *top of mind*. At a minimum, they want them to be in the *evoked set*, a small list of brand names (typically five or less) that comes to mind when a product or service category (e.g., airlines [United, American,

EXHIBIT 10.1 Message strategy objectives and methods.

Objective: What the Advertiser Hopes to Achieve	Method: How the Advertiser Plans to Achieve the Objective
Promote brand recall: To get consumers to recall its brand name(s) first; that is, before any of the competitors' brand names	Repetition Slogans and jingles
Link a key attribute to the brand name: To get consumers to associate a key attribute with a brand name and vice versa	Unique selling proposition (USP)
Persuade the consumer: To convince consumers to buy a product or service through high-engagement arguments	Reason-why ads Hard-sell ads Comparison ads Testimonials Demonstration Advertorials Infomercials
Affective association: To get the consumer to feel good about the brand	Feel-good ads Humor ads Sexual-appeal ads
Scare the consumer into action: To get consumers to buy a product or service by instilling fear	Fear-appeal ads
Change behavior by inducing anxiety: To get consumers to make a purchase decision by playing to their anxieties; often, the anxieties are social in nature	Anxiety ads Social anxiety ads
Define the brand image: To create an image for a brand by relying predominantly on visuals rather than words and argument	Image ads
Leverage social disruption and cultural contradictions: To leverage disruption and cultural contradictions in society to the brand's advantage. Get consumers to see the brand as a way to resolve these tensions and contradictions.	Tie brand to social/cultural movement as a way to resolve cultural contradictions
Situate the brand in a social context: To give the brand the desired social meaning	Slice-of-life ads Product placement/short Internet films Light-fantasy ads
Transform consumption experiences: To create a feeling, image, or mood about a brand that is activated when the consumer uses the product or service	Transformational ads

© Cengage Learning

parity products (those with few major objective differences between brands—e.g., laundry soaps) and other "low-involvement" goods and services, the first brand remembered is often the most likely to be purchased. First-remembered brands are often the most popular brands. In fact, consumers may actually infer popularity, desirability, and even superiority from the ease with which they recall brands. The most easily recalled brand may be seen as the leading brand (most popular, highest market share), even when it isn't. Cognitive psychologists have shown that humans infer how common something is (frequency) by how easily they remember it. So, consumers will actually believe brand X's market share to be higher because it comes to mind so quickly. If people think a brand is the leading brand, it can actually become the leading brand. For things purchased routinely, you can't expect consumers to deliberate and engage in extensive consideration of product attributes. Instead, in the real world of advertising and brand promotion, you rely on recall of the brand name, recall of a previously made judgment (e.g., *I like Tide*) to get the advertised brand in the shopping cart. Sometimes, the simplest strategy is the best strategy. This is what we termed mindshare advertising in Chapter 5.

Clearly, there is a large advantage in simple brand recall in routinely purchased product categories, like consumer package goods.

So, how do advertisers promote easy recall?

There are two popular methods: repetition and memory aids—slogans, jingles, and point-of-purchase branding (see Insights Online [Exhibit 10.2] for some interesting examples and discussion).

Delta], soft drinks [Coke, Pepsi], or toothpaste [Crest, Colgate]) is mentioned. So, if someone says "soft drink," the folks in Atlanta (The Coca-Cola Company headquarters) want you to say "Coke," preferably before any other brand name but certainly in the first group mentioned before a pause to think of others.

Again, the odds of being either top of mind or in the evoked set increase with recall. In the case of

Method A: Repetition. Repetition is a tried-and-true way of gaining easier retrieval of brand names from consumer's memory. Advertisers do this by buying a lot of ads and/or by frequently repeating the brand name within the ad itself. This is typically a strategy for television

and radio but can be accomplished visually in print, with promotional placement in television shows and movies, and online. The idea is that things said (or shown) more often will be remembered more easily than things said (or shown) less frequently. So the advertiser repeats the brand name over and over again. Then, when the consumer stands in front of, say, the laundry detergent, the advertised brand name is recalled from memory.

The more accessible (easier to remember) brand names are retrieved first and fastest from memory, making them (all else being equal) more likely to end up in the shopping cart. Getting into the consumer's evoked set gets you close to actual purchase, and achieving top of mind gets you even closer.

Does repetition always work? No, of course it doesn't. There are plenty of times when consumers remember one brand, and then buy another. They may actually hate the most easily remembered brand and never buy it. This type of advertising plays a pure probability game—being easily recalled tilts the odds of being purchased in favor of the advertisers willing to pay for the recall that repetition buys.

We think the all-time record for most brand mentions in a single ad might be a tie: either "Kibbles and Bits, Kibbles and Bits, I gotta get me some Kibbles and Bits" over and over and over (see Exhibit 10.3), or the endless "Meow, Meow, Meow, Meow" for Meow Mix. Can you think of one with more? If you can, please let us know, we actually collect ridiculous stuff like this.

Visual repetition is also important. The very frequent image of the Geiko Gecko, paired with frequent use of the word, makes this campaign one of the most successful of all time. It has repetition, verbal–visual pairing, and no doubt owns a big piece of the mind of American consumers. Although psychologists are less sure about how repeated images function in recall as they are about words, there is a general belief that they are related. In the case of Geiko–Gecko pairing, image is linked to words, and we know that helps.

Repetition strategies are being used on the Internet as well: Familiar names are placed so that consumers will see and hear them again and again. In fact, many IBP efforts work in this way. The more streaming of Internet content there is, the more this happens. Also, think visuals. Think sports arenas: Seeing a name over and over (and having it in a TV shot) is certainly one of the ideas behind named arenas such as Qualcomm Stadium, AT&T Park, and Minute Maid Park. It is less clear that

EXHIBIT 10.3 This ad may hold the all-time record for most brand mentions in a single 30-second ad: "Kibbles and Bits, Kibbles and Bits . . ."

Kibbles 'n Bits is a registered trademark of Del MonteCorporation. © Del Monte Foods 2004.

this does any good at all, but just in case, big advertisers are willing to take the chance. Sometimes corporate egos need big arenas.

Method B: Slogans and Jingles. Slogans are one small step up from raw repetition in degree of complexity. Here, slogans and jingles are used to enhance the odds of recalling the brand name. The basic mechanism at work here is still memory, and the goal is still brand-name recall. Slogans are linguistic devices that link a brand name to something memorable by means of the slogan's simplicity, meter, rhyme, or some other factor. Jingles do the same thing, just set to a melody. Examples are numerous: "You Deserve a Break Today"; "You're in Good Hands with Allstate"; "Like a Good Neighbor, State Farm Is There"; "Get Met, It Pays"; and "It Keeps on Going and Going and Going." Slogans and jingles provide rehearsal—that is, encourage repetition because they are catchy, or prone to repeating—and the inherent properties of the slogan or jingle provide a retrieval cue for the brand name.

Also consider a practical application of the human need to complete or "close" a verse: For example, when you say, "Like a good neighbor," you pretty much are compelled to complete the phrase with "State Farm is there." As you know, slogans and jingles are hard to get out of your head. That's the idea.

Method C: Point-of-Purchase Branding. Part of remembering is being reminded. In the contemporary advertising IBP world, marketers often use point-of-purchase displays that help trigger, or cue, the brand name (and maybe an ad) from memory. That is the main idea behind point-of-purchase advertising—to provide a memory trigger. The in-store visual triggers retrieval of the brand name, and maybe memories of the actual ad itself, importantly, at the point-of-purchase decision—when it goes in the cart or stays on the shelf.

The aisle itself (its look, smell, etc.) or the packaging may cue the category. That is, on the shopper's highly repeated and routinized path down this aisle, the aisle itself and the packaging may prompt recollections about the category (say, detergent) and may make the heavily advertised brand (say, Tide) come right to mind. Efforts are underway to make on-line browsing more store-like on this dimension or better.

Evaluation of repetition, slogans, and jingles is typically done through day-after-recall (DAR) tests and tracking studies emphasizing recall (e.g., "name three detergents"). In other words, these ads are evaluated with the most traditional ad copy research there is: simple recall measures. This is one time when the method of evaluation actually makes perfect sense: You are trying to get recall; you test for recall.

─────── LO ③ ───────

Strategic Implications of Repetition, Slogans, and Jingles

- **Extremely resistant to forgetting.** These methods make it difficult to forget the brand. Once established, the residual amount of impact from the campaign can be huge. If some advertisers stopped advertising today, you would remember their slogans, jingles, and names for a long, long time.

- **Efficient for consumer.** For routinely purchased items, consumers rely on a simple and easy decision rule: Buy what you remember. So, this kind of advertising works well in repeat-purchase and low-involvement items.

- **Long-term commitment/expense.** To achieve an adequate level of recall, advertisers have to sign on for a lot of advertising. It takes lots and lots of repetition, particularly early on, or a very memorable slogan or jingle. Once advertisers have achieved a high recall level, they can fine-tune their spending so that they are spending just enough to stay where they want. But they have to get there first, and it can be a very expensive trip.

- **Competitive interference.** This is less a problem with repetition, but consumers may learn a slogan or jingle only to associate it with the wrong brand. This has happened more times than you might imagine. For example, "It keeps on going, and going, and going . . . ." It's Duracell, right? Wait, maybe it's Eveready? Not absolutely sure? Not good. This is why it is absolutely vital to firmly link brand name to slogan. You don't want to pay for your competitor's success.

- **Creative resistance.** Creatives generally hate this type of advertising. Can you imagine why? These ads are rarely called creative and don't usually win a lot of creative awards. So creatives are less likely to enjoy working on them. Thus, the client paying the bills is less likely to get the "hot" or even senior creative teams. A lot of rookies get these assignments.

10-2b Objective #2: Link Key Attribute(s) to the Brand Name

Sometimes advertisers want consumers to remember the brand and associate it with one or at most two attributes. (See Insights Online [Exhibit 10.4] for a rather humorous example.) This type of advertising is most closely identified with the **unique selling proposition (USP)** style, a type of ad that strongly emphasizes a supposedly unique quality (or qualities) of the advertised brand. It is more complicated than simple brand recall, and a bit more challenging. It is one step up from Objective #1 in complexity. It requires more of the consumer, a little more thought, a little more learning. So, it requires more from those planning and making the ads. The ads provide a reason to buy, but don't require the consumer to think too much about that reason, just associate it with the brand name. In fact, many experts believe these ads work best if consumers don't think too much about the claim, just associate the two: the name and the claim. The primary mechanisms are memory and learning. The appeal may be through words (copy) or visuals (art direction).

Method: USP. The idea of emphasizing one and only one brand attribute is a very good idea—sometimes two are used if they are complementary, such as "strong but

EXHIBIT 10.5 Brand + attribute. It's just right. Do you suppose anyone else is using that idea in this space?

gentle." Look at the ad in Exhibit 10.5; it uses this technique. Ads that try to link several attributes to a brand while working to establish recall generally fail—they are too confusing and give too much information. Too much is attempted. Sometimes this type of advertising relies on a soft logic. The ad makes sense, but don't think too much about it: Listerine is strong, Ivory is pure, Angel Soft is just right. Evaluation of the USP method is typically done through recall tests, communication tests, and tracking studies. Did the consumer remember the USP? Sometimes price is the USP, but as you might imagine, a lot of advertisers use that as a claim, and it can be pretty crowded space.

Strategic Implications of the USP Method

- *Big carryover.* USP advertising is very efficient. Once this link has been firmly established, it can last a very long time. An investment in this kind of advertising can carry you through some lean times.

- *Very resistant.* This type of advertising can be incredibly resistant to competitive challenge. Generations of consumers have been born, lived, and died remembering that Ivory is pure. Being the first to claim an attribute can be a huge advantage.

Professionals will often say "Brand X owns that space" (meaning that attribute). For example, "Ivory owns the purity space," "Cheer owns the all-temperature space."

- *Long-term commitment and expense.* If advertisers are going to use the USP method, they have to be in it for the long haul. You can't keep switching strategies and expect good results. Pick an attribute and stay with it. If advertisers would just do this one thing, a lot more would be successful.

- *Some creative resistance.* Creatives tend not to hate this quite as much as simple repetition, but it does seem to get old with them pretty fast. Don't expect the best or most experienced creative teams.

10-2c **Objective #3: Persuade the Consumer**

This style of advertising is about arguments. In this type of advertising, we move up from linking one or possibly two attributes to a brand name using soft logic and simple learning to actually posing one or more (usually more) logical arguments to an engaged consumer. This is high-engagement advertising. That is, it assumes an actively engaged consumer, paying attention and considering the arguments. Its goal is to convince the consumer through arguments that the advertised brand is the right choice. The advertiser says, in effect, you should buy my brand because of *x*, *y*, and *z* reasons. These arguments have typically been verbal (copy) but have in the past few decades employed more visual arguments as well. As detailed below, there are several forms of this type of advertising.

For this general type of advertising to work as planned, the consumer has to think about what the advertiser is saying. The consumer must "get" the ad, understand the argument, and generally agree with it. In a pure persuasion ad, there is an assumed dialogue between the ad and the consumer, and some of the dialogue contains the consumer disagreeing and counterarguing with a message. As mentioned in Chapter 7, some research has found counterarguments to be the single most common consumer response to these types of ads. Actually, the most common response is no response at all, consumers just ignore it. Again, remember: Consumers ignore the vast majority of advertising. Further, the inherent wordiness, its antiquated style, and that it is now speaking to the most distracted population in history are the reasons such advertising has become less popular. Every year several people actually die due to distraction, like walking in front of a bus, or texting while driving; so given that, what do you think the future of high engagement, rational argument ads, is?

Method A: Reason-Why Ads. In a reason-why ad, the advertiser reasons with the potential consumer. The ad points out to the consumer that there are good reasons why this brand will be satisfying and beneficial. Advertisers are usually relentless in their attempt to reason with consumers when using this method. They begin with some claim, like "Seven great reasons to buy Brand X," and then proceed to list all seven, finishing with the conclusion (implicit or explicit) that only a moron would, after such compelling evidence, do anything other than purchase Brand X. Other times, the reason or reasons to use a product can be presented deftly. Psychologists have shown that humans value conclusions they have reached more than those made for them. So, really great reason-why ads will often give the reasons why, but let the consumer actually make the (obvious by then) conclusion that the advertised brand is best. Yet, the biggest trick to this method is making sure that the reasons make sense and that consumers actually care. Sometimes, the reason-why ad includes the reason why the choice actually matters. Price advertising can be a reason-why. There is a great deal of price advertising, and for that reason it is hard to make that claim unique. Wise advertisers have argued that value is a superior claim than price; someone may beat you on the objectively lower price,

but you can always claim that your brand is a better value. Look at the Kia ad in Exhibit 10.6, what are the reasons why a consumer should buy? Do they make sense? Will they work?

Strategic Implications of Reason-Why Ads

- *Permission to buy.* Gives consumers reasons for purchasing the advertised brand.

- *Socially acceptable defense.* We all know that we sometimes have to defend our purchase decisions to friends and family. These types of ads are chock full of reasons why the purchase was a smart idea.

- *High level of involvement.* Consumers have to be paying attention for these ads to work. They have to engage with these ads. How much of the time do you think that actually happens? Sometimes consumers get swamped with too much information and just do something simple like buy what they did last time, or what a friend or *Consumer Reports* recommended.

- *Potential for counterarguments.* This type of advertising might actually convince consumers why *not* to buy the advertised brand. Remember, consumers like to argue with ads.

- *Legal/regulatory challenges/exposure.* The makers of these ads tend to get dragged into court or summoned by a regulatory body quite a bit. You'd better make sure that all your reason-why ads can stand up in court. Some haven't.

- *Some creative resistance.* Creatives are often ho-hum on these type of ads.

(See Insights Online [Exhibit 10.7] to decide whether the Volkswagen Super Bowl ad is a Reason-Why ad.)

Method B: Hard-Sell Ads. Hard-sell ads are a subcategory of reason-why ads: reason why with urgency. They are characteristically high pressure and urgent, thus "hard." Phrases such as "act now," "limited time offer," "your last chance to save," and "one-time-only sale" are representative of this method. The idea is to create a sense of urgency so that consumers will act quickly. Sometimes these are done as IBP, and include "call or click *now*." Of course, many consumers have learned to ignore or otherwise discount these messages. We've all seen "Going Out of Business Sale" signs that remained up and the store open for months and even years. As one of our editors

EXHIBIT 10.6 Kia uses reason-why.

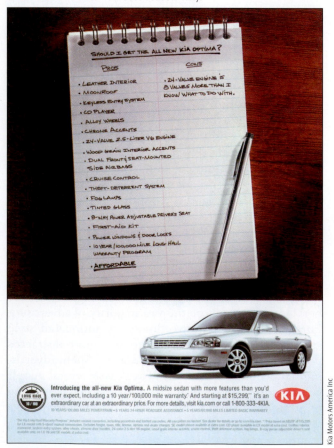

Introducing the all-new Kia Optima. A midsize sedan with more features than you'd ever expect, including a 10 year/100,000 mile warranty.* And starting at $15,299,** it's an extraordinary car at an extraordinary price. For more details, visit kia.com or call 1-800-333-4KIA.

10 YEARS/100,000 MILES POWERTRAIN • 5 YEARS 24-HOUR ROADSIDE ASSISTANCE • 5 YEARS/60,000 MILES LIMITED BASIC WARRANTY

INSIGHTS ONLINE

10.8 Go online to see the AdAge feature, "Which Is Best: Hard-Sell or Soft-Sell Advertising? This Article Debates the Two Approaches."

noted, this happens all the time. She lived in NYC; on the stretch of Fifth Avenue from 42nd to 48th she once (in four years of living and working in Midtown) saw only one electronics store that *didn't* have a "Going Out of Business" sign. Cry "*wolf*" too many times and no one believes any more. What marketers attempt to deceive, surely you must be kidding?

Strategic Implications of Hard-Sell Approaches

- *"Permission to buy now."* The sale was about to end.
- *Socially acceptable defense.* "I had to act," "It was on sale that day only," "It was such a good deal."
- *Low credibility.* A lot of consumers know this is just a scam, and that "last chance" almost never means last chance.
- *Legal/regulatory challenges/exposure.* The makers of these ads tend to face the same legal and regulatory problems as the reason-why ads.
- *Some creative resistance.* Again, these are not the kind of ads creatives beg for.

(See Insights Online [Exhibit 10.8] for more information about Hard-Sell ads.)

Method C: Comparison Ads. **Comparison advertisements** are another form of advertising designed to persuade the consumer. Comparison ads try to demonstrate a brand's ability to satisfy consumers by comparing its features to those of competitive brands. Comparisons can be an effective and efficient means of communicating a large amount of information in a clear, interesting, and convincing way, or they can be extremely confusing and create a situation of information overload in which the market leader usually wins. Comparison advertising as a technique has traditionally been used by marketers of convenience goods such as pain relievers, laundry detergents, and household cleaners. Advertisers in a wide range of product categories have tried comparison advertising from time to time. Every now and

then, there are exceptions to this typically mundane class; two come immediately to mind—the classic: Avis "We're Number 2: We Try Harder," and the recent Mac versus PC ads (see Exhibit 10.9). This Apple campaign was brilliant in that it made all the right technical and performance comparisons (rarely more than one or two per ad) and did it in an amusing, interesting, and absolutely wonderful way. It drew on person–company stereotypes to contextualize the comparison. Once again, Apple was very smart.

Evaluation of comparison ads is typically done through tracking studies that measure attitudes, beliefs, and preferences over time.

Using comparison in an advertisement can be direct and name competitors' brands, or it can be indirect and refer only to the "leading brand" or "Brand X." Here are a few rules gleaned from consumer research:

- Direct comparison by a low-share brand (say Apple) to a high-share brand (say Windows) increases receivers' attention and increases their intent to purchase the low-share brand (Apple).
- Direct comparison by a high-share brand to a low-share brand does not attract additional attention to the high-share brand but actually helps the low-share brand. This is not good. Direct comparison is more effective if members of the target audience have not demonstrated clear brand preference in their product choices.[1]

EXHIBIT 10.9 One of the best comparison ads of all time.

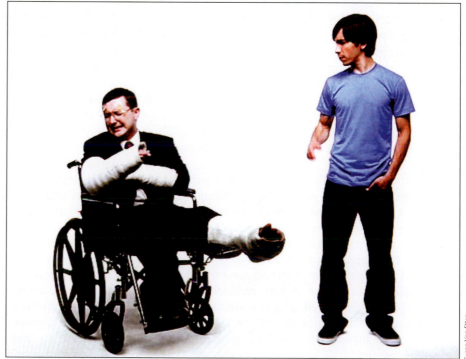

Susan Van Etten

For these reasons, established market leaders almost never use comparison ads. These ads are almost always used by the underdog brand, the brand that wishes to be seen in the company of the market leader.

Strategic Implications of Comparison Ads

- Can help a low-share brand.
- Provides social justification (to others) for purchase of the less popular brand.
- Gives permission to buy. Lets the consumer work through and then come to his or her own conclusion that it really is the best brand. (Consumer-generated conclusions are more powerful than those made on behalf of the advertiser.)
- Significant legal/regulatory exposure. Companies love to file complaints to agencies such as the NAD for these types of ads. Factor in legal costs.
- Not done much outside the United States; in much of the world, comparison advertising is either outlawed, not done by mutual agreement, or simply considered in such poor taste as to be never done.
- Not for established market leaders.
- These ads are sometimes evaluated as more offensive and less interesting than noncomparative ads. They have a tendency to turn some consumers off.

Method D: Testimonials. Testimonials are another type of persuade-the-consumer ads. A frequently used message tactic is to have a spokesperson who champions the brand in an advertisement, rather than simply providing information. When an advocacy position is taken by a spokesperson in an advertisement, it is known as a **testimonial**. The value of the testimonial lies in the authoritative presentation of a brand's attributes and benefits by the spokesperson. There are three basic versions of the testimonial message tactic.

The most conspicuous version is the *celebrity testimonial*. Sports stars and supermodels are widely used. The belief is that a celebrity testimonial will increase an ad's ability to attract attention and produce a desire in receivers to emulate or imitate the celebrities they admire.

Whether this is really true or not, the fact remains that celebrities remain popular in contemporary advertising. Of course, there is the ever-present risk that a celebrity will fall from grace, as several have in recent years, and potentially damage the reputation of the brand for which he or she was once the champion.

Expert spokespeople for a brand are viewed by the target audience as having expert product knowledge. A spokesperson portrayed as a doctor, lawyer, scientist, gardener, or any other expert relevant to a brand is intended to increase the credibility of the message being transmitted. There are also real experts.

EXHIBIT 10.10 Dave Mirra is known as the Miracle Boy of freestyle BMX riding. What type of audience might find his testimonials persuasive?

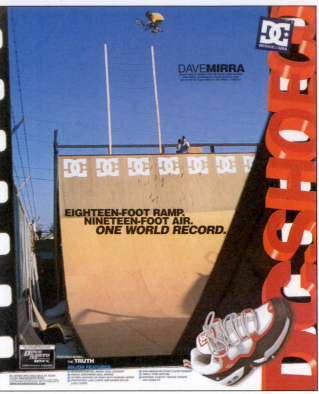

Advertising for the Club, a steering-wheel locking device that deters auto theft, uses police officers from several cities to demonstrate the effectiveness of the product. Some experts can also be celebrities. This is the case when Michael Jordan gives a testimonial for Nike basketball shoes or Dave Mirra for BMX-riding shoes. Check out Dave in Exhibit 10.10. (See Insights Online [Exhibit 10.11] for yet another example.)

There is also the *average-user testimonial*. Here, the spokesperson is not a celebrity or portrayed as an expert but rather as an average user speaking for the brand. The philosophy is that the target market can relate to this person. Solid theoretical support for this testimonial approach comes from reference-group theory. An interpretation of reference-group theory in this context suggests that consumers may rely on opinions or testimonials from people they consider similar to themselves, rather than on objective product information. Simply put, the consumer's

> ### INSIGHTS ONLINE
>
> **10.11** Go online to see the AdAge feature, "Nationwide Insurance Uses *Pretty Woman* Julia Roberts's Voice-Over while Ditching Its Past 'World's Greatest Spokesperson Campaign'. Do You Think This a Smart Move?"

logic in this situation is, "That person is similar to me and likes that brand; therefore, I will also like that brand." In theory, this sort of logic frees the receiver from having to scrutinize detailed product information by simply substituting the reference-group information. Of course, in practice, the execution of this strategy is rarely that easy. Consumers are very sophisticated at detecting this attempt at persuasion. Evaluation is usually through tracking studies and communications tests.

Strategic Implications of Testimonial Advertising

- Very popular people can generate popularity for the brand.
- People perceived to be very similar to the consumer, or an expert, can be powerful advocates for the brand.
- Consumers often forget who likes what, particularly when stars promote multiple goods and services.
- Can generate more popularity for the star than for the brand.

Celebrities, being human, are not as easy to manage as cartoon characters: think Tony the Tiger versus Tiger Woods (see Insights Online [Exhibit 10.12] for another notable example).

Method E: Demonstration. How close an electric razor shaves, how green a fertilizer makes a lawn, and how easy an exercise machine is to use are all product features that can be demonstrated by using a method known simply as demonstration. "Seeing is believing" is the motto of this school of advertising. When it's done well, the results are striking. In Exhibit 10.13 a demonstration is offered. Do you see it? Do you believe it? Evaluation of demonstration ads is typically done through tracking studies that measure attitudes, beliefs, and brand preferences over time.

Strategic Implications of Demonstration Ads

- Inherent credibility of "seeing is believing."
- Can be used as social justification; helps the consumer defend his or her decision to buy.
- Provides clear permission to buy. ("I saw a test; it was the best.")
- Fairly heavy regulatory/legal exposure.

Method F: Infomercials. With the **infomercial**, an advertiser typically buys from 5 to 60 minutes of television time and runs an information/entertainment program that is really an extended advertisement. Real estate investment programs, weight-loss and fitness products, motivational programs, and cookware have dominated the infomercial format. The program usually has a host who provides information about a product and typically brings on guests to give testimonials about how successful they have been using the featured product. Most infomercials run on cable or satellite channels, although networks have sold early-morning and late-night time as well.

Strategic Implications of Infomercials

- Long format gives advertisers plenty of time to make their case.
- As network ratings fall, day-parts (e.g., Sunday mornings 9–11) that were previously unaffordable have now opened up, making infomercials better deals for advertisers.
- Has the advantage of looking like an entertainment show, when it's really an ad.

EXHIBIT 10.13 Straight demonstration of a product benefit by Curad. www.curadusa.com.

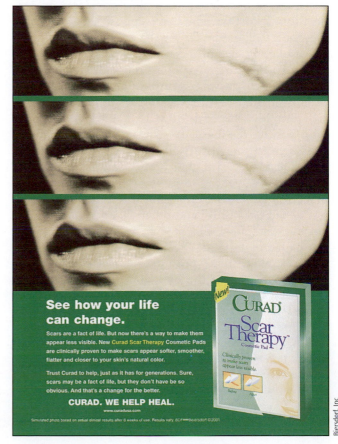

See how your life can change.

Scars are a fact of life. But now there's a way to make them appear less visible. New Curad Scar Therapy Cosmetic Pads are clinically proven to make scars appear softer, smoother, flatter and closer to your skin's natural color.

Trust Curad to help, just as it has for generations. Sure, scars may be a fact of life, but they don't have to be so obvious. And that's a change for the better.

CURAD. WE HELP HEAL.
www.curadusa.com

Simulated photo based on actual clinical results after 8 weeks of use. Results vary. BDF****Beiersdorf ©2001

Biersdorf, Inc

- The genre of ads has a somewhat negative public image, which doesn't help build credibility or trust in the advertised brand.

There are other persuade-the-consumer formats, including ads posing as newspaper articles (advertorials), but all have the same basic mechanism at their core—here's why you should buy this—providing supportive arguments for purchase.

10-2d Objective #4: Affective Association: Get the Consumer to Feel Good about the Brand

Now, things are getting a little more sophisticated and fun. Advertisers want consumers to like their brand. They believe that brand liking leads to purchase. But rather than providing the consumer with hard reasons to like the brand, these ads work more through feelings. Again, this is another pretty big step up in complexity.

There are several well-known approaches to getting the consumer to like one's brand. Let's look at some of the general approaches; most specific examples are merely finer distinctions within these more general categories.

Method A: Feel-Good Ads. These ads are supposed to work through affective (feeling) association or pre-decision distortion. They are supposed to either link the good feeling elicited by the ad with the brand or by leveraging the propensity for humans to distort information in the favor of liked brands without even knowing they are doing so. Although the actual theory and mechanics of this seemingly simple association are complex, the basic idea is that by creating ads with positive feelings, advertisers will lead consumers to associate those positive feelings with the advertised brand, leading to a higher probability of purchase.

Of course, getting from liking the ad to liking the brand can be one big leap. Recent research by Stanford researcher Baba Shiv[2] and others has demonstrated an enrichment effect that occurs when the consumer thinks of a brand with attached positive emotions. The consumer will actually, prior to conscious consideration, bias information in the direction of the emotionally enriched brand. They don't even know they are doing this. So if you can get a brand to be liked, even just a little and not even consciously, you can get more purchases. The evidence on how well this method works in practice is mixed. It may be that positive feelings are transferred to the brand, or it could be that they actually interfere with remembering the message or the brand name. From an advertising and IBP perspective, how do you get good results from this method? Well, if you

can create advertising that makes consumers connect positive emotions with the brand, you will have some success. The key is not to make the ad liked, but to make the brands liked. Liking the ad doesn't necessarily mean liking the brand. But message strategy development is a game of probability, and liking the ad may lead to a higher probability of purchase. There are many practitioners who believe in the method's intuitive appeal. We believe you must clearly associate the brand name and/or image with the feeling. Lots of ads don't do this—not even close. You may love ads for Miller Lite but be a PBR drinker. You may think, "Nice ads—wish they made a better beer."

Some feel-good advertising campaigns do work. Sometimes, feel-good ads try to get the consumer *not* to think about certain things. United Airlines could show how often its planes depart and arrive on schedule. Of course, why would they want to? Instead, it has shown successful business meetings and the happy reunion of family members, which create a much richer message, a wider field of shared meanings. And you don't have to think about being stuck at O'Hare with a rude ticket agent. The emotions become the product attribute linked to the brand. Sometimes it works beautifully. Consider Kodak's highly successful print and television campaign that highlighted the "Memories of Our Lives" with powerful scenes: a son coming home from the military just in time for Christmas dinner and a father's reception dance with his newly married daughter. Here, Kodak makes it clear that it is in the memory business, and Kodak memories are good memories. Kodak did this type of advertising for about 100 years. Unfortunately, they didn't weather the transition to digital very well, but 100 years is a good run. In Exhibit 10.14, Martex attempts to evoke warm feelings associated with the relationship between a father and son.

Recently, there has been progress in understanding the mechanisms involved in feel-good advertising.[3] It is becoming clearer that thought and feelings are, at some basic level, separate systems. Feelings are believed to be a more "primitive" system. That is, they emanate from a part of the brain that responds quickly to stimuli in the environment. The classic example is that a loud noise frightens us (feeling), even before we know what we are frightened of (thought). So emotions are faster than thought, and sometimes even stronger. There is also evidence that as the media environment gets more cluttered, the affective (or feeling) ads may actually do better than thought-based ads that require a great deal of processing. Feeling ads may have a leg up in the contemporary media environment. Evaluation of feel-good ads is typically done by measuring attitude change via pre- and post-exposure tests, tracking studies, theater dial-turning tests, and communication tests.

EXHIBIT 10.14 A touching ad for Martex Bath & Bedding. www.martex.com.

OUR KIDS
ARE FULL OF SURPRISES.
FROM TOWELS TO TOYBOXES,
THEY TREAT EVERYTHING
LIKE AN ADVENTURE.
SAME WITH YOU AND
YOUR KIDS, RIGHT?

M A R T E X
BATH & BEDDING | IN TOUCH WITH YOU.

Strategic Implications of Feel-Good Advertising

- Eager creatives. Creatives win awards and advance their careers with this style of advertising.

- May perform better in cluttered media environment.

- May generate competing thoughts and connections. An emotional ad about family and business travel may get viewers to think about their lives and their time on the road—but not really make any enduring connections to the brand. Your expensive emotional ad may make Joe or Mary consumer a better (or guilty) parent, but not a customer.

(See Insights Online [Exhibit 10.15] for an interesting discussion.)

Method B: Humor Ads. The goal of a humor ad is pretty much the same as that of other feel-good ads, but humor is a different animal. Generally, the goal of humor in advertising is to create in the receiver a pleasant and memorable

10.15 Go online to see the AdAge feature, "The 'Sunny Side' of Volkswagen's Feel-Good Super Bowl Teaser Spot."

association with the brand. Recent advertising campaigns as diverse as those for ESPN ("This Is SportsCenter"), California Milk Processor Board ("Got Milk?"), and Las Vegas ("What Happens in Vegas, Stays in Vegas") have all successfully used humor as the primary message theme. But research suggests that the positive impact of humor is not as strong as the intuitive appeal of the approach. Quite simply, humorous versions of advertisements often do not prove to be more persuasive than non-humorous versions of the same ad. Funny ads are usually great entertainment but may often be pretty bad business investments.

How many times have you been talking to friends about your favorite ads, and you say something like, "Remember the one where the guy knocks over the drink, and then says . . . ." Everybody laughs, and then maybe someone says something like, "I can't remember who it's for, but what a great ad." Wrong, this is not a great ad. You remember the gag, but not the brand. Not good. You and your friends didn't pay for the ad. How come with some funny ads you can recall the brand? The difference may be that in the ads you recall, the payoff for the humor is an integral part of the message strategy. Thus, it better ensures the memory link between humor and brand. If the ad is merely funny and doesn't link the joke (or the punch line) to the brand name, then the advertiser may have bought some very expensive laughs. Clients rarely consider this funny.

A great example of an explicitly linked payoff is the Bud Light "Give Me a Light" campaign of the early 1980s. "Miller Lite" was quickly becoming the generic term for light beer. To do something about this, Bud Light came up with the series of "Give Me a Light" ads to remind light beer drinkers that they had to be a little more specific in what they were ordering. The ads showed customers ordering "a light" and instead getting spotlights, landing lights, searchlights, lights in Wrigley Field, and all sorts of other types of lights. The customer in the ad would then say, "No, a Bud Light." The ads not only were funny but also made the point perfectly: Say "Bud Light," not just "a light," when ordering a beer. In addition, the message allowed thousands of customers and would-be comedians in bars and restaurants to repeat the line in person, which amounted to a lot of free advertising. The campaign, by Needham, Harper and Steers-Chicago (now DDB Chicago), was a huge success. Why? Because the punch line was firmly linked to the brand name, and the ad actually got consumers to repeat the tag line in actual consumer practice.

Evaluation of humorous ads is typically done through pre- and post-exposure tests, dial-turning attitude tests, and tracking studies that measure attitudes, beliefs, and preferences over time. In Exhibit 10.16, the SKY ad "There is more to watch in HDTV" is

Wright's Media

pretty funny if you've seen *The Shining*. "*Here's Johnny!*" in HD? Does this ad work? Will it sell Sky subscriptions? Why? Does the humor effectively connect to the brand?

Strategic Implications of Humor Advertising

- If the joke is integral to the copy platform, humor can be very effective. If it is not, it is just expensive entertainment.

- Very eager creatives. Creatives love to do funny ads. Funny ads win awards and advance careers.

- Humorous messages may adversely affect comprehension. Humor can actually interfere with memory processes: The consumer doesn't remember what brand the ad was for; happens all the time.

- Very funny messages can wear out very quickly, leaving no one laughing, especially the advertiser.[4] It's like hearing the same joke over and over. Advertisers who use this technique have to keep changing the gag. Think Geico.

Because you have to keep the gag fresh, these ad campaigns can be very expensive.

Method C: Sex-Appeal Ads. Sex ads are a type of feelings-based advertising. Because they are directed toward humans, ads tend to focus on sex from time to time. Not a big surprise: Humans tend to think about sex from time to time. Sex ads are thought not to require much thought, just arousal and affect (feelings). But does sex sell?

In a literal sense, the answer is no, because nothing, not even sex, *makes* someone buy something. However, sexual appeals are attention-getting and occasionally arousing, which may affect how consumers feel about a brand. The advertiser is trying to get attention and link some degree of sexual arousal and positive feelings

to the brand. Sometimes this work, but the commonly held notion that "sex sells" is more over-simplification than reality.

Can you use sex to help create a brand image? Sure you can. Calvin Klein and many other advertisers have used sexual imagery successfully to mold brand image. But these are for products such as clothes and perfumes, which emphasize how one looks, feels, and smells. The context for the sex appeal is congruent; it fits, it makes sense. If you are trying to link a sexy image in an ad with a sexy brand image for lingerie or perfume or other relevant goods and services, it can work. Does the same appeal work as well for cars, telephones, computer peripherals, and file cabinets? How about breakfast cereals? In general, no. As recently noted by Professor Tom Reichert at the University of Georgia,[5] traditional wisdom in the ad business was that the use of sex is "amateurish and sophomoric, and a desperate—not to mention ineffective—attempt to rescue plummeting sales." The research on the topic generally confirms that sex-appeal ads can be effective when the context is appropriate, but a distraction or worse when it not. Think about it: A really hot ad comes on at night, you watch. What are you thinking about during the ad? The brand? You may remember the hot model in considerable detail and not remember a thing about the brand, unless that "heat" maps onto the meaning of the brand. Victoria's Secret wants to get you to link sex to their brand, and they have been very successful doing just that. On the other hand, some condom ads emphasize security, or effectiveness, while others emphasize the obvious link between buying some and getting some.

The ad shown in Exhibit 10.17 uses a sex-appeal message. How effective do you think this ad is in fulfilling the objective of instilling brand meaning and preference? Is it on target strategically? Is it demeaning, a bit silly, or just a little sexy?

Evaluation of sex-appeal ads is typically done through communication tests, focus groups, pre- and post-exposure tests, and tracking studies that measure attitudes, beliefs, and preferences over time. When using sex appeal, clients sometimes order more focus groups and communication tests to make sure that they are not going over some invisible and always-moving line.

Strategic Implications of Sexual-Appeal Advertising

- Higher attention levels.

- Higher arousal and affect (feeling). This can be good if it can be tied to brand meaning, bad if it can't.

- Possible poor memorability of brand due to interference at the time of exposure. In other words, the viewer is thinking about something else.

EXHIBIT 10.17 Why does/doesn't sex help sell Guess? Explain the role of sex in terms of the Guess brand.

- Product-theme continuity excludes many goods and services.
- Legal, political, and regulatory exposure.

10-2e **Objective #5: Scare the Consumer into Action**

The strategy here is to scare the consumer into acting. Fear appeals are typically designed to elicit a specific feeling (fear) as well as a specific thought (buy x to prevent y). Fear is an extraordinarily powerful emotion and may be used to get consumers to take some very important action. But this fear must be coupled with some degree of thought in order for it to work. That's why we place this strategy a bit higher up the ladder in terms of its degree of complexity. It is generally considered hard to use effectively and is fairly limited in application. It is only used in few product and service categories.

Method: Fear-Appeal Ads. A fear appeal highlights the risk of harm or other negative consequences of not using the advertised brand or not taking some recommended action. Usually it's a little bit of fear designed to induce a little bit of thought, and then action. Getting the balance right is the tricky part. The intuitive belief about fear as a message tactic is that fear will motivate the receiver to buy a product that will reduce or eliminate the portrayed threat. For example, Radio Shack spent $6 million to run a series of ads showing a dimly lit unprotected house, including a peacefully sleeping child, as a way to raise concerns about the safety of the receiver's valuables as well as his or her family. The campaign used the theme

"If Security Is the Question, We've Got the Answer." The ad closed with the Radio Shack logo and the National Crime Prevention Council slogan, "United Against Crime."[6] Similarly, the ad in Exhibit 10.18 for Body Alarm cuts right to the chase: It capitalizes on fears of not being able to cry for help during a bodily attack. ADT has had a long-running campaign showing a vulnerable woman (often single, sometimes with a child) being saved by the ADT security team from sure victimization.

The contemporary social environment has provided advertisers with an ideal context for using fear appeals. In an era of drive-by shootings, carjackings, gang violence, and terrorism, Americans fear for their personal safety. Manufacturers of security products such as alarm and lighting security systems leverage this fearful environment.[7] Other advertisers have recently tried fear appeals. One such advertiser, the Asthma Zero

EXHIBIT 10.18 Fairly scary. Get the point?

Mortality Coalition, urges people who have asthma to seek professional help and uses a fear appeal in its ad copy: "When those painful, strained breaths start coming, keep in mind that any one of them could easily be your last."[8]

Traditional wisdom holds that intense fear appeals actually short-circuit persuasion and result in a negative attitude toward the advertised brand.[9] Other researchers argue that the tactic is generally beneficial to the advertiser.[10] Our review of the research, plus our own professional experience, leads us to believe that to be successful, a fear-appeal ad must have a very clear benefit from acting in a very specific way, at any fear level. Fear ads must offer a "way out" of harm's way. The ideal fear-appeal ad would thus be one that is entirely believable[11] (one that people can't easily say doesn't apply to them or seems unlikely to be a real threat) and offers a very clear (completely obvious) and very easy way to avoid the bad thing threatened by the ad. Evaluation of fear-appeal ads is typically done through tracking studies that measure attitudes, beliefs, and preferences over time; pre- and post-exposure tests; and communication tests.

Strategic Implications of Fear-Appeal Advertising

- You must have a plausible threat to motivate consumers.

- You must have a completely clear and easy-to-discern link between the alleviation of the threat and the use of the advertised brand.

- Some fear ads are simply ridiculous and have low impact.

10-2f Objective #6: Change Behavior by Inducing Anxiety

Anxiety is fear's cousin. Anxiety is not quite outright fear, but it is uncomfortable and can last longer. Although it's hard to keep people in a state of outright fear, people can feel anxious for a bad long time. People try to avoid feeling anxious. They try to minimize, moderate, and alleviate anxiety. They use all sorts of mechanisms to avoid anxiety from thought to behavior. Often people will buy or consume things to help them in their continuing struggle with anxiety. They might watch television, drink, exercise, eat, or take medication. They might also buy mouthwash, deodorant, condoms, a safer car, life insurance, or a retirement account, and advertisers know this. Advertisers pursue a change-behavior-by-inducing-anxiety objective by playing on consumer anxieties. The ads work through both thought and feelings. Regrettably, this is one of the most effective types of advertising

around. It is also probably advertising's greatest sin against humanity.

Method A: Anxiety Ads. There are many things to be anxious about. Advertisers realize this and use many settings to demonstrate why you should be anxious and what you can do to alleviate the anxiety. Social, medical, and personal-care products frequently use anxiety ads. The message conveyed in anxiety ads is that (1) there is a clear and present problem, and (2) the way to avoid this problem is to buy the advertised brand. Anxiety ads tout the likelihood of being stricken by gingivitis, athlete's foot, calcium deficiency, body odor, heart disease, and on and on. The idea is that these anxiety-producing conditions are out there, and they may affect you unless you take the appropriate action.

Method B: Social Anxiety Ads. This is a subcategory of anxiety ads where the danger is negative social judgment, as opposed to a physical threat. Procter & Gamble (P&G) has long relied on such presentations for its household and personal-care brands. In fact, P&G has used this approach so consistently over the years that in some circles, the anxiety tactic is referred to as the P&G approach. When Head & Shoulders dandruff shampoo is advertised with the theme "You Never Get a Second Chance to Make a First Impression," the audience realizes that Head & Shoulders could spare them the embarrassment of having dandruff. One of the more memorable P&G social anxiety ads is the scene where a husband and wife are busily cleaning the spots off the water glasses before dinner guests arrive because they didn't use P&G's Cascade dishwashing product, which, of course, would have prevented the glasses from spotting. Most personal-care products have used this type of appeal. Look at the ad for Enutrition in Exhibit 10.19. Is this anxiety motivating? Will it drive women to the site? Is it a nice or ethical thing to do?

Anxiety ads are often used in the context of important social roles, and the consumer's perceived inadequacy in that role. Billions of dollars have been made selling products by first making mothers feel a little more inadequate about their mothering skills, or father's about their ability to adequately provide for the family, or one's desirability, then offered a packed solution by the advertiser. May God have mercy on our souls.

This type of ads works by pointing to anxieties that reside right on the surface of consumers in these roles, or are just slightly latent, or beneath the surface. We tend to worry about the things we care most about and the things where the standards of adequacy and excellence are unknowable. What makes a great

EXHIBIT 10.19 But, hey, have a good day.

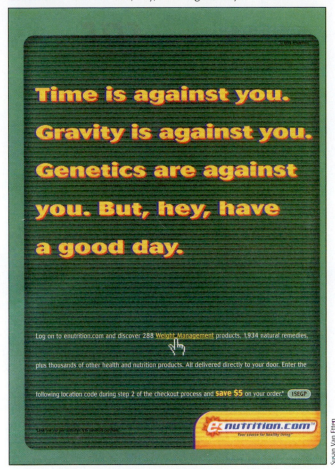

Susan Van Etten

husband, father, mother, worker, and so on? We are not quite sure. So, advertisers go to that anxiety and irritate it a bit, and then offer the consumer the way to feel better. It's really kind of a nasty thing to do, but it seems to work so well. Fortunately, some degree of self-awareness comes to smart companies. Evaluation of anxiety ads is typically done by measuring attitudes and beliefs through tracking studies and communication tests.

Strategic Implications of Anxiety Advertising

- Can generate perception of widespread (and thus personal) threat and motivate action (buying and using the advertised product). These ads have a pretty good track record of working.

- The brand can become the solution to the ever-present problem, and this results in long-term commitment to the brand. Once a solution (brand) is found, the consumer doesn't have to think about it again.

- Efficient. A little anxiety goes a long way.

- If the anxiety-producing threat is not linked tightly enough to your brand, you may increase category demand and provide business for your competitors, particularly the market leader. If total category share goes up, market leaders get most of it. Still, if the creative is good and the link to the specific brand is strong, it is a good method for any size player.

- Ethical issues. There is more than enough to feel anxious about without advertisers adding more.

- These ads have historically been disproportionately targeted at women. Critics note the inherent unfairness and sexism. They are absolutely right.

10-2g Objective #7: Define the Brand Image

The term "brand image" refers to the meaning of a brand, but at the level of impression, the quick take-away of what the brand is all about. It is expressed in visual terms (image) because brand images typically rely on the visual impression a brand makes with only a glance. Truly iconic brands have the ability to convey their essential meaning with just the swoosh (Nike), or the red circle (Coke), or the stylized and familiar written brand name (Tide). Not surprisingly, defining brand image is typically achieved visually. Brand images are important for several reasons. For one, they allow for an enormously efficient form of communication in a crowded media environment. The McDonald's golden arches deliver a lot of meaning with just a glance. Second, once established (and properly maintained), they create clear differentiation of one brand from another. Finally, they are not very dependent on any one language and are thus perfect for the transnational company. What is Skyy's brand image? Look carefully at Exhibit 10.20 and think about how this particular ad advances that image.

Method: Image Ads. Image advertising attempts to distill the brand's essential meaning with a very sparse use of words and heavy reliance on visuals. Image ads don't tend to contain much hard product information. They may use images to point to a brand quality or attribute or evoke a certain set of feelings about the brand. But, whether feelings or thoughts, or both, the idea is to define brand meaning in an efficient visual manner.

Evaluation of image ads is typically done through qualitative methods, and sometimes associative tests are used, along with attribute-related attitude tracking studies done over time. As we've said before, the evaluation of visual communication is still not where it should be. Further, these ads are often figurative rather than literal and require evaluation methods like the Zaltman (ZMET) metaphor-based techniques

EXHIBIT 10.20 What is Skyy's image, and how does this ad project it?

SKYY Spirits

(discussed in Chapter 7). They are also heavily dependent upon the maker of the ad being completely in touch with the contemporary culture so that the audience "gets" the ad. It is the skillful use of this social and cultural knowledge that turns brands into very successful brands, or even brand icons.[12]

Brand managers must work closely with advertising professionals to make sure that (1) the desired brand identity is really understood by all parties, and (2) how that typical verbal description is translated into a visual. Think about the most successful brands in the world. They are almost all "iconic," meaning that their essential meaning is captured and efficiently transmitted visually. The *Marlboro Man* is said to be a perfect icon of what the brand means. Apple, Nike, McDonald's, and Coke come to mind. To get to that iconic status requires an enduring and very cultural connected creative effort. It requires management wise enough to either help in this effort or trust the creatives.

Strategic Implications of Image Advertising

- Generally, less counterarguments generated by consumers.
- Relatively little or no legal/regulatory exposure. Hard to litigate the truth or falsity of a picture.

- Iconic potential.
- Very common in some categories (e.g., fashion, fragrance). Your image can get lost in the competitive cloud.
- Can be quickly rejected if advertised image rings untrue or poorly matches what the consumer currently thinks of the brand, particularly through direct experience.
- Don't tend to copy-test well. Why? Well, once again, existing copy-test procedures are designed predominately for words, not images.
- Managerial resistance. Client often argues for more words.
- Creatives tend to love them; you can get great people on your communication team.

10-2h Objective #8: Give the Brand the Desired Social Meaning

Now we are getting squarely into social and cultural branding, the type we discussed in Chapter 5.

Maybe you haven't given it much thought, but if you're ever going to understand advertising, you have to get this: Objects have social and cultural meanings. Billions of dollars are spent annually in efforts to achieve very specific social meanings for advertised brands. As an advertising and brand messaging professional, you have to try to make material objects (and services like FedEx) that already carry some meaning, have the meaning you want them to have. How do you do it?

Advertisers have long known that when they place their brand in the right social setting, either in an ad, a branded promotion in a real environment, or a product placement in a television, show, movie, or video game, their brand takes on some of the characteristics of its surroundings. The social setting and the brand rub off on each other. That is what is meant by giving the brand social meaning.

Most watches keep good time. But a Casio is different than a Tag Heuer, a Rolex, and so on. They all do the same thing. They are, as far as keeping time, the same. So, a watch is not just a watch. A watch is a way of communicating social status, wealth, fashion, and a sense of self. For men, it is one of the most accepted statements of social identity. In the watch category, these kinds of ads are common because the brands so heavily rely on desired social meaning. Think of fashion ads, same thing. Many categories rely on this objective to sell.

Let us say it again: Objects have social meaning; they are not just things. Good social meaning advertising can let the advertiser shape that meaning. If done well, these can be very effective ads.

Method A: Slice-of-Life Ads. A brand placed in a social context gains social meaning by association. Slice-of-life advertisements depict an ideal usage situation for the brand. The social context surrounding the brand rubs off and gives the brand a social meaning. Consumers may, of course, reject or significantly alter that meaning, but often they accept it. Think about it. You put the brand into a social setting and transfer meaning from that social setting to the brand. Look at Exhibit 10.21 for Louis Boston. Think about it, about how it works. Walk through the process that gives this brand a meaning through the slice-of-life technique.

Evaluation of slice-of-life ads is typically done through tracking studies that measure attitudes, beliefs, and preferences over time; pre- and post-exposure tests; and communication tests.

Strategic Implications of Slice-of-Life Ads

- Generally, fewer counterarguments made by consumers.
- Legal/regulatory advantages. Advertisers' attorneys like pictures more than words because determining the truth or falsity of a picture is much tougher than words. Have you ever noticed how heavily regulated industries tend to use lots of pictures and little copy (other than mandated warning labels)?

To get to that iconic status requires an enduring and very cultural connected creative effort. It requires management wise enough to either help in this effort or trust the creatives.

- Iconic potential. To make their brands another Coca-Cola is many advertisers' dream. Socially embedding your brand in everyday life gives you this chance.
- Creation of brand-social realities. You may be able to create the perfect social world for the brand, and its space in it.
- Fairly common. Unless the creative is outstanding (particularly visually) and you are generally willing to spend a reasonable amount for repetition, these ads can get lost in the clutter. In certain categories, such as fashion, a lot of ads are of this type.
- These ads don't tend to copy-test well. This is because so much of copy-testing is still designed around remembering words and verbal claims. Copy-testing has simply not caught up with the new reality of the prominence of visual forms of advertising and brand promotion.
- Creatives tend to love these ads (at least, art directors do); you will get some top-flight creative folks on the job.

Method B: Branded Entertainment: Product Placement.
In the age of new media, we have gone well beyond a few product placements in movies and TV shows to a more and more broad-spectrum and integrated set of methods to bring brand messages to consumers. These methods are often gathered under one umbrella called Madison & Vine. It began as a conference to bring together Hollywood (the famous intersection of "Hollywood and Vine") and the advertising industry (traditionally based along New York's Madison Avenue, although agencies are now all over the place): thus "Madison & Vine." Madison & Vine then became a book, an *Ad Age* column, and now encompasses a wide array of nontraditional IBPs. Recording, gaming, and cell phone industries are involved as well now. The most important

EXHIBIT 10.21 By carefully constructing a social world within the frame of the ad into which the product is carefully placed, meaning is transferred to the product. "Background" and product meanings merge. This is the sophistication behind "slice-of-life" adverting. www.louisboston.com.

development is how many major advertisers are now involved in producing movies that are really brand promotions, TV shows that are really brand promotions, cell phone content that is really brand promotion, TV spots for new musical recordings that are also ads for the product, and so on. We will dig deeper into this topic in Chapter 16, but for now we'll focus on a common form and one that is in this strategic set: product placement and integration.

One way to integrate the product into a desired setting is to place the product in a television show or film. An actor picks up a can of Coke, rather than just any soda, and hopefully the correct image association is made. Even more explicit are short films (usually less than 10 minutes) made for the Internet. A few years ago, BMW released six such films showing its cars in dramatic contexts. The most famous was a film starring Madonna and directed by her former husband, British film director Guy Ritchie (*Lock, Stock, and Two Smoking Barrels; Snatch*). The films were all made by hot directors and had amazing story content; yet they were also a way of demonstrating the product by placing it in a deliberately and carefully created social world. BMW sales responded very nicely and executives believed it was a much better media buy than network television, where getting lost in the crowd is so easy. Ford alone spends nearly $2 billion a year on national advertising. What would BMW have to spend just to get noticed in that environment? BMW eventually pulled these films from their website, either because the models in the films were getting outdated as new models were out, or for some other reason we simply don't know. However, since that time, the idea, or similar ones, has really caught on. Exhibit 10.22 shows how Johnson & Johnson (J&J) used the documentary film *Babies: A Day in the Life* to advance its brands. What do you think about this technique? Why would J&J do this? Why do you think this medium is a good way to spend J&J funds to sell their brands?

You can follow the evolving saga of this on adage.com/madisonandvine, so we will mention just a few other examples. Ford Motor Company has decided to be partners in the new motion picture studio Our Stories Films, a joint venture of Ford, entrepreneur and BET founder Robert L. Johnson, and movie moguls Bob and Harvey Weinstein to produce what Ford has called "the black Walt Disney." Their initial goal is to produce three to five "African-American family films." According to *Advertising Age*, Ford will have "script integration, sponsorships, and promotions." According to theory, everyone wins: Ford gets its cars into movies, the cost of producing the films is partially underwritten by the car company, and Robert L. Johnson serves an African-American audience.

Advertisers want their brands to become integral parts of a desired social reality, a media-created world

EXHIBIT 10.22 Documentary film is used effectively by several companies, including Johnson & Johnson.

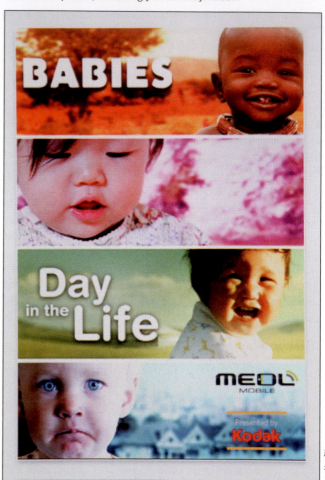

where the brand is absolutely normal and expected, almost invisible. Some contemporary theories of memory suggest that this would indeed be best over time, as the source of the brand image becomes disassociated from the brand memory. In other words, consumers believe Degree is a very popular brand among the desired target market, part of their world. Recent research has, however, suggested that the effects of placement are strongest with so-called low involvement goods and services, lower priced, the result of fairly quick decision making. When consumers actually have to consider a major purchase, like a car, the effects of brand promotion appear to be much weaker and may even backfire.

Strategic Implications of Branded Entertainment

- Low counterargument, if placement not too obvious.
- May reduce defensive measures by consumers, such as source discounting.

- May actually increase consumers' estimates about how many other people use the brand, thus making it appear more prevalent and popular than it actually is.

- A perceived cost advantage over very expensive network TV.

- Non-standardized rate structure; hard to price these; deals done in private.

- May not be very effective for high involvement categories.

- Science is unclear as to how well this technique works.

10-2i Objective #9: Leverage Social Disruption and Cultural Contradictions

We are now way up the sophistication scale. As mentioned in Chapter 3, some really great brands have used advertising to successfully leverage social disruption (youth revolution, second-wave of American feminism in the 1970s, the post-punk culture and energy, and now angry populism). The idea is to find a point where the social fabric is frayed (usually gender, race, age, politics, labor, economy, other opportunity inequities) and suggest that your brand gets it and is the unofficially sanctioned brand of the counter-culture. Among the brands that have been said to have achieved enormous success through this are: Marlboro (independence and reassertion of rigid gender/labor roles in the post–World War II period), Virginia Slims (second wave of American feminism), Mountain Dew (disaffected Gen-X slackers), Pepsi (1960s youth revolution), and so on.[13]

Most advertisers tend to ignore, or even deny the existence of major social disruptions. So, while this strategy has succeeded with a few amazingly successful brands, most advertisers appear to not employ it. Maybe more should. The worry seems to be that the brand becomes associated with an unpleasant event. The Apples, Marlboros, Pepsis, Mountain Dews, have bet on it and won, other less iconic brands appear too conservative to risk it.

Method: Tie Brand to Social/Cultural Movement. Sometimes this is done very explicitly (Pepsi), other times very implicitly. Pabst Blue Ribbon (PBR) became the working-class hero beer of west coast bike messenger culture (see Exhibit 10.23). PBR management was smart enough to notice and then capitalize on it through all sorts of promotional activities. Red Bull is said to have done something pretty similar. What do you think are the current social

EXHIBIT 10.23 Pabst Blue Ribbon—Heineken. An amazing job of leveraging the social dynamics of the times.

Susan Van Etten

tensions that could be appropriated for selling brands through advertising and brand promotion?

This is a very sophisticated and typically difficult method. The reason it is difficult is not in the execution but being culturally attuned enough to know in the present what various target marketers are conflicted about, and how to offer a brand as a solution, even a partial one. This is different than merely chasing trends; it is seeing the cultural land beneath your feet shifting in significant ways, before it is obvious to everyone. What would you say are the ones going on these days: populist anger, distrust of the very rich, widening income inequality, or a diminished future? Think about how you could leverage those (or others) to a brand's advantage.

10-2j Objective #10: Transform Consumption Experiences

We view this as the most sophisticated strategy going. But, it is also very hard to do well.

You know how it's sometimes hard to explain to someone else just exactly why a certain experience was so special, why it was so good? It wasn't just this or that; the entire experience was somehow better than the sum of the individual parts. Sometimes that feeling is at least partly due to your expectations of what something will be like, your positive memories of previous experiences, or both.

Sometimes advertisers try to provide that anticipation and/or familiarity bundled up in a positive memory of an advertisement or other brand communication, to be activated during the consumption experience itself, and recalled positively after the experience. That's right: The advertiser is trying to help create positive memories of brand usage even before the consumer has used the brand, and (more commonly) weave those memories of actual use together with advertiser-supplied "memories" in a way that the advertising can effectively shape consumer memories of brand usage. The advertising or promotional experience is thus said to have *transformed* the actual consumption experience, both at the time of consumption and in the consumer's memory.

Method: Transformational Ads. The idea behind transformational advertising is that it can actually make the consumption experience better. For example, after years of transformational advertising by McDonald's (an early user), the experience of actually eating at McDonald's may be "transformed" or made better by virtue of what you know and feel about McDonald's each time you walk in. Transformational advertising attempts to create a brand feeling, expectation, and mood that are activated when the consumer uses the product or service. Actual usage is thus transformed, made better. Transformational ads that are effective are said to connect the experience of the advertisement so closely with the brand experience that consumers cannot help but think of material from the ads (or in a more general sense, the memory of many things from many ads) when they think of the brand. Think about the transformational potential in the Guess ad in Exhibit 10.17. How does this evocative ad potentially transform the Guess clothing experience? The idea is to get this situation, this quasi-fantasy to map onto the consumer's memory of the brand. When they slide into those jeans at the store fitting room, and then later at home, does some of the created memory, that quasi-fantasy, travel with the pants?

What if you sign up for a trip to go to a theme park, take a cruise, or purchase anything that sells an experience? It could be a retail store, say Nordstrom or Tiffany. Prior to taking that cruise or going to that theme park, you saw an ad (or received a video) that shows the ideal trip to that location, the perfect experience. What is seen becomes part of memory.

EXHIBIT 10.24 Smart marketing.

AP Images/PRNewsFoto/Disney Cruise Line

Then, maybe after going, you get some type of similar one, but maybe this time it included photos or video of your trip there—great moments. Those also become part of long-term memory. If, as researchers have shown, it is possible to create false memories of brands that don't even exist, isn't it possible that over time commercial content and actual experience begin to merge in memory, and the consumers remember things as they and the advertisers want them to? What if Disney sent you a video of a perfect trip to the Magic Kingdom before you went, and one after you returned? Maybe in a year or two those memories would merge in a fashion that benefits Disney. Then, when you remember your time at the park, the hotel, the cruise, the store, you remember a blend of things: some from your actual experience, some from what was provided by the marketer. This has benefits for your feelings toward the brand, your recommendations to others, increases the likelihood to repurchase, and actually may shape, or transform, actual future consumption experiences. Product placements in movies and television shows, and other forms of branded entertainment, can accomplish the same thing. Traditional ads can do this as well (Exhibit 10.24).

Evaluation of transformational ads and other forms of IBP are typically done through field studies, tracking studies, ethnographic (on-site, qualitative) methods, and communication tests. On rare occasions, small-scale experiments are conducted.

Strategic Implications of Transformational Advertising

- Can be extremely powerful due to a merging of ad and brand experience.
- Fosters long-term commitment.
- Can ring absolutely false and hurt the brand.
- Ethical issues. Some believe that this manipulation of experience is unethical.

10-3 IN THE END

In the end, message development is where the advertising and branding battle is usually won or lost. It's where real creativity exists. It's where the agency has to be smart and figure out just how to turn the wishes of the client into effective advertising. It is where the creatives have to get into the minds of consumers, realizing that the advertisement will be received by different people in different ways. It is where advertisers merge culture, mind, and brand. Great messages are developed by people who can put themselves into the minds (and culture) of their audience members and anticipate their response, leading to the best outcome: selling the advertised brand.

SUMMARY

 Identify 10 objectives of message strategy.

Advertisers can choose from a wide array of message strategy objectives as well as methods for implementing these objectives. Three fundamental message objectives are promoting brand recall, linking key attributes to the brand name, and persuading the customer. The advertiser may also wish to create an affective association in consumers' minds by linking good feelings, humor, and sex appeal with the brand itself. Such positive feelings associated with the advertised brand can lead consumers to a higher probability of purchase. The advertiser may try to scare the consumer into action or change behavior by inducing anxiety, using negative emotional states as the means to motivate purchases. Transformational advertising aims to transform the nature of the consumption experience so that a consumer's experience of a brand becomes connected to the glorified experiences portrayed in ads. A message may also situate the brand in an important social context to heighten the brand's appeal. Finally, advertisers seek to define a brand's image by linking certain attributes to the brand, mostly using visual cues.

 Identify methods for executing each message strategy objective.

Advertisers employ any number of methods to achieve their objectives. To get consumers to recall a brand name, advertisers use repetition, slogans, and jingles. When the advertiser's objective is to link a key attribute to a brand, USP ads emphasizing unique brand qualities are employed. If the goal is to persuade a consumer to make a purchase, reason-why ads, hard-sell ads, comparison ads, testimonials, demonstrations, and infomercials all do the trick. Feel-good ads, humorous ads, and sexual-appeal ads can raise a consumer's preferences for one brand over another through affective association. Fear-appeal ads, judiciously used, can motivate purchases, as can ads that play on other anxieties. Transformational ads attempt to enrich the consumption experience. With slice-of-life ads, product placement, and short Internet films, the goal is to situate a brand in a desirable social context. Finally, ads that primarily use visuals work to define brand image.

 Discuss the strategic implications of various methods used to execute each message strategy objective.

Each method used to execute a message strategy objective has pros and cons. Methods that promote brand recall or link key attributes to a brand name can be extremely successful in training consumers to remember a brand name or its specific, beneficial attributes. However, these methods require long-term commitment and repetition to work properly, and advertisers can pay high expense while generating disdain from creatives. Methods used to persuade consumers generally aim to provide rhetorical arguments and demonstrations for why consumers should prefer a brand, resulting in strong, cognitive loyalty. However, these methods assume a high level of involvement and are vulnerable to counterarguments that neutralize their effectiveness—more-sophisticated audiences tune them out altogether, rejecting them as misleading, insipid, or dishonest. Methods used in creating affective association have short-term results and please creatives; however, the effect on audiences wears out quickly and high expense dissuades some advertisers from taking the risk. Methods designed to play on fear or anxiety are compelling, but legal and ethical issues arise, and most advertisers wish to avoid instigating consumer panic. Finally, methods that transform consumption experiences, situate the brand socially, or define brand image have powerful enduring qualities but often get lost in the clutter or can ring false to audiences.

KEY TERMS

unique selling proposition (USP)
comparison advertisements
testimonial
infomercial

ENDNOTES

1. Conclusions in this list are drawn from William R. Swinyard, "The Interaction between Comparative Advertising and Copy Claim Variation," *Journal of Marketing Research*, vol. 18 (May 1981), 175–186; Cornelia Pechmann and David Stewart, "The Effects of Comparative Advertising on Attention, Memory, and Purchase Intentions," *Journal of Consumer Research*, vol. 17 (September 1990), 180–191; and Sanjay Petruvu and Kenneth R. Lord, "Comparative and Noncomparative Advertising: Attitudinal Effects under Cognitive and Affective Involvement Conditions," *Journal of Advertising*, vol. 23 (June 1994), 77–90.

2. Baba Shiv and Antoine Bechara, "Revisiting the Customer Value Proposition," in Barbara Loken, Rohini Ahluwalia, and Michael J. Houston (Eds.), *Brands and Brand Management: Contemporary Research Perspectives* (New York and London: Routledge, 2010), 189–206.

3. See Michel Tuan Pham, Joel B. Cohen, John W. Pracejus, and G. David Hughes, "Affect Monitoring and the Primacy of Feelings in Judgment," *Journal of Consumer Research*, vol. 28 (September 2001), 167–188.

4. This claim is made by Video Storyboards Tests, based on its extensive research of humor ads, and cited in Kevin Goldman, "Ever Hear the One about the Funny Ad?" *The Wall Street Journal*, November 2, 1993, B11.

5. Tom Reichert, *The Erotic History of Advertising* (Amherst, NY: Prometheus, 2004).

6. Jeffrey D. Zbar, "Fear!," *Advertising Age*, November 14, 1994, 18.

7. Ibid.

8. Emily DeNitto, "Healthcare Ads Employ Scare Tactics," *Advertising Age*, November 7, 1994, 12.

9. Irving L. Janis and Seymour Feshbach, "Effects of Fear Arousing Communication," *Journal of Abnormal Social Psychology*, vol. 48 (1953), 78–92.

10. Michael Ray and William Wilkie, "Fear: The Potential of an Appeal Neglected by Marketing," *Journal of Marketing*, vol. 34, no. 1 (January 1970), 54–62.

11. E. H. H. J. Das, J. B. F. de Wit, and W. Strobe, "Fear Appeals Motivate Acceptance of Action Recommendations: Evidence for a Positive Bias in the Processing of Persuasive Messages," *Personality and Social Psychology Bulletin*, vol. 29 (2003), 650–664.

12. Douglas B. Holt, "What Becomes an Icon Most?" *Harvard Business Review*, March 2003.

13. For a good discussion, see Thomas C. O'Guinn and Albert Muniz, Jr. , "The Social Brand: Towards a Sociological Model of Brands," in Barbara Loken, Rohini Ahluwalia, and Michael J. Houston (Eds.), *Brands and Brand Management: Contemporary Research Perspectives* (New York and London: Routledge, 2010), 133–159.

CHAPTER 11
Executing the Creative

After reading and thinking about this chapter, you will be able to do the following:

1 Identify the main members of a creative team and how the creative brief guides their efforts.

2 Detail the elements of copywriting for print media, including the headline, subhead, and body copy.

3 Detail the elements of copywriting for television and video and for radio.

4 Describe the common copywriting approaches for digital or interactive ads.

5 Identify the components of art direction that are essential in creative execution of print ads.

6 Describe the production process in creating a television commercial.

The heart and soul of advertising is the creative, period. Talk all you want about copy-testing and consumer insight, but when it really comes down to it, advertising works best when it projects as much of the desired brand meaning as possible to the consumer.

Creative is about giving meaning to the brand. It is through this art that meaning is shaped and brought to life. The rest is merely planning.

Chapter 9 ("Managing Creativity in Advertising and IBP") and Chapter 10 ("Creative Message Strategy") provided insights into the creative process itself and the way firms try to stimulate and energize the creative effort in advertising and integrated brand promotion (IBP). These chapters also highlighted specific message objectives and strategies and detailed the methods associated with each. Now, in this chapter, we'll turn our focus to how this all comes together.

 LO **1**

11-1 THE CREATIVE TEAM AND THE CREATIVE BRIEF

When big ad agencies roamed the earth uncontested, a creative team usually meant an art director and a copywriter. These days, it can be a lot of folks. It often includes a **media planner** and/or an **account planner**. Media planners have joined the creative team because media are evolving so fast and are now so varied and so important to the shaping of the message that someone has to be driving that bus and informing the creative team of those realities on an ongoing basis. This is particularly true as creatives struggle with the challenge of trying to use social media networks and new mobile marketing options as places to communicate. What sort of message fits in those media? Media planners can

Put simply, creative is about giving meaning to the brand. It is through this art that meaning is shaped and brought to life. The rest is merely planning.

be a big help here. Account planners, usually armed with a lot of consumer research, get involved so that the consumer has a voice in the creative planning.

As you read in Chapter 9 ("Managing Creativity in Advertising and IBP"), creativity is the magic in advertising and IBP. At this stage in the process, executing the creative, the entire **creative team**—copywriters, art directors, media planners, and account planners—is driven by the creative brief. The **creative brief**, which can be thought of as the unique creative thought behind a campaign, has been described as the "ignition" for the creative team.[1] During this process, copywriters, in addition to their role in creating the "language" of the messages, also sometimes suggest the idea for the visuals. Likewise, art directors sometimes come up with the headline or tagline. Media planners convey what is possible through the ever-expanding media choices, and account planners try to keep the profile of the target consumer in the team's mind (see Insights Online [Exhibit 11.1] for an interesting discussion).

11-2 COPYWRITERS AND ART DIRECTORS

So, let's consider the two most traditional job descriptions in the world of creative advertising and discuss what they were and what they are becoming: copywriters and art directors.

Word versus image purists have had a long-running war. The advertising industry reflected this through artificial separation of the domains for decades. In reality, images and words overlap constantly. This doesn't mean that copywriting and art directing are one and the same. There are special skill sets involved with each, but one must recognize that knowing how to do it all isn't bad.

Copywriting is the process of crafting the meaning of a brand through words. Copywriting requires far more than the ability to string product descriptions together in coherent sentences. One apt description of copywriting is that it is a never-ending search for ideas combined with a never-ending search for new and different ways to express those ideas. Copywriting has to be crafted to its medium or media, and in today's explosion of media, that could be anything from a fully stylized,

copy-laden magazine ad to dialogue in a branded entertainment film or even a brand "shout out" in social media. You can learn techniques—some of them principles, some of them hints and tips. But even if you don't plan to be a copywriter, knowing something about the craft is essential to any working understanding of advertising.

Imagine you're a copywriter on the MasterCard account. You've sat through meeting after meeting in which your client, account executives, and researchers have presented a myriad of benefits one gets from using a MasterCard for online purchases. You've talked to customers about their experiences. You've even gone online to try the card out for yourself. All along, your boss has been reminding you that the work you come up with must be as inspiring as the work that focuses on building interest for the brand and properly defining it. Now your job is to take all the analytics—charts, numbers, and strategies—and turn them into a simple, emotionally involving, thoughtful campaign such as the one in Exhibit 11.2. You are to make MasterCard

EXHIBIT 11.2 Take all the charts, numbers, and strategies and turn them into a simple, emotionally involving, thoughtful campaign.

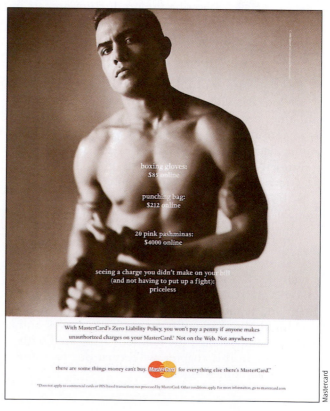

Mastercard

mean something—something that is consistent with the brand DNA and its positioning—and you have to do it in a way that is interesting and compelling to consumers.

Effective copywriters are well-informed, astute advertising decision makers with creative talent. Copywriters are able to comprehend and then incorporate the complexities of marketing strategies, consumer behavior, and advertising strategies into powerful communication. They must do this in such a way that the copy does not interfere with, but rather enhances, the visual aspects of the message.

An astute advertiser will go to great lengths to provide copywriters with as much information as possible about the objectives for a particular advertising effort. The responsibility for keeping copywriters informed lies with the client's brand managers, filtered through the account executives and creative directors in the ad agency or brand communication firm. Without this information, copywriters are left without guidance and direction, and they must rely on intuition about what sorts of information are relevant and meaningful to a target audience. Effective brand communication relies on a good creative brief.

The creative brief serves as the guide used in the copywriting process to specify the message elements that must be coordinated during the preparation of copy (see Exhibit 11.3). These elements include main brand claims, creative devices, media that will be used, special creative needs a brand might have, and what we want the message recipients to think once they receive the message.[2] Part of the typical copywriting challenge is creating excitement around what can otherwise be dull product features.

Some of the key elements considered in devising a creative brief are the following:

1. The single most important thought you want a member of the target market to take away from the advertisement
2. The product features to be emphasized
3. The benefits a user receives from these features
4. The media chosen for transmitting the information and the length of time the advertisement will run (this one is getting tougher to know)

EXHIBIT 11.3 A sample creative brief.

Creative Brief	
Agency	Creative Stupor, Austin
Client	Jake's Fried Chicken
Brand	Jake's Fried Chicken Restaurants
Project	Best Fried Chicken Anywhere.
Date	June 12, 2012
Author	Blake N. Milton
Purpose	To remind fried chicken lovers of Jake's chicken's USP: *High Fat and Proud of It.*
Creative opportunity	To leverage the under-served segment of don't care about my arteries give me the real thing.... Unapologetic comfort food.
Media mix	Open
Message objective	Brand recall USP: *Real fried chicken; forget the guilt.*
Tone	In your face, dripping down your chin.
Key consumer opportunity	Give consumer permission to indulge with Jake's Fried Chicken.
Message	*You want it; go for it.*
Reason to believe	You already know it; know you have permission. Besides: Jake told you so.

Tom O'Guinn

5. The suggested mood or tone for the ad or promotion
6. The production budget for the ad or brand promotion[3]

There are times, however, when these considerations can be modified or even disregarded. For example, sometimes a brilliant creative execution demands a different medium or a creative thought may require a completely different mood than the one specified in the creative brief. A creative brief is best thought of as a starting point. Once the creative brief is devised and adapted, the creative team can get on with the task of crafting the actual advertisement. It is also around the creative brief that arguments often occur. A lot of creatives believe the brand managers (clients) who derive it, are either completely clueless about advertising, have put impossible constraints on them, or should just be ignored all together. If there is one place in this whole process where things could be greatly improved it is in the formulation, translation, negotiation, revision and ultimate execution of this typically one-page document.

11-3 **COPYWRITING**

Copywriting ought to be strategic in its execution of the objectives of the creative brief.

LO ②

11-3a **Copywriting for Print Advertising**

In preparing copy for a print ad, the first step in the copy development process is deciding how to use (or not use) the three separate components of print copy: the headline, the subhead, and the body copy. (Slogans and taglines are also part of the copywriting process, but we consider that effort separately later in the chapter.) Be aware that the full range of components applies most directly to print ads that appear in magazines, newspapers, or direct mail pieces. These guidelines also apply to other "print" media such as billboards, transit advertising, specialty advertising, and websites.

The Headline. The **headline** in an advertisement is the leading sentence(s), usually at the top or bottom of the ad, that attracts attention, communicates a key selling point, or achieves brand identification. Many headlines fail to attract attention, and the ad itself then becomes another bit of clutter in consumers' lives. Lifeless headlines do not compel the reader to examine other parts of the ad. Simply stated, a headline can either motivate a reader to move on to the rest of an ad or lose the reader for good. And be aware, there are certain ads where the creative execution depends completely on the headline and the entire ad is carried by the headline. Look at the headline in Exhibit 11.4.

The Subhead. A **subhead** consists of a few words or a short sentence and usually appears above or below the headline. It offers the opportunity to include important brand information not included in the headline. The subhead in the ad for Clorox in Exhibit 11.5 is an example of a subhead conveying important brand information not communicated in the headline. A subhead serves basically the same purpose as a headline—to communicate key selling points or brand information quickly. A subhead is normally in print smaller than the headline but larger than the body copy. In most cases, the subhead is lengthier than the headline and can be used to communicate more complex selling points. The subhead should reinforce the headline and stimulate a more complete reading of the entire ad.

The Body Copy. Body copy is the textual component of an advertisement and tells a more complete story of a brand. Effective body copy is written in a fashion

EXHIBIT 11.4 A headline that creates curiosity motivates the reader to continue reading, perhaps after a slight disconcerting pause.

that takes advantage of and reinforces the headline and subhead, is compatible with and gains strength from the visual, and is interesting to the reader. Whether body copy is interesting is a function of how accurately the copywriter and other decision makers have assessed various components of message development and how good the copywriter is. Even the most elaborate body copy will be ineffective if it is "off creative strategy." It will not matter if it's very clever but has little to do in advancing the strategy. The biggest problem is that very few people ever read the body copy. Look at Exhibit 11.5 again: Do you really have enough time on your hands to read all that copy about bleach? Does anyone? Really? This is one reason words have been declining in ads for decades.

There are several standard techniques for preparing body copy. The **straight-line copy** approach explains in straightforward terms why a reader will benefit from use of a brand. This technique is used many times in conjunction with a benefits message strategy. Body copy that uses **dialogue** delivers the selling points of a message to the audience through a character or characters in the ad. Dialogue can also depict two people in the ad having a conversation, a technique often used in slice-of-life messages. A **testimonial** uses dialogue as if the spokesperson is having a one-sided conversation with the reader through the body copy.

EXHIBIT 11.5 Subheads include important brand information not included in the headline. Where is the subhead in this Clorox ad? What does the subhead accomplish that the headline does not? www.clorox.com

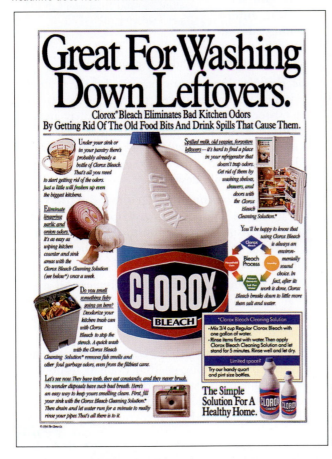

The Clorox Company

Narrative is a method for preparing body copy that simply displays a series of statements about a brand. A person may or may not be portrayed as delivering the copy. It is difficult to make this technique lively for the reader, so the threat of writing a dull ad using this technique is ever present. **Direct response copy** is, in many ways, the least complex of copy techniques. In writing direct response copy, the copywriter is trying to highlight the urgency of acting immediately. (See Insights Online [Exhibit 11.6] for an interesting example.) Hence, the range of possibilities for direct response copy is more limited. In addition, many direct response advertisements rely on sales promotion devices, such as coupons, contests, and rebates, as a means of stimulating

action. Giving deadlines to the reader is also a common approach in direct response advertising.

These techniques for copywriting establish a general set of styles that can be used as the format for body copy. Again, be aware that any message objective can be employed within any particular copy technique. There are a vast number of compatible combinations.

LO

11-3b Copywriting for Television and Video

Relative to the print media, television presents totally different challenges for a copywriter. It is obvious that the audio and visual capabilities of television and video offer different opportunities for a copywriter. Compared to print media, however, video media have inherent limitations for a copywriter. In print media, a copywriter can write longer and more involved copy to better communicate complex brand features. For consumer goods such as automobiles or home entertainment systems, a brand's basis for competitive differentiation and positioning may lie with complex, unique functional features. In this case, print media provide a copywriter the time and space to communicate these details, complete with illustrations. In addition, the printed page allows a reader to dwell on the copy and process the information at a personalized, comfortable rate. These advantages do not exist in most video media, certainly not broadcast television.

Writing Copy for Television (Video)

Great print can make you famous. Great TV can make you rich.

—Anonymous[4]

Television has always been a vastly creative forum for the copywriter and art director. In the current era of social media (YouTube and interactive websites), the addition of online video transmission offers the same opportunities as television. The comments in this section apply to ads that show up on social media sites or may even have been created for transmission to mobile devices. The ability to create a mood or demonstrate brand values gives television and video wonderful capabilities; it also offers you the ability to really screw up in magnificent fashion for a very large and expensive audience (no pressure here!). Obviously, copy for television must be highly sensitive to the ad's visual aspects. Television is a visual medium; you should try not to let the words get in the way.

The opportunities inherent to television as an advertising medium represent challenges for the copywriter as well. Certainly, television's inherent capabilities do much to bring a copywriter's words to life. But the action qualities can create problems. First, the copywriter must remember that words do not stand alone. Visuals, special effects, and sound techniques may ultimately convey a message far better than the cleverest turn of phrase. Second, television commercials represent a difficult timing challenge for the copywriter. It is necessary for the copy to be precisely coordinated with the visuals. If the visual portion was one continuous illustration, the task would be difficult enough. Contemporary television ads, however, tend to be heavily edited (i.e., lots of cuts), and the copywriting task can be a nightmare. The copywriter not only has to fulfill all the responsibilities of proper information inclusion (based on creative platform and strategy decisions) but also has to carefully fit all the information within, between, and around the display. To make sure this coordination is precise, the copywriter, producer, and director assigned to a television advertisement work closely together to make sure the copy supports and enhances the video element. The road map for this coordination effort is known as a **storyboard**. A storyboard is an important-shot-by-important-shot sketch depicting in sequence the visual scenes and copy that will be used in the advertisement. The procedures for coordinating audio and visual elements through the use of storyboards will be presented later in the chapter when television production is discussed in more detail. (See Insights Online [Exhibit 11.7] for more information.)

Guidelines for Writing Television Copy. Writing copy for television advertising has its own set of unique opportunities and challenges. The following are some general guidelines:

- *Use the video.* Allow the video portion of the commercial to enhance and embellish the audio portion. Given the strength and power of the visual presentation in television advertising, take advantage of its impact with copy.

- *Support the video.* Make sure that the copy doesn't simply hitchhike on the video. If all the copy does is verbally describe what the audience is watching, an opportunity to either communicate additional information or strengthen the video communication has been lost.

- *Coordinate the audio with the video.* In addition to strategically using the video, it is essential that the audio and video do not tell entirely different stories.

- *Sell the brand as well as entertain the audience.* Television ads can sometimes be more entertaining than television programming. A temptation for the copywriter and art director is to get caught up in the excitement of a good video presentation and forget that the main purpose is to deliver persuasive

communication. How many times have you seen a great, entertaining ad and then have no idea what brand the ad was promoting?

- *Be flexible.* Due to media-scheduling strategies, commercials are produced to run as 15-, 20-, 30-, or 60-second spots. The copywriter may need to ensure that the audio portion of an ad is complete and comprehensive within varying time lengths. Also, consider how the ad would play in the small formats of mobile devices.

- *Use copy judiciously.* If a television ad is too wordy, it can create information overload and interfere with the visual impact. Ensure that every word is a working word and contributes to the impact of the message.

- *Reflect the brand personality and image.* All aspects of an ad, copy and visuals, should be consistent with the personality and image the advertiser wants to build or maintain for the brand.

- *Build campaigns.* When copy for a particular advertisement is being written, evaluate its potential as a sustainable idea. Can the basic appeal in the advertisement be developed into multiple versions placed in other media that form a campaign?[5]

11-3c Writing Copy for Radio

Some writers consider radio the ultimate forum for copywriting creativity. Because the radio is restricted to an audio-only presentation, a copywriter is freed from some of the harsher realities of visual presentations. Yet it has been said that radio *is* actually visual. The copywriter must (inevitably) create images in the minds of listeners. The creative potential of radio rests in its ability to stimulate a "theater of the mind," which allows a copywriter to create images and moods for audiences that transcend those created in any other medium.

Despite these creative opportunities, the drawbacks of this medium should not be underestimated. Few radio listeners ever actively listen to radio programming (talk radio is an exception), much less the commercial interruptions. Radio may be viewed by some as the theater of the mind, but others have labeled it audio wallpaper—wallpaper in the sense that radio is used as a filler or unobtrusive accompaniment to reading, driving, household chores, or homework. If it were absent, the average person would miss it, but the average person would be hard pressed to recall the radio ads aired during their drive home last night.

The most reasonable view of copywriting for radio is to temper the enthusiasm of the theater-of-the-mind perspective and the pessimism of the audio-wallpaper view. (Of course, "reasonable" creative perspectives often are mind-numbingly dull.) A radio copywriter should recognize the unique character of radio and exploit the opportunities it offers. First, radio adds the dimension of sound to the basic copywriting effort, and sound (other than voices) can become a primary tool in creating copy. Second, radio can conjure images in the mind of the receiver that extend beyond the starkness of brand "information" actually being provided. Radio copywriting should, therefore, strive to stimulate each receiver's imagination. (See Insights Online [Exhibit 11.8] for an interesting example.)

Writing copy for radio begins the same way that writing copy for print begins. The copywriter reviews components of the creative brief to take advantage of and follow through on the marketing and advertising strategies integral to the brand's market potential. Let's consider formats for radio ads and guidelines for copy preparation the copywriter can turn to for direction.

Guidelines for Writing Radio Copy. The unique opportunities and challenges of the radio medium warrant a set of guidelines for the copywriter to increase the probability of effective communication. The following are a few suggestions for writing effective radio copy:

- *Capture attention and get to the point early.* The first five seconds can capture or lose the radio listener—grab attention. Then get to the main point and stick with it.

- *Use common, familiar language.* The use of words and language easily understood and recognized by the receiver is even more important in radio than in print copy preparation. Esoteric language or phrases will confuse and ultimately lose the listener.

- *Use short words and sentences.* The probability of communicating verbally increases if short, easily processed words and sentences are used. Long, involved, elaborate verbal descriptions make it difficult for the listener to follow the copy.

- *Stimulate the imagination.* Copy that can conjure up concrete and stimulating images in the receiver's mind can have a powerful impact on recall.

- *Repeat the brand name.* Because the impression made by a radio ad is fleeting, it may be necessary to repeat the brand name several times before it registers. The same is true for location if the ad is being used to promote a retail organization.

- *Stress the main selling point or points.* The premise of the advertising should always revolve around the creative brief. The urge to get "wild and crazy" with a radio ad to attract and hold attention needs to take a back seat to strategic goals. If the main selling points of a brand are mentioned only in passing, there is little reason for the listener to believe or remember them.

- *Use sound and music with care.* By all means, a copywriter should take advantage of all the creative audio capabilities afforded by the radio medium, including the use of sound effects and music. Although these devices can contribute greatly to attracting and holding the listener's attention, care must be taken to ensure that they do not overwhelm the copy and therefore the persuasive impact of the commercial.

- *Tailor the copy to the time, place, and specific audience.* Take advantage of any unique aspect of the advertising context. If the ad is created for a particular geographic region, use colloquialisms unique to that region as a way to tailor the message. The same is true with time-of-day factors or unique aspects of the audience.[6]

LO **4**

11-3d Copywriting for Digital/Interactive Media

In digital and interactive media, *audience* has a significantly different meaning than it does in traditional one-way (noninteractive) media. Audience members often seek out the ads or other online IBP material, rather than the other way around, and they are doing it in much smaller formats like a computer screen or smartphone display. In addition, cyberads can pop up as one moves from Web page to Web page (more on this in Chapter 14). The media—computers and mobile devices—are fundamentally more user-directed than print, television, or radio. This means that consumers approach (and read) cyberads somewhat differently than other ads. Most have more incentive to read the copy than traditional print advertising. Further, much digital and interactive media copy is direct response, thus totally dictating copy style. There are those who argue that the copywriting in digital and interactive media is of lower quality—particularly if you use the standards of traditional print and broadcast media as criteria. But digital and interactive media copywriters are trying to meet the demands of vastly different audiences and often real-time media creation (as in tweets).[7] At this point, we believe that the basic principles of good print and broadcast copywriting just discussed generally apply. But the copy should assume a more active and engaged audience and has to adapt the creative brief objectives to the smaller format and potentially real-time challenges of the reception environment. Still, remember that odds are that receivers are not there for your ads. Consider the Virgin Atlantic Facebook ad website in Exhibit 11.9. Think about it—does it compare with traditional copywriting, or is it cyberwriting? Why?

Common Copywriting Approaches to Digital/Interactive Advertising

In this time of screaming technological advances, I find that what is considered old and near death is also what will never be replaced by technology. Mainly, that is good old fashioned creativity.

—Tracy Wong[8]

Digital/interactive ads are truly hybrids between print and broadcasting advertisements. On the one hand, the receiver encounters the message in a print format either at a website, in an email, at a blog, or from social media communication. On the other hand, the message is delivered electronically similar to television or radio. And, as the quote highlights, just because this sort of copy delivery is made possible by technological advances, it does not mean that creativity is abandoned. The common approaches to copywriting are as follows[9]:

- At a **long-copy landing page**, a website designed to sell a product directly, the copy might equal the equivalent of a four- to eight-page letter to a potential customer. The brand and its benefits are described in great detail with visuals included throughout.

- A **short-copy landing page** is simply a brand offer that may be accessed by a consumer through a key word search and has the length and look of a magazine ad. Its components will resemble a magazine ad as well with headline, subhead, and body copy.

- A **long-copy email** is designed to offer the receiver all sorts of incentives to buy the product and usually offers a link to a short-copy landing page.

EXHIBIT 11.9 Look at this ad; do you see anything different about the copy in it compared to a magazine ad?

- A **teaser email** is a short message designed to drive readers to a long-copy landing page where they can order the brand directly.

- A **pop-up/pop-under ad**, discussed in Chapter 14, refers to those sometimes annoying little ads that involuntarily show up while you are surfing. The **pop-up/pop-under copy** in this sort of ad resembles a series of headlines and subheads without much or any body copy. Such an ad usually makes a special offer or drives the receiver to a website.

- **Social media copy** rarely has headlines or subheads but rather is more like pure copywriting. "Tweets" about a brand or brand "call outs" in a blog are subtle references to the brand that hope to build awareness and positive affinity (due to the association with the social media communication). The reality is that in many cases the advertiser is not in total control of the copy here. Even when a tweet emanates from the firm, the tweeter is offering a free-form discussion of the brand—the same with a blog entry.

11-3e Slogans/Taglines

Copywriters are often asked to come up with a good slogan or tagline for a product or service. A **slogan** or **tagline** is a short phrase that is in part used to help establish an image, identity, or position for a brand or an organization but is most often used to increase memorability of the key benefit of a brand.[10] A slogan is established by repeating the phrase in a firm's advertising and other public communication as well as through salespeople and event promotions. Slogans are often used as a headline or subhead in print advertisements or as the tagline at the conclusion of radio and television advertisements. Slogans typically appear directly below the brand or company name, on the brand website, or spoken in broadcast commercials, as "You're in Good Hands" does in every Allstate insurance ad or digital application. Some classic and memorable ad slogans and taglines are listed in Exhibit 11.10.

A good slogan or tagline can serve several positive and important purposes for a brand or a firm. First, a slogan can be an integral part of a brand's image and personality. BMW's slogan, "The Ultimate Driving Machine," does much to establish and maintain the personality and image of the brand. Second, if a slogan is carefully and consistently developed over time, it can act as shorthand identification for the brand and provide information on important brand benefits. The long-standing slogan

EXHIBIT 11.10 Classic and memorable slogans used for brands and organizations.

Brand/Company	Slogan
Allstate Insurance	You're in Good Hands with Allstate.
American Express	Don't Leave Home Without It.
AT&T (Consumer)	Reach Out and Touch Someone.
AT&T (Business)	AT&T. Your True Choice.
Beef Industry Council	Real Food for Real People.
Best Buy	Turn on the Fun.
BMW	The Ultimate Driving Machine.
Budweiser	This Bud's for You.
Chevrolet Trucks	Like a Rock.
Cotton Industry	The Fabric of Our Lives.
De Beers	Diamonds Are Forever.
Ford	Have You Driven a Ford Lately?
Goodyear	The Best Tires in the World Have Goodyear Written All Over Them.
Harley-Davidson	The Legend Rolls On.
Lincoln	What a Luxury Car Should Be.
Maybelline	Maybe She's Born with It. Maybe It's Maybelline.
Microsoft (Online)	Where Do You Want to Go Today?
Panasonic	Just Slightly Ahead of Our Time.
Prudential Insurance	Get a Piece of the Rock.
Rogaine	Stronger Than Heredity.
Sharp	From Sharp Minds Come Sharp Products.
Toshiba	In Touch with Tomorrow.
VH1	Music First.
Visa	It's Everywhere You Want to Be.
Volkswagen	Drivers Wanted.

© Cengage Learning

for De Beers Diamonds, "Diamonds Are Forever," communicates the benefits of the product and the brand. A good slogan also provides continuity across different media and between advertising campaigns. Nike's "Just Do It" slogan gave the firm an underlying theme for a wide range of campaigns and other promotions. In this sense, a slogan is a useful tool in helping to bring about thematic IBP for a firm.

11-3f **The Copy Approval Process**

"The client has some issues and concerns about your ads." This is how account executives announce the death of your labors: "issues and concerns." To understand the portent of this phrase, picture the men lying on the floor of that Chicago garage on St. Valentine's Day. Al Capone had issues and concerns with these men.

I've had account executives beat around the bush for 15 minutes before they could tell me the bad news. "Well, we had a good meeting."

"Yes," you say, "but are the ads dead?"

"We learned a lot?"

"But are they dead?"

"Wellll,... They're really not dead. They are just in a new and better place."

—Luke Sullivan[11]

The final step in copywriting is getting the copy approved. For many copywriters, this is the most dreaded part of their existence—as the quote above reveals. During the approval process, the proposed copy is likely to pass through the hands of a wide range of client and agency people, many of whom are ill prepared to judge the quality of the copy. And there are those who argue convincingly that the approval process stifles creativity as the creative team strives for approval rather than creative excellence.[12] The challenge at this stage is to keep the creative potency of the copy intact. As David Ogilvy suggests in his commandments for advertising, "Committees can criticize advertisements, but they can't write them."[13]

The copy approval process usually begins within the creative department at the advertising agency. A copywriter submits a draft copy to either a senior writer or creative director, or both. From there, the redrafted copy is forwarded to the account management team. The main concern at this level is to evaluate the copy on legal grounds. After the account management team has made recommendations, a meeting is likely held to present the copy, along with proposed visuals, to the client's product category manager, brand manager, and/or marketing staff. Inevitably, the client representatives feel compelled to make recommendations for altering the copy. In some cases, these recommendations realign the copy in accordance with important marketing strategy objectives. In other cases, the recommendations are amateurish and problematic. From the copywriter's point of view, they are rarely welcome, although the copywriter usually has to act as if they are.

Depending on the assignment, the client, and the traditions of the agency, the creative team may also decide to turn to various forms of copy research to resolve any differences. Typically, copy research is either developmental or evaluative. **Developmental copy research** (see Chapter 7) can actually help copywriters at the early stages of copy development by providing audience interpretations and reactions to the proposed copy. **Evaluative copy research** (see Chapter 7) is used to judge the copy after it has been produced. Here, the audience expresses its approval or disapproval of the copy used in an ad. Copywriters are not fond of these evaluative report cards. In our view, they are completely justified in their suspicion; for many reasons, state-of-the-art evaluative copy research just isn't very good.

Finally, the copy should always be submitted for final approval to the advertiser's senior executives. Many times, these executives have little interest in evaluating advertising plans, and they leave this responsibility to middle managers. In some firms, however, top executives get very involved in the approval process. The various levels of approval for the copy are summarized in Exhibit 11.11. For the advertiser, it is best to recognize that copywriters, like other creative talent in an agency, should be allowed to exercise their creative expertise with guidance but not overbearing interference. Copywriters typically provide energy, originality, and distinctiveness to an often dry marketing strategy.

EXHIBIT 11.11 The copy approval process.

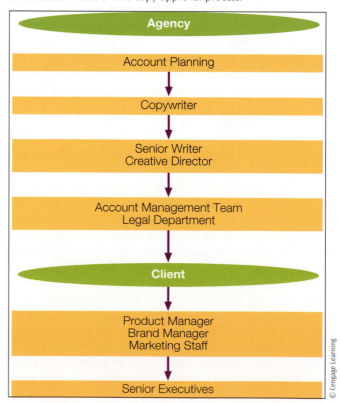

© Cengage Learning

LO ⑤

11-4 ART DIRECTION

At this point, we can turn our attention to the process of art direction. In the discussion of copywriting just completed, the issue of coordinating the copy with visuals was raised several times. Now, we want to focus on the process of how the visual elements of an advertisement and IBP materials are developed.

A hundred years ago advertisers largely relied on words to persuade consumers. They argued with consumers, attempted to reason with them, pleaded with them, and cajoled them. Then sometime in the early 20th century, particularly noticeable after about 1910, advertisers began to move away from all words and toward pictures. This trend would extend throughout the 20th century and into the 21st. Now, advertising has become mostly visual. There are several reasons for the rise of the visual in advertising. Among them are (1) improved technologies, which facilitate better and more affordable illustration and the opportunity to rotate visuals nearly instantaneously in digital media; (2) the inherent advantage of pictures to quickly demonstrate the values of a brand; (3) the ability to build brand "images" through visuals; (4) the legal advantage of pictures over words in that the truth or falsity of a picture is almost impossible to determine; (5) the widely held belief that pictures, although just as cultural as words, permit a certain type of global portability that words do not; and (6) pictures allow advertisers to place brands in desired social contexts, thus transferring important social meaning to them.

11-4a Illustration, Design, and Layout

We'll begin with a discussion of three primary visual elements of a print or digital ad: illustration, design, and layout. We'll then identify aspects of each that should be specified, or at least considered, as a print or digital/interactive ad is being prepared. An advertiser must appreciate the technical aspects of coordinating the visual elements in an ad with the mechanics of the layout and ultimately with the procedures for print production or Web placement. Today, art directors and their designers are using Adobe's InDesign software to create highly illustrative print and digital ads that are suitable for presentation on new tablet devices or e-readers like the iPad.[14] This new software offers major improvements in the quality and speed of the illustration, layout, and design processes (www.adobe.com/products/indesign/).

Initially, the art director, copywriter, and in the current era a media planner and account planner (the contemporary creative team as identified at the outset of the chapter) decide on the general purpose and therefore content of an advertising visual. Then the art director, usually in conjunction with a graphic designer, takes this raw idea for the visual and develops it further. Art directors, with their specialized skills and training, coordinate the design and illustration components of the ad. The creative director oversees the entire process. The copywriter is still in the loop to achieve word/visual coordination.

Illustration. **Illustration**, in the context of print and digital advertising, is the actual drawing, painting, photography, or computer-generated art that forms the picture in an advertisement. Illustration is the look of the ad. For example, consider how creating the desired social context for a brand advances the slice-of-life method of socially situating. Consider how a unique selling proposition (USP) strategy would be advanced by communicating a certain brand feature visually. A primary role of illustration, along with the headline, is to attract and hold attention, as discussed earlier. With all the advertising clutter, this is no easy task. In some advertising situations (e.g., the very early stages of a new product launch or for very-low-involvement repeat-purchase items), just being noticed by consumers may be enough. In most cases, however, being noticed is a necessary, but not sufficient, goal. An illustration is made to communicate with a particular target audience and, generally, must support other components of the ad to achieve the intended communication impact. So, what do you think of the impact of the Spanx ad in Exhibit 11.12? Will it get noticed? Will the brand be remembered? So, is this guy Spanx's idea of their male target? Is this going to work? What about the other design elements in the ad?

One traditional role of art direction is to make the brand "heroic." Visual techniques such as backlighting, low-angle shots, and dramatic use of color can communicate heroic proportions and qualities. Professionals even call this the "hero" or "beauty shot." Does the illustration in Exhibit 11.13 make Polo Blue heroic? Is it a good beauty shot? Would a white space background have made it pop more, made the brand more heroic, large, powerful? Or did the art director need the blue background to reinforce the name brand "Blue?" Thoughts, please.

Perhaps the most straightforward illustration is one that simply displays brand features, benefits, or both. Even though a print ad is static, the product can be shown in use through an "action" scene or even through a series of illustrations. The benefits of product use can be demonstrated with before-and-after shots or by demonstrating the result of having used the product.

Brand image is projected through illustration. The myriad of ways this is done is beyond enumeration, but the illustration interacts with the packaging, associated brand imagery (e.g., the brand logo), and evoked

EXHIBIT 11.12 Will this illustration get this ad noticed?

feelings, which all contribute. The "mood" of an ad can help this along—created by color tones and highlighting. Whether these goals are achieved with an ad depends on the technical execution of the illustration.

EXHIBIT 11.13 The art direction for this ad tries to make the brand "heroic."

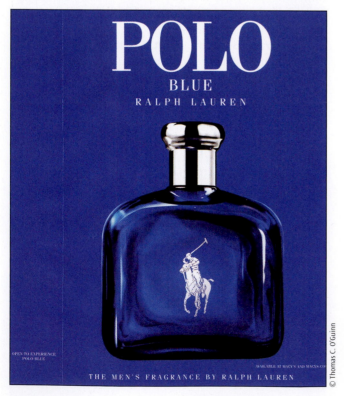

The lighting, color, tone, and texture of the illustration can have a huge impact.

Just as a headline can stimulate examination of the illustration, the illustration can stimulate reading of the body copy. Because body copy generally carries essential selling messages, any tactic that encourages reading is useful. The Beck's ad in Exhibit 11.14 tries to create curiosity and interest. It is working very hard to get you to read the body copy. Does it work? Will someone who sees this ad be so intrigued by the visual that they actually read the copy? Without reading the copy, does this ad makes any sense? Normally, an illustration and headline need to be fully coordinated and play off each other for this level of interest to occur. One caution is to avoid making the illustration too clever a stimulus for motivating copy reading. Putting cleverness ahead of clarity in choosing an illustration can confuse the receiver and cause the body copy to be ignored. As one expert puts it, such ads win awards but can camouflage the benefit offered by the product.[15]

As described earlier, advertisers often try to situate their brands within a type of social setting, thereby linking it with certain "types" of people and certain lifestyles. Establishing desired social contexts is a highly prized function of modern art direction. Look at the Motorola ad in Exhibit 11.15 and then think about what it would mean if the product were divorced from the social context as it is in Exhibit 11.16. See what we mean? Context can be everything. Is the phone really *motodelic*, or is the context of the ad? Do the girl and the chair come with the phone?

EXHIBIT 11.14 This ad tries to get you to read the body copy. Does it work?

Design. **Design** is "the structure itself and the plan behind that structure" for the aesthetic and stylistic aspects of a print advertisement.[16] Design represents the effort on the part of the creative team to physically arrange all the components of a printed or digital/interactive advertisement in such a way that order and beauty are achieved—order in the sense that the illustration, headline, body copy, and special features of the ad are easy to read; beauty in the sense that the ad is visually pleasing to a reader. Even cyberspace ads (which we will consider specifically in a few pages) have to have visual appeal along with all the interactive options they present.

There are aspects of design that directly relate to the potential for an ad to communicate effectively based on its artistic form. As such, design factors are highly relevant to creating effective print advertising and we will consider those now.

EXHIBITS 11.15 AND 11.16 Context is (almost) everything. When you remove the advertised brand from the advertiser-created content, it isn't the same, is it?

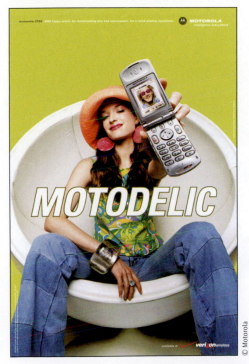

Principles of Design. Principles of design govern how a print advertisement should be prepared. The word *should* is carefully chosen in this context. It is used because, just as language has rules of grammar and syntax, visual presentation has rules of design. The **principles of design** relate to each element within an advertisement and to the arrangement of and relationship between elements as a whole.[17] Principles of design suggest the following:

- A design should be in balance.
- The proportion within an advertisement should be pleasing to the viewer.
- The components within an advertisement should have an ordered and directional pattern.
- There should be a unifying force within the ad.
- One element of the ad should be emphasized above all others.

We will consider each of these principles of design and how they relate to the development of an effective advertisement. Of course, as surely as there are rules, there are occasions when the rules need to be broken. An experienced designer knows the rules and follows them but is also prepared to break the rules to achieve the desired creative outcome. But first you learn the rules (see Insights Online [Exhibit 11.17 for an interesting example).

Balance. **Balance** in an ad is an orderliness and compatibility of presentation. Balance can be either formal or informal. **Formal balance** emphasizes symmetrical presentation—components on one side of an imaginary vertical line through the ad are repeated in approximate size and shape on the other side of the imaginary line. Formal balance creates a mood of seriousness and directness and offers the viewer an orderly, easy-to-follow visual presentation.

Informal balance emphasizes asymmetry—the optical weighing of nonsimilar sizes and shapes. Exhibit 11.18 shows a Harley-Davidson advertisement using a range of type sizes, visuals, and colors to create a powerful visual effect that achieves informal balance. Informal balance in an ad should not be interpreted as imbalance. Rather, components of different sizes, shapes, and colors are arranged in a more complex relationship providing asymmetrical balance to an ad and a visually intriguing presentation to the viewer. Think about how this Harley ad draws your eyes to the bike.

Proportion. **Proportion** has to do with the size and tonal relationships between different elements in an advertisement. Whenever two elements are placed in proximity, proportion results. Proportional considerations include the relationship of the width of an ad to its depth, the width of each element to the depth of each element, the size of one element relative to the size of every other, the space between two elements and the relationship of that space to a third element, and the amount of light area as opposed to the amount of dark area. Ideally, factors of proportion vary so as to avoid monotony in an ad. Further, the designer should pursue pleasing proportions, which means the viewer will not detect mathematical relationships between elements. In general, unequal dimensions and distances make for some of the liveliest designs in advertising. Look at the Parmalat ad in Exhibit 11.19. How does the use of proportion draw you to the brand,

EXHIBIT 11.18 This ad uses informal balance for creative effect.

First Base Imaging, London

EXHIBIT 11.19 Proportion, when expertly controlled, can result in an inspired display of the oversized versus the undersized. www.parmalat.com.

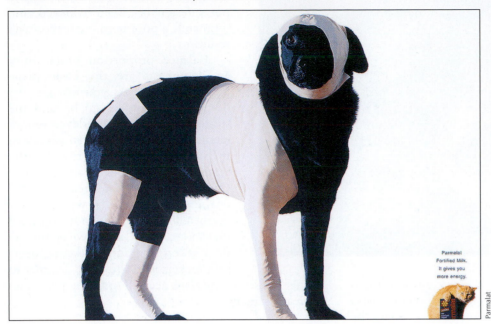

Parmalat
Fortified Milk.
It gives you
more energy.

body copy, and illustration. Several design techniques contribute to unity. The border surrounding an ad keeps the ad elements from spilling over into other ads or into the printed matter next to the ad.

Another construct of unity is the axis. In every advertisement, an axis will naturally emerge. The **axis** is a line, real or imagined, that runs through an ad and from which the elements in the advertisement flare out. A single ad may have one, two, or even three axes running vertically and horizontally. An axis can be created by blocks of copy, by the

and the payoff in the bottom right corner? Small can be powerful.

Order. **Order** in an advertisement is also referred to as a sequence or, in terms of its effects on the reader, "gaze motion." The designer's goal is to establish a relationship among elements that leads the reader through the ad in some controlled fashion. A designer can create a logical path of visual components to control eye movement. The eye has a "natural" tendency to move from left to right, from up to down, from large elements to small elements, from light to dark, and from color to noncolor. Exhibit 11.20 is an example of an ad that takes advantage of many of these tendencies. The bright lights on top of the Land Rover and the white headlines against a dark background initially attract the gaze. The eye then moves down the shape of the car, and the headlights bring the gaze down to the body copy and logo. The natural tendency for the eye to move from top to bottom leads the eye to a final shot of the Land Rover. Order also includes inducing the reader to jump from one space in the ad to another, creating a sense of action. The essential contribution of this design component is to establish a visual format that results in a focus or several focuses.

Unity. Ensuring that the elements of an advertisement are tied together and appear to be related is the purpose of **unity**. Considered the most important of the design principles, unity results in harmony among the diverse components of an advertisement: headline, subhead,

EXHIBIT 11.20 The order of elements in this ad for the Land Rover controls the reader's eye, moving it from the top of the ad through the body copy and logo, then down to the product shot at the bottom. www.landrover.com.

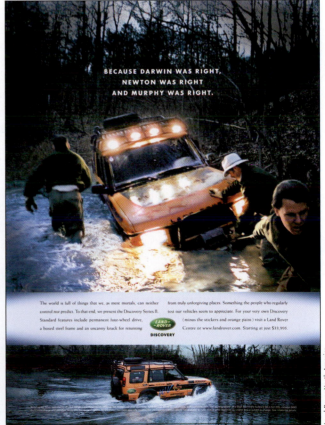

BECAUSE DARWIN WAS RIGHT,
NEWTON WAS RIGHT
AND MURPHY WAS RIGHT.

The world is full of things that we, as mere mortals, can neither control nor predict. To that end, we present the Discovery Series II. Standard features include permanent four-wheel drive, a boxed steel frame and an uncanny knack for returning from truly unforgiving places. Something the people who regularly test our vehicles seem to appreciate. For your very own Discovery (minus the stickers and orange paint) visit a Land Rover Centre or www.landrover.com. Starting at just $33,995.

LAND-ROVER
DISCOVERY

EXHIBIT 11.21 There are three prominent visual elements here.

FOR ONCE,
SKIN THAT'LL
ACTUALLY LOOK BETTER
WITH AGE.

MAKES YOU HATE IT,
DOESN'T IT.

The secret lies in the centuries old process of vegetable tanning. Of soaking the hides for 40 days in wooden drums, in bark and seeds extracted from the forests of Asia and Africa. But with leather this good, there's just one problem. In a few years, the bag on your shoulder may look better than you

HIDESIGN
years behind its time

Reprinted with permission from Hidesign

placement of illustrations, or by the items within an illustration, such as the position and direction of a model's arm or leg. Elements in an ad may violate the axes, but when two or more elements use a common axis as a starting point, unity is enhanced. A design can be more forceful in creating unity by using either a three-point layout or a parallel layout. A **three-point layout structure** establishes three elements in the ad as dominant forces. The uneven number of prominent elements is critical for creating a gaze motion in the viewer. The Hidesign ad in Exhibit 11.21 features three prominent elements. Walk through them. **Parallel layout structure** employs art on the right-hand side of the page and repeats the art on the left-hand side. This is an obvious and highly structured technique to achieve unity. Check out the parallel layout in this Epiphone guitar ad (Exhibit 11.22). Think about why this type of look works well for this brand. Don't you see a lot of this design around places where young people hang out? Why is that?

Emphasis. At some point in the decision-making process, someone needs to decide which major component—the headline, subhead, body copy, or illustration—will be emphasized. The key to good design relative to emphasis is that one item is the primary but not the only focus in an ad.

If one element is emphasized to the total exclusion of the others, then a poor design has been achieved, and ultimately a poor communication will result.

Balance, proportion, order, unity, and emphasis are the basic principles of design. As you can see, the designer's objectives go beyond the strategic and message-development elements associated with an advertisement. Design principles relate to the aesthetic impression an ad produces. Once a designer has been informed of the components that will make up the headline, subhead, body copy, and illustration to be included in the ad, then advertising and marketing decision makers *must* allow the designer to arrange those components according to the principles of creative design.

Layout. In contrast to design, which emphasizes the structural concept behind a print ad, layout is the mechanical aspect of design—the physical manifestation of design concepts. A **layout** is a drawing or digital rendering of a proposed print advertisement (digital interactive ads are digitized from the start, of course) showing where all the elements in the ad are positioned. An art director uses a layout to work through various alternatives for visual presentation and sequentially develop the print ad to its final stages. It is part and

EXHIBIT 11.22 Here, the visual layout on the left is repeated on the right. www.epiphone.com.

i can't tell you

but i can   play it for you

Epiphone

Client: The Epiphone Company, a division of Gibson Guitar Corp

parcel of the design process and inextricably linked to the development of an effective design.

An art director typically proceeds through various stages in the construction of a final design for an ad. The following are the different stages of layout development, in order of detail and completeness, that an art director typically uses.

Thumbnails. **Thumbnails** are the first drafts of an advertising layout. The art director will produce several thumbnail sketches to work out the general presentation of the ad. Although the creative team refines the creative concept, thumbnails represent placement of elements—headline, images, body copy, and tagline. Headlines are often represented with zigzag lines, and body copy with straight, parallel lines. An example of a thumbnail is shown in Exhibit 11.23 for S.F. Water. Typically, thumbnails are drawn at one-quarter the size of the finished ad. It tells you enough, right?

Rough Layout. The next step in the layout process is the **rough layout**. Unlike a thumbnail sketch, a rough layout is done in the actual size of the proposed ad and is usually created with a computer layout program, such as InDesign. This allows the art director to experiment with different headline fonts and easily manipulate the placement and size of images to be used in the ad.

Comprehensive. The comprehensive layout, or **comp**, is a polished version of the ad—but not the final

version. Now for the most part computer-generated, a comp is a representation of what the final ad will look like. At this stage, the final headline font is used, the images to be used—photographs or illustrations—are digitized and placed in the ad, and the actual body copy is often included on the ad. Comps are generally printed in full color if the final ad is to be in color. Comps produced in this way make it very easy for the client to imagine (and approve) what the ad will look like when it is published. The client will make one last approval of the digital file before it is sent to the printer. Changes that a client requests, prior to the ad being sent to the printer, are still easily and quickly made. The stages of layout development discussed here provide the artistic blueprint for a print advertisement. We now turn our attention to the matter of typography in print production.

Typography in Print Production. The issues associated with typography have to do with the typeface chosen for headlines, subheads, and body copy, as well as the various size components of the type (height, width, and running length). Designers agonize over the type to use in a print ad because decisions about type affect both the readability and the mood of the overall visual impression. For our purposes, some knowledge of the basic considerations of typography is useful for an appreciation of the choices that must be made.

Categories of Type. Typefaces have distinct personalities, and each can communicate a different mood and image. A **type font** is a basic set of typeface letters. For those of us who do word processing on computers, the choice of type font is a common decision. In choosing type for an advertisement, however, the art director has thousands of choices based on typeface alone.

There are six basic typeface groups: blackletter, roman, script, serif, sans serif, and miscellaneous. The families are divided by characteristics that reflect the personality and tone of the font. **Blackletter**, also called *gothic*, is characterized by the ornate design of the letters. This style is patterned after hand-drawn letters in monasteries where illuminated manuscripts were created. You can see blackletter fonts used today in very formal documents, such as college diplomas. **Roman** is the most common group of fonts used for body copy because of its legibility. This family is characterized by the use of thick and thin strokes in the creation of the letterforms. **Script** is easy to distinguish by the linkage of the letters in the way that cursive handwriting is connected. Script is often found on wedding invitations and documents that are intended to look elegant or of high quality. **Serif** refers to the strokes or "feet" at the ends of the letterforms. Notice the serifs that are present in these letters as you read. Their presence

EXHIBIT 11.23 A thumbnail showing the transition from idea to advertisement.

helps move your eye across the page, allowing you to read for a long time without losing your place or tiring your eyes. **Sans serif** fonts, as the name suggests, do not have serifs, hence the use of the French word *sans*, meaning "without." Sans serif fonts are typically used for headlines and not for body copy. **Miscellaneous (type)** includes typefaces that do not fit easily into the other categories. Novelty display, garage, and deconstructed fonts all fall into this group. These fonts were designed specifically to draw attention to themselves and not necessarily for their legibility. The following example displays serif and sans serif type:

> This line is set in serif type.
> This line is set in sans serif type.

Type Measurement. There are two elements of type size. **Point** refers to the size of type in height. In the printing industry, type sizes run from 6 to 120 points. Now, with computer layout programs such as QuarkXPress, the range is much larger, between 2 and 720 points. **Picas** measure the width of lines. A pica is 12 points wide, and each pica measures about one-sixth of an inch. Layout programs make it very easy for the art director to fit copy into a designated space on an ad by reducing or enlarging a font with a few strokes on the keyboard.

Readability. It is critical in choosing type to consider readability. Type should facilitate the communication process. The following are some traditional recommendations when deciding what type to use (however, remember that these are only guidelines and should not necessarily be followed in every instance):

- Use capitals and lowercase, NOT ALL CAPITALS.
- Arrange letters from left to right, not up and down.
- Run lines of type horizontally, not vertically.
- Use even spacing between letters and words.

Different typefaces and styles also affect the mood conveyed by an ad. Depending on the choices made, typefaces can connote grace, power, beauty, modernity, simplicity, or any number of other qualities.

11-4b Art Direction and Production in Digital/Interactive Media

We've referenced art direction and production in digital/interactive media in the previous sections. But, cyberspace has its own space qualities. It is its own medium, too. It's not television or radio, but ads produced for television or radio can certainly be transmitted over the Web. In that case, the considerations for radio and television production hold. But when an ad is prepared primarily with the characteristics of headline, body copy, and illustration—like an email, banner, pop-up, or even a website—digital/interactive ads are closer to print than to anything. Even though the basic principles of art direction (design and concept) apply, the cyber media are fundamentally different in the way the audience comes to them, navigates them, and responds to them. This difference presents one of the real challenges of electronic advertising.

In most respects, cyberproduction does not differ significantly from print production, but it does differ from print in how aspects of production are combined with programming language, such as HTML, and with each other. Advances in streaming audio and digital video keep art direction and production in cyberspace a fast-moving target. Still, many cyberads may be either produced in traditional ways and then digitized and combined with text or created entirely with computer design packages. All media have to find their own way, their own voice. This is not just an aesthetic matter. It's figuring out what works, which has something to do with design. How the information is laid out matters. If you go back and look at the first few years of television advertising, you have to say that they really didn't fully understand the medium or the ways audiences would use this new technology. The ads went on forever and seemed to be written for radio. In fact, many of the early TV writers were radio writers. They tried to make television radio.

This same phenomenon seems to be happening with websites. At first, Web ads looked more like print ads than something truly cyber. Yet, unlike print ads, websites have the ability to change almost immediately. If a client wants to change a copy point, for example, it can happen many times in one afternoon. And Web consumers demand change. Although frequent changes may seem time-consuming and expensive, they ensure return visits from audiences. More importantly, digital/interactive ads offer the viewer direct interaction by clicking on the ad or a link in an email: an opportunity that can't be missed.

Web pages are often very busy, with lots of information crammed into small spaces. In short, the Web is not print *or* television: It is electronic and fluid and must be thought of in this way. In terms of design, this means trying to understand why people come to various sites, who they are, what they are looking for, what they expect to encounter, and what they expect in return for their very valuable click. One of the most valuable lessons out there right now is the case of **consumer-generated content (CGC)**: where people are making their own ads for their favorite brands. Firms are starting to specifically encourage customers to offer suggestions (called "crowdsourcing") as a way to energize the creative process.[18] One Apple cyberad that was incredibly popular on the Web was not made by Apple's high-priced ad agency—a college kid did it. YouTube and other venues have allowed consumers to say, "Hey, it's my brand too . . . I get it more than you do . . . here's my ad."

11-4c Art Direction and Production in Television Advertising

In many ways, television was simply made for advertising. It is everywhere, serving as background to daily life. But as background, it tends to be ignored or only half paid attention to. If you consider the 10 message strategies detailed in Chapter 10, use of the TV medium would dictate very different strategies. In some cases, you need high attention levels, which are difficult to get; in other strategies, you might actually prefer lower levels of attention and the counterarguing that comes with it. Sometimes, it's just about leaving impressions, or setting moods, or getting you to notice; sometimes it tells stories. But in all of these cases, the visual is important—whether it's the main feature or plays a key supportive role.

The Creative Team in Television Advertising. Due to its complexity, television production involves a lot of people. These people have different but often overlapping expertise, responsibility, and authority. This makes for tremendous organizational skills. At some point, individuals who actually shoot the film or the tape are brought in to execute the copywriter's and art director's concepts. They are, more and more, also in contact with a media planner and/or account planner, making sure that what is being done for TV is consistent with, compatible with, or can do double duty with other media forms; such as longer TV ads on the Internet or visual captures that end up in print or on websites. The account planner is there to make sure that the consumer's values and interests continue to be represented.

At this point, the creative process becomes intensely collaborative: The film director applies his or her craft and is responsible for the actual production. The creative team (i.e., the art director, copywriter, media director, and account planner) rarely relinquishes control of the project, even though the film director may prefer that. Getting the various players to perform their particular specialties at just the right time, while avoiding conflict with other team members, is an ongoing challenge in TV ad production. Someone has to be in charge on the set, and that is usually the chief creative on site.

Creative Guidelines for Television Advertising. Just as for print advertising, there are general creative principles for television advertising.[19] These principles are not foolproof or definitive, but they certainly represent good advice and provide organizational structure. Again, truly great creative work has at one time or another violated some or all of these conventions, but the decision to venture off guidelines was no doubt guided by the creative brief—so all is well.

- *Use an attention-getting and relevant opening.* The first few seconds of a television commercial are crucial. A receiver can make a split-second assessment of the relevance and interest a message holds. An ad can either turn a receiver off or grab his or her attention for the balance of the commercial with the opening. Remember, remote controls and DVRs are ubiquitous. It is incredibly easy to avoid commercials, so you, as an advertiser, must have a good hook to suck viewers in. Ads just don't get much time to develop. There is the belief that "slower" ads (ads that take time to develop) don't wear out as quickly as the hit-and-run ads. So, if you have a huge (almost inexhaustible) supply of money, an ad that "builds" might be best. If you don't, go for the quick hook. In Exhibit 11.24, the TV spot opens with a shot of "ManMom" sitting at a table with two young men and a bag of Combos. It's hard not to wonder what's going to come next.

- *Emphasize the visual.* The video capability of television should be highlighted in every production effort. To some degree, this emphasis is dependent on the creative concept, but the visual should carry the selling message even if the audio portion is ignored by the receiver.

- *Coordinate the audio with the visual.* The images and copy of a television commercial must reinforce each other. Divergence between the audio and visual portions of an ad only serves to confuse and distract the viewer.

- *Persuade as well as entertain.* It is tempting to produce a beautifully creative television advertisement rather than a beautifully effective television advertisement. Creating an entertaining commercial is an inherently praiseworthy goal except when the entertainment value of the commercial completely overwhelms its persuasive impact.

- *Show the brand.* Unless a commercial is using intrigue and mystery surrounding the brand, the brand should be highlighted in the ad. Close-ups and shots of the brand in action help receivers recall the brand and its appearance. The client really likes this.

EXHIBIT 11.24 If the first seconds of this ad draw you in, there's a pretty good chance you'll stick around for the slogan at the end. "Combos. What your mom would feed you if your mom were a man."

"Grace" :30
(A very manly-looking mother, Man Mom, sits at a table with her two grown-up sons. There's a bag of Cheddar Cheese Pretzel Combos on the table. One of the sons reaches for the Combos)
Man Mom: Ahem.
(The son quickly retracts his arm)
Son: Sorry, mom.
(All three join hands to say grace)
Man Mom: We thank you for this bounty of pretzels filled with creamy-tasting cheddar cheese that we're about to receive. And please, please let Dallas cover the spread this weekend.
(The son opens the bag of Combos, takes some and then passes the bag to Man Mom. Cut to Combos end treatment)
Anncr. (VO): Combos. What your mom would feed you if your mom were a man.

LO ⑥

11-5 THE PRODUCTION PROCESS IN TELEVISION ADVERTISING

The television production process can best be understood by identifying the activities that take place before, during, and after the actual production of an ad. These stages are referred to as preproduction, production, and postproduction, respectively. By breaking the process down into this sequence, we can appreciate both the technical and the strategic aspects of each stage.

11-5a Preproduction

The **preproduction** stage is that part of the television production process in which the advertiser and the advertising agency carefully work out the precise details of how the creative planning behind an ad can best be brought to life with the opportunities offered by television. Exhibit 11.25 shows the sequence of six events in the preproduction stage.

Storyboard and Script Approval. As Exhibit 11.26 shows, the preproduction stage begins with storyboard and script approval. A storyboard is a shot-by-shot sketch depicting, in sequence, the visual scenes and copy that will be used in an advertisement. A **script** is the written version of an ad; it specifies the coordination of the copy elements with the video scenes. The script is used by the producer and director to set the location and content of scenes, by the casting department to choose actors and actresses, and by the producer in budgeting and scheduling the shoot. Exhibit 11.26 is part of a storyboard from the Miller Lite "Can Your Beer Do This?" campaign. This particular spot was entitled "Ski Jump" and involved rigging a dummy to a recliner and launching the chair and the dummy from a 60-meter ski jump. The storyboard gives the creative team and the client an overall idea of the look and feel of the ad.

The art director and copywriter are significantly involved at this stage of production. It is important that the producer discusses the storyboard and script with the creative team and fully understands the creative concept and objectives for the advertisement before production begins. Because it is the producer's responsibility to solicit bids for the project from production houses, the producer must be able to fully explain to bidders the requirements of the job so that cost estimates are as accurate as possible.

Budget Approval. Once there is agreement on the scope and intent of the production as depicted in the storyboard and script, the advertiser must give budget approval. The producer needs to work carefully with the creative team and the advertiser to estimate the approximate cost of the shoot, including production staging, location costs, actors, technical requirements, staffing, and a multitude of other considerations. It is essential that these discussions be as detailed and comprehensive as possible, because it is from this budget discussion that the producer will evaluate candidates for the directing role and solicit bids from production houses to handle the job.

Assessment of Directors, Editorial Houses, Music Suppliers. A producer has dozens (if not hundreds) of directors, postproduction editorial houses, and

EXHIBIT 11.25 Sequence of events in the preproduction stage of television advertising.

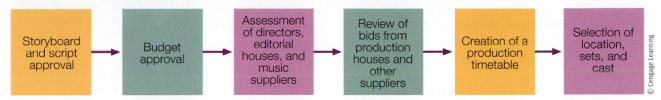

Storyboard and script approval → Budget approval → Assessment of directors, editorial houses, and music suppliers → Review of bids from production houses and other suppliers → Creation of a production timetable → Selection of location, sets, and cast

© Cengage Learning

music suppliers from which to choose. An assessment of those well suited to the task takes place early in the preproduction process. The combination of the creative talents of ad agencies and production houses can produce creative, eye-catching ads. Directors of television commercials, like directors of feature films, develop specializations and reputations. Some directors are known for their work with action or special effects. Others are more highly skilled in working with children, animals, outdoor settings, or shots of beverages flowing into a glass ("pour shots").

The director of an advertisement is responsible for interpreting the storyboard and script and managing the talent to bring the creative concept to life. A director specifies the precise nature of a scene, how it is lit, and how it is filmed. Choosing the proper director is crucial to the execution of a commercial. Aside from the fact that a good director commands a fee anywhere from $8,000 to $25,000 per day, the director can have a tremendous effect on the quality and impact of the presentation. An excellent creative concept can be undermined by poor direction. Among the now-famous feature film directors who have made television commercials are Ridley Scott (Apple), John Frankenheimer (AT&T), Woody Allen (Campari), Spike Lee (Levi's, Nike, the Gap, Barney's New York), and Federico Fellini (Coop Italia).

Similarly, editorial houses and music suppliers (and musicians) have particular expertise and reputations. The producer, the director, and the agency creative team actively review the work of suppliers that are particularly well suited to the production. In most cases,

EXHIBIT 11.26 How does this storyboard for a Miller Lite Beer ad save the advertiser time and money during the television production process?

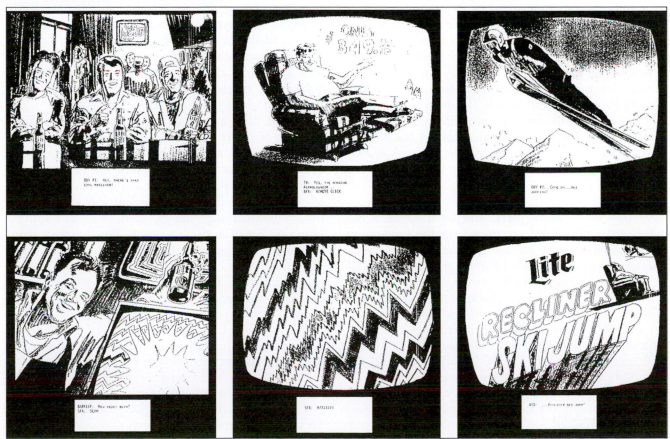

Miller Brewing Company

geographic proximity to the agency facilities is important, as members of the agency team try to maintain a tight schedule. Because of this need, editorial and music suppliers have tended to cluster near agencies in Chicago, New York, and Los Angeles.

Review of Bids from Production Houses and Other Suppliers. Production houses and other suppliers, such as lighting specialists, represent a collection of specialized talent and also provide needed equipment for ad preparation. The expertise in production houses relates to the technical aspects of filming a commercial. Producers, production managers, sound and stage specialists, camera operators, and others are part of a production house team. The agency sends a bid package to several production houses. The package contains all the details of the commercial to be produced and includes a description of the production requirements and a timetable. An accurate timetable is essential because many production personnel work on an hourly or daily compensation rate. Costs vary from market to market, but production expenses typically run into the hundreds of thousands of dollars.

Most agencies send out a bid package on a form developed by the agency. By using a standardized form, an agency can make direct comparisons between production house bids. The producer reviews each of the bids and revises them if necessary. From the production house bids *and* the agency's estimate of its own costs associated with production (travel, expenses, editorial services, music, on-camera talent, and agency markups), a production cost estimate is prepared. Once the advertiser has approved the estimate, one of the production houses is awarded the job. The lowest production bid is not always the one chosen. Aside from cost, there are creative and technical considerations. A hot director costs more than last year's model. The agency's evaluation of the reliability of a production house also enters into the decision.

Selection of Location, Sets, and Cast. Once a bid has been approved and accepted, both the production house and the agency production team begin to search for appropriate, affordable locations if the commercial is to be shot outside a studio setting.

A delicate stage in preproduction is casting. Although not every ad uses actors and actresses, when an ad calls for individuals to perform roles, casting is crucial. Every individual appearing in an ad is, in a very real sense, a representative of the advertiser and the brand (think about "Flo," the Progressive Insurance gal). This is another reason why the agency creative team stays involved. Actors and actresses help set the mood and tone for an ad and affect the image of the brand.

The successful execution of various message strategies depends on proper casting. For instance, a slice-of-life message requires actors and actresses with whom the target audience can readily identify. Testimonial message tactics require a search for particular types of people, either celebrities or common folks, who will attract attention and be credible. The point to remember is that successfully casting a television commercial depends on much more than simply picking people with good acting abilities. Individuals must be matched to the brand, the nature of the audience, and the scene depicted in the ad (see Insights Online [Exhibit 11.27] for an interesting case involving Dove's real beauties).

Production. The **production stage** of the process, or the **shoot**, is where the storyboard and script come to life and are filmed. The actual production of the spot may also include some final preparations before the shoot begins. The most common final preparation activities are lighting checks and rehearsals. An entire day may be devoted to *prelight*, which involves setting up lighting or identifying times for the best natural lighting to ensure that the shooting day runs smoothly. Similarly, the director may want to work with the on-camera talent along with the camera operators to practice the positioning and movement planned for the ad. This work, known as *blocking*, can save a lot of time on a shoot day, when many more costly personnel are on the set.

Shoot days are the culmination of an enormous amount of effort beginning all the way back at the development of the creative brief. They are the execution of all the well-laid plans by the advertiser and agency personnel. The set on a shoot day is a world all its own. For the uninformed, it can appear to be little more than high-energy chaos, or a lot of nothing going on between camera setups. For the professionals involved, however, a shoot has its own tempo and direction.

A successful shoot depends on the effective management of a large number of diverse individuals—creative performers, highly trained technicians, and skilled laborers. Logistical and technical problems always arise, not to mention the ever-present threat of a random event (a thunderstorm or intrusive noise) that disrupts filming and tries everyone's patience. There is a degree of tension and spontaneity on the set that is a necessary part of the creative process but must be kept at a manageable level. Much of the tension stems from trying to execute the various tasks of production correctly and at the proper time.

Another dimension to this tension, however, has to do with expense. As pointed out earlier, most directors, technicians, and talent are paid a daily rate plus overtime after 10 hours. Daily shooting expenses, including director's fees, can run from $80,000 to $120,000 for just an average production, so the agency and the advertiser, understandably, want the shoot to run as smoothly and quickly as possible.

There is the real problem of not rushing creativity, however, and advertisers often have to learn to accept the pace of production. For example, a well-known director made a Honda commercial in South Florida, where he shot film for only one hour per day—a half-hour in the morning and a half-hour at twilight. His explanation? "From experience you learn that cars look flat and unattractive in direct light, so you have to catch the shot when the angle [of the sun] is just right."[20] Despite the fact that the cameras were rolling only an hour a day, the $9,000-per-hour cost for the production crew was charged all day for each day of shooting. Advertisers have to accept, on occasion, that the television advertising production process is not like an assembly line production process.

SUMMARY

 Identify the main members of a creative team and how the creative brief guides their efforts.

Effective creative execution depends on the input of the creative team: art director, copywriter, account planner, and media planner. The creative team will have access to a wide variety of inputs, including the client's, and information sources, such as market research. A creative brief is used as a device to assist the creative team overall and the copywriter in particular in dealing with this challenge. Key elements in the creative brief include brand features and benefits that must be communicated to the audience, the mood or tone appropriate for the audience, and the intended media for the ad.

 Detail the elements of copywriting for print media, including the headline, subhead, and body copy.

The three unique components of print copy are the headline, subhead, and body copy. Headlines need to motivate additional processing of the ad. Good headlines communicate information about the brand or make a promise about the benefits the consumer can expect from the brand. If the brand name is not featured in the headline, then that headline must entice the reader to examine the body copy or visual material. Subheads can also be valuable in helping lead the reader to and through the body copy. A subhead appears above or below the main headline and carries additional information beyond the headline. In the body copy, the brand's complete story can be told. Effective body copy must be crafted carefully to engage the reader, furnish supportive evidence for claims made about the brand, and avoid clichés and exaggeration that the consumer will dismiss as hype.

 Detail the elements of copywriting for television and video and radio.

Several formats can be considered in preparing television ad copy. These are demonstration, problem and solution, music and song, spokesperson, dialogue, vignette, and narrative. To achieve effective copy in the television medium, it is essential to coordinate the copy with the visual presentation, seeking a synergistic effect between audio and video. Entertaining to attract attention should again not be emphasized to the point that the brand name or selling points of the ad get lost. Developing copy consistent with the heritage and image of the brand is also essential. Finally, copy that can be adapted to various time lengths and modified to sustain audience interest over the life of a campaign is most desirable.

Four basic formats can be used to create radio copy. These are the music format, the dialogue format, the announcement format, and the celebrity announcer format. Guidelines for writing effective radio copy start with using simple sentence construction and language familiar to the intended audience. When the copy stimulates the listener's imagination, the advertiser can expect improved results as long as the brand name and the primary selling points don't get lost. When using music or humor to attract and hold the listener's attention, the copywriter must take care not to shortchange key selling points for the sake of simple entertainment.

 Describe the common copywriting approaches for digital/interactive ads.

Digital/interactive ads are hybrids between print and broadcasting advertisements. The receiver does encounter a message in a print format either at a website, in an email, at a blog, or from social media communication. But the message is delivered electronically similar to television or radio. Common approaches to copywriting include long-copy landing page, short-copy landing page, long copy email, teaser email copy, pop-up/pop-under ad copy, and social media copy. Copywriting in each of these digital/interactive formats may or may not employ the elements of headline and subhead or even body copy (in the case of pop-ups and pop-unders). But there are "copy" elements in each case that communicate brand information.

5 Identify the components of art direction that are essential in creative execution of print ads.

In print ad design, all the verbal and visual components of an ad are arranged for maximum impact and appeal. Several principles can be followed as a basis for a compelling design. These principles feature issues such as balance, proportion, order, unity, and emphasis. The first component of an effective design is focus—drawing the reader's attention to specific areas of the ad. The second component is movement and direction—directing the reader's eye movement through the ad. The third component is clarity and simplicity—avoiding a complex and chaotic look that will deter most consumers.

The layout is the physical manifestation of all design planning for print ads. An art director uses various forms of layouts to bring a print ad to life. There are several predictable stages in the evolution of a layout. The art director starts with a hand-drawn thumbnail, proceeds to the digitized rough layout, and continues with a tight comprehensive layout that represents the look of the final ad. With each stage, the layout becomes more concrete and more like the final form of the advertisement. In the last stage, the digitized ad is sent out for placement in print media.

 6 Describe the production process in creating a television commercial.

The intricate process of TV ad production can be broken into three major stages: preproduction, production, and postproduction. In the preproduction stage, scripts and storyboards are prepared, budgets are set, production houses are engaged, and a timetable is formulated. Production includes all those activities involved in the actual filming of the ad. The shoot is a high-stress activity that usually carries a high price tag. The raw materials from the shoot are mixed and refined in the postproduction stage. Today's editors work almost exclusively with computers to create the final product—a finished television ad. If all this sounds expensive, it is!

KEY TERMS

media planner	pop-up/pop-under copy	thumbnails
account planner	social media copy	rough layout
creative team	slogan/tagline	comp
creative brief	developmental copy research	type font
copywriting	evaluative copy research	blackletter
headline	illustration	roman
subhead	design	script
straight-line copy	principles of design	serif
dialogue	balance	sans serif
testimonial	formal balance	miscellaneous (type)
narrative	informal balance	point
direct response copy	proportion	pica
storyboard	order	consumer-generated
long-copy landing page	unity	content (CGC)
short-copy landing page	axis	preproduction
long copy email	three-point layout structure	script
teaser email	parallel layout structure	production stage/shoot
pop-up/pop-under ad	layout	

ENDNOTES

1. Mario Pricken, *Creative Advertising* (London: Thames & Hudson, Ltd., 2008), 8.

2. Tom Altsteil and Jean Grow, *Advertising Creative: Strategy, Copy and Design*, 2nd ed. (Los Angeles: Sage Publications, 2010), 53.

3. The last two points in this list were adapted from the classic perspectives of A. Jerome Jewler, *Creative Strategy in Advertising*, 3rd ed. (Belmont, CA: Wadsworth, 1989), 196.

4. Cited in Luke Sullivan, *Hey Whipple, Squeeze This: A Guide to Creating Great Ads* (Hoboken, NJ: John Wiley and Sons, 2012), 103.

5. The last three points in this list were adapted from Kennett Roman and Jane Maas, *The New How to Advertise*, 6. Michael Learmonth,

"Lowered Expectations: Web Redefines 'Quality,'" *Advertising Age*, February 22, 2010, 8.

6. Tom Alsteil and Jean Grow, *Advertising Creative: Strategy, Copy and Design*, 2nd ed. (Los Angeles: Sage Publications, 2010), 218–219.

7. Michael Learmonth, "Lowered Expectations: Web Redefines 'Quality'" *Advertising Age*, February 22, 2010, 8.

8. Quoted in Christy Ashley and Jason D. Oliver, "Creative Leaders: Thirty Years of Big Ideas," *Journal of Advertising*, vol. 39, no. 1 (Spring 2010), 126.

9. Content in this section is drawn from Robert W. Bly, *The Copywriter's Handbook*, 3rd ed. (New York: Henry Holt and Company, 2006), 263–264.

10. John R. Rossiter, "Defining the Necessary Components of Creative, Effective Ads," *Journal of Advertising*, vol. 37, no. 4 (Winter 2008), 141.

11. Luke Sullivan, *Hey Whipple, Squeeze This: A Guide to Creating Great Ads*, 182.

12. Jean Halliday, "How GM Stifled 'Passion and Creativity' in Its Marketing Ranks," *Advertising Age*, June 12, 2009, 13.

13. David Ogilvy, *Ogilvy on Advertising* (New York: Vintage Books, 1985).

14. Nat Ives, "How to Make Over a Magazine for the iPad: Popular Science," *Advertising Age*, May 31, 2010, 6.

15. Tony Antin, *Great Print Advertising* (New York: Wiley, 1993), 38.

16. This discussion is based on Roy Paul Nelson, *The Design of Advertising*, 7th ed. (Boston: McGraw-Hill 1996), 136.

17. Ibid., 149.

18. Garrick Schmitt, "Can Creativity Be Crowdsourced?" *Advertising Age*, April, 16, 2009, 14.

19. Tom Altsteil and Jean Grow, *Advertising Creative: Strategy, Copy and Design*, 2nd ed. (Los Angeles: Sage Publications, 2010), 228–229.

20. Jeffrey A. Trachtenberg, "Where the Money Goes," *Forbes*, September 21, 1987, 180.

PART 4

Placing the Message in Conventional and "New" Media

O nce again we transition to a new and totally different area of advertising and integrated brand promotion (IBP), "Placing the Message in Conventional and 'New' Media." We are now at the point where reaching the target audience is the key issue.

Beyond the basic and formidable challenge of effectively choosing the right media to reach the right target audience(s), contemporary advertisers and promotion professionals are demanding even more from the media placement decision: synergy and integration. Throughout the first three parts of the text, the issue of IBP has been raised whenever the opportunity existed to create coordinated communications. But nowhere is IBP more critical than at the media placement stage. This challenge has been made more complex in the last 10 years as media beyond traditional mass media—new digital media such as email, websites, blogs, mobile, and social media networks—manifest themselves as opportunities to reach consumers. The challenge is to ensure that if diverse communications media options are chosen—traditional combined with new media—there is still a cohesive strategy guiding the overall communication program.

CHAPTER

12

Media Planning Essentials Maintaining integration is indeed a challenge in the contemporary media environment. Chapter 12, "Media Planning Essentials," begins with a discussion of the major changes that have altered and now define the contemporary media landscape, particularly the role of social media and advertisers' use of social media networks. We offer a framework of what has remained the same in considering the coordination of new and old media but also consider what has to be taken into account for each on its own terms. Next, the fundamentals of media planning are explained, followed by the details. Next, we discuss how the complex communications environment impacts the entire process of media strategy and planning, followed by particular attention to IBP's impact.

CHAPTER

13

Media Planning: Newspapers, Magazines, TV, and Radio Chapter 13, "Media Planning: Newspapers, Magazines, TV, and Radio," offers an analysis of the major traditional media options available to advertisers. Even in an environment where all sorts of new media options are available, the vast majority of the creative effort—and money—is still spent on print and broadcast advertising campaigns. Despite the many intriguing opportunities that new media options offer, print and broadcast media will likely form the foundation of most advertising campaigns. "New" media simply can't do what "old" media do—the creative execution opportunities are simply superior in old media in many ways. But we also raise the issue that these traditional media are turning to new, digital media opportunities as well. Both print and broadcast media have embraced digital options, offering advertisers new opportunities to reach audiences and drive audiences to a more interactive experience with brands. The chapter follows a sequence in which the advantages and disadvantages of each medium are discussed, followed by considerations of costs, buying procedures, and audience measurement techniques.

CHAPTER

14

Media Planning: Advertising and IBP in Digital and Social Media Advertisers are energized and somewhat mystified on just how to take full advantage of the digital and social media options that the contemporary technology environment offers. Chapter 14, "Media Planning: Advertising and IBP in Digital and Social Media," describes the new media landscape and the advertising and IBP opportunities it offers. You will learn that it is crucial to understand how consumers think, feel, and act regarding social media, online advertising, and e-commerce. This chapter was written by Angeline Close of the University of Texas at Austin and describes the full complement of digital and social media opportunities and challenges facing advertisers—as well as the "dark side" of social media. You will learn about how advertisers are trying to not just use but embrace consumer blogs, Pinterest, Facebook, Instagram, Twitter, LinkedIn, MySpace, Digg, HowSocial, Groupon, Vine, and other social media to enhance their online presence. Newer sites Pheed, Thumb, Medium, Conversations, Chirpify, and Flavyr are also considered. You will learn about the full complement of the different types of digital ads, paid search, e-tail, and the emergence of social e-commerce. This chapter concludes with a valuable discussion of synergizing digital and social media with other IBP tools.

CHAPTER 12
Media Planning Essentials

After reading and thinking about this chapter, you will be able to do the following:

1 Describe measured versus unmeasured media and about how much each represents of total advertising and IBP dollars.

2 Describe the basic ideas and essential terms in media planning.

3 Understand the meaning of competitive media assessment and share of voice.

4 Discuss media efficiency.

5 Discuss what makes social media different.

6 Discuss the basics of branded entertainment.

7 Discuss the benefits and the realities of media planning models.

8 Discuss making the buy.

After all the research is done, the message strategies determined, and the ads created, the people in charge of media placement have their say. While not the most glamorous part of the advertising world, media planning is where the big money is spent, and big money saved or wasted. It is where the advertiser can win or lose. And it is where a lot has changed.

The subsequent chapter discusses how things are done now in digital and social media. In this chapter, we offer you some of the things that have endured, the essential ideas and concepts that remain the same. Also, traditional media are not dead. If you think they are, try to buy some network television time. Bring a lot of money.

--- LO **1** ---

12-1 MEASURED AND UNMEASURED MEDIA

A lot has changed in media land, but not everything. There are still some ideas, names, concepts, and principles that are just as they always were.

Advertising requires money, usually a lot of it. True, there are some big brands that do very little mass advertising (e.g., Starbucks), but the vast majority do.

So, what kind of money are we talking?

Exhibit 12.1 shows the amount of dollars spent in advertising—by several major brands.

The truth is that for most goods and services, you have to have access to a considerable amount of money to play at the national or international level. This is an enormous barrier to small companies.

Sure, we can give examples of the small brand that broke through on a wing and a prayer, but the truth is there are a lot more Goliaths than Davids. (See Insights Online [Exhibit 12.2] for a notable example.)

12-1a Where the Money Goes: The Big Pie

So, how is this money spent?

Typically, expenditures are divided into two types: measured media and unmeasured media, or above-the-line and below-the-line promotions.

Let us explain.

Think of all the money used to promote a brand as a big pie. The big pie (see Exhibit 12.3) includes mass media advertising, direct mail, point-of-purchase promotion, coupons, promotional emails, buzz marketing, product placement, brand integration in computer games, and everything spent to promote a good or service. Traditionally, companies would make the distinction between (1) **above-the-line promotion**, which meant traditional **measured media** advertising, and (2) **below-the-line promotion**, which is everything else. For consumer package goods companies, below-the-line promotion might be desirable retail shelving, in-store promotions, coupons, and events; for durable goods (say cars), it might be for dealer incentives and financing incentives. Below-the-line promotion is also referred to as **unmeasured media**. It's not that it is really unmeasured, but it is just called "unmeasured."

Measured media include network TV, cable TV, spot TV, syndicated TV, network Spanish TV, the Internet (excluding broadband video and paid search), Net radio, spot radio, local radio (500 stations, top-28 markets), magazines (Sunday, consumer, business-to-business, and 30 local magazines), 250 local newspapers, Spanish newspapers, national newspapers (*The Wall Street Journal, USA Today, The New York Times*), and Outdoor (200-plus markets). Unmeasured media is everything else: paid Internet search, coupons, product placement, events, and the like.

After all the research is done, the message strategies determined, and the ads created, the people in charge of the media placement function have their say. While not the most glamorous part of the advertising world, it is where the big money is spent.

 INSIGHTS ONLINE

12.2 Go online to see the AdAge feature, "Abbott Pharmaceuticals Invests $365 Million on Media."

This is a very big pie. Let's call everything companies invest to promote the brand the total brand promotions pie. The most recent data (2011, reported in 2013) reveal that measured media account for 56 percent and unmeasured account for 44 percent of total up-front investing. This ratio, despite all the talk of new media, has remained fairly stable for the last few years.

If you break things down a bit more, you can see the relative standing of the different measured media (see Exhibit 12.4). Television in all its forms is still king by a long way. The Internet and online advertising/social media advertising account for a big spike in measured media investing. It is more than double all outdoor advertising, on the heels of radio (which has been around since the 1920s), and climbing.

--- LO **2** ---

12-2 **THE BASIC IDEAS AND TERMS**

Media planning determines where and when the advertiser's money is spent (see Insights Online [Exhibit 12.5] for an interesting example). Hardly glamorous, it is, however, vital. A lot of people enter the ad industry through the media department. It has traditionally been a job of numbers, schedules, deadlines, and relatively low salaries. But as the world of media has opened up, it has become considerably more interesting and desirable, if not better paying. Now, with the merger of movies, music, gaming, and other entertainment, media planning has become more than it was but still involves a lot of numbers, schedules, and deadlines.

EXHIBIT 12.1 Look at how much these top brands spend on advertising and promotion per year.

Show Me the Money: Spending by selected advertisers, 2011 (in millions of USD).

Apple (excluding iTunes)	542,877
Blue Moon (Miller Coors)	10,173
Crest	228,608
JCPenney	438,173
Mountain Dew (PepsiCo)	23,621
McDonald's	962,875
Sephora	19,149
Target	682,995
Taco Bell (YUM)	250,583
U.S. Army	47,096

Advertising Age, Marketer Tree, http://adage.com/datacenter/marketertrees 2012update/#276

EXHIBIT 12.3 This approximate ratio has not changed as much as you might expect.

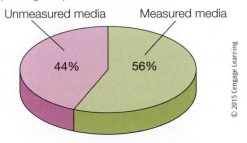

Unmeasured media 44% — Measured media 56%

© 2015 Cengage Learning

EXHIBIT 12.4 Spending on Media by Top 100 advertisers, 2011 (Measured Media). This is where the money goes.

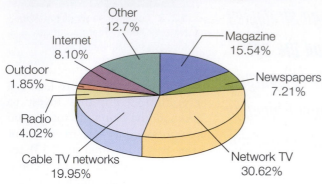

Other 12.7%
Internet 8.10%
Outdoor 1.85%
Radio 4.02%
Cable TV networks 19.95%
Network TV 30.62%
Magazine 15.54%
Newspapers 7.21%

Advertising Age, Ad Spending Totals by Medium, http://adage.com /datacenter/datapopup.php?article_id=235494

Media planning requires creativity and strategic thinking. Sure, you need to know how to do the basic math and know the key terms, but you should never let the raw numbers and techno-buzzwords obscure the strategy. What you really need to understand is what you are trying to do with media, why you are doing it, and the key aspects of the various tools at your disposal.

A **media plan** specifies the media in which advertising messages will be placed to reach the desired target audience. A **media class** is a broad category of media, such as television, radio, or newspapers. A **media vehicle** is a particular option for placement within a media class. For example, *Newsweek* is a media vehicle within the magazine-media class. The **media mix** is the blend of different media that will be used to effectively reach the target audience.

A media plan includes strategy, objectives, media choices, and a media schedule for placing a message. And remember: Everything must fit together. The advertising plan (Chapter 7) is developed during the planning stage of the advertising effort and is the driving force behind a media plan. Market and advertising research determines that certain media options hold the highest potential for shaping the consumer behavior (Chapter 5) of the target audience. The message strategy (Chapter 10) has enormous implications for where to place the messages, that is, in which media. Thus, in reality, the media planning process takes place soon after the overall development of the advertising plan.

12-2a Media Strategies, Objectives, and Data

The true power of a media plan rests in the media strategy. What are you trying to do with your media: buy simple awareness, counter a competitor's claims, reposition your brand, react to good or bad media publicity, or establish an image and good feel surrounding your brand? You have to know this before you start thinking about actual media buys. You need to match message objectives with media choices.

This strategy is then tactically executed in media terms of message weight, reach, frequency, continuity, audience duplication, and newer terms associated with branded entertainment and e-advertising; such as click-throughs. But don't miss the big picture; you should always know and pay close attention to the fundamental qualities of each medium and specific vehicle in terms of what your brand is trying to do. To be really good, you need to be able to see the media buys in the strategic context of brand communication and consumer behavior goals.

Perhaps the most obvious media objective is that the vehicle chosen *reaches the target audience*. Recall that a target audience can be defined by demographics, geography, lifestyle, attitude dimensions, or usage category.

With the old/traditional media, the media planner will be instructed to reach a target, something like "housewives 18–49 who hate cooking, long for the day when their children are out of the house, and need a vacation from their husbands." Now, most media are bought and sold with much broader variables: age, income, geography, family size—in other words, very basic demographics associated with the total audience of a particular vehicle, say *Newsweek*. All that other stuff helps the creative but doesn't do much for the media buyer. You really can't call a salesperson at *Newsweek* and say, "Give me just those women who meet this very specific profile." So media planners are often put in the awkward and unenviable position of trying to deliver very specific audience characteristics based on inadequate data from media organizations. Most of the time, there is simply no way to identify which television shows are watched by "women who believe their husbands are way too needy" *and* "regularly shop at Lululemon." Those data are not routinely collected in a single source and are not available. No matter how many times you tell account executives and creatives this, they seem to still think these data exist. No, generally speaking, they don't, not in traditional media. Traditional media buyers have to use their creativity to figure out what the next best thing would be. A lot of the creativity involved in media planning is trying to find that next best thing.

But new media has changed that. Because just about everything is tracked in new media at the individual level, this problem no longer exists, at least not to the extent it used to. If advertisers effectively leverage new media they can reach incredible levels of individual consumer specificity. This incredible mass of detailed consumer information is now called **Big Data**. Social networking sites and search engines know all your search behavior; they know if you have a GPS-enabled device, where you go, when you go; they search your email, and they can target you down to the store, the time of day, and sometimes who you are with. From analyzing your emails (which you gave them permission to do when you signed up for some social media services), they can make some assumptions about how you feel about certain things without ever asking you a single question. They may then **micro-target** you with various messages, pay to optimize your smartphone browser for their benefit, or place an ad on your smartphone for a store you will pass in two blocks. The only thing really limiting the new media right now is that they still have not developed the actual ads, promotional contacts, messaging, and integrated brand communications (IBC) to really leverage all these data. But they probably will. But even now, these data can be used brilliantly in media planning.

In old/traditional media, a media research organization can increase the precision and usefulness of traditional media buys. An example of the type of information supplied is shown in Exhibit 12.6, where market statistics for four brands of men's aftershave and cologne are compared: Eternity for Men, Jovan Musk, Lagerfeld, and Obsession for Men. The most revealing data are contained in columns C and D. Column C shows each brand's strength relative to a demographic variable, such as age or income. Column D provides an index indicating that particular segments of the population are heavier users of a particular brand. Specifically, the number expresses each brand's share of volume as a percentage of its share of users. An index number above 100 shows particular strength for a brand. The strength of Eternity for Men as well as Obsession for Men is apparent in both the 18–24 and the 25–34 age cohorts. In magazines (their known specialty) and other print, Standard Rate and Data Service provides the exposure data (www.srds.com/portal/main?action=LinkHit&frameset=yes&link=ips).

Even more sophisticated data have become available. Research services such as A. C. Nielsen's Homescan and Information Resources' BehaviorScan are referred to as **single-source tracking services**, which offer information not only on demographics but also on brands, purchase size, purchase frequency, prices paid, and media exposure. With demographic, behavioral, and media-exposure correlates provided by research services like these, advertising and media planners can address issues such as the following:

- How many members of the target audience have tried the advertiser's brand, and how many are repeat purchasers?

- What appears to affect brand sales more—increased amounts of advertising or changes in advertising copy?

- What other products do buyers of the advertiser's brand purchase regularly?

- What television programs, magazines, and newspapers reach the largest number of the advertiser's audience?

Another critical element in setting advertising objectives is determining the **geographic scope** of media placement. Media planners need to identify media that cover the same geographic area as the advertiser's distribution system. Obviously, investing money on the placement of ads in media that cover geographic areas where the advertiser's brand is not distributed is wasteful.

Some analysts suggest that when certain geographic markets demonstrate unusually high purchasing tendencies by product category or by brand, then geo-targeting should be the basis for the media placement decision. **Geo-targeting** is the placement of ads in geographic regions where higher purchase tendencies for a brand are evident. For example, in one geographic area the average consumer purchases of Prego spaghetti sauce were 36 percent greater than the average consumer purchases nationwide. With this kind of information, media buys can be geo-targeted to reinforce high-volume users.[1]

Reach refers to the number of people or households in a target audience that will be exposed to a media vehicle or schedule at least one time during a given period of time. It is often expressed as a percentage. If an advertisement placed on the hit network television program *American Idol* is watched at least once by 10 percent of the advertiser's target audience, then the reach is said to be 10 percent. Media vehicles with broad reach are ideal for consumer convenience goods, such as toothpaste and cold remedies. These are products with fairly simple features, and they are frequently purchased by a broad cross section of the market. Broadcast television, cable television, and national magazines have the largest and broadest reach of any of the media, due to their national and even global coverage. But their audiences have been shrinking.

Frequency is the average number of times an individual or household within a target audience is exposed to a media vehicle in a given period of time (typically a week or a month). For example, say an

EXHIBIT 12.6 Commercial research firms can provide advertisers with an evaluation of a brand's relative strength within demographic segments. This typical data table from Mediamark Research shows how various men's aftershave and cologne brands perform in different demographic segments. www.mediamark.com.

Aftershave Lotion & Cologne for Men

BASE: MEN	TOTAL U.S. '000	Eternity for Men A '000	B % DOWN	C % ACROSS	D INDEX	Jovan Musk A '000	B % DOWN	C % ACROSS	D INDEX	Lagerfeld A '000	B % DOWN	C % ACROSS	D INDEX	Obsession for Men A '000	B % DOWN	C % ACROSS	D INDEX
All Men	92674	2466	100.0	2.7	100	3194	100.0	3.4	100	1269	100.0	1.4	100	3925	100.0	4.2	100
Men	92674	2466	100.0	2.7	100	3194	100.0	3.4	100	1269	100.0	1.4	100	3925	100.0	4.2	100
Women	—	—	—	—	—	—	—	—	—	—	—	—	—	—	—	—	—
Household Heads	77421	1936	78.5	2.5	94	2567	80.4	3.3	96	1172	92.4	1.5	111	2856	72.7	3.7	87
Homemakers	31541	967	39.2	3.1	115	1158	36.3	3.7	107	451	35.5	1.4	104	1443	36.8	4.6	108
Graduated College	21727	583	23.7	2.7	101	503	15.8	2.3	67	348	27.4	1.6	117	901	23.0	4.1	98
Attended College	23842	814	33.0	3.4	128	933	29.2	3.9	113	*270	21.3	1.1	83	1283	32.7	5.4	127
Graduated High School	29730	688	27.9	2.3	87	1043	32.7	3.5	102	*460	36.3	1.5	113	1266	32.2	4.3	101
Did Not Graduate H.S.	17374	*380	15.4	2.2	82	*715	22.4	4.1	119	*191	15.0	1.1	80	*475	12.1	2.7	65
18–24	12276	754	30.6	6.1	231	*391	12.2	3.2	92	*7	0.5	0.1	4	747	19.0	6.1	144
25–34	20924	775	31.4	3.7	139	705	22.1	3.4	98	*234	18.5	1.1	82	1440	36.7	6.9	162
35–44	21237	586	23.8	2.8	104	1031	32.3	4.9	141	*311	24.5	1.5	107	838	21.3	3.9	93
45–54	14964	*202	8.2	1.4	51	*510	16.0	3.4	99	*305	24.0	2.0	149	481	12.3	3.2	76
55–64	10104	*112	4.6	1.1	42	*215	6.7	2.1	62	*214	16.9	2.1	155	*245	6.2	2.4	57
65 or over	13168	*37	1.5	0.3	10	*342	10.7	2.6	75	*198	15.6	1.5	110	*175	4.4	1.3	31
18–34	33200	1529	62.0	4.6	173	1096	34.3	3.3	96	*241	19.0	0.7	53	2187	55.7	6.6	156
18–49	62950	2228	90.4	3.5	133	2460	77.0	3.9	113	683	53.9	1.1	79	3315	84.5	5.3	124
25–54	57125	1563	63.4	2.7	103	2246	70.3	3.9	114	850	67.0	1.5	109	2758	70.3	4.8	114
Employed Full Time	62271	1955	79.3	3.1	118	2141	67.0	3.4	100	977	77.0	1.6	115	2981	76.0	4.8	113
Employed Part-time	5250	*227	9.2	4.3	163	*141	4.4	2.7	78	*10	0.8	0.2	14	*300	7.7	5.7	135
Sole Wage Earner	21027	554	22.5	2.6	99	794	24.9	3.8	110	332	26.2	1.6	115	894	22.8	4.3	100
Not Employed	25153	*284	11.5	1.1	42	912	28.6	3.6	105	*281	22.2	1.1	82	643	16.4	2.6	60
Professional	9010	*232	9.4	2.6	97	*168	5.3	1.9	54	*143	11.3	1.6	116	504	12.8	5.6	132
Executive/Admin./Mgr.	10114	*259	10.5	2.6	96	*305	9.6	3.0	88	*185	14.6	1.8	134	353	9.0	3.5	82
Clerical/Sales/Technical	13212	436	17.7	3.3	124	*420	13.2	3.2	92	*231	18.2	1.7	128	741	18.9	5.6	132
Precision/Crafts/Repair	12162	624	25.3	5.1	193	*317	9.9	2.6	76	*168	13.2	1.4	101	511	13.0	4.2	99
Other Employed	23022	631	25.6	2.7	103	1071	33.5	4.7	135	*261	20.6	1.1	83	1173	29.9	5.1	120
H/D Income																	
$75,000 or More	17969	481	19.5	2.7	101	*320	10.0	1.8	52	413	32.5	2.3	168	912	23.2	5.1	120
$60,000–74,999	10346	*368	14.9	3.6	134	*309	9.7	3.0	87	*142	11.2	1.4	100	495	12.6	4.8	113
$50,000–59,999	9175	*250	10.2	2.7	103	*424	13.3	4.6	134	*153	12.1	1.7	122	*371	9.4	4.0	95
$40,000–49,999	11384	*308	12.5	2.7	102	*387	12.1	3.4	99	*134	10.6	1.2	86	580	14.8	5.1	120
$30,000–39,999	12981	*360	14.6	2.8	104	542	17.0	4.2	121	*126	10.0	1.0	71	*416	10.6	3.2	76
$20,000–29,999	13422	*266	10.8	2.0	75	*528	16.5	3.9	114	*164	12.9	1.2	89	*475	12.1	3.5	84
$10,000–19,999	11867	*401	16.3	3.4	127	*394	12.3	3.3	96	*67	5.3	0.6	41	*481	12.3	4.1	96
Less than $10,000	5528	*31	1.3	0.6	21	*291	9.1	5.3	153	*69	5.4	1.2	91	*194	4.9	3.5	83

Based on "GfK MRI, GfK MRI Men's Women's Personal Care Products Report," *GfK MRI*, Spring 1997, 16.

advertiser places an ad on a weekly television show with a 20 rating (20 percent of households) four weeks in a row. The show has an (unduplicated) reach of 43 (percent) during the four-week period. So, frequency is then equal to 20 × 4/43, or 1.9. This means that an audience member had the opportunity to see the ad an average of 1.9 times.

Advertisers often struggle with the dilemma of increasing reach at the expense of frequency, or vice versa. At the core of this struggle are the concepts of effective frequency and effective reach. **Effective frequency** is the number of times a target audience needs to be exposed to a message before the objectives of the advertiser are met—either communications objectives or sales impact. Many factors affect the level of effective frequency. New brands and brands laden with features may demand high frequency. Simple messages for well-known products may require less frequent exposure for consumers to be affected. Although most analysts agree that one exposure will typically not be enough, there is debate about how many exposures are enough. A common industry practice is to place effective frequency at three exposures, but analysts argue that as few as two or as many as nine exposures are needed to achieve effective frequency.

Effective reach is the number or percentage of consumers in the target audience that are exposed to an ad some minimum number of times. The minimum-number estimate for effective reach is based on a determination of effective frequency.

If effective reach is set at four exposures, then a media schedule must be devised that achieves at least four exposures over a specified time period within the target audience. With all the advertising clutter (too many ads) that exists today, effective reach is likely a much higher number; some experts have advocated six as a minimum.

Message weight is another media measure; it is the total mass of advertising delivered. Message weight is the gross number of advertising messages or exposure opportunities delivered by the vehicles in a schedule. Media planners are interested in the message weight of a media plan because it provides a simple indication of the size of the advertising effort being placed against a specific market.

Message weight (at least in traditional media) is typically expressed in terms of gross impressions. **Gross impressions** represent the sum of exposures to the entire media placement in a media plan. Planners often distinguish between two types of exposure. *Potential ad impressions*, or *opportunities* to be exposed to ads, are the most common and refer to exposures by the media vehicle carrying advertisements (e.g., a program or publication). *Message impressions*, on the other hand, refer to exposures to the ads themselves. Information on ad exposure probabilities can be obtained from a number of companies. This information can pertain to particular advertisements, campaigns, media vehicles, product categories, ad characteristics, and target groups.

For example, consider a media plan that, in a one-week period, places ads on three television programs and in two national newspapers. The sum of the exposures to the media placement might be as follows:

	Gross Impressions	
	Media Vehicle	**Advertisement**
Television		
Program A audience	16,250,000	5,037,500
Program B audience	4,500,000	1,395,000
Program C audience	7,350,000	2,278,500
Sum of TV exposures	28,100,000	8,711,000
Newspapers		
Newspaper 1	1,900,000	376,200
Newspaper 2	450,000	89,100
Sum of newspaper exposures	2,350,000	465,300
Total gross impressions	**30,450,000**	**9,176,300**

The total gross impressions figure is the media weight.

Of course, this does not mean that 30,450,000 separate people were exposed to the programs and newspapers or that 9,176,300 separate people were exposed to the advertisements. Some people who watched TV program A also saw program B and read newspaper 1, as well as all other possible combinations. This is called **between-vehicle duplication** (remember, "vehicles" are shows, newspapers, magazines—things that carry ads). It is also possible that someone who saw the ad in newspaper 1 on Monday saw it again in newspaper 1 on Tuesday. This is **within-vehicle duplication**. That's why we say that the total *gross* impressions number contains audience duplication. Data available from services such as Simmons Media Research Bureau report both types of duplication so that they may be removed from the gross impressions to produce the *unduplicated* estimate of audience, or *reach,* as discussed above. (You should know, however, that the math involved in such calculations is fairly complex.)

Another way of expressing media weight is in terms of gross rating points (GRP). GRP is the product of reach times frequency (GRP = $r \times f$). When media planners calculate the GRP for a media plan, they multiply the rating (reach) of each vehicle in a plan times the number of times an ad will be inserted in the media vehicle and sum these figures across all vehicles in the plan. Exhibit 12.7 shows the GRP for a combined magazine and television schedule. The GRP number is used as a relative measure of the intensity of one media plan versus

EXHIBIT 12.7 Gross rating points (GRP) for a media plan.

Media Class/ Vehicle	Rating (reach)	Number of Ad Insertions (frequency)	GRP
Television			
American Idol	25	4	100
Law & Order	20	4	80
Good Morning America	12	4	48
Days of Our Lives	7	2	14
Magazines			
People	22	2	44
Travel & Leisure	11	2	22
News & World Report	9	6	54
Total			**362**

© Cengage Learning

another. Whether a media plan is appropriate is ultimately based on the judgment of the media planner.

The message weight objective provides only a broad perspective for a media planner. What does it mean when we say that a media plan for a week produced more than 30 million gross impressions? It means only that a fairly large number of people were potentially exposed to the advertiser's message. It provides a general point of reference. When Toyota introduced the Avalon in the U.S. market, the $40 million introductory ad campaign featured 30-second television spots, newspaper and magazine print ads, and direct mail pieces. The highlight of the campaign was a nine-spot placement on a heavily watched Thursday evening TV show, costing more than $2 million. The message weight of this campaign in a single week was enormous—just the type of objective Toyota's media planners wanted for the brand introduction.[2]

Continuity is the pattern of placement of advertisements in a media schedule. There are three strategic scheduling alternatives: continuous, flighting, and pulsing. **Continuous scheduling** is a pattern of placing ads at a steady rate over a period of time. Running one ad each day for four weeks during the soap opera *General Hospital* would be a continuous pattern. Similarly, an ad that appeared in every issue of *Redbook* magazine for a year would also be continuous. **Flighting** is another media-scheduling strategy. Flighting is achieved by scheduling heavy advertising for a period of time, usually two weeks, then stopping advertising altogether for a period, only to come back with another heavy schedule.

Flighting is often used to support special seasonal merchandising efforts or new product introductions or as a response to competitors' activities. The financial advantages of flighting are that discounts might be gained by concentrating media buys in larger blocks. Communication effectiveness may be enhanced because a heavy schedule can achieve the repeat exposures necessary to achieve consumer awareness. For example, the ad for Reddi-wip® in Exhibit 12.8 was run heavily in December issues of magazines to take advantage of seasonal dessert-consumption patterns. We're guessing they know that people like whipped cream during the holiday season.

Finally, **pulsing** is a media-scheduling strategy that combines elements from continuous and flighting techniques. Advertisements are scheduled continuously in media over a period of time, but with periods of much heavier scheduling (the flight). Pulsing is most appropriate for products that are sold fairly regularly all year long but have certain seasonal requirements, such as clothing.

EXHIBIT 12.8 An example of a print ad that was flighted during December—a month in which whipped-cream dessert toppings figure prominently. www.reddi-wip.com.

ConAgra Foods, Inc

12-2b **Continuity and the Forgetting**

Although many may not know it, industry media continuity practices were actually strongly influenced by academic research in the area of human memory. When people first started trying to understand how and when to place ads, the idea of forgetting soon came into play. It makes sense. Very early in advertising's history, this very useful piece of psychological research was recognized. It turns out that people's forgetting is fairly predictable; that is, all else being equal, we know at about what interval things fade from people's memory. It seems to obey a mathematical function pretty well; thus it is often called the **forgetting function**. The original work for this was done more than a century ago by psychologist Hermann Ebbinghaus in the late 19th century and most notably in the advertising world by Hubert Zielske in 1958. In his very famous study, Zielske sent food ads to two randomly selected groups of women. One received the ad every 4 weeks for 52 weeks (13 total exposures); the other received the ad once every week for 13 straight weeks (13 total exposures).

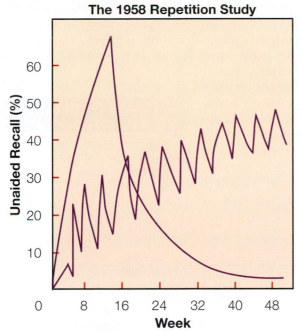

The 1958 Repetition Study

Source: Based on Hubert A. Zielske, "The Remembering and Forgetting of Advertising," *Journal of Marketing*, American Marketing Association, January 23, 1959, 239-243. Reprinted in R. Batra, J. Myers, and D. Aaker, *Advertising Management*, 4th ed. (Upper Saddle River, NJ: Prentice Hall, 1992.)

Exhibit 12.9 shows what happened. The group that received all 13 ads in the first 13 weeks (called a flighting schedule) scored much higher in terms of peak unaided recall, but the level of recall fell off very fast, and by halfway through the year was very low. The group that got the ads at an evenly spaced schedule (called a continuous schedule) never attained as high a level of recall as the other group but finished much higher at the end of the year and had an overall higher average recall.

This research has been very influential in terms of guiding industry media planners for several decades. The real-world implications are pretty clear. If you need rapid and very high levels of recall—say for the introduction of a new product, a strategic move to block the message of a competitor, or a political ad campaign, where there is only one day of actual shopping (election day)—use a flighting (sometimes called "heavy-up") schedule. A continuous schedule would be more broadly effective and would be used for established brands with an established message.

We do, however, offer a note of caution here. As you know, the idea of recall and its measurement have received considerable criticism from both industry managers and academic researchers. We agree with this criticism; simple memory measures are inadequate at best in most advertising situations. As discussed earlier, they are most appropriate when a simple outcome like brand name recall is sought. In that case, forgetting (or not forgetting) is an important factor in advertising success or failure.

12-2c Length or Size of Advertisements

Beyond whom to reach, how often to reach them, and in what pattern, media planners must make strategic decisions regarding the length of an ad in electronic media or the size of an ad in print media. Certainly, the advertiser, creative director, art director, and copywriter have made determinations in this regard as well. Television advertisements (excluding infomercials) can range from 10 to 60 seconds, and sometimes even two minutes, in length. Is a 60-second television commercial always six times more effective than a 10-second spot? Of course, the answer is no. Is a full-page newspaper ad always more effective than a two-inch, one-column ad? Again, not necessarily. Some research shows an increase in recognition scores of print advertising with increasing image size. Some call this the **square root law**; that is, "the recognition of print ads increases with the square of the illustration."[3] So a full-page ad should be twice as memorable as a quarter-page ad. Such "laws" should not be considered laws but rather general guidelines; they show a general relationship but are not completely precise. Still, advertisers use full-page newspaper ads when a product claim, brand image, or market situation warrants it.

The decision about the length or size of an advertisement depends on the creative requirements for the ad, the media budget, and the competitive environment within which the ad is running. From a creative standpoint, ads attempting to develop an image for a brand may need to be longer in broadcast media or larger in print media to offer more creative opportunities. On the other hand, a simple, straightforward message announcing a sale may be quite short or small, but it may need heavy repetition. From the standpoint of the media budget, shorter and smaller ads are, with few exceptions, much less expensive. If a media plan includes some level of repetition to accomplish its objectives, the lower-cost option may be mandatory. From a competitive perspective, matching a competitor's presence with messages of similar size or length may be essential to maintain the share of mind in a target audience.

LO ③

12-3 COMPETITIVE MEDIA ASSESSMENT

Even though media planners normally do not base an overall media plan on how much competitors are investing or where competitors are placing their ads, a competitive media assessment can provide a useful perspective. A competitive media assessment is particularly important for product categories in which all the competitors are focused on a narrowly defined target audience. This condition exists in several product categories in which heavy-user segments dominate consumption—for example, snack foods, soft drinks, beer and wine, and chewing gum. Brands of luxury cars and financial services also compete for common-buyer segments.

When a target audience is narrow and attracts the attention of several major competitors, an advertiser must assess its competitors' IBP investing and the relative share of voice its brand is getting. **Share of voice** is a calculation of any one advertiser's brand expenditures relative to the overall spending in a category:

$$\text{Share of voice} = \frac{\text{one brand's advertising expenditures in a medium}}{\text{total product category advertising expenditures in a medium}}$$

This calculation can be done for all advertising by a brand in relation to all advertising in a product category, or it can be done to determine a brand's share of product category spending on a particular advertising medium, such as network television or magazines. For example, athletic-footwear marketers invest approximately $310 million per year in measured advertising media. Nike and Reebok are the two top brands, with approximately $160 million and $55 million, respectively, in annual expenditures in measured advertising media. The share-of-voice calculations for both brands follow:

$$\text{Share of voice, Nike} = \frac{\$160 \text{ million} \times 100}{\$310 \text{ million}} = 51.6\%$$

$$\text{Share of voice, Reebok} = \frac{\$55 \text{ million} \times 100}{\$310 \text{ million}} = 17.7\%$$

Together, both brands dominate the product category advertising with a nearly 70 percent combined share of voice. Yet Nike's share of voice is nearly three times that of Reebok.

Research data, such as that provided by Competitive Media Reporting, can provide an assessment of share of voice in up to 10 media categories. A detailed report shows how much a brand was advertised in a particular media category versus the combined media category total for all other brands in the same product category. Knowing what competitors are investing in a medium and how dominant they might be allows an advertiser to strategically schedule within a medium. Some strategists believe that scheduling in and around a competitor's schedule can create a bigger presence for a small advertiser.[4] (See Insights Online [Exhibit 12.10] to consider the media strategies of Dominos and Pizza Hut.)

LO ④

12-4 MEDIA EFFICIENCY

The advertiser and the agency team determine which media class is appropriate for the current effort. These criteria give a general orientation to major media and the inherent capabilities of each media class.

Each medium under consideration in a media plan must be scrutinized for the efficiency with which it performs. In other words, which media deliver the largest target audiences at the lowest cost? A common measure of media efficiency is **cost per thousand (CPM)**, which is the dollar cost of reaching 1,000 (the M in CPM comes from the Roman numeral for 1,000) members of an audience using a particular medium. The CPM calculation can be used to compare the relative efficiency of two media choices within a media class (magazine versus magazine) or between media classes (magazine versus radio). The basic measure of CPM is fairly straightforward; the dollar cost for placement of an ad in a medium is divided by the total audience and multiplied by 1,000. Let's calculate the CPM for a full-page black-and-white ad in the Friday edition of *USA Today*:

$$\text{CPM} = \frac{\text{cost of media buy} \times 1,000}{\text{total audience}}$$

$$\text{CPM for } USA\ Today = \frac{\$72,000 \times 1,000}{5,206,000} = \$13.83$$

These calculations show that *USA Today* has a CPM of $13.83 for a full-page black-and-white ad. But this calculation shows the cost of reaching the

12.11 Go online to see the AdAge feature, "Change Is in the Air with Media Planning."

entire readership of *USA Today*. (See Insights Online [Exhibit 12.11] to learn more about media planning.)

12-4a Internet Media

We cover other issues related to Internet media in Chapter 14. Many Internet portals post their advertising rates. The most important thing to remember is that these media are fundamentally different in one very major way with a few exceptions, they are "pull" media. With pull media, the consumer goes looking for the advertiser or advertising and thus "pulls" the advertised brand toward them. This is just the opposite of the traditional "push" media (e.g., a 30-second television ad) in which the brand is "pushed" at the consumer.

by three nodes rather than the traditional two: marketer–consumer–consumer (see Exhibit 12.12). Consumers talk to other consumers and like to talk about stuff—consumer stuff. Now, through the Internet, they can do this, for almost no cost, instantaneously, and with the power of huge numbers. Marketers can use the Internet for fairly small sums relative to traditional media. Nielsen estimates that two-thirds of Internet users visit a social network or blog site, and that this collectively accounts for about 10 percent of total Internet traffic. So, clearly, it is important.

We know social media are used to discuss brands, and we know that marketers use these media to create buzz and eventual sales for their brands. But how social media are counted and then priced is still an emerging story. Several companies track conversations about brands on the Web, analyze the data, and report various metrics, such as **net promoter scores** (essential good mentions–bad mentions), net volume (how much conversation about a brand occurs in a given period), and so on. Exhibit 12.13 shows brand-chat volume for a one-week period.

— LO ⑤ —

12-5 SOCIAL MEDIA: WHAT IS DIFFERENT

12-5a Social Networking

Facebook, Twitter, and others have revolutionized the way we think about mediated communication. From the earliest work on brand communities, Muniz and O'Guinn noted that this new paradigm is represented

— LO ⑥ —

12-6 MEDIA CHOICE AND INTEGRATED BRAND PROMOTIONS

A final complicating factor in the media environment is that more firms are adopting an IBP perspective, which relies on a broader mix of communication tools. As you know, IBP is the use of various promotional tools, including advertising, in a coordinated manner to build and maintain brand awareness, identity, and preference. Promotional options such as event sponsorship, direct marketing, branded entertainment, sales promotion, and public relations are drawing many firms away from traditional mass media advertising. But even these new approaches still require coordination with the advertising that remains.

12-6a Branded Entertainment

Scott Donaton at *Advertising Age* refers to the combination and meaningful merger of entertainment media

EXHIBIT 12.12 The World Wide Web has made us rethink the brand–consumer relationship.

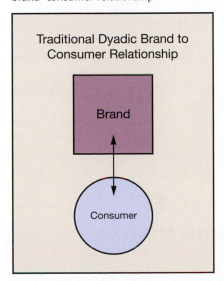

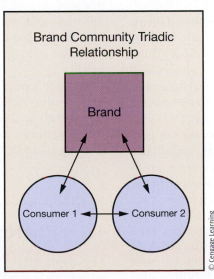

© Cengage Learning

EXHIBIT 12.13 Advertisers now calculate the level of brand conversations on the Internet and social media.

Rank	Brand	Conversation Volume	Positive Conversations
1	Apple	921,267	74.6%
2	Microsoft	574,004	78.9%
3	Fox	496,865	61.4%
9	AT&T	476,450	62.1%
24	Dannon	415,751	65.2%
4	Disney	334,655	86.5%
6	Sony	306,763	85.9%
5	Nintendo	303,326	84.3%
7	BlackBerry	264,768	86.9%
8	Ford	237,433	87.6%
15	ABC	220,226	71.7%
19	ESPN	178,039	68.0%
21	Glade	165,085	82.6%
16	UPS	160,202	69.3%
13	Canon	144,291	89.7%

© Cengage Learning

EXHIBIT 12.14 This is how Starbucks invests their promotion budgets. The very cool and popular Morning Joe show on MSNBC is brought to you by Starbucks. Starbucks is always on the set, almost always mentioned, and directly promoted, and when you go to a Starbucks you see Exhibit 12.14.

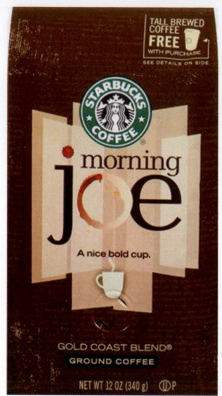

Starbucks Coffee Company

and advertising as "Madison & Vine." Even though this is covered elsewhere, let us just say a few things about this very exciting turn of events. This concept is also referred to as branded entertainment. It began, actually long ago, with simple product placements in movies, radio, and then television shows. It actually goes back to the 1920s and 1930s, but it really began to escalate in the late 1980s. The basis for the idea was that traditional advertising was no longer cost effective and that the cost of making and promoting films and music was also out of control. Hollywood, the record industry, and advertising all had a stake in finding a better, less regulated, less expensive, accountable, and more effective means of marketing communications. Thus, Madison & Vine was born: a recognized, full-fledged attempt to merge media in the form of branded entertainment on television, in games, in retail settings called brandscapes (think of stores such as NikeTown), on mobile phones—all across the board. We discussed the basic mechanism in Chapter 10, but it also is important to consider branded entertainment from the media side of things.

For clients seeking branded entertainment opportunities, there typically are three primary approaches. The most straightforward and least expensive is product placement. A character on television might be seen drinking Diet Pepsi, driving a Cadillac, or dropping off a FedEx package. A more sophisticated approach involves storyline integration, such as putting a UPS delivery truck in an EA Sports NASCAR game, or Starbucks fully integrated on the most popular news discussion show around, *Morning Joe* on MSNBC and at your local Starbucks, as seen in Exhibit 12.14. Original

content, as when the cavemen graduated to their own primetime show or BMW produced short online film clips featuring their vehicles, is the most expensive, but potentially most compelling, form of branded entertainment. Yet, as Lawson notes, measuring the value of these various forms of branded entertainment is difficult. "We're trying to find meaningful ways to measure this sort of stuff," Lawson says. "Ultimately, the clients still want that, and as they invest more money in that area, they will want to feel more comfortable knowing that their message is getting out there in a meaningful way."[5]

In terms of media measurement, IAG gives scores to the most recalled brand placement.

Nielsen is also in the interactive game. The company measures, among other things, the number of placements in shows (see Chapter 7).

LO 7

12-7 PLANNING MODELS

The explosion of available data on markets and consumers has motivated media planners to rely heavily on electronic databases, computers, and software to assist with the various parts of the media planning effort. Nearly all of the major syndicated research services offer electronic data to their subscribers, including advertisers, agencies, and media organizations. These databases contain information helpful in identifying target markets and audiences, estimating or projecting media vehicle audiences and costs, and analyzing competitive advertising activity, among many others. Such software often produces summary reports, tabulations, ranking, reach–frequency analysis, optimization, simulation, scheduling, buying, flowcharts, and a variety of graphical presentations.

Advertisers that use a mix of media in their advertising campaigns often subscribe to a variety of electronic data services representing the media they use or consider using. However, the various syndicated services do not provide standardized data, reports, and analyses that are necessarily comparable across media categories. Also, individual syndicated service reports and analyses may not offer the content and depth that some users prefer. Nor do they typically analyze media categories that they do not measure. Media software houses offer hundreds of specialized and standardized software products that help advertisers, agencies, and media organizations worldwide develop and evaluate markets, audiences, and multimedia plans. Exhibit 12.15 shows typical screens from one such computer program. The first screen is reach and cost data for spot TV ads, and the second screen is the combined reach and cost data for spot TV and newspaper ads.

EXHIBIT 12.15 The explosion of data about markets and consumers has caused advertisers to rely more on computerized media planning tools.

ADplus(TM) RESULTS: SPOT TV (30S)
Walt Disney World
Off-Season Promotion
Monthly
Target: 973,900
Jacksonville DMA Adults

Message/vehicle = 32.0%

Frequency (f) Distributions

f	VEHICLE % f+	% f+	MESSAGE % f	% f+
0	5.1	-	9.1	-
1	2.0	94.9	7.5	90.9
2	2.2	92.9	8.1	83.4
3	2.3	90.7	8.1	75.2
4	2.4	88.3	7.8	67.1
5	2.4	85.9	7.2	59.3
6	2.5	83.5	6.6	52.1
7	2.5	81.0	6.0	45.5
8	2.5	78.5	5.3	39.5
9	2.5	76.0	4.7	34.2
10+	73.5	73.5	29.5	29.5
20+	49.8	49.8	6.1	6.1

Summary Evaluation

	VEHICLE	MESSAGE
Reach 1+ (%)	94.9%	90.9%
Reach 1+ (000s)	923.9	885.3
Reach 3+ (%)	90.7%	75.2%
Reach 3+ (000s)	882.9	732.8
Gross rating points (GRPs)	2,340.0	748.8
Average frequency (f)	24.7	8.2
Gross impressions (000s)	22,789.3	7,292.6
Cost-per-thousand (CPM)	6.10	19.06
Cost-per-rating point (CPP)	59	186

Vehicle List	RATING	AD COST	CPM-MSG	ADS	TOTAL COST	MIX %
WJKS-ABC-AM	6.00	234	12.51	30	7,020	5.1
WJXT-CBS-AM	6.00	234	12.51	30	7,020	5.1
WTLV-NBC-AM	6.00	234	12.51	30	7,020	5.1
WJKS-ABC-DAY	5.00	230	14.76	60	13,800	9.9
WJXT-CBS-DAY	5.00	230	14.76	60	13,800	9.9
WTLV-NBC-DAY	5.00	230	14.76	60	13,800	9.9
WJKS-ABC-PRIM	10.00	850	27.27	30	25,500	18.4
WJXT-CBS-PRIM	10.00	850	27.27	30	25,500	18.4
WTLV-NBC-PRIM	10.00	850	27.27	30	25,500	18.4
			Totals: 19.06	360	138,960	100.0

ADplus(TM) RESULTS: DAILY NEWSPAPERS (1/2 PAGE), SPOT TV (30S)
Walt Disney World
Off-Season Promotion
Monthly
Target: 973,900
Jacksonville DMA Adults

Message/vehicle = 28.1%

Frequency (f) Distributions

f	VEHICLE % f	% f+	MESSAGE % f	% f+
0	1.2	-	4.0	-
1	0.8	98.8	4.9	96.0
2	0.9	98.0	5.9	91.1
3	0.9	97.2	6.5	85.2
4	1.0	96.2	6.7	78.7
5	1.1	95.2	6.8	72.0
6	1.1	94.2	6.6	65.2
7	1.2	93.0	6.3	58.6
8	1.3	91.8	5.9	52.4
9	1.3	90.6	5.5	46.5
10+	89.3	89.3	41.0	41.0
20+	73.3	73.3	9.6	9.6

Summary Evaluation

	VEHICLE	MESSAGE
Reach 1+ (%)	98.8%	96.0%
Reach 1+ (000s)	962.6	934.6
Reach 3+ (%)	97.2%	85.2%
Reach 3+ (000s)	946.5	829.7
Gross rating points (GRPs)	3,372.0	948.0
Average frequency (f)	34.1	9.9
Gross impressions (000s)	32,839.9	9,232.3
Cost-per-thousand (CPM)	10.96	38.99
Cost-per-rating point (CPP)	107	380

Vehicle List	RATING	AD COST	CPM-MSG	ADS	TOTAL COST	MIX %
1 Daily Newspapers		Totals:	114.00	80	221,040	61.4
Times-Union	42.00	8,284	104.93	20	165,680	46.0
Record	4.00	866	115.18	20	17,320	4.8
News	3.20	926	153.95	20	18,520	5.1
Reporter	2.40	976	216.35	20	19,520	5.4
2 Spot TV (30s)		Totals:	19.00	360	138,960	38.6
WJKS-ABC-AM	6.00	234	12.51	30	7,020	2.0
WJXT-CBS-AM	6.00	234	12.51	30	7,020	2.0
WTLV-NBC-AM	6.00	234	12.51	30	7,020	2.0
WJKS-ABC-DAY	5.00	230	14.76	60	13,800	3.8
WJXT-CBS-DAY	5.00	230	14.76	60	13,800	3.8
WTLV-NBC-DAY	5.00	230	14.76	60	13,800	3.8
WJKS-ABC-PRIM	10.00	850	27.27	30	25,500	7.1
WJXT-CBS-PRIM	10.00	850	27.27	30	25,500	7.1
WTLV-NBC-PRIM	10.00	850	27.27	30	25,500	7.1
		Totals:	38.99	440	360,000	100.0

EXHIBIT 12.16 A media flowchart gives an advertiser a visual representation of the overall media plan.

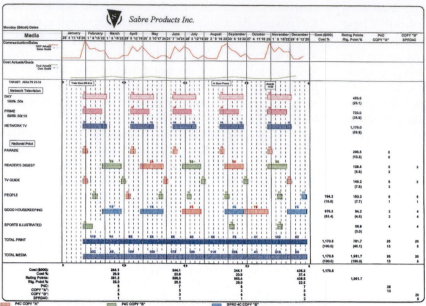

Telmar Information Services Corp., FlowMaster for Windows ™, New York, 1999. Reprinted with permission.

Computerization and modeling can never substitute for planning and judgment by media strategists. Computer modeling does, however, allow for the assessment of a wide range of possibilities before making costly media buys. It can, and does, save advertisers money.

One of the most important aspects of the media-scheduling phase involves creating a visual representation of the media schedule. Exhibit 12.16 shows a media schedule flowchart that includes both print and electronic media placement. With this visual representation of the schedule, the advertiser has tangible documentation of the overall media plan.

LO 8

12-8 MAKING THE BUY

Once an overall media plan and schedule are in place, the focus must turn to **media buying**. Media buying entails securing the electronic media time and print media space specified in the schedule. An important part of the media-buying process is the agency of record. The **agency of record** is the advertising agency chosen by the advertiser to purchase time and space. The agency of record coordinates media discounts and negotiates all contracts for time and space. Any other agencies involved in the advertising effort submit insertion orders for time and space within those contracts.

Each spring, television programming and ad executives participate in a ritual called the "**upfronts**." The upfronts is a period where the television networks reveal their fall line-ups and presell advertising on them. About 75 percent of prime-time television advertising is bought this way, in advance. Only the remaining 25 percent is really "in play" for the season. There are all sorts of unofficial rules in this ritual. Viewed from the outside, it's much like a typical American trying to understand cricket. Let's just say it's played a bit like poker—you can see some cards for free; others will cost you. Whatever the best game metaphor, it looks like the TV networks are not getting as much premium pricing as they used to. Why? It's the TV clutter, TiVo, branded entertainment, competition from computer-delivered entertainment, and its very high price. Several media soothsayers predict the end of the upfronts within the next decade. Personally, we think they will probably still be around.

Rather than using an agency of record, some advertisers use a **media-buying service**, which is an independent organization that specializes in buying large blocks of media time and space and reselling it to advertisers. Some agencies and companies have developed their own media-buying units (e.g., GM's GM planworks) to control both the planning and the buying processes. Regardless of the structure used to make the buys, media buyers evaluate the audience reach, CPM, and timing of each buy. The organization responsible for the buy also monitors the ads and estimates the actual audience reach delivered. If the expected audience is not delivered, then media organizations have to *make good* by repeating ad placements or offering a refund or price reduction on future ads. For example, making good to advertisers because of shortfalls in delivering the 1998 Winter Olympics prime time cost CBS an estimated 400 additional 30-second spots.[6] (See Insights Online [Exhibit 12.17] if you are interested in a career in media planning, advertising, digital, or other types of IBP.)

SUMMARY

 Describe measured versus unmeasured media and about how much each represents of total advertising and IBP dollars.

Measured media include network TV, cable TV, spot TV, syndicated TV, network Spanish TV, the Internet (excluding broadband video and paid search), Net radio, spot radio, local radio (500 stations, top 28 markets), magazines (Sunday, consumer, business-to-business, and 30 local magazines), 250 local newspapers, Spanish newspapers, national newspapers (*The Wall Street Journal, USA Today, The New York Times*), and Outdoor (200-plus markets). They represent a little more than half of all dollars spent on IBP (56 percent in 2011). Unmeasured media are everything else: paid Internet search, coupons, product placement, events, and the like (44 percent in 2011).

2 **Describe the basic ideas and essential terms in media planning.**

Although many important changes are taking place in the advertising industry, the components of the media planning process remain essentially the same. A media plan specifies the media vehicles that will be used to deliver the advertiser's message. Developing a media plan entails setting objectives such as effective reach and frequency and determining strategies to achieve those objectives. Media planners use several quantitative indicators, such as CPM, to help them judge the efficiency of prospective media choices. The media planning process culminates in the scheduling and purchase of a mix of media vehicles expected to deliver the advertiser's message to specific target audiences at precisely the right time to affect their consumption decisions. Although media planning is a methodical process, it cannot be reduced to computer decision-making models and statistical measurements; data quality and human and personal factors prohibit media planning from being an exact science.

3 **Understand the meaning of competitive media assessment and share of voice.**

Competitive media assessment is simply determining how much your brand is spending on IBP relative to the category as a whole. Share of voice is a calculation of any one advertiser's brand expenditures relative to the overall spending in a category.

4 **Discuss media efficiency.**

Media efficiency is traditionally evaluated in terms of the cost of reaching a certain number of prospective consumers. Traditionally, this has been in CPM, but today there are also cost-per-click on the Internet (see Chapter 14) and other measures. The basic idea remains the same: how much to reach how many?

5 **Discuss what makes social media different.**

Lots of things, but one basic thing is that this is where consumers talk to lots of other consumers, and that changes everything about the way we think about media.

6 **Discuss the basics of branded entertainment.**

Branded entertainment is where advertisers create entertainment vehicles for promoting their brands. They are not traditional ads, and we believe consumers don't see them as ads, but just how effective they are remains to be seen.

7 **Discuss the benefits and the realities of media planning models.**

Most media buys are determined through the use of computerized planning models. These mathematically optimize media schedules for cost efficiency. They are, however, no substitute for applying strategic planning principles to the media buy. You need to be able to explain why you are buying what you are buying.

8 **Discuss making the buy.**

There are several critical points such as the upfronts, and there are terms such as *agency of record* and *media-buying services* that must be understood.

KEY TERMS

above-the-line promotion	media mix	frequency
measured media	Big Data	effective frequency
below-the-line promotion	micro-target	effective reach
unmeasured media	single-source tracking services	message weight
media plan	geographic scope	gross impressions
media class	geo-targeting	between-vehicle duplication
media vehicle	reach	within-vehicle duplication

continuity

continuous scheduling

flighting

pulsing

forgetting function

square root law

share of voice

cost per thousand (CPM)

net promoter scores

media buying

agency of record

upfronts

media-buying service

ENDNOTES

1. This section and the example are drawn from Erwin Ephron, "The Organizing Principle of Media," *Inside Media*, November 2, 1992.

2. Bradley Johnson, "Toyota's New Avalon Thinks Big, American," *Advertising Age*, November 14, 1994, 46.

3. John R. Rossiter, "Visual Imagery: Applications to Advertising," in *Advances in Consumer Research* (Provo, UT: Association for Consumer Research, 1982), 101–106.

4. Andrea Rothman, "Timing Techniques Can Make Small Ad Budgets Seem Bigger," *The Wall Street Journal*, February 3, 1989, B4; see also

Robert J. Kent and Chris T. Allen, "Competitive Interference Effects in Consumer Memory for Advertising: The Role of Brand Familiarity," *Journal of Marketing*, July 1994, 97–105.

5. Brooke Capps, "The Man Who Brought UPS to NASCAR and Geico Cavemen to Hollywood," *Advertising Age*, May 3, 2007.

6. "CBS Faces Olympics Make-Goods," www.adage.com, February 19, 1998.

CHAPTER 13
Media Planning: Newspapers, Magazines, TV, and Radio

After reading and thinking about this chapter, you will be able to do the following:

1 Understand the changes taking place in the traditional mass media of newspapers, magazines, TV, and radio relative to new digital media options.

2 Detail the pros and cons of newspapers as a media class, identity newspaper advertising categories, and consider the future of newspapers as a medium.

3 Detail the pros and cons of magazines as a media class, identity magazine advertising categories, and consider the future of magazines as a medium.

4 Detail the pros and cons of TV as a media class, identity TV advertising categories, describe audience measurement for TV, and consider the future of television as a medium.

5 Detail the pros and cons of radio as a media class, identity radio advertising categories, and consider the future of radio as a medium.

LO 1

13-1 THE PRESENT AND FUTURE OF TRADITIONAL MASS MEDIA

In Chapters 1 and 2 we discussed that the advertising industry as a whole continues to evolve and change in significant ways. Nowhere is the change more tangible or dramatic than in the traditional media of newspapers, magazines, TV, and radio. For 75 years, choosing media to deliver advertising messages has been a straightforward process. Advertisers would work with agencies to develop messages for brands. Then agencies would negotiate for airtime with TV and radio networks or for space with newspapers and magazines. Most of these media options were owned by a few big media companies.

Well, it just doesn't work like that anymore. The last two decades have witnessed unprecedented change in media options and applications. Consumers have turned to multiple new sources of information and entertainment and are more active in their media choice and patronage. User-generated content from viral videos, augmented reality messages, wikis, and social media sites now offer noncommercial information about brands and brand experiences—and we predict this change will continue because it empowers consumers. As a result, advertisers are turning more often to digital media that offer new, different, and cost-effective ways to reach target markets—including when those target markets are on the move with their mobile devices. In addition, digital media allow advertisers to make rapid changes in campaigns—changes that might take months to accomplish with traditional media. And let's not forget that a digital campaign can be a global campaign if the advertiser chooses to make it so—a monumental task in traditional media.

These changes in media options are effecting not only advertisers' perceptions of how to develop effective campaigns but also the way they are spending their money on media. Digital/interactive advertising is now a $36 billion industry, or about 10 percent of total U.S. spending on advertising *and* promotion, up from just 4 percent in 2004.[1] The other important change is that media companies are catching on to the fact that the old traditional way of delivering content through traditional mass media is fading. One example is that total advertising dollars spent on newspapers by advertisers has dropped from 23 percent of all ad spending to just 13 percent—taking literally billions of dollars of revenue away from newspaper publishers.[2] Now, Google and Yahoo! offer precisely targeted local ads (the power of newspapers in the past), craigslist.com has free classified ads, and news information is free *everywhere* on the Web. In response, newspaper companies are making aggressive moves into interactive media to shore up flagging revenues—with varying degrees of success.[3]

Big traditional media companies in TV, radio, newspapers, and magazines *have* to get into new media because of the way advertisers are setting their media strategies. Consider the way Delta Air Lines designs ad campaigns. First, the company enlists the services of traditional ad agency SS&K and digital marketing company Publicis Modem. The two agencies work out the message, images, and story line for Delta campaigns. Then SS&K develops a traditional media campaign (primarily print media—see Exhibit 13.1) and Publicis designs different ads for online media, including banner ads and emails to frequent fliers. The new digital media campaign also includes a social networking site and the purchase of paid search terms so that Delta will list high on any Google or Yahoo! consumer searches.[4]

The media environment is by no means settled into any predictable structure, and the media companies on all sides of the "digital divide" are scrambling to properly position themselves for the new ways consumers seek out brand information. Despite the shift to digital media, traditional media still command the majority of all ad dollars. So, no matter how sexy digital/interactive media are, they must synergize with traditional newspapers, magazines, TV, and radio to work most effectively. The discussions that follow give you an overview of traditional mass media so that you'll be aware of the options available to plan brand advertising strategies. The next chapter, Chapter 14, "Media Planning: Advertising and IBP in Digital Media," addresses digital media with respect to social media and related topics.

13-2 MEDIA STRATEGY

If the consumer doesn't see the message, no matter how creative or brilliant, it is not an effective message. Perhaps the media function is underrated compared to the creative with this crucial point in mind. Media

EXHIBIT 13.1 Delta Air Lines uses both the traditional medium of magazines and a wide variety of digital/interactive media in its advertising campaigns.

© Delta Air Lines, Inc

decisions are critically important for two reasons. One, advertisers need media to reach audiences that are likely in need of the information or to buy their brands. Two, when advertisers choose media, these choices ultimately determine which media companies earn the billions of dollars invested on newspaper, magazine, TV, and radio advertising slots.

In Chapter 12, "Media Planning Essentials," you gained an overall perspective on all classes of media. This chapter focuses on the challenges advertisers face in evaluating the major print and broadcast media options as key ways to reach audiences. As the discussion of media planning in the previous chapter emphasized, even great advertising can't achieve communications and sales objectives if the media placement misses the target audience.

Our discussion of print, TV, and radio media will concentrate on several key aspects of using these major traditional mass media. With respect to the print media—newspapers and magazines—we'll first consider the advantages and disadvantages of the media themselves. Both newspapers and magazines have inherent capabilities and limitations that advertisers must take into consideration in building a media plan. Next, we'll look at the types of newspapers and magazines from which advertisers can choose. Finally, we will identify buying procedures and audience measurement techniques.

After we look at the print media, we will consider TV and radio in the same way. First, the types of TV and radio options are described. Next, the advantages and disadvantages of TV and radio are considered and the buying procedures and audience measurement techniques are identified. Finally, the future of TV and radio in the context of new digital, satellite, and broadband technology is considered.

As we begin our examination of traditional media, let's not lose perspective—over 70 percent of all advertising dollars in the United States still go to traditional print, radio, and TV media![5] In addition, the vast majority of the creative effort—and money—is expended on print and broadcast ad campaigns. Despite the many intriguing opportunities that new digital media might offer, traditional media will likely form a significant foundation for most advertising campaigns. There are certain objectives advertising can achieve—particularly creative goals—only with these traditional mass media that digital media simply cannot match. The discussions in this chapter will demonstrate why these media represent such rich and necessary communication alternatives for advertisers.

13-3 PRINT MEDIA—STRATEGIC PLANNING CONSIDERATIONS

You might think that the print media—newspapers and magazines—are lifeless lumps and lack impact compared to dynamic broadcast media options like Spike TV or the Discovery Channel. Think again. Consider the problems that faced the Absolut Vodka brand. At one point in its illustrious history, Absolut was on the verge of extinction. The Swedish brand was selling only 12,000 cases a year in the United States—not enough to register a single percentage point of market share. The name Absolut was seen as gimmicky; bartenders thought the bottle was ugly and hard to pour from; consumers gave no credibility to vodka produced in Sweden.

TBWA ad agency in New York set about the task of overcoming these liabilities of the brand and decided to rely on print ads *alone*—primarily because spirits ads were banned from broadcast at the time. The agency took on the challenge of developing magazine and newspaper ads that would build awareness, communicate quality, achieve credibility, and avoid the Swedish clichés etched in the minds of American consumers. The firm came up with one of the most famous and

successful print campaigns of all time. The concept was to feature the strange-shaped Absolut bottle as the hero of each ad, in which the only copy was a two-word tagline always beginning with *Absolut* and ending with a "quality" word such as *perfection* or *clarity*. The two-word description evolved from the original quality concept to a variety of clever combinations. "Absolut Centerfold" appeared in *Playboy* and featured an Absolut bottle with all the printing removed, and "Absolut Wonderland" was a Christmas-season ad with the bottle in a snow globe like the ones that feature snowy Christmas scenes.

In the end, the Absolut campaign was not only a creative masterpiece but also a resounding market success—using print media alone, without the flashier TV or digital media. Absolut has become one of the leading imported vodkas in the United States. The vodka with no credibility and the ugly bottle became sophisticated and fashionable with a well-conceived and well-placed print campaign.[6] To this day, the Absolut brand still relies heavily on magazine advertising in the IBP mix with continued success. Exhibit 13.2

EXHIBIT 13.2 In a world of new media and digital/interactive media, Absolut vodka has relied for many years on magazines to effectively reach its target audience with high quality and carefully targeted print ads.

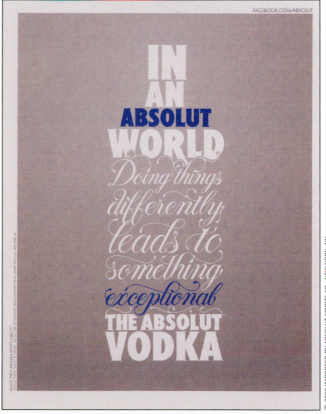

13.3 Go online to see the AdAge feature, "Video Interview with Absolut Creative Legend on Traditional Media Agency Compensation."

is an example of the type of ad Absolut has been running in magazines over these many years. (For an interesting interview with Absolut's Lee Clow about creatives' compensation, see Insights Online [Exhibit 13.3].)

LO ②

13-3a Newspapers and Digital Newspapers

The newspaper is a medium accessible to a wide range of advertisers; digital newspapers provide new legs to synergize with the traditional paper flagship. Most newspapers feature an iPad or other tablet app, as well as apps for smartphones. Thus, the advertising-based or subscription-based business models must be updated as subscriptions to the paper versions decline, while digital subscriptions are on the upswing. Annual investment in newspaper advertising stands at about $22 billion—only behind network TV. Exhibit 13.4 shows the top 10 advertisers in newspapers. Newspapers, with the exception of national newspapers like *USA Today* or *The Wall Street Journal,* are ideally suited to reach a geographic area—precisely the type of audience local retailers want to reach.

Newspapers must reinvent themselves, grow digital legs, and revamp their business model to stay competitive. There are some sad truths about the status of newspapers as a medium—especially the ones that are myopic in their ways. Since the 1980s, newspapers across the United States have been suffering circulation and subscription declines. Note that this decline in readership and circulation is reflected in the fact that 9 out of 10 of the advertisers in Exhibit 13.5 have reduced their newspaper spending—significantly.

What may be worse is that the percentage of adults reading daily newspapers is also declining. Only about 23 percent of adults in the United States read a printed daily newspaper, compared with about 78 percent in 1970.[7] Much of the decline in both circulation and readership comes from the fact that newspapers have been losing patronage to TV news programs and Internet news sites. Although shows such as *Good Morning America* and *CNN News* cannot provide the breadth of coverage that newspapers can, they still offer news, and

EXHIBIT 13.4 Top 10 newspaper advertisers (U.S. dollars in millions).

Advertiser	2011	2010	Percent Change
Macy's	$428.8	$469.7	−8.7
Fry's Electronics	214.2	226.8	−5.5
AT&T	193.6	215.1	−10.0
Procter & Gamble	182.2	198.0	−8.0
Verizon Communications	164.2	291.2	−43.6
News Corp	158.7	236.4	−32.9
Bankrate	153.2	115.1	33.2
General Motors	152.0	245.7	−38.1
Sears Holding Corp.	146.2	157.2	−7.0
Target Corp.	127.3	142.8	−10.9

"100 Leading National Advertisers, Spenders by Medium," *Advertising Age,* June 25, 2012, 20.

they offer it in a lively multisensory format. On the Internet, news seekers can access news 24/7, not just when a newspaper is delivered. Newspapers' foray into digital media has been somewhat successful. Mobile or digital readers of newspapers have grown, but digital or mobile readership of newspapers has not been great enough to offset the overall decline in newspaper readership. The final backbreaker is newspaper ad revenue. Given the decline in print newspaper readership, global ad revenue has declined 41 percent since 2007 (see Insights Online [Exhibit 13.5] for an interesting perspective on this).[8]

Advantages of Newspapers. Printed newspapers may have lost some of their luster during the past four decades, but they still do reach about a quarter of U.S. households, representing about 50 million adults. And, as mentioned earlier, the newspaper is still an excellent medium for retailers targeting local geographic markets. But broad reach isn't the only attractive feature of newspapers as a medium. Newspapers offer other advantages to advertisers:

Geographic Selectivity. Daily newspapers in cities and towns across

13.5 Go online to see the AdAge feature, "The 100 Leading National Advertisers Shows Traditional Media Still Rules; It Is Synergizing with Digital, but Traditional Is Still the Heartbeat of Advertising."

the United States offer advertisers the opportunity to reach a geographically well-defined target audience—particularly densely populated urban markets. Some newspapers are beginning to run zoned editions, which target even more narrow geographic areas within a metropolitan market. Zoned editions are typically used by merchants doing business in the local area.

Timeliness. The newspaper is timely even in its printed form. Because of the short time needed for producing a typical newspaper ad and the regularity of daily publication, the newspaper allows advertisers to reach audiences in a timely way. This doesn't mean on just a daily basis. Newspaper ads can take advantage of events or a unique occurrence in a community on a weekly or monthly basis as well.

Creative Opportunities. Even though the newspaper page does not offer the breadth of creative options available in the broadcast media, there are things advertisers can do in a newspaper that represent important creative opportunities. Since the newspaper page offers a large and relatively inexpensive format, advertisers can provide a lot of information to the target audience at relatively low cost. This is important for products or services with extensive or complex features that may need lengthy and detailed copy. The Tire America ad in Exhibit 13.6 needs just such a large format to provide detail about tire sizes and prices. Also notice the large amount of detailed information Tire America is able to provide about not just tires but the many other services available to residents in the local area.

Credibility. Newspapers still benefit from the perception that "if it's in the paper it must be the truth." As an example, this credibility element played a key role in the decision by Glaxo Wellcome and Smith-Kline Beecham to announce their megamerger (creating the $73 billion GlaxoSmithKline Corporation) using newspapers.[9]

Audience Interest and Demographics. Regular newspaper readers are truly interested in the information they are reading and staying current with local and or world happenings. Even though overall print readership may be down in the United States, apps are growing in popularity, and many readers still remain interested. Newspaper readers are relatively upscale; newspapers reach a higher percentage of highly educated and affluent consumers (in both the print and Web versions) than do broadcast or cable TV. In addition, many readers buy a newspaper specifically to see

EXHIBIT 13.6 The newspaper medium offers a large format to advertisers. This is important when an advertiser has a large amount of detailed information to offer consumers as Tire America does in this ad.

Tire America

what's on sale at stores in the local area, making this an ideal environment for local merchants. And newspapers are still an option for local classified advertising despite options like craigslist (online classifieds), which have cut into newspaper classifieds revenue quite dramatically.

Cost. In terms of both production and space, newspapers offer a low-cost alternative to advertisers. The cost per contact may be higher than with TV and radio options, but the absolute cost for placing a black-and-white ad is still within reach of even a small advertising budget.

Disadvantages of Newspapers. Newspapers offer advertisers many good opportunities. Like every other media option, however, newspapers have some significant disadvantages.

Limited Segmentation. Although newspapers can achieve good geographic selectivity and reach upscale consumers, the ability to target a specific audience with any precision is limited. Newspapers simply cut across too broad an economic, social, and demographic audience to allow for the isolation of specific targets. The placement of ads within certain sections can achieve minimal targeting by gender, but even this effort is somewhat fruitless. Some newspapers are developing special sections to enhance their segmentation capabilities—food sections, personal health sections, and the like. Many papers have developed sections on e-business and e-film reviews to target specific audiences. In addition, more and more newspapers are being published to serve specific ethnic groups, which is another form of segmentation. The industry feels it has made great progress in this regard and is approaching advertisers with the argument that newspaper advertising, if purchased strategically, can rival the targeting capability of many magazines.

Creative Constraints. The opportunities for creative executions in printed newspapers are certainly outweighed by the creative constraints. First, newspapers have comparatively poor reproduction quality. Led by *USA Today,* most newspapers now print some pages in color. But even the color reproduction does not enhance the look of most products in advertisements. For advertisers whose brand images depend on accurate, high-quality reproduction (color or not), newspapers simply have severe limitations compared to other media options. Second, newspapers are a unidimensional medium—no sound, no action. For brands that demand a broad creative execution, this medium is often not the best choice.

Cluttered Environment. The average printed newspaper is filled with headlines, subheads, photos, and announcements—not to mention the news stories. This presents a terribly cluttered environment for an advertisement. To make things worse, most advertisers in a product category try to use the same sections

to target audiences. For example, home equity loan and financial services ads are in the business section, and women's clothing ads are in the metro or local sections.

Short Life. In most U.S. households, newspapers are read quickly and discarded (or hopefully recycled). The way advertisers can overcome this limitation is by buying several insertions in each daily issue, buying space several times during the week, or both. This way, even if a reader doesn't spend much time with the newspaper, multiple exposures are a possibility. The newspaper has creative limitations, but what the average newspaper does, it does well. If an advertiser wants to reach a local audience with a simple black-and-white ad in a timely manner, then the newspaper is an excellent choice.

Categories of Newspaper Advertising. Advertisers have several options when it comes to the types of ads that can be placed in newspaper: display advertising, inserts, and classified advertising.

Display Advertising. Advertisers of goods and services rely most on display advertising. **Display advertising** in newspapers includes the standard components of a print ad—headline, body copy, and often an illustration—to set it off from the news content of the paper. An important form of display advertising is co-op advertising sponsored by manufacturers. In **co-op advertising** (also discussed in Chapter 1), a manufacturer pays part of the media bill when a local merchant features the manufacturer's brand in advertising. Co-op advertising can be done on a national scale as well. Intel invests heavily in co-op advertising with computer manufacturers who feature the "Intel Inside" logo in their print ads.

Inserts. Inserts do not appear on the printed newspaper page but rather are folded into the newspaper before distribution. There are two types of insert advertisements. The first is a **preprinted insert**, which is an advertisement delivered to the newspaper fully printed and ready for insertion into the newspaper.

The second type of insert ad is a **free-standing insert (FSI)**, which contains cents-off coupons for a variety of products and is typically delivered with Sunday newspapers. Pizza Hut is a heavy user of free-standing inserts to offer consumers coupons. Pizza Hut free-standing insert ads stand out to the newspaper reader for two reasons. First, it is a separate large-format page which helps attract attention. Second, free-standing inserts are often printed on higher quality paper than the newspaper itself and can use bright, attractive colors to highlight the Pizza Hut products.

Classified Advertising. You are no doubt aware that **classified advertising** is newspaper advertising that appears as all-copy messages under categories such as sporting goods, employment, and automobiles. Many classified ads are taken out by individuals, but real estate firms, automobile dealers, and construction firms also buy classified advertising. In the past 10 years, literally billions of dollars in classified advertising has shifted from traditional newspaper posting to digital placement on sites like craigslist.

The Future of Newspapers. Earlier in the chapter, we talked about the fact that newspaper circulation has been in a long, sustained downward trend, and that traditional print readership is following the same pattern. To survive as a viable advertising medium, newspapers will have to evolve with the demands of both audiences and advertisers, who provide them with the majority of their revenue. Primarily, newspapers will have to exploit their role as a source for local news—which some new media like the Web cannot do very effectively. Some analysts refer to this opportunity for newspapers as **hyper-localism**, where people will get their global and national news from the Web but turn to local newspapers for sale on paint at the local hardware store.[10]

Many analysts feel that another important transition for newspapers to make is to adopt a pay-for-inquiry advertising model.[11] A **pay-for-inquiry advertising model** is a payment scheme in which the medium, in this case newspapers, gets paid by advertisers based solely on the inquiries an advertiser receives in response to an ad. Radio, TV, and the Internet (pay-per-click) have been using pay-for-inquiry models of various types for several years. Some feel that newspaper publishers have little to lose by switching to such a model since they are losing advertising to the Internet anyway. To compete in the future as a viable advertising medium, newspapers will have to do the following:

- Continue to provide in-depth coverage of issues that focus on the local community.
- Continue to provide some coverage of national and international news for readers who want both global and local news.
- Borrow from the Internet's approach to advertisers—be accountable to advertisers and offer local advertisers a pay-per-inquiry model for ad costs.
- Maintain and expand their role as the best local source for consumers to find specific information on advertised product features, availability, and prices (hyper-localism).
- Provide consumers/buyers the option of shopping through an online newspaper computer service not unlike eBay or craigslist.

- Use bloggers to cover events and take advantage of local social networking.
- Become more mainstream in IBPs relating to new media.

13-3b **Magazines**

Like newspapers, magazines have been struggling in a changing media world as well. Spending on magazine advertising still commands about $24 billion annually, but that is down from around $34 billion in advertising revenue at the peak of magazines' popularity.[12] That loss of several billion dollars in annual revenue has created some casualties. Illustrious magazine titles like *Signature, Mode,* and even the *Gourmet Magazine,* founded in 1940, have ceased publication. But advertisers still find that magazines "work hard" in reaching target customers effectively and efficiently.

No doubt, many of the most popular and successful magazines are ones you read yourself—*People, Sports Illustrated, Elle,* and *Car and Driver* make the annual list of leading magazines. Exhibit 13.7 shows the top 10 advertisers in magazines. One key change to note is that Time Warner is spinning off its Time Inc. (with *Time* magazine) in a complete legal and structural separation from Time Warner. Some may see this as a symbol of print's downgrading in the future of media. Note once again that as with newspapers, spending in magazines by several top advertisers is down, reflecting

EXHIBIT 13.7 Top 10 magazine advertisers (U.S. dollars in millions).

Advertiser	2011	2010	Percent Change
Procter & Gamble	$1,050.1	$1,076.8	−2.5
L'Oreal	709.4	581.6	22.0
Pfizer	406.8	335.4	21.3
Time Warner	281.2	258.9	8.6
Johnson & Johnson	247.7	293.4	−15.6
Coty	243.3	226.8	7.3
General Motors	223.9	409.6	−45.3
Campbell Soup Co.	218.0	220.9	−1.3
Nestle	213.3	287.6	−25.8
Moet Hennessy Louis Vuitton	209.4	186.5	12.3

"100 Leading National Advertisers, Spenders by Medium," *Advertising Age,* June 25, 2012, 20.

the general decline in advertising placement in traditional media.

Like newspapers, magazines have advantages and disadvantages, offer various ad costs and buying procedures, and measure their audiences in specific ways. (For an interesting look at the history of traditional advertising, see Insights Online [Exhibit 13.8].)

Advantages of Magazines. In addition to being synergistic with digital media, magazines have some advantages relative to newspapers or even broadcast media: audience selectivity, audience interest, creative opportunity, and a long life.

Audience Selectivity. The key advantage of magazines relative to other media is their ability to target a highly selective audience. This selectivity can be based on demographics (for instance, *AARP The Magazine* targets retirement-aged Americans and is the top circulated magazine in the United States), lifestyle (*Game Informer, Real Simple, Muscle & Fitness*), or special interests, as shown in Exhibit 13.9. Here *Flyfisher* magazine, published by the Federation of Fly Fishers, reaches a highly selective audience for advertising by offering content of special interest to a select readership. The audience segment can be narrowly defined, as is the one that reads *Modern Bride,* or it may cut across a variety of interests, like *Time* or *People* readers. Magazines also offer geographic selectivity on a regional basis, as does *Southern Living,* or city magazines, such as *Atlanta,* which highlight happenings in major metropolitan areas. Celebrity-oriented tabloid magazines like *US Weekly* are also popular. Another magazine trend deals with food and cooking, such as *Bon Appetit, Cooking Light,* and *Every Day with Rachel Ray.*

Audience Interest. Perhaps more than any other medium, magazines attract an audience because of content. Although TV programming can attract audiences through interest as well, magazines have the additional advantage of voluntary exposure to the advertising. Parents seek out publications that address the joys and challenges of parenting in a wide range of strong-circulation magazines like *American Baby.* When a magazine attracts a highly interested readership, advertisers, in turn, find a highly receptive audience for their brand messages. The Escort radar detector ad in Exhibit 13.10 appeared in *Car and Driver* magazine. This specialized product can reach its specialized target market because reader interest in *Car and Driver* magazine content attracts them to the magazine and results in exposure for the Escort brand.

EXHIBIT 13.9 Specialty magazines like *Flyfisher* (www .fedflyfishers.org) help advertisers target highly specialized markets with efficiency and effectiveness.

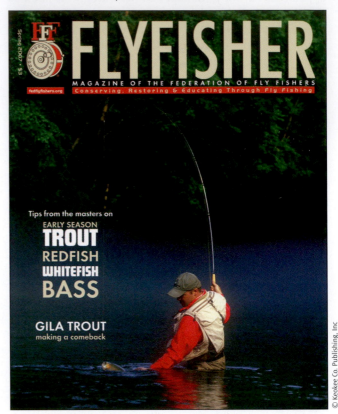

Creative Opportunities. Magazines offer a wide range of creative opportunities. Because of the ability to vary the size of an ad, use color, use white space, and play off the special interests of the audience, magazines represent a favorable creative environment. Also, because the paper quality of most magazines is high, color reproduction can be outstanding—another creative opportunity.

These factors are precisely why Infiniti invests nearly $60 million annually in magazine advertising. A case in point was when the firm introduced its full-size QX56 SUV, magazines offered the perfect combination of audience selectivity and high-quality visual presentation to effectively advertise the brand.[13] In an attempt to expand the creative environment even further, some advertisers have tried various other creative techniques: pop-up ads, scratch-and-sniff ads, ads with perfume scent strips, and even ads with small computer chips that flash lights and play music.

Long Life. Many magazines are saved issue to issue by their subscribers. This means that, unlike newspapers, a magazine can be reexamined over a week or a month. Some magazines are saved for long periods for future reference, such as *Architectural Digest, National Geographic,* and *Travel & Leisure.* In addition to multiple subscriber exposure, this long life increases the

EXHIBIT 13.10 An advantage of magazines: Specialized magazine content attracts audiences with special interests and those audiences attract advertisers. This ad by Escort Radar appeared in *Car and Driver* magazine.

Cordless Freedom · Elegant Design · High Performance

CORDLESS
SOLO S2

Auto
RADAR & LASER DETECTION

No Cord.
No Compromise.

The battery-powered SOLO S2 is the most powerful combination of cordless convenience and long range radar/laser detection ever. With its breakthrough technology and elegant design, SOLO S2 provides the freedom of a cordless detector with the performance you expect from ESCORT. It's so advanced, RadarTest.com called it *"an engineering miracle!"*

SOLO S2 is easily moved from one vehicle to another and it's perfect for travel. It provides long range protection on every radar and laser signal, while virtually eliminating false alarms.

Take our "no risk" 30-day test drive. SOLO S2. No cord. No compromise. Order yours today at **www.EscortRadar.com** or call toll-free **1-888-8 ESCORT** (1-888-837-2678)
SOLO S2 · $329.95

ESCORT.
FOLLOW NO ONE

Escort Inc. Used with permission

Clutter. Magazines are not quite as cluttered as newspapers, but they still represent a fairly difficult context for message delivery. The average magazine is about half editorial and entertainment content and half advertising material, but some highly specialized magazines, like *Bride,* can have as much as 80 percent of their pages devoted to advertising. And given the narrowly defined audiences, this advertising tends to be for brands in direct competition with each other. In addition to this clutter, there is another sort of clutter that has recently begun to plague magazines. As soon as a new market segment is recognized, there is a flood of "me too" magazines. The teen magazine market suffered precisely this problem from 2000 to 2005. Traditional titles like *People, Cosmopolitan, Elle,* and *Vogue* suddenly found themselves amid a glut of tweenybopper magazines including *Teen People, Teen Vogue, Cosmo Girl,* and *Elle Girl.* One example of a magazine published during this cluttered era for magazines is *Boy Crazy!* (see Exhibit 13.12). *Boy Crazy!* was just one of a dozen

INSIGHTS ONLINE

13.11 Go online to see the AdAge feature, "A Chart of Top Magazines as Ranked by Ad Dollars."

EXHIBIT 13.12 In the consumer magazine category, publishers try to appeal to narrowly defined target audiences. *Boy Crazy!* is one of the many titles targeted to teen girls.

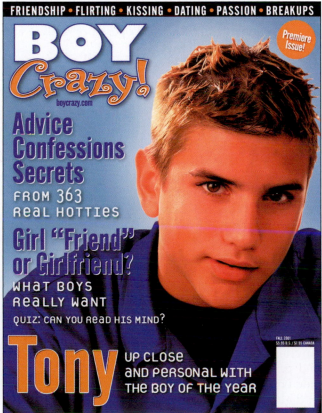

FRIENDSHIP · FLIRTING · KISSING · DATING · PASSION · BREAKUPS

BOY Crazy!
boycrazy.com

Premiere Issue!

Advice Confessions Secrets
FROM 363 Real Hotties

Girl "Friend" or Girlfriend?
WHAT BOYS REALLY WANT
QUIZ: CAN YOU READ HIS MIND?

Tony
UP CLOSE AND PERSONAL WITH THE BOY OF THE YEAR

FALL 2001
$3.95 U.S. / $7.95 CANADA

AP/ Topic Gallery

chance of **pass-along readership** as people visit the subscriber's home (or professional offices) and look at magazines. (See Insights Online [Exhibit 13.11] for a chart of the top magazines ranked by ad dollars.)

Disadvantages of Magazines. The disadvantages of magazines as a media choice have to do with the fact that although having selectivity is good, being too selective in their reach can be problematic and actually attract too many advertisers.

Limited Reach and Frequency. The tremendous advantage of selectivity discussed in the previous section actually creates a limitation for magazines. The more narrowly defined the interest group, the less overall reach a magazine will have. Since most magazines are published monthly or perhaps every two weeks, there is little chance for an advertiser to achieve frequent exposure using a single magazine. To overcome this limitation, advertisers often use several magazines targeted at the same audience. For example, many readers of *Better Homes and Gardens* may also be readers of *Architectural Digest.* By placing ads in both publications, an advertiser can increase both reach and frequency within a targeted audience.

magazines targeted to teen girls carrying content on young celebrity men and their lifestyles. This may be good in terms of coverage but it may devalue individual ads, and the magazines in which they appear may reach fewer consumers than the advertiser expected (note that two of the newer teen girl magazines have already failed).

Long Lead Times. Advertisers are required to submit their ads as much as 90 days in advance of the date of publication. If the submission date is missed, there can be as much as a full month's delay in placing the next ad. And once an ad is submitted, it cannot be changed during that 90-day period, even if some significant event alters the communications environment.

Cost. Even though the cost per contact in magazines is not nearly as high as in some media (direct mail in particular), it is more expensive than most newspaper space and many times the cost per contact in the broadcast media. The absolute cost for a single insertion can be prohibitive. For magazines with large circulations, such as *AARP* (47 million) and *Good Housekeeping* (4.4 million), the cost for a one-time, full-page, four-color ad can run from $100,000 to about $250,000.

The Future of Magazines. Magazines have had a slight drop (down 3 percent in 2013 from 2012 according to AdAge Datacenter from ZenithOptimedia). Magazines must synergize with digital apps and platforms for mobile, tablet, and computer devices to stay competitive. It is a must based on online and mobile consumer behavior and the need to stay current. Especially for news magazines, hybrid models let magazines be as current as newspapers. Readership has stabilized on the print side and is growing significantly through digital devices. Also, ad revenues are either up slightly or down slightly, depending on the year. Recent stats find the number of adults who read magazines (both print and digital combined) on a monthly basis grew to nearly $1.2 billion (including subscription and pass-along readership) aided by a 47 percent jump in digital readership.[14]

Two important factors need to be considered as influences on magazines as an advertising medium in the future. First, magazines will, like other traditional media, have to continue to adapt to new media options. In the late 1990s, magazines rushed to publish online, with more than 250 magazines offering online versions. These e-versions were touted as having several advantages to both the publisher and the subscriber, but the initial experience with digizines was less than successful. Now, with the advent and widespread use of tablet devices, digital magazine readership is up as cited above. Tablet devices like the Apple iPad pictured in Exhibit 13.13 offer easier and better reading experiences than the digizines that had to be accessed by desktop or laptop computers. But some perspective is needed here as well. The nearly 50 percent rise in digital readership still only amounts to 13.5 million. In addition, magazine publishers have to worry about cannibalizing their print circulation, which would lower advertising revenue possibilities from that format.[15]

The second factor affecting the future of magazines is that publishers are exploring other ways to take advantage of the interactive digital environment beyond digital version publications. In an effort to generate additional revenue, some magazines are starting to make the products advertised in the publication available for sale online—thus earning a margin on the sales. *Maxim* opened Shop Maxim Online, which allowed readers direct access to products seen in the publication and *Maxim* received a cut of sales. The project has met with marginal success, but the model seems to be viable for other publishers to try.[16]

EXHIBIT 13.13 The introduction of new and better tablet readers, like the Apple iPad, has provided magazine publishers with opportunities to expand readership.

PRNewsFoto/Netflix

13-4 TELEVISION AND RADIO: STRATEGIC PLANNING CONSIDERATIONS

When you say the word *advertising*, the average person thinks of TV and radio advertising. It's easy to understand why. Television advertising can be advertising at its very best. With the benefit of sight and sound, color and music, action and special effects, TV advertising can be the most powerful advertising of all because it has advantages over all other media. In many parts of the world, particularly in the United States, TV is the medium most widely used by consumers for entertainment and information. Radio advertising also has key advantages. The ability to reach consumers in multiple locations and the creative power of radio rank as important communications opportunities. Advertisers readily appreciate the power of TV and radio advertising and invest billions of dollars a year in these media (see Insights Online [Exhibit 13.14] for actual spending amounts).

 LO 4

13-4a Television

To many, TV is the medium that defines what advertising is. With its multisensory stimulation, TV offers the chance for advertising to be all that it can be. Television presents two extraordinary opportunities to advertisers. First, the diversity of communication possibilities allows for outstanding creative expression of a brand's value. Dramatic color, sweeping action, and spectacular sound effects can cast a brand in an exciting and unique light—especially in an era of widescreen and high-definition TV (HDTV). Second, once this expressive presentation of a brand is prepared, it can be disseminated to millions of consumers through multiple channels—broadcast, cable, satellite, and interactive means—often at a fraction of a penny per contact despite a relatively higher upfront investment. For instance, a 30-second Super Bowl spot is on average $2.75 million. Divide that by the reach and the fact that it is a time when consumers look forward to watching versus skipping ads, and it sounds much more of a smart investment. Plus, TV is easily synergized with digital. Sites like Hulu even have a place where you can watch ads for fun, as some TV ads are downright hilarious.

Americans love their TV, and most homes have TVs in multiple rooms—bedrooms, kitchens, and kid's rooms if the parents give in to pesterpower. These opportunities have not been lost on advertisers. The United States is one of the few countries that allows DTC pharmaceutical advertising on TV and in other media. In the United States, advertisers invest about $70 billion annually in TV advertising for media time alone—this does not include the many billions of dollars spent on production costs. Global spending on TV advertising is about $200 billion.[17] To fully appreciate all that TV means to advertisers, we need to understand much more about this complex medium that is growing digital legs.

INSIGHTS ONLINE

13.14 Go online to see the AdAge feature, "Chart Shows U.S. Spending Is Led by TV, Radio, Magazines, Outdoor, then Internet."

Television Categories. It is a common mistake to classify TV as a single type of broadcast medium. The reality is that during the past 20 years, several distinct versions of TV have evolved, from which consumers can choose news and entertainment programming and advertisers can choose to reach those consumers. There are four categories of basic TV: network, cable, syndicated, and local TV (we'll get to Web and interactive TV such as Apple TV shortly). Exhibit 13.15 shows the spending in these four TV categories for 2010 and 2011. Let's examine the nature of each of the four categories for TV advertising.

Network Television. Network TV broadcasts programming over airwaves to affiliate stations across the United States under a contract agreement. "Broadcast" is a bit of a misnomer since programming from these networks can be delivered on-air, over cable, through satellite transmission, or by mobile apps to smartphones and tablets. The method of delivery does not change the fact that advertisers can buy time within these "broadcast" programs to reach audiences in hundreds of markets. Estimates are that network TV reaches more than 90 percent of U.S. households. Exhibit 13.16 shows the top 10 advertisers on network TV.

EXHIBIT 13.15 Total measured advertising spending. Spending by advertisers on the four major TV categories (U.S. dollars in millions).

	2011	2010	Percent Change
Network TV	$24.8	$24.8	0.0
Spot TV	15.6	16.3	−4.6
Syndicated TV	4.7	4.1	15.4
Cable TV	23.0	21.3	7.8

"100 Leading National Advertisers, Spenders by Medium," *Advertising Age*, June 25, 2012, 20.

EXHIBIT 13.16 Top 10 U.S. network television advertisers (U.S. dollars in millions). Spending by advertisers on the four major TV categories (U.S. dollars in millions).

Advertiser	2011	2010	Percent Change
AT&T	$739.6	$869.8	−15.0
Procter & Gamble	649.0	702.2	−7.6
Verizon Communications	647.7	603.6	7.3
General Motors	627.2	679.4	−7.7
Ford Motor Co.	513.7	575.2	−10.7
Pfizer	469.5	508.0	−7.6
Time Warner	451.4	411.0	9.8
Sprint Nextel Corp.	437.8	453.1	−3.4
McDonald's Corp.	415.2	380.6	9.1
Fiat	399.3	161.7	146.9

"100 Leading National Advertisers, Spenders by Medium," *Advertising Age*, June 25, 2012, 20.

Despite speculation throughout the last decade that alternative TV options (discussed next) would ultimately undermine network TV, the broadcast networks still continue to flourish—mostly due to innovative programming. For example, episodes of *American Idol* regularly draw audiences in the range of 30 million viewers, and the Super Bowl now draws 120 million viewers, with a 30-second spot costing about $3 million. Regular programming costs are somewhat more reasonable. Thirty seconds on *Two and a Half Men* costs about $250,000 and on *The Office* costs about $140,000.[18] No other TV option gives advertisers the breadth of reach of network TV. But the point is that broadcast networks are alive and well, delivering huge audiences and attracting solid advertising revenues.

Cable Television. From its modest beginnings as community antenna TV (CATV) in the 1940s, cable TV has grown into a worldwide communications force. **Cable TV** transmits a wide range of programming to subscribers through wires rather than over airwaves. In the United States, about 60 million basic-cable subscribers (nearly 58 percent of all U.S. households) are wired for cable reception and receive dozens of channels of sports, entertainment, news, music video, and home-shopping programming.[19] Cable's power as an ad option has grown enormously during the past decade as cable's share of the prime-time viewing audience has grown, and advertisers now invest about $20 billion for ad time on cable.

Aside from more channels and hence more programming, two other aspects distinguish cable from network TV. First is the willingness of cable networks to invest in original programming. Cable networks are investing record dollar amounts in new, highly specific programming to continue to attract well-defined audiences. Programs like TNT's *The Closer* and Nickelodeon's *SpongeBob SquarePants* attract specific and very large target audiences.[20] Another example of station-specific programming that attracts a well-defined audience is the Speed Channel (see Exhibit 13.17). The Speed Channel offers motorsports enthusiasts programming and commentary 24/7 on motorsports events, personality updates, and technical tips. Second, there is huge potential revenue from **video on demand (VOD)**. Data shows that VOD will grow to be used by 66 percent of all households by 2016.[21] Of course, the challenge for cable is to grab its fair share of these households. Consumers can acquire VOD through satellite dishes and mobile devices as well. The main point remains, however, that consumers are turning to VOD, and advertisers will have to discover ways to reach consumers with advertising in the context of the "no-ad" VOD environment.

EXHIBIT 13.17 Part of the power and success of cable TV comes from offering very specific programming through a wide range of cable networks. An example is the Speed Channel, which offers all forms of motor sports programming and commentary.

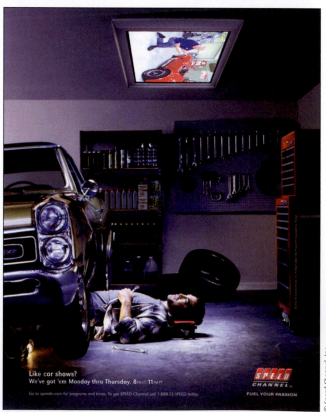

Syndicated Television. **Television syndication** is either original programming or programming that first appeared on network TV. It is then rebroadcast on either network or cable stations with pending distribution on the Internet. Syndicated programs provide advertisers with proven programming that typically attracts a well-defined, if not enormous, audience. There are several types of TV syndication. **Off-network syndication** refers to programs that were previously run in network prime time. The popular off-network syndicated shows *Home Improvement* and *Seinfeld* command significant ad dollars—in the range $150,000 to $200,000 for a 30-second ad. Less popular shows are more affordable, with prices set between about $25,000 and $60,000. **First-run syndication** refers to programs developed specifically for sale to individual stations. The most famous first-run syndication show is *Star Trek: The Next Generation*. **Barter syndication** takes both off-network and first-run syndication shows and offers them free or at a reduced rate to local TV stations, with some national advertising presold within the programs. Local stations can then sell the remainder of the time to generate revenues. This option allows national advertisers to participate in the national syndication market conveniently. Two of the most widely recognized barter syndication shows are *Jeopardy* and *Wheel of Fortune*.

Local Television. **Local TV** is the programming other than the network broadcast that independent stations and network affiliates offer local audiences. Completely independent stations air old movies, sitcoms, or children's programming. Network affiliates get about 90 hours of programming a week from the major networks, but they are free to air other programming beyond that provided by the network. News, movies, syndicated programs, and community-interest programs typically round out the local TV fare. Local TV commands significant advertising dollars—in the range of $15 billion annually[22]—and local TV providers should be encouraged. A majority of mobile device users indicate that they want to tune into live, local news broadcasts on their smartphones and tablets.[23]

Satellite. Programming transmitted to audiences via **satellite** transmission is another popular option for consumers. The most widely accessed satellite programming is available from DirecTV and DISH Network. As stated earlier, satellite providers offer programming from major media companies. Another version of satellite transmission is direct transmission or **closed circuit**. The distinction is the technology for delivery. The best known of the closed-circuit programming comes from the CNN Airport Network, which transmits news and weather programming

directly to airport terminals around the world. While satellite transmission used to be the province of rural America, it has become mainstream as a way for consumers to receive their TV programming and therefore as a way for advertisers to reach target markets. DirecTV is now the second largest media company in the United States—larger than Disney or CBS—with annual revenues exceeding $22 billion.[24] The popularity of satellite transmission among consumers is the result of extensive programming, VOD options, and high-quality video transmission.

Web/Tablet/Smartphone TV. Of course, the next evolution of TV transmission is underway with programs being accessed by consumers over the Web, as tablet and smartphone downloads, or through smartphone reception. Referred to as "TV everywhere," this capability is still emerging, and it may be premature to call this a TV "category." But the capability has advertisers excited, and we need to consider the potential here. Bear with us if, by the time you read this, delivery of video through the Web and mobile devices has changed dramatically.

First, let's consider the distribution of video over the Web. Tracking data indicate that hundreds of billions of video streams of TV programming occurred each year with Hulu adding another billion or so streams through its video-sharing site. Major media players like Fox, CBS, NBC, and ABC all have platforms to stream programming through the Web. Advertisers are anxious to place ads on Web broadcasts. CBS sold nearly $500 million in digital advertising in 2012, and estimates are that Web video advertising attracted about $20 billion in revenue overall that year.[25]

Finally, cell or smartphone TV seems to have huge potential. Verizon Wireless's V CAST Mobile TV started with distribution in 25 markets in 2007 and has been aggressively expanded. Broadcast shows need to be watched as scheduled—there is no on-demand viewing (yet). With a 2.2-inch display, 20 available channels, and a monthly fee of $15 dollars for the cell phone (in addition to voice and text fees), there seems to be good potential for generating ad revenue. Smartphone manufacturers have sold millions of iPhones with the capability of playing video, and this allows advertisers to reach viewers "everywhere," further increasing advertisers' opportunities.

Advantages of Television. Throughout the book, we have referred to the unique capability of TV as an advertising medium. There must be some very good reasons why advertisers such as AT&T, Nike, and Procter & Gamble invest hundreds of millions of dollars annually in TV advertising. The specific advantages of this medium are as follows.

Creative Opportunities. The overriding advantage of TV compared to other media is the ability to send a message using both sight and sound. With recent advances in transmission and reception equipment, households now have brilliantly clear visuals and stereo-enhanced audio to further increase the impact of TV advertising. Now, with HDTV capabilities becoming mainstream, all sorts of new creative opportunities present themselves.

Coverage, Reach, and Repetition. Television, in one form or another, reaches more than 98 percent of all households in the United States—an estimated 300 million people. These households represent every demographic segment in the United States, which allows advertisers to achieve broad coverage. We have also seen that the cable and satellite TV option provides reach to hundreds of millions of households throughout the world. With the new mobile TV options just discussed, coverage and reach capabilities are enhanced even more. Further, no other medium allows an advertiser to repeat a message as frequently as TV. (See Insights Online [Exhibit 13.18] for information about Time Warner's move to cut its ties to the magazine industry.)

Cost per Contact. For advertisers that sell to broadly defined mass markets, TV offers a cost-effective way to reach millions of members of a target audience. The average prime-time TV program reaches 11 million households, and top-rated weekly shows can reach more than 60 million households. This brings an advertiser's cost-per-contact figure down to an amount unmatched by any other media option—literally fractions of a penny per contact.

Audience Selectivity. Television programmers are doing a better job of developing shows that attract well-defined target audiences. **Narrowcasting** is the development and delivery of specialized programming to well-defined audiences. Cable and satellite TV are far and away the most selective TV options. They provide not only well-defined programming but also entire networks—such as MTV and ESPN—built around the concept of attracting selective audiences.

Disadvantages of Television. Television has great capabilities as an advertising medium, but it is not without limitations. Some of these limitations are serious enough to significantly detract from the power of TV advertising.

INSIGHTS ONLINE

13.18 Go online to see the AdAge feature, "Time Warner Will No Longer Be a Magazine Company."

Fleeting Message. One problem with the sight and sound of a TV advertisement is that it is gone in an instant. The fleeting nature of a TV message, as opposed to a print ad (which a receiver can contemplate), makes message impact difficult. Some advertisers invest huge amounts of money in the production of TV ads to overcome this disadvantage.

High Absolute Cost. Although the cost per contact of TV advertising is the best of all traditional media, the absolute cost may be the worst. The average cost of airtime for a single 30-second TV spot during prime time is about $100,000, with the most popular shows, like *Monday Night Football*, commanding as much as $500,000 for a 30-second spot.[26] Remember this is prime-time pricing. Off-prime-time slots go for a more modest $20,000 to $50,000 for 30 seconds. In addition, the average cost of producing a quality 30-second TV spot is around $300,000 to $400,000. These costs make TV advertising prohibitively expensive for many advertisers. Of course, large national consumer products companies—for which TV advertising is best suited anyway—find the absolute cost acceptable for the coverage, reach, and repetition advantages discussed earlier.

Poor Geographic Selectivity. Although programming can be developed to attract specific audiences, program transmission cannot target small geographic areas nearly as well. This is especially true for satellite subscribers. For a national advertiser that wants to target a city market, the reach of a TV broadcast is too broad. Similarly, for a local retailer that wants to use TV for reaching local segments, the TV transmission is likely to reach a several-hundred-mile radius—which will increase the advertiser's cost with little likelihood of drawing patrons.

Poor Audience Attitude and Attentiveness. Since the inception of TV advertising, consumers have bemoaned the intrusive nature of the commercials. Just when a movie is reaching its thrilling conclusion, on come the ads. The involuntary and frequent intrusion of advertisements on TV has made TV advertising the most distrusted form of advertising among consumers. In one of the few surveys tracking consumer sentiment, only 17 percent of consumers surveyed felt that TV advertising affected them in their purchase of a new car, compared with 48 percent who claimed that direct mail advertising was a factor in their decision.[27] But be aware that it is not fundamentally the job of TV advertising to motivate an immediate purchase. Image building and awareness are the key achievements for TV ads.

Along with—and perhaps as a result of—this generally bad attitude toward TV advertising, consumers have developed ways of avoiding exposure. Making a trip to the refrigerator or conversing with fellow viewers are the preferred low-tech ways to avoid exposure. On the low-tech side, **channel grazing**, or using a remote control to monitor programming on other channels while an advertisement is being broadcast, is the favorite way to avoid commercials.

The most common way to avoid TV advertising is with digital video recorders (DVRs) like TiVo. **Digital video recorders (DVRs)** use computer hard drives to store up to 140 hours of TV programming. Consumers use the devices to skip commercials and watch only the programming itself. Indeed, the overwhelming reason consumers use DVRs *is* to skip commercials. A survey of DVR users revealed that 81 percent of them invested in a DVR primarily to skip commercials, and they claim to fast-forward through 75 percent of the ads that appear in the programming that they watch.[28] Obviously, widespread use of DVRs has advertisers looking for ways to get exposure for their brands on TV. More brand placement within programming and those annoying little "runners" at the bottom of the screen during programs are ways to reach DVR users.

Clutter. All the advantages of TV as an advertising medium have created one significant disadvantage: clutter. The major TV networks run about 15 minutes of advertising during each hour of prime-time programming, and cable channels carry about 14 minutes of advertising per hour.[29] Research has found that 65 percent of a surveyed group of consumers felt that they were "constantly bombarded with too much" advertising.[30] Critics of TV advertising have also raised an issue beyond clutter. There are those who feel that TV advertising has a unique power over its viewers. As such, there is occasionally a call for banning certain types of advertising.

Measuring Television Audiences. Television audience measurements identify the size and composition of audiences for different TV programming. Advertisers choose where to buy TV time based on these factors. These measures also set the cost for TV time. The larger the audience or the more attractive the composition, the more costly the time will be.

The following are brief summaries of the information used to measure TV audiences.

TV Households. **TV households** is an estimate of the number of households that are in a market and own a TV. Since more than 98 percent of all households in the United States own a TV, the number of total households and the number of TV households are virtually the same, about 120 million.

Households Using TV. Households using TV (HUT), also referred to as sets in use, is a measure of the number of households tuned to a TV program during a particular time period.

Program Rating. A **program rating** is the percentage of TV households that are in a market and are tuned to a specific program during a specific time period. Expressed as a formula, program rating is:

$$\text{Program rating} = \frac{\text{TV households tuned to a program}}{\text{Total TV households in the market}}$$

A **ratings point** indicates that 1 percent of all the TV households in an area were tuned to the program measured. If an episode of *CSI* is watched by 19.5 million households, then the program rating would be calculated as follows:

$$\textit{CSI} \text{ rating} = \frac{19,500,000}{95,900,000} = 20 \text{ rating}$$

The program rating is the best-known measure of TV audience, and it is the basis for the rates TV stations charge for advertising on different programs. Recall that it is also the way advertisers develop their media plans from the standpoint of calculating reach and frequency estimates, such as gross rating points.

Share of Audience. **Share of audience** provides a measure of the proportion of households that are using TV during a specific time period and are tuned to a particular program. If 65 million households are using their TVs during the *CSI* time slot, and *CSI* attracts 19.5 million viewers, then the share of audience is:

$$\textit{CSI} \text{ share} = \frac{\text{TV households tuned to a program}}{\text{Total TV households using TV}}$$

$$= \frac{19,500,000}{65,000,000} = 30 \text{ share}$$

The Future of Television. The future of TV is exciting for several reasons. First, the emerging digital interactive era will undoubtedly affect TV as an advertising medium. As discussed earlier, the prospects include greater viewer participation in programming as currently happens with *American Idol* and *The Voice*. Equally as important, though, is that technology is creating the ability to transmit advertising to a wide range of new mobile devices from smartphones to tablets, to maybe smart watches. And remember the "TV everywhere" concept raised earlier in the chapter. Estimates are that global mobile advertising through such devices will reach $10 billion in the United States and nearly $25 billion worldwide by 2016.[31] And recall the discussion from Chapter 2 regarding the growth of broadband access. Broadband has made it possible to stream TV programming and therefore TV advertising via the Internet to either PCs or mobile devices. Advertisers are still considering the implications of this mode of communication and how well it serves as a way to send persuasive communications. Some analysts believe that while TV programming works well on the Web, so far TV advertising does not.[32] The issue relates to "ad loads" that consumers are willing to tolerate while watching TV on their TVs (about 22 per hour) versus the much lighter ad load (about 6 per hour) for Web transmission. This lighter ad load is seen as unsustainable in order for Web TV to achieve profitability—but will heavier loads kill Web viewership? Also, consumers especially dislike ads that interrupt in any way their online/mobile experience.[33]

While you will do a "deep dive" on social networks in the next chapter, the interaction TV advertisers are fostering between TV broadcasts and social media commentary needs to be mentioned. With social TV, advertisers are driving brand recognition from TV advertising to social media—and vice versa. You have seen advertisers implore you to "like" their brand on Facebook or tweet on Twitter about the brand. The "partnership" between TV and social media has many possibilities. Analysts say that TV can benefit the most by virtue of advertisers using social media as a "megaphone" for brands—engaging consumers in social media driven by TV advertising.[34] The pioneering effort in social TV was Fox Network's *Glee*, and the program continues to be a leader. But other notable efforts include Current TV's on-air tweets during programming.[35]

Finally, consolidation in the industry cannot be ignored. Comcast has acquired about $20 billion in cable companies and still counting. Similarly, Rupert Murdoch has been expanding the DirecTV empire of cable holdings and media holdings that generates billions of dollars in revenue from literally every corner of the earth. And let's not forget traditional media giants CBS, Time Warner, and Disney, all of which in their own right have great broadcast media power. The issue is the extent to which these big and powerful media companies can end up controlling programming content. It is not automatically the case that big media companies shape programming in a biased way, but that is the concern of media watchdogs.

Although it is hard to predict what the future will hold, one thing seems sure—TV will hold its own as an entertainment and information medium for households. The convenience, low cost, and diversity of programming make TV an ideal medium for consumers. With the addition of technologies that allow TV programming through a variety of mobile devices, TV would seem destined to reach a wider variety of markets. As a result, TV, despite its limitations, will continue to be an important part of the IBP mix for many advertisers.

13-4b Radio

Radio may seem like the least glamorous and most inconspicuous of the major media. This perception does not jibe with reality. Radio plays an integral role in the media plans of some of the most astute advertisers. Because of the unique features of radio, advertisers invest about $8 billion annually in radio advertising to reach national and local audiences.[36] There are good reasons why advertisers of all sorts use radio to reach target audiences. Let's turn our attention to the different radio options available to advertisers.

Radio Categories. Radio offers an advertiser several options for reaching target audiences. The basic split of national and local radio broadcasts presents an obvious geographic choice. More specifically, though, advertisers can choose among the following categories, each with specific characteristics: networks, syndication, AM versus FM, satellite, and Internet/mobile.

Networks. **Radio networks** operate much like TV networks in that they deliver programming via satellite to affiliate stations across the United States. Network radio programming concentrates on news, sports, business reports, and short features. Some of the more successful radio networks that draw large audiences are ABC, CNN, and AP News Network.

Syndication. **Radio syndication** provides complete programs to stations on a contract basis. Large syndicators offer stations complete 24-hour-a-day programming packages that totally relieve a station of any programming effort. Aside from full-day programming, they also supply individual programs, such as talk shows. Large syndication organizations such as Westwood One place advertising within programming, making syndication a good outlet for advertisers.

AM versus FM. AM radio stations send signals that use amplitude modulation (AM) and operate on the AM radio dial at signal designations 540 to 1600. AM was the foundation of radio until the 1970s. Today, AM radio broadcasts, even the new stereo AM transmissions, cannot match the sound quality of FM. Thus, most AM stations focus on local community broadcasting or news and talk formats that do not require high-quality audio. Talk radio has, in many ways, been the salvation of AM radio. FM radio stations transmit using frequency modulation (FM). FM radio transmission is of a much higher quality. Because of this, FM radio has attracted the wide range of music formats that most listeners prefer. AM/FM broadcast is now available via the Web and through smartphones, providing mobile advertising opportunities to advertisers.

Satellite Radio. Of course one of the newest options in radio is satellite radio, which is transmitted from satellites circling the earth. Currently, satellite radio costs a consumer anywhere from $99 to $200 to set up and then about $10 per month for a subscription. The advantages of satellite radio have to do with variety of programming, more crisp and clear sound reproduction, access to radio in places where broadcast does not reach, and *no ads* (on most music stations). The two leading satellite radio providers, Sirius and XM Satellite Radio, merged in 2008 to avoid joint bankruptcy. The new company Sirius/XM radio has about 24 million subscribers and provides 135 channels of news, sports, music, and entertainment programming in the United States and Canada (see Exhibit 13.19).[37] Satellite radio is primarily installed in consumers' vehicles, although there is some in-home installation as well. It remains to be seen whether consumers like the variety and quality offered by satellite radio enough to pay the subscription fee or whether they will prefer to keep "free" radio and listen to ads.

Internet/Mobile Radio. Internet radio has a wide and enthusiastic following. Sites like Pandora (the runaway leader) and Rhapsody allow listeners to access radio stations or build their own radio "stations" that play listeners' preferred music genres. And, unlike satellite radio, there is no fee. Recently, Internet radio providers have adopted technology to allow access through all varieties of smartphones. Mobile access once again provides advertisers the opportunity to reach target audiences while they are at the gym, on the train, jogging, or taking a walk in the park.

Types of Radio Advertising. Advertisers have three basic choices in radio advertising: local spot radio advertising, network radio advertising, or national spot radio advertising. Local spot radio advertising attracts 80 percent of all radio advertising dollars in a year. In **local spot radio advertising**, an advertiser places advertisements directly with individual stations rather than with a network or syndicate. Local spot radio dominates the three classes of radio advertising because there are more than 10,000 individual radio stations

in the United States, giving advertisers a wide range of choices. And local spot radio reaches well-defined geographic audiences, making it the ideal choice for local retailers.

Network radio advertising is advertising placed within national network programs. Since there are few network radio programs being broadcast, only about $600 million a year is invested by advertisers in this format.

The last option, **national spot radio advertising**, offers an advertiser the opportunity to place advertising in nationally syndicated radio programming. An advertiser can reach millions of listeners nationwide on more than 5,000 radio stations by contracting with Clear Channel's Premiere Radio Networks.

Advantages of Radio. Even though radio may not be the most glamorous or sophisticated of the major media options, it has some distinct advantages over newspapers, magazines, and TV.

Cost. On both a per-contact and absolute basis, radio is often the most cost-effective medium available to an advertiser. A full minute of network radio time can cost between $5,000 and $10,000—an amazing bargain compared with the other media we've discussed. In addition, production costs for preparing radio ads are quite low; an ad often costs nothing to prepare if the spot is read live during a local broadcast.

Reach and Frequency. Radio has the widest exposure of any medium with over 90 percent of the population

EXHIBIT 13.19 Satellite radio provider Sirius/XM is gaining wider acceptance among radio listeners. Subscription fees and new car sales are boosting subscription numbers and the benefit of "access anywhere" is appealing to consumers.

SIRIUS// 100 STREAMS OF SATELLITE RADIO

commercials_OFF
music_ON

SIRIUS it's_ON

over the age of 12 (241 million people in the United States) listening to radio in some form on a weekly basis.[38] It reaches consumers in their homes, cars, offices, and backyards and, now with mobile access, even while they exercise. The wireless and portable features of radio provide an opportunity to reach consumers that exceeds all other media. The low cost of radio time gives advertisers the opportunity to frequently repeat messages at low absolute cost and cost per contact.

Target Audience Selectivity. Radio can selectively target audiences on a geographic, demographic, and psychographic/lifestyle basis. The narrow transmission of local radio stations gives advertisers the best opportunity to reach well-defined geographic audiences. For a local merchant with one store, this is an ideal opportunity. Radio programming formats and different **dayparts** (i.e., times during the day) also allow target audience selectivity. In addition, various radio formats such as hard rock, oldies, new age, easy listening, country, classical, news, and talk radio formats all attract different audiences.

Flexibility and Timeliness. Radio is the most flexible medium because of short closing periods for submitting an ad. This means an advertiser can wait until close to an air date before submitting. With this flexibility, advertisers can take advantage of special events or unique competitive opportunities in a timely fashion. Also, on-air personalities can read altered copy on the day of a scheduled ad.

Creative Opportunities. Even though radio may be unidimensional in sensory stimulation, it can still have powerful creative impact. Radio has been described as the "theater of the mind." Ads such as the folksy tales of Tom Bodett for Motel 6 or the eccentric humor of Stan Freberg are memorable and can have tremendous impact on the attitude toward a brand. In addition, the musical formats that attract audiences to radio stations can also attract attention to radio ads. Research has discovered that audiences who favor certain music may be more prone to listen to an ad that uses songs they recognize and like.

Disadvantages of Radio. As good as radio can be, it also suffers from some severe limitations as an advertising medium. Advertising strategists must recognize these disadvantages when deciding what role radio can play in an integrated marketing communications program.

Poor Audience Attentiveness. Just because radio reaches audiences almost everywhere doesn't mean that everyone is paying attention. Radio is often described as "verbal wallpaper." It provides a comfortable background distraction while a consumer does something else—hardly an ideal level of attentiveness for advertising communication. Consumers who are listening and traveling in a car often switch stations when an ad comes on and divide their attention between the radio and the road.

Creative Limitations. Although the theater of the mind may be a wonderful creative opportunity, taking advantage of that opportunity can be difficult indeed. The audio-only nature of radio communication is a tremendous creative compromise. An advertiser whose product depends on demonstration or visual impact is at a loss when it comes to radio. And like its TV counterpart, a radio message creates a fleeting impression that is often gone in an instant.

Fragmented Audiences. The large number of stations that try to attract the same audience in a market has created tremendous fragmentation. Think about your own local radio market. There are probably four or five different stations that play the kind of music you like. Or consider that in the past few years, more than 1,000 radio stations in the United States have adopted the talk-radio format. This fragmentation means that the percentage of listeners tuned to any one station is likely very small.

Chaotic Buying Procedures. For an advertiser who wants to include radio as part of a national advertising program, the buying process can be sheer chaos. Since national networks and syndicated broadcasts do not reach every geographic market, an advertiser has to buy time in individual markets on a station-by-station basis. This could involve dozens of negotiations and individual contracts.

The Future of Radio. Three factors must be considered with respect to the future of radio. First, the prospects for subscription satellite radio should not be underestimated—especially with recent court ruling that may pave the way for broadband providers to start charging for Internet radio access. Satellite radio does away with radio advertising clutter and offers listeners multiple, detailed choices to match their listening preferences. This is a huge advantage along with the increased audio quality. The key issue is whether radio listeners will be willing to pay for an entertainment medium that has been free from its inception.

Second, radio will be affected by emerging technologies much in the same way that TV will be affected. High-definition radio, HD radio, is becoming a reality, and big firms like Clear Channel now offer dozens of digital channels. There are no subscription fees, but an HD receiver will cost a radio fan about $50, which, while fairly reasonable, may still present a barrier to adoption and use. Finally, there has been a large degree of consolidation going on in the traditional radio market. Led by Clear Channel Communications, fewer big competitors now own more and more radio stations. Through an aggressive period of acquisitions in the early 2000s, Clear Channel now owns approximately 850 radio stations in all regions of the United States

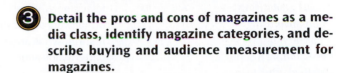

INSIGHTS ONLINE

13.20 Go online to see the AdAge feature, "A Chart of Media Companies That Lead TV, Radio, Newspaper, Cinema, Internet, and Out of Home."

and generates about $7 billion in revenue. Consolidation provides both opportunities and liabilities for both consumers and advertisers. Opportunities for consumers relate to the consistency of quality in the radio programming available and advertisers have an easier time buying and placing radio spots. (See Insights Online [Exhibit 13.20] for a chart that lists the largest companies by medium.)

SUMMARY

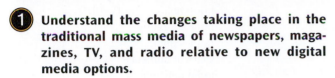 Understand the changes taking place in the traditional mass media of newspapers, magazines, TV, and radio relative to new digital media options.

The changes in the advertising industry are tangible and dramatic with respect to advertisers' use of the traditional media of newspapers, magazines, TV, and radio. For decades, advertisers would work with their advertising agencies to develop messages for their brands and then the agencies would negotiate for airtime with TV and radio networks or for space in newspapers and magazines. Most of these media options were owned by a few big media companies. Now, advertisers are fast adopting the belief that digital and interactive media—primarily Internet ads and mobile device ads—offer a more cost-effective and timely way to reach target markets. In addition, digital media allow advertisers to rapidly make changes in campaigns that might take months to accomplish with traditional media. Also, if the advertiser chooses, an Internet campaign can easily be a global campaign—a monumental task in traditional media. Advertisers are shifting literally billions of dollars out of traditional media in preference for digital media.

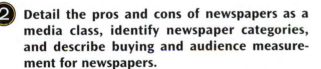 Detail the pros and cons of newspapers as a media class, identify newspaper categories, and describe buying and audience measurement for newspapers.

Newspapers can be categorized by target audience, geographic coverage, and frequency of publication. As a media class, newspapers provide an excellent means for reaching local audiences with informative advertising messages. Precise timing of message delivery can be achieved at modest expenditure levels. But for products that demand creative and colorful executions, this medium simply cannot deliver. Newspaper costs are typically transmitted via rate cards and are primarily a function of a paper's readership levels. Newspapers are struggling to survive in the digital age and are looking for ways to adopt pay-for-inquiry advertising models to attract advertisers back to the medium. In addition, traditional newspapers are offering digital editions, which could be successful on e-readers and tablet devices.

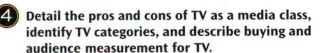 Detail the pros and cons of magazines as a media class, identify magazine categories, and describe buying and audience measurement for magazines.

Three important magazine categories are consumer, business, and farm publications. Because of their specific editorial content, magazines can be effective in attracting distinctive groups of readers with common interests. Thus, magazines can be superb tools for reaching specific market segments. Also, magazines facilitate a wide range of creative executions. Of course, the selectivity advantage turns into a disadvantage for advertisers trying to achieve high-reach levels. Costs of magazine ad space can vary dramatically because of the wide range of circulation levels achieved by different types of magazines. Like newspapers, magazines are adapting to the digital/interactive era. Paid electronic subscriptions with access through a variety of mobile devices is just beginning to take hold as options for magazines.

4 Detail the pros and cons of TV as a media class, identify TV categories, and describe buying and audience measurement for TV.

The four basic forms of TV are network, cable, syndicated, and local TV. Television's principal advantage is obvious: Because it allows for almost limitless possibilities in creative execution, it can be an extraordinary tool for affecting consumers' perceptions of a brand. Also, it can be an efficient device for reaching huge audiences; however, the absolute costs for reaching these audiences can be staggering. Lack of audience interest and involvement certainly limit the effectiveness of commercials in this medium, and digital devices like DVRs that allow the viewer to skip commercials make TV advertising nonexistent for many. As with any medium, advertising rates will vary as a function of the size and composition of the audience that is watching—yet audience measurement for TV is not an exact science, and its methods are often disputed. The spread of broadband access to more consumers both at home and through mobile devices is allowing transmission of TV programming in new and different ways. Advertisers are taking advantage of this opportunity to reach target markets beyond just in-home TV advertising.

Detail the pros and cons of radio as a media class, identify radio categories, and describe audience measurement for radio.

Advertisers can choose from three basic types of radio advertising: local spot, network radio, or national spot advertising. Radio can be a cost-effective medium, and because of the wide diversity in radio programming, it can be an excellent tool for reaching well-defined audiences. Poor listener attentiveness is a drawback to radio, and the audio-only format places obvious constraints on creative execution. Satellite radio, which is subscriber-based, does away with advertising entirely on its music stations. Radio ad rates are driven by considerations such as the average number of listeners tuned to a station at specific times throughout the day. Buying and placing ads for radio is becoming easier due to ever-increasing consolidation in the industry. Like the other traditional mass media, radio is taking advantage of mobile transmission through smartphones and tablet devices. And, again, advertisers find this new access attractive in reaching target markets.

KEY TERMS

display advertising
co-op advertising
preprinted insert
free-standing insert (FSI)
classified advertising
hyper-localism
pay-for-inquiry advertising model
pass-along readership
network TV
cable TV
video on demand (VOD)

television syndication
off-network syndication
first-run syndication
barter syndication
local TV
satellite and closed-circuit
narrowcasting
channel grazing
digital video recorder (DVR)
dayparts
TV households

households using TV (HUT)
program rating
ratings point
share of audience
radio networks
radio syndication
local spot radio advertising
network radio advertising
national spot radio advertising

ENDNOTES

1. "100 Leading National Advertisers 2012, U.S. Spending Totals," *Advertising Age*, June 25, 2012, 22; "U.S. Interactive Marketing Forecast, 2009–2014," *Forrester Research, Inc.*, July 30, 2009, 7.

2. Ibid.

3. Jennifer Saba, "Analysis: In Scare for Newspapers, Digital Ad Growth Stalls," *Reuters*, June 7, 2012, www.reuters.com, accessed June 7, 2012.

4. Emily Steel, "Advertising's Brave New World," *The Wall Street Journal*, May 25, 2007, B1, B3.

5. "100 Leading National Advertisers 2012, U.S. Spending Totals," *Advertising Age*, June 25, 2012, 22.

6. Historical information about the Absolut Vodka campaign was adapted from information in Nicholas Ind, "Absolut Vodka in the U.S.," in *Great Advertising Campaigns* (Lincolnwood, IL: NTC Business Books, 1993), 15–32.

7. Data on newspaper readership are available at the Newspaper Association of America and the Pew Research Center for the People & the Press websites, www.nnn-naa.com and www.people-press.org. Data cited here were drawn from those sites on April 9, 2010, and February 19, 2013. Data on current newspaper readership released on September 27, 2012.

8. "Taxing Times," *The Economist*, November 10, 2012, 61.

9. David Goetzl, "GlaxoSmithKline Launches Print Ads," *Advertising Age*, January 8, 2001, 30.

10. Michael Kinsley, "The World in 2010," *The Economist*, January 2010, 50.

11. Nat Ives, "Pay-for-Inquiry Ad Model Gains Modest Traction at Newspapers," *Advertising Age*, February 8, 2010, 2, 21; Rance Crain, "Newspapers Ought to Embrace the Pay-per-Inquiry Ad Model," *Advertising Age*, February 12, 2010, 12.

12. "100 Leading National Advertisers 2012, U.S. Spending Totals," *Advertising Age*, June 25, 2012, 20.

13. Jean Halliday, "Auto Industry Pushes Print's Creative Limits," *Advertising Age*, March 8, 2004, 4.

14. Emma Brazilian, "Digital-Only Magazine Readership Up Nearly 50 Percent. GfK MRI Finds Overall Readership Increases Slightly," *Adweek*, November 28, 2012, www.adweek.com, accessed February 19, 2013.

15. Nat Ives, "Pubs Flirt with Kindle but Don't Carry a Torch," *Advertising Age*, January 25, 2010, 4.

16. Nat Ives, "Magazines Dabble in E-commerce," *Advertising Age*, December 11, 2006, 18.

17. Domestic U.S. ad spending data taken from "100 Leading National Advertisers 2012, U.S. Spending Totals," *Advertising Age*, June 25, 2012, 22; Global TV ad spending projections taken from Michael Bush, "Magna Predicts Global Ad Spending Rise of 6% in 2010," *Advertising Age*, December 8, 2009, 4.

18. Brian Steinberg, "TV Ad Prices: 'Idol' No Match for Football," *Advertising Age*, October 22, 2012, 18, 20.

19. Data drawn from the National Cable & Telecommunications Association, Industry Statistics, www.ncta.com, accessed February 20, 2013.

20. Jeanine Poggi, "Why Cable Has Become More Like Broadcast TV," *Advertising Age*, May 14, 2012, 16.

21. Brian Steinberg, "The Endangered DVR: VOD Could Make It Obsolete," *Advertising Age*, September 17, 2012, 12.

22. Ken Wheaton, "Showing Signs of Strength, Local TV Should Face the Future," *Advertising Age*, January 18, 2010, 12.

23. Ibid.

24. "100 Leading Media Companies 2012," *Advertising Age,* October 1, 2012, 38.

25. Ibid.

26. Brian Steinberg, "TV Ad Prices: 'Idol' No Match for Football," *Advertising Age,* October 22, 2012, 18, 20.

27. Jean Halliday, "Study Claims TV Advertising Doesn't Work on Car Buyers," *Advertising Age,* October 13, 2003, 8.

28. Brian Steinberg, "The Future of TV," *Advertising Age,* November 30, 2009, 18.

29. Andrew Green, "Clutter Crisis Countdown," *Advertising Age,* April 21, 2003, 22.

30. 2004 Yankelovich Partners poll, cited in Gary Ruskin, "A 'Deal Spiral of Disrespect,'" *Advertising Age,* April 26, 2004, 18.

31. "Mobile Fact Pact 2012," *Advertising Age,* August 20, 2012, 6.

32. Thomas Morgan, "TV Works on the Web, but TV Advertising Does Not," *Advertising Age,* April 2, 2010, www.adage.com, accessed April 3, 2010.

33. John McDermott, "Mobile Ads More Disruptive Than TV Spots: Consumers Especially Dislike Ads That Interrupt the App Experience," *Advertising Age,* December 12, 2012, www.adage.com, accessed December 15, 2012.

34. Mike Mikho, "Why Social Media Needs TV and TV Needs Social Media," *Advertising Age,* October 15, 2012, www.adage.com, accessed October 15, 2012.

35. Simon Dumenco, "Believe the Hype? Four Things Social TV Can Actually Do," *Advertising Age,* April 16, 2012, 4.

36. "100 Leading National Advertisers 2012, U.S. Spending Totals," *Advertising Age,* June 25, 2012, 20.

37. Liana Baker, "Sirius XM Subscriber Numbers Miss, Shares Fall," *Reuters,* November 1, 2011, www.reuters.com, accessed February 20, 2013.

38. Laurie Panas-Brackett, "New Report from Arbitron Shows Young Radio Listeners on the Rise," *princetonmarketing.net,* September 26, 2011, www.princetonmarketing.net, accessed February 20, 2013.

CHAPTER 14

Media Planning: Advertising and IBP in Digital and Social Media

After reading and thinking about this chapter, you will be able to do the following:

(1) Understand the role of digital and social media in advertising and IBP along with the options available to brands through digital or social media.

(2) See the importance in virtual identity for consumers and brands online.

(3) Understand the basics of digital advertising and e-search.

(4) Know the basics of e-commerce as related to IBP and how it can stem from e-advertising, social media, and e-search.

(5) Note the advantages of digital and social media for implementing advertising and IBP campaigns, along with noting the dark side of social media, such as security and privacy concerns.

(6) See how to synergize with different IBP tools.

LO (1)

14-1 YOU'VE BEEN POKED— THE ROLE OF DIGITAL AND SOCIAL MEDIA AS A SYNERGISTIC IBP TOOL

The role of digital and social media in advertising is a big one, and one that is here to stay and grow with new technology such as mobile media. New media bring new vernacular to consumers. Friend me. Facebook graph search him. Tweet that. LinkedIn him for a job lead. Groupon. Re-tweet that. Facetime tonight? Skype interview. Unfriend her. These online terms and brands have changed the way of online consumer behavior, advertising, and branding—and they way you can search for and obtain a career in advertising or otherwise.[1] Hence, it is crucial to understand how consumers think, feel, and act regarding social media, online advertising, and e-commerce. Online advertisers want to know where and why consumers go online, how that relates to where they go offline, as well as what makes them tick.

In the ad for Subaru in Exhibit 14.1, the brand understands that their target market is forward thinking and green, so in a brilliant move, Subaru uses digital advertising to link their car brand to a community event. The ad leverages their event sponsorship of the Wagathon Walkathon in Austin. Further, this digital/traditional/event sponsorship/ PR move fits well in Austin due to a match of Subaru's target market of eco-friendly, outdoorsy, yet urban-of-sorts lifestyle consumers. Business practitioners like Subaru are looking for solutions as to how to understand consumer lifestyles, attitude, affect, emotion, and online consumer behavior so that they can maximize online and offline customer experiences. Further, digital marketers can create events with sponsors to help instill brand loyalty with offline, experiential marketing. Not just mainstream commercial brands but nonprofit organization managers too seek to understand online consumer behavior so that they can raise awareness and make online giving easy.

New media bring new vernacular to consumers. Friend me. Facebook graph search him. Tweet that.

Online advertisers know the importance of not just incorporating but also embracing consumer blogs, Pinterest, Facebook, Instagram, Twitter, LinkedIn, MySpace (the new cooler one from Justin Timberlake and friends), Digg, HowSocial, Groupon, Vine, and other social media to enhance their online presence. Newer ones include Pheed, Thumb, Medium, Conversations, Chirpify, and Flavyr. And e-dating sites can be created social media style. Some of these companies even put the social media feel into professional communications, such as email

or newsletters. Yet, questions remain as how to leverage these online branding tools to increase the consumer experience and hence the value of the websites. Some of the world's leading brand visionaries, as well as new brands, align their corporate websites and social media objectives to enhance their return on investment for digital advertising (see Insights Online [Exhibit 14.2] for more specific information).[2]

14-1a **Social Media and Web 2.0**

Web 2.0 distinguishes the progression of the Internet to interactive online communication, participation, and engagement.[3] The first-generation Internet was one-way messaging and online information retrieval;

EXHIBIT 14.1 Subaru uses digital advertising to link their car brand to an event—the Wagathon Walkathon in Austin, a locale that fits well with their target market of eco-friendly yet urban consumers.

Web 2.0 describes what people are doing with technology and how they are using it.[4] Users can now create information and post comments while adding (or subtracting with a negative post) value to socially embedded websites. This content is called **user-generated content (UGC)** or **consumer-generated media (CGM)**.[5] Web 2.0 depends on mass collaboration as individuals simultaneously create value for themselves and others.[6] In a marketing context, there is a focus on brands and organizations "liked" and mentioned through network effects. Similarly, organizations reach and interact with existing customers online while becoming part of customer conversations.[7] The Internet still holds the power of curiosity.[8]

14-1b Media Types in Social Media

Social media are media that are designed to connect people and their networks with other people, brands, organizations, or other entities. Examples include Twitter, Pinterest, YouTube, Facebook, and MySpace. There are three media types in social media: earned, owned, and paid.[9] **Earned media** is the incremental exposure that your brand earns through viral engagement and interactions with the brand. For instance, Facebook likes, check-ins, or shares are earned media. One note with earned media is that the brand does not pay for the buzz; hence it is not technically advertising as advertising traditionally is paid. The second type is owned media; **owned media** are brand assets or objects created within social networks by your organization, such as a Facebook page or an application. **Paid media** are advertisements that can be purchased on a social network or other digital platforms. Note that, in theory, any advertisement by the traditional definition is "paid" per se. This is not to be confused with paid traditional advertising that leverages a call to action to like the brand on Twitter, Pinterest, Facebook, or other social media sites, as DKNY subtly does in their ad in Exhibit 14.4 on the bottom with the social media icons. It is a smart idea to integrate social media, or even a QR code (although the efficacy of QR codes seems to have worn off due to lack of consumer convenience). Here, in the context of social media, note that some brand integration can be officially paid to the site such as Facebook, while others are not paid; for example, earned media is when your Facebook friend raves about his or her DKNY perfume. There is a big difference when we think about the inherent bias; thus, earned media in social networks

is king in our eyes. (See Insights Online [Exhibit 14.3] for more on how digital marketing is going to continue to change the nature of advertising.)

14-1c Options via Digital or Social Media: Definitions and Categories

Definitions of Social Media. **Social media** are "media designed to facilitate dissemination of content through social interaction between individuals, groups and organizations using Internet and web-based technologies to enable the transformation of broadcast monologues (one to many) into social dialogues (many to many)."[10] A second definition of social media is "a group of Internet-based applications that build on the ideological and technological foundations of Web 2.0, and that allows for the creation and exchange of

EXHIBIT 14.4 DKNY uses digital and social media in the Be Delicious campaign. They use a QR code for consumers to scan to view how to join their core club.

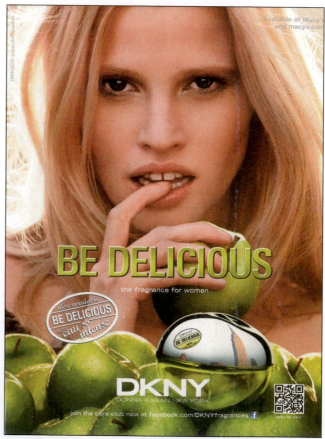

user-generated content."[11] Regardless of the definition you prefer, the core of social media is individual empowerment and democratization of knowledge. This is because you are a content producer—sometimes even create ads for Super Bowl advertisers such as Doritos. Social media are accessible, in that they are simple to find and use for a broad audience and are scalable, as network effects play a key role.[12]

Social Media Categories. Here are some brief descriptions of social media categories, along with their use for integrated brand promotion (IBP) and digital advertising or messaging. Specifically, here is an overview of social networking, blogs and micro-blogs, video and picture sharing, and social news websites.[13,14]

Social Networking Websites. Social networking sites and apps are services on which users can create an individual profile page, find and add friends and contacts, send messages, and update their personal profiles to notify friends, contacts, or colleagues about themselves.[15] On some social networking websites, users can join networks organized by workplace, school, or college. Social networking websites often combine several other social media technologies into one platform; for example, Facebook gives users the opportunity to post status updates (i.e., micro-blogs), notes (i.e., blogs), pictures, and videos. Often, users are able to tag other users in their networks in such posts, creating additional links between users and content. The most popular social networking sites with a generally social orientation are Facebook, Google+, Pinterest, and MySpace. There are also social networking sites with more specific foci, such as LinkedIn and Plaxo, that specifically target professional and business networking.

Blogs. Slang for "Web logs," **blogs** are sites maintained and written by individuals but hosted and technically owned by an organization that provides access to Web space and a content management system.[16] Bloggers maintain regular posts that may include text, graphics, videos, or links to other blogs and Web pages. These are usually posted in chronological order. Blogs often focus on news and views on particular subjects. Many blogs permit readers to leave comments. Some of the most popular blog sites are Blogger, LiveJournal, and WordPress. A blog is a virtual journal of sorts that is often updated and intended for public access. Topics include fashion, art, culture, celebrity, and business, among others. Key characteristics of the blog are its journal form and its informal style. **Micro-blogs** are social networking services that enable users to post and read short messages. Posters are restricted by the number of characters in the message. The best known is Twitter, through which users can send messages known

as "tweets"—text-based posts of up to 140 characters displayed on the author's profile page and delivered to the author's subscribers, who are known as followers. Senders can restrict delivery to those in their circle of friends or, by default, allow open access to any site visitors. Users can send and receive tweets via the Twitter website and also through text messaging on cell phones and external applications that can access the site. Twitter has gained much prominence in the Super Bowl, as some advertisers such as Coca-Cola contacted Twitter for permissions to exceed the post limit to accommodate Tweets into the Super Bowl campaign.

Video and Photo Sharing Websites. A favorite of many consumers to show their Starbucks cups with misspelled names, new purchases, family, friends, and pets, as well as some stupidly funny sightings such as a baby monkey riding on a pig's back or a goat that sounds like a yelling human (juxtaposed over Taylor Swift music), these websites allow users to watch, upload, and share videos. Typically, unregistered users can watch videos already posted to the site, while registered users are permitted to upload videos and comment on other users' videos.[17] The best known of the **video sharing websites**, or social media sites that have consumers and companies upload videos and watch others' videos for free, is YouTube, which dominates market share. We may see the convergence of video and photo sharing sites. We predict video will get more popular, as the digital millennials such as you and your classmates enter the agencies and workforce with your comfort and experience with video. Plus, now that many smartphones such as the iPhone have video recording capability, video is becoming more convenient and mainstream. **Photo sharing sites** operate in much the same way as video sharing websites but with content based on still images instead of video. Some popular picture sharing websites are Instagram (bought out for $1 *billion* by Facebook in 2013—wow!), Pinterest, Photobucket, SlickPic, Flickr, Webshots, dotPhoto, Picasa, and the more traditional platforms of Yahoo Images and Google Images. A picture is worth a thousand words, an old adage says. Who doesn't love a good photo? We have a hunch that photographs that look authentic (versus a Photoshopped image that we are accustomed to) may pop out and cut the clutter—catching our eye. Birkenstock, the hippy cool, comfy shoe brand, thinks so too as evidenced by their casual cool "Be Naturally Good" campaign seen in Exhibit 14.5. In this series of ads, the art direction reminds us of a photograph you would take in your backyard. It looks Pinterest-esque; it reminds us of a photo you would see from a friend's posting to a photo sharing site.

EXHIBIT 14.5 Birkenstock, a German shoe brand since 1774, uses the look and feel of Pinterest with their "Be Naturally Good" campaign. It is further synergized well with QR codes and facebook.com/birkenstock.

LO 2

14-2 CONSUMER AND BRAND VIRTUAL IDENTITY

14-2a Consumer Virtual Identity

Virtual identity is how the consumer or brand uses images and text online to construct or showcase its identity. This concept is crucial to understand as it relates to IBP, social media, and digital advertising. Online identity, in the virtual world and in the on-ground world, is increasingly becoming an important pseudo-image for today's connected consumer. Avatars are consumer-generated images that an online user portrays, which may or may not accurately coincide with the consumers' "real identity". In one of the author's dissertation research on e-dating, there is startling evidence that consumers' online identity in some drastic cases was highly exaggerated from their "real identity" and instead displayed their desired identity.[19] They may exaggerate to enhance their sense of self-concept (perhaps even lying to themselves) or more drastically to lure an unknowing potential dating partner.[20] Findings of dissimilarity are also found in the context of avatars, or cartoon-based pictorial representations of the image an online consumer wishes to portray. In some cases, such avatars are brands, designers, sports teams, or other nonhuman images. While depersonalized compared to an avatar that is purported to look like the consumer, these nonhuman avatars or mascots, like the Florida Gator, the Georgia Bulldawg, or the University of Texas Longhorn, are attractive and represent an image transfer from the brand to the person adopting that image.

It is unhealthy to fully understand online identity without considering the notion that there is more than one world in today's consumer's mind. There is the "real world," which, for many, consists of work, family, social activities, and shopping at bricks-and-mortar stores and service providers. Some of this is difficult, if not impossible, to do online. Until someone invents an application that can put gas in one's car or bring one's child to day care, such interactions in the real world are necessary. Consumers have their "real-world" image. The twist is that this image is not necessarily congruent with their image in the virtual world. Behind the screen, a consumer may create a new identity, a new attitude, and in a sense become a different person while online. We must understand that virtual identities are indeed real to consumers. Understanding this concept can help consumer-minded businesses and organizations cater better to customer wants.

Social news websites are sites that allow people to discover and share content from anywhere on the Internet by submitting links and stories to a central service.[18] Most often, social news services allow visitors to vote and comment on submitted links and stories. The best known of these social news websites are Reddit, Digg, Propeller, and Newsvine. Social news sites are wonderful for raising reach and can even help get the right story or video to viral status (a good thing, despite the scary name). Like a virus, viral marketing spreads quickly, and the word gets out. Social news sites are most valuable when they maintain a stable community to add links and vote on them (see Insights Online [Exhibit 14.6] for an interesting example).

INSIGHTS ONLINE

14.6 Go online to see the AdAge feature, "Another Plus of Digital Media Is Real-Time Advertising, Such as Oreo's Super Bowl Super Event Marketing Savvy Move during the Blackout."

14-2b Social Media as a Brand Management Tool: Brand Image and Visibility

We will discuss social media definitions and issues primarily from a consumer (user) context, because as a digital advertiser, you need to have knowledge of online consumer behavior to create an effective advertising strategy. Social media are important tools for brand managers who are keenly interested in establishing and maintaining a brand image, reputation, or position. Especially during times of crisis (e.g., after an oil spill), companies are expected to communicate directly with the impacted consumers and their communities. Social media are a vast net that can be as visible as you make it, depending on your breadth and depth of use and your privacy settings. There are various categories ranging from networking to picture sharing. Web 2.0 is interactive and social. It leaves a trail of your digital footprints that future employers, spouses, and yes, even your parents can plausibly see. There are many advantages to the use of social media for both individuals and brands. A predominant concern relates to privacy, so brand managers must keep their consumers' identities as a trusted component of their relationship. Brands should leverage social media as a digital advertising opportunity that can target by consumer lifestyle. Managers too should use social media as a way to monitor and build a brand image, reputation, and position and communicate with customers and their networks.

From a brand manager perspective, key questions suggested by Botha and Mills (2012) remain[21]: How do we find out what is being said about a brand via social media? What is being said about competing brands? How is that different from our brand? Is our brand more or less visible in some social media than others, and how does that differ from our competitors? Are we "liked"? Brand managers must track what is being said by consumers, interpret consumer-generated information, and respond to social media posts and comments. This entails spending time scanning Facebook, following Twitter feeds, looking at Pinterest pins, and reading comments on YouTube.[22] This sounds prone to error and is time-consuming. Thus, here is a tool that can collect brand visibility information for you; the tool is called How Sociable. This tool, via subscription, monitors a brand's activity across many social media platforms so that a person does not have to rigorously check social media to monitor a brand. In addition to monitoring electronic word of mouth, managers are keenly interested in metrics from any social media and social media ads. There are questions around social media measurement, such as, What is a like really worth? Some metrics from Internet advertising do apply to social media. For instance, site stickiness, or how long someone spends on a site, is a relevant metric. Bounce rate, or the percentage of people who come from or go to another site after clicking on your site, is also relevant. Another metric more specific to social media is engagement with the social media site.

Let's not forget the hybrid nature of shopping these days. So, a further metric for advertisers and brand marketers is sales in bricks-and-mortar stores as well as digital e-commerce sales. Gucci understands this; check out the stunning art direction in Exhibit 14.7 by Gucci's agency. The ad focuses on the product—a good thing as the products are beautiful and they are not overshadowed by celebrity or other background art. The innovative thing about this ad, while again subtle, is that it directs consumers, who may not have a Gucci store in their city, to the Gucci "digital flagship store" at Gucci.com. Thus, digital media and e-commerce work well here with traditional print media. Again, it is *not* a question of traditional or digital; it is how to seamlessly integrate both.

EXHIBIT 14.7 Gucci employs stunning art direction and photography in their ad showing their new styles. On the second page of this two-page spread, there is a call to action for consumers to visit their digital flagship store at Gucci.com.

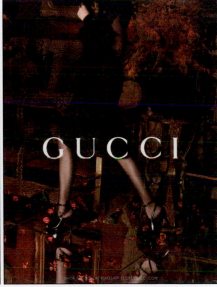

Gucci

LO ③

14-3 BASICS OF DIGITAL ADVERTISING AND ONLINE SEARCH

14-3a Digital Advertising

Much of digital advertising is based on **pay-per-click (PPC)**. PPC is an advertising revenue model where the advertiser is charged by the number of people who click on, or tap, the ad to pull it up for more information or to see the ad in entirety. Thus, when you see an online ad and click on it, the advertiser is charged. This is nice, compared to traditional advertising, because the advertiser can pay for a pulled exposure rather than a message pushed to all watching that TV channel or reading that magazine. A second model of advertising payment works via bidding for specific ad words in search engines and social media. It is a good idea, if possible, to bid higher than Facebook's suggested bid amount to reach your target audience who, in turn, will engage with your ads at a faster pace (low frequency). As with traditional media, it is smart to keep reach and frequency in check so as not to spark consumer resistance. The goal is to get a high effective exposure rate and engagement rate, not to annoy consumers.

For social media advertising to be effective, the brand page must have a fan base. That is, consumers must be motivated to find your page and "like it." A smart way to do this is to give an incentive—a chance to win something, a first look at new products, or special offers. This online consumer base can be served by an IBP campaign that is more interactive in nature, another advantage of social media. Develop a strong portfolio of assets upon which you can build your campaigns and drive interaction within Facebook. In order to capitalize in social ads and sponsored stories, you must have a scalable fan base. With a larger network, there is a higher exposure rate, which can in turn enhance engagement with the ad and brand.

Types of Digital Ads. There are several types of digital ads, including social media ads, display/banner ads, and pop-up and pop-under ads.

Social Media Ads. Note that even within one social media site, such as Facebook, there are different types of ads. Facebook has **sponsored stories** that are ad-like stories that can be promoted with payment. **Post ads** are ads in a post and tend to have higher relative response rates because they are within a consumer's post to his or her network. **Web ads** in digital and social media are intended to drive traffic off of the site where the digital ad is run. **App ads** are ads associated with a third-party application (such as FarmVille); these tend

to generate consumer loyalty and can provide consumer data for more accurate key word targeting.

Some key words are very expensive, but slight variations of those words can be much more affordable and still reach the type of consumer the brand can best speak to. Like traditional media, digital media need to be in line with both the brand/IBP or campaign objectives and addressed to a specific target market. Recently, Facebook collapsed their 27 or so social media ad buys (it was too many options for media buyers) into a few. So differentiated social media ad "types," such as sponsored stories, are now sold more in a package/value added deal with other social media ad buys.[23] (See Insights Online [Exhibit 14.8] for more information.)

Display/Banner Ads. **Display/banner ads** are paid placements of advertising on sites that contain copy or images. One feature of a display/banner ad is that consumers can click on the ad (this is the "click-through" defined earlier). Thus, the challenge of creating and placing display/banner ads is not only to catch people's attention but also to entice them to visit the marketer's home page and stay for a while. The ability to create curiosity and provide the viewer resolution to that curiosity can have an important impact on learning and brand attitude.[24] The downside to display and banner ads is the clutter.

A more targeted option is to place these ads on sites that attract specific market niches. A pricing evaluation service for these types of ads is offered by Interactive Traffic. The **I-Traffic Index** is an index that computes a site's advertising value based on traffic, placement and size of ads, ad rates, and evaluations of the site's quality. Firms such as Forrester Research assess the costs of display/banner ads on a variety of sites and provide an estimate to advertisers of the audience delivered. For example, there are sites that speak to consumers with an interest in events related to culture, art, theater, and symphony in their areas. These events have to be promoted within a specific time window; thus, it is crucial that event ads be placed in specific outlets such as cultural calendars, event sites, local happenings sections of local media, and in related outlets that reach the specific psychographic or lifestyle. The Austin Symphony, in Exhibit 14.9, does a nice job of synergizing traditional print media with social media to help reposition the symphony as a more fabulous event suitable for a fun and unique girls' night out.

Pop-Up/Pop-Under Ads. **Pop-under ads** are ads that are present under the active window and are only visible once the surfer closes that window. Most find these a nuisance. Losing popularity because of the annoyance factor, a **pop-up ad** is an ad that opens in a separate

EXHIBIT 14.9 Events are a social occurrence as most go with friends or loved ones. The symphony is trying to stay hip with trendsetter socialites with Twitter- and Facebook-leveraged messages encouraging girls' nights out or nights out on the town with friends.

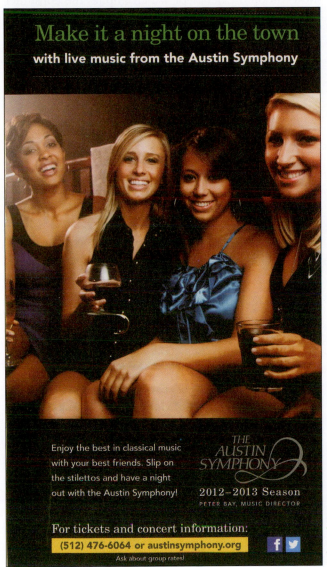

14-3b E-Search

Online awareness and social media tactics are means to enhance online advertising effectiveness and consumer search. **E-search** is electronic search; it refers to how consumers look for ideas, brands, and information online for purchases or entertainment. To show its power, consider election years and online political advertising: some say elections were won in part by how some candidates used online and social media advertising to speak to younger voters. With respect to political advertising, planners consider how online videos and ads can impact voter assessment. After seeing an ad, consumers' motivations may be sparked to use the Internet or their smartphone to obtain more information on voting records, politicians, or for their preferred brands.

Paid Search and Search Engine Optimization. Paid search is the process by which advertisers pay websites and portals to place ads in or near relevant search results based on key words. For example, if you Google "running shoes," you will find links to Onlineshoes.com and Zappos.com next to the search results as sources for purchasing running shoes. Paid search has grown astronomically. Advertisers spent more than $15 billion a year in 2009; now, it is well over $31 billion or so.[26] One catalyst for growth in paid search is the success of Google, which pushed the concept from its beginning, although all sites can accommodate paid search. Paid-search technology can fine-tune a Web user's search to more relevant and specific websites. The top key words that lead Internet users to advertiser sites are health and medical, education, food and beverage, and government. In one month, Americans conduct more than 61 billion searches for key words or phrases,[27] and most of these are conducted on Google sites. Paid search is valued by firms as they try to improve the efficiency of the Internet as an IBP tool. Another key paid search concept is **search engine optimization (SEO)**. SEO is a process whereby the volume and quality of traffic to a website from search engines are improved based on surfers' profiles. Basically, the goal is that the higher a site is presented in search results, the more likely surfers are to visit that site—but the more it will cost. (See Insights Online [Exhibit 14.10] for an interesting perspective on whether Facebook is making the most of possible connections.)

window while a page is loading. The more times people click on these ads, the more money can be charged for the privilege of advertising. When they became common in 2003, they were instantly despised; 80 percent of surfers said that pop-ups were annoying, and about 65 percent felt that display/banner ads were annoying.[25] Thus, we do not recommend them due to consumer resistance and because many service providers are offering blockers that greatly reduce an advertiser's ability to get a pop-up onto a user's screen. The movement now is toward ads that load before a viral video or other desired online content. An **interstitial** is an ad that loads while you browse; they appear on a site after a page has been requested but before it has loaded and stay onscreen long enough for the message to be registered.

INSIGHTS ONLINE

14.10 Go online to see the AdAge feature, "Graph Search Is the Latest Change; Is Facebook Ever Going to Grow Up?"

LO 4

14-4 IMPORTANCE OF IBP IN E-TAIL: EMERGENCE OF SOCIAL E-COMMERCE AND BIG DATA

Big data refers to a huge volume of structured and unstructured data that is much too large to analyze or process using traditional ways. Big data is all the rage, with software sites like Collusion that help you track who is tracking you, and even block some of them. According to the Collusion developers, thousands of organizations collect your online browsing data, which in turn creates a network of connections among the sites you visit. Collusion helps you by graphing the spread of your online data from the sites to these trackers; this is done visually in real time to expose these connections. An option is to block some of these links. Keep in mind however, that the goal of tracking online consumer behavior is essentially to help bring more relevant, and even useful or appreciated ads or reminders that are specific to your wants and needs. For instance, I am looking for a SUV, so I went to Chevy Tahoe's website and to Cadilliac's site. Knowing this,

the ads I get by these brands are appreciated, as I am interested in learning about these brand's and their new models. In a way, it is trying to help make push advertising more pull advertising, in that the consumer first shows an online behavior which implies the consumer is interested.[28]

Digital advertising or social media plugs may spark consumers to browse e-tail sites, place items or service tickets into virtual shopping carts, and hopefully convert cart placements into sales turned relationships. Here we provide some statistics on e-commerce's projected growth. The e-commerce and online shopping landscape has grown substantially in size and scope over the last decade. Hundreds of millions of online buyers bring e-commerce revenues of US $680 billion a year.[29] The increase in the number of online shoppers, increasing revenues, and emergence of new forms of e-commerce and shopping highlight the need to understand the online shopping process. An understanding of the online shopping process is important to online advertisers and for online retailers. Further, knowing the conditions in which trust makes a consumer click on an ad, watch an online ad, or patronize an e-tailer is important.[30] Amazon.com, featured in Exhibit 14.11, is especially interested in online

EXHIBIT 14.11 Amazon.com/Fashion is a new initiative from the top e-tailer. E-search is a big part of Amazon's business. Here, their ad notes their new free return policy and how consumers can e-search hundreds of top fashion brands.

consumer behavior as it enters into a more specific market for them—fashion. Amazon has traditionally been known for e-tailing goods such as books, movies, and other consumer household products, so a repositioning to focus on the emerging fashion component of the brand is a change. Keeping up with Zappos, an early innovator of the free-return shipping model, the Amazon campaign shows the new fashionable side of the e-tailer along with the e-service and e-search component. Together, these can help reduce e-shopping cart abandonment.

14-5 ADVANTAGES OF DIGITAL AND SOCIAL MEDIA FOR IMPLEMENTING ADVERTISING AND IBP CAMPAIGNS, AS WELL AS THE DARK SIDE

Social media have many challenges and opportunities.[31] Here, we start with the pros, then turn to the cons—or even the dark side of social media.

14-5a Advantages of Digital and Social Media

Several unique characteristics of the Internet offer advantages for advertising over traditional media options. Advantages of digital and social media include interactivity, target market selectivity, integration, and ease of use, and it is a way to engage and integrate brands with consumers' lifestyles that they have shared in their open book—or **digital footprint**, the trail of social media posts, videos, photos, status updates, and online information on a person, organization, or brand. A plus to digital and social media is the sheer volume and popularity of going online in general, and specifically the frequency with which consumers check social media. Another plus is the breadth in social media sites. Consumers have accounts in various types of social media. In the United States, 67 percent of all adults use one or more social networking sites; while slightly more women (71 percent) versus men (62 percent) use social media, there are no major differences among races. Younger consumers age 18–29 are the highest social media consumers (83 percent), second to the 30–49-year-olds (77 percent). Only 32 percent of consumers aged 65 and over use social media.[32]

Interactivity. **Interactivity**, or two-way communications that can feed off one another, is an advantage

of digital media. A consumer can go to a site or click through from a display/banner ad and take a tour of the brand's features and values. A **click-through** is a measure of the number of page elements (hyperlinks) that have actually been requested (i.e., "clicked through" from the display/banner ad to the link). If advertisers can attract surfers to the brand website, there is the opportunity to convert that surfer to a buyer if the site is set up for e-commerce. Design components of various digital or mobile or tablet ad formats can have an important effect on click-through and sales potential.[33] Social media provide new and important opportunities for advertisers with respect to interactivity. You can even design your own engagement ring at Mondera.com, make your own Nikes at mynikeid.com, and design your own car at most auto brand sites.

Integration. Digital and mobile advertising is most easily integrated and coordinated with other forms of promotion. The integration of Web activities with other components of the marketing mix is one of the easiest integration tasks in the IBP process. This is due to the flexibility and deliverability of Web advertising discussed earlier. Social media also provide a seamless interface with the most traditional of IBP tools—television. Television ratings for live events, such as the Grammys and the Oscars, have spiked in recent years as viewers tweet and post on Facebook to alert friends to the awards and to their reactions to the proceedings.[34]

Investing in Internet Digital Advertising. On a cost-per-thousand (CPM) basis, the cost of Web ads for the most part compares favorably with ads placed in traditional media. It is important to compare absolute cost and CPM for ads placed in traditional media and on the Web. The real attraction of digital is not found in raw numbers and CPMs but rather in terms of highly segmentable and highly motivated audiences. The Internet is ideally suited for niche marketing—finding consumers most likely interested in the brand offering. This aspect of the Internet as an advertising option has always been its great attraction: the ability to identify segments and deliver almost-customized (or in the case of email, actually customized) messages directly. With respect to banner ads specifically, in the early 2000s, about 90 percent of agencies priced banner ads on a CPM basis, whereas a smaller number used click-throughs (i.e., the number of times an ad visitor goes to the advertiser's site) as the basis for pricing; today, this has greatly changed because cost per click (hence, CPC) models can be more accountable, assuming no click fraud is going on.[35]

Engagement via a Digital Footprint. Companies, non-profits, and human brands alike can engage others via their online presence. For the sport (tennis) company

Babolat, as shown in Exhibit 14.12, the integration of their print campaign with Facebook and a QR code that brings the consumer to the product's website is a way to engage via hybrid channels. With social media, you can be an open book if you so choose and consciously or unconsciously share the brands you use or like. By checking in (I am at the University of Texas today, Facebook friends!), branded places become part of your Web 2.0 storyline. Posting photos of you in your Chevy in a Braves hat with a PowerAde in hand is another way brands are benefitting in an organic way from social media. We all have a story, or our personal book, and when documented online it leaves a digital footprint. The question is, how much of your book do you choose to share in social media? What aspects of your identity do you share with your social media world and how are those shaped by brands? Or, do you choose to stay away from social media, and keep a closed book when it comes to your digital footprint? Your personal information is readily available online if you so choose in social media. With graph search in Facebook, the e-search is easier than ever. You may

EXHIBIT 14.12 Babolat uses digital media to launch their new Aeropro Drive racket. Leveraged with QR code and a celebrity endorser, lefty tennis professional Rafael Nadal, the ad also uses a social media call to action via facebook.com/babolat.

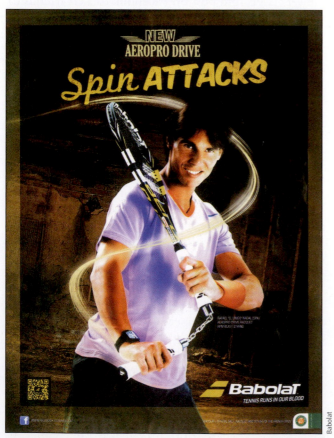

have your resume on LinkedIn and have your sorority formal photos on Facebook. You may have selected to "like" Lady Gaga, Radiohead, or Staind. You may also publicly "like" brands like Vans, Puma, Lululemon, Apple, Nike, and Tom's. These self-confessions, evolving technology, and Web 2.0 tools (e.g., social networking, blogging) make it simple to share your life story—your open book. It is your choice to share your life information in social media (I'm engaged!)—or not.[36,37,38] Women share a picture of their engagement ring, and new parents may show the first ultrasound (It's a boy!). Or, on sadder days, you may share news of a grandparent's passing, or that you lost a pet or bombed a test. In this way, you are reaching out to your network to help you cope through tough times and congratulate your milestones. There is something to be said for maintaining a strong network of friends, family, and professionals, and social media is a tool to make this easier to manage in large numbers. Brands can use this to integrate themselves into your life story. Your online history of what you post becomes a digital paper trail, available for you and others to reflect back on. The information that you share creates a "digital footprint," defined as your profile of personal information, accessible online to a spectrum of people.[39,40] Note that this spectrum of audience in social media is based on your privacy settings. You may choose to post to all of your social media connections, friends of friends, or in your entire network. In some cases, future employers and spouses (and parents!) follow your digital footprint, so it is important to keep in line with your true and aspirational self. It is also important to consider privacy aspects of social media. (See Insights Online [Exhibit 14.13] for an interesting perspective.)

▶ INSIGHTS ONLINE

14.13 Go online to see the AdAge feature, "Digital Measurement Helps Give Us More Accurate Messages but Still Faces Online Resistance."

14-5b **Privacy Issues and the Dark Side of Digital and Social Media**

One cannot have an intelligent conversation about digital and social media without discussing the role of authenticity, privacy, security, and related fears about one's personal and financial information.

The Dark Side. It is harder to judge authenticity behind a screen.[41] The thought of having one's identity stolen by online or digital means, or **cyber-identity theft**,[42] is enough to inhibit some consumers from shopping and banking online. It is key to explore consumer perception of both privacy and security because security refers to how safe the site or app is and privacy is more about how the host maintains consumer data and online consumer behavior. Establishing the highest standards for privacy and security are important for online brand managers. Doing so can help e-tailers make sure that they are accurately addressing concerns that their customers have that could be preventing them from completing online transactions. Today's brand managers have a wealth of resources at their fingertips to help establish their brand's identity and to connect with their customers. Facebook, Twitter, LinkedIn, and other social networking sites are not just tools for consumers to connect with each other (C2C). Instead, we must look at social networks as a brand management tool. Just as touch points with the brand are key at live events (e.g., sponsor signage at a sporting event), virtual touch points are a tool to help leverage those on-ground consumer relationships.

While social networking can never replace the authenticity of a handshake and personalized service, these virtual touch points can reinforce extant relationships or spark a new interest or unrealized need—such as for a waterproof smartphone case. A feature of some media is that it allows for e-search with QR codes that can help consumers find a product, information, or service. As in the Otter Box ad in Exhibit 14.14, the use of QR codes in advertising is a topic that scholars are examining in terms of efficacy. Do you take the time to scan QR codes you may see in ads? Why or why not?

Online Resistance. We suspect that there is some **online resistance**, which is an attitude or behavior against the digital movement at times. For some consumers, and for the authors as well, social networks are designed as a vehicle that connects us with people who have at one point graced our lives. Be it our marketing and advertising students, high school pals, current colleagues, or yes, parents, it is this constant connection with people that draws consumers to log on for hours on end to social networking sites. In fact, Facebook is the most visited site in the United States. Make these vehicles another way to market to us and sell to us, and we may resist. There could be the perception that marketers and advertisers are stomping on consumers' sacred territory. That said, if done correctly (i.e., precise targeting in a nonintrusive manner), there can be some subtle synergies from online advertisers that can actually enhance one's social networking experience. For example, after one of the authors changed her Facebook status from "in a relationship" to "engaged," a sidebar on the social media

EXHIBIT 14.14 Otter Box uses digital media to speak to a relevant target audience of iPhone owners in their iProtection campaign. Note the call to e-search for your perfect case by scanning a QR code or going to their site.

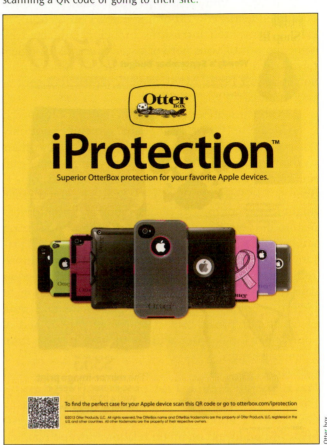

Otter box

site appeared from a wedding dress vendor, then honeymoon destinations, jewelers, and florists galore. This is life stage marketing at its finest—the dress is one of the first things on the newly engaged woman's mind, and Facebook and their advertisers were right there to assist in the search.

Privacy and Information in Social Media. Marketplace exchanges embedded with social media may be more publicly visible. For instance, when you order photos from Walgreen's via a Facebook app, you may choose to have this visible on your Facebook page. This makes a usually more private purchase more socially embedded. The e-environment lends itself to casual information sharing. Privacy involves the control of information disclosure and unwanted intrusions into a consumer's environment.[43,44] Privacy in this era now entails control over personal exchanges that use information technology to enhance autonomy or minimize vulnerability and which can minimize covert marketing practices online.[45,46] Often, online consumers do not use the privacy tools available to them, such as clearing out needless cookies, reading privacy policies, or paying attention to logos that show the site has been endorsed or is a member of a third-party privacy endorser, known as a **privacy seal**.[47,48,49] Such consumer apathy toward online privacy protection can lead to unwanted intrusions or being contacted by someone out of your networks (or circles, as Google+ terms them). The landscape changes so quickly that you may not be as aware of your digital footprint as you should.

Do you remember each of your digital footprints? If not, you are not alone. Few people remember not only self-posted information but also details posted by others to their online profiles. Especially as online users gain multiple social networking accounts (e.g., Google+, Twitter, Facebook, LinkedIn, MySpace, Pinterest), they might forget comments, photographs, and other information in their digital footprint. Although it may seem unlikely that a reputable business would use or sell private information that identifies customers, a minimal compilation of anonymous information (e.g., zip code, date of birth) could generate enough information to identify someone. Thus, it is important to take note of which companies respect consumer privacy and of your opt-in or opt-out settings for you to hear from business partners.

Main Social Media Platforms and Disclosure.

Disclosure on each of these main platforms (e.g., Google+, Facebook/Instagram, LinkedIn, Pinterest) helps you build and maintain relationships and conduct business. Yet it is important for you to stay smart—and safe—with what you post, to whom, and when. "We are in Hawaii for a week" is not designed to say "Come rob us this week!" Common use of social networking brings disclosure issues to different audiences. There are some vulnerabilities to be aware of: consumers' loss of information control, privacy intrusions due to friends' behaviors, and digital vigilance. Unauthorized viewers, employers, and third-party applications can gain access to social media profiles.[50] For instance, that ex who is no longer your Facebook friend may be friends with your friend. Or, a future employer may want to check out your digital profile upon deciding whether or not to interview or hire you. Most U.S. employers check out candidates' social media profiles—most often without their consent—before making hiring decisions. Is your social media digital footprint ready for employers to see? If not, you may try to find ways to keep your social media activity private. Realizing that future employers do not want to see spring break trips, fraternity parties, and your brother's new dog, you may keep your settings private. Graduates often need to conceal their social networking profiles during job searches to avoid misunderstandings and to disassociate from a

nonprofessional image.[51] Now there are different social media platforms which you may use for different images in different contexts. For one, the LinkedIn platform is more appropriate for sharing your resume, your skills, your employment history, and any professional accolades. The group setting in LinkedIn is wonderful to help you find, make, and maintain connections in your industry. Via social media, it is simple and convenient to post to these specific audiences when something of interest comes about relevant to these groups only. A second social media platform that crosses professional and personal boundaries is Pinterest. Pinterest is reminiscent of the days when consumers would rip out ads or articles of interest to pin to their corkboard. You can post articles relevant to business or pleasure. Pinterest is also a wonderful shopping tool. Love that iPad case? Pin it up to your Pinterest page for your friends to check out. Social media brings the social back into e-commerce. Meanwhile, the Google+ and Facebook platforms may not be as appropriate, as many of those circles or friends are from high school, family, college, and so on and would likely not appreciate a status post that speaks directly to a niche professional audience. Google+ is the sixth most popular social media site (behind Facebook, Twitter, LinkedIn, Pinterest, and the new MySpace).[52] Facebook is larger in terms of world users than most of the world's nations and has about 750 million different visitors per month.[53] Facebook has the highest social media brand visibility score. The second most visited is Twitter, with 250 million different visitors per month[54]—impressive, but not on Facebook's tails.

14-6 SYNERGIZING WITH OTHER IBP TOOLS

It is a must-do to synergize a brand's digital presence with the other marketing tools in your toolkit. Not every communication or sales objective needs a hammer (national advertising); some objectives are much better suited to a precise, small screwdriver (a local event sponsorship). Most times, you will need both tools, at least, to get the job done. Case in point: see the Fiat ad in Exhibit 14.15. It shows the changing trend is to drive (no pun intended) interested car consumers to the auto brand's virtual showroom instead of, or as a means to, the dealership. For consumers, this gives a chance to get to know the brand's models and specs and to feel more empowered before the sometimes daunting task of car shopping with a salesperson. Thus, Fiat uses a few marketing tools and makes sure

EXHIBIT 14.15 Fiat notes that digital is important in car advertising in order to get attention and to drive, no pun intended, interested parties to their dealership site. They note with their convertible ad that nothing turns heads like going topless.

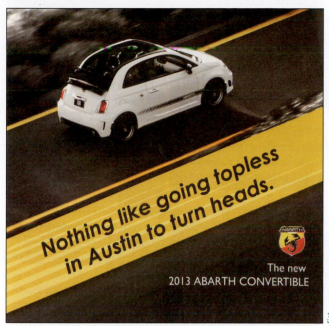

Nothing like going topless in Austin to turn heads.

The new
2013 ABARTH CONVERTIBLE

the tools are used synergistically. Consider synergizing digital media with other tools in your toolkit, such as advergaming, sales promos, coupons, contests, and other price deals.

14-6a Video Games and Advergaming

Consumers spent $24.75 billion on video games and related accessories the last year data was available. Of this, almost a third was digital content purchases. Games are rated "E" for everyone and "T" for teen, but the vast majority (73 percent) are coded for everyone. Thus, while some games get media attention for violence, most games are not particularly violent. Those birds don't seem particularly angry or violent and are a pop culture hit seen on lunchboxes and T-shirts; we wouldn't be shocked if they get their own cartoon TV show in the near future. *Angry Birds* aside, those video games that are violent can be *quite* violent; thus are a legitimate concern for public policy as well as parents.

You may be surprised that the "gamer" stereotype may not be accurate. So, do you envision a 16-year-old boy wearing a hoodie, on his game system, eating a bowl of cereal as the typical gamer? Could be. But the average game player is age 30, and the most frequent game buyer is age 35. Almost half of the players are

women. This is an attractive demographic and psychographic as gamers are relatively young, digital, on social media, and have peer influence. The peer influence may be seen via social media. Note the success of social media app games such as *Words with Friends, Angry Birds With Friends*, or *FarmVille* from gaming companies Zynga and Rovio. Social media and gaming are synergizing (just as marketing, advertising, and PR seem to be blurring definitional lines). Gaming has become more social; over 60 percent play with others virtually or in person. The growing advergaming market is in mobile gaming, because one in three gamers play on their smartphone.[55]

Different than an ad shown during a game, advertising and brand placement within video games is called **advergaming**. Cicchirillo and Lin note some points and differences of types of advergames.[56] Advergames are designed with the intent of promoting and marketing a brand; the game content centers around the brand. Note that there are levels of brand promotion within an advergame. Advergaming brand integration can occur at an associative (lowest), illustrative (medium), or demonstrative (highest) level.[57] An associative advergame brand integration merely makes a brand association during the game; for example, consider a Toyota billboard in the scenery of an auto-racing game. Advergaming is often at the associative level; it is done primarily via embedded billboards and posters in video games. For example, the auto-racing game from Electronic Arts, *Need for Speed: Carbon,* is full of ads on billboards, storefronts, and the racing cars themselves.

An illustrative advergame brand integration integrates a brand spokesperson or personality as a main character within the game; for example, the Pillsbury Doughboy would be a character in an advergame at the illustrative level. A demonstrative advergaming brand integration features the brand, service, or product as a key part of the game. In some demonstrative advergames, the game has consumers learn about and virtually use the products within the game to advance to higher levels of the game. Axe, a Unilever brand, launched one of its man-spray products via a demonstrative advergame. In this SIM-like game, the player navigated a virtual world in search of the man-spray (more accurately a body spray marketed toward teenage guys who traditionally would think of body sprays as girly). In this game, the man-spray was needed to win the girl in the advergame.

A question for advertisers to address is the effectiveness of in-game placement at each level. Although there is some evidence of a positive effect on brand recall, there is also evidence that repeated playing of the game can have a negative effect on players' attitudes toward embedded brands,[58] which could be due to a wear-out effect, also seen in some traditional advertising research.

Cicchirillo and Lin note that advergames are under ethical scrutiny; especially, ethical concerns to advergaming are greatest when geared toward children.[59] Often, as many as one in three advergames ask the player, presumably a child, to pass the game along to a friend. Hence, when considering this emerging, and plausibly fun, tool, think about the appropriateness of targeting children with the content, how they may not be able to yet process the content as more than a video game, and if it is appropriate to ask children to pass along the brand message to their friends. Perhaps this tool is best used for prosocial messages toward adolescents (e.g., anti-cyber bullying, peer pressure, the role of sports, and a healthy lifestyle). There is a difference in the way advergames tool may be put to use by for-profit and nonprofit marketers,[60] as the nonprofit marketers may seek to create awareness of a social cause or to prompt a positive change in consumer behavior.

14-6b Sales Promotion

The digital and interactive options on the Internet are ideally suited to executing various aspects of sales promotion as part of the IBP effort. Coupon distribution and contests are the leading tools that are well suited to digital/interactive implementation, but sampling and trial offers can be promoted as well. The newer online sales promotion ideas are flash sales, more accurately sales events. E-tailers such as Rue La La and Gilt (now launching Gilt Man) have daily sample sale events. Such emerging forms of sales promotion enhance trial use and give consumers opportunities to check out new products from favorite as well as new brands, without the pressure of a salesperson.

Coupons. Companies such as Retail-Me-Not from Austin, Texas, share online coupon codes with the world for e-commerce. Other **social couponing** sites, or sites that give or sell price discounts under the condition that a set number of other consumers buy or download the deal, like Groupon, distribute coupons via the sites of other commercial online services. E-centives simply allows users to print coupons on their home printers and then take them to the store for redemption. The company charges clients anywhere from $3 to $15 per thousand coupons distributed. The average cost to manufacturers for coupons distributed via freestanding inserts or in magazines is $7 per thousand. However, only a small portion of those coupons are even clipped (2–3 percent redemption

rate), whereas with online coupons the manufacturer is paying only per thousand clipped, or in this case printed, by consumers. This makes digital distribution more effective in getting the coupons into the hands of consumers.

Contests and Sweepstakes. Sites like iwon.com and LuckySurf.com run ongoing contests to try to gain the loyalty of Web users. But firms like Pepsi and Disney partner with portals like Yahoo! to run contests that draw attention to the brand over the Web along with similar promotions being run off-line. Pepsi partnered with Yahoo! for an under-the-bottle-cap promotion that allowed users to earn points or discounts from under-the-cap awards on bottles of brands across the Pepsi line. The contest was also launched on network TV and local spot radio. Drinkers of Pepsi brands were able to redeem points online and accumulate enough points to purchase goods or get discounts from merchants like Sony Music and Foot Locker.

Sampling, Trial Offers, Price-Off Deals. Firms can use their websites or email communications to offer consumers a wide range of sales promotion special deals. Samples, trial offers, and price-offs (discounts) can be offered over the Internet either with email campaigns, pop-up or banner ads, or directly at the company website. Surfers merely need to click through on an interactive ad, respond to an email, or visit the website to explore and take advantage of the offer. One advantage of using the Internet for these sales promotion techniques is that the firm acquires the consumer's email information for new prospects and achieves a de facto opt-in contact.

14-6c Public Relations and Publicity

Companies can use the Web to disseminate information about the firm in a classic public relations sense. Web organizations like Business Wire (www.businesswire.com) and PR Newswire (www.prnewswire.com) offer services where firms can request the dissemination of a press release over the Internet. These are often highly targeted press releases. Cost of the service varies by topic category—business, entertainment, news, or sports. Generally, a domestic national press release is $525 for 400 words and $135 for a 100-word release. Global distribution is $1,995. Business Wire is also able to provide a targeted email distribution of the release for 50 cents per destination—a little pricey for most companies to consider. These press releases can be picked up by major news services and online newspapers like the Huffington Post.

EXHIBIT 14.16 BMW is a leader in digital media. In their ads for the BMW X5 with xDrive, the ads show the dealer site, but the true focus, as it should be in product marketing for luxury goods, is on the product. Note the four distinct views of their SUV.

SAND. GRAVEL. ASPHALT. ICE.
YOU'LL FORGET THERE'S
A DIFFERENCE.

When you're on the road, you shouldn't be focused on what kind of road it is. And with the BMW X5 you won't. That's because it comes with xDrive, BMW's intelligent all-wheel-drive system that automatically adjusts to any road condition—so you don't have to. Add to that, no-cost maintenance for 4 years or 50,000 miles and room to seat seven, and it becomes clear the BMW X5 can take you anywhere. Comfortably.

THE BMW X5 WITH xDRIVE.

NO-COST MAINTENANCE

4 YRS / 50K MILES¹

BMW of Austin | 7011 McNeil Drive | Austin, TX 78729 | 512-343-3500 | bmwofaustin.com

¹Whichever comes first. For complete details on BMW Ultimate Service,® visit bmwusa.com/ultimateservice.
©2013 BMW of North America, LLC. The BMW name, model names and logo are registered trademarks.

14-6d Direct Marketing, E-Commerce, and M-Commerce

The Internet is extremely well suited to implementing a direct marketing IBP effort. Aside from the direct contact through email, mobile marketing, or virtual mail, direct marketing efforts can be coordinated with traditional media advertising campaigns through television, radio, newspapers, and magazines by directing consumers to either company websites or e-commerce sites that sell a variety of brands. One of the major shifts in the auto industry is in changing from a direct marketing model to a salesperson model; traditionally, a consumer would have to go to a dealer to get pricing and other info. Now, the consumer is more empowered with sites such as KellyBlueBook.

com to get pricing information and other sites for consumer reviews. Still, auto brands such as Subaru and BMW drive consumers to their dealer websites, or to the brand sites—as Exhibit 14.16 shows. On BMW's site, a digital leader, consumers can design their own BMW with their choice of color, interior, sport package, rims, audio, and other features. This is a way to use e-commerce to engage consumers prior to the dealer visit.

Email. The strength of email marketing is due to inherent cost and media advantages. For one, email is one of the least expensive marketing tools and provides the highest return on investment relative to other forms of online marketing.[61] Second, email marketing is fast, flexible, and up-to-date.[62] Third, email's further edge over other communication media is the wide variety of scopes for design (e.g., pictures, sounds, flash animations, or videos).[63] Fourth, and perhaps a most desirable quality, is the ability of enhanced campaign effectiveness measurement (e.g., via tracking click-through rates).[64] In consideration of the above-named advantages, advertisers are increasingly recognizing email marketing as an effective digital tool.

Despite these benefits, there are some disadvantages associated with email marketing. First, spammers have compromised privacy and tainted the general attitude toward email marketing messages. The second veritable challenge confronting marketers is information overload and consumers' desire to cut through online clutter. The thousands of emails and embedded information that reach consumers daily exceed the limited processing capacity of the human memory.[65] To overcome this limitation, advertisers can combat information overload with eye-catching and attention-getting advertising design. Combining style with the interactive nature of email videos, embedding a video in email can be an effective marketing tool—that is, if there are no technical inhibitors preventing the video from downloading promptly and easily, which is the third limitation. A fourth limitation to email, specific to

BMW

email with video, is that it may reach the recipient in a place where the video could disturb others with the sound. Despite these limitations, video online has demonstrated itself as favorable to consumers and as a preferred form of media—especially if it goes viral.

Viral Video. While it sounds like a disease, viral is a good thing in industry lingo. The top viral brand messages have over 100 million views. Consumers or advertisers can encourage viral marketing. **Viral marketing** is the process of consumers marketing to consumers over the Internet through electronic or in-person word of mouth transmitted through emails and electronic mailing lists. YouTube is often the host of video-based viral marketing. A venue for viral campaigns is online videos of either television ads or follow-ons to television ads; Super Bowl ads are often leaked or posted officially in a viral manner before the game to generate buzz. What are your favorite viral videos? Ours are the goats that sound like screaming humans; these are especially fabulous when juxtaposed over some Taylor Swift, Usher, or Christiana Aguilera songs. Most viral videos, like the goats, have a humor appeal. As of writing, the top viral video content were[66]: (1) The Harlem Shake—Miami Heat edition; (2) PlayStation 4; (3) What Most Schools Don't Teach—from Code.org, this message from Mark Zuckerberg of Facebook and Bill Gates of Microsoft shares why you should learn to code; (4) The Harlem Shake–Red Bull Skydiving edition; (5) Separators–Oreo's viral campaign from one of our favorite agency Wieden+Kennedy in Portland, OR. This shows that the top viral videos currently are plugging brands (Miami Heat, Sony, Code.org, Red Bull, and Oreo) in innovative ways. Did we mention that the Harlem Shake–Miami Heat edition had 22,285,751 views—*in a single week?*

Viral is good. Use it or lose out on the viral movement.

Mobile Marketing. Mobile marketing is the process of reaching consumers on Internet-enabled mobile devices like smartphones, iPods, and tablet e-readers. As you can see in Insights Online [Exhibit 14.17], we are in midst of an exciting mobile marketing movement. Even though mobile marketing is really a phenomenon brought about by mobile, wireless access through smartphones, MP3 players, laptops, and tablet devices, it represents a form of direct marketing as well by virtue of wireless technology. Almost 86 percent of the world's population now has a mobile device; at last count there were over 6 billion mobile subscriptions worldwide.[67] Because most people in the world are mobile subscribers, marketers can initiate direct marketing campaigns if they are opt-in (in theory desired by the consumer). For example, it can be helpful to get a text from Pizza Hut on a Friday night for free breadsticks with a pizza order that weekend—if you were going to order a pizza that night anyway. That said, it can be annoying and intrusive—even costing the consumer if they don't have unlimited texts.

It is not only that email campaigns, text messaging, or sales promotions will reach mobile users directly on their devices, but also firms can sponsor mobile videos that are downloaded on video handsets. IBP communications through mobile devices achieve surprisingly high recall and effectiveness if the consumer prefers to enable location. This way, any messages you get can be from local businesses. Again, this brings a new privacy issue. Most consumers with smartphones get messages, albeit some unwanted, to their phones, which is an industry to watch for changes in with geo-cashing, opt-in laws, and other pending mobile guidelines. As we write, the industry review board Interactive Advertising Bureau is working on mobile measurement guidelines, and industry reports based on big data with Facebook are creating new exposure rate metrics for social media.[68] In sum, mobile and other digital or social media tools seem to work due to their inherent arousal.[69]

INSIGHTS ONLINE

14.17 Go online to see the AdAge feature, "The Mobile Marketing Movement."

SUMMARY

1 **Understand the role of digital and social media in advertising and IBP along with the options available to brands through digital or social media.**

In sum, the role of digital and social media in advertising and IBP is a crucial one. Web 2.0 distinguishes the progression of the Internet to interactive online communication, participation, and engagement. There is an array of creative and strategic options to brands available through digital or social media.

2 **See the importance in virtual identity for consumers and brands online.**

To best execute in digital platforms, it is key to understand online consumer behavior, namely the importance of virtual identity for consumers and brands online. Brands can measure their online reputation score and should manage their brand identity and online reputation.

 3 **Understand the basics of digital advertising and e-search.**

Digital advertising and e-search have progressed, so know the basics of them and the pricing models such as CPC. The basics of e-commerce relate to IBP, and it can stem from e-advertising, social media, and/or e-search.

4 **Know the basics of e-commerce as related to IBP and how it can stem from e-advertising, social media, and e-search.**

E-commerce can be leveraged by understanding e-search and online advertising; digital advertisers should look for ways to enhance click-through and conversions to sales.

 5 **Note the advantages of digital and social media for implementing advertising and IBP campaigns, along with noting the dark side of social media, such as security and privacy concerns.**

The advantages of digital and social media for implementing advertising and IBP campaigns include target market flexibility, interactivity, consumer engagement, and the ability to leverage a consumer's digital footprint with a brand relationship among others. The main dark side issues about social media are privacy, security, and authenticity concerns.

 6 **See how to synergize with different IBP tools.**

Digital and social media have many advantages for implementing advertising and IBP campaigns and synergize with different IBP tools such as advergaming, sponsorship, events, viral video, mobile marketing, email, sampling, POP, and traditional media.

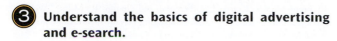
KEY TERMS

Web 2.0	pay-per-click (PPC)	big data
user-generated content (UGC)	sponsored stories	digital footprint
consumer-generated media (CGM)	post ads	interactivity
earned media	Web ads	click-through
owned media	app ads	cyber-identity theft
paid media	display/banner ads	online resistance
social media	I-Traffic Index	privacy seal
blog	pop-under ad	advergaming
micro-blogs	pop-up ad	social couponing
video sharing websites	interstitial	viral marketing
photo sharing sites	e-search	mobile marketing
social news websites	paid search	
virtual identity	search engine optimization (SEO)	

ENDNOTES

1. Angeline Close, ed., *Online Consumer Behavior: Theory and Research in Social Media, Advertising, and E-tail* (New York/London: Routledge/Taylor & Francis Group, 2012).

2. Ibid.

3. Elsamari Botha and Adam J. Mills, "Managing New Media: Tools for Brand Management in Social Media," in Angeline G. Close (Ed.), *Online Consumer Behavior: Theory and Research in Social Media, Advertising, and E-tail* (New York/London: Routledge/Taylor & Francis Group, 2012), 83–100.

4. Ibid.

5. Pierre Berthon, Leyland Pitt, D. Cyr, and Colin Campbell, "E-readiness and Trust: Macro and Micro Dualities for e-Commerce in a Global Environment," *International Marketing Review,* vol. 25, no. 6 (2008), 700–714.

6. Don Tapscott and Anthony D. Williams, *Wikinomics: How Mass Collaboration Changes Everything* (New York: Penguin, 2007).

7. Angeline Close, ed., *Online Consumer Behavior: Theory and Research in Social Media, Advertising, and E-tail* (New York/London: Routledge/Taylor & Francis Group, 2012).

8. Satya Menon and Dilip Soman, "Managing the Power of Curiosity for Effective Web Advertising Strategies," *Journal of Advertising,* vol. 31, no. 3 (Fall 2002), 1–14.

9. Angeline Close, ed., *Online Consumer Behavior: Theory and Research in Social Media, Advertising, and E-tail* (New York/London: Routledge/Taylor & Francis Group, 2012).

10. Ibid.

11. Andreas M. Kaplan and Michael Haenlein, "Users of the World, Unite! The Challenges and Opportunities of Social Media," *Business Horizons,* vol. 53, no. 1 (2010), 59–68.

12. Dan Zarella, *The Social Media Marketing Book* (North Sebastopol, CA: O'Reilly Media, 2010).

13. Angeline Close, ed., *Online Consumer Behavior: Theory and Research in Social Media, Advertising, and E-tail* (New York/London: Routledge/Taylor & Francis Group, 2012).

14. Elsamari Botha and Adam J. Mills, "Managing New Media: Tools for Brand Management in Social Media," in Angeline G. Close (Ed.), *Online*

Consumer Behavior: Theory and Research in Social Media, Advertising, and E-tail (New York/London: Routledge/Taylor & Francis Group, 2012), 83–100.

15. Ibid.

16. Ibid.

17. Ibid.

18. Ibid.

19. Angeline Close, *E-Dating and Information Technology,* Doctoral Dissertation, Athens, GA: The University of Georgia Press, 2006.

20. Ibid.

21. Elsamari Botha, Mana Farshid, and Leyland Pitt, "How Sociable? An Exploratory Study of University Brand Visibility in Social Media," *South African Journal of Business Management,* vol. 42, no. 2 (2011), 15–23.

22. Ibid.

23. Source: http://techcrunch.com/2013/06/06/facebook-simplifies-ads/.

24. Satya Menon and Dilip Soman, "Managing the Power of Curiosity for Effective Web Advertising Strategies," *Journal of Advertising,* vol. 31, no. 3 (Fall 2002), 1–14.

25. Stephen Baker, "Pop-Up Ads Had Better Start Pleasing," *BusinessWeek,* December 8, 2003, 40.

26. IAB, Interactive Advertising Bureau, IAB.com, accessed January 2013.

27. Search Engine Watch, http://searchenginewatch.com/article/2067271/Worldwide-Internet-Now-Serving-61-Billion-Searches-per-Month, accessed March 2013.

28. http://www.techspot.com/news/48254-collusion-for-chrome-lets-users-visualize-website-trackers-third-parties.html

29. J. P. Morgan, http://www.ipaydna.biz/J.P.-Morgan-Report-US,-Global-e-Commerce-Industry-Set-For-Significant-Growth--n-31.htm, accessed March 2013.

30. Pierre Berthon, Leyland Pitt, D. Cyr, and Colin Campbell, "E-readiness and Trust: Macro and Micro Dualities for e-Commerce in a Global Environment," *International Marketing Review,* vol. 25, no. 6 (2008), 700–714.

31. Andreas M. Kaplan and Michael Haenlein, "Users of the World, Unite! The Challenges and Opportunities of Social Media," *Business Horizons,* vol. 53, no. 1 (2010), 59–68.

32. Pew Internet & American Life Project, http://pewinternet.org/Commentary/2012/March/Pew-Internet-Social-Networking-full-detail.aspx, accessed March 2013

33. Kelli S. Burns and Richard J. Lutz, "The Function of Format," *Journal of Advertising,* vol. 35, no. 1 (Spring 2006), 53–63.

34. Andrew Hampp, "Live TV's Alive as Ever, Boosted by Social Media," *Advertising Age,* February 15, 2010, 1–2.

35. Fuyuan Shen, "Banner Advertisement Pricing, Measurement, and Pretesting Practices: Perspectives from Interactive Agencies," *Journal of Advertising,* vol. 31, no. 3 (Fall 2002), 59–68.

36. Ereni Marcos, Lauren L. Labrecque, and George R. Milne, "Web 2.0 and Consumers' Digital Footprint: Managing Privacy Disclosure Choices in Social Media," in Angeline G. Close (Ed.), *Online Consumer Behavior: Theory and Research in Social Media, Advertising, and E-tail* (New York/London: Routledge/Taylor & Francis Group, 2012), 157–184.

37. George R. Milne and Shalini Bahl, "Are There Differences between Consumers' and Marketers' Privacy Expectations? A Segment- and Technology-Level Analysis," *Journal of Public Policy & Marketing,* vol. 29, no. 1 (2010), 138–149.

38. Amit Poddar, Jill Mostellar, and Pam Scholder-Ellen, "Consumers' Rules of Engagement in Online Information Exchanges," *Journal of Consumer Affairs,* vol. 43, no. 3 (2009), 419–448.

39. Mary Madden, Susannah Fox, Aaron Smith, and Jessica Vitak, "Digital Footprints: Online Identity Management and Search in the Age of Transparency," 2007, http://pewresearch.org/pubs/663/digital-footprints.

40. Ereni Marcos, Lauren L. Labrecque, and George R. Milne, "Web 2.0 and Consumers' Digital Footprint: Managing Privacy Disclosure Choices in Social Media," in Angeline G. Close (Ed.), *Online Consumer Behavior: Theory and Research in Social Media, Advertising, and E-tail* (New York/London: Routledge/Taylor & Francis Group, 2012), 157–184.

41. Lauren I. Labrecque, Shabnam H. A. Zanjani, and George R. Milne, "Authenticity in Online Communications: Examining Antecedents and Consequences," in Angeline G. Close (Ed.), *Online Consumer Behavior: Theory and Research in Social Media, Advertising, and E-tail* (New York/London: Routledge/Taylor & Francis Group, 2012), 133–156.

42. Angeline G. Close, G. M. Zinkhan, and R. Z. Finney, *Cyber Identity Theft.* American Marketing Association, 2007.

43. Goodwin, Cathy, "Privacy: Recognition of a Consumer Right," *Journal of Public Policy & Marketing,* vol. 10, no. 1 (1991), 149–166.

44. Ereni Marcos, Lauren L. Labrecque, and George R. Milne, "Web 2.0 and Consumers' Digital Footprint: Managing Privacy Disclosure Choices in Social Media," in Angeline G. Close (Ed.), *Online Consumer Behavior: Theory and Research in Social Media, Advertising, and E-tail* (New York/London: Routledge/Taylor & Francis Group, 2012), 157–184.

45. Milne, George R., Andrew Rohm, and Shalini Bahl, "Consumers' Protection of Online Privacy and Identity," *Journal of Consumer Affairs,* vol. 38, no. 2 (2004), 217–232.

46. Ereni Marcos, Lauren L. Labrecque, and George R. Milne, "Web 2.0 and Consumers' Digital Footprint: Managing Privacy Disclosure Choices in Social Media," in Angeline G. Close (Ed.), *Online Consumer Behavior: Theory and Research in Social Media, Advertising, and E-tail* (New York/London: Routledge/Taylor & Francis Group, 2012), 157–184.

47. George R. Milne, Shalini Bahl, and Andrew Rohm, "Toward a Framework for Assessing Covert Marketing Practices," *Journal of Public Policy & Marketing,* vol. 27, no. 1 (2008), 57–62.

48. Anthony D. Miyazaki "Online Privacy and the Disclosure of Cookie Use: Effects on Consumer Trust and Anticipated Patronage," *Journal of Public Policy and Marketing,* vol. 27, no. 1 (Spring 2008), 19–33.

49. Anthony D. Miyazaki and Sandeep Krishnamurthy, "Internet Seals of Approval: Effects on Online Privacy Policies and Consumer Perceptions," *Journal of Consumer Affairs,* vol. 36, no. 1 (2002), 28–49.

50. Ereni Marcos, Lauren L. Labrecque, and George R. Milne, "Web 2.0 and Consumers' Digital Footprint: Managing Privacy Disclosure Choices in Social Media," in Angeline G. Close (Ed.), *Online Consumer Behavior: Theory and Research in Social Media, Advertising, and E-tail* (New York/London: Routledge/Taylor & Francis Group, 2012), 157–184.

51. Ibid.

52. EbizMBA, "Top 15 Most Popular Social Networking Sites," http://www.ebizmba.com/articles/social-networking-websites, accessed March 2013.

53. Ibid.

54. Ibid.

55. Industry Facts, Entertainment Software Association, 2013, www.theesa.com/facts, accessed March 2013.

56. Vincent Cicchirillo and J. Lin. "Stop Playing with Your Food: A Comparison of For-Profit and Non-Profit Food Related Advergames," *Journal of Advertising Research,* vol. 51, no. 3 (2011), 484–498.

57. Ibid.

58. Cauberghe Verolien and Patrick De Pelsmacker, "Advergames: The Impact of Brand Prominence and Game Repetition on Brand Responses," *Journal of Advertising,* vol. 39, no. 1 (Spring 2010), 5–18.

59. Vincent Cicchirillo and J. Lin. "Stop Playing with Your Food: A Comparison of For-Profit and Non-Profit Food Related Advergames," *Journal of Advertising Research,* vol. 51, no. 3, (2011), 484–498.

60. Ibid.

61. Oleg Pavlov, Nigel Melville, and Robert Plice, "Toward a Sustainable Email Marketing Infrastructure," *Journal of Business Research,* vol. 61, no. 11 (2008), 1191–1199.

62. Debbie Du Frene, Brian Engelland, Carol Lehman, and Rodney Pearson, "Changes in Consumer Attitudes Resulting from Participation in a Permission E-Mail-Campaign," *Journal of Current Issues and Research in Advertising,* vol. 27, no. 1 (2005), 65–77.

63. Vincent Cicchirillo and J. Lin. "Stop Playing with Your Food: A Comparison of For-Profit and Non-Profit Food Related Advergames," *Journal of Advertising Research,* vol. 51, no. 3, (2011), 484–498.

64. Nigel Melville, Aaron Stevens, Robert Plice, and Oleg Pavlov, "Unsolicited Commercial E-Mail: Empirical Analysis of a Digital Commons," *International Journal of Electronic Commerce,* vol. 10, no. 4 (2006), 143–168.

65. Jacob Jacoby, "Information Load and Decision Quality: Some Contested Issues," *Journal of Marketing Research,* vol. 14, no. 4 (1997), 569–573.

66. Viral Video Chart. Powered by Visable Measures. *AdAge,* http://adage.com/article/the-viral-video-chart/bill-gates-mark-zuckerberg-jack-dorsey-land-profit-code-org-viral-chart/240165/, accessed March 2013.

67. Global mobile statistics, http://mobithinking.com/mobile-marketing-tools/latest-mobile-stats/a#subscribers, accessed March 2013.

68. Resolution Media and Kenshoo Social, *Metrics that Matter: Introducing Exposure Rate, A New Facebook Advertising KPI,* Industry Report, June 2012.

69. S. S. Sundar and S. Kalyanaraman, "Arousal, Memory, and Impression Formation Effects of Animation Speed in Web Advertising," *Journal of Advertising,* vol. 33, no. 1 (Spring 2004), 7–17.

PART 5

Integrated Brand Promotion

Part 5 of the text brings us to the end of our journey in the study of advertising and integrated brand promotion (IBP). This part highlights the full range of communication tools a firm can use in creating an IBP campaign. Throughout the text, we have been emphasizing that IBP is key to effective brand development. You will find that the variety and breadth of communication options discussed here represent a tremendous opportunity for marketers to be creative and break through the clutter in today's marketplace. Each of the tools discussed in Part 5 has the unique capability to influence the audience's perception of and desire to own a brand while ensuring that consistency with advertising is maintained. This part of the text brings you the latest emerging techniques in support media, product placement, branded entertainment, and influencer marketing and the role social media play across all the options.

CHAPTER

15

Sales Promotion, Point-of-Purchase Advertising, and Support Media All the techniques of both consumer and trade sales promotion are discussed. Coupons, price-off deals, premiums, contests, sweepstakes, sampling, trial offers, refunds, rebates, frequency programs, and point-of-purchase displays are highlighted for the consumer market, while incentives, allowances, trade shows, and cooperative advertising are presented in this chapter as they relate to trade and business promotion. Coverage of sales promotion and new media provides the most forward-thinking discussion of using new distribution and communication techniques for sales promotion as well as the use of mobile or location marketing for point-of-purchase promotions. The chapter concludes with extensive treatment of the wide array of out-of-home support media available to advertisers, including outdoor signage, billboards, transit advertising, aerial advertising, cinema advertising, packaging, and good old (and new media) directory advertising.

CHAPTER

16

Event Sponsorship, Product Placements, and Branded Entertainment This chapter highlights the thought-provoking issue of the convergence of Madison & Vine—that is, the phenomenon of advertising, branding, and entertainment converging to provide consumers a wider array of "touch points" with brands. The chapter continues from here to review the growing allure of event sponsorships with emphasis on the experiential impact of events on consumers and the "leverage" events can have on communication to other important constituents like salespeople and employees. Product placements on television, in movies, and in video games are discussed as a way to embed brand images "authentically" in consumer lifestyle activities. The chapter then takes a deep dive into the provocative subject of branded entertainment. If you had any lingering doubts about the power of IBP, the topics discussed in this chapter will dispel those.

CHAPTER

17

Integrating Direct Marketing and Personal Selling Consumers' persistent desire for greater convenience and marketers' never-ending search for competitive advantage continue to create an emphasis on direct marketing in IBP programs. With direct marketing, the opportunity exists not only to communicate to a target audience but also to seek an immediate response. You will learn why direct marketing continues to remain popular among consumers, what media are used by direct marketers to deliver their messages, and how direct marketing creates special challenges for achieving IBP. In the excitement and, indeed, drama of digital media options, we sometimes forget the powerful role personal selling has across many IBP strategies. The chapter provides a perspective on this important IBP process, including the basic types of personal selling.

CHAPTER

18

Public Relations, Influencer Marketing, and Corporate Advertising Chapter 18 is a chapter that has new and exciting material with full coverage of "influencer" marketing and new issues in corporate advertising (fueled by corporate social responsibility). This chapter begins with a discussion of the expanding role public relations is now playing in the overall IBP effort of many firms and differentiates between proactive (creating "buzz" for a brand) and reactive (damage control) public relations strategies. You will learn that public relations is an important option in IBP, but rarely will it ever take the lead role. The coverage of influencer marketing is the best and most contemporary you will find anywhere. Professional influencer programs, peer-to-peer programs, buzz and viral marketing, cultivating "connectors"—it's all here. This chapter concludes with a wide-ranging and complete discussion of corporate advertising. Various forms of corporate advertising are identified, and the way each can be used as a means for building the reputation of an organization in the eyes of key constituents is discussed. In the current era, corporate advertising is being used more frequently as a way to demonstrate a firm's social and environment commitments.

CHAPTER 15

Sales Promotion, Point-of-Purchase Advertising, and Support Media

After reading and thinking about this chapter, you will be able to do the following:

1. Explain the importance and growth of modern sales promotion.

2. Describe the sales promotion techniques used in the consumer market.

3. Describe the sales promotion techniques used in the trade channel and business markets.

4. Identify the risks to the brand of using sales promotion.

5. Understand the role and techniques of point-of-purchase advertising.

6. Describe the role of support media in a comprehensive IBP strategy.

15-1 THE ROLE OF SALES PROMOTION, POINT-OF-PURCHASE ADVERTISING, AND SUPPORT MEDIA

Sales promotion, point-of-purchase (P-O-P) advertising, and support media (like billboards, transit advertising, and packaging) offer advertisers a wide range of opportunities to communicate to consumers that are vastly different from traditional mass media or digital media. These IBP tools work in ways that traditional media and digital media don't. Consider these ways of attracting you to brands. You walk into a hotel room and a sensor sets the lights and the room temperature, switches on the TV to ESPN at the right volume—the loyalty program on your smartphone knows all this. You're on your way home from work and you get a text message that the local grocery store has a special on Sobe Water, which you drink—the grocery store scanner knows this. Or, you drive by a billboard and it flashes, "Hi Lucy, you need an

oil change in 312 miles." The billboard can talk to your car GPS and computer. This is not futuristic, Orwellian speculation. All the technology is in place for these kinds of sales promotions and P-O-P IBP campaigns to take place. The potential for knowing when and where consumers are is blurring the lines between advertising and promotions. Google, for instance, knows that a large percentage of consumer mobile searches are local in nature and uses this information to make location-based sales promotions a timely and potent IBP tool.[1] There is an old saying in marketing that P-O-P is the "last three feet of marketing." With new technologies, that old saying may have to be changed to the "last three blocks or last three miles of marketing." But also keep in mind that while P-O-P plays a role at the point of purchase, it is not and can never be the leading tool in IPB. The more complex and information-rich tools of IBP are really what create brand loyalty and competitive advantage.

This chapter will explore all the possibilities and opportunities that sales promotion, P-O-P advertising, and other support media offer to the advertiser.

INSIGHTS ONLINE

15.1 Go online to see the AdAge feature, "Bacon Flavored Scope? An April Fool's Promotion?"

These are traditional tools of promotion, but they are being adapted quickly to new technologies available for forward-thinking IBP campaigns (see Insights Online [Exhibit 15.1] for an interesting example).

15-2 SALES PROMOTION DEFINED

Sales promotion is often a key component within an IBP campaign—particularly campaigns seeking short-term sales effects. Sales promotions like dealer incentives, consumer price discounts, and samples can attract attention and give new energy and word-of-mouth buzz to the overall advertising and the IBP effort. While mass media advertising is designed to build a brand image over time, sales promotion is designed to make things happen in the short run, particularly with new mobile or location-based techniques as just described. Used properly, sales promotion is capable of almost instant demand stimulation, like the kind that contests and sweepstakes can create. The "message" in a sales promotion features price reduction, free samples, a prize, or some other incentive for consumers to try a brand or for a retailer to feature the brand in a store. The Glad Tall Kitchen Bag package featured in Exhibit 15.2 is a classic example of a sales promotion, a free sample in this case, that could attract consumers' attention and get them to either try the product for the first time or switch brands.

Defined, **sales promotion** is the use of incentive techniques that create a perception of greater brand value among consumers, the trade, and business buyers. The intent is to generate a short-term increase in sales by motivating trial use, encouraging larger purchases, or stimulating repeat purchases. **Consumer-market sales promotion** can be either price promotions or not and includes the following:

- coupons/e-coupons
- price-off deals
- premiums
- contests and sweepstakes
- sampling and trial offers
- rebates
- loyalty/frequency programs
- gift cards

EXHIBIT 15.2 Sales promotion often creates the perception of greater value for the consumer. Here, the promise of a free sample inside the Glad Tall Kitchen Bag package is just such a sales promotion offer.

INSIGHTS ONLINE

15.3 Go online to see the AdAge feature, "Heinz Baked Beans Has a Cool and Creative Consumer Promotion That Gives Buyers a Musical Spoon That Fits with Each Flavor of Beans."

All these incentives are ways of inducing household consumers to try or eventually purchase a firm's brand rather than a competitor's brand. Notice that some incentives reduce price, offer a reward, or encourage a trip to the retailer. (See Insights Online [Exhibit 15.3] to find out how Heinz used sounds and shapes to entice customers.)

Trade-market sales promotion uses the following ways of motivating distributors, wholesalers, and retailers to stock and feature a firm's brand in their store merchandising programs:

- P-O-P displays
- incentives
- allowances
- cooperative advertising
- sales training

Business-market sales promotion is designed to cultivate buyers in organizations or corporations who are making purchase decisions about a wide range of products, including computers, office supplies, and consulting services. Techniques used for business buyers are similar to the trade-market techniques and include the following:

- trade shows
- premiums
- incentives
- loyalty/frequency programs

LO ①

15-3 THE IMPORTANCE AND GROWTH OF SALES PROMOTION

Sales promotion is designed to affect demand differently than advertising does. As we have learned, most advertising is designed to have awareness-, image-, and preference-building effects for a brand over the long run. The role of sales promotion, on the other hand, is primarily to elicit an immediate purchase from a customer group. Coupons, samples, rebates, contests and sweepstakes, and similar techniques offer household consumers, trade buyers, or business buyers an immediate incentive to choose one brand over another, as exemplified in Exhibit 15.4. Here AAA is offering

EXHIBIT 15.4 Marketers use a wide range of incentives in the sales promotion category to attract attention to a brand. Here, AAA is offering a price-off deal when consumers book a vacation through a AAA travel agent.

what is referred to as a price-off deal to consumers who book a vacation through AAA.

Other sales promotions, such as frequency programs (e.g., airline frequent-flyer programs), provide an affiliation value for a brand, which increases a consumer's ability and desire to identify with a particular brand. Sales promotions featuring price reductions, such as coupons, are effective in the convenience goods category (toothpaste, garbage bags, etc.), where frequent purchases, brand switching, and a perceived homogeneity (similarity) among brands characterize consumer behavior.

Sales promotions are used across all consumer goods categories and in the trade and business markets as well. When a firm determines that a more immediate response than advertising can accomplish is needed—whether the target customer is a household, business buyer, distributor, or retailer—sales promotions are designed to provide that effect. The goals for sales promotion versus those of advertising are compared in

EXHIBIT 15.5 Sales promotion and advertising serve different purposes in IBP. What would you describe as the key differences between the two based on the features listed here?

Purpose of Sales Promotion	Purpose of Advertising
Stimulate short-term demand	Cultivate long-term demand
Encourage brand switching	Encourage brand loyalty
Induce trial use	Encourage repeat purchases
Promote price orientation	Promote image/feature orientation
Obtain immediate, often measurable results	Obtain long-term effects, often difficult to measure

© Cengage Learning

INSIGHTS ONLINE

15.6 Go online to see the AdAge feature, "Viggle Uses Promotion via V-gifts, Where Brands Deliver Freebees to Users of Their App."

Exhibit 15.5. Notice the key differences in the goals for these different forms of promotion. Sales promotion encourages more immediate and short-term responses, whereas the purpose of advertising is to cultivate an image, loyalty, and repeat purchases over the long term. (See Insights Online [Exhibit 15.6] to more fully explore this concept.)

15-3a The Importance of Sales Promotion

The importance of sales promotion should not be underestimated. Sales promotion may not seem as stylish and sophisticated as mass media advertising or as exciting as new digital media opportunities, but expenditures on this tool are impressive. Big consumer products firms began shifting dollars out of media advertising and into promotions several years ago. The chairman and CEO of Procter & Gamble told analysts that the firm's advertising and IBP spending was shifting "and it's shifting from measured media to in-store, to the Internet, and to trial activity [i.e., product sampling]."[2] The development and management of an effective sales promotion program requires a major commitment by a firm. During any given year, it is typical that as much as 30 percent of brand management time is spent on designing, implementing, and overseeing sales promotions.

When a firm determines that a more immediate response than advertising can accomplish is needed— whether the target customer is a household, business buyer, distributor, or retailer—sales promotions are designed to provide that effect.

15-3b Growth in the Use of Sales Promotion

As mentioned above, many marketers have shifted the emphasis of their promotional spending during the past several years. Some has made its way to the Internet and mobile marketing, as we saw in the last chapter, and still more spending has found its way to consumer, trade, and business sales promotions. There are several reasons why many marketers have been shifting funds from mass media advertising to sales promotions. Let's consider these reasons now.

Demand for Greater Accountability. In an era of cost cutting and shareholder scrutiny, companies are demanding greater accountability across all functions, including marketing, advertising, and promotions. When activities are evaluated for their contribution to sales and profits, it is often difficult to draw specific conclusions regarding the effects of advertising. But the more immediate effects of sales promotions are typically easier to document. Various studies have shown that only 18 percent of TV advertising campaigns produced a short-term positive return on investment (ROI) on promotional dollars. Conversely, other studies have shown that P-O-P in-store displays have been shown to positively affect sales by as much as 35 percent in some product categories.[3]

Short-Term Orientation. Several factors have created a short-term orientation among managers. Pressures from stockholders to increase quarter-by-quarter revenue and profit per share are one factor. A bottom-line mentality is another. Many organizations are developing marketing plans—with rewards and punishments for manager performance—that are based on short-term revenue generation. This being the case, companies are seeking tactics that can have short-term effects. There is some sound reasoning behind the strategy, though. If a customer stops in for free fries, he or she might also buy a burger and drink—an immediate effect on sales. And a free product also presents the chance to "convert the curious into loyalists." McDonald's, for example, claims that at least half the customers who come in for free coffee wind up buying something else.[4]

Consumer Response to Promotions. The precision shopper in the contemporary marketplace is demanding greater value across all purchase situations, and that trend is battering over-priced brands. These precision shoppers search for extra value in every product purchase. Coupons, premiums, price-off deals, and other sales promotions increase the value of a brand in these shoppers' minds. Be careful here—coupons, price reduction, and value seeking do not necessarily mean consumers are choosing the *lowest*-priced item. Sales promotion techniques act as an incentive to purchase the brand *featuring* a promotion, even if another brand has a lower basic price. (See Insights Online [Exhibit 15.7] for an example of a special promotion used by Coca-Cola that became as noteworthy as its product.)

Proliferation of Brands. Each year, thousands of new brands are introduced into the consumer market. The drive by marketers to design products for specific market segments to satisfy ever more narrowly defined needs has caused a proliferation of brands that creates a mind-dulling maze for consumers. Consider this case of brand proliferation—in one 12-month period, Coca-Cola's new head of marketing launched 1,000 (not a typo) new drinks or new variations of existing brands worldwide (Has anybody tried Coca-Cola Blak? Has anybody even heard of Coca-Cola Blak?).[5] At any point in time, consumers are typically able to choose from about 60 spaghetti sauces, 100 snack chips, 50 laundry detergents, 90 cold remedies, and 60 disposable diaper varieties. As you can see in Exhibit 15.8, gaining attention in this blizzard of brands is no easy task. Because of this proliferation and "clutter" of brands, marketers turn to sales promotions—contests, coupons, premiums, loyalty programs, P-O-P displays—to gain some attention for their individual brands.

Increased Power of Retailers. Big retailers like Target, Home Depot, and Costco now dominate retailing in the United States. These powerful retailers have responded quickly and accurately to the new environment for retailing, where consumers are demanding more and better products and services at lower prices. Because of these consumer demands, retailers are, in turn, demanding more deals from manufacturers. Many of the deals are delivered in terms of trade-oriented sales promotions: P-O-P displays, slotting fees (payment for shelf space), case allowances, and co-op advertising allowances. In the end, manufacturers use more and more sales promotions to gain and maintain good relations with the powerful retailers—a critical link to the consumer. And retailers use the tools of sales promotion as competitive strategies against each other.

Clutter. A nagging and traditional problem in the advertising process is clutter. Many advertisers target the same customers because their research has led them to the same conclusion about whom to target. The result is that advertising media are cluttered with ads all seeking the attention of the same people. When consumers encounter a barrage of ads, they tune out (remember the discussion in Chapter 5). And clutter is getting worse, not better, across all media—including the Internet, where pop-ups and banners clutter nearly every website. One way to break through the clutter is to feature a sales promotion. In print ads, the featured deal is often a coupon. In television and radio advertising, sweepstakes, premium, and rebate offers can attract viewers' and listeners' attention. The combination of advertising and creative sales promotions has proven to be a good way to break through the clutter.

EXHIBIT 15.8 As you can see by this shelf of spaghetti sauces, getting the consumer to pay attention to any one brand is quite a challenge. Sales promotion techniques often provide the answer for gaining attention. Notice the P-O-P promotion attached to the shelves.

LO ②

15-4 SALES PROMOTION DIRECTED AT CONSUMERS

U.S. consumer-product firms have made a tremendous commitment to sales promotion in their overall marketing plans. During the 1970s, consumer-goods marketers allocated only about 30 percent of their budgets to sales promotion, with about 70 percent allocated to mass media advertising. Now we see that for many consumer-goods firms, the percentages are just the opposite, with nearly 75 percent of promotional budgets being spent on various forms of promotion and P-O-P materials. With this sort of investment in sales promotion and P-O-P as part of the IBP process, let's examine in detail the objectives for sales promotion in the consumer market and the wide range of techniques that can be used.

15-4a Objectives for Consumer-Market Sales Promotion

To help ensure the proper application of sales promotion, specific strategic objectives should be set. The following basic objectives can be pursued with sales promotion in the consumer market.

Stimulate Trial Purchase. When a firm wants to attract new users, sales promotion tools can reduce the consumer's risk of trying something new. A reduced price, offer of a rebate, or a free sample may stimulate trial purchase. Exhibit 15.9 illustrates an attempt by Peet's Coffee to stimulate trial use of its brand by offering a very low price on a sampler pack of coffees—along with free shipping. Note that this promotion is trying to get consumers to try a *brand of coffee* for the first time—not the *product category* of coffee. Recall the discussions in Chapters 2 and 4 (primary versus selective demand stimulation) highlighting the fact that advertising and promotion cannot *initiate* product category use in mature product categories, like coffee, but can only affect brand choice among people who already use the product category.

Stimulate Repeat Purchases. In-package coupons good for the next purchase, or the accumulation of points with repeated purchase, can keep consumers loyal to a particular brand. Loyalty or frequent purchase programs are the best techniques for pursuing this objective (more detail on these shortly). The most prominent frequency programs are found in the airline and hotel industries. Or consider that loyalty "punch

EXHIBIT 15.9 One objective for sales promotion is to stimulate trial use of a brand. Here, Peet's Coffee & Tea is offering consumers a low-risk opportunity to try a variety of coffees, which can be ordered online or by using a toll-free number.

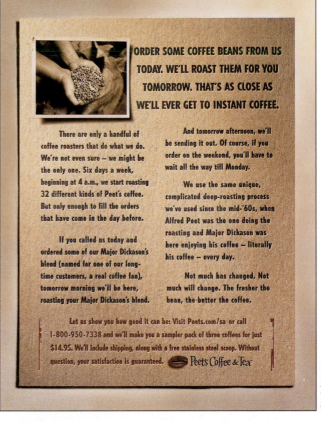

Vitro Robertson

card" at your favorite coffee shop—same idea. Firms try to retain their most loyal and lucrative customers by enrolling them in frequency programs.

Stimulate Larger Purchases. Price reductions or two-for-one sales can motivate consumers to stock up on a brand, thus allowing firms to reduce inventory or increase cash flow. Shampoo is often double-packaged with a bottle of conditioner to offer extra value to consumers. Pepsi and Coke regularly offer discounts on three or more 12 packs purchased at the same time. Encouraging consumers to buy in larger quantities offers several benefits to both the manufacturer and retailer. Both get increased dollar volume and both realize the benefit of faster inventory turnover.

Introduce a New Brand. Because sales promotion can attract attention and motivate trial purchase, it is commonly used for new brand introduction. One of the most successful uses of sales promotions to introduce a new brand was when the makers of Curad bandages introduced their new kid-size bandage by distributing 7.5 million sample packs in Mc-Donald's Happy Meal sacks. The promotion was a huge success, with initial sales exceeding estimates by 30 percent. (See Insights Online [Exhibit 15.10] for another notable example.)

Combat or Disrupt Competitors' Strategies. Because sales promotions often motivate consumers to buy in larger quantities or try new brands, they can be used to disrupt competitors' marketing strategies. If a firm knows that one of its competitors is launching a new brand or initiating a new advertising campaign, a well-timed sales promotion offering deep discounts or extra quantity can disrupt the competitors' strategy. Add to the original discount an in-package coupon for future purchases, and a marketer can severely compromise competitors' efforts.

Contribute to Integrated Brand Promotion. In conjunction with advertising, direct marketing, public relations, and other programs being carried out by a firm, sales promotion can add yet another type of communication to the mix. Sales promotions suggest an additional value, with price reductions, premiums, or the chance to win a prize. This is a different message within the overall communications effort a firm can use in its IBP effort.

15-4b **Consumer-Market Sales Promotion Techniques**

Several sales promotion techniques are used to stimulate demand and attract attention in the consumer market. Some of these are coupons, price-off deals, premiums, contests and sweepstakes, samples and trial offers, gift cards, rebates, and frequency (continuity) programs.

Coupons. A **coupon** entitles a buyer to a designated reduction in price for a product or service. Coupons are the oldest and most widely used form of sales promotion. Annually, about 360 billion coupons are distributed to American consumers, with redemption rates ranging from 2 percent for gum purchases to nearly 45 percent for disposable diaper purchases. Overall, U.S. consumers redeem more than 3 billion coupons annually.[6] Exhibit 15.11 shows coupon-redemption rates for several product categories. One counterintuitive fact that advertisers should be aware of is that more affluent households dominate coupon usage with 41 percent of heavy coupon-using households having incomes greater than $70,000.[7]

Any discussion of coupons as a promotional tool would not be complete without a discussion of online couponing. The most famous and highly visible site for online couponing is Groupon—although there are many sites offering coupons. The impact of online couponing is actually not very compelling. While Groupon has over 150 million subscribers, the company is losing money—lots of money. Also, consumers are highly oriented to the old fashioned process

EXHIBIT 15.11 Percentage of purchases made with coupons in various product categories.

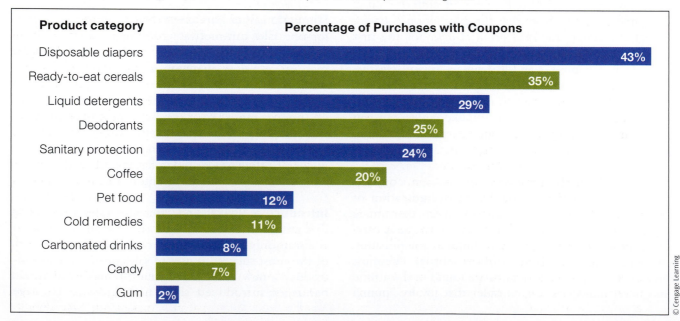

of clipping coupons from newspapers. So, for the time being, the future of couponing online is not clear.[8]

There are five primary advantages to the coupon as a sales promotion tool:

- The use of a coupon makes it possible to give a discount to a price-sensitive consumer while still selling the product at full price to other consumers.

- The coupon-redeeming customer may be a competitive-brand user, so the coupon can induce brand switching.

- A manufacturer can control the timing and distribution of coupons. This way a retailer is not implementing price discounts in a way that can damage brand image.

- A coupon is an excellent method of stimulating repeat purchases. Once a consumer has been attracted to a brand, with or without a coupon, an in-package coupon can induce repeat purchase.

- Coupons can get regular users to trade up within a brand array. For example, users of low-priced disposable diapers may be willing to try the premium version of a brand with a coupon.

The use of coupons is not without its problems. There are administrative burdens and risks with coupon use:

- Although coupon price incentives and the timing of distribution can be controlled by a marketer, the timing of redemption cannot. Some consumers redeem coupons immediately; others hold them for months.

- Heavy redemption by regular brand buyers merely reduces a firm's profitability.

- Couponing entails careful administration. Coupon programs include much more than the cost of the face value of the coupon. There are costs for production and distribution and for retailer and manufacturer handling. In fact, the cost for handling, processing, and distribution of coupons is typically equal to about two-thirds of the face value of the coupon.

- Fraud is a chronic and serious problem in the couponing process. The problem relates directly to misredemption practices. There are three types of misredemption that cost firms money: redemption of coupons by consumers who do not purchase the couponed brand; redemption of coupons by salesclerks and store managers without consumer purchases; and illegal collection or copying of coupons by individuals who sell them to unethical store merchants, who in turn redeem the coupons without the accompanying consumer purchases.

Price-Off Deals. The price-off deal is another straightforward technique. A **price-off deal** offers a consumer cents or even dollars off merchandise at the P-O-P through specially marked packages. The typical price-off deal is a 10 to 25 percent price reduction. The reduction is taken from the manufacturer's profit margin rather than the retailer's (another point of contention in the power struggle). Manufacturers like the price-off technique because it is controllable. Plus, the price off, judged at the P-O-P, can affect a positive price comparison against competitors. Consumers like a price-off deal because it is straightforward and automatically increases the value of a known brand. Regular users tend to stock up on an item during a price-off deal. Retailers are less enthusiastic about this technique. Price-off promotions can create inventory and pricing problems for retailers. Also, most price-off deals are snapped up by regular customers, so the retailer often doesn't benefit from new business.

Premiums and Advertising Specialties. **Premiums** are items offered free, or at a reduced price, with the purchase of another item. Many firms offer a related product free, such as a free granola bar packed inside a box of granola cereal. Service firms, such as a car wash or dry cleaner, may use a two-for-one offer to persuade consumers to try the service.

There are two options available for the use of premiums. A **free premium** provides consumers with an item at no cost. The item can be included in the package of a purchased item, mailed to the consumer after proof of purchase is verified, or simply given away at the P-O-P or at an event. The most frequently used free premium is an additional package of the original item or a free related item placed in the package (e.g., free conditioner with the purchase of shampoo).

A **self-liquidating premium** requires a consumer to pay most of the cost of the item received as a premium. For example, Snapple can offer a "Snapple Cooler" with the purchase of six bottles of Snapple for $6.99—the cost of the cooler to Snapple. Self-liquidating premiums are particularly effective with loyal customers. However, these types of premiums must be used cautiously. Unless the premium is related to a value-building strategy for a brand, it can serve to focus consumer attention on the premium rather than on the benefits of the brand. Focusing on the premium rather than the brand erodes brand equity. For example, if consumers buy a brand just to get a really great looking T-shirt at $4.99, then they won't purchase the brand again until there is another great premium available at a low price.

Advertising specialties have three key elements: a message placed on a useful item, given free to consumers, with no obligation to make a purchase. Popular advertising specialties are baseball caps, T-shirts, coffee mugs, pens, and calendars. Advertising specialties allow a firm to tout its company or brand name with a target customer in an ongoing fashion. Many of us have ball caps or coffee mugs that carry brand names.

Contests and Sweepstakes. Contests and sweepstakes can draw attention to a brand like no other sales promotion technique. Technically, there are important differences between contests and sweepstakes. In a **contest**, consumers compete for prizes based on skill or ability. Winners in a contest are determined by a panel of judges or based on which contestant comes closest to a predetermined criterion for winning, such as picking the total points scored in the Super Bowl. Contests tend to be somewhat expensive to administer because each entry must be judged against winning criteria.

A **sweepstakes** is a promotion in which winners are determined purely by chance. Consumers need only to enter their names in the sweepstakes as a criterion for winning. Sweepstakes often use official entry forms as a way for consumers to enter the sweepstakes. Other popular types of sweepstakes use scratch-off cards. Instant-winner scratch-off cards tend to attract customers. Gasoline retailers, grocery stores, and fast-food chains commonly use scratch-off-card sweepstakes as a way of building and maintaining store traffic. Sweepstakes can also be designed so that repeated trips to the retail outlet are necessary to gather a complete set of winning cards. In order for contests and sweepstakes to be effective, advertisers must design them in such a way that consumers perceive value in the prizes and find playing the games intrinsically interesting.

Contests and sweepstakes often create excitement and generate interest for a brand, but the problems of administering these promotions are substantial. Consider these challenges to effectively using contest and sweepstakes in the IBP effort:

- There will always be regulations and restrictions on contests and sweepstakes. Advertisers must be sure that the design and administration of a contest or sweepstakes complies with both federal and state laws. Each state may have slightly different regulations. The legal problems are complex enough that most firms hire agencies that specialize in contests and sweepstakes to administer the programs.

- The game itself may become the consumer's primary focus, while the brand becomes secondary. Like other sales promotion tools, this technique thus fails to build long-term consumer affinity for a brand.

- It is hard to get any meaningful message across in the context of a game. The consumer's interest is focused on the game rather than on any feature of the brand.

- Administration of a contest or sweepstakes is sufficiently complex that the risk of errors in administration is fairly high and can create negative publicity.

- If a firm is trying to develop a quality or prestige image for a brand, contests and sweepstakes may contradict this goal.

Sampling and Trial Offers. **Sampling** is a sales promotion technique designed to provide a consumer with an opportunity to use a brand on a trial basis with little or no risk. To say that sampling is a popular technique is an understatement. Most consumer-product companies use sampling in some manner, and they invest approximately $2.2 billion a year on the technique. Surveys have shown that consumers are very favorable toward sampling, with 43 percent indicating that they would consider switching brands if they liked a free sample that was being offered.[9]

Sampling is particularly useful for new products but should not be reserved for new products alone. It can be used successfully for established brands with weak market share in specific geographic areas. Ben & Jerry's "Stop & Taste the Ice Cream" tour gave away more than a million scoops of ice cream in high-traffic urban areas in an attempt to reestablish a presence for the brand in weak markets.[10] Six techniques are used in sampling:

- **In-store sampling** is popular for food products (Costco) and cosmetics (Macy's). This is a preferred technique for many marketers because the consumer is at the P-O-P and may be swayed by a direct encounter with the brand. Increasingly, in-store demonstrators are handing out coupons as well as samples, as any trip to Costco will verify.

- **Door-to-door sampling** is extremely expensive because of labor costs, but it can be effective if the marketer has information that locates the target segment in a well-defined geographic area. Some firms enlist the services of newspaper delivery people, who package the sample with daily or Sunday newspapers as a way of reducing distribution costs.

- **Mail sampling** allows samples to be delivered through the postal service. Again, the value here is that certain zip-code markets can be targeted. A drawback is that the sample must be small enough to be economically feasible to mail. Specialty sampling firms provide targeted geodemographic door-to-door distribution as an alternative to the postal service.

- **On-package sampling**, a technique in which the sample item is attached to another product package, is useful for brands targeted to current customers. Attaching a small bottle of Ivory conditioner to a regular-sized container of Ivory shampoo is a logical sampling strategy.

- **Mobile sampling** is carried out by logo-emblazoned vehicles that dispense samples, coupons, and premiums to consumers at malls, shopping centers, fairgrounds, and recreational areas.

Sampling has its critics. Unless the brand has a clear value and benefit over the competition, a trial of the brand is unlikely to persuade a consumer to switch brands. This is especially true for convenience goods because consumers perceive a high degree of similarity among brands, even after trying them. The perception of benefit and superiority may have to be developed through advertising in combination with sampling. In addition, sampling is expensive. This is especially true in cases where a sufficient quantity of a product, such as shampoo or laundry detergent, must be given away for a consumer to truly appreciate a brand's value. Finally, sampling can be a very imprecise process. Despite the emergence of special agencies to handle sampling programs, a firm can never completely ensure that the product is reaching the targeted audience and not just consumers in general.

Trial offers have the same goal as sampling—to induce consumer trial use of a brand—but they are used for more expensive items. Exercise equipment, appliances, watches, hand tools, and consumer electronics are typical of items offered on a trial basis. Trial offers can be free for low-priced products, as we saw with Peet's Coffee. Or trials can be offered for as little as a day to as long as 90 days for more expensive items like vacuum cleaners or computer software. The expense to the firm can be formidable. Segments chosen for this sales promotion technique must have high sales potential.

Gift Cards. Gift cards represent an increasingly popular form of sales promotion. Manufacturers or retailers offer either free or for-purchase debit cards that provide the holder with a preset spending limit. The cards are designed to be colorful and memorable. A wide range of marketers, including luxury car manufacturers like Lexus and retailers like the Gap, have made effective use of gift cards. The really good news about gift cards is that gift card holders tend to use them freely to pay the full retail price for items, which means retailers and brand marketers earn higher profit margins from gift card purchases. Exhibit 15.12 shows a Starbucks gift card as a promotional tool. Once a consumer visits a Starbucks and uses the card, the extra benefit can be that repeat visits will occur and brand loyalty is achieved. Firms like Starbuck's often find that loyal shoppers use a gift card as a way to introduce friends and family to a brand they like, and one of the hottest trends for shoppers in this mobile world is to go to a website, purchase a card, and then have it delivered via email—instant gratification![11]

EXHIBIT 15.12 Firms use gift cards as a way to draw attention to the brand and as a way for loyal customers to introduce their friends to the brand's offerings.

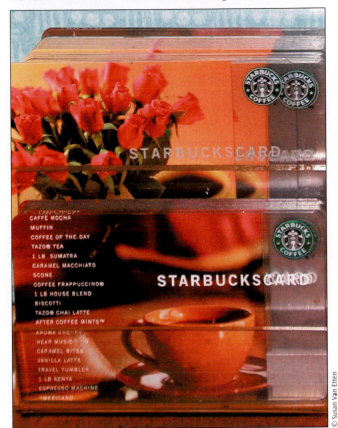

© Susan Van Etten

Rebates. A **rebate** is a money-back offer requiring a buyer to mail in a form (although many are redeemed instantly at checkout) requesting the money back from the manufacturer rather than from the retailer (as in couponing). The rebate technique has been refined throughout the years and is now used by a wide variety of marketers for products as diverse as computers (Dell) to mouthwash (Warner-Lambert). Rebates are particularly well suited for increasing the quantity purchased by consumers, so rebates are commonly tied to multiple purchases.

Another reason for the popularity of rebates is that relatively few consumers actually take advantage of the rebate offer after buying a brand. The best estimate of consumer redemption of rebate offers is that only 60 percent of buyers ever bother to fill out and then mail in the rebate request—resulting in an extra $2 billion in revenue for the manufacturers and retailers who offer rebates.[12]

Frequency (Continuity) Programs. In recent years, one of the most popular sales promotion techniques among consumers has been frequency programs. **Frequency programs**, also referred to as continuity programs or loyalty card programs, offer consumers discounts or free product rewards for repeat purchase or patronage of the same brand, company, or retailer. These programs were pioneered by airline companies. Frequent-flyer programs such as Delta Air Lines' SkyMiles, frequent-stay programs such as Marriott's Rewards program, and frequent-renter programs such as Hertz's #1 Club are examples of such loyalty-building activities. Research shows that loyalty programs tend to benefit larger firms more than smaller firms in highly competitive markets.[13] So, if you run a small coffee shop or flower store, launching a frequent buyer program might not have the big effect on loyalty you would hope for. Frequency programs have worked their way into new media as well. Seventy-three percent of online buyers reported using a loyalty card of some sort when shopping online.[14]

LO ③

15-5 SALES PROMOTION DIRECTED AT THE TRADE CHANNEL AND BUSINESS MARKETS

Sales promotions can also be directed at members of the trade—wholesalers, distributors, and retailers—and business markets. For example, Hewlett-Packard designs sales promotion programs for its retailers, like Best Buy, in order to ensure that the HP line gets proper attention and display. But HP will also have sales promotion campaigns aimed at business buyers like Accenture or IHC HealthCare. The purpose of sales promotion as a tool does not change from the consumer market to the trade or business markets. It is still intended to stimulate demand in the short term and help *push* the product through the distribution channel or cause business buyers to act more immediately and positively toward the marketer's brand. Firms spend big money to attract businesses to their brands with sales promotions.

15-5a Objectives for Promotions in the Trade Channel

As in the consumer market, trade-market sales promotions should be undertaken with specific objectives in mind. Generally speaking, when marketers devise incentives for the trade market, they are executing a **push strategy**; that is, sales promotions directed at the trade help push a brand into the distribution channel until it ultimately reaches the consumer. Four primary objectives can be identified for these promotions.

Obtain Initial Distribution. Because of the proliferation of brands in the consumer market, there is fierce competition for shelf space. Sales promotion incentives can help a firm gain initial distribution and shelf placement. Like consumers, members of the trade need a reason to choose one brand over another when it comes to allocating shelf space. A well-conceived promotion incentive may sway them.

Increase Order Size. One of the struggles in the channel of distribution is over the location of inventory. Manufacturers prefer that members of the trade maintain large inventories so that the manufacturer can reduce inventory-carrying costs. Conversely, members of the trade would rather make frequent, small orders and carry little inventory. Sales promotion techniques can encourage wholesalers and retailers to order in larger quantities, thus shifting the inventory burden to the trade channel.

Encourage Cooperation with Consumer-Market Sales Promotions. It does a manufacturer little good to initiate a sales promotion in the consumer market if there is little cooperation in the channel. Wholesalers may need to maintain larger inventories, and retailers may need to provide special displays or handling during consumer-market sales promotions. To achieve synergy, marketers often run trade promotions simultaneously with consumer promotions.

Increase Store Traffic. Retailers can increase store traffic through special promotions or events. Door-prize drawings, parking-lot sales, or live radio broadcasts from the store are common sales promotion traffic builders. Burger King has become a leader in building traffic at its 7,000 outlets with special promotions tied to Disney movie debuts. Beginning with a *Beauty and the Beast* tie-in promotion, Burger King has set records for generating store traffic with premium giveaways. The *Pocahontas* campaign distributed 55 million toys and glasses. Manufacturers, in addition to retailers, can also design sales promotions that increase store traffic for retailers. A promotion that generates a lot of interest within a target audience can drive consumers to retail outlets. For example, Honda could run a spring-time promotion for its lawnmower line featuring corporate representatives at stores like Lowes and Home Depot and support its retailers with a special promotion.

15-5b Trade-Market Sales Promotion Techniques

The sales promotion techniques used within the trade market are incentives, allowances, trade shows, sales-training programs, and cooperative advertising.

Incentives. Incentives to members of the trade include a variety of tactics not unlike those used in the consumer market. Awards in the form of travel, gifts, or cash bonuses for reaching targeted sales levels can induce retailers and wholesalers to give a firm's brand added attention. Consider this incentive ploy: The Volvo national sales manager put together an incentive program for dealerships, in which the leading dealership in the nation would win a trip to the Super Bowl, including dinner with Hall of Fame footballer Lynn Swann. But the incentive does not have to be large or expensive to be effective. Weiser Lock offered its dealers a Swiss Army knife with every dozen cases of locks ordered. The program was a huge success. A follow-up promotion featuring a Swiss Army watch was an even bigger hit.

Another form of trade incentive is referred to as push money. **Push money** is carried out through a program in which retail salespeople are offered a monetary reward for featuring a marketer's brand with shoppers. The program is quite simple. If a salesperson sells a particular brand of, say, a refrigerator for a manufacturer as opposed to a competitor's brand, the salesperson will be paid an extra $50 or $75 "bonus" as part of the push money program.

One risk with incentive programs for the trade is that salespeople can be so motivated to win an award or extra push money that they may try to sell the brand to every customer, whether it fits that customer's needs or not. Also, a firm must carefully manage such programs to minimize ethical dilemmas. An incentive technique can look like a bribe unless it is carried out in a highly structured and open fashion.

Allowances. Various forms of allowances are offered to retailers and wholesalers with the purpose of increasing the attention given to a firm's brands. Allowances are typically made available to wholesalers and retailers about every four weeks during a quarter. **Merchandise allowances**, in the form of free products packed with regular shipments, are payments to the trade for setting up and maintaining displays. The payments are typically far less than the amount manufacturers would have to spend to maintain the displays themselves.

In recent years, shelf space has become so highly demanded, especially in supermarkets, that manufacturers are making direct cash payments, known as **slotting fees**, to induce food chains to stock an item. The slotting fee for a new brand is sometimes called a "product introduction fee." The proliferation of new products has made shelf space such a precious commodity that these fees now run in the hundreds of thousands of dollars per product. And manufacturers pay these fees willingly. Research shows that shelf facings have a strong impact on consumer evaluation particularly among frequent users of a brand and for brands with low market share.[15] Another form of allowance is called a bill–back allowance. **Bill-back allowances** provide retailers a monetary incentive for featuring a marketer's brand in either advertising or in-store displays. If a retailer chooses to participate in either an advertising campaign or a display bill-back program, the marketer requires the retailer to verify the services performed and provide a bill for the services. A similar program is the **off-invoice allowance**, in which advertisers allow wholesalers and retailers to deduct a set amount from the invoice they receive for merchandise. This program is really just a price reduction offered to the trade on a particular marketer's brand. The incentive for the trade with this program is that the price reduction increases the margin (and profits) a wholesaler or retailer realizes on the off-invoiced brand.

Sales-Training Programs. An increasingly popular trade promotion is to provide training for retail store personnel. This method is used for consumer durables and specialty goods, such as computers, mobile devices, home theater systems, heating and cooling systems, security systems, and exercise equipment. The increased complexity of these products has made it important for manufacturers to ensure that the proper factual information and persuasive themes are reaching consumers at the P-O-P. For personnel at large retail stores, manufacturers can hold special classes that feature product information, demonstrations, and training about sales techniques.

Cooperative (Co-Op) Advertising. **Cooperative advertising** as a trade promotion technique is also referred to as vertical cooperative advertising and provides dollars directly to retailers for featuring company's brand in local advertising. (Such efforts are also called vendor co-op programs.) Manufacturers try to control the content of this co-op advertising in two ways. They may set strict specifications for the size and content of the ad and then ask for verification that such specifications have been met. Alternatively, manufacturers may send the template for an ad, into which retailers merely insert the names and locations of their stores. Such an ad is featured in Exhibit 15.13. Notice that the Hublot watch ad elements are national (even international), with the co-op sponsorship of the California retailer highlighted in the lower left. With this ad, Hublot controls the look and feel of the ad and insures that the image of the brand is supported.

15-5c Business-Market Sales Promotion Techniques

Often the discussion of sales promotion focuses only on consumer and trade techniques. It is a major oversight to leave the business market out of the discussion.

EXHIBIT 15.13 Here is a classic example of co-op advertising by a manufacturer in support of a retailer. Hublot is being featured by a California retailer in a magazine ad. Manufacturers will provide the ad template for the retailer to run, featuring the firm's brand.

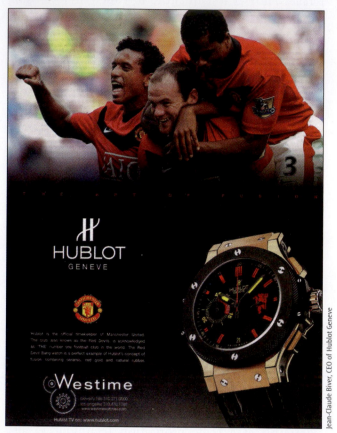

Jean-Claude Biver, CEO of Hublot Geneve

The Promotional Product Association estimates that several billion dollars a year in sales promotion is targeted to the business buyer. The following are the primary forms of sales promotion used in the business market.

Trade Shows. **Trade shows** are events where several related products from many manufacturers are displayed and demonstrated to members of a trade. Literally every industry has trade shows, from ones featuring gourmet products to those highlighting computer technology products. Advertisers are finding that a trade show is an efficient way to reach interested current and potential buyers, with the brand right at hand for discussion and actual use. The Promotional Products Association International reports that when trade show visitors receive a promotional item from a firm at a trade show booth, more than 70 percent of the visitors remember the name of the company that gave them the item.[16]

At a typical trade show, company representatives staff a booth that displays a company's products or service programs. The representatives are there to explain the products and services and perhaps make an important contact for the sales force. Trade shows can be critically important to a small firm that cannot afford advertising and has a sales staff too small to reach all its potential customers. Through the trade-show route, salespeople can make far more contacts than they could with direct sales calls.

Business Gifts. Estimates are that nearly half of corporate America gives business gifts. These gifts are given as part of building and maintaining a close working relationship with suppliers. Business gifts that are part of a promotional program may include small items like logo golf balls, jackets, or small items of jewelry. Extravagant gifts or expensive trips that might be construed as "buying business" are not included in this category of business-market sales promotion.

Premiums and Advertising Specialties. As mentioned earlier, the key chain, ball cap, T-shirt, or calendar that reminds a buyer of a brand name and slogan can be an inexpensive but useful form of sales promotion. Although business buyers are professionals, they are not immune to the value perceptions that an advertising specialty can create. In other words, getting something for nothing appeals to business buyers as much as it does to household consumers. Will a business buyer choose one consulting firm over another to get a sleeve of golf balls? Probably not. But advertising specialties can create awareness and add to the satisfaction of a transaction nonetheless.

Trial Offers. Trial offers are particularly well suited to the business market. First, since many business products and services are of high cost and often result in a significant time commitment to a brand (i.e., many business products and services have long life), trial offers provide a way for buyers to lower the risk of making a commitment to one brand over another. Second, a trial offer is a good way to attract new customers who need a good reason to try something new. The chance to try a new product for 30 days with no financial risk can be a compelling offer.

Frequency Programs. The high degree of travel associated with many business professions makes frequency programs an ideal form of sales promotion for the business market. Airline, hotel, and restaurant frequency programs are dominated by the business-market traveler. But frequency programs for the business market are not restricted to travel-related purchases. Retailers of business products like Staples, OfficeMax, and Costco have programs designed to reward the loyalty of the business buyer. Costco has teamed with American Express to offer business buyers an exclusive Costco/American Express credit card.

Among the many advantages of the card is a rebate at the end of the year based on the level of buying—the greater the dollar amount of purchases, the greater the percentage rebate.

15-6 THE RISKS OF SALES PROMOTION

The discussion so far has demonstrated that sales promotion techniques can be used to pursue important sales objectives. As we have seen, there are a wide range of sales promotion options for the consumer, trade, and business markets. But there are also significant risks associated with sales promotion, and these risks must be carefully considered.

15-6a Creating a Price Orientation

Since most sales promotions rely on some sort of price incentive or giveaway, a firm runs the risk of having its brand perceived as cheap, with no real value or benefits beyond the low price. Creating this perception in the market contradicts the concept of IBP. If advertising messages highlight the value and benefit of a brand only to be contradicted by a price emphasis in sales promotions, then a confusing signal is being sent to the market. At one point, Chrysler dealers challenged corporate management on just this point, arguing that escalating price incentives on various vehicles were "wrecking" the brand.[17]

15-6b Borrowing from Future Sales

Management must admit that sales promotions are typically short-term tactics designed to reduce inventories, increase cash flow, or show periodic boosts in market share. The downside is that a firm may simply be borrowing from future sales. Consumers or trade buyers who would have purchased the brand anyway may be motivated to stock up at the lower price. This results in reduced sales during the next few time periods of measurement. This can play havoc with the measurement and evaluation of the effect of advertising campaigns or other image-building communications. If consumers are responding to sales promotions, it may be impossible to tease out the effects of advertising.

15-6c Alienating Customers

When a firm relies heavily on sweepstakes or frequency programs to build loyalty among customers, particularly their best customers, there is the risk of alienating these customers with any change in the program. Airlines suffered just such a fate when they tried to adjust the mileage levels needed for awards in their frequent-flyer programs. Ultimately, many of the airlines had to give concessions to their most frequent flyers as a conciliatory gesture.

15-6d Managerial Time and Expense

Sales promotions are both costly and time-consuming. The process is time-consuming for the marketer and the retailer in terms of handling promotional materials and protecting against fraud and waste in the process. As we have seen in recent years, funds allocated to sales promotions are taking dollars away from advertising. Advertising is a long-term, franchise-building process that should not be compromised for short-term gains.

15-6e Legal Considerations

With the increasing popularity of sales promotions, particularly contests and premiums, there has been an increase in legal scrutiny at both the federal and state levels. Legal experts recommend that before initiating promotions that use coupons, games, sweepstakes, and contests, a firm check into lottery laws, copyright laws, state and federal trademark laws, prize notification laws, right of privacy laws, tax laws, and FTC and FCC regulations. The best advice for staying out of legal trouble with sales promotions is to carefully and clearly state the rules and conditions related to the program so that consumers are fully informed.

15-7 POINT-OF-PURCHASE ADVERTISING

Annual expenditures on P-O-P advertising are estimated to be more than $23 billion per year.[18] Why this huge investment in in-store promotional materials? First, consider that P-O-P is the only medium that places advertising, brands, and a consumer together in the same place at the same time. Then, think about these results. Research conducted by the trade association Point-of-Purchase Advertising International (http://www.popai.com) indicates that 76 percent of all product selections involve some final deliberation by consumers at the P-O-P.[19] In addition, in an early study on the effects of P-O-P sponsored by K-Mart and Procter & Gamble, the research showed that P-O-P advertising boosted the sales of coffee, paper towels, and toothpaste by 567 percent, 773 percent, and 119 percent, respectively.[20] With results such as these, it is plain to see why P-O-P advertising is one of the fastest-growing categories in today's marketplace.

15-7a Point-of-Purchase Advertising Defined

Point-of-purchase (P-O-P) advertising refers to materials used in the retail setting to attract shoppers' attention to a brand, convey primary brand benefits, or highlight pricing information. P-O-P displays may also feature price-off deals or other consumer sales promotions. A corrugated-cardboard dump bin and an attached header card featuring the brand logo or related brand information can be produced for pennies per unit. When the bin is filled with a brand and placed as a freestanding display at retail, sales gains may follow.

Effective deployment of P-O-P advertising requires careful coordination with the marketer's sales force. Gillette found this out when it realized it was wasting money on lots of P-O-P materials and displays that retailers simply ignored.[21] Gillette sales representatives visited about 20,000 stores per month and were in a position to know what retailers were and were not using. Gillette's marketing executives finally woke up to this fact when their sales representatives told them, for example, that 50 percent of the shelf signs being shipped to retailers from three separate suppliers were going directly to retailers' garbage bins. Representatives helped redesign new display cards that mega-retailers such as Walmart approved for their stores and immediately put into use. Now any time Gillette launches a new P-O-P program, it tracks its success carefully.[22] Having a sales force that can work with retailers to develop and deliver effective P-O-P programs is a critical element for achieving IBP.

15-7b Objectives for Point-of-Purchase Advertising

The objectives of P-O-P advertising are similar to those for sales promotion in general. The goal is to create a short-term impact on sales while preserving the long-term image of the brand being developed and maintained by advertising for the brand. Specifically, the objectives for P-O-P advertising are as follows:

- Draw consumers' attention to a brand in the retail setting.
- Maintain purchase loyalty among brand-loyal users.
- Stimulate increased or varied usage of the brand.
- Stimulate trial use by users of competitive brands.

These objectives are self-explanatory and follow closely on the objectives of sales promotion. Key to the effective use of P-O-P is to maintain the brand image being developed by advertising. But remember from the discussions of consumer decision making in Chapter 5 (Advertising, Integrated Brand Promotion, and Consumer Behavior), that consumers bring to the point of purchase a wide range of experiences and prior knowledge which affects their choices.

15-7c Types of Point-of-Purchase Advertising and Displays

A myriad of displays and presentations are available to marketers. P-O-P materials generally fall into two categories: **short-term promotional displays**, which are used for six months or less; and **permanent long-term displays**, which are intended to provide P-O-P presentation for more than six months. Within these two categories, marketers have a wide range of choices:

- *Window and door signage:* Any sign that identifies or advertises a company or brand or gives directions to the consumer.
- *Counter/shelf unit:* A smaller display designed to fit on counters or shelves.
- *Floor stand:* Any P-O-P unit that stands independently on the floor.
- *Shelf talker:* A printed card or sign designed to mount on or under a shelf.
- *Mobile/banner:* An advertising sign suspended from the ceiling of a store or hung across a large wall area.
- *Cash register:* P-O-P signage or small display mounted near a cash register designed to sell impulse items such as gum, lip balm, or candy.
- *Full line merchandiser:* A unit that provides the only selling area for a manufacturer's line; often located as an end-of-aisle display.
- *End-of-aisle display or gondola:* Usually a large display of products placed at the end of an aisle. (See Exhibit 15.14.)
- *Dump bin:* A large bin with graphics or other signage attached.
- *Illuminated sign:* Lighted signage used outside or in-store to promote a brand or the store.
- *Motion display:* Any P-O-P unit that has moving elements to attract attention.
- *Interactive unit:* A computer-based kiosk where shoppers get information such as tips on recipes or how to use the brand. Can also be a unit that flashes and dispenses coupons.

EXHIBIT 15.14 End-of-aisle displays are used to attract shoppers' attention to a brand and also provide marketers with extra shelf space for their brands.

Bonnie Kamin/PhotoEdit

- *Overhead merchandiser:* A display rack that stocks products and is placed above the cash register. The cashier can reach the product for the consumer. The front of an overhead merchandiser usually carries signage.

- *Cart advertising:* Any advertising message adhered to a shopping cart.

- *Aisle directory:* Used to delineate contents of a store aisle; also provides space for an advertising message.

- *Retail digital signage:* The newest P-O-P device available is retail digital signage. These are video displays that have typically been ceiling- or wall-mounted and are now being moved to end-of-aisle caps or given strategic shelf placement to relay special pricing or new product introductions.

This wide array of in-store options gives marketers the opportunity to attract shoppers' attention, induce purchase, and provide reinforcement for key messages that are being conveyed through other components of the IBP plan. Retailers are increasingly looking to P-O-P displays as ways to differentiate and provide ambience for their individual stores, which means that the kind of displays valued by Whole Foods versus Walgreens versus Albertson's versus Target (to name just a few) will often vary considerably. Once again, it is the marketer's field sales force that will be critical in developing the right P-O-P alternative for each retailer stocking that marketer's products. Without the retailers' cooperation, P-O-P advertising has virtually no chance to work its magic. (See Insights Online [Exhibit 15.15] for an interesting example of how ALDI used its lobby as a P-O-P display.)

▶ **INSIGHTS ONLINE**

15.15 Go online to see the AdAge feature, "Agency McCann Turns a Retail Lobby in ALDI to a Pop-Up Holiday Shop Full of Ingredients to Bake a Holiday Pie in an Innovative P-O-P."

15-7d P-O-P Advertising and Mobile or Location Marketing

We have considered mobile marketing in several contexts throughout the book, including highlighting the firm Foursquare. There are those who argue that the new P-O-P advertising *is* mobile marketing.[23] Mobile marketing through smartphones and other mobile devices adds another dimension to the retailers' in-store or near-store marketing. What a billboard used to do—alert the consumer to a nearby location—a smartphone can now do. And, when the consumer is in front of a store shelf, sensors can identify the location and let the marketer send one last message to try to convert the browsing into a purchase. The full breadth of potential for location marketing and P-O-P is still being explored—particularly consumers' attitude and reaction toward the practice. But, the technology offers compelling possibilities.

15-7e P-O-P Advertising and the Trade and Business Markets

Although we have focused our discussion of the use of P-O-P advertising as a technique to attract consumers, this promotional tool is also strategically valuable to manufacturers as they try to secure the cooperation in the trade and business markets. Product displays and information sheets offered to retailers often encourage retailers to support one distributor or manufacturer's brand over another. P-O-P promotions can help win precious shelf space and exposure in a retail setting. From a retailer's perspective, a P-O-P display can enhance the atmosphere of the store and make the shopping experience easier for customers. Brand manufacturers and distributors obviously share that interest. When a retailer is able to move a particular brand off the shelf, it in turn positively affects both the manufacturer's and distributor's sales.

LO 6

15-8 SUPPORT MEDIA

This section discusses traditional support media: outdoor signage and billboard advertising, transit and aerial advertising, cinema advertising, directory advertising, and packaging. We placed this section in this chapter because these supportive IBP tools are more similar to sales promotion and P-O-P devices than they are to the major media covered in Chapters 12 and 13.

Support media are used to reinforce or supplement a message being delivered via some other media vehicle; hence the name *support media*. Support media are especially productive when used to deliver a message near the time or place where consumers are actually contemplating product selections, like the billboards along a highway advertising gas stations, restaurants, or motels. Since these media can be tailored to local markets, they can have value to any organization that wants to reach consumers in a particular venue, neighborhood, or metropolitan area.

the United States has actually been increasing fairly steadily and now stands at about $8 billion per year.[24] Outdoor advertising offers several distinct advantages. This medium provides an excellent means to achieve wide exposure for a message and a brand in specific local markets. Size of the display is a powerful attraction of this medium, especially when combined with special lighting and moving features. Billboards can be captivating when clever creative is conceived for the board to highlight the brand or company name. Billboards created for a retail store in Minneapolis have even wafted a mint scent throughout the city as part of a candy promotion for Valentine's Day. Billboards also offer around-the-clock exposure for an advertiser's message and are well suited to showing off a brand's distinctive packaging or logo.

Billboards are especially effective when they reach viewers with a message that speaks to a need or desire that is immediately relevant. For instance, we all know that billboards are commonly deployed by fast-food restaurants along major freeways to help hungry travelers know where to exit to enjoy a Whopper or Big Mac. Exhibit 15.16 features a clever example of putting outdoor signage in the right place at the right time to maximize its appeal. The German eyeglass company that sponsored this billboard has created a clever, entertaining, and timely communication. The product categories that rely most heavily on outdoor advertising are local services (like gas stations), real estate and insurance companies, hotels, financial institutions, and automobile dealers and services.

15-8a **Outdoor Signage and Billboard Advertising**

Billboards, posters, and outdoor signs are perhaps the oldest forms of advertising. Posters first appeared in North America not as promotional pieces, but rather were used during the Revolutionary War to keep the civilian population informed about the war's status. In the 1800s, they became a promotional tool, with circuses and politicians among the first to adopt this new medium. Today, the creative challenge posed by outdoor advertising is as it has always been—to grab attention and communicate with minimal verbiage and striking imagery.

In recent years, total spending on outdoor advertising in

EXHIBIT 15.16 Here is a clever and entertaining example of how a billboard can deliver the right message at the right time.

David Auerbach Opticians

Billboards have obvious drawbacks. Long and complex messages simply make no sense on billboards; some experts suggest that billboard copy should be limited to no more than six words. In addition, the impact of billboards can vary dramatically depending on their location, and assessing locations is tedious and time-consuming. To assess locations, companies may have to send individuals to the site to see if the location is desirable. This activity, known in the industry as **riding the boards**, can be a major investment of time and money. Considering that billboards are constrained to short messages, often fade into the landscape, and are certainly not the primary focus of anyone's attention, their costs may be prohibitive for many advertisers.

Despite the cost issue and frequent criticism by environmentalists that billboards represent a form of visual pollution, there are advocates for this medium who contend that important technological advances will make outdoor advertising an increasingly attractive alternative in the future. The first of these advances offers the prospect of changing what has largely been a static medium to a dynamic medium. Digital and wireless technologies have found their way into billboards with remarkable consequences. As an example, Coca-Cola has even purchased 14- by 48-foot LED screens in 27 markets so that they can run their own ads exclusively 24 hours a day.[25] Digital billboard displays let advertisers rotate their messages on a board at different times during the day.[26] This capability is especially appealing to local marketers—like television stations and food sellers—whose businesses are very time-sensitive. For example, FreshDirect uses this technology to change the messaging for its food-delivery service—morning, noon, and night—on the billboard outside New York City's Queens Midtown Tunnel. Ultimately, billboard time may be sold in dayparts like radio or television, making them more appealing to time-sensitive advertisers.

15-8b Out-of-Home Media Advertising: Transit, Aerial, Cinema

A variety of support media are referred to as out-of-home media advertising. **Out-of-home media advertising** includes various advertising venues that reach primarily local audiences. **Transit advertising** is a close cousin to billboard advertising, and in many instances it is used in tandem with billboards. This is a popular advertising form around the world. Transit ads can appear in many venues, including on backs of buildings, in subway tunnels, throughout sports stadiums, and on taxis, buses, and trucks. Transit ads also appear as signage on terminal and station platforms

EXHIBIT 15.17 The story is the same around the world. Mass transit has become an advertising vehicle too.

© Chris T. Allen

or actually envelop mass transit vehicles, as exemplified in Exhibit 15.17. One of the latest innovations in out-of-home media is digital signage that can deliver customized messages by neighborhood using wireless Internet technology. Such digital messages can be seen in retail settings (covered earlier in the chapter) or on taxi tops. We've come a long way from the circus poster.

Transit advertising is especially valuable when an advertiser wishes to target adults who live and work in major metropolitan areas. The medium reaches people as they travel to and from work, and because it taps into daily routines repeated week after week, transit advertising offers an excellent means for repetitive message exposure. In large metro areas such as New York City—with its 200 miles of subways and 3 million subway riders—transit ads can reach large numbers of individuals in a cost-efficient manner. When working with this medium, an advertiser may find it most appropriate to buy space on just those train or bus lines that consistently haul people belonging to the demographic segment being targeted. This type of demographic matching of vehicle with target audience derives more value from limited ad budgets. Transit advertising can also be appealing to local merchants because their messages may reach a passenger as he or she is traveling to a store to shop.

Transit advertising works best for building or maintaining brand awareness. But, as with outdoor billboards, lengthy or complex messages simply cannot be worked into this medium. Also, transit ads can easily go unnoticed in the hustle and bustle of daily life. People traveling to and from work via a mass transit system are certainly one of the hardest audiences to engage with an advertising message. They can be bored, exhausted, absorbed by their thoughts about the day, or occupied by some other medium.

When advertisers can't break through on the ground or under the ground, they can always look to the sky. **Aerial advertising** can involve airplanes pulling signs or banners, skywriting, or those majestic blimps. For several decades, Goodyear had blimps all to itself; now, the availability of smaller, less-expensive blimps has made this medium more popular to advertisers. For example, Virgin Lightships (now owned and operated by Van Wagner Airship Group) has created a fleet of small blimps that can be rented for advertising purposes for around $200,000 per month that include huge, full-color 30- by 70-foot LED screens that can display brand images, advertising, and potentially live TV broadcast feeds. Aerial billboards, pulled by small planes or jet helicopters equipped with screeching loudspeakers (bring back any spring break memories?), have also proliferated in recent years, as advertisers look for new ways to connect with consumers.

Cinema advertising includes those (somewhat annoying) ads that run in movie theaters before the film and other advertising appearing off-screen within a theater. Although consumers often claim that they are not particularly favorably inclined to watching advertising before a film they paid to see, research shows that 63 percent of movie goers surveyed actually don't mind the ads before the film, and firms continue to invest in this form of out-of-home advertising.[27] Cinema advertising is not just on-screen. Off-screen ads advertising and promotion include sampling, concession-based promotion (the ad on the side of your popcorn box), and lobby-based advertising.

15-8c Directory Advertising

Directory advertising includes all the local phone directory and local business advertising books published by a variety of firms—the most well known being the Yellow Book. The last time you reached for a phone directory to appraise the local options for Chinese or Mexican food, you probably didn't think about it as a traditional support medium. However, directory advertising plays an important role in the media mix for many types of organizations, as evidenced by the $8 billion spent in this medium annually.[28]

A phone directory can play a unique and important role in consumers' decision-making processes. Whereas most support media keep the brand name or key product information in front of a consumer, directory advertising helps people follow through on their decision to buy. By providing the information that consumers need to actually find a particular product or service, a directory can serve as the final link in a buying decision. Because of their availability and consumers' familiarity with this advertising tool, directories provide an excellent means to supplement awareness-building and

interest-generating campaigns that an advertiser might be pursuing through other media.

On the downside, the proliferation and fragmentation of phone directories can make this a challenging medium to work in. Many metropolitan areas are covered by multiple directories, some of which are specialty directories designed to serve specific neighborhoods, ethnic groups, or interest groups. Selecting the right set of directories to get full coverage of large sections of the country can be a daunting task. In addition, working in this medium requires long lead times; and throughout the course of a year, information in a directory ad can easily become dated. There is also limited flexibility for creative execution in the traditional paper format.

Growth in the use of mobile devices has also clouded the future of printed directories. Access to online directories offers consumers a fast(er) and more convenient way of not just finding a phone number but also getting the location of a desired store or service.

15-8d Packaging

Why consider the brand package as an element of support media? It is not a medium in the classic sense, but it carries important brand information nonetheless, and that information carries a message. In the simplest terms, **packaging** is the container or wrapping for a product. Classic quotes from consultants describe packaging as "the last five seconds of marketing" and "the first moment of truth."[29] Although the basic purpose of packaging seems fairly obvious, it can also make a strong positive contribution to the promotional effort. One of the best historical incidents of the power of packaging is when Dean Foods created the "Milk Chug," the first stylish, single-serving milk package. Dean Foods officials noted that "One thing milk didn't have was the 'cool' factor like Pepsi and Coke."[30] Twelve months after introduction of the new package, sales of white milk increased 25 percent and chocolate and strawberry flavors saw increases as much as 50 percent. In addition, the Point-of-Purchase Advertising Institute has research to show that more than 70 percent of supermarket purchases now result from in-store decisions.[31] As Exhibit 15.18 demonstrates, packaging adds another strategic dimension and can serve an important role in IBP.

Promotional Benefits of Packaging to the Advertiser. Packaging provides several strategic benefits to the brand manufacturer. First, there is a general effect on IBP strategy. The package carries the brand name and logo and communicates the name and symbol to a consumer. In the myriad of products displayed at the retail level, a well-designed package can attract a buyer's

EXHIBIT 15.18 An attractive attention-grabbing package, like these Gatorade packages, can serve important IBP purposes. An effective package can attract attention in the store and also serve as a constant brand name reminder for the user.

© Terri Miller/E-Visual Communications, Inc.

attention and induce the shopper to more carefully examine the product. Several firms attribute renewed success of their brands to package design changes. Kraft Dairy Group believes that significant package changes helped its Breyer's ice cream brand make inroads in markets west of the Mississippi. A package consulting firm came up with a package with a black background, a radically different look for an ice cream product.

Additional value of packaging has to do with creating a perception of value for the product—remember that the "value" message is a key part of IBP communication. The formidable packaging surrounding computer software is made more substantial simply to add tangibility to an intangible product. Similarly, when consumers are buying image, the package must reflect the appropriate image. The color, design, and shape of a package have been found to affect consumer perceptions of a brand's quality, value, and image—and their willingness to pay a premium price over other brands.[32] Perrier, one of the most expensive bottled waters on the market, has an aesthetically pleasing bottle compared to the rigid plastic packages of its competitors. Perfume manufacturers often have greater packaging costs than product costs to ensure that the product projects the desired image.

SUMMARY

 Explain the importance and growth of modern sales promotion.

Sales promotions use diverse incentives to motivate action on the part of consumers, members of the trade channel, and business buyers. They serve different purposes than mass media advertising does, and for some companies, sales promotions receive substantially more funding. The growing reliance on these promotions can be attributed to the heavy pressures placed on marketing managers to account for their spending and meet sales objectives in short time frames. Deal-prone shoppers, brand proliferation, the increasing power of large retailers, and media clutter have also contributed to the rising popularity of sales promotion.

 Describe the sales promotion techniques used in the consumer market.

Sales promotions directed at consumers can serve various goals. For example, they can be employed as means to stimulate trial, repeat, or large-quantity purchases. They are especially important tools for introducing new brands or for reacting to a competitor's advances. Coupons, price-off deals, gift cards, and premiums provide obvious incentives for purchase. Contests and sweepstakes can be excellent devices for stimulating brand

interest. A variety of sampling and trial offer techniques are available to get a product into the hands of the target audience with little or no risk to the consumer. Rebates and frequency (continuity) programs provide rewards for repeat purchase.

3 **Describe the sales promotion techniques used in the trade channel and business markets.**

Sales promotions directed at the trade can also serve multiple objectives. They are a necessity in obtaining initial distribution of a new brand. For established brands, they can be a means to increase distributors' order quantities or obtain retailers' cooperation in implementing a consumer-directed promotion. Incentives and allowances can be offered to distributors to motivate support for a brand. Sales-training programs and cooperative advertising programs are additional devices for effecting retailer support. In the business market, professional buyers are attracted by various sales promotion techniques. Frequency (continuity) programs are very valuable in the travel industry and have spread to business-product advertisers. Trade shows are an efficient way to reach a large number of highly targeted business buyers. Gifts to business buyers are a form of sales promotion that is unique to this market. Finally, premiums, advertising specialties, and trial offers have proven to be successful in the business market.

Identify the risks to the brand of using sales promotion.

There are important risks associated with heavy reliance on sales promotion. Offering constant deals for a brand can erode brand equity and reputation, and sales resulting from a promotion may simply be borrowing from future sales. Constant deals can also create a customer mindset that leads consumers to abandon a brand as soon as a deal is retracted. Sales promotions are expensive to administer and fraught with legal complications. Sales promotions yield their most positive results when carefully integrated with an overall advertising plan.

Understand the role and techniques of point-of-purchase advertising.

Point-of-purchase (P-O-P) advertising refers to materials used in the retail setting to attract shoppers' attention to a firm's brand, convey primary brand benefits, or highlight pricing information. The effect of P-O-P can be to reinforce a consumer's brand preference or change a consumer's brand choice in the retail setting. P-O-P displays may also feature price-off deals or other consumer and business sales promotions. A myriad of displays and presentations are available to marketers. P-O-P materials generally fall into two categories: short-term promotional displays, which are used for six months or less, and permanent long-term displays, which are intended to provide P-O-P

presentation for more than six months. In trade and business markets, P-O-P displays encourage retailers to support one manufacturer's brand over another; they can also be used to gain preferred shelf space and exposure in a retail setting. Recently, new technologies have made P-O-P a mobile marketing device as deals and offers can be sent to consumers via mobile devices like smartphones, iPods, and iPads.

 Describe the role of support media in a comprehensive IBP strategy.

The traditional support media include billboard, transit, aerial, cinema, and directory advertising. Billboards and transit advertising are excellent means for carrying simple messages into specific metropolitan markets. Street furniture is becoming increasingly popular as a placard for brand builders around the world. Aerial advertising can also be a great way to break through the clutter and target specific geographic markets in a timely manner. Directory advertising can be a sound investment because it helps a committed customer locate an advertiser's brand. Again, new technologies have allowed for digitization of billboard, transit, and aerial ads. Cinema advertising is becoming more prevalent, and despite consumer protests, most consumers are not vehemently opposed to ads in theaters. Finally, packaging can be considered in the support media category because the brand's package carries important information for consumer choice at the P-O-P, including the brand logo and the "look and feel" of the brand.

KEY TERMS

sales promotion
consumer-market sales promotion
trade-market sales promotion
business-market sales promotion
coupon
price-off deal
premiums
free premium
self-liquidating premium
advertising specialties
contest
sweepstakes
sampling
in-store sampling

door-to-door sampling
mail sampling
on-package sampling
mobile sampling
trial offers
rebate
frequency programs
push strategy
push money
merchandise allowances
slotting fees
bill-back allowances
off-invoice allowance
cooperative advertising

trade shows
point-of-purchase (P-O-P) advertising
short-term promotional displays
permanent long-term displays
support media
riding the boards
out-of-home media advertising
transit advertising
aerial advertising
cinema advertising
directory advertising
packaging

ENDNOTES

1. Kunar Patel, "Forget Foursquare: Why Location Marketing Is the New Point-of-Purchase," *Advertising Age,* March 22, 2010, 1, 19.

2. Bradley Johnson, "Leading National Advertisers Report: Spending up $3.1% to $105 Billion," *Advertising Age,* June 25, 2007, S-2.

3. Jack Neff, "TV Doesn't Sell Packaged Goods," *Advertising Age,* May 24, 2004, 1, 30; Cara Beardi, "Pop-Ups Sales Results," *Advertising Age,* July 23, 2001, 27.

4. Kate MacArthur, "Give It Away: Fast Feeders Favor Freebies," *Advertising Age,* June 18, 2007, 10.

5. Dean Foust, "Queen of Pop," *BusinessWeek,* August 7, 2006, 44–450.

6. The Seekers, "A Study of Coupon Usage," *Newspaper National Network LP,* November 2010, 2.

7. Daniel Bortz, "The Best Couponing Strategies for the Everyday Saver," *U.S. News & World Report,* September 19, 2012, www.usnews.com, accessed October 19, 2012.

8. "The Dismal Scoop on Groupon," *The Economist,* October 22, 2011, 81.

9. Patricia O'Dell, "Steady Growth," *PromoMagazine.com,* December 1, 2009.

10. Betsy Spethmann, "Branded Moments," *Promo Magazine,* September 2000, 84.

11. Patricia Odell, "2012 Trends Report: The Outlook for Marketing Growth in Key Promotional Categories," *Chief Marketer,* www.chiefmarketer.com, accessed September 1, 2012.

12. Promo Magazine Staff, "Coupon Use Skyrocketed in 2009," *Promo Magazine.com,* January 27, 2010, 34.

13. Yuping Liu and Rong Yang, "Competing Loyalty Programs: Impact of Market Saturation, Market Share, and Category Expandability," *Journal of Marketing,* vol. 73 (January 2009), 93–108.

14. Allison Enright and Elisabeth A. Sullivan, "Marketers, Come on Down," *Marketing News,* July 30, 2010, 14.

15. Pierre Chandon, J. Wesley Hutchinson, Eric T. Bradlow, and Scott H. Young, "Does In-Store Marketing Work? Effects of the Number and Position of Shelf Facings on Brand Attention and Evaluation at the Point of Purchase," *Journal of Marketing,* vol. 73 (November 2009), 1–17.

16. Data available at Promotional Products Association International website, www.ppai.org.

17. Jean Halliday, "Dealers: Chrysler Is Wrecking Brands," *Advertising Age,* June 12, 2006, 1, 39.

18. Richard Alan Nelson and Rick Ebel, "Super Charged," *pubs.ppai.org,* Table 4, www.pubs.ppai.org, accessed September 1, 2012.

19. Patricia O'Dell, "P-O-P Vital as More Shoppers Decide in Store: Study," *Chiefmarketer.com,* May 11, 2012, www.chiefmarketer.com, accessed September 1, 2012.

20. Data cited in Lisa Z. Eccles, "P-O-P Scores with Marketers," *Advertising Age,* September 26, 1994.

21. Nicole Crawford, "Keeping P-O-P Sharp," *Promo Magazine,* January 1998, 52, 53.

22. Jack Neff, "P&G Trims Fat Off Its $2B Trade-Promotion System," *Advertising Age,* June 5, 2006, 8.

23. Kunur Patel, "Forget Foursquare: Why Location Marketing Is the New Point-of-Purchase," *Advertising Age,* March 22, 2010, 1, 19.

24. ZenithOptimedia, "U.S. Ad Spending Forecast through 2013, Publicis Groupe's ZenithOptimedia Advertising Expenditure Forecasts, June 2012," *adage.com/datacenter,* accessed December 23, 2012.

25. Natalie Zmuda, "Coca-Cola Gets Hands-on with Its Own Digital Billboards," *Advertising Age,* February 18, 2010, 12.

26. "Sexy Signage," *The Economist,* January 26, 2013, 62.

27. Jack Loechner, "After the Popcorn, Before the Show," Center for Media Research, www.mediapost.co, June 18, 2010.

28. ZenithOptimedia, "U.S. Ad Spending Forecast through 2013, Publicis Groupe's ZenithOptimedia Advertising Expenditure Forecasts, June 2012," adage.com/datacenter, accessed December 23, 2012.

29. Don Hootstein, "Standing Out in the Aisles," *Marketing at Retail,* June 2007, 22–24.

30. Catherine Arnold, "Way Outside the Box," *Marketing News,* June 23, 2003, 13–14.

31. *An Integrated Look at Integrated Marketing: Uncovering P.O.P's Role as the Last Three Feet in the Marketing Mix* (Washington, DC: Point-of-Purchase Advertising Institute, 2000), 10.

32. Don Hootstein, "Standing Out in the Aisles," *Marketing at Retail,* June 2007, 22–24.

CHAPTER 16

Event Sponsorship, Product Placements, and Branded Entertainment

After reading and thinking about this chapter, you will be able to do the following:

1 Justify the growing popularity of event marketing and sponsorship as a modern means of experiential brand promotion.

2 Summarize the uses and appeal of product placements in venues like TV, movies, and video games.

3 Explain the benefits and challenges of connecting with event venue or entertainment properties in building a brand.

4 Discuss the challenges presented by the ever-increasing variety of communication and branding tools for achieving integrated brand promotion via the consumer experience.

16-1 THE ROLE OF EVENT SPONSORSHIP, PRODUCT PLACEMENTS, AND BRANDED ENTERTAINMENT IN IBP

This chapter discusses an array of tools and tactics that marketers use to create unique experiences with and for consumers. Events, product placements, and branded entertainment offer the advertiser some of the most exciting opportunities for integrated brand promotion (IBP) (see Insights Online [Exhibit 16.1] for an interesting example). Consider these highly innovative and highly successful campaigns using product placement and branded entertainment. To bring some life to a boring product category, Healthy Choice enlisted the help of the Second City improv group to create an entertaining and engaging campaign for the *Fresh Mixers* brand of microwave lunch specialties. What resulted was Healthy Choice *Fresh Mixers Working Lunch*—a live improv comedy show at lunchtime across every U.S. time zone that spoofed tedious office meetings and included the characters eating Fresh Mixers

(brand placement). Similarly, Procter & Gamble (P&G) wanted to liven up the promotion for an old (some say tired) brand—Folgers Coffee—so that the younger 20-something segment would take notice. So, the P&G team and its agency Saatchi and Saatchi came up with a Web-based film where Folgers exists to help bedraggled office workers deal with the dreaded "Yellow People." Yellow People are those annoying but seemingly ever-present people who confront you first thing in the morning when you get to work or school. Chatter about the film spread across the blogosphere, website hits increased dramatically, and when the film was posted on YouTube it immediately attracted over 300,000 views. The Healthy Choice and Folgers campaigns were both huge successes and gained exposure to attention to the brands in innovative and entertaining ways.

The dynamic nature of events, product placement, and branded entertainment make them potent additions to any IBP campaign. But their dynamic nature also means that the rules for success are hard to pin down. But a new order does appear to be emerging from this innovative environment, built around the central premise that the fields of advertising, branding, and entertainment are converging and collapsing on one another. More than ever before, brand builders want to be embedded in the entertainment that their target consumers enjoy.

This chapter first assesses event sponsorship, one of marketers' longtime favorites.[1] Next, the IBP tactic of product placement is considered. This is the strategy where brands are prominently featured in television shows, films, and even video games. Finally, we'll examine a newer form of brand building, branded entertainment, and assess what's new and different about it. When it comes to building brands there are very few limits on what one can try with branded entertainment, and often quirky, edgy, or off-the-wall may be just what the doctor ordered to gain attention for a brand. Before we get to the specific applications, let's review briefly the forces that have sparked this brave new world of advertising and IBP.

16-2 THE CONVERGENCE OF MADISON & VINE

Marketers have embraced diverse means for brand building, and the list of options continues to grow.[2] Yet think about what techniques like events, product placement, and branded entertainment have in common. Whether it's laughing at lunchtime along with Second City Improv or scanning videos on YouTube (like the Folgers "Yellow People"), we see brands coupled with entertainment. Advertising, branding, and entertainment are converging at an accelerating rate, and because of the advertising–entertainment linkage, this convergence is sometimes slotted under the heading of **Madison & Vine**, which refers to two renowned avenues representing the advertising and entertainment industries, respectively. Why the accelerating convergence? There are many reasons.

An important issue propelling this search for new ways to reach consumers is the erosion in effectiveness of traditional broadcast media. By now you have been sensitized to the many forces that are working to undermine "old school" media. One is simply a question of options. People have an ever-expanding set of options to fill their leisure time, from playing video games to surfing the Web to "always on" social networking. Does anyone under the age of 55 watch network television anymore? Even if they do, there is

growing concern among advertisers that soon we will all have digital video recorder (DVR) set-top technology that will make watching TV ads a thing of the past. As noted in Exhibit 16.2, one version of DVR capability is TiVo Central which offers an array of features, but in the minds of many consumers, the best feature is that it lets you skip commercials. With the integration of inexpensive DVR systems into cable and satellite boxes, DVR penetration has accelerated. As you know, people are time shifting their viewing, often recording programming during the week, with catch-up scheduled for the weekends. This so-called appointment viewing is just not going to be advertiser friendly.

In the "**Chaos Scenario**" predicted several years ago by *Advertising Age*'s Bob Garfield, a mass exodus from the traditional broadcast media was coming. As we saw in Chapter 13, Bob was right. Advertisers' dollars have been diverted from traditional media because audience fragmentation, consumers' desire to control their information environment, and ad-avoidance hardware are undermining their value. With reduced funds available, the networks will have less to invest in the quality of their programs, leading to further reductions in the size of their audiences. This then causes even faster advertiser defections, and on and on in what Garfield calls an "inexorable death spiral" for traditional media. He predicted a brave new world where "marketing—and even branding—are conducted without reliance on the 30-second [television] spot or the glossy [magazine] spread."[3]

EXHIBIT 16.2 DVRs, like this TiVo unit, automatically find and record your favorite shows and allow you to pause live TV, watch in slow motion, and create your own instant replays. Unfortunately for advertisers, they also let you fast-forward through advertising.

TiVo, Inc.

Well, as we know, the changing communication environment has not resulted in an "inexorable death spiral" for traditional media. Traditional media have been growing ad revenues nicely over the last few years since the recession of 2008–2009 and still attract over $200 million annually in advertisers' dollars. Television programs like *American Idol* draw about 50 million viewers weekly. And as we saw in Chapter 13, there are things you can do in traditional media creatively that you just cannot do with other IBP techniques. But Garfield's point is still well taken. Billions of advertising dollars have been freed up to move to other brand-building tools. As discussed in Chapter 14, digital and social media marketing in their many forms will continue to surge because of this new money. But according to a Trendwatch survey, the brand-building options most preferred by marketers with the money they shift from old-school advertising are events and experiential marketing.[4]

Why events and experiential marketing? Well, the reasons are many, and this chapter will explain and celebrate those reasons. But it is important to stress that the collection of tools and tactics featured in this chapter are surging in popularity not just because advertisers *must* find new ways to connect with their consumers. Event sponsorship, product placements, and branded entertainment are popular with marketers because they can work in numerous ways to assist with a brand-building agenda beyond the capabilities of traditional media. In theory, these things can foster brand awareness and even liking through a process known as mere exposure.[5] In addition, the meaning-transfer process discussed in Chapter 5 can change people's perceptions of the brand. That is, the fun and excitement of Daytona Beach at spring break can become part of your feelings about the brands that were there with you. The brand evokes that pleasant memory. Similarly, consumers' sense of self may be influenced by the events they attend (as in a NASCAR race or a sporting event), and brands associated with such venues may assist in embellishing and communicating that sense of self.[6] But enough with the justifications for now. Let's get to the specific applications.

Event sponsorship, product placements, and branded entertainment are popular with marketers because they can work in numerous ways to assist with a brand-building agenda beyond the capabilities of traditional media.

involves a marketer providing financial support to help fund an event, such as a rock concert, tennis tournament, or hot-dog-eating contest. In return, that marketer acquires the rights to display a brand name, logo, or advertising message on-site at the event. If the event is covered on TV, the marketer's brand and logo will most likely receive exposure with the television audience as well. As you might suspect, sports sponsorships draw the biggest share of advertising dollars when it comes to events. Event spending has continued to grow at about 8 percent a year and now exceeds $27 billion in the United States, and it is estimated to be approaching the $50 billion level as an aggregate worldwide.[7]

Even in the face of bankruptcy, recession, and retrenchment, the Big Three automakers in the United States remain aggressive with their event sponsorship. General Motors, one of the world's foremost old-school ad spenders, typifies this commitment to events. GM has experimented with a number of ways to "get closer" to its prospective customers. Most entail sponsoring events that get consumers in direct contact with its vehicles, or events that associate the GM name with causes or activities that are of interest to its target customers. For example, GM has sponsored a traveling slave-ship exhibition, a scholarship program for the Future Farmers of America, the Woodward Dream Cruise hot-rod show (in hometown Detroit), and a week of fashion shows in New York City. GM has also launched a movie theater on wheels that travels to state fairs, fishing contests, and auto races to show its 15-minute film about the Silverado pickup truck. Like many marketers large and small, GM has been shifting more and more of its budget out of the measured media and into events.[8] Similarly, Fortune, publisher of the widely known *Fortune* magazine, has begun sponsoring series of high-profile, theme-based events (e.g., The Most Powerful Women Summit) around the world as a way to not only gain attention for the magazine but also diversify the revenue stream for the publisher.[9] (See Insights Online [Exhibit 16.3] for another interesting example of event sponsorship.)

LO 1

16-3 EVENT SPONSORSHIP

One of the time-tested and increasingly popular means for reaching targeted groups of consumers on their terms is event sponsorship. **Event sponsorship**

▶ INSIGHTS
ONLINE

16.3 Go online to see the AdAge feature, "The IOC Olympic Council Limits Athletes Competing in the Olympics from Appearing in Ads Just before, during, or after the Olympics; Gatorade Is Not an Official Sponsor of the Olympic Event, but Makes a Presence."

16-3a Who Uses Event Sponsorship?

Event sponsorship can take varied forms. The events can be international in scope, as in the FIFA World Cup with big-name sponsors like Adidas, McDonald's, Coke, Sony, Hyundai, and Visa. Or they may have a distinctive local flavor, like the Smucker's Stars on Ice tour, which targets more local audiences. Events provide a captive audience for a sponsor, may receive radio and television coverage, and often are reported in the print media and covered online. Hence, event sponsorship can yield face-to-face contact with real consumers and receive simultaneous and follow-up publicity—all good things for a brand.

The list of companies participating in various forms of event sponsorships seems to grow every year. Jeep, Best Buy, Reebok, Atlantic Records, Revlon, Heineken, Citibank, and a host of other companies have sponsored tours and special appearances for recording artists such as Faith Hill, Tim McGraw, Jewel, Jay-Z, Sting, Sheryl Crow, Elton John, and 50 Cent. Soon after ESPN launched the X Games to attract younger viewers, a host of sponsors signed on, including Taco Bell, Levi Strauss, Kellogg's, Gatorade, and Activision. These brand builders are looking for benefits through unique associations with something new and hip via a process that anthropologist Grant McCracken has labeled "the movement of meaning."[10] (See Insights Online [Exhibit 16.4] for a notable example about Under Armor.)

And the world is much engaged with football—no, not that kind of football. English professional soccer has become one of the darlings of the sports business because of the valuable marketing opportunities it supports. For example, Manchester United of the English Premier Soccer League surpasses the New York Yankees in its ability to generate revenues. In this world of big-time sports, global companies like Pepsi, Nike, and Vodafone pay huge amounts to have their names linked to the top players and teams. Regarding the FIFA World Cup, Nike's marketing VP says simply—"It's the No. 1 event in all of sports."[11] Nike should know.

Sports sponsorships truly come in all shapes and sizes, including organizations like Professional Bull Riders and the World Hunting Association. Advertisers thus have diverse opportunities to associate their brands with the distinctive images of various participants, sports, and even nations. For another example, examine Exhibit 16.5. Here, United Airlines has taken a major role in sponsoring the Olympics but just not any Olympics. United is focused on the Paralympics ski team, which may

INSIGHTS ONLINE

16.4 Go online to see the AdAge feature "Under Armor Unveils Anthem to Kick Off Its Biggest Global Ad Push."

EXHIBIT 16.5 Firms often choose to sponsor major events as an opportunity to provide visibility for their brand. Here, United Airlines has taken a major sponsorship role in both the U.S. Olympic team and the Paralympics ski team.

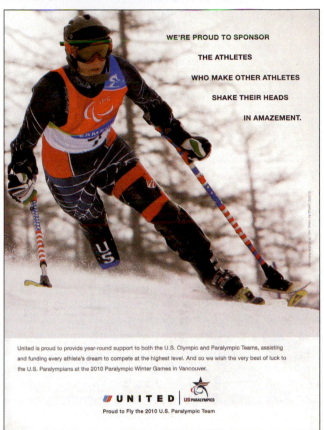

WE'RE PROUD TO SPONSOR

THE ATHLETES

WHO MAKE OTHER ATHLETES

SHAKE THEIR HEADS

IN AMAZEMENT.

United is proud to provide year-round support to both the U.S. Olympic and Paralympic Teams, assisting and funding every athlete's dream to compete at the highest level. And so we wish the very best of luck to the U.S. Paralympians at the 2010 Paralympic Winter Games in Vancouver.

UNITED | US PARALYMPICS

Proud to Fly the 2010 U.S. Paralympic Team

United Airlines

carry extra weight with consumers in terms of feeling good about the United brand.

16-3b Finding the Sweet Spot for Event Sponsorship

You know enough about advertising and IBP at this point to know that the major sweet spot in event sponsorship comes when significant overlap is achieved between an event's participants and the marketer's target audience. If the event has big numbers of fans and/or participants, then that's even better. Moreover, marketers stand to gain the most in supporting an event as its exclusive sponsor. However, exclusivity can be extremely pricey, if not cost prohibitive, except in those situations where one finds a small, neighborhood event with passionate supporters just waiting to be noticed. Consider, for example, the World Bunco Association (WBA), which was chartered in 1996. Bunco is a dice game, usually played in groups of 8, 12, or 16. It's especially popular with middle-aged women, sort of a ladies' version of "poker night." Bunco is a game of chance, so its leaves players with lots of time for eating, drinking, and intimate conversation about everything from a daughter's new baby to the recipe for yummy Snickers Salad (a concoction of Cool Whip, marshmallow crème, cream cheese, chopped Snickers bars, and just a touch of apple to make it good for you).

"So where is the sponsorship opportunity?" you ask. Consider a few facts: Approximately 14 million women in the United States have played Bunco, and 4.6 million play regularly. Six out of 10 women say that recommendations from their Bunco group influence their buying decisions.[12] In addition, about a third of all regular Bunco players suffer from frequent heartburn, and it just so happens that 70 percent of frequent heartburn sufferers are women. Can you see where this is going now?

The makers of Prilosec OTC, an over-the-counter heartburn medication, discovered Bunco and went to work learning about the women who play it regularly. They attended Bunco parties, listened to country music, camped in RVs, and watched a lot of NASCAR races. Naturally, they entered into a partnership with the World Bunco Association to sponsor the first Bunco World Championship. With a $50,000 first prize, associated fund-raising for the National Breast Cancer Foundation, and lots of favorable word of mouth from regional Bunco tournaments, the World Championships caught on fast. It wasn't long before cable TV caught Bunco fever and began covering the championship matches, where the Prilosec OTC purple tablecloths made it a branded experience. As you can see in Exhibit 16.6, the Bunco World Tour packed plenty of excitement. And Prilosec definitely hit the sweet spot with the target audience being the primary participants in the event.

The Bunco World Championship was an opportunity for a brand like Prilosec OTC and illustrates an attractive scenario. Again, this is a scenario where there is excellent overlap between the lifestyles of event enthusiasts and benefits that your product can deliver. Supporting Bunco allowed Prilosec OTC to connect with its core customer in a fun and meaningful way, and the unique connection between Prilosec OTC and Bunco fostered brand loyalty and favorable word of mouth. There is much to be said for the sponsorship opportunity that your brand can uniquely own, and it doesn't have to be the soccer World Cup or the Olympics to have a huge positive impact on a brand.

16-3c Assessing the Benefits of Event Sponsorship

In the early days of event sponsorship, it often wasn't clear what an organization was receiving in return for its sponsor's fee. Traditionally, many critics contend that sponsorships, especially those of the sporting kind, can be ego-driven and thus a waste of money.[13] Company presidents are human, and they like to associate with sports stars and celebrities. This is fine, but when sponsorship of a golf tournament, for example, is motivated mainly by a CEO's desire to play in the same foursome as Paula Creamer or Phil Mickelson, the company is really just throwing money away.

One of the things fueling the growing interest in event sponsorship is that many companies have found ways to make a case for the effectiveness of their sponsorship dollars. Boston-based financial services company John Hancock has been a pioneer in developing detailed estimates of the advertising equivalencies of its sponsorships. John Hancock began sponsoring a college football bowl game in 1986 and soon after had a means to judge the value of its sponsor's fee. Hancock employees scoured magazine and newspaper articles about their bowl game to determine name exposure in print media. Next they factored in the number of times that the John Hancock name was mentioned in pregame promos and during the television broadcast. Early on, Hancock executives estimated that they received the equivalent of $5.1 million in advertising exposure for their $1.6 million sponsorship fee. However, as the television audience for the John Hancock bowl dwindled in subsequent years, Hancock's estimates of the bowl's value also plunged. Subsequently, Hancock moved its sports sponsorship dollars into other events, like the Boston Marathon and Major League Baseball. The famous John Hancock signature is now a fixture at Dodger Stadium and Fenway Park.

Improving one's ability to gauge the effectiveness of dollars spent will generally drive more spending on any IBP tool.[14] Enter a familiar player—Nielsen Media Research—and its Sponsorship Scorecard.

EXHIBIT 16.6 Passionate event participants often become passionate advocates for a brand that sponsors their event. That's what happened for the Prilosec brand when it sponsored the Bunco World Championship.

Nielsen developed this service to give advertisers a read on the impact of their signage in sports stadiums. In one assessment for Fleet Bank in Boston's Fenway Park, Nielsen calculated that Fleet signage received 84 impressions of at least five seconds each during a telecast of the Red Sox/Yankees game.[15] That's the rough equivalent of fourteen 30-second TV spots. But don't get sold on Fenway—in a head-to-head comparison during the World Series, Coors Field delivered 2.4 billion gross impressions for its top five sponsors, versus a measly 791,000 for Fenway.[16]

As we see illustrated in both the John Hancock and Fleet Bank examples, the practice of judging sponsorship spending through media impressions is a popular approach. Establishing **media impressions** entails creating a metric that lets a marketer judge sponsorship spending in a direct comparison to spending in the traditional measured media. But gross impressions only tell part of the story. Sponsorships provide a unique opportunity to foster brand loyalty. When marketers connect their brand with the potent emotional experiences often found at rock concerts, in soccer stadiums, at the Bunco table, or on Fort Lauderdale beaches, positive feelings may be attached to the sponsor's brand that linger well beyond the duration of the event. Judging whether your brand is receiving this loyalty dividend is another important aspect of sponsorship assessment. Getting a good read on the return from one's sponsorship dollars will require a mix of qualitative and quantitative approaches. This is true of most advertising expenditures. But, researchers have found that with respect to community-based events (like local marathons or music events), attendees who are more community-minded come away from the event with a more positive opinion of the sponsor, which contributes to an increased intention to buy the sponsors' brands.[17]

Since various types of events attract well-defined target audiences, marketers should also monitor event participants to ensure they are reaching their desired target. Such is the case for the sponsor Accenture featured in Exhibit 16.7. Accenture, a business consulting firm, knows that its target audience not only enjoys the game of golf, but also enjoys watching the game of golf on television. As such, Accenture has sponsored the Match Play Championship PGA golf tour event for many, many years. And, as you will read in the next section, such big-name sponsorships as a PGA golf tour event help Accenture leverage its brand name recognition.

16-3d Leveraging Event Sponsorship

As noted above, one way to justify event sponsorship is to calculate the number of viewers who will be exposed to a brand either at the event or through media coverage of the

EXHIBIT 16.7 One of the best uses of event sponsorship is reaching a well-defined target audience that may be hard to reach through other IBP tools, particularly advertising. Accenture, the business consulting firm, has teamed up with the PGA golf tour to reach its target market of business decision makers.

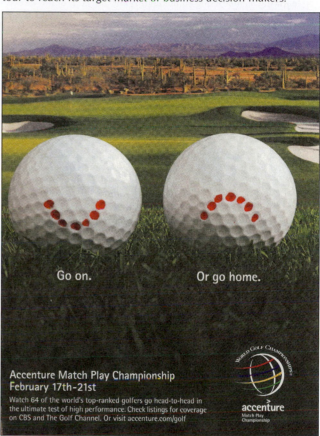

Go on. Or go home.

Accenture Match Play Championship
February 17th–21st
Watch 64 of the world's top-ranked golfers go head-to-head in the ultimate test of high performance. Check listings for coverage on CBS and The Golf Channel. Or visit accenture.com/golf

accenture
Match Play
Championship

© Accenture

event, and then assess whether the sponsorship provides a cost-effective way of reaching the target segment. This approach assesses sponsorship benefits in direct comparison with traditional advertising media. Some experts now maintain, however, that the benefits of sponsorship can be fundamentally different from anything that traditional media might provide. Finding ways to leverage the sponsorship is especially critical. Any collateral communication or activity reinforcing the link between a brand and an event is referred to as **leveraging** or activating a sponsorship (see Insights Online [Exhibit 16.8] for a notable example).[18]

Events can be leveraged as ways to entertain important clients, recruit new customers, motivate the firm's salespeople, and generally enhance employee morale. Events provide unique opportunities for face-to-face contact with key customers. Marketers commonly use

INSIGHTS ONLINE

16.8 Go online to see the AdAge feature, "Chevy and Bud Light Platinum Join Up with Justin Timberlake to Sponsor the Grammys Event via the 'Find New Roads' Campaign."

EXHIBIT 16.9 Guidelines for effectively using event sponsorship as an IBP tool.

Guidelines for Event Sponsorship

1. **Match the brand to the event**. Be sure that the event matches the brand personality. Stihl stages competitions at Mountain Man events featuring its lumbering equipment. Would the Stihl brand fare as well sponsoring a boat race or a triathlon? Probably not.

2. **Tightly define the target audience**. Closely related to point number one is the fact that the best event in the world won't create impact for a brand if it's the wrong target audience. Too often the only barometer of success is the number of bodies in attendance. Far more important is the fact that the brand is getting exposure to the right audience. This is what JBL and TREK accomplished with the mountain bike tour sponsorship.

3. **Stick to a few key messages**. Most events try to accomplish too much. People are there to experience the event and can accommodate only a limited amount of persuasion. Don't overwhelm them. Stick to a few key messages and repeat them often.

4. **Develop a plot line**. An event is most effective when it is like great theater or a great novel. Try to develop a beginning, a middle, and an exciting ending. Sporting events are naturals in this regard, which explains much of their popularity. In nonsporting events, the plot line needs to be developed and delivered in small increments so that the attendees can digest both the event and the brand information.

5. **Deliver exclusivity**. If you are staging a special event, make it by invitation only. Or, if you are a featured sponsor, invite only the most important customers, clients, or suppliers. The target audience wants to know that this event is special. The exclusivity provides a positive aura for the brand.

6. **Deliver relevance**. Events should build reputation, awareness, and relationships. Trying to judge the success of an event in terms of sales is misleading and shortsighted. Don't make the event product-centric; make it a brand-building experience for the attendees.

7. **Use the Internet**. The Internet is a great way to promote the event, maintain continuous communication with the target audience, and follow up with the audience after an event. Plus, it's a good way to reach all the people who can't attend the event in person. For golf fans, pga.com gets viewers involved with each event on the PGA tour and gives sponsors another chance to reach the target audience.

8. **Plan for the before and after**. Moving prospects from brand awareness to trial to brand loyalty doesn't happen overnight. The audience needs to see the event as part of a broad exposure to the brand. This is the synergy that needs to be part of the event-planning process. The event must be integrated with advertising, sales promotions, and advertising specialty items.

Based on Laura Shuler, "Make Sure to Deliver When Staging Events," *Marketing News*, September 13, 1999, 12.

this point of contact to distribute specialty advertising items so that attendees will have a branded memento to remind them of the rock concert or their New York City holiday. Marketers may also use this opportunity to sell premiums such as T-shirts and hats, administer consumer surveys as part of their marketing research efforts, or distribute product samples.

Another very different way of leveraging the impact of event sponsorship has also been discovered by researchers. When an event sponsor fits a consumer's image and sense of self, a **consumer–event congruity** occurs where consumer participation in the event enhances the persuasiveness of the event and, in turn, causes the participants to think more positively about the sponsor and increases the desire to patronize the sponsor.[19] A checklist of guidelines for selecting the right events and maximizing their benefits for the brand is outlined in Exhibit 16.9.

As you will see again in Chapter 18, a firm's event participation may also be the basis for public relations activities that then generate additional media coverage. A great example of this comes from the 2010 Winter Olympics where P&G, the maker of Pampers, partnered with Team USA to introduce a new line of Pampers Swaddlers and Cruiser Diapers. Olympic athletes like Chad Hedrick and Noelle Pikus-Pace competed in Vancouver with their families in the stands. They also received limited-edition, specially branded Team USA diapers to keep their little ones dry. These athletes and their families then shared the sights and sounds of the Winter Olympics with everybody back home via photos and videos posted on Pampers.com. Babies, the Olympics, and a beautiful city like Vancouver make for a lot of great stories. It's the kind of story that news media are also eager to cover—much to the delight of Pampers's brand managers. (See Insights Online [Exhibit 16.10] for yet another interesting example of how Google Chrome appealed to families.)

INSIGHTS ONLINE

16.10 Go online to see the AdAge feature, "A Celebrity Baby from *Family Guy*, the Adult Cartoon, Works with Google Chrome to Promote the Browser as a Seamless Experience among Multiple Consumer Technology Devices."

LO 2

16-4 PRODUCT PLACEMENTS

As noted early in this chapter, the fields of advertising, branding, and entertainment are converging and collapsing on one another. Brand builders aspire to be embedded in any form of entertainment that their target consumers enjoy. And even though event sponsorship has been around for decades, brand builders are also looking elsewhere to help put on the show. Indeed, in today's world of advertising and IBP, no show seems to be off limits. Brands can now be found whenever and wherever consumers are being entertained, whether at a sporting event, in a movie theatre, on the Internet, or in front of a TV set or video game console. If it entertains an audience, some brand will want to be there, on the inside.

Product placement is the practice of placing any branded product into the content and execution of an established entertainment vehicle. These placements are purposeful and paid for by the marketer to expose and/or promote a brand. Product placement has come a long way since E.T. nibbled on Reese's Pieces in the movie *E.T. the Extra-Terrestrial*. But that product (or brand) placement foreshadowed much that has followed. The genie, as they say, is now definitely out of the bottle.

In today's world, product-placement agencies work with marketers to build bridges to the entertainment industry. Working collaboratively, agents, marketers, producers, and writers find ways to incorporate the marketer's brand as part of the show. The show can be of almost any kind. Movies, short films on the Internet, and reality TV are great venues for product placements. Video games, novels, and magazines offer great potential. There may be an opportunity for a brand to be involved anywhere and anytime people are being entertained.

16-4a On Television

Television viewers have become accustomed, maybe even numb, to product placements. Soap operas and reality shows have helped make product placements seem the norm: Vietnam Airlines saves the day with transportation to Cambodia for contestants on *The Amazing Race,* and text a vote for your favorite on *Dancing with the Stars* via AT&T. But the tactic has spread like wildfire. On Time Warner's WB network, a shiny orange Volkswagen Beetle convertible played an important role in the teen superhero drama *Smallville.* Ray Romano chased his wife around the grocery store, knocking over a display of Ragu products, in an episode of *Everybody Loves Raymond.* The final episode of NBC's long-running comedy *Frasier* included a special moment where Niles gave his brother a little gift to cheer him up. That gift? Pepperidge Farm Mint Milano cookies. Nothing says lovin' like Pepperidge Farm!

There's even a school of thought contending that product placements can be television's savior.[20] Recall Bob Garfield's Chaos Scenario discussed previously in this chapter, with its "inexorable death spiral" for the traditional media like TV. So, if consumers won't watch ads on TV, why not turn the programming itself into an ad vehicle? When Randy has a sip of Coke on *American Idol,* or when contestants get rewarded with a Pringles snack on an episode of *Survivor,* these brands are in effect receiving an implicit endorsement. There is no telling where this trend is headed, but it is hard to put the genie back into the bottle. Product placement isn't needed to save TV, but it certainly provides advertisers another reason to invest in this traditional medium.

16-4b At the Movies

The car chase is a classic component of many action/adventure movies and in recent years has been seized as a platform for launching new automotive brands.[21] If you'd like to immerse yourself in a superb example of branded entertainment, download *The Italian Job,* a movie starring the lovable Mini Cooper, like the one on display in Exhibit 16.11. The Mini proves to be the perfect getaway car, as it deftly maneuvers in and out of tight spots throughout the movie. BMW has been a pioneer in the product-placement genre, starting with its Z3 placement in the 1995 James Bond thriller *GoldenEye.* Toyota tried to rev up sales of its boxy Scion brand through a featured role in the made-for-the-Internet film *On the D.L.* And Audi touted its futuristic RSQ concept car in the science fiction feature film *I, Robot.* As they say, birds of a feather flock together.

It is not just automakers that have discovered product placements in movies and films. White Castle, American Express, Nokia, and the Weather Channel—to name just a few—have joined the party as well. *Talladega Nights: The Ballad of Ricky Bobby,* starring Will Ferrell, featured a cornucopia of product placements for everything from Applebee's to Old Spice.[22] All this activity is supported by research indicating that persons under 25 years old are most likely to notice product placements in films and are also willing to try products they see in movies and films.[23]

As we have emphasized throughout, young consumers are increasingly difficult to reach via traditional broadcast media. Although they are likely to soon get their fill of product placements at the movies, in the near term this looks like a good tactic for reaching an age cohort that can be hard to reach.

16-4c In Video Games

As you read in Chapter 14, when product placements occur in video games the strategy is referred to as advergaming. There is good reason marketers are spending over $24 billion a year on this venue to reach their target audiences. Brand placement in video games has wide reach and helps reach the unreachable. Consider these numbers: According to Nielsen Research, 56 percent of U.S. households (about 60 million households) have at least one current-generation gaming console.[24] Moreover, most analysts conclude that around 40 percent of the hard-core players are in the 18 to 34 age cohort—highly sought after by advertisers because of their discretionary spending but expensive to reach via conventional media. Now factor in that video games are not only an attractive entertainment option but also a form of entertainment where players rarely wander off during a commercial break. With all those focused eyeballs in play, is it any wonder that marketers want to be involved?

Billboard ads and virtual products have become standard fare in games like *True Crime: Streets of L.A.*, starring Puma-wearing Nick Kang. In the Ubisoft game *Splinter Cell: Chaos Theory,* secret agents sneak past Diet Sprite vending machines as they track down terrorists. And Tony Hawk must be a Jeep fan because Wranglers, Grand Cherokees, and Liberties are always on the scene in his games. Nielsen research has established that the majority of players see brand placements as adding to the quality of play, and because of the repetitive brand exposures in games, they affect purchase intent more than old-style media do. The next big thing for marketers is Web-enabled consoles that allow more dynamic ad placements and precise tracking of where and how often players pause to take a closer look.[25] Whether you call it "gamevertising" or "advergaming," you can expect to see more of brands like these in the virtual world: LG Mobile, Coca-Cola, BMW, Sony, Old Spice, Levi Strauss, Nokia, Callaway Golf, Ritz Bits, Target, Radio Shack, the U.S. Army, and more.

16-4d What We Know about Product Placement

The business of product placements has evolved at warp speed during the past decade. An activity that was once rare, haphazard, and opportunistic has become more systematic and, in many cases, even strategic. Even though product placement will never be as tidy as crafting and running a 30-second TV spot, numerous case histories make several things apparent about using this tool, both in terms of challenges and opportunities.[26]

Integrate the Placement within the IBP Campaign. First, product placements can add the greatest value when they are integrated with other elements of an advertising plan. No big surprise here; it's always about the synergy. As with event sponsorship, the idea is to leverage the placement. One should avoid isolated product placement opportunities but rather create connections to other elements of the advertising plan. For instance, a placement combined with a well-timed public relations campaign can yield synergy: novel product placements create great media buzz, and that often translates into consumers picking up the buzz and sharing it with their peer group. Recent research suggests that brands stand to gain the most from product placements when consumers are engaged enough to make it a part of their daily conversation.[27] So if you want to get people talking about your brand, give them something to talk about! Favorable word of mouth is always a great asset for a brand and helps in building momentum. This can make product placements just the right thing to complement other advertising initiatives that energize the launch of a new product. We have seen this used on numerous occasions in the launch of new car models and brands.

Make the Placement Look Authentic. Another factor affecting the value of any placement has to do with the elusive concept of authenticity. **Authenticity** refers to the quality of being perceived as genuine and natural. Authenticity is emerging as a powerful influence on brand loyalty among consumers.[28] As advertisers and their agents look for more and more chances to write their brands into the script of shows, it is to be expected that some of these placements will come off as phony. For example, when Eva Longoria plugs a new Buick at a shopping mall during an episode of *Desperate Housewives,* the scene looks phony and contrived. No way would Longoria or her character in this TV show ever stoop to such an unflattering activity. Conversely, when Kramer argues with a homeless man in the TV show *Seinfeld* about returning his Tupperware containers, the spoof is perfect and adds to the comedic moment. Brands want to be embedded (naturally) in the entertainment, not detract from it. This is authenticity and is often a difficult goal to achieve.

Develop the Right Industry Relationships. But like so many other things in the advertising business, success with product placements is fostered through developing deep relationships with the key players in this dynamic business. You need to have the right people looking for the right opportunities that fit with the strategic objectives that have been established for the brand. This too is not a new idea for the business of advertising. As was emphasized in Chapter 8, advertising is a team sport, and the best team wins most of its games. You want to be part of a team where the various members understand each other's goals and are working to support one another. Good teams take time to develop. They also move product placement from an opportunistic and haphazard endeavor to one that supports IBP. That's always the right thing.

Don't Expect Quantifiable ROI. Finally, much like event sponsorship, product placements present marketers with major challenges in terms of measuring the success or ROI of the activity. Here again the collective wisdom seems to be that calculating media impressions for placements does not tell the whole story regarding their value—we agree with this completely. Product placements can vary dramatically in the value they offer to the marketer. One key item to look for is the celebrity connection in the placement.[29] When Tom Cruise puts on Wayfarer shades in one of his movies or reaches for a Red Stripe beer as he did in *Top Gun,* the implied endorsement can drive sales of the product.[30] Astute users of product placements are always looking

for plot connections that could be interpreted by the audience as an implied brand endorsement from the star of the show.

In the next section we will turn our attention to branded entertainment, another topic that is closely related to everything considered in this chapter thus far. To set the stage, one way to see branded entertainment is as a natural extension and outgrowth of product placement. Branded entertainment raises the stakes but also raises the potential payout. With product placement, the question is: "What shows are in development that we might fit our brand into?" With branded entertainment, one option for advertisers is to create their own shows, so they never have to worry about finding a place for their brand. This guarantees that the brand will be one of the stars of the show.

16-5 BRANDED ENTERTAINMENT

For a stock-car racing fan, there is nothing quite like being at the Lowe's Motor Speedway on the evening of the Coca-Cola 600. It's NASCAR's longest night. But being there live is a rare treat, and so the NASCAR Sprint Cup Series gets plenty of coverage on television, making it among the most popular televised sporting events in North America. If you've never watched a NASCAR race, you owe it to yourself to do so, because even though NASCAR is all about the drivers and the race, every race is also a colossal celebration of brands. There are the cars themselves—as in Exhibit 16.12—carrying the logos large and small of something like 800 NASCAR sponsors. The announcers keep you informed throughout via the Old Spice Lap Leaders update and the Visa Race Break. We are told that Home Depot is the Official Home Improvement Warehouse of NASCAR and UPS is the Official Delivery Service of NASCAR. At commercial breaks there are the beer ads with Budweiser and Miller shouting at each other, and we rejoin the race to follow the Budweiser or Miller Lite car around the track. None of this comes as any surprise because NASCAR openly and aggressively bills itself as the best marketing opportunity in sports. Said another way, a NASCAR race is a fantastic example of branded entertainment.

It's not hard to understand why Gillette or Budweiser would be willing to shell out millions of dollars to be a featured brand in the NASCAR Sprint Cup Series. Huge television audiences will yield hundreds of thousands of media impressions, especially for those cars (and brands) leading the race. A hundred thousand fans in the stands will make your brand a focal point, and many will visit a branded showcase before or after the race to meet the car and driver.

EXHIBIT 16.12 Brands are the real stars of NASCAR races.

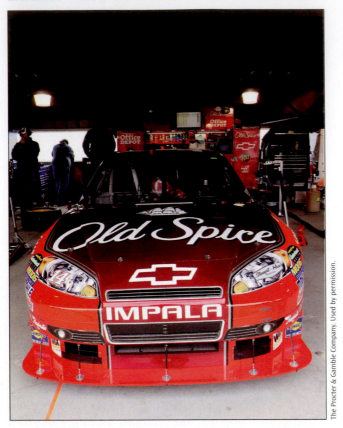

The Procter & Gamble Company. Used by permission.

In addition, general industry research indicates that NASCAR fans are unusually loyal to the brands that sponsor cars and have absolutely no problem with marketers plastering their logos all over their cars and their drivers. Indeed, many NASCAR fans often wear those logos proudly. Moreover, the data say that race fans are three times more likely to purchase a product promoted by their favorite NASCAR driver relative to the fans of all other sports.[31] One NASCAR marketing executive put it something like this: "Our teams and drivers have done a wonderful job communicating to fans that the more Old Spice they buy, the faster Tony Stewart is going to go." Obviously, this entails impressing and connecting with consumers in a most compelling way, making the Gillette car or the Bud car or the Viagra car or the Lowe's car all great icons of branded entertainment.

NASCAR is truly a unique brand-building "vehicle" with numerous marketing opportunities for brands large and small. But we use it here as an exemplar of something bigger, something more pervasive, and something that is growing in popularity as a way to support and build brands in the IBP program. Although it has been called many things, we have settled on the label *branded entertainment*. **Branded entertainment** entails the development and support of any

entertainment property (e.g., TV show, theme park, short film, movie, or video game) where a primary objective is to feature a firm's brand or brands in an effort to impress and connect with consumers in a unique and compelling way.

What distinguishes branded entertainment from product placement is that in branded entertainment, the entertainment would not exist without the marketer's support, and in many instances, it is marketers themselves who create the entertainment property. BMW's efforts in product placement versus branded entertainment provide a perfect example. The appearance of the Z3 in the 1995 James Bond thriller *GoldenEye* is a nice example of product placement. But BMW did not stop there. In 2001, BMW and its ad agency Fallon Minneapolis decided it was time to make their own movies with BMW vehicles as the star of the show. The result was a series of original, Web-distributed short films like *Beat the Devil*, starring Clive Owen, James Brown, Marilyn Manson, and, most especially, the BMW Z4. The success of these custom-made BMW films helped launch the new era of branded entertainment.

Many have followed BMW's lead in developing their own forms of entertainment as a means to feature brands. Goen Group developed a reality show, the *Million Dollar Makeover Challenge*, starring its diet pill Trimspa. Unilever helped produce two specials to promote its Axe body wash that ran on MTV and SpikeTV. *The Fairway Gourmet*, featured on PBS, promoted images of the good life, courtesy of the Hawaii Visitors & Convention Bureau. In the digital era, Chipotle (the restaurant chain) captured the attention of the Grammy's TV audience by creating an animated film *Back to the Start* which featured the restaurant's practice of doing business only with farmers dedicated to humane practices.[32] At last count, the film attracted over 7 million views on YouTube. By creating shows themselves (often with their ad agencies), marketers seek to attract a specific target audience with a carefully tailored story that shows their brands at their best. This is something quite different from trying to find a special place for one's brand in an existing show. As others have suggested, "clients often enter the (general) realm of entertainment marketing via small product placements that eventually develop into larger promotional programs."[33] On the path of brand building, it is natural to evolve from the simple product placement to the more elaborate enterprise of branded entertainment. Taking branded entertainment to perhaps its ultimate manifestation, a Bollywood film titled *Zindagi Na Milegi Dobara* (roughly translated to mean "You Only Live Once") was essentially a feature-length tourism advertisement for the country of Spain. The three main characters embarked on an adventure-filled holiday across Spain. By the time the film was released in its final form, one analyst remarked, "People talk about 'in-movie advertising.' In this case, the whole fricking movie was 'in-movie advertising!'" Within a month after the movie's release, visa applications to visit Spain had doubled and the number of Indian tourists to Spain jumped 65 percent the following year.[34]

Returning to the NASCAR example, today's NASCAR racing circuit could not exist without big brands like Gillette, Budweiser, Toyota, and Old Spice sponsoring racing teams and their drivers. Without the brands, there would be no NASCAR. As exemplified by a NASCAR race, in today's world of brand building, it is often impossible to disentangle the brand building from the entertainment. That's a great scenario for brand builders, because, among other things, it makes their efforts DVR-proof. You can't skip the brands in a NASCAR race. (See Insights Online [Exhibit 16.13] for an example of how Oreo caught people's attention during Pride Week.)

16-5a Where Are Product Placement and Branded Entertainment Headed?

It is easy to understand the surging popularity of product placements and branded entertainment. Reaching the unreachable through a means that allows your brand to stand out and connect with the consumer can only mean more interest from marketers. But there are always complicating and countervailing forces. No one can really say how rapidly advertising dollars will flow into branded entertainment in the next decade although current estimates suggest that annually about $4 billion finds its way to branded entertainment and product placement combined.[35] Several forces could work to undermine that dollar flow, however.

One of the obvious countervailing forces is instant oversaturation. Like any other faddishly popular promotional tactic, if advertisers pile on too quickly, a jaded consumer and a cluttered environment will be the result.[36] Some will argue that creative collaboration can always yield new opportunities for branded entertainment (as in Healthy Choice's *Working Lunch*), but you have to acknowledge at some point that yet another motion picture featuring another hot automobile

will start to feel a little stale. Indeed, we may already be there.

A related problem involves the processes and systems that currently exist for matching brands with entertainment properties. Traditional media provide a well-established path for reaching consumers. Marketers like that predictability. Branded entertainment is a new and often unpredictable path. As noted by a senior executive at Fallon Minneapolis, a pioneer in branded entertainment with BMW Films, "For every success you have several failures, because you're basically using a machete to cut through the jungle . . . with branded entertainment, every time out, it's new."[37] Lack of predictability causes the process to break down.

Finally, there is a concern about playing it straight with consumers. For example, Ralph Nader's Commercial Alert consumer advocacy group has charged that TV networks deceive the public by failing to disclose the details of product-placement deals. The group's basic argument seems to be that since many product placements are in fact "paid advertisements," consumers should be advised as such. It is conceivable that a federal agency could call for some form of disclosure when fees have been paid to place brands in U.S. TV shows, although now that the practice has become so prevalent, we expect that consumers already perceive that there is money changing hands behind the scenes. Consumers are generally pretty savvy about this sort of thing.

16-5b What's Old Is New Again

It turns out that marketers, media moguls, ad agencies, and entertainers have much in common. They do what they do for business reasons. And they have and will continue to do business together. That's reality. It has been reality for decades. Smart advertisers have always recognized this, and then go about their business of trying to reach consumers with a positive message on behalf of their brands. No firm has managed this collaboration better throughout the years than Procter & Gamble, and to close this section, we take a then-and-now look at P&G initiatives to acknowledge that. Even though it is enjoying a huge surge of popularity recently, branded entertainment has been around for decades.

In 1923, P&G was on the cutting edge of branded entertainment in the then-new medium of radio. (Try if you dare to imagine a world without television or Facebook—how did people survive?) To promote their shortening product Crisco, they helped create a new radio program called *Crisco Cooking Talks*. This was a 15-minute program that featured recipes and advice to encourage cooks, like the one in Exhibit 16.14 who is taking notes about a new recipe being offered,

EXHIBIT 16.14 In the 1920s, P&G was an innovator in the new medium of radio, reaching consumers with the first branded entertainment program, *Crisco Cooking Talks.*

An enduring relationship is clearly something to strive for. Long-term relationships beget trust, and when partners trust each other, they also look out for each other. So although P&G does not have direct control over the content of *Top Model,* it is able to ask for brand inserts and sometimes influence the show's content because of the relationship. However, P&G has learned to not push too hard to get its brand featured. That can detract from the entertainment value of the programming, which wouldn't help anyone. To maintain the right balance, the CoverGirl brand receives strong integration into the plot in just a few episodes per season.

Authenticity of the brand integration is always desirable, and CoverGirl definitely gets that on *Top Model.* For example, each season the finalists must prepare to be photographed for a magazine ad. This is after all what models get paid to do: appear in ads. So it's perfectly natural that this is part of the show, and it's perfectly natural that the magazine ad will be for CoverGirl, as this is a brand that stands for "enhancing your natural beauty." The content of the show and the essence of the brand become completely intertwined, with an implied endorsement from *America's Next Top Model,* like Eva in Exhibit 16.15. It doesn't

EXHIBIT 16.15 P&G has continued its use of branded entertainment. Every winner of the *Top Model* competition goes on to be CoverGirl model for P&G, delivering an instant brand endorsement from a new celebrity.

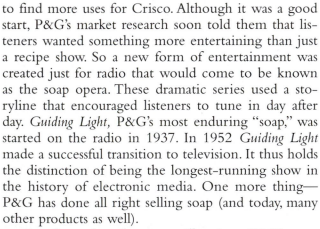

to find more uses for Crisco. Although it was a good start, P&G's market research soon told them that listeners wanted something more entertaining than just a recipe show. So a new form of entertainment was created just for radio that would come to be known as the soap opera. These dramatic series used a storyline that encouraged listeners to tune in day after day. *Guiding Light,* P&G's most enduring "soap," was started on the radio in 1937. In 1952 *Guiding Light* made a successful transition to television. It thus holds the distinction of being the longest-running show in the history of electronic media. One more thing—P&G has done all right selling soap (and today, many other products as well).

Fast-forward to the new millennium. P&G's consumer has changed, and new forms of IBP are necessary. Today P&G works with partners like NBC Digital Networks and Starcom MediaVest Group to ensure that its brands are embedded in the entertainment venues preferred by its targeted consumers. A great example is the integration of P&G's CoverGirl brand in the CW Network's *America's Next Top Model,* hosted by former CoverGirl Tyra Banks. In this CoverGirl/*Top Model* relationship, we see exemplified many best practices for branded entertainers.

get any better than that in the brave new world of brand building.

Like many other marketers, P&G Productions is also moving to the Web to create original content. According to *Advertising Age,* this tracks with the trend of Madison & Vine moving to Silicon Valley.[38] One of P&G's recent "Webisodes" is the series *A Parent Is Born* (see Exhibit 16.16). This series was an online documentary following Suzie and Steve on their emotional journey to parenthood. Each of its 12 episodes was about five minutes in length and tracked the experience for Suzie and Steve from finding out the sex of their baby through baby showers and childbirth class to the grand finale where the newborn (baby Leo) comes home. Now you're thinking—who'd be interested in watching this sort of thing? The obvious answer—expecting couples—who, by the way, will soon be prime prospects for P&G's Pampers brand of disposable diapers. Therein lies the appeal of the Webisode—it is relatively inexpensive to produce, and brands get total control in developing the content so as to meet their specific objectives and appeal to their specific target audience. And as we have seen over and over again, like with the *Working Lunch* example that began the chapter, marketers will always prefer the IBP tools that take them right to their target audience.

EXHIBIT 16.16 P&G created its own Web-based documentary series, *A Parent Is Born,* as a way to feature the firm's brands—particularly the Pampers brand of disposable diapers.

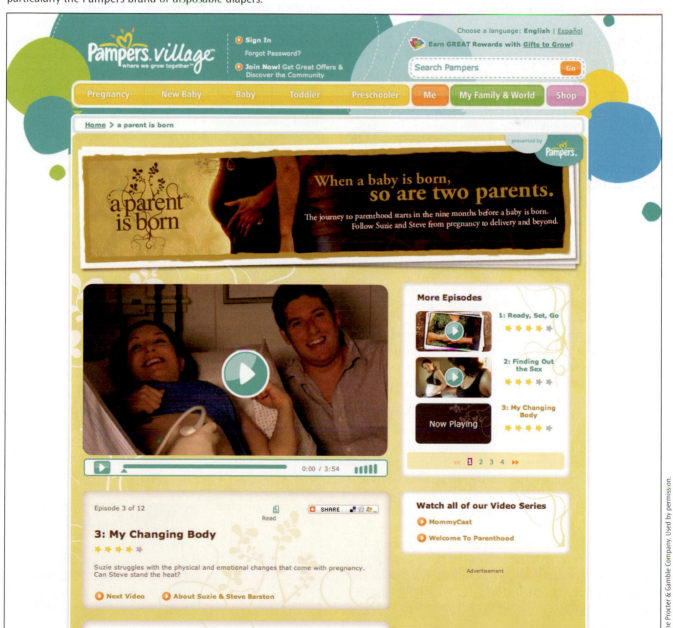

LO 4

16-6 THE COORDINATION CHALLENGE

The choices for delivering messages to a target audience continue to evolve. As you have seen, marketers and advertisers are constantly searching for new, cost-effective ways to break through the clutter and connect with consumers. Today, everything from advertising in restrooms to sponsoring a marathon to advergaming to producing short films for the Internet is part of the portfolio.

In concluding this chapter, a critical point about the explosion of advertising and IBP tools needs to be reinforced. Advertisers have a vast and ever-expanding array of options for delivering messages to their potential customers. From cable TV to national newspapers, from high-tech billboards to online contests and giveaways, the variety of options is staggering. The keys to success for any campaign are choosing the right set of options to engage a target segment and then coordinating the placement of messages to ensure coherent and timely communication.

Actually, even in this era of a hyper-focus on integration, many factors work against coordination in IBP. As advertising and IBP have become more complex, organizations often become reliant on diverse functional specialists. For example, an organization might have separate managers for advertising, event sponsorship, branded entertainment, and digital development. Specialists, by definition, focus on their specialty and can lose sight of what others in the organization are doing. Specialists also want their own budgets and typically argue for more funding for their particular area. This competition for budget dollars often yields rivalries and animosities that work against coordination. Never underestimate the power of competition for the budget. It is exceedingly rare to find anyone who will volunteer to take less of the budget so that someone else can have more.

Coordination is further complicated by the fact that there can be an incredible lack of alignment around who is responsible for achieving the integration.[39] Should the client accept this responsibility? Or should integration be the responsibility of a "lead" agency? Ad agencies often see themselves in this lead role but have not played it to anyone's satisfaction.[40] One vision of how things should work has the lead agency playing the role of an architect and general contractor. The campaign architect is charged with drawing up a plan that is media neutral and then hiring subcontractors to deliver those aspects of the project that the agency itself is ill suited to handle. The plan must also be profit neutral. That is, the budget must go to the subcontractors who can deliver the work called for in the master plan.[41] Here again the question becomes, Will the "architect/general contractor" really spread the wealth, if by doing so it forfeits wealth? Life usually doesn't work that way. But one thing is for sure: When it is not clear who is accountable for delivering an integrated campaign, there is little chance that synergy or integration will be achieved.

Remember finally that the objective underlying the need for coordination is to achieve a synergistic effect. Individual media can work in isolation, but advertisers get more for their dollars if various media and IBP tools build on one another and work together. Even savvy marketers like American Express are challenged by the need for coordination, and especially so as they cut back on their use of the 30-second TV spot and venture into diverse IBP tools. For instance, to launch its *Blue* card, AmEx employed an innovative mix, starting with Blue-labeled water bottles given away at health clubs and Blue ads printed on millions of popcorn bags. The company sponsored a Sheryl Crow concert in New York's Central Park and transformed L.A.'s House of Blues jazz club into the "House of Blue," with performances by Elvis Costello, Stevie Wonder, and Counting Crows. Print ads and TV have also been used to back the Blue, but AmEx's spending in these traditional media was down by more than 50 percent relative to previous campaigns. Making diverse components like these work together and speak to the targeted consumer with a "single voice" is the essence of advertising and IBP. AmEx appears to have found a good formula: The Blue card was the most successful new-product launch in the company's history.[42] (See Insights Online [Exhibit 16.17] for a great example of coordination by Nike.]

The coordination challenge does not end here. Chapters that follow will add more layers of complexity to this challenge. Topics to come include direct marketing, personal selling, public relations, influencer marketing, and corporate advertising. These activities entail additional contacts with a target audience that *should* reinforce the messages being delivered through broadcast, print, digital, and support media. Integrating these efforts to speak with one voice represents a marketer's best and maybe only hope for breaking through the clutter to engage with a target segment in today's crowded marketplace. But these next chapters offer more diversity in IBP applications, which makes the "one voice" goal even more of a challenge.

INSIGHTS ONLINE

16.17 Go online to see the AdAge feature, "Nike Sets the Pace for Taking Sport Marketing beyond Entertainment."

SUMMARY

 Justify the growing popularity of event marketing and sponsorship as a modern means of experiential brand promotion.

The list of companies sponsoring events grows with each passing year, and the events include a wide variety of activities. Of these various activities, sports attract the most sponsorship dollars. Sponsorship can help in building brand familiarity; it can promote brand loyalty by connecting a brand with powerful emotional experiences, and in most instances it allows a marketer to reach a well-defined target audience. Events can also facilitate face-to-face contacts with key customers and present opportunities to distribute product samples, sell premiums, and conduct consumer surveys.

 Summarize the uses and appeal of product placements in venues like TV, movies, and video games.

Product placements have surged in popularity during the past decade and there are many reasons to believe that advertisers will continue to commit more resources to this activity. Like any other advertising tactic, product placements offer the most value when they are connected to other elements of the advertising plan. One common use of the placement is to help create excitement for the launch of a new product. Implicit celebrity endorsements and authenticity are key issues to consider when judging placement opportunities. High-quality placements are most likely to result from great collaboration among marketers, agents, producers, and writers. As always, the best team wins.

 Explain the benefits and challenges of connecting with an event venue or entertainment properties in building a brand.

Brand builders want to connect with consumers, and to do so they are connecting with the entertainment business. Even though not everyone can afford a NASCAR sponsorship, in many ways NASCAR sets the standard for celebrating brands in an entertaining setting. Many marketers, such as BMW, P&G, and Unilever, are now developing their own entertainment properties to feature their brands. However, the rush to participate in branded entertainment ventures raises the risk of oversaturation and consumer backlash, or at least consumer apathy. As with any tool, while it is new and fresh, good things happen. When it gets old and stale, advertisers will turn to the next "big thing."

 Discuss the challenges presented by the ever-increasing variety of communication and branding tools for achieving integrated brand promotion via the consumer experience.

The tremendous variety of media options we have seen thus far represents a monumental challenge for an advertiser who wishes to speak to a customer with a single voice. Achieving this single voice is critical for breaking through the clutter of the modern advertising environment. However, the functional specialists required for working in the various media have their own biases and sub-goals that can get in the way of integration. We will return to this issue in subsequent chapters as we explore other options available to marketers in their quest to win customers.

KEY TERMS

Madison & Vine	media impressions	product placement
Chaos Scenario	leveraging	authenticity
event sponsorship	consumer-event congruity	branded entertainment

ENDNOTES

1. Richard Tedesco, "Marketers Are Still Staging Events—Budget Cuts Be Damned," promomagazine.com/eventmarketing, January 1, 2009.

2. Kunur Patel, "All the World's a Game, and Brands Want to Play Along," *Advertising Age,* May 31, 2010, 4.

3. Bob Garfield, "The Post Advertising Age," *Advertising Age,* March 26, 2007, 1, 12–14.

4. Dan Lippe, "Events Trail Only Ads in Alignment with Brands," *Advertising Age,* March 19, 2007, S-2.

5. Bettina Cornwell, Clinton Weeks, and Donald Roy, "Sponsor-Linked Marketing: Opening the Black Box," *Journal of Advertising* (Summer 2005), 21–42.

6. Chris Allen, Susan Fournier, and Felicia Miller, "Brands and Their Meaning Makers," in Curtis P Haugtvedt, Paul Herr, and Frank R Kardes (Eds.), *Handbook of Consumer Psychology* (Hillsdale, NJ: LEA Publishing, 2008), Chapter 31.

7. Patricia Odell, "Sponsorship Spending Struggles to Recover," promomagazine.com/news/sponsorship, January 28, 2010; ZenithOptimedia U.S. Ad Spending Forecast through 2013, *Advertising Age Data Center,* www.adage.com/datacenter, accessed September 23, 2012.

8. Emily Steel, "Measured Media Lose in Spending Cuts," *The Wall Street Journal,* March 14, 2007, B3; Mike Spector and Gina Chon, "The Great Texas Truck Fair," *The Wall Street Journal,* October 20, 2006, B1, B10.

9. Nat Ives, "Events Businesses Are Paying Off for Publishers," *Advertising Age,* March 5, 2012, 9.

10. Grant McCracken, "Culture and Consumption: A Theoretical Account of the Structure and Movement of the Cultural Meaning of Consumer Goods," *Journal of Consumer Research,* vol. 13 (June 1986), 71–84.

11. Jeremy Mullman, "World Cup Kicks Off International Marketing Games on Epic Scale," *Advertising Age,* May 17, 2010, 4.

12. Ellen Byron, "An Old Dice Game Catches On Again, Pushed by P&G," *The Wall Street Journal,* January 30, 2007, A1, A13.

13. Amy Hernandez, "Research Studies Gauge Sponsorship ROI," *Marketing News,* May 12, 2003, 16; Ian Mount, "Exploding the Myths of Stadium Naming," *Business 2.0,* April 2004, 82, 83.

14. Kate Fitzgerald, "Events No Longer Immune to Marketer Demand for ROI," *Advertising Age,* March 19, 2007, S-3.

15. Rich Thomaselli, "Nielsen to Measure Sports Sponsorship," *Advertising Age,* May 3, 2004, 14.

16. "Coors Field Serves 2.4B Total Ad Impressions during World Series," mediabuyerplanner.com/entry, November 20, 2007.

17. Angeline Close, R. Zachary Finney, Russell Lacey, and Julie Sneath, "Engaging the Consumer through Event Marketing: Linking Attendees with the Sponsor, Community, and Brand," *Journal of Advertising Research,* vol. 46, no. 3 (2006), 420–433.

18. Bettina Cornwell, Clinton Weeks, and Donald Roy, "Sponsor-Linked Marketing: Opening the Black Box," *Journal of Advertising,* vol. 34 (Summer 2005), 21–42.

19. Angeline Close, Anjala Krishen, and Michael S. LaTour, "This Event Is Me!: How Consumer-Event Congruity Leverages Sponsorship," *Journal of Advertising Research,* vol. 49, no. 3 (2009), 271–284.

20. Marc Graser, "TV's Savior?" *Advertising Age,* February 6, 2006, S-1, S-2.

21. Marc Graser, "Automakers: Every Car Needs a Movie," *Advertising Age,* December 11, 2006, 8.

22. Kate Kelly and Brian Steinberg, "Sony's 'Talladega Nights' Comedy Is Product-Plug Rally," *The Wall Street Journal,* July 28, 2006, A9, A12.

23. Emma Hall, "Young Consumers Receptive to Movie Product Placements," *Advertising Age,* March 29, 2004, 8; Federico de Gregorio and Yongjun Sung, "Understanding Attitudes Toward and Behaviors in Response to Product Placement," *Journal of Advertising,* vol. 39 (Spring 2010), 83–96.

24. Nielsen Newswire, "Trends in U.S. Video Gaming—The Rise of Cross-Platform," March 9, 2012, www.nielsen.com, accessed March 9, 2013.

25. John Gaudiosi, "In-Game Ads Reach the Next Level," *Business 2.0,* July 2007, 36, 37.

26. Cristel Russell and Michael Belch, "A Managerial Investigation into the Product Placement Industry," *Journal of Advertising Research,* vol. 45 (March 2005), 73–92.

27. Federico de Gregorio and Yongjun Sung, "Understanding Attitudes Toward and Behaviors in Response to Product Placement," *Journal of Advertising,* vol. 39 (Spring 2010), 83–96.

28. Rance Crain, "Want to Really Serve Consumers? Offer Them an Experience," *Advertising Age,* December 10, 2012, 26.

29. James Karrah, Kathy McKee, and Carol Pardun, "Practitioners' Evolving Views on Product Placement Effectiveness," *Journal of Advertising Research,* vol. 43 (June 2003), 138–149.

30. Christina Passariello, "Ray-Ban Hopes to Party Like It's 1983 by Re-launching Its Wayfarer Shades," *The Wall Street Journal,* October 27, 2006, B1, B4.

31. Rich Thomaselli, "Nextel Link Takes NASCAR to New Level," *Advertising Age,* October 27, 2003, S-7.

32. Jack Neff and Natalie Zumba, "The Rise of Branded Experiences," *Advertising Age,* January 7, 2013, 13.

33. Cristel Russell and Michael Belch, "A Managerial Investigation into the Product Placement Industry," *Journal of Advertising Research,* vol. 45 (March 2005), 82, 83.

34. Neil Munshi, "Spain's Starring Role in Bollywood Movie a Boon to Tourism" *Advertising Age,* February 6, 2012, 6.

35. Richard Alan Nelson and Rick Ebel, "Super Charged," pubs.ppai.org, June 27, 2012, www.pubs.ppai.org, accessed September 1, 2012.

36. Larry Dobrow, "Is It Time to Put an End to Brand Integration?" adage.com, May 21, 2009.

37. Kate MacArthur, "Branded Entertainment, Marketing Tradition Tussle," *Advertising Age,* May 10, 2004, 6.

38. Andrew Hampp, "How Madison & Vine Moved to Silicon Valley," *Advertising Age,* March 15, 2010, 4.

39. Burt Helm, "Struggles of a Mad Man: Saatchi & Saatchi CEO Kevin Roberts," *BusinessWeek,* December 3, 2007, 44–50.

40. Joe Cappo, *The Future of Advertising* (Chicago, IL: McGraw-Hill, 2003), Chapter 8.

41. Ibid., 153, 154.

42. Suzanne Vranica, "For Big Marketers Like AmEx, TV Ads Lose Starring Role," *The Wall Street Journal,* May 17, 2004, B1, B3.

CHAPTER 17
Integrating Direct Marketing and Personal Selling

After reading and thinking about this chapter, you will be able to do the following:

1 Identify the three primary purposes served by direct marketing and explain its growing popularity.

2 Distinguish a mailing list from a marketing database and review the many applications of each.

3 Describe the prominent media used by direct marketers in delivering their messages to the consumer.

4 Explain the key role of direct marketing and personal selling in complementing other advertising activities.

In this chapter, we examine direct marketing and explain how it is used to complement other forms of advertising and integrated brand promotion (IBP). In addition, we conclude this chapter with an introduction to the field of personal selling. Personal selling brings the human element into the marketing/advertising/IBP process and shares many important features with direct marketing. For instance, as with direct marketing, an organization's sales personnel are looking to develop a dialogue with customers that can result in product sales in the short run and repeat business over the long run. Trial purchases are desirable, but a satisfied customer who comes back to purchase again and again (and encourages friends and family to do likewise) is the ultimate goal. Personal selling, which features direct contact and response to consumer feedback, is ideally suited to encouraging brand loyalty.

 LO **1**

17-1 THE EVOLUTION OF DIRECT MARKETING

With the growing concern about fragmenting markets and the diminishing effectiveness of traditional media in reaching those markets, more and more ad dollars will be moved into other options like direct marketing programs.[1] The Direct Marketing Association (DMA) provides some stats on the direct marketing industry.[2] Marketers invested approximately $168.5 *billion* on direct marketing. Direct marketing generates $2.05 trillion in incremental sales and 8.7 percent of total U.S. gross domestic product. Direct marketing provides jobs in the United States; it accounts for a total of 9.2 million U.S. jobs. Before we examine the evolution of direct marketing and look deeper at the reasons for its popularity, we need a clear understanding of what people mean when they use the term *direct marketing*. While there are lots of ways to describe direct marketing, the definition from the DMA provides a starting point:

> **Direct marketing** *is an interactive system of marketing, which uses one or more advertising media to affect a measurable response and/or transaction at any location.*[3]

When examined piece by piece, this definition offers an excellent way to understand the scope and purpose of direct marketing.[4]

Direct marketing is *interactive* in that the advertiser is attempting to develop an ongoing dialogue with customers. (See Insights Online [Exhibit 17.1] for an example of how Converse uses Facebook to do this.) Direct marketing programs are commonly planned with the notion that one contact will lead to another and then another so that the marketer's message can become more focused and refined with each interaction. The DMA's definition also notes that multiple media can be used in direct marketing programs. This is an important point for two reasons. First, we do not want to equate direct mail and direct marketing. Any medium (including mobile media) can be used in executing direct marketing programs, not just the mail. Second, as we have noted before, a combination of media is likely to be more effective than any one medium alone.

Another key aspect of direct marketing programs is that they often are designed to produce immediate, measurable response. In many cases, direct marketing programs are designed to produce an immediate sale (recall the discussion from Chapter 1 on direct versus delayed response advertising). In a magazine or television ad, a customer might be asked to call or go online for Proactiv skin care, a Ninja juicer, Snuggie, ShamWOW, or a Slap-Chop—some recent top infomercial products. Because of this emphasis on immediate response, direct marketers are in a position to judge the effectiveness of a particular program. On the Web, banner ads implore you to order now through an app or site. And on your smartphone, a message may offer you an outstanding opportunity to place an order and get that phone skin you have been wanting.

The final phase of the DMA's definition notes that a direct marketing transaction can take place anywhere. The key idea here is that customers do not have to make a trip to a retail store for a direct marketing

program to work. Follow-ups can be made by mail, over the telephone, on a mobile device, or via a computer on the Internet. At one time the thinking was that Web-based direct marketers such as Amazon and eToys.com would ultimately provide so much convenience for shoppers that traditional retail stores might fall by the wayside. It now seems clear that consumers like the option of contacting companies and evaluating the products in many ways. So smart retailers (see Exhibit 17.2) make themselves available in both the physical and virtual worlds. As the Best Buy ad in Exhibit 17.2 shows, Best Buy is alerting consumers to the fact that if they do their shopping through online direct marketers only, they won't have the option of returning an item to a store near them for a refund or exchange. But at Best Buy, you can buy online or in the store and still return an item to the store—a great advantage over online only. Customers are free to choose where and how they want to shop—but online alone does have its drawbacks. And as we will see later in the chapter regarding e-commerce, retailers from

EXHIBIT 17.2 Among other things, pure-play e-tailers like Amazon realize that when consumers are dissatisfied with their purchases, many want a physical store where they can return the merchandise for a refund or exchange. In this ad, BestBuy.com has some fun with this issue in the context of online shopping. At Best Buy, if *Folksongs from Romania* is not what you thought you ordered, you can return it to one of their stores.

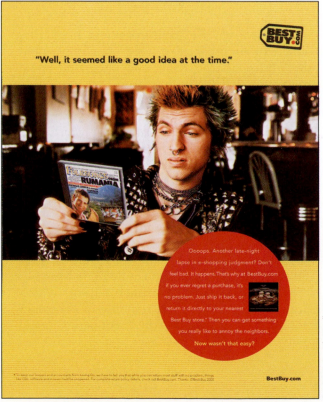

Target to Lululemon to Nordstrom are building their online and mobile presence to respond to consumers' desire to take advantage of the conveniences of direct marketing via the Web, social media, and mobile consumer technology.[5] The best e-tailers, such as Zappos.com (Spanish for shoes), have two-way free shipping, to keep e-tailing more consumer friendly.

17-1a Direct Marketing—A Look Back

From Johannes Gutenberg and Benjamin Franklin to Richard Sears, Alvah Roebuck, Les Wunderman, and Lillian Vernon, the evolution of direct marketing has involved some of the great pioneers in business. As Exhibit 17.3 shows, the practice of direct marketing today is shaped by the successes of many notable

mail-order companies and catalog merchandisers.[6] Among them, none is more exemplary than L.L. Bean. Bean founded his company in 1912 on his integrity and $400. His first product was a unique hunting shoe made from a leather top and rubber bottom sewn together. Other outdoor clothing and equipment soon followed in the Bean catalog.

A look at the L.L. Bean catalog of 1917 (black and white, just 12 pages) reveals the fundamental strategy underlying Bean's success. It featured the Maine Hunting Shoe and other outdoor clothing with descriptive copy that was informative, factual, and low-key. On the front page was Bean's commitment to quality. It read: "Maine Hunting Shoe—guarantee. We guarantee this pair of shoes to give perfect satisfaction in every way. If the rubber breaks or the tops grow hard, return

EXHIBIT 17.3 Direct marketing milestones over the years.

c. 1450	Johannes Gutenberg invents movable type.
1667	The first gardening catalog is published by William Lucas, an English gardener.
1744	Benjamin Franklin publishes a catalog of books on science and industry and formulates the basic mail-order concept of customer satisfaction guaranteed.
1830s	A few mail-order companies began operating in New England, selling camping and fishing supplies.
1863	The introduction of penny postage facilitates direct mail.
1867	The invention of the typewriter gives a modern appearance to direct mail materials.
1872	Montgomery Ward publishes his first "catalog," selling 163 items on a single sheet of paper. By 1884 his catalog grows to 240 pages, with thousands of items and a money-back guarantee.
1886	Richard Sears enters the mail-order business by selling gold watches and makes $5,000 in his first six months. He partners with Alvah Roebuck in 1887, and by 1893 they are marketing a wide range of merchandise in a 196-page catalog.
1912	L. L. Bean founds one of today's most admired mail-order companies on the strength of his Maine Hunting Shoe and a guarantee of total satisfaction for the life of the shoe.
1917	The Direct Mail Advertising Association is founded. In 1973 it becomes the Direct Mail/Direct Marketing Association.
1928	Third-class bulk mail becomes a reality, offering economies for the direct mail industry.
1950	Credit cards first appear, led by the Diners' Club travel and entertainment card. American Express enters in 1958.
1951	Lillian Vernon places an ad for a monogrammed purse and belt and generates $16,000 in immediate business. She reinvests the money in what becomes the Lillian Vernon enterprise. Vernon recognizes early on that catalog shopping has great appeal to time-pressed consumers.
1953	Publishers Clearing House is founded and soon becomes a dominant force in magazine subscriptions.
1955	Columbia Record Club is established, and eventually becomes Columbia House—the music-marketing giant.
1967	The term *telemarketing* first appears in print, and AT&T introduces the first toll-free 800 service.
1983	The Direct Mail/Direct Marketing Association drops Direct Mail from its name to become the DMA, as a reflection of the multiple media being used by direct marketers.
1984	Apple introduces the Macintosh personal computer.
1992	The number of people who shop at home surpasses 100 million in the United States.
1998	The Direct Marketing Association, www.the-dma.org, eager to adapt its members' bulk mailing techniques for the Internet, announces it will merge with the Association for Interactive Media, www.interactivehq.org.
2003	U.S. consumers register more than 10 million phone numbers in the first four days of the national Do Not Call Registry.

Adapted from the DMA's "Grassroots Advocacy Guide for Direct Marketers" (1993), Direct Marketing Association, Inc.; Rebecca Quick, "Direct Marketing Association to Merge with Association of Interactive Media," *The Wall Street Journal*, October 12, 1998, B6.

EXHIBIT 17.4 A good guarantee never goes out of fashion.

Susan Van Etten

them together with this guarantee tag and we will replace them, free of charge. Signed, L.L. Bean."[7] Bean realized that long-term relationships with customers must be based on trust, and his guarantee policy was aimed at developing and sustaining that trust when he could not interact with customers face-to-face. As an astute direct marketer, Bean also showed a keen appreciation for the importance of building a good mailing list. For many years he used his profits to promote his free catalog via advertisements in hunting and fishing magazines. Those replying to the ads received a rapid response and typically became Bean customers. Bean's obsession with building mailing lists is nicely captured by this quote from his friend, Maine native John Gould: "If you drop in just to shake his hand, you get home to find his catalog in your mailbox."[8] Today, L.L. Bean is still a family-operated business that emphasizes the basic philosophies of its founder. Quality products, understated advertising, and sophisticated customer-contact and distribution systems sustain the business. But Bean's 100-percent-satisfaction guarantee remains at the heart of the relationship between Bean and its customers, as seen as on its homepage in Exhibit 17.4.

17-1b Direct Marketing Today

Direct marketing today is rooted in the legacy of mail-order giants and catalog merchandisers such as L.L. Bean, Sears, and JCPenney, and to a lesser extent, although popular (especially for men), Victoria's Secret. Today, direct marketing has broken free from its mail-order heritage to become a tool used by all types of organizations throughout the world. Although many types of businesses and not-for-profit organizations are using direct marketing, it is common to find that such direct marketing programs are often not carefully integrated with an organization's other advertising and IBP efforts. Integration should be the goal for advertising and direct marketing. Again and again the evidence supports our thesis that integrated programs are more effective than the sum of their parts.[9]

Because direct marketing now encompasses many different types of activities, it is important to remember the defining characteristics spelled out in the DMA definition given earlier. Direct marketing involves an attempt to interact or create a dialogue with the customer (see Insights Online [Exhibit 17.5] for an interesting example); multiple media are often employed in the process, and direct marketing is characterized by the fact that a measurable

INSIGHTS ONLINE

17.5 Go online to see the AdAge feature, "Old School Payphones in NYC Serve as a Direct Marketing Means to Inform New Yorkers on a Story Specific to the Neighborhood, in a Pro-Community Campaign by Ad Agency Droga5."

response is immediately available for assessing a program's impact. With these defining features in mind, we can see that direct marketing programs are commonly used for three primary purposes.

As you might imagine, the most common use of direct marketing is as a tool to close the sale with a customer. This can be done as a stand-alone program, or it can be coordinated with a firm's other advertising. Telecommunications giants such as AT&T, Sprint, and Verizon make extensive use of the advertising/direct marketing combination. High-profile mass media campaigns build awareness for their latest offer, followed by systematic direct marketing follow-ups to close the sale.

A second purpose for direct marketing programs is to identify

Direct marketing involves an attempt to interact or create a dialogue with the customer; multiple media are often employed in the process, and direct marketing is characterized by the fact that a measurable response is immediately available for assessing a program's impact.

prospects for future contacts and, at the same time, provide in-depth information to selected customers. Any time you respond to an offer for more information or for a free sample, you've identified yourself as a prospect and can expect follow-up sales pitches from a direct marketer. The Adkins ad in Exhibit 17.6 is a marketer's attempt to initiate a dialogue with prospective customers. Here, the firm is trying to engage the prospective customer with the offer of a rebate, coupons, a free starter kit, and the chance to interact with the company via a toll-free number or at the firm's website.

Direct marketing programs are also initiated as a means to engage customers, seek their advice, furnish helpful information about using a product, reward customers for using a brand, and in general foster brand loyalty. The manufacturer of Valvoline motor oil ran one of the classic programs to build loyalty for its brand by encouraging young car owners to join the Valvoline Performance Team.[10] To join the team, young drivers filled out a questionnaire that entered them into the Valvoline database. "Team" members received posters, special offers on racing-team apparel, news about racing events that Valvoline sponsored, and promotional reminders at regular intervals that reinforced the virtues of Valvoline for the driver's next oil change.

EXHIBIT 17.6 When firms use direct marketing, they need to engage the customer. Here, Adkins is offering the customer a rebate, coupons, a free sample, and two ways to begin a dialogue—toll-free number or website visit.

17-1c What's Driving the Growing Popularity of Direct Marketing?

The growth in popularity of direct marketing is due to a number of factors Some of these have to do with changes in consumer lifestyles and technological developments that in effect create a climate more conducive to the practice of direct marketing (see Insights Online [Exhibit 17.7] for an interesting example). In addition, direct marketing programs offer unique advantages vis-à-vis conventional mass media advertising, leading many organizations to shift more of their marketing budgets to direct marketing activities.

From the consumer's standpoint, direct marketing's growing popularity might be summarized in a single word—*convenience*. Dramatic growth in the number of dual-income and single-person households has reduced the time people have to visit retail stores. Direct marketers provide consumers access to a growing range of products and services in their homes, thus saving many households' most precious resource—time.

More liberal attitudes about the use of credit and the accumulation of debt have also contributed to the growth of direct marketing. Credit cards are the primary means of payment in most direct marketing transactions. The widespread availability of credit cards makes it ever more convenient to shop from the comfort of one's home. Third-party pay systems like PayPal have also contributed to the ease of payment in direct marketing.

Developments in telecommunications have also facilitated the direct marketing transaction. After getting off to a slow start in the late 1960s, toll-free telephone numbers have exploded in popularity to the point where there is no company website or a catalog that does not include an 800 number for interacting with the seller. Whether one is requesting a Bowflex demonstration video, ordering a bikini from Victoria's Secret, or planning a luxury cruise, the preferred mode of access for some consumers is chat or the 800 number when the consumer has questions or needs customer service, because these are real-time forms of communication.

Another key development having an impact on the growth of direct marketing is the Web, computers, and mobile devices. The diffusion of computer technology sweeping through modern societies has been a tremendous boon to direct marketers. The computer and mobile devices now allow consumers convenient access to shopping, and firms are even better able to track, keep records on, and interact with millions of customers with relative ease. As we will see in an upcoming discussion, Web interactions between firms using direct marketing for modest dollar amounts are fueling the growth of direct marketing's most potent tool—the marketing database—to better serve customers and make for more efficient transactions or, hopefully, relationships.

And just as the computer has provided marketers with the tool they need to handle databases of customer information, it too has provided convenience-oriented consumers with the tool they need to comparison shop with a point and click. What could be more convenient then pulling up shopping agent mySimon to check prices on everything from board shorts to snowboards? Or, in the mobile version, shoppers can browse in Best Buy or Home Depot stores and then do a price comparison online in a hybrid shopping format. (See

Insights Online [Exhibit 17.8] to learn about an innovative new tool being developed by Google.)

The appeal of direct marketing is enhanced further by the persistent emphasis of marketing managers on producing measurable effects. For instance, in direct marketing, it is common to find calculations such as **cost per inquiry (CPI)** or **cost per order (CPO)** being featured in program evaluation. These calculations simply divide the number of responses to a program by that program's cost. When calculated for every program an organization conducts over time, CPI and CPO data tell an organization what works and what doesn't in its competitive arena. These sorts of specific metrics just can be gathered for many IBP tools.

This emphasis on producing and monitoring measurable effects is realized most effectively through an approach called *database marketing.* Working with a database, direct marketers can target specific customers, track their actual purchase behavior over time, and experiment with different programs for affecting the purchasing patterns of these customers. Obviously, those programs that produce the best outcomes become the candidates for increased funding in the future. Let's look into database marketing.

LO 2

17-2 DATABASE MARKETING

If any ambiguity remains about what makes direct marketing different from marketing in general or other IBP techniques, that ambiguity can be erased by knowing about the database. The one characteristic of direct marketing that distinguishes it from other tactics generally is its emphasis on database development. Knowing who the best customers are along with what and how often they buy is a direct marketer's secret weapon. This knowledge accumulates in the form of a marketing database.

Databases used as the centerpieces in direct marketing campaigns take many forms and can contain many different layers of information about customers. At one extreme is the simple mailing list that contains nothing more than the names and contact information of possible customers; at the other extreme is the customized marketing database that augments names and contact info with various additional information about customers' characteristics, past purchases, and product preferences. Understanding this distinction between mailing lists and marketing databases is important in appreciating the scope of database marketing.

17-2a **Mailing Lists**

A **mailing list** is simply a file of names and addresses that an organization might use for contacting prospective or prior customers. Mailing lists are plentiful, easy to access, and inexpensive. For example, CD-ROM directories available for a few hundred dollars provide a cheap and easy way to generate mailing lists. More-targeted mailing lists are available from a variety of suppliers. The range of possibilities is mind-boggling, including groupings like subscribers to *Mickey Mouse Magazine,* kindergarten teachers, new home buyers, physical fitness trainers, Lord & Taylor credit card purchasers, or even the number of archaeologists in the United States!

Each time you subscribe to a magazine, order from a catalog, register your automobile, fill out a warranty card, redeem a rebate offer, apply for credit, join a professional society, or log in at a website, the information you provided about yourself goes on another mailing list. These lists are freely bought and sold through many means, including over the Internet. Sites such as Worldata and InfoUSA allow firms to buy names and addresses or email address lists. What's out there is remarkable, as can be seen in Exhibit 17.9—the Web screen for database provider InfoUSA.com. InfoUSA maintains information and has databases on 17 million businesses and 210 million consumers (they have missed many people). From these databases, a firm can order mailing lists based on geography, demographics, lifestyle, and specific behaviors (e.g., people who purchased an SUV in the last year).

Two broad categories of lists should be recognized: the internal, or house, list versus the external, or outside, list. **Internal lists** are simply an organization's records of its own customers, subscribers, donors, and inquirers. **External lists** are purchased from a list compiler or rented from a list broker (like InfoUSA). At the most basic level, internal and external lists facilitate the two fundamental activities of the direct marketer: Internal lists are the starting point for developing better relationships with current customers, whereas external lists help an organization cultivate new business.

17-2b **List Enhancement**

Name-and-address files, email addresses, or mobile device contacts, no matter what their source, are merely the starting point for database marketing. The next step in the evolution of a database is list enhancement. Typically this involves augmenting an internal list by combining it with other externally supplied lists or databases. External lists can be appended or merged with a house list.

One of the most straightforward list enhancements entails simply adding or appending more names and addresses to an internal list. Proprietary name-and-address files may be purchased from other companies

EXHIBIT 17.9 Firms start the direct marketing process by first defining the target market, then enlisting the services of database firms like InfoUSA. InfoUSA gathers and maintains information on 17 million businesses and 210 million consumers.

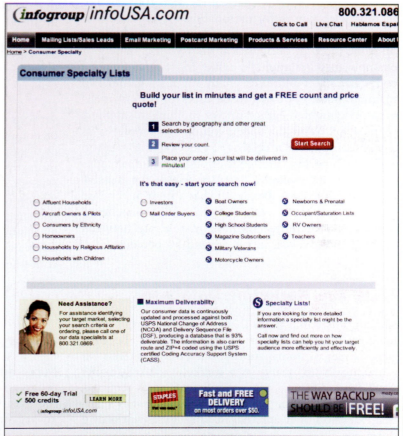

that operate in noncompetitive businesses. With today's computer capabilities, adding these additional households to an existing mailing list is simple. Many well-known companies such as American Express, Bloomingdale's, and Hertz sell or rent their customer lists for this purpose.

A second type of list enhancement involves incorporating information from external databases into a house list. Here the number of names and contact information remains the same, but an organization ends up with a more complete description of who its customers are. Typically, this kind of enhancement includes any of four categories of information:

- *Demographic data*—the basic descriptors of individuals and households available from the Census Bureau.
- *Geo-demographic data*—information that reveals the characteristics of the neighborhood in which a person resides.
- *Psychographic data*—data that allow for a more qualitative assessment of a customer's general lifestyle, interests, and opinions.
- *Behavioral data*—information about other products and services a customer has purchased; prior purchases can help reveal a customer's preferences.

List enhancements that entail merging existing records with new information rely on software that allows the database manager to match records based on some piece of information the two lists share. For example, matches might be achieved by sorting on zip codes and street addresses. Many suppliers gather and maintain databases that can be used for list enhancement. Highlighted earlier, one of the biggest suppliers is InfoUSA. With the sheer volume of people in its database, and literally dozens of pieces of information about each person, InfoUSA offers exceptional capabilities for list enhancement. Because of the massive size of the InfoUSA database, it has a high match rate (60 to 80 percent) when it is merged with clients' internal lists. A more common match rate between internal and external lists is around 50 percent.

17-2c The Marketing Database

Mailing lists come in all shapes and sizes, and by enhancing internal lists they obviously can become rich sources of information about customers. But for a mailing list to qualify as a marketing database, one important additional type of information is required. Although a marketing database can be viewed as a natural extension of an internal mailing list, a **marketing database** also includes information collected directly

from individual customers. Developing a marketing database involves pursuing dialogues with customers and learning about their individual preferences and behavioral patterns. This can be potent information for hatching marketing programs that will hit the mark with consumers.

Aided by the dramatic escalation in processing power that comes from every new generation of computers, marketers see the chance to gather and manage more information about every individual who buys, or could buy, from them. Their goal might be portrayed as an attempt to cultivate a kind of cybernetic intimacy with the customer. A marketing database represents an organization's collective memory, which allows the organization to make the kind of personalized offer that once was characteristic of the corner grocer in small-town America. For example, working in conjunction with the Ohio State University Alumni Association, Lands' End created a special autumn promotion to offer OSU football fans all their favorite gear just in time for the upcoming session. Print ads in the September issue of the OSU alumni magazine set the stage for a special catalog of merchandise mailed to Buckeye faithful. Lands' End had similar arrangements with other major universities to tap into fall football frenzy. Database marketing at its best puts an offer in the hands of the consumer that is both relevant and timely. That's cybernetic intimacy.

Database marketing can also yield important efficiencies that contribute to the marketer's bottom line. As suggested in Exhibit 17.10, the cover of a targeted Cabela's catalog for women, many multichannel retailers like Cabela's find it useful to create several targeted versions of their base or master catalogs, with seasonal or demographic points of emphasis. Why? The gender or age-specific versions run about 100 pages, versus more than 1,000 pages for some of Cabela's master catalogs. A customer or household receives the targeted version catalog based on its profile in Cabela's database and the time of year. These streamlined catalogs are a great way to make timely offerings to targeted households in a cost-effective manner, which is even more convenient for the consumer. In a nutshell, that's what database marketing is all about.

17-2d Marketing Database Applications

Many different types of customer-communication programs are driven by marketing databases. One of the greatest benefits of a database is that it allows an organization to quantify how much business the organization is actually doing with its current best

EXHIBIT 17.10 Firms are able to "slice and dice" their databases to create tailored communications with target customers. Here, rather than sending a 300- or 400-page master catalog to women, Cabela's produces a much shorter, perhaps 30-page catalog for its current and potential female customers.

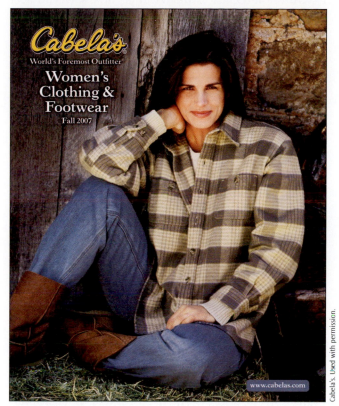

Cabela's. Used with permission.

customers. A good way to isolate the best customers is with a recency, frequency, and monetary (RFM) analysis. An **RFM analysis** asks how recently and how often a specific customer is buying from a company, and how much money he or she is spending per order and over time. With this transaction data, it is a simple matter to calculate the value of every customer to the organization and identify customers that have given the organization the most business in the past. Past behavior is an excellent predictor of future behavior, so yesterday's best customers are likely to be any organization's primary source of future business.

Reinforcing and recognizing your best customers is an essential application of the marketing database. This application may be nothing more than a simple follow-up letter that thanks customers for their business or reminds them of the positive features of the brand to reassure them that they made the right choice. Since date of birth is a common piece of information in a marketing database, it naturally follows that another great time to contact customers is on their birthday. Sunglass Hut International has used a birthday card mailing as part of its program to stay in a dialogue with its best customers for many years. Of course, everyone likes a little birthday present too, so along with the card, Sunglass Hut includes a Customer Appreciation Check for $20 good at any Sunglass Hut store nationwide. Sunglass Hut executives maintain that this birthday card promotion, targeted to current best customers identified from their marketing database, is one of their best investments of advertising/ IBP dollars.

To recognize and reinforce the behaviors of preferred customers, marketers in many fields are offering frequency-marketing programs that provide concrete rewards to frequent customers, as discussed in the last chapter as a separate IBP sales promotion technique. **Frequency-marketing programs** have three basic elements: a *database*, which is the collective memory for the program; a *benefit package*, which is designed to attract and retain customers; and a *communication strategy*, which emphasizes a regular dialogue with the organization's best customers.

The casino industry is renowned for its application of frequency-marketing principles, and Harrah's Entertainment has set the standard for program innovation.[11] Harrah's "Total Rewards" program started out as a way for its 27 million members to accumulate points that could be cashed in for free meals and other casino amenities. This is a good, simple approach, which was quickly copied by the competition. Harrah's subsequently upgraded its program on a number of dimensions. Now Harrah's has 10 million active members in its Total Rewards program, and they know a lot about each one. Whether you are a golfer, like down pillows, or prefer a room close to the elevator, as well as what games you play, are all in the database. This information helps Harrah's tailor 250 million direct mail pieces per year and 8 million email messages per month to its Total Rewards members. This Total Rewards group generates $6.4 billion and 80 percent of Harrah's gaming revenue annually. That's why companies need to know their best customers.

Another common application for the marketing database is **cross-selling**. Since most organizations today have many different products or services they hope to sell, one of the best ways to build business is to identify customers who already purchase some of a firm's products and create marketing programs aimed at these customers but featuring other products. If they like our ice cream, perhaps we should also encourage them to try our frozen yogurt. If they have a checking account with us, can we interest them in a credit card? If customers dine in our restaurants on Fridays and Saturdays, with the proper incentives perhaps we can get them to dine with us midweek, when we really need the extra business. A marketing database can provide a myriad of opportunities for cross-selling.

A final application for the marketing database is a natural extension of cross-selling—pursuing new customers. Once an organization gets to know who its current customers are and what they like about various products, it is in a much stronger position to go out and seek new customers. Knowledge about current customers is especially valuable when an organization is considering purchasing external mailing lists to append to its marketing database. If a firm knows the demographic characteristics of current customers—knows what they like about products, knows where they live, and has insights about their lifestyles and general interests—the selection of external lists will be much more efficient. The basic premise here is simply to try to find prospects who share many of the same characteristics and interests with current customers. And what's the best vehicle for coming to know the current, best customers? Marketing database development.

17-2e **The Privacy Concern**

One large dark cloud looms on the horizon for database marketers: consumers' concerns about invasion of privacy. It is easy for marketers to gather a wide variety of information about consumers, and this is making the general public nervous. Many consumers are uneasy about the way their personal information is being gathered and exchanged by businesses and the government without their knowledge, participation, or consent. Of course, the Internet only amplifies these concerns because the Web makes it easier for all kinds of people and organizations to get access to personal information. In addition, there has been a recent surge in database development merging offline data like credit rating, savings levels, and home value with individuals' online search activities.[12] It's a pretty safe assumption these days that if you are online, some database somewhere is capturing your every click. And, in addition to information gained for databases for mailing purposes, what about the ability of firms to track your mobile device via geo-targeting? This can help brands offer discounts or promotions to shops nearby, to alert you where your friends are, to help you save money, or be aware of a new promotion.

In response to public opinion, state and federal lawmakers have proposed and sometimes passed legislation to limit businesses' access to personal information. For instance, consumers' desire for privacy was clearly the motivation for the launch of the

Federal Trade Commission's Do Not Call Registry (recall the discussions on similar topics in Chapter 4). It proved to be a popular idea with consumers but has many opponents in business, including the DMA.[13] The DMA estimated that the list would cost telemarketers on the order of $50 billion in lost sales. However, clever marketers have found ways to circumvent the "do not call" list with tactics like the lead card.[14] The lead card asks unsuspecting consumers to send in a postcard to receive free information about a product or service. By replying this way, consumers unknowingly forfeit their protection from telemarketers that "do not call" was supposed to provide.

As suggested by Exhibit 17.11, many in business are keenly aware of consumers' concerns about the privacy of their personal information. As consumer concerns about privacy grew, organizations like ZeroKnowledge emerged to provide consulting to firms on issues regarding consumer privacy. Companies can address customers' concerns about privacy if they remember two fundamental premises of database marketing. First, a primary goal for developing a marketing database is to get to know customers in such a way that an organization can offer them products and services that better meet their needs. The whole point of a marketing database is to keep junk mail (and junk digital communications) to a minimum by targeting only exciting and relevant programs to relevant current and potential customers. If customers are offered something they value, as with Harrah's Total Rewards members, they will welcome being in the database.

Second, developing a marketing database is about creating meaningful, long-term relationships with customers. If you want people's trust and loyalty, would you collect personal information from them and then sell it to a third party behind their back? We hope not! When collecting information from customers, an organization must help them understand why it wants the information and how it will use it. If the organization is planning on selling this information to a third party, it must get customers' permission. If the organization pledges that the information will remain confidential, it must honor that pledge. Integrity is fundamental to all meaningful relationships, including those involving direct marketers and their customers. Recall that it was his integrity as much as anything else that enabled L.L. Bean to launch his successful career as a direct marketer. It will work for you too. By the way, if you are one of those people who would like to do more to protect the privacy of your personal information, start with a visit to www.ftc.gov/privacy.

EXHIBIT 17.11 This eerily Orwellian ad paints a dark picture of our future if database direct marketers go unchecked. There is definitely something about the Web and mobile devices that has heightened people's concerns about who is in control of their personal information and who is watching them.

17-3 MEDIA APPLICATIONS IN DIRECT MARKETING

LO **3**

Because mailing lists and marketing databases are the focal point for originating most direct marketing programs, information and arguments need to be communicated to customers in implementing these programs. As we saw in the definition of direct marketing offered earlier in this chapter, multiple media can be deployed in program implementation, and some form of immediate, measurable response is typically an overriding goal for the marketer. The immediate response desired may be an actual order for services or merchandise, a request for more information, or the acceptance of a free trial offer. (See Insights Online [Exhibit 17.12] for an example of how MINI and

> **INSIGHTS ONLINE**
>
> **17.12** Go online to see the AdAge feature, "MINI Uses Driving Dogs from Their Agency DraftFCB to Market Direct to Consumers with the Nonprofit SPCA—Letting Adoptees Drive Around with a Free Cardboard Car Bed for Their New Rescue Dog."

DraftFCB promoted both dog adoptions and car sales.) Because advertising conducted in direct marketing campaigns is typified by this emphasis on immediate response, it is commonly referred to as **direct response advertising**.

As you probably suspect, **direct mail** and **telemarketing** are the direct marketer's traditional media. However, all conventional media, such as magazines, radio, and television, can be used to deliver direct response advertising; nowadays, a wide array of companies are also deploying email as a most economical means of interacting with customers, whether on smartphones, tablets, or computers. In addition, a transformation of the traditional television commercial—the infomercial—remains popular in direct marketing. Let's begin our examination of these media options by considering the advantages and disadvantages of the dominant devices—direct mail and telemarketing.

17-3a　Direct Mail

Direct mail has some notable faults as an advertising medium, not the least of which is cost. It can cost 15 to 20 times more to reach a person with a direct mail piece than it would to reach that person with a television commercial or newspaper advertisement because of the cost-per-contact advantages of mass media discussed in Chapter 13. In addition, in a society where people are constantly on the move, mailing lists are commonly plagued by bad addresses. Each bad address represents advertising dollars wasted. And direct mail delivery dates, especially for bulk, third-class mailings, can be unpredictable. When precise timing of an advertising message is critical to its success, direct mail can be the wrong choice.

But there will be times when direct mail is the right choice. The advantages of direct mail stem from the selectivity of the medium. When an advertiser begins with a database of prospects, direct mail can be the perfect vehicle for reaching those prospects with little waste. Also, direct mail is a flexible medium that allows message adaptations on literally a household-by-household basis—personal salutations and the like.

Direct mail as a medium also lends itself to testing and experimentation. With direct mail it is common to test two or more different appeal letters using a modest budget and a small sample of households. The goal is to establish which version yields the largest response. When a winner is decided, that form of the letter is backed by big-budget dollars in launching the organization's primary campaign.

In addition, the array of formats an organization can send to customers is substantial with direct mail. It can mail large, expensive brochures or include technology. It can use pop-ups, foldouts, scratch-and-sniff strips, or a simple, attractive postcard, as in Exhibit 17.13. Here, Fleece and Flannel, a small retailer of western clothing, was able to put together an attractive postcard campaign for a local mailing area. The postcard announced the grand opening of the store in a highly cost-effective, efficient manner. If a product can be described in a limited space with minimal graphics, there really is no need to get fancy with the direct mail piece.

It is also worth considering the effectiveness of direct mail pieces. Many of us refer to direct mail as "junk mail," and we have the impression that it can't be very effective. Well, the data suggest otherwise to some extent. Envelope-size direct mail garners a response rate of about 3.4 percent, and catalogs earn a response from the recipient at a rate of 4.3 percent. While that does not seem very high, consider that the response to email direct marketing is a paltry 0.12 percent (or nearly none).[15]

17-3b　Telemarketing

Telemarketing is probably the direct marketer's most invasive tool. As with direct mail, contacts can be selectively targeted, the impact of programs is easy to track, and experimentation with different scripts and delivery formats is simple and practical. Because telemarketing involves real, live person-to-person dialogue, no medium produces better response rates—about 13 percent to all calls.[16] On the other hand, telemarketing is expensive on a cost-per-contact basis. Further, telemarketing does not share direct mail's flexibility in terms of delivery options. When you reach people in their home or workplace, you have a limited amount of time to convey information and request some form of response.

You already know the biggest concern with telemarketing. It is a powerful yet highly intrusive medium that must be used with discretion. High-pressure telephone calls at inconvenient times can alienate customers. Telemarketing will give best results over the long run if it is used to maintain constructive dialogues with existing customers and qualified prospects. And remember, consumers have the option of signing up for the Do Not Call Registry, which blocks marketers from using this technique with those households.

EXHIBIT 17.13 This postcard for Fleece and Flannel announces the grand opening of its new store in Livingston, Montana. In that part of the world, it's perfectly natural to select a fly-fishing guide and guru to serve as your spokeswoman and target a local area of shoppers with a direct mail campaign.

Courtesy of Colette Stewart, Owner of Montana Fleece and Flannel, Livingston, MT

17-3c Email

Perhaps the most controversial tool deployed of late by direct marketers has been unsolicited or "bulk" email. Commonly referred to as spam, this junk email can get you in big trouble with consumers. In a worst-case scenario, careless use of the email tool can earn one's company the label of a "spammer," which because of the community-oriented character of the Internet can then be a continuing source of negative buzz. But is this discouraging companies from deploying this tool? Hardly. Recent studies document that over 90 percent of all emails received by business email servers are essentially spam—although it is hard to estimate how many are direct marketing appeals.[17]

There is a school of thought that says some consumers are not averse to receiving targeted email advertisements and that as the Internet continues to evolve as an increasingly commercial medium, those companies that observe proper etiquette on the Net (dare we say "Netiquette"?) will be rewarded through customer loyalty. The key premise of netiquette is to get the consumer's permission to send information about specific products or services, or, to use the current buzzword, they must "opt in." This opt-in premise has spawned a number of e-marketing service providers who claim to have constructed email lists of consumers who have "opted in" for all manner of products and services. They contend that the future of direct marketing will be in reaching those people who have already said "Yes." But, as cited earlier, the unsolicited email generates a pathetic 0.12 percent response rate.

Our advice is to stay away from the low-cost temptations of bulk email. The quickest way to get flamed and damage your brand name is to start sending out bulk emails to people who do not want to hear from you. As one analyst said, "most consumers view their personal email addresses and mobile phones as personal property. Violating that space ticks people off, no question."[18] Instead, through database development, ask your customers for permission to contact them via email. Honor their requests. Don't abuse the privilege by selling their email addresses to other companies, and when you do contact them, have something important to say. Seth Godin, whose 1999 book *Permission Marketing* really launched the "opt-in" mindset, puts it this way: "The best way to make your [customer] list worthless is to sell it. The future is, this list is mine and it's a secret."[19] Isn't it funny—you can imagine L.L. Bean feeling exactly the same way about his customer list a century ago.

One other issue needs to be addressed here. It is important to not confuse email with e-commerce. E-commerce is any purchase transaction consummated between a consumer and a marketer. Marketers encourage e-commerce by encouraging people to visit their website. (See an interesting example in Insights Online [Exhibit 17.14].) One option, of course, is email, which we see is not very successful. But motivating consumers (and business buyers) to visit the firm's site through direct mail, an infomercial, or a traditional media ad is contributing to huge growth in e-commerce. E-commerce sales now stand at about $252 billion annually and are expected to grow to over $320 billion by 2016—but likely not fueled by email direct marketing.[20]

17-3d Direct Response Advertising in Other Media

Direct marketers have experimented with many methods in trying to convey their appeals for a customer response. In magazines, a popular device for executing a direct marketer's agenda is the bind-in insert card. Thumb through a copy of any magazine and you will see how effective these light-cardboard inserts are at stopping the reader and calling attention to themselves. Insert cards not only promote their product but also provide tempting offers like $25 off your next order at Coldwater Creek or a free sample of Scope mouthwash.

When AT&T introduced the first 800 number in 1967, it simply could not have known how important this service would become to direct marketing. Newspaper ads from *The Wall Street Journal* provide toll-free numbers for requesting everything from really cheap online trading services to leasing a Learjet. If you watch late-night TV, you may know the 800 number to call to order that Snuggie for you and your dog (sales to date: people—18 million; dogs—only 2 million).[21] Finally, magazine ads like the Bose ad shown in Exhibit 17.15 are commonly used to provide a toll number to initiate contact with customers. Bose has built nearly its entire business around ads like these in magazines encouraging consumers to interact with the company via a toll-free number. As these diverse examples indicate, toll-free numbers make it possible to use nearly any medium for direct response purposes.

EXHIBIT 17.15 There is nothing fancy about this Bose ad—some enticing information and a big, bold toll-free number so that the consumer can interact with the company—good, sound, direct marketing.

No. It won't make your morning coffee.

But it might make your day.

The Bose® Wave® music system

An all-in-one music system with built-in CD player, FM/AM tuner, clock and alarm. You control them all with a convenient credit card-style remote.

Free shipping with your order.

"...you'll think you're listening to a...sound system that costs five times more."
– *Forbes FYI*

To experience it for yourself with a risk-free, 30-day home trial:
1-800-925-9738
ext. TW519
www.Bose.com/WMS

Take advantage of our easy payment plan with no interest charges from Bose.

BOSE
Better sound through research®

© 2010 Bose Corporation

17-3e Infomercials

The infomercial is a novel form of direct response advertising that merits special mention. An **infomercial** is fundamentally just a long television advertisement made possible by the lower cost of ad space on many cable and satellite channels. They range in length from 2 to 60 minutes, but the common length is 30 minutes. Although producing an infomercial is more like producing a television program than it is like producing a 30-second commercial, infomercials are all about selling. There appear to be several keys to the successful use of this unique vehicle.[22] Infomercials typically appear during low-cost time periods (check out programming on Saturday and Sunday mornings).

A critical factor is testimonials from satisfied users. Celebrity testimonials can help catch a viewer as he or she is channel surfing past the program, but celebrities aren't necessary, and, of course, they add to the production costs. Whether testimonials are from celebrities or from regular folks, without them your chances of producing a profitable infomercial diminish hugely.

Another key point to remember about infomercials is that viewers are not likely to stay tuned for the full 30 minutes. An infomercial is a 30-minute direct response sales pitch, not a classic episode of *NCSI* or *The Simpsons*. The implication here is that the call to action should come not at the end of the infomercial only; most of the audience could be long gone by minute 28 into the show. A good rule of thumb in a 30-minute infomercial is to divide the program into 10-minute increments and try close a sale three times. Each closing should feature the toll-free number or the Web address that allows the viewer to order the product or request more information. And an organization should not offer information to the customer unless it can deliver speedy follow-up; same-day response should be the goal in pursuing leads generated by an infomercial.

Many different types of products and services have been marketed using infomercials. CD players, self-help videos, home exercise equipment, kitchen appliances, and Annette Funicello Collectible Bears have all had success with the infomercial. Although it is easy to associate the infomercial with things such as the Ronco Showtime Rotisserie & BBQ (yours for just four easy payments of $39.95!), many familiar brands have experimented with this medium. Brand marketers such as Quaker State, Primestar, Lexus, Monster, Disney, Hoover, Kal Kan, and yes, even Mercedes-Benz have all used infomercials to help inform consumers about their offerings.

How does one explain the growing appeal of the infomercial for all manner of marketers? Data generated by TiVo's StopWatch service are revealing.[23] They show that bare-bones direct response ads for products like Perfect Pushup exercise equipment are among the least likely to be zapped. That kind of result will get lots of scrutiny from all corners of the advertising business.

LO ④

17-4 CLOSING THE SALE WITH DIRECT MARKETING AND/OR PERSONAL SELLING

As we have pointed out repeatedly, the wide variety of options available to marketers for reaching customers poses a tremendous challenge with respect to coordination and integration. Organizations are looking to achieve the synergy that can come when various advertising and IBP options reach the consumer with a common and compelling message. However, to work in various media, functional specialists both inside and outside an organization need to be employed.

It then becomes a very real problem to get the advertising manager, special events manager, sales promotion manager, and Web designer to work in harmony. And now we need to add to the list of functional specialists the direct marketing or database manager.

The evolution and growing popularity of direct marketing raise the challenge of achieving integrated communication to new heights. In particular, the development of a marketing database commonly leads to interdepartmental rivalries and can create major conflicts between a company and its advertising agency. The marketing database is a powerful source of information about the customer; those who do not have direct access to this information will be envious of those who do. In addition, the growing use of direct marketing campaigns must mean that someone else's budget is being cut. Typically, direct marketing programs come at the expense of conventional advertising campaigns or the use of other IBP techniques. Since direct marketing takes dollars from activities that have been the staples of the traditional ad agency business, it is easy to see why pure advertising agencies view direct marketing with some disdain.

There are no simple solutions for achieving integrated communication, but one classic approach is the establishment of a marketing communications manager, or "marcom" manager for short. A **marcom manager** (some firms now fold these duties into the chief marketing officer role) plans an organization's overall communications program and oversees the various functional specialists inside and outside the organization to ensure that they are working together to deliver the desired message to the customer, which ultimately yields a product sale. Of course, the pivotal role for direct marketing programs in this process is to establish dialogue with customers, and then close the sale.

17-4a The Critical Role of Personal Selling

This brings us to the field of personal selling, yet another unique functional specialization in the business world. **Personal selling** is the face-to-face communications and persuasion process. Products that are higher priced, complicated to use, require demonstration, must be tailored to user needs, involve a trade-in, or are judged at the point of purchase are heavily dependent on personal selling. Household consumers and business buyers are frequently confronted with purchase decisions that are facilitated by interaction with a salesperson. In many decision contexts, only a qualified and well-trained salesperson can address the questions and concerns of a potential buyer. Fail to get the dialogue right at this critical stage of the

purchase process, and all other advertising efforts will end up being wasted. And, as convenient and controllable as consumers find the direct marketing access to firms discussed thus far, they also really like to interact with sales people. While Apple has sold millions of iMac computers online, its retail shops are jammed and really quite old fashioned when it comes to selling. Apple makes a trip to an Apple store personal and trains its salespeople down to the last psychological detail. For example, Apple sales staff are instructed to *never* correct customers if they mispronounce the names of its gadgets or apps.[24]

There are many different types of sales jobs. A salesperson can be engaged in order taking, creative selling, or supportive communication. The discussion that follows demonstrates that the communication task for each type of selling varies dramatically.

The least complex type of personal selling is order taking. Its importance, however, should not be underestimated. **Order taking** involves accepting orders for merchandise or scheduling services. Order takers deal with existing customers who are lucrative to a business due to the low cost of generating additional revenues from them. Order takers can also deal with new customers, which means that the order takers need to be trained well enough to answer the basic questions a new customer might have about a product or service. Order takers are responsible for communicating with buyers in such a way that a quality relationship is maintained. This type of selling rarely involves communicating large amounts of information. However, a careless approach to this function can be a real turn-off for the loyal consumer and can end up damaging the relationship.

Creative selling requires considerable effort and expertise. Situations where creative selling takes place range from retail stores through the selling of services to business and the sale of large industrial installations and component parts. **Creative selling** is the type of selling where customers rely heavily on the salesperson for technical information, advice, and service. In a retail setting like the one illustrated in Exhibit 17.16, stores selling higher-priced items and specialty goods must have a trained sales staff and emphasize customer and product knowledge. The services of an insurance agent, stockbroker, media representative, or real estate agent represent another type of creative selling. These salespeople provide services customized to the unique needs and circumstances of each buyer.

The most complex and demanding of the creative selling positions are in business-to-business markets. Many times, these salespeople have advanced degrees in technical areas like chemical engineering, computer science, or any of the medical professions. Technical salespeople who deal in large-dollar purchases and

EXHIBIT 17.16 Point of purchase is where the salesperson plays a critical role in determining the consumer's ultimate choice. Also, the salesperson can provide valuable information about product differences that can result in a sale.

Jeff Greenberg/PhotoEdit

to speed on the profile of that targeted new buyer. One key issue: This consumer had become Web savvy and likely would come to the showroom with lots of background research on the car. So step one for the salesperson: Find out what the customer already knows about the car. Don't rehash what she already knows. Surprise her and excite her with something new.

Finally, when a sales force is deployed for the purpose of supportive communication, it is not charged directly with closing the sale. Rather, the objective is to provide information to customers, offer services, and generally to foster goodwill. The **missionary salesperson** calls on accounts with the express purpose of monitoring the satisfaction of buyers and updating buyers' needs but may provide product information after a purchase. Many firms also use direct marketing tools like telephone and email reminders to complement the efforts of the missionary salesperson in maintaining a dialogue with key customers.

complex corporate decisions for specialized component parts, medical equipment, or raw materials have tremendous demands placed on them. They are often called on to analyze the customer's product and production needs and carry this information back to the firm so that product design and supply schedules can be tailored for each customer.

Another noteworthy form of creative selling that has emerged in recent years is system selling. **System selling** entails selling a set of interrelated components that fulfill all or a majority of a customer's needs in a particular area. System selling has emerged because of the desire on the part of customers for "system solutions." Large industrial and government buyers, in particular, have come to seek out one or a small number of suppliers that can provide a full range of products and services needed in an area. Rather than dealing with multiple suppliers, these buyers then "system buy" from a single source. This trend in both buying and selling emphasizes the customer-relationship-management aspects of selling.

Creative selling tasks call for high levels of preparation, expertise, and contact with the customer and are primary to the process of relationship building. This doesn't happen by chance. Companies work hard to train their salespeople to be ready to address the needs of specific target markets. Take, for example, Honda and its launch of the Honda Fit.[25] This was an important launch for Honda because Fit represented the company's first true entry-level vehicle since the 1970s. But the buyers of entry-level vehicles have changed dramatically since the 1970s, and Honda was keen to bring its 7,500 U.S. sales associates up

17-4b Customer Relationship Management

Salespeople can play a critical role as well in cultivating long-term relationships with customers—which often is referred to as a **customer relationship management (CRM)** program. As an example, Merck spends 12 months training its sales representatives not only in knowledge of pharmaceuticals but also in trust-building techniques. Reps then are required to take regular refresher courses. Similarly, General Electric went so far as to station its own engineers full time at Praxair, Inc., a user of GE electrical equipment, to help the firm boost productivity.[26]

Likewise, salespeople are also instrumental in ensuring customer satisfaction. Salespeople no longer simply approach customers with the intention of making a sale. Rather, they are problem solvers who work in partnership with customers. The salesperson is in the best position to analyze customer needs and propose the right solution on a case-by-case basis. By accepting this role, the sales force helps determine ways in which a firm can provide total customer satisfaction through its entire market offering. The great thing about satisfied consumers is they come back and buy again and again, which ultimately is the mechanism that sustains any business.

17-4c A Case in Point

To wrap things up for this chapter, let's consider an example of what happens for a company when it strikes just the right balance among advertising, brand building, direct marketing, and personal selling. Let's start with a quiz. Who's number one in the specialty bedding business? No, it's not Crazy Larry's Mattress Barn or the House of Pillows. Think instead *the Sleep Number Bed* by Select Comfort.

The Select Comfort story represents a real metamorphosis from a tiny niche brand to a market leader.[27] For years, Select Comfort promoted its air mattresses with late-night infomercials along the lines of the Ronco Showtime Rotisserie & BBQ. Some consumers found value in the product as a good option to pull out of the closet and blow up when friends dropped in for the night. But that's hardly a mainstream market, and Select Comfort was looking for more. Thus, the company invented a new brand, the Sleep Number bed, where the user can adjust the firmness of the mattress with a simple remote control using a numerical range from 1 to 100. The ad featuring the really big remote in Exhibit 17.17 for the Sleep Number bed is typical of the print advertising that Select Comfort added to its IBP mix as the firm moved away from infomercials only. But the company had a lot of work to do in building this brand. First, it had to overcome the perception that this is just a *very* expensive air mattress. Second, it had to shed the association with late-night and Sunday morning cable TV to be accepted as a high-quality product found in upscale shopping malls across the United States.

A lot of things changed in building the Sleep Number brand. Although Select Comfort did not abandon its heritage as a direct marketer, new ad campaigns also included a healthy mix of newspaper advertising and local and prime-time TV spots. Often these ads would feature the first point of difference for the mattress: Couples sharing a bed could each adjust their side to just the right level of firmness (typically less than 50 for gals and more than 50 for guys). Patented technology in the remote control made this a sustainable point of difference.

Once basic awareness was established for the brand, Select Comfort next proceeded with the communication objective of associating the bed with deep, restorative sleep. And while all this brand building was taking place, targeted consumers continuously received direct mail pieces that were seeking to close the sale. A person typically doesn't buy a $1,000 mattress online or over the phone, but a visit to one of the company's 400 or so retail stores is another matter. There, well-trained sales personnel patiently helped each customer find his or her sleep number, while reinforcing the importance of deep, restorative sleep. Of course, it is also the job of that salesperson to work to close the sale.

The Select Comfort example typifies a theme developed throughout this book. Each marketer must find the right balance of IBP tools and tactics to get its points across to targeted consumers. Different tools and tactics play various roles in the process from building brand awareness to communicating key brand benefits, and ultimately to closing the sale. If the various media and programs an organization employs are sending different messages or mixed signals, the organization is only hurting itself. All the functional specialists who are part of the marketing and sales team must be working as a team. To achieve the synergy that will allow it to overcome the clutter of today's marketplace, and, for example, move to the top spot in the specialty bedding market, an organization has no choice but to pursue advertising and IBP.

EXHIBIT 17.17 Weary travelers in the Minneapolis airport are encouraged to find their sleep number when they encounter this extra large poster ad from Select Comfort in Concourse D.

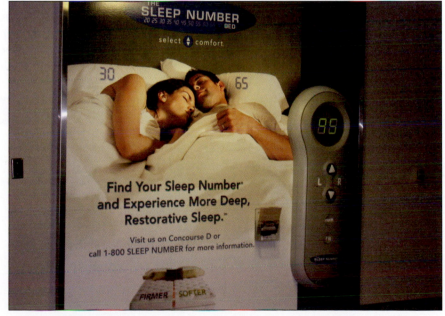

Chris T. Allen

SUMMARY

 Identify the three primary purposes served by direct marketing and explain its growing popularity.

Many types of organizations are increasing their expenditures on direct marketing. These expenditures serve three primary purposes: direct marketing offers potent tools for closing sales with customers, for identifying prospects for future contacts, and for offering information and incentives that help foster loyalty. The growing popularity of direct marketing can be attributed to several factors. Direct marketers make consumption convenient: credit cards, 800 numbers, and the Internet take the hassle out of shopping. In addition, today's computing power, which allows marketers to build and mine large customer information files, has enhanced direct marketing's impact. The emphasis on producing and tracking measurable outcomes is also well received by marketers in an era when everyone is trying to do more with less.

 Distinguish a mailing list from a marketing database and review the many applications of each.

A mailing list is a file of names and addresses of current or potential customers, such as lists that might be generated by a credit card company or a catalog retailer. Internal lists are valuable for creating relationships with current customers, and external lists are useful in generating new customers. A marketing database is a natural extension of the internal list but includes information about individual customers and their specific preferences and purchasing patterns. A marketing database allows organizations to identify and focus their efforts on their best customers. Recognizing and reinforcing preferred customers can be a potent strategy for building loyalty. Cross-selling opportunities also emerge once a database is in place. In addition, as one gains keener information about the motivations of

current best customers, insights usually emerge about how to attract new customers.

 Describe the prominent media used by direct marketers in delivering their messages to the customer.

Direct marketing programs emanate from mailing lists and databases, but there is still a need to deliver a message to the customer. Direct mail and telemarketing are common means used in executing direct marketing programs. Email has recently emerged as a low-cost alternative. Because the advertising done as part of direct marketing programs typically requests an immediate response from the customer, it is known as direct response advertising. Conventional media such as television, newspapers, magazines, and radio can also be used to request a direct response by offering an 800 number or a Web address to facilitate customer contact.

 Explain the key role of direct marketing and personal selling in complementing other advertising activities.

Developing a marketing database, selecting a direct mail format, and producing an infomercial are some of the tasks attributable to direct marketing. These and other related tasks require more functional specialists, who further complicate the challenge of presenting a coordinated face to the customer. In addition, many products and services must be supported by well-trained sales personnel. Here again, the message consumers hear in advertising for any brand needs to be skillfully reinforced by the sales team. Fail to get the dialogue right at this final, critical stage of the purchase process, and all other advertising efforts will end up being wasted. The sales force plays a critical role in the process because theirs is the job of closing the sale, while at the same time ensuring customer satisfaction.

KEY TERMS

direct marketing
cost per inquiry (CPI)
cost per order (CPO)
mailing list
internal lists
external lists
marketing database
RFM analysis

frequency-marketing programs
cross-selling
direct response advertising
direct mail
telemarketing
infomercial
marcom manager
personal selling

order taking
creative selling
system selling
missionary salesperson
customer relationship management
   (CRM)

ENDNOTES

1. Bianco, "The Vanishing Mass Market," *BusinessWeek*, July 12, 2004, 61–68.

2. Direct Marketing Association, http://www.the-dma.org/aboutdma/whatisthedma.shtml, accessed April, 2013.

3. Bob Stone, *Successful Direct Marketing Methods* (Lincolnwood, IL: NTC Business Books, 1994), 5.

4. The discussion to follow builds on that of Stone, *Successful Direct Marketing Methods*.

5. Phil Wahba and Dhanya Skariachan, "Insight: How U.S. Retailers Are Building Up Their Online Muscle," *Reuters*, December 24, 2012, www.Reuters.com, accessed March 14, 2013.

6. The historical data here was drawn from Edward Nash, "The Roots of Direct Marketing," *Direct Marketing Magazine*, February 1995, 38–40; Cara Beardi, "Lillian Vernon Sets Sights on Second Half-Century," *Advertising Age*, March 19, 2001, 22.

7. Allison Cosmedy, *A History of Direct Marketing* (New York: Direct Marketing Association, 1992), 6.

8. Ibid.

9. Daniel Klein, "Disintegrated Marketing," *Harvard Business Review*, March 2003, 18, 19; Michael Fielding, "Spread the Word," *Marketing News*, February 15, 2005, 19, 20; Michael Fielding, "Direct Mail Still Has Its Place," *Marketing News*, November 1, 2006, 31, 33.

10. Edward Nash, "The Roots of Direct Marketing," *Direct Marketing Magazine*, February 1995, 38–40.

11. Michael Bush, "Why Harrah's Loyalty Effort Is Industry's Gold Standard," *Advertising Age*, October 5, 2009, 8.

12. Michael Learmonth, "Holy Grail of Targeting Is Fuel for Privacy Battle," *Advertising Age*, March 22, 2010, 1, 21.

13. Ira Teinowitz and Ken Wheaton, "Do Not Market," *Advertising Age*, March 12, 2007, 1, 44.

14. Jennifer Levitz and Kelly Greene, "Marketers Use Trickery to Evade No-Call Lists," *The Wall Street Journal*, October 26, 2007, A1, A14.

15. "DMA Releases 2012 Response Rate Report," June 14, 1012, www.thedma.org, accessed September 1, 2012.

16. Ibid.

17. Mathew Schwartz, "U.S. Extends Spam Lead," www.informationweek.com, accessed July 14, 2010.

18. Maureen Morrison, "Consumers Balance on Verge of 'Offer Anarchy,'" *Advertising Age*, February 13, 2012, 24.

19. Jodi Mardesich, "Too Much of a Good Thing," *Industry Standard*, March 19, 2001, 85.

20. Lauren Indvik, "U.S. Online Retail Sales to Reach $327 Billion by 2016," February 27, 2012, www.mashable.com, accessed August 31, 2012; data from Forrester Research Inc.

21. Katherine Rosman, "As Seen on TV… and in Aisle 5," *The Wall Street Journal*, January 28, 2010, D1, D4.

22. Thomas Mucha, "Stronger Sales in Just 28 Minutes," *Business 2.0*, June 2005, 56–60; Elizabeth Holmes, "Golf-Club Designer Hopes to Repeat TV Success," *The Wall Street Journal*, January 30, 2007, B4.

23. Brian Steinberg, "How to Stop Them from Skipping: TiVo Tells All," *Advertising Age*, July 16, 2007, 1, 33.

24. Schumpeter, "The Art of Selling," *The Economist*, October 22, 2011, 84.

25. Jacqueline Durett, "Road Warriors," *Sales & Marketing Management*, September 2006, 46–48.

26. Daniel Tynan, "The 10 Biggest CRM Mistakes," *Sales & Marketing Management*, December 2005, 30–33.

27. Willow Duttge, "Counting Sleep," *Advertising Age*, June 5, 2006, 4, 50.

CHAPTER 18

Public Relations, Influencer Marketing, and Corporate Advertising

After reading and thinking about this chapter, you will be able to do the following:

1 Explain the role of public relations (PR) as part of an organization's overall advertising and IBP strategy.

2 Detail the objectives and tools of public relations.

3 Describe two basic strategies motivating an organization's public relations activities.

4 Illustrate the strategies and tactics used in influencer marketing programs.

5 Discuss the applications and objectives of corporate advertising.

Public relations and corporate advertising are exciting topics to conclude our look at advertising and integrated brand promotion (IBP). Public relations (PR), in particular, brings to life the whole idea of "buzz building" for a brand that is increasingly popular in marketing today. PR can be used to activate social media, engage mainstream media, highlight celebrity spokespersons, bond with a community, or stage a branded experience via an event. And when there is skillful teamwork among client, PR firm, digital agency, design experts, and talent agencies, the result is often blowing the doors off a brand campaign. As many have proven, there is a convergence taking place among the skill sets of marketers, advertisers, and public relations professionals.[1] In this chapter we will take you through the fundamentals of buzz building and sponsored events as a PR strategy while adding public relations savvy to your IBP tool kit.

One can argue that we've entered an exciting new, sexy, pro-social, community, and digital era for public relations. PR and buzz building have never been hotter. Public relations has moved well beyond its traditional role of simply managing goodwill or "relations" with a firm's many publics, which can take the form of damage control in the face of negative publicity. It is more about corporate communications and image management in times of noncrisis. The traditional functions are still important, but there's much more going on in PR circles today.

Another major topic in this chapter—influencer marketing—will emphasize public relations activities as a dedicated brand-building agenda in a digital and social media environment. Influencer marketing, as a special case of public relations, focuses on monitoring the digital environment and managing how consumers view a firm and its brands. In this era of social media, blogs, and overall digital communications between consumers, a firm can monitor, understand, and better respond to what consumers are saying to each other about the firm's brands. And PR is also the tool for implementing helpful pro-social public service announcements (PSAs). The Ad Council is an amazing nonprofit organization in New York City that has helped give the United States social icons such as Woodsy the Owl, Rosie the Riveter, McGruff the Crime Dog,

Smokey the Bear, and catchy copy such as "Click It or Ticket" (to promote seat belt wearing), "Buzzed Driving Is Drunk Driving," and "Only YOU can prevent forest fires." What about smoking? Antismoking campaigns in the United States are old news, but the latest PSA is focusing on social smoking—the habit of having a "ciggy" with friends or with a cocktail every so often (see Insights Online [Exhibit 18.1] for a humorous example). Consumer behavior research notes that social smokers don't have an identity of a smoker per se, so an agency like BBDO can help debunk this myth.

Last but not least, corporate advertising is also considered in this final chapter. Corporate advertising typically uses major media to communicate a unique, broad-based message that is distinct from more product-specific brand building. Corporate advertising contributes to the development of an overall image for a firm without touting specific products or services. Corporate advertising has a lot to do with the trustworthiness and reputation of a firm. As consumers are becoming increasingly informed and sophisticated, they are also demanding a higher standard of conduct from the companies they patronize. When a company has established trust and integrity, it is much easier to build productive relationships with consumers.

LO 1

18-1 PUBLIC RELATIONS

The role of **public relations** is to foster goodwill between a firm and its many constituent groups. These constituent groups include customers, stockholders, suppliers, employees, government entities, citizen action groups, and the public. The firm's public relations function seeks to highlight positive events like outstanding quarterly sales and profits (to stockholders) or noteworthy community service programs (to government entities and the general public). PR is also used strategically for damage control when adversity strikes. All organizations at some point face adversity (think Carnival Cruises and faulty ships, BP and oil spills, Nike and Tiger Woods and Lance Armstrong). In addition, new techniques in public relations have fostered a bolder, more aggressive, proactive role for PR in many IBP campaigns.

18-1a   A New Era for Public Relations?

In the last five years, public relations may have entered a whole new era. Advertiser spending on public relations and word of mouth (we'll discuss this factor later) grew by 12.4 percent in 2012 alone, with spending exceeding $6 billion.[2] What's more, employment of PR managers and specialists is expected to grow over 20 percent by 2020.[3] There are many forces at work that support a growing role for PR activities as part of the advertising and IBP campaigns for all sorts of products and services. Among these are familiar things like increasingly sophisticated and connected consumers who are talking to each other more and more about brands, online and off. As noted by Stephen Brown, a prolific and provocative writer on the subject of branding, we are living in a different world from the one that operated in the heyday of mass marketing.[4] As he notes, we have evolved to an intensely commercial world where TV shows feature stories about marketing and consumer psychology, stand-up comics perform skits about shopping routines and brand strategies, and documentaries like *Who Killed the Electric Car?* and *Beer Wars,* with General Motors and Budweiser playing the villains, make great antibrand entertainment. Industry gossip, executive screw-ups, and product critiques are bloggers' standard fodder. It is a brand-obsessed world.

And as you already know, the consumer is increasingly in control in this brand-obsessed world, using tools like blogs, Pintrest, Facebook, YouTube, Twitter, and whatever will be invented next week to exert that control via new media.[5] It's a world where marketers must monitor the brand buzz and become part of the dialogue in an effort to rescue or revive their brands. Some agencies, such as Digitas, have brand buzz rooms full of TVs and computers exclusively devoted to a client, such as AMEX. It is an emerging job opportunity for ad/PR grads to help a company or brand monitor its image via social media and respond accordingly. Mass media advertising has never been about dialogue—but digital media now do offer the opportunity for firms to be part of the dialogue. Now it is about a story—and how the brand is a part of the story of the consumer's life.

Via social media and other forms of viral or pass-along readership, consumers are spreading the word about brands as never before. Even though marketers have always believed that the most powerful influence in any consumer's decision is the recommendations of friends and family, they have never known exactly what to do about it. Some clues about what to do were provided by Malcolm Gladwell in his bestseller *The Tipping Point,* wherein he makes the case that people he labels as "mavens" and "connectors" are critically important in fostering social epidemics. The key idea here is that these mavens and connectors can be located, and if you give them useful information or interesting stories about your brand, they may share it with their networks. That sharing is a more robust phenomenon when there exists a medium like the Internet that allows one to spread the word to thousands of one's close, personal friends with a single click.

People talk about brands. The challenge is to give them interesting things to talk about, things that brings a firm's brand into the conversation in a positive way. Marketers are starting to get it. PR isn't just about managing goodwill; it can be about finding ways to get your brand into the day-to-day conversations of key consumers. Hilton Worldwide (the hotel company) did just that when it enlisted PR specialists to help gain attention for the opening of the Conrad New York Hotel. Hilton was only one of 60 sponsors of the Tribeca Film festival. But Hilton used the event as a way to showcase its new property. Hilton brought in the "Pop-up Conrad Concierge" (a mobile service facility) to various film festival locations around New York. Using their PR agency's digital social intelligence system, Hilton monitored brand conversations across several social media sites and filtered them by location and event attendance. Then, voila! The Pop-up Conrad Concierge team showed up and brought Conrad-branded umbrellas and snacks for folks waiting in line—a tremendous example of engaging the consumer with the brand.[6]

In today's dynamic marketplace, where there are lots of online and offline conversations about brands, a brand builder needs to take a proactive stance in influencing at least some of those conversations. As always, it takes a strong team effort to ensure integration, and research is demonstrating that PR expertise needs to be well represented as part of any contemporary marketing, advertising, and IBP team.[7]

Public Relations and Damage Control. Lance Armstrong is LIVESTRONG no more; sometimes a little damage control is needed (or a lot). Public relations has always been an important and unique contributor in that PR serves a role that no other promotional tool can. Public relations is the one and only tool that can provide damage control for bad publicity. Such public relations problems can arise from either a firm's own activities or from external forces completely outside a firm's control. Let's consider a classic public relations debacle to illustrate the nature of damage control.

Intel is one of the great success stories of American industry. Intel had risen from relative techno-obscurity as an innovative computer technology company to one of the largest corporations in the world with one of the most visible brands (Who doesn't know "Intel Inside"?).

Sales have grown from $1.3 billion to over $50 billion annually in only 30 years. But all this success did not prepare Intel for the one serious public relations challenge that the firm encountered during its rapid ascent. At one point, Intel introduced its new-generation chip, the now well-known Pentium. But shortly after its introduction, Pentium users were discovering a flaw in the chip. During certain floating-point operations, some Pentium chips were actually producing erroneous calculations—even though the error showed up in only the fifth or sixth decimal place, power users in scientific laboratories require absolute precision and accuracy in their calculations.

Having a defect in a high-performance technology product such as the Pentium chip was one thing, and how Intel handled the problem was another. Intel's initial "official" response was that the flaw in the chip was so insignificant that it would produce an error in calculations only once in 27,000 years. But then IBM, which had shipped thousands of PCs with Pentium chips, challenged the assertion that the flaw was insignificant, claiming that processing errors could occur as often as every 24 days. IBM announced that it would stop shipment of all Pentium-based PCs immediately.

From this point on, the Pentium situation became a runaway public relations disaster. Every major newspaper, network newscast, and magazine carried the story of the flawed Pentium chip. Even the cartoon series *Dilbert* got in on the act, running a whole series of cartoon strips that spoofed the Intel controversy (see Exhibit 18.2). One observer characterized the Pentium situation this way: "From a public relations standpoint, the train has left the station and is barreling out of Intel's control."[8] For weeks Intel did nothing but publicly argue that the flaw would not affect the vast majority of users.

Finally, Intel decided to provide a free replacement chip to any user who believed he or she was at risk. In announcing the $475 million program to replace customers' chips, Andy Grove, then Intel's highly accomplished CEO, admitted publicly that "the Pentium processor divide problem has been a learning experience for Intel"[9]—perhaps the greatest understatement in the history of PR.

The story of Intel and its Pentium chip is now a piece of history. But it highlights that firms large and small encounter PR problems, and that's not going to change. Indeed, as consumers become more informed and connected, the bad news just travels faster and lingers longer.[10] This bad news can take many forms. For Taco Bell it was a YouTube video of rats running amok at its Greenwich Village restaurant.[11] You can close the restaurant, but that video is still out there. Johnson & Johnson walked into a PR firestorm by suing the Red Cross (that most revered of helping organizations) for logo infringement.[12] That's a hard case to win in the

EXHIBIT 18.2 When Intel did not respond quickly and positively to problems with its newest high-performance chip, the press unloaded a barrage of negative publicity on the firm. The publicity was so widespread that even *Dilbert* got into the act with this parody of Intel's PR decision making.

court of public opinion, and it was definitely a self-inflicted wound by J&J. And poor Colonel Sanders must be rolling over in his grave. Marketers at KFC have had a history of dreaming up popular promotions but then doing a poor job of coordinating with their store managers. That's exactly what happened when KFC corporate offered a discount coupon but local franchisees didn't have the product to deliver—everyone got agitated. Everyone, that is, except Chick-fil-A and Church's, whose sales grew at KFC's expense.[13] Chick-fil-A is not a gay-friendly brand, though, as its management has taken a side against gay marriage. That in itself caused some serious PR crises for the delicious chicken sandwich maker. That is a shame, because that company offers some wonderful scholarships to college and high school student employees. We should think about this and the decision to take a side on a controversial issue—especially one that has little if anything to do with one's product.

Companies need to learn how to handle the bad news. No company is immune. And even though many public relations episodes must be reactive, a firm can be prepared with public relations materials to conduct an orderly and positive relations-building campaign with its constituents. To fully appreciate the potential of public relations, we will next consider the objectives and tools of public relations and basic public relations strategies.

── LO ②──

18-1b Objectives for Public Relations

Even though reacting to a crisis is a necessity, it is always more desirable to take a proactive approach. The key is to have a structured approach to public relations, including a clear understanding of objectives for PR. Within the broad guidelines of image building, damage control, and establishing relationships with constituents, it is possible to identify six primary objectives of public relations:

- *Promoting goodwill.* This is an image-building function of public relations. Industry events or community activities that reflect favorably on a firm are highlighted. When Hilton provided movie festival attendees with umbrellas and snacks while waiting in line to attend film screenings, goodwill for the brand was no doubt enhanced. (See Insights Online [Exhibit 18.3] for a great example of a pro-social PR campaign.)

- *Promoting a product or service.* Press releases, events, or brand "news" that increase public awareness of a firm's brands can be pursued through public relations. Large pharmaceutical firms such as Merck and GlaxoSmithKline issue press releases when they discover new drugs or achieve FDA approval. Likewise, Starbucks champions sustainable production of its green coffee through its C.A.F.E. Practices and encourages you to learn more, as in Exhibit 18.4. Starbucks management argues that the firm has been working for years to develop and apply a comprehensive set of environmental, social, and economic guidelines for the ethical and sustainable growing of coffee. In turn, they believe

EXHIBIT 18.4 Starbucks actively promotes economic and social responsibility as a core brand value with the way the firm sources its coffee supplies.

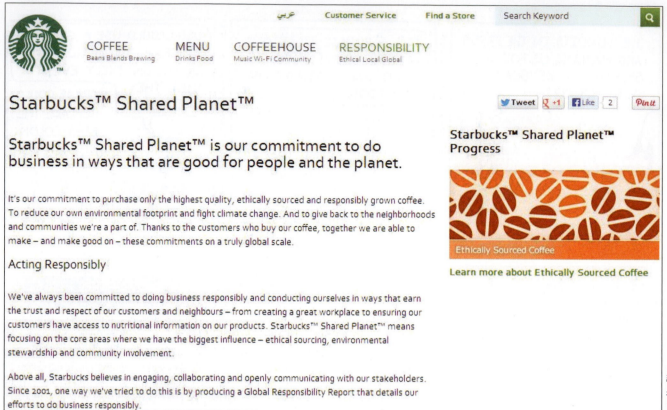

Susan Van Etten

that when coffee is bought this way, it helps foster a better future for farmers and a more stable climate for the planet.

- **_Preparing internal communications._** Disseminating information and correcting misinformation within a firm can reduce the impact of rumors and increase employee morale. For events such as reductions in the labor force or mergers of firms, internal communications can do much to dispel rumors circulating among employees and in the local community. As Nike experiences recurring PR problems related to its outsourcing of manufacturing to Third-World countries, it is imperative that management keep U.S.-based employees informed of the details of its practices and processes so that they (who may be challenged by friends and neighbors) can provide accurate information.

- **_Counteracting negative publicity._** This is the damage-control function of public relations, as discussed earlier. The attempt here is not to cover up negative events but rather to prevent the negative publicity from damaging the image of a firm and its brands. When a lawsuit was filed against NEC alleging that one of its cellular phones had caused cancer, McCaw Cellular Communications used public relations

activities to inform the public and especially cellular phone users of scientific knowledge that argued against the claims in the lawsuit. Also, one industry's public relations problems are another industry's golden opportunity, as the ad in Exhibit 18.5 shows. Here the firm Jabra, which offers a full line of hands-free devices for using cellular phones, is able to promote its brand with only a slightly veiled reference to health concerns of cellular phone use.

- **_Lobbying._** The public relations function can assist a firm in dealing with government officials and pending legislation. Microsoft reportedly spent billions on such lobbying efforts when antitrust violations were leveled at the company in Europe. Industry groups also maintain active and aggressive lobbying efforts at both the state and federal levels. As an example, the beer and wine industry has lobbyists monitoring legislation that could restrict beer and wine advertising.

- **_Giving advice and counsel._** Assisting management in determining what (if any) position to take on public issues, preparing employees for public appearances, and helping management anticipate public reactions are all part of the advice and counsel function of public relations.

EXHIBIT 18.5 The PR problems in the cellular phone industry created great opportunities for another industry. When medical research results suggested that extensive cell phone use could be linked to brain cancer, firms develop accessories to offer users more remote proximity to the cell handset. In this ad, Jabra is alluding to the negative publicity in the cell industry and the medical research as the basis for its brand appeal.

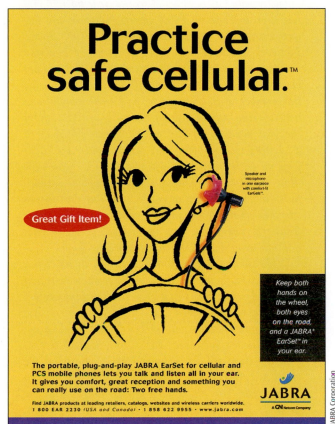

18-1c **The Tools of Public Relations**

There are several means by which a firm can pursue the objectives just cited. The goal is to gain as much control over the PR process as possible. By using the tools discussed in the following sections, a firm can integrate its public relations efforts with other brand communications.

Press Releases. One important tactical tool is the press release. Indeed, a narrow view of public relations envisions the PR department writing press releases and working with key contacts in the traditional and digital media to get them interested in the release, with the hope that a story of some kind will follow. Having a file of information that makes for good news stories puts the firm in a position to take advantage of press coverage. The following are

some typical categories of information that make for a good story:

- New products launches
- New scientific discoveries
- New personnel
- New corporate facilities
- Innovative corporate practices, such as energy-saving programs or employee benefit programs
- Annual shareholder meetings
- Charitable and community service activities

The only drawback to press releases is that a firm often doesn't know if or when the item will (if ever) appear in the news. Also, journalists are free to edit or interpret a news release, which may alter its intended message. To help minimize unintended outcomes, it's key to develop working relationships with editors or bloggers from publications the organization deems critical to its press release program. As with most communication endeavors, know your audience! Target felt strongly enough about cultivating relationships with journalists that it relocated one of its PR specialists from Minneapolis to Phoenix to cultivate local-media relationships there and in other western U.S. markets.[14] Although public relations should not be defined by the press release ritual, this is still an important skill set.

Press releases are vital to community building and event marketing. Here is an example of an event press release. Note how it brings in the value of the event to the sponsor, brand, athletes, and most important, community. Here, Jackie Tyson of Peloton Sports in Alpharetta, Georgia, shows an example of how to write one after a sponsored event:

SALT LAKE CITY, UTAH—Two months after the completion of the Larry H. Miller Tour of Utah professional stage race, event organizers confirmed that new records were set for economic impact, national audiences, and media coverage. A quantitative research study reveals that out-of-state spectators contributed $14 million in direct economic impact for the state of Utah. Tour organizers also confirmed that national television viewership almost doubled from last year, media impressions grew by nearly 50 percent and the Tour earned $8.5 million in publicity value.

"The Tour of Utah has enjoyed tremendous growth this year. Judging by the excitement of the crowds, the cycling fans who tuned in online and on FOX Sports Network, and the positive feedback from the key stakeholders, the Tour of Utah has a solid foundation in place for the future. It is great to hear partners like the Utah Sports Commission confirm

that the Tour of Utah has become one of the largest sporting events in the state. The gears have already started turning for 2013," said Steve Miller, President of the Tour of Utah.

The research included measurement of economic impact, sponsorship awareness and spectator profiles related to the cycling event, which took place August 7–12, 2012. Data was collected by crowd intercept surveys at all start and finish host venue locations during race week—Ogden, Miller Motorsports Park in Tooele, Lehi, Salt Lake City, Snowbird Ski and Summer Resort and Park City.

Dr. Angeline Close of the University of Texas at Austin led a research team and collected and processed completed surveys during race week. They found that Tour fans stayed 4.3 consecutive nights for the event, and that 14% of the total attendance traveled from outside the state of Utah to watch the race. Of the estimated fans who traveled from out of state, the majority confirmed they visited Utah specifically to watch the Tour of Utah. The average daily expenditure for out-of-state spectators was calculated to be $353 per person, based on five factors: lodging, food/beverage, transportation, retail/groceries, and other sightseeing/ entertainment. A total of $12–14 million in economic impact was directly linked to out-of-state fans.

The method divided spectators into three distinct groups—out-of-state fans, Utah residents who traveled more than 50 miles to attend a stage, and local residents who wanted to watch the event. Only visitor dollars from out-of-state fans were tabulated in the final report, so that the analysis aligned in a similar fashion with other Utah sporting event studies conducted by the Utah Sports Commission, one of the Tour of Utah's top partners.

"Utah has a solid reputation for hosting some of the best international sporting events in the world, showcasing Utah as the State of Sport for winter and summer. The Larry H. Miller Tour of Utah has grown significantly in just the past two years and has become a centerpiece for summer, now one of the largest outdoor sporting events for our state," said Jeff Robbins, president and CEO of the Utah Sports Commission.

The Utah Sports Commission is focused on sport development to grow Utah's economy and leverage the state's world-class sports assets to enhance Utah's position in the global sports marketplace. In 2011–2012, the Sports Commission partnered with 44 world-class sporting events across the state. An estimated $1.8 million in funding was provided to sports events, resulting in an estimated $146 million in economic impact to the state of Utah. Twenty-seven of these events hosted also had a major national and

international television component to them generating an estimated $46 million in media value to the state.

The Tour of Utah also generates solid exposure for Utah across multiple media channels. Media coverage of the 2012 Larry H. Miller Tour of Utah grew 49% from the year before, with an estimated 37.2 million media impressions and $8.5 million in earned publicity value. It is also the second year for national television coverage on FOX Sports Network and live webcasting to a worldwide audience. FOX Sports Network aired 12 hours of live coverage over the six days of racing, reaching an average of 67 million homes. Live coverage was a significant factor in raising the number of households to 637,000 people who watched the race daily, an increase of 75% from the year before. The Tour of Utah web site received 113,000 visits during race week, with 362,530 page views. In addition, 64% of site visits viewed the Tour Tracker® component, which provided start-to-finish audio and video coverage of the race on the web site and with various mobile applications. The Tour Tracker® experience was viewed in 123 countries and had more than 10,500 mobile downloads.

The Tour of Utah gained attention in its eighth year in 2012 for increased race mileage, more elevation gain, and stronger international field of competition. The race route covered 543 miles of diverse and mountainous terrain with 38,500 feet of elevation gain. Mileage increased 33% and vertical feet of climbing increased 25% from 2011, solidifying the event as "America's Toughest Stage Race™." Seven of this year's 17 professional teams competed at the Tour de France, including the BMC Racing Team, which featured 2012 overall Tour of Utah winner Johann Tschopp of Switzerland.

The Utah Sports Commission supports the Tour of Utah as it looks to expand in 2013 to the southern part of the state. An exploratory committee has received positive feedback from more than seven communities interested in hosting the multi-day stage race in Southern Utah. The Larry H. Miller Tour of Utah continues to be free to all spectators, making professional cycling one of the most unique professional sports in the world today.

Note that the press release covers the basic who, what, when, where, and most importantly why. A good press release for an event shows the economic impact on sponsors, to help leverage their investment and attract future sponsors for the event. A sport press release should also include key athletes, teams, and, if post-event, the winners. Like a USP, the press release should end with something that makes the event unique; in this case, it is that it was a fabulous spectator event that is free! Note that a press release is often in a media outlet, in a story-like manner. Yet, a press release is distinct from a feature story—a related PR tool.

Feature Stories. Although a firm cannot write a feature story for a newspaper or any other medium, it can invite journalists to do an exclusive story on the firm when there is a noteworthy event. A feature story is different from a press release in that it is typically more controllable, detailed, and lengthy. A feature story, as opposed to a news release, offers a single journalist the opportunity to do a fairly lengthy piece with exclusive rights to the information. Jupiter Communications, a leading research organization that tracks Internet usage and generates statistics about the Internet, has a simple philosophy when it comes to using feature stories as a public relations tool. Says Jupiter's CEO, "It is our goal to get every research project we do covered somewhere. We know this is the cheapest and maybe most effective, way to market ourselves."[15]

Company Newsletters/e-Newsletters. In-house publications such as newsletters (either printed or digital or both) can disseminate positive information about a firm through its employees. As members of the community, employees are proud of their firm's achievements. Newsletters can also be distributed to important constituents in the community, such as government officials, the chamber of commerce, or the tourism bureau. Suppliers often enjoy reading about an important customer, so newsletters can be mailed and emailed to this group as well. As in other areas, firms have discovered that the Internet is an excellent way to distribute information that traditionally has been the focus of printed newsletters.

Interviews and Press Conferences. Interviews with key executives or staged press conferences can be highly effective public relations tools. Often they are warranted in a crisis management situation. But firms also call press conferences to announce important scientific breakthroughs or explain the details of a corporate expansion or a new product launch. No one did this better than Steve Jobs each and every time Apple had big news about a new product. The press conference has an air of credibility because it uses a news format to present salient information.

Sponsored Events. As was discussed in Chapter 16 and highlighted earlier by the Hilton example, event marketing and sponsoring events can also serve as an essential PR or community-building component for a brand. Sponsorships run the gamut from supporting community events, such as the Tour de Georgia or the Tour of Utah cycling race to mega-events such as the

Olympics or World Cup. At the local level, prominent display of the corporate name and logo offers residents the chance to see that an organization is dedicated to supporting their community. Further, event marketing offers VIP sponsors and their clients a special experience, often via luxurious skyboxes, dining, and gift bags exclusively for sponsors and friends. While market resistance may occur due to advertising, it is rare to not like event sponsors, as they make the event of your choosing more financially beneficial to the consumer—and provide value added in forms of products, entertainment, or coupons to try the product or service. Also, events add to the local economy, again making them good for communities by providing jobs and more business for local hotels, restaurants, retailers, and other local service providers.

Another form of sponsorship is the fundraiser. Fundraisers for nonprofit organizations of all sorts give positive visibility to corporations. For many years, Chevrolet has sponsored college scholarships through the NCAA by choosing the best offensive and defensive player in televised football games. The scholarships are announced with much fanfare at the conclusion of the game. This sort of publicity for Chevrolet can also make a favorable impression.

Publicity. **Publicity** is essentially free media exposure about a firm's activities or brands. The public relations function seeks to monitor and manage publicity but obviously can never actually control what the media chooses to say or report. This lack of control was demonstrated earlier in the chapter with the examples of Intel, Taco Bell, and KFC. Politics is another walk of life where the tone of one's publicity can be hard to manage. Organizations (or politicians) need to be prepared to take advantage of events that make for good publicity and to counter events that are potentially damaging to their reputation (see Insights Online [Exhibit 18.6] for a notable example). And you can be sure that politicians running for or holding prominent positions have a team of PR experts.

The appeal of publicity—when the information is positive—is that it tends to carry heightened credibility. Publicity that appears in news stories on television and radio and in newspapers and magazines assumes an air of believability because of the credibility of the media context. Publicity that appears

INSIGHTS ONLINE

18.6 Go online to see the AdAge feature, "American Political Leaders Including Hilary Clinton and Obama Are Featured in a Controversial Pakistani Ad on Religion, despite Hilary's Insistence that Neither She Nor the U.S. Government Had Anything to Do with the Video."

on the Web is not quite so credible—most consumers question the authority and expertise of bloggers, although stories appearing at sites like Reuters or Associated Press are more believable. Not-for-profit organizations often use publicity in the form of news stories and public interest stories as ways to gain widespread visibility at little or no cost, given their often constrained budgets.

But publicity is not always completely out of the company's control. For instance, during the Academy Awards, a bracelet worn by actress Julia Roberts caused quite a stir. After Roberts won the award for best actress, she stood smiling (which we all know she does so well) and waving to the cameras, and suddenly the whole world wanted to know about the snowflake-design Van Cleef & Arpels bracelet that adorned her right (waving) wrist. What a lucky break for the designers? Not really. The whole episode was carefully planned by Van Cleef's PR agency, Ted, Inc. The agency lobbied hard to convince Roberts that the bracelet and matching earrings were stunning with her dress, knowing that if she won the Oscar, she would be highly photographed waving that pretty bracelet.[16] (See Insights Online [Exhibit 18.7] for another interesting example.)

LO 3

18-1d Basic Public Relations Strategies

Given the breadth of possibilities for using public relations as part of a firm's overall advertising and IBP effort, it's good to revisit the possibilities in simple terms. Public relations strategies can be categorized as either proactive or reactive. **Proactive public relations strategy** is guided by marketing objectives, seeks to publicize a company and its brands, and should serve to build goodwill (and buzz) for the brand. **Reactive public relations strategy** focuses on problems to be solved rather than on opportunities and requires a company to take defensive measures. Think BP again.

Proactive Strategy. In developing a proactive PR strategy, a firm acknowledges opportunities to use public relations efforts to accomplish something positive,

as the "Tools of Public Relations" discussion revealed. Companies often rely heavily on their public relations firms to help them put together a proactive strategy. In fact, in the modern era, analysts believe that marketers will increasingly turn to their PR specialists as a way to converge brand equity with corporate reputation.[17] As an example, the biotechnology industry is often the subject of much controversy in the press regarding genetically altered food and seed products. A prime example is Monsanto, portrayed as the evil empire in the documentary film *Food, Inc.* The advertisement in Exhibit 18.8 from the biotechnology industry attempts to take a proactive approach to dealing with the controversies by presenting a positive image and information. In this ad, the industry portrays itself as not only a protector of the land but also a protector of that most revered of all professions—the American farmer. In a recent Super Bowl ad, Dodge also focused on the American farmer and the related values in an emotional appeal.

In many firms, the positive aspects of employee achievements, corporate contributions to the community, and the organization's social and environmental

EXHIBIT 18.8 The biotechnology industry is taking a proactive PR approach to the controversies surrounding the industry and its processes.

programs go unnoticed by important constituents. To implement a proactive strategy, a firm needs to develop a comprehensive public relations program. The key components of such a program are as follows:

1. *A public relations audit.* A **public relations audit** identifies the characteristics of a firm or the aspects of the firm's activities that are positive and newsworthy. Information is gathered in much the same way as information related to advertising strategy is gathered. Corporate personnel and customers are questioned to provide information. This information may include descriptions of company products and services, market performance of brands, profitability, goals for products, market trends, new product introductions, important suppliers, important customers, employee programs and facilities, community programs, and charitable activities.

2. *A public relations plan.* Once the firm is armed with information from a public relations audit, the next step is a structured plan. A **public relations plan** identifies the objectives and activities related to the public relations communications issued by a firm. The components of a public relations plan include the following:

   a. *Situation analysis.* This section of the public relations plan summarizes the information obtained from the public relations audit. Information contained here is often broken down by category, such as product performance or community activity.

   b. *Program objectives.* Objectives for a proactive PR program stem from the current situation. Objectives should be set for both short-term and long-term opportunities. Public relations objectives can be as diverse and complex as advertising objectives. The focal point is not sales or profits per se. Rather, factors such as the credibility of product performance (i.e., placing products in verified, independent tests) and the stature of the firm's research and development efforts (highlighted in a prestigious trade publication article) are legitimate types of PR objectives.

   c. *Program rationale.* In this section, it is critical to identify the role the public relations program will play relative to all the other communication efforts—particularly advertising and community involvement—being undertaken by a firm. This is the area where an IBP perspective is clearly articulated for the public relations effort.

   d. *Communications vehicles.* This section of the plan specifies precisely what means will be used

to implement the public relations plan. The tools discussed earlier in the chapter—press releases, interviews, newsletters, blogs, websites—constitute the communications vehicles through which objectives can be implemented. There will likely be discussion of precisely how press releases, interviews, and company newsletters and the Web can be used.

   e. *Message content.* Analysts suggest that public relations messages should be researched and developed in much the same way that advertising messages are researched and developed. Focus groups and in-depth interviews are being used to fine-tune PR communications. For example, a pharmaceutical firm learned that calling obesity a "disease" rather than a "condition" increased the overweight population's receptivity to the firm's press release messages regarding a new anti-obesity drug.[18] And, in the new digital era, firms are keenly aware that the message content will likely be passed along through social media. One expert in PR strategy said, "Back in the old days, our agency would write a fantastic piece of content, like a white paper (a firm's position or strategy related to a situation) and think that was the end. Today audiences take that content and post it, comment on it and share and give it additional life."[19]

A proactive public relations strategy has the potential for making an important supportive contribution to a firm's IBP effort. Carefully placing positive information targeted to potentially influential constituents—such as members of the community or stockholders—supports the overall goal of enhancing the image, reputation, and perception of a firm and its brands.

Reactive Strategy. Going on Oprah to defend your side in a sports cheating scandal can be an example of both publicity and a reactive PR strategy. In this case, timing is everything. It took the CEO of Carnival Cruise Lines three entire days to make an official announcement after over 3,000 customers were stranded on their faulty cruise line. This is simply not acceptable. A reactive PR strategy may seem like a contradiction in terms, but as stated earlier, firms must implement a reactive strategy when events outside the control of the firm create negative publicity. Coca-Cola was able to rein in negative publicity by acting swiftly after an unfortunate incident occurred in Europe. Seven days after a bottling problem caused teens in Belgium and France to become sick after drinking Coke, the firm acted quickly and pulled all Coca-Cola products from the market, with an apology from the CEO.[20] Coca-Cola's quick actions could not prevent negative consequences in terms of product sales. That would call for new marketing programs tailored to meet the needs of consumers on a country-by-country basis. The reactive PR program relied heavily on IBP strategies, including free samples; dealer incentive programs; and beach parties featuring sound and light shows, DJs, and cocktail bars with free Cokes to win back the critical teen segment.[21] In the end it was a complete and integrated effort that restored consumers' trust and rebuilt the business across Europe.

It is difficult to organize for and provide structure around reactive PR. Since the events that trigger a reactive effort are unpredictable, a firm must simply be prepared to act quickly and thoughtfully. Two steps help firms implement a reactive public relations strategy:

1. **The public relations audit.** The public relations audit that was prepared for the proactive strategy helps a firm also prepare its reactive strategy. The information provided by the audit gives a firm what it needs to issue public statements based on current and accurate data.

2. **The identification of vulnerabilities.** In addition to preparing current information, the other key step in a reactive strategy is to recognize areas where the firm has weaknesses in its operations or products that can negatively affect its relationships with important constituents. From a public relations standpoint, these weaknesses are called *vulnerabilities.* If aspects of a firm's operations are vulnerable to criticism, such as environmental issues related to manufacturing processes, then the public relations function should be prepared to discuss the issues in a broad range of forums with many different constituents. Leaders at Pepsi, Quaker Oats, and Philip Morris were taken somewhat by surprise when shareholders challenged the firms on their practices with respect to genetically modified foods. Even though the concern was among a minority of shareholders, there were enough concerned constituents to warrant a proxy vote on the issue of genetically modified foods.[22] Executives at these firms now understand that pursuing any form of genetically modified foods will always be one of their vulnerabilities.

18-1e A Final Word on Public Relations

Public relations is a prime example of how a firm (or an individual) can identify and then manage aspects of communication in an integrated and synergistic manner to diverse audiences. Without recognizing public relations activities as a component of the firm's overall IBP communication effort, misinformation or disinformation could compromise more mainstream communications such as advertising. The coordination of public relations into an integrated program is a matter of recognizing and identifying the process as critical to the overall IBP effort and, as always, getting the right set of players on your IBP team. Modern marketing managers feel that social media is a "sweet spot" for public relations. As one manager said, "Social media is recognized as a place for relationships—and that, historically and intrinsically, is the province of public relations."[23] As such, let's discuss how social media are being used for various PR strategies.

—————— LO **4** ——————

18-2 INFLUENCER MARKETING

If public relations is the discipline devoted to monitoring and managing how people view us, then it can also be thought of as a discipline devoted to monitoring and managing what consumers are saying to one another about us. Moreover, as noted earlier in this chapter, consumers have become increasingly predisposed to talk about brands, both online and offline. Since we know they are likely to talk about our brands anyway, it seems prudent to follow the advice of Bonnie Raitt from her album *Luck of the Draw.* As Bonnie says (and sings) in her 1990s blues-rock hit: "Let's give them something to talk about!"

That basic idea, "give them something to talk about," underlies the evolution of an important new communication discipline that we will represent under the general label of influencer marketing. As defined by Northlich, a leader in influencer marketing programming, **influencer marketing** refers to a series of personalized marketing techniques directed at individuals or groups who have the credibility and capability to drive positive word of mouth in a broader and salient segment of the population. The idea is to give the influencer something to talk about. In addition, it is useful to distinguish between professional and peer-to-peer influencer programs. Both can provide one of the most valued assets for any brand builder—an advocacy message from a trusted source. (See Insights Online [Exhibit 18.9] for an interesting example.)

INSIGHTS ONLINE

18.9 Go online to see the AdAge feature, "Twitter Is a Tool to Highlight Everyday Consumers as Important Brand Influencers, as Oreo—the Latest Master of Real-Time Marketing—Shows with Its Twitter Follower, Who Also Follows Kit Kat Online, via a Clever Tic-Tac-Toe Design."

18-2a **Professional Influencer Programs**

If you're a pet owner, it's likely you've made many visits to the vet. And while visiting the vet, perhaps you asked a few questions about the best products to feed your puppy or kitten. Pet owners always want to do the right thing for their four-legged friends. If you've lived this scenario, you know what comes next. The vet is ready to talk about proper feeding, and not only that, he or she may be ready with product samples or informational brochures describing the benefits of a particular brand of pet food. Coincidence? Not at all. The makers of IAMS and Hill's Science Diet know that vets are key influencers in the decision about what to feed one's pet, especially for devoted pet owners who don't mind paying a little extra to get the best. These brands target vets with influencer marketing programs to try to earn their recommendation, and thus the vet becomes the influence in the decision process for the firm's brand.

Many professionals are in this position where their advice about products is highly valued by consumers. Your doctor, dentist, neonatal nurse, auto mechanic, and hair stylist all have the credibility to influence product choices in their specific areas of expertise. Sometimes the opportunity is obvious, as with the example of vets and pet food. But more and more we are seeing creative programming that takes influencer programming into new territory. An excellent example is that of Select Comfort, which targets many different types of health care professionals with an influencer program for its Sleep Number bed.

One particular group of health care professionals targeted by Select Comfort is occupational therapists (OTs). Persons in this field provide therapy to individuals with serious physical challenges, and they commonly receive promotional materials for things like the Moen bathtub grab bar, which makes it easier for persons with physical challenges to bathe safely. But are OTs experts on sleep? It doesn't matter. Many of their patients are likely to value their opinions, and all health care professionals commonly hear complaints from their patients about having trouble sleeping. So what advice can the OT provide to help a person sleep better?

Obviously, if you're Select Comfort, you'd like the OT to encourage patients to have a look at the Sleep Number bed. The first step is to get that OT to try and use the bed herself. Thus, Select Comfort offers special promotions to encourage OTs to

Influencer marketing refers to a series of personalized marketing techniques directed at individuals or groups who have the credibility and capability to drive positive word of mouth in a broader and salient segment of the population.

purchase Sleep Number beds for their own bedrooms. Next, the OT needs tools to follow through on their potential advocacy. This is no problem. Like most professionals, OTs belong to associations and subscribe to journals. Name and address files from such sources allow a company to start building an OT marketing database. Once an OT expresses any kind of interest in the Sleep Number bed, she is sent an advocacy kit. Some key elements of that kit are displayed in Exhibit 18.10. These materials include everything from a lengthy demonstration DVD to hand-out brochures and even prescription pads so the OT can write clients a prescription for a Sleep Number bed. Marketers at Select Comfort cannot control what the OT says to her patient about the Sleep Number bed. But they can put materials in her hands that will make it easy for her to become an advocate, if she believes such advocacy is justified. That's the nature of influencer marketing.

Think of influencer marketing as systematic seeding of conversations involving a consumer, the influencer, and the brand. Professionals in any field of endeavor take their role very seriously, so influencer programs directed to them must be handled with great care. Several points of emphasis should be kept in mind when developing programs for professionals. First, their time is money, so any program that wastes their time will be a waste of money and not be implemented. However, tactics designed to encourage professionals to try the product themselves can be very valuable. Also, messaging with professionals needs to provide intellectual currency and help the professionals learn important benefits of the brand and potentially increase their perceived expertise with their clients. For example, health care professionals' concerns will be better addressed through clinical studies than celebrity endorsements. Additionally, programs directed at professionals require a long-term commitment. For them to be advocates, trust first must develop, and any marketer must show patience and persistence to earn that trust.

18-2b **Peer-to-Peer Programs**

Peer-to-peer programs typically have a very different tone than programs for professionals. In peer-to-peer programs, the idea is to give influencers something fun or provocative to talk about. Think of it as an emphasis on "social currency" for peer-to-peer programs versus "intellectual currency" for professionals. A great guiding

EXHIBIT 18.10 Firms need to try to encourage key influencers to recommend the firm's brand. Here, Select Comfort, maker of the Sleep Number bed, provides an information kit to health care professionals that includes a DVD and brochures that carefully document the benefits of the Sleep Number bed. There is even a prescription pad that allows the therapist to put his or her recommendation in writing.

in marketing parlance, is the process of encouraging consumers to talk to each other about a firm's brand or marketing activities. **Buzz marketing** can be defined as creating an event or experience that yields conversations that include the brand. Buzz marketing occurs when a firm's marketing activities gain widespread media coverage and become a source of conversation in households, between friends, or at work. Buzz marketing depends on that old-fashioned way people communicate with each other—face to face (see Insights Online [Exhibit 18.11] for an interesting example).

Viral marketing is the process of consumers marketing to consumers via the Web (e.g., via blogs, Facebook, Twitter, or forwarding YouTube links) or through personal contact stimulated by a firm marketing a brand. Viral marketing occurs when word of mouth in digital media reaches high levels of activity. Also, firms are anxious to encourage positive word of mouth among consumers, which is much easier in this era of social media. If a consumer is excited about a new purchase, it is not unusual to see a comment show up on a Facebook page or for a blast of tweets to go out to friends and relatives. But new digital media are not the only way to create word-of-mouth buzz. Researchers have identified that approximately 30 percent of online word of mouth is stimulated by old traditional media—particularly consumers talking about TV ads they have seen recently.[26] The idea behind both buzz and viral marketing strategies is to target a handful of carefully chosen trendsetters or connectors as your influencers and let them spread the word (see Insights Online [Exhibit 18.12] for an interesting example).

principle for peer-to-peer programs is "Do something remarkable" to get people talking about your brand.[24] To promote Virgin Mobile's "Nothing to Hide" campaign, Richard Branson descended into Times Square on a giant cell phone while performing a striptease act—pretty remarkable. To promote a book launch German publisher Eichborn attached tiny banners to 200 flies and let them buzz around at a book fair[25]—pretty odd, but pretty remarkable. Just follow that advice from Bonnie Raitt: Giving them something to talk about is always a good starting point. Creating buzz about a brand or having a brand go "viral" in terms of consumer conversations are key peer-to-peer programs (see Insights Online [Exhibit 18.11] for a great example). Additionally, there is the process of cultivating "connectors" for a firm's brand. Let's examine these peer-to-peer phenomena in detail.

Buzz and Viral Marketing. Two hot concepts in this area of peer-to-peer influence are buzz and viral marketing. Essentially, both of these refer to efforts to stimulate word of mouth involving key targets that might otherwise be impervious to more traditional advertising and promotional tools. **Word of mouth,**

Buzz and viral marketing both depend on high levels of contact between consumers; it is often the case that these programs are fielded in cities like New York, London, and Los Angeles, because that's where you

INSIGHTS ONLINE

18.11 Go online to see the AdAge feature, "A Cider Brand Purposely Stages Consumer Complaints by Putting Twigs in the Cases of Cider to Show How the Cider Is in Touch with Nature and to Generate Buzz."

INSIGHTS ONLINE

18.12 Go online to see the AdAge feature, "Dove and Their Agency Ogilvy & Mather Got a Lot of Buzz for Their Real Campaign for Beauty Featuring Non-Modelesque Women; Now, in a Comical Spot Reducing a Man to His Hair, the Agency Is Asking, Are Guys Allowed to Have Great Hair?"

find the trendsetters. Consider this scene at the cafés on Third Street Promenade in and around Los Angeles. A gang of sleek, impossibly attractive bikers pulls up and, guess what, they seem *genuinely* interested in getting to know you over an iced latte—their treat, no less! Sooner or later the conversation turns to their Vespa scooters glinting in the sun, and they eagerly pull out a pad and jot down an address and phone number—for the nearest Vespa dealer. The scooter-riding, latte-drinking models are on the Vespa payroll, and they're paid to create buzz about the scooters by engaging hip café dwellers in conversation and camaraderie.[27]

Taking Buzz to the Next Level. Publicity stunts can be thought of as buzz builders, and there is nothing new about them. In 1863, P. T. Barnum orchestrated a wedding between two of his circus stars to boost attendance at the circus. The remarkable thing about this circus wedding was that the bride and the groom were both just 3 feet tall. P. T. Barnum knew how to create a buzz; he just didn't call it that. (See Insights Online [Exhibit 18.13] for another interesting example of creating buzz through an attention-getting stunt.)

> ### INSIGHTS ONLINE
>
> **18.13** Go online to see the AdAge feature, "In a Horrifying PSA against Domestic Violence, Makeup Vlogger Does a Covert Makeup Tutorial on YouTube to Teach Ladies How to Conceal Bruises and Injuries on Your Face after Being Beaten in a Domestic Violence Situation."

But as you might expect, there is a lot that separates old-school publicity stunts from today's practice of influencer marketing. For one thing, there is the level of experience and sophistication of organizations like Northlich and Keller Fay Group when it comes to assisting clients with influencer programming. For instance, Keller Fay has developed a tracking system that can estimate the number of word-of-mouth conversations taking place on a daily basis. Another familiar name and key supplier in this space is Nielsen BuzzMetrics. BuzzMetrics provides services to clients for tracking word-of-mouth activity across the Internet. And the Word of Mouth Marketing Association (WOMMA), founded by Andy Sernovitz, is a great resource for learning about the art and science of buzz building. The WOMMA website is a fantastic resource for learning more about all the topics in this section, and Sernovitz's five keys for success with influencer marketing are featured in Exhibit 18.14.

The point is, it's no longer just about the publicity stunt, and with billions of brand conversations happening every day, lots of brand builders, from Kodak to Kashi, want to be involved.[28] In addition, new research has found that word-of-mouth communications that result

EXHIBIT 18.14 To generate buzz, five T's are the keys: Talkers, Topics, Tools, Talking, and Tracking.

Talkers. Much like our point about connectors, Andy Sernovitz asserts that you have to find the people who are predisposed to talk about brands in general, and/or your brand in particular. Often you need to be on the Internet to find these people. Find them and get to know them.

Topics. Next, of course, you have to give them something to talk about. This can't be a marketing message or a mission statement. There needs to be a mystery or a cool story or some breaking news that you are sharing to get people talking. Maybe the best at doing this is Steve Jobs at Apple. He definitely has a knack for stirring up interest and conversation with his suspenseful product announcements and his implied promise that our next great thing is just around the corner.

Tools. Make good use of the tools that promote a viral conversation. You can post a story on a Web page and some will find it there, but in the end it just sits there. You put the exact same story on a blog and it's linkable, portable, built to travel across the Internet. Suddenly lots of people are sharing the story.

Taking Part. Stop thinking in terms of one-way communication; start thinking in terms of dialogue. If you want favorable word-of-mouth, you need to be part of the conversation, not ignore it. Dell was slow to take part in a conversation about problems consumers had getting service. Basically, they ignored the conversation. When blogger Jeff Jarvis had big problems with his Dell and couldn't get the company's attention he coined the phrase "Dell Hell," which became a lightning rod for conversation about Dell on the Internet. You've got to be tuned in if you ever want to join the conversation.

Tracking. Word-of-mouth on the Internet is very measurable. With blogs, people write things down in full view. This is an opportunity for any company to know what people are saying about their brands and why they are saying it. Lots of companies are paying close attention to what consumers are saying about their brands. Even Dell is now among them.

Sources: Andy Sernovitz, *Word of Mouth Marketing: How Smart Companies Get People Talking* (Chicago, IL: Kaplan Publishing, 2006); Piet Levy, "Tease Please," *Marketing News,* April 30, 2009, 6.

in brand referrals by the influencers have a strong impact on new customers for the brand—much more so than traditional marketing techniques.[29]

Cultivating Connectors. One specific area where we see dramatic advancements in peer-to-peer marketing is in the activity of identifying and cultivating connectors. Meet Donna Wetherell. Donna is an outgoing mom and works at a customer-service call center where she knows about 300 coworkers by name. She likes to talk about shopping and lots of different brands. She always seems to have lots of extra coupons for the brands she likes, so much so that her coworkers call her the coupon lady. Donna is a connector, one of 600,000 that P&G enrolled for its influencer program called Vocalpoint.[30]

That's right, your chatty next-door neighbor, who seems to know everyone and loves to talk about her favorite brands in person and on social media, could be one of these highly coveted connectors. For its connector database, P&G focused on women who had large social networks. They searched for them over the Internet at sites like iVillage.com. It seems connectors liked the idea of being the first to receive new product samples and to feel that their voice was being heard by a big company.

Once a connector database like P&G's is developed, it again becomes a matter of giving your connectors something to talk about. That's the part they enjoy. But in the end it's not always a simple thing to get consumers talking about a product like dishwashing detergent, so here's what P&G execs asserted: "We do tremendous research behind it to give them a reason to care."[31] Just as with professional programs, you can't force someone to be an advocate for your brand. You can identify people who have big social networks, but they're not going to compromise their relationships with others by sharing dull stories or phony information. You must give them something interesting to talk about.

Developing connector databases, finding the conversation starters, tracking the buzz online and off—that's the new era of influencer marketing. And it doesn't hurt to have a little of the P. T. Barnum flair as part of the process either. An area that once was very mysterious, that is, word-of-mouth marketing, is becoming increasingly demystified and in some ways made more scientific. Firms like BzzAgent of Boston, Massachusetts, are a logical outgrowth of this movement. BzzAgent has recruited hundreds of thousands of "agents" that are ready to go to work buzzing for your brand. According to the firm's website, when you are a BzzAgent, you will tell others about products you like, try new products, and then "Get people talking by sharing your honest opinion through face-to-face conversations and online

via sites including Facebook, Twitter and blogs. Remember to always disclose that you're a BzzAgent and to keep the spam in the can. Bzz is no place for excessive, repetitive or unauthentic posts."[32] You would have to expect that if it's marketing and it works, then firms like BzzAgent will come up with ways to help firms use it.

18-3 CORPORATE ADVERTISING

Corporate advertising is not designed to promote the benefits of a specific brand but instead is intended to establish a favorable attitude toward a company as a whole. A variety of highly regarded and successful firms use corporate advertising to enhance the image of the firm and affect consumers' attitudes. This perspective on corporate advertising is gaining favor worldwide. Firms with the stature of General Electric, Toyota, and Hewlett-Packard are investing in corporate ad campaigns. Exhibit 18.15 shows a corporate campaign for Elkay, a high-end manufacturer of sinks and other plumbing fixtures. Notice how this ad fits the description of corporate advertising perfectly. Elkay is not featuring any one of its products in particular. But rather this interesting and attractive ad

EXHIBIT 18.15 Firms often use corporate advertising as a way to generate name recognition and a positive image for the firm as a whole rather than any of its products in particular. Here, Elkay touts the company name rather than any specific product features.

Delight in everyday perfection.

ELKAY
elkay.com

specialty collection sinks. Style that endures.

is designed to draw attention to the Elkay name and the general nature of its product line.

18-3a The Scope and Objectives of Corporate Advertising

Corporate advertising is a significant force in the overall advertising carried out by organizations around the world. Billions of dollars are invested annually in media for corporate campaigns. Interestingly, most corporate campaigns run by consumer-goods manufacturers are undertaken by firms in the shopping-goods category, such as appliance and auto marketers. Studies have also found that larger firms are much more prevalent users of corporate advertising than smaller firms are. Presumably, these larger firms have broader communications programs and more money to invest in advertising, which allows the use of corporate campaigns. Apple is another company that has historically relied on corporate campaigns (see Exhibit 18.16) to support its numerous subbrands. The billboard in Exhibit 18.16 is a classic example of Apple's corporate campaign strategy.

The brand logo and slogan for Apple appear, but no mention of product features is included. Recently, with the proliferation of individual product types, Apple has a need to prepare separate brand campaigns for the iPhone, iPad, and iMac.

Magazines and television are well suited to corporate advertising, although as the Apple billboard demonstrates, other media can accomplish the task as well. Corporate advertising appearing in magazines has the advantage of being able to target particular constituent groups with image- or issue-related messages. Magazines also provide the space for lengthy copy, which is often needed to achieve corporate advertising objectives and the high-quality reproduction which can add a positive aura to a corporate campaign. Television is a popular choice for corporate campaigns because the creative opportunities provided by television can deliver a powerful, emotional message. IBM has long used both television and magazine ads (see Exhibit 18.17) in a corporate campaign designed to reaffirm its image as an innovator. Notice in this ad that IBM relies on featuring the futuristic vision

EXHIBIT 18.16 Corporate image advertising is meant to build a broad image for the company as a whole. Here Apple's "Think Different" slogan does just that.

Michael Newman/PhotoEdit

EXHIBIT 18.17 IBM has always felt that the company's image as an innovator is important in the face of competition from the likes of Apple and Samsung. This is one of the ads in a corporate image campaign designed to unify the image of the firm as a futuristic innovator with its technology.

of the firm's approach to technological innovation—a very positive image for a corporate campaign.

The objectives for corporate advertising should be focused. In fact, corporate advertising shares similar purposes with proactive public relations when it comes to what companies hope to accomplish. Here are some of the possibilities for a corporate campaign:

- To build the image of the firm among customers, shareholders, the financial community, and/or the general public
- To boost employee morale or attract new employees
- To communicate an organization's views on social, political, or environmental issues
- To better position the firm's products against competition, particularly foreign competition
- To play a role in the overall advertising and IBP strategy of an organization, providing a platform for more brand-specific campaigns

Notice that corporate advertising is not always targeted at the consumer. A broad range of constituents can be targeted with a corporate advertising effort. For example, when GlaxoWellcome and SmithKline Beecham merged to form a multibillion dollar pharmaceutical behemoth, the newly created firm, known as GlaxoSmithKline, launched an international print campaign aimed at investors who had doubts about the viability of the new corporate structure. The campaign was all about image and led with the theme: "Disease does not wait. Neither will we."[33]

18-3b Types of Corporate Advertising

Three basic types of corporate advertising dominate the campaigns run by organizations: image advertising, advocacy advertising, and cause-related advertising. Each is discussed in the following sections. We then consider green marketing, which can be considered as a special case of any of these first three.

Corporate Image Advertising. The majority of corporate advertising efforts focus on enhancing the overall image of a firm among important constituents—typically customers, employees, and the general public. When IBM promotes itself as the firm providing "Solutions for a small planet" or when General Mills advances its motto "Nourishing Lives," the goal is to enhance the overall image of the firm.

Bolstering a firm's image may not result in immediate effects on sales, but as we saw in Chapter 5, attitude can play an important directive force in consumer decision making. When a firm can enhance its overall image, it may well affect consumer predisposition in brand choice. Energy giant Shell Oil developed a series

of television, print, online, and outdoor ads to tout their efforts to "unlock" cleaner sources of energy and let the world know that Shell is "ready to help tackle the challenge of the new energy future."[34] Launched in the spring of 2010, just as BP oil was gushing into the waters of the Gulf of Mexico, the campaign also seemed to be saying that where BP has failed (remember the BP "Beyond Petroleum" slogan?), Shell plans to succeed. It's a bold promise. Only time will tell if Shell delivers on the promise.

Advocacy Advertising. **Advocacy advertising** attempts to establish an organization's position on important social or political issues. Advocacy advertising is meant to influence public opinion on issues of concern to a firm. Typically, the issue featured in an advocacy campaign is directly relevant to the business operations of the organization. For example, Burt's Bees' advocacy for a Natural Standard for Personal Care Products is perfectly aligned with its business model: No other company features natural ingredients in their products like Burt's Bees.

Cause-Related Advertising. **Cause-related advertising** features a firm's affiliation with an important social or societal cause—examples are reducing poverty, increasing literacy, conserving energy, protecting the environment, and curbing drug abuse—and takes place as part of the cause-related marketing efforts undertaken by a firm. The goal of cause-related advertising can be to enhance the image of the firm by associating it with social issues of importance to its constituents; this tends to work best when the firm confronts an issue that truly connects to its business. The ad in Exhibit 18.18, in which General Electric shows its commitment to "Better Health for More People," highlights the firm's commitment to improving people's health with its technology products. This campaign helps establish the firm as a socially conscious marketer while also helping society deal with an important problem.

Cause-related marketing is becoming increasingly common. There are several reasons for this. First, research supports the wisdom of such expenditures. In a consumer survey conducted by Cone, a Boston-based brand strategy firm, 91 percent of respondents said they have a more favorable impression of companies that support good causes and also said they believed that the causes a company supports can be a valid reason for switching brands.[35] Other studies indicate that support of good causes can translate into brand preference with the important qualifier that consumers will judge a firm's motives.[36] If the firm's support is perceived as disingenuous, cause-related expenditures are largely wasted.

EXHIBIT 18.18   In this cause-related corporate advertising campaign, General Electric highlights its commitment to developing products designed to provide "Better Health for More People" through the firm's "healthy imagination" program. In this ad, the focus is on National Women's Health Week.

finding homes for orphan animals, with free food and grant support for rescue shelters.[38] Campbell's Soup, Avon, and Yoplait have ongoing programs that generate funding to support research for a breast cancer cure. Home Depot promotes water conservation in areas of desperate need through its "Use Water Wisely" campaign; Nick at Nite funded an initiative called "National Family Dinner Day."[39] To advance the cause of families spending more time together, Nick at Nite networks ran the program by shutting off for the dinner hour on Nick at Nite Family Day to help make their point. These examples illustrate the wide variety of programs that can be launched to support a cause.

Green Marketing. It is heartening to observe that numerous companies have sparked to the idea of supporting any number of causes. One area in particular seems to offer special opportunities in the years ahead. Like so many things, this one has numerous labels, but "green marketing" is probably the most popular. **Green marketing** refers to corporate efforts that embrace a cause or a program in support of the environment. Such efforts include shoe boxes made out of 100 percent recycled materials at Timberland and the "Dawn Saves Wildlife" program sponsored by Procter & Gamble. General Electric and its "Ecomagination" campaign was another high-profile exemplar of this movement. In funding this corporate campaign, GE took the stance that it is simply a good business strategy to seek real solutions to problems like air pollution and fossil-fuel dependency.[40] They are demonstrating that going green can really be a great business strategy. Surveys show that environmental issues are of major concern to consumers, and a formidable segment is acting on this concern.[41] The green movement looks sustainable for some time.

In addition, the Internet once again is changing the game. It is no longer possible for companies to pay lip service to environmental causes but hide their true motives. "Green sites" like Green Seal and EnviroLink can assist in determining who is really doing what to protect the environment. Or just Google *greenwashing* and you'll find 2 million more sites to explore. Some of the "green claims" out there (see the Eco-Smart Hummer and Eco-Conscious Barbie) are so absurd they are almost funny. Motivated and well-informed consumers are hard to fool. Hopefully, companies will realize that it doesn't pay to make token gestures on behalf of the planet. Firms really only need to follow the one immutable law of branding to get it right when it comes to green marketing: Underpromise and overdeliver. Here's hoping that you too are getting on board the green bandwagon. It ain't easy being green, as Kermit the Frog would say.[42]

One would also like to think that the trend toward greater social responsibility by businesses is simply a matter of people wanting to do the right thing. For instance, Whirlpool Corporation is a Habitat Cornerstone Partner and assisted in the massive rebuilding effort needed in the wake of Hurricane Katrina. Jeff Terry, who manages the program of donations and volunteering on behalf of Whirlpool, says of the experience: "The first time you do this work it will change your life."[37] Sure, Whirlpool's participation in this program brings the company a lot of favorable publicity, but its people's hearts also appear to be in the right place. That makes the program a win–win activity for everyone involved.

The range of firms participating in cause-related marketing programs continues to grow. Pedigree has built its dog food brand through a commitment to

SUMMARY

 Explain the role of public relations (PR) as part of an organization's overall advertising and IBP strategy.

Public relations focuses on communications that can foster goodwill between a firm and constituent groups such as customers, stockholders, employees, government entities, and the general public. Businesses utilize public relations activities to highlight positive events associated with the organization; PR strategies are also employed for damage control when adversity strikes. Public relations has entered a new era, as changing corporate demands and new techniques have fostered a bolder, more aggressive role for PR in IBP campaigns.

 Detail the objectives and tools of public relations.

An active public relations effort can serve many objectives, such as building goodwill and counteracting negative publicity. Public relations activities may also be orchestrated to support the launch of new products or communicate with employees on matters of interest to them. The public relations function may also be instrumental to the firm's lobbying efforts and in preparing executives to meet with the press. The primary tools of public relations experts are press releases, feature stories, company newsletters, interviews and press conferences, and participation in the firm's event sponsorship decisions and programs.

 Describe two basic strategies motivating an organization's public relations activities.

When companies perceive public relations as a source of opportunity for shaping public opinion, they are likely to pursue a proactive public relations strategy. With a proactive strategy, a firm strives to build goodwill with key constituents via aggressive programs. The foundation for these proactive programs is a rigorous public relations audit and a comprehensive public relations plan. The plan should include an explicit statement of objectives to guide the overall effort. In many instances, however, public relations activities take the form of damage control. In these instances the firm is obviously in a reactive

mode. Although a reactive strategy may seem a contradiction in terms, it certainly is the case that organizations can be prepared to react to bad news. Organizations that understand their inherent vulnerabilities in the eyes of important constituents will be able to react quickly and effectively in the face of hostile publicity.

 Illustrate the strategies and tactics used in influencer marketing programs.

We know that consumers are predisposed to talk about brands, and what they have to say is vital to the health and well-being of those brands. Hence it is no surprise that marketers are pursuing strategies to proactively influence the conversation. Influencer marketing refers to tools and techniques that are directed at driving positive word of mouth about a brand. In professional programs, important gatekeepers like veterinarians or any type of health care professional may be a focal point. In peer-to-peer programs, the new mantra has become finding the connectors. But whether it's professional or peer to peer, the marketer is always challenged to give the influencers something meaningful or provocative that they will want to talk about.

 Discuss the applications and objectives of corporate advertising.

Corporate advertising is not undertaken to support an organization's specific brands but rather to build the general reputation of the organization in the eyes of key constituents. This form of advertising serves goals such as enhancing the firm's image and building fundamental credibility for its line of products. Corporate advertising may also serve diverse objectives, such as improving employee morale, building shareholder confidence, or denouncing competitors. Corporate ad campaigns generally fall into one of three categories: image advertising, advocacy advertising, or cause-related advertising. Corporate advertising may also be orchestrated in such a way to be very newsworthy, and thus it needs to be carefully coordinated with the organization's ongoing public relations programs.

KEY TERMS

public relations	public relations plan	corporate advertising
publicity	influencer marketing	advocacy advertising
proactive public relations strategy	word-of-mouth	cause-related advertising
reactive public relations strategy	buzz marketing	green marketing
public relations audit	viral marketing	

ENDNOTES

1. Matthew Schwartz, "New Influence," *Advertising Age,* October 26, 2009, S4, S5; Michael Bush, "Growth of Social Media Shifts PR Chiefs toward Center of Marketing Departments," *Advertising Age,* September 21, 2009, 7.

2. Julie Liesse, "Forecast for 2013: PR Pros' Predictions," *Public Relations,* November 12, 2012, C6.

3. Matthew Schwartz, "Directing Traffic at the New Branding Crossroads," *Public Relations,* November 12, 2012, C5.

4. Stephen Brown, "Ambi-brand Culture," in Jonathan Schroeder and Miriam Salzer-Morling (Eds.), *Brand Culture* (New York: Routledge, 2006), 50–66.

5. Frank Rose, "Let the Seller Beware," *The Wall Street Journal,* December 20, 2006, D10; Jack Neff, "Lever's CMO Throws Down the Social Media Gauntlet," *Advertising Age,* April 13, 2009, 1, 20.

6. Matthew Schwartz, "Directing Traffic at the New Branding Crossroads," *Public Relations,* November 12, 2012, C5.

7. Claire Stammerjohan, Charles M. Wood, Yuhmiin Chang, and Esther Thorson, "An Empirical Investigation of the Interaction between Publicity, Advertising, and Previous Brand Attitudes and Knowledge," *Journal of Advertising,* vol. 34 (Winter 2005), 55–67; Jonah Bloom, "With PR on the Rise, Here's a Refresher Course in the Basics," *Advertising Age,* May 11, 2009, 22.

8. James G. Kimball, "Can Intel Repair the Pentium PR?" *Advertising Age,* December 19, 1994, 35.

9. Barbara Grady, "Chastened Intel Steps Carefully with Introduction of New Chip," *Computerlink,* February 14, 1995, 11.

10. Pete Blackshaw, *Satisfied Customers Tell Three Friends: Angry Customers Tell 3,000* (New York: Doubleday, 2008).

11. Kate MacArthur, "Taco Hell: Rodent Video Signals New Era in PR Crises," *Advertising Age,* February 26, 2007, 1, 46.

12. Jack Neff, "J&J Targets Red Cross, Blunders into PR Firestorm," *Advertising Age,* August 13, 2007, 1, 22.

13. Emily York, "Grilled Chicken a Kentucky Fried Fiasco," *Advertising Age,* May 11, 2009, 1, 30.

14. Natalie Zmuda, "Target Gets Local with On-the-Field Team of PR Pros," *Advertising Age,* February 13, 2012, 12.

15. Andy Cohen, "The Jupiter Mission," *Sales and Marketing Management,* April 2000, 56.

16. Beth Snyder Bulik, "Well-Heeled Heed the Need for PR," *Advertising Age,* June 11, 2001, S2.

17. Matthew Schwartz, "Directing Traffic at the New Branding Crossroads," *Public Relations,* November 12, 2012, C5.

18. Geri Mazur, "Good PR Starts with Good Research," *Marketing News,* September 15, 1997, 16.

19. Julie Liesse, "Forecast for 2013: PR Pros' Predictions," *Public Relations,* November 12, 2012, C6.

20. Kathleen V. Schmidt, "Coke's Crisis," *Marketing News,* September 27, 1999, 1, 11.

21. Amie Smith, "Coke's European Resurgence," *Promo Magazine,* December 1999, 91.

22. James Cox, "Shareholders Get to Put Bio-Engineered Foods to Vote," *USA Today,* June 6, 2000, 1B.

23. Julie Liesse, "The Digital Sweet Spot," The PR Factor 2010, *Advertising Age,* November 29, 2010, S4.

24. Michael Krauss, "To Generate Buzz, Do Remarkable Things," *Marketing News,* December 15, 2006, 6.

25. "Pretty Fly Campaign," adage.com, October 29, 2009.

26. Simon Dumenco, "In Praise of the Original Social Media: Good Ol' Television," *Advertising Age,* May 17, 2010, 30; Ed Keller, "All Media Are Social: The Unique Roles of TV, Print and Online in Driving Word of Mouth," *MediaBizBloggers.com,* July 15, 2010.

27. Gerry Khermouch and Jeff Green, "Buzz-z-z Marketing," *BusinessWeek,* July 30, 2001, 50–56.

28. Michael Bush, "How Marketers Use Online Influencers to Boost Branding Efforts," adage.com, December 21, 2009.

29. Michael Trusov, Randolph E. Bucklin, and Koen Pauwels, "Effects of Word-of-Mouth versus Traditional Marketing: Findings from an Internet Social Networking Site," *Journal of Marketing,* vol. 73 (September 2009), 90–102.

30. Robert Berner, "I Sold It through the Grapevine," *BusinessWeek,* May 29, 2006, 32–34.

31. Ibid, 34.

32. Descriptions taken from the BzzAgent website accessed at www.bzzagent.com (accessed March 16, 2013).

33. David Goetzl, "GlaxoSmithKline Launches Print Ads," *Advertising Age,* January 8, 2001, 30.

34. Michael Bush, "Shell Breaks Industry Silence with Aggressive Campaign," *Advertising Age,* June 28, 2010, 10

35. Stephanie Thompson, "Raising Awareness, Doubling Sales," *Advertising Age,* October 2, 2006, 4.

36. Michael J. Barone, Anthony D. Miyazaki, and Kimberly A. Taylor, "The Influence of Cause-Related Marketing on Consumer Choice," *Journal of the Academy of Marketing Science,* vol. 28, no. 2 (2000), 248–262.

37. Ibid..

38. James Tenser, "The New Samaritans," *Advertising Age,* June 12, 2006, S-1, S-6.

39. Bob Liodice, "Ten Companies with Social Responsibility at the Core," *Advertising Age,* April 19, 2010, 88.

40. James Tenser, "The New Samaritans," *Advertising Age,* June 12, 2006, S-1, S-6; Natalie Zmuda and Emily York, "Cause Effect: Brands Rush to Save World One Good Deed at a Time," *Advertising Age,* March 1, 2010, 1, 22.

41. Mya Frazier, "Going Green? Plant Deep Roots," *Advertising Age,* April 30, 2007, 1, 54–55; Jack Neff, "Green-Marketing Revolution Defies Economic Downturn," *Advertising Age,* April 20, 2009, 1, 23.

42. Aubrey Fowler and Angeline G. Close. "It Ain't Easy Being Green: Bridging the Gap among Macro, Meso, and Micro Agendas," *Journal of Advertising,* vol 41, no 4 (December 2012), 119–132.

3P's creativity framework Indicates creativity is fostered by three inputs: people, process, and place.

A

above-the-line promotion Traditional measured media advertising: any message broadcast to the public through conventional means such as television, the Internet, radio, and magazines.

accessibility How easy (quick) it is to remember something.

accessibility bonus A psychological phenomenon in which easily remembered brands are also believed to be more prevalent (common), more popular, and better.

account executive (AE) The liaison between an advertising agency and its clients; the nature of the account executive's job requires excellent persuasion, negotiation, and judgment skills in order to both successfully alleviate client discomfort and sell highly effective, groundbreaking ideas.

account planner A relatively recent addition to many advertising agencies; it is this person's job to synthesize all relevant consumer research and use it to design a coherent advertising strategy.

account planning A system by which, in contrast to traditional advertising research methods, an agency assigns a coequal account planner to work alongside the account executive and analyze research data. This method requires the account planner to stay with the same projects on a continuous basis.

account services A team of managers that identifies the benefits a brand offers, its target audiences, and the best competitive positioning and then develops a complete promotion plan.

account team A group of people comprising many different facets of the advertising industry (direct marketing, public relations, graphic design, etc.) who work together under the guidance of a team leader to both interface with other members of the account team and team members of their own respective specialties.

Action for Children's Television (ACT) A group formed during the 1970s to lobby the government to limit the amount and content of advertising directed at children.

advergaming Advertising and brand placement within video games.

advertisement A specific message that an organization has placed to persuade an audience.

advertiser Business, not-for-profit, or government organization that uses advertising and other promotional techniques to communicate with target markets and to stimulate awareness and demand for its brands.

advertising A paid, mass-mediated attempt to persuade.

advertising agency An organization of professionals who provide creative and business services to clients related to planning, preparing, and placing advertisements.

advertising campaign A series of coordinated advertisements and other promotional efforts that communicate a single theme or idea.

advertising clutter An obstacle to advertising resulting from the large volume of similar ads for most products and services.

advertising plan A plan that specifies the thinking and tasks needed to conceive and implement an effective advertising effort.

advertising response function A mathematical relationship based on marginal analysis that associates dollars spent on advertising and sales generated; sometimes used to help establish an advertising budget.

advertising specialties A sales promotion having three key elements: a message, placed on a useful item, given to consumers with no obligation.

advertising substantiation program An FTC program initiated in 1971 to ensure that advertisers make available to consumers supporting evidence for claims made in ads.

advocacy advertising Advertising that attempts to influence public opinion on important social, political, or environmental issues of concern to the sponsoring organization.

aerial advertising Advertising that involves airplanes (pulling signs or banners), skywriting, or blimps.

affirmative disclosure An FTC action requiring that important material determined to be absent from prior ads must be included in subsequent advertisements.

agency of record The advertising agency chosen by the advertiser to purchase media time and space.

AIO *See* **lifestyle research.**

app ads An ad within a Web, tablet, or smartphone application (i.e., app) that is associated with a third party.

appropriation The use of pictures or images owned by someone else without permission.

attitude An overall evaluation of any object, person, or issue that varies along a continuum, such as favorable to unfavorable or positive to negative.

attitude study A method of obtaining customer feedback that measures target markets' feelings and opinions about a company's product, as well as that of the competing brand.

audience A group of individuals who may receive and interpret messages sent from advertisers through mass media.

authenticity The quality of genuineness inherent in something. Advertisers value product placement with a high degree of apparent authenticity, as more blatant approaches are easily detected by consumers, resulting in possible disgust or irritation and achieving the opposite of the advertiser's aim.

axis A line, real or imagined, that runs through an advertisement and from which the elements in the ad flare out.

B

balance An orderliness and compatibility of presentation in an advertisement.

barter syndication A form of television syndication that takes both off-network and first-run syndication shows and offers them free or at a reduced rate to local television stations, with some national advertising presold within the programs.

behavioral targeting The process of database development made possible by online tracking markers that advertisers place on a Web surfer's hard drive to track that person's online surfing and shopping behavior.

beliefs The knowledge and feelings a person has accumulated about an object or issue.

below-the-line promotion A promotional effort that includes in-store promotions, coupons, dealer discounts, and product placement.

benefit segmentation A type of market segmenting in which target segments are delineated by the various benefit packages that different consumers want from the same product category.

between-vehicle duplication Exposure to the same advertisement in different media.

Big Data Term used to refer to massive data that have become available through social media. These include email surveillance and analysis, frames per second (fps) tracking, and capturing every single click, location, and word users of smartphones create.

bill-back allowances A monetary incentive provided to retailers for featuring a marketer's brand in either advertising or in-store displays.

blackletter A style patterned after monastic hand-drawn letters characterized by the ornate design of the letters. Also called *gothic*.

blog (short for Web log) A personal journal on a website that is frequently updated and intended for public access. Such sites are emerging as new and sophisticated sources of product and brand information.

brainstorming An organized approach to idea generation; for effective brainstorming, it is necessary to learn about the material in question beforehand, foster a safe environment free of destructive criticism, and openly discuss disagreements that may arise.

brand A name, term, sign, symbol, or any other feature that identifies one seller's good or service as distinct from those of other sellers.

brand advertising Advertising that communicates the specific features, values, and benefits of a particular brand offered for sale by a particular organization.

brand ambassador A consumer who actively recommends a brand to others.

brand awareness An indicator of consumer knowledge about the existence of the brand and how easily that knowledge can be retrieved from memory.

brand communities Groups of consumers who feel a commonality and a shared purpose grounded or attached to a consumer good or service.

branded entertainment Embedding one's brand or brand icons as part of any entertainment property (e.g., a sporting event) in an effort to impress and connect with consumers in a unique and compelling way.

brand equity Developed by a firm that creates and maintains positive associations with the brand in the mind of consumers.

brand extension An adaptation of an existing brand to a new product area.

branding The strategy of developing brand names so that manufacturers can focus consumer attention on a clearly identified item.

brand loyalty A decision-making mode in which consumers repeatedly buy the same brand of a product as their choice to fulfill a specific need.

brand platform The key idea on which the brand rests.

brand promise A statement of the key value of the brand. What does it promise to the consumer?

brand switching An advertising objective in which a campaign is designed to encourage customers to switch from their established brand.

build-up analysis A method of building up the expenditure levels of various tasks to help establish an advertising budget.

business markets The institutional buyers who purchase items to be used in other products and services or to be resold to other businesses or households.

business-market sales promotion Promotion designed to cultivate buyers from large corporations who are making purchase decisions.

buzz marketing The process of creating events or experiences that yield conversations that include the brand or product advertisers are trying to sell.

C

cable TV A type of television that transmits a wide range of programming to subscribers through wires rather than over airwaves.

cause-related advertising Advertising that identifies corporate sponsorship of philanthropic activities.

cease-and-desist order An FTC action requiring an advertiser to stop running an ad within 30 days so a hearing can be held to determine whether the advertising in question is deceptive or unfair.

celebrity endorsements Advertisements that use an expert or celebrity as a spokesperson to endorse the use of a product or service.

chain of needs Customer needs lead to products; new needs are created by the unintended side effects of modern times and new products; even newer products solve additional and even newer needs.

channel grazing Using a television remote control to monitor programming on other channels while an advertisement is being broadcast.

Chaos Scenario As predicted by Bob Garfield, the mass exodus of advertising revenue from traditional broadcast media due to audience fragmentation and ad-avoidance hardware, which in turn reduces funding for the affected media and serves to limit their product quality, reducing audience size. This of course accelerates diversion of advertising dollars even further until there is little reliance on these media at all for marketing.

cinema advertising Includes ads that run in movie theaters before the film and other advertising appearing off-screen within a theater.

classified advertising Newspaper advertising that appears as all-copy messages under categories such as sporting goods, employment, and automobiles.

click-through A measure of the number of page elements (hyperlinks) that have actually been requested (i.e., "clicked through" from the display/banner ad to the link).

client The company or organization that pays for advertising. Also called the *sponsor*.

cognitive dissonance The anxiety or regret that lingers after a difficult decision.

cognitive responses The thoughts that occur to individuals at that exact moment in time when their beliefs and attitudes are being challenged by some form of persuasive communication.

cognitive style The unique preference of each person for thinking about and solving a problem. Cognitive style pioneer Carl Jung proposed three different dimensions in which thinking differs: sensing versus intuiting, thinking versus feeling, and extraverted versus introverted.

commission system A method of agency compensation based on the amount of money the advertiser spends on the media.

communication test A type of pretest message research that simply seeks to see if a message is communicating something close to what is desired.

community A group of people loosely joined by some common characteristic or interest.

comp A polished version of an ad.

comparison advertisements Advertisements in which an advertiser makes a comparison between the firm's brand and competitors' brands.

competitive field The companies that compete for a segment's business.

competitor analysis In an advertising plan, the section that discusses who the competitors are, outlining their strengths, weaknesses, tendencies, and any threats they pose.

concept test A type of developmental research that seeks feedback designed to screen the quality of a new idea, using consumers as the final judge and jury.

consent order An FTC action asking an advertiser accused of running deceptive or unfair advertising to stop running the advertisement in question, without admitting guilt.

consideration set The subset of brands from a particular product category that becomes the focal point of a consumer's evaluation.

consultants Individuals who specialize in areas related to the promotional process.

consumer behavior Those activities directly involved in obtaining, consuming, and disposing of products and services, including the decision processes that precede and follow these actions.

consumer–brand relationship The affiliation between consumer and brand. While obviously not the same as human-to-human relationships, consumers do have connections to material objects and services; some of these are brands.

consumer culture A way of life centered around consumption.

consumer–event congruity When an event sponsor fits a consumer's image and sense of self.

consumer-generated content (CGC) Advertisements for products produced either in part or completely by their end users. The recent explosion of consumer-generated content is largely due to the advent of content-sharing Internet websites (like YouTube) that essentially enable anyone to post (and view) video content.

consumer-generated media (CGM) A type of UGC that is specific to media, such as a video or photo post.

consumer insights Knowledge of how consumers think about, use, or otherwise view brands, good, or services within the context of their lives. These insights are typically derived through ethnographic methods.

consumerism The actions of individual consumers to exert power over the marketplace activities of organizations.

consumer markets The markets for products and services purchased by individuals or households to satisfy their specific needs.

consumer-market sales promotion A type of sales promotion designed to induce household consumers to purchase a firm's brand rather than a competitor's brand.

consumer packaged goods Typically low-priced items such as paper towels, batteries, toothpaste, laundry products, and frozen or canned food.

consumer sales promotion A type of sales promotion aimed at consumers that focuses on price-off deals, coupons, sampling rebates, and premiums.

contest A sales promotion that has consumers compete for prizes based on skill or ability.

continuity The pattern of placement of advertisements in a media schedule.

continuous scheduling A pattern of placing ads at a steady rate over a period of time.

conversion A process where consumers go on from trying a brand to buying it a second time.

co-op advertising *See* **cooperative advertising.**

cooperative advertising The sharing of advertising expenses between national advertisers and local merchants. Also called *co-op advertising.*

copywriting The process of expressing the value and benefits a brand has to offer, via written or verbal descriptions.

corporate advertising Advertising intended to establish a favorable attitude toward a company as a whole, not just toward a specific brand.

corrective advertising An FTC action requiring an advertiser to run additional advertisements to dispel false beliefs created by deceptive advertising.

cost per inquiry (CPI) The number of inquiries generated by a direct marketing program divided by that program's cost.

cost per order (CPO) The number of orders generated by a direct marketing program divided by that program's cost.

cost per thousand (CPM) The dollar cost of reaching 1,000 members of an audience using a particular medium.

coupon A type of sales promotion that entitles a buyer to a designated reduction in price for a product or service.

creative abrasion The clash of ideas, abstracted from the people who propose them, from which new ideas and breakthroughs can evolve. *Compare* **interpersonal abrasion.**

creative boutique An advertising agency that emphasizes copywriting and artistic services to its clients.

creative brief A document that outlines and channels an essential creative idea and objective.

creative selling The act of assisting and persuading customers regarding purchasing decisions; creative selling typically involves products in which customers require extensive knowledge about the product before buying, such as specialty goods or higher-priced items (e.g., sports equipment, cookware, insurance, or real estate).

creative services A group that develops the message that will be delivered through advertising, sales promotion, direct marketing, event sponsorship, or public relations.

creative team The copywriters and art directors responsible for coming up with the creative concept for an advertising campaign.

creativity The ability to consider and hold together seemingly inconsistent elements and forces, making a new connection; creativity is essential in the advertising world because successful marketing demands a constant seamless synthesis of the product and entirely different ideas or concepts.

cross-selling Marketing programs aimed at customers that already purchase other products.

crowdsourcing The online distribution of certain tasks to groups (crowds) of experts, enthusiasts, or even consumers.

culture What people do—the ways they eat, groom themselves, celebrate, mark their space and social position, and so forth.

customer relationship management (CRM) The continual effort toward cultivating and maintaining long-term relationships with customers; many companies have recognized trust and rapport are key elements to repeated sales and thus train their sales teams to emphasize each particular customer's needs rather than the bottom line.

customer satisfaction Good feelings that come from a favorable post-purchase experience.

cyber-identity theft Having one's identity stolen by online or digital means.

D

dailies Newspapers published every weekday; also, in television ad production, the scenes shot during the previous day's production.

database agency Agency that helps customers construct databases of target customers, merge databases, develop promotional materials, and then execute the campaign.

dayparts Segments of time during a television broadcast day.

deception Making false or misleading statements in an advertisement.

defamation When a communication occurs that damages the reputation of an individual because the information was untrue.

delayed response advertising Advertising that relies on imagery and message themes to emphasize the benefits and satisfying characteristics of a brand.

demographic segmentation Market segmenting based on basic descriptors like age, gender, race, marital status, income, education, and occupation.

design The structure (and the plan behind the structure) for the aesthetic and stylistic aspects of a print advertisement.

designers Specialists intimately involved with the execution of creative ideas and efforts.

developmental copy research A type of copy research that helps copywriters at the early stages of copy development by providing audience interpretations and reactions to the proposed copy.

dialogue Advertising copy that delivers the selling points of a message to the audience through a character or characters in the ad.

dialogue balloons A type of projective technique that offers consumers the chance to fill in the dialogue of cartoonlike stories, as a way of indirectly gathering brand information.

differentiation The process of creating a perceived difference, in the mind of the consumer, between an organization's brand and the competition.

digital footprint The trail of social media posts, videos, photos, status updates, and online information on a person, organization, or brand.

digital/interactive agency An advertising or IBP agency that specializes in digital/interactive campaigns using the Web or wireless transmission.

digital video recorder (DVR) A computer-like hard drive that can store up to 140 hours of television programming.

direct mail A direct marketing medium that involves using the postal service to deliver marketing materials.

direct marketing According to the Direct Marketing Association, "An interactive system of marketing which uses one or more advertising media to affect a measurable response and/or transaction at any location."

direct marketing agency Agency that maintains large databases of mailing lists; some of these firms can also design direct marketing campaigns either through the mail or by telemarketing. Also called a **direct response agency**.

directory advertising Includes all the local phone directory and local business advertising books published by a variety of firms.

direct response Copy research method measuring actual behavior of consumers.

direct response advertising Advertising that asks the receiver of the message to act immediately.

direct response agency Also called direct marketing agency.

direct response copy Advertising copy that highlights the urgency of acting immediately.

display advertising A newspaper ad that includes the standard components of a print ad—headline, body copy, and often an illustration—to set it off from the news content of the paper.

display/banner ads Advertisements placed on World Wide Web sites that contain editorial material.

door-to-door sampling A type of sampling in which samples are brought directly to the homes of a target segment in a well-defined geographic area.

E

earned media The incremental exposure that your brand earns through viral engagement and interactions with the brand.

e-business A form of e-advertising or promotion in which companies selling to business customers rely on the Internet to send messages and close sales.

economies of scale The ability of a firm to lower the cost of each item produced because of high-volume production.

effective frequency The number of times a target audience needs to be exposed to a message before the objectives of the advertiser are met.

effective reach The number or percentage of consumers in the target audience that are exposed to an ad some minimum number of times.

embedded Tightly connected to a context.

emergent consumers A market segment made up of the gradual but constant influx of first-time buyers.

e-search Stands for electronic search; how consumers look for ideas, brands, and information online for purchases or entertainment.

ethics Moral standards and principles against which behavior is judged.

ethnocentrism The tendency to view and value things from the perspective of one's own culture.

evaluative copy research A type of copy research used to judge an advertisement after the fact—the audience expresses its approval or disapproval of the copy used in the ad.

evaluative criteria The product attributes or performance characteristics on which consumers base their product evaluations.

event-planning agencies Experts in finding locations, securing dates, and putting together a "team" of people to pull off a promotional event.

event sponsorship Providing financial support to help fund an event, in return for the right to display a brand name, logo, or advertising message on-site at the event.

extended problem solving A decision-making mode in which consumers are inexperienced in a particular consumption setting but find the setting highly involving.

external facilitator An organization or individual that provides specialized services to advertisers and agencies.

external lists Mailing lists purchased from a list compiler or rented from a list broker and used to help an organization cultivate new business.

external position The competitive niche a brand pursues.

external search A search for product information that involves visiting retail stores to examine alternatives, seeking input from friends and relatives about their experiences with the products in question, or perusing professional product evaluations.

eye-tracking system A type of physiological measure that monitors eye movements across print ads.

F

Federal Trade Commission (FTC) The government regulatory agency that has the most power and is most directly involved in overseeing the advertising industry.

fee system A method of agency compensation whereby the advertiser and the agency agree on an hourly rate for different services provided.

fieldwork Research conducted outside the agency, usually in the home or site of consumption.

first-run syndication Television programs developed specifically for sale to individual stations.

flighting A media-scheduling pattern of heavy advertising for a period of time, usually two weeks, followed by no advertising for a period, followed by another period of heavy advertising.

focus group A brainstorming session with a small group of target consumers and a professional moderator, used to gain new insights about consumer response to a brand.

forgetting function Idea that people's forgetting is fairly predictable and seems to obey a mathematical function.

formal balance A symmetrical presentation in an ad—every component on one side of an imaginary vertical line is repeated in approximate size and shape on the other side of the imaginary line.

frame-by-frame test Copy research method that works by getting consumers to turn dials (like/dislike) while viewing television commercials in a theater setting.

free premium A sales promotion that provides consumers with an item at no cost; the item is either included in the package of a purchased item or mailed to the consumer after proof of purchase is verified.

free-standing insert (FSI) A newspaper insert ad that contains cents-off coupons for a variety of products and is typically delivered with Sunday newspapers.

frequency The average number of times an individual or household within a target audience is exposed to a media vehicle in a given period of time.

frequency-marketing programs Direct marketing programs that provide concrete rewards to frequent customers.

frequency programs A type of sales promotion that offers consumers discounts or free product rewards for repeat purchase or patronage of the same brand or company.

fulfillment centers Centers that ensure customers receive the product ordered through direct mail.

full-service agency An advertising agency that typically includes an array of advertising professionals to meet all the promotional needs of clients.

G

geodemographic segmentation A form of market segmentation that identifies neighborhoods around the country that share common demographic characteristics.

geographic scope Scope of the geographic area to be covered by advertising media.

geotargeting The placement of ads in geographic regions where higher purchase tendencies for a brand are evident.

global advertising Developing and placing advertisements with a common theme and presentation in all markets around the world where the firm's brands are sold.

government officials and employees One of the five types of audiences for advertising; includes employees of government organizations, such as schools and road maintenance operations, at the federal, state, and local levels.

Great Depression A period (1929–1941 for the United States) in which the vast majority of people in many countries suffered from a severe economic decline.

green marketing Corporate efforts that embrace a cause or program in support of the environment. Green marketing is currently of particular importance, as the public is becoming increasingly aware and concerned about the urgency of environmental issues.

gross domestic product (GDP) A measure of the total value of goods and services produced within an economic system.

gross impressions The sum of exposures to all the media placement in a media plan.

H

habit A decision-making mode in which consumers buy a single brand repeatedly as a solution to a simple consumption problem.

headline The leading sentence(s), usually at the top or bottom of an ad, that attracts attention, communicates a key selling point, or achieves brand identification.

heavy users Consumers who purchase a product or service much more frequently than others.

household consumers The most conspicuous of the five types of audiences for advertising; most mass media advertising is directed at them.

households using TV (HUT) A measure of the number of households tuned to a television program during a particular time period.

hyper-localism The process where people will get their global and national news from the Web but turn to local newspapers for items on sale at local stores.

I

identity Who one perceives themselves to be.

illustration In the context of advertising, the drawing, painting, photography, or computer-generated art that forms the picture in an advertisement.

implicit memory measures Techniques used to obtain feedback that determines consumers' recognition of products (and thus marketing success), characterized by questions or tasks that do not explicitly make reference to the advertisement in question. The perceived advantage of this type of test is a more subconscious, unadulterated response.

increasing income inequality This refers to the fact that in the United States the wealthiest have been pulling away from the rest of us at a faster rate.

Industrial Revolution A major change in Western society beginning in the mid-18th century and marked by a rapid change from an agricultural to an industrial economy.

industry analysis In an advertising plan, the section that focuses on developments and trends within an industry and on any other factors that may make a difference in how an advertiser proceeds with an advertising plan.

inelasticity of demand Strong loyalty to a product, resulting in consumers being less sensitive to price increases.

influencer marketing A series of personalized marketing techniques directed at individuals or groups who have the credibility and capability to drive positive word of mouth in a broader and salient segment of the population.

infomercial A long advertisement that looks like a talk show or a half-hour product demonstration.

informal balance An asymmetrical presentation in an ad—nonsimilar sizes and shapes are optically weighed.

in-house agency The advertising department of a firm.

inquiry/direct response measures A type of posttest message tracking in which a print or broadcast advertisement offers the audience the opportunity to place an inquiry or respond directly through a reply card or toll-free number.

institutional advertising Corporate advertising that takes place in the trade channel. This form of advertising is used most prominently by retailers.

in-store sampling A type of sampling that occurs at the point of purchase and is popular for food products and cosmetics.

integrated brand promotion (IBP) The use of various promotional tools, including advertising, in a coordinated manner to build and maintain brand awareness, identity, and preference.

integrated marketing communications (IMC) The process of using promotional tools in a unified way so that a synergistic communications effect is created.

interactive media Media that allow consumers to call up games, entertainment, shopping opportunities, and educational programs on a subscription or pay-per-view basis.

interactivity Two-way communications that can feed off one another and is an advantage of digital media.

internal lists An organization's records of its customers, subscribers, donors, and inquirers, used to develop better relationships with current customers.

internal position The niche a brand achieves with regard to the other similar brands a firm markets.

internal search A search for product information that draws on personal experience and prior knowledge.

international advertising The preparation and placement of advertising in different national and cultural markets.

interpersonal abrasion The clash of people, often resulting from an inability to regard idea feedback as separate from personal feedback, from which communication shuts down and new ideas get slaughtered. *Compare* **creative abrasion**.

interstitial An ad that loads while you browse; they appear on a site after a page has been requested but before it has loaded and stay onscreen long enough for the message to be registered.

involvement The degree of perceived relevance and personal importance accompanying the choice of a certain product or service within a particular context.

IRI BehaviorScan Supplier of single-source data testing.

I-Traffic Index An index that computes a site's advertising value based on traffic, placement and size of ads, ad rates, and evaluations of the site's quality.

L

layout A drawing of a proposed print advertisement, showing where all the elements in the ad are positioned.

leveraging Any collateral communication or activity reinforcing the link between a brand and an event.

libel Defamation that occurs in print and would relate to magazine, newspaper, direct mail, or Internet reports.

life-stage A circumstantial variable, such as when a family's youngest child moves away from home, which changes the consumption patterns of the family.

lifestyle research (AIO) Survey-based knowledge derived through questions about consumers' activities, interests, and opinions (AIO). It is used to help develop messages and target profiles of consumers.

lifestyle segmentation A form of market segmenting that focuses on consumers' activities, interests, and opinions.

limited problem solving A decision-making mode in which consumers' experience and involvement are both low.

local advertising Advertising directed at an audience in a single trading area, either a city or state.

local spot radio advertising Radio advertising placed directly with individual stations rather than with a network or syndicate.

local TV Television programming other than the network broadcast that independent stations and network affiliates offer local audiences.

logo A graphic mark that identifies a company and other visual representations that promote an identity for a firm.

long-copy email Copy written for an email message designed to offer the receiver incentives to buy the product and usually offers a link to a short-copy landing page.

long-copy landing page Website copy designed to sell a product directly; the copy might equal the equivalent of a four- to eight-page letter to a potential customer.

long interview A one-on-one interview with a consumer in which the interviewer probes to get at deeper connections between brands, consumption practices, and consumers' real lives. They are typically in the 0:30- to 1-hour. range.

M

Madison & Vine A reference to continually converging advertising and entertainment, coined from the names of two renowned avenues that represent the two industries, respectively.

mailing list A file of names and addresses that an organization might use for contacting prospective or prior customers.

mail sampling A type of sampling in which samples are delivered through the postal service.

marcom manager A marketing communications manager who plans an organization's overall communications program and oversees the various functional specialists inside and outside the organization to ensure that they are working together to deliver the desired message to the customer.

market analysis Complements the industry analysis, emphasizing the demand side of the equation, where an advertiser examines the factors that drive and determine the market for the firm's product or service.

market segmentation The process of breaking down a large, widely varied market into submarkets that are more similar than dissimilar in terms of consumer characteristics.

marketing The process of conceiving, pricing, promoting, and distributing ideas, goods, and services to create exchanges that benefit consumers and organizations.

marketing database A mailing list that also includes information collected directly from individual customers.

marketing mix The blend of the four responsibilities of marketing—conception, pricing, promotion, and distribution—used for a particular idea, product, or service.

markup charge A method of agency compensation based on adding a percentage charge to a variety of services the agency purchases from outside suppliers.

meaning What an advertisement intends or conveys.

measured media Media that are closely measured to determine advertising costs and effectiveness: television, radio, newspapers, magazines, and outdoor media.

media buying Securing the electronic media time and print media space specified in a given account's schedule.

media-buying service An independent organization that specializes in buying media time and space, particularly on radio and television, as a service to advertising agencies and advertisers.

media class A broad category of media, such as television, radio, or newspapers.

media impressions Instances in which a product or brand is exposed to potential consumers by direct newspaper, television, radio, or magazine coverage (rather than the payment of these media as venues in which to advertise). The effectiveness of sponsorship spending is often judged by the comparison of media impressions to traditional media advertising, such as commercials.

media mix The blend of different media that will be used to effectively reach the target audience.

media plan A plan specifying the media in which advertising messages will be placed to reach the desired target audience.

media planner An advertising agency (although on occasion an in-house person) with expertise in buying and scheduling media for ad placements.

media planning and buying services Services related to media planning or buying that are provided by advertising agencies or specialized media-buying organizations.

media specialists Organizations that specialize in buying media time and space and offer media strategy consulting to advertising agencies and advertisers.

media vehicle A particular option for placement within a media class (e.g., *Newsweek* is a media vehicle within the magazine media class).

members of a trade channel One of the five types of audiences for advertising; the retailers, wholesalers, and distributors targeted by producers of both household and business goods and services.

members of business organizations One of the five types of audiences for advertising; the focus of advertising for firms that produce business and industrial goods and services.

merchandise allowances A type of trade-market sales promotion in which free products are packed with regular shipments as payment to the trade for setting up and maintaining displays.

message weight A sum of the total audience size of all the media specified in a media plan.

micro-blogs Social networking services that enable users to post and read short messages, for instance, Twitter. Posters are restricted by the number of characters in the message.

micro-targeting Refers to the practice of delivering customized messages down to the individual level or near the individual level.

mindshare brands Brands that are promoted and purchased largely through memory of the brand name and sometimes one simple quality or attribute.

miscellaneous In regard to font styles, a category that includes display fonts that are used not for their legibility but for their ability to attract attention. Fonts like garage and novelty display belong to this category.

missionary salesperson A person who proactively contacts customers after a purchase has been made, in order to ensure customer satisfaction and foster goodwill, by asking if the customer has questions about the product, providing additional information, and checking to see if the customer's current needs have changed (and may present an opportunity for further sales).

mobile marketing Directing advertising and IBP campaigns to consumers' mobile devices—smartphones, iPods, and e-readers.

mobile sampling A type of sampling carried out by logo-emblazoned vehicles that dispense samples, coupons, and premiums to consumers at malls, shopping centers, fairgrounds, and recreational areas.

monopoly power The ability of a firm to make it impossible for rival firms to compete with it, either through advertising or in some other way.

N

narrative Advertising copy that simply displays a series of statements about a brand.

narrowcasting The development and delivery of specialized television programming to well-defined audiences.

national advertising Advertising that reaches all geographic areas of one nation.

National Advertising Review Board (NARB) A body formed by the advertising industry to oversee its practice.

national spot radio advertising Radio advertising placed in nationally syndicated radio programming.

need state A psychological state arising when one's desired state of affairs differs from one's actual state of affairs.

net promoter scores Number of recommendations for a brand.

network radio advertising Radio advertising placed within national network programs.

network TV A type of television that broadcasts programming over airwaves to affiliate stations across the United States under a contract agreement.

niche marketing The practice of narrowly targeting a relatively small segment of a market in which the consumers are typically willing to pay a premium price for the brand.

normative test scores Scores that are determined by testing an ad and then comparing the scores to those of previously tested, average commercials of its type.

O

objective-and-task approach A method of advertising budgeting that focuses on the relationship between spending and advertising objectives by identifying the specific tasks necessary to achieve different aspects of the advertising objectives.

off-invoice allowance A program allowing wholesalers and retailers to deduct a set amount from the invoice they receive for merchandise.

off-network syndication Television programs that were previously run in network prime time.

online resistance An attitude or behavior against the digital movement at times. For some consumers, and for the authors as well, social networks are designed as a vehicle that connects us with people who have at one point graced our lives.

on-package sampling A type of sampling in which a sample item is attached to another product package.

order The visual elements in an ad that affect the reader's "gaze motion" through the ad.

order taking The practice of accepting and processing needed customer information for prearranged merchandise purchase, or scheduling services that a consumer will purchase once rendered. While their role in the transaction process rarely involves communicating large amounts of information, order takers must be able to answer customer questions and be accommodating and considerate.

out-of-home media advertising The combination of transit and billboard advertising.

owned media Brand assets or objects created within social networks by your organization, such as a Facebook page or an application.

P

packaging The container or wrapping for a product; packaging serves as an important vessel for product information and user appeal, as it is often viewed by the customer in a potential buying situation.

paid media Media that are paid for on social media or other media; advertisements that can be purchased on a social network or other digital platforms.

paid search The process by which advertisers pay websites and portals to place ads in or near relevant search results based on key words.

parallel layout structure A print ad design that employs art on the right-hand side of the page and repeats the art on the left-hand side.

pass-along readership People other than the primary subscriber who read a publication.

pay-for-inquiry advertising model A payment scheme in which a media company gets paid by advertisers based solely on the inquiries an advertiser receives in response to an ad.

pay-for-results A compensation plan that results when a client and its agency agree to a set of results criteria on which the agency's fee will be based.

pay-per-click (PPC) An advertising revenue model where the advertiser is charged by the number of people who click on, or tap, the ad to pull it up for more information or to see the ad in entirety.

percentage-of-sales approach An advertising budgeting approach that calculates the advertising budget based on a percentage of the prior year's sales or the projected year's sales.

permanent long-term displays P-O-P materials intended for presentation for more than six months.

personal selling The face-to-face communications and persuasions process, often used with products that are higher-priced, complicated to use, must be tailored to individual user needs, involve a trade-in, or are judged at the point of purchase.

phishing A form of email spam with which spammers try to entice Web users to enter personal information on fake websites that are forged to look like authentic sites such as a bank, the IRS, or other organizations that will get the email users' attention.

photo sharing websites They operate in much the same way as video sharing websites but with content based on still images instead of video; an example is Pintrest.

physiological assessment The interpretation of certain biological feedback generated from viewers who are exposed to an ad. Although physiological assessment has advanced with devices such as MRIs and PT scans, its overall value is still questionable.

pica A measure of the width or depth of lines of type.

pilot testing A form of message evaluation consisting of experimentation in the marketplace.

point A measure of the size of type in height.

point-of-entry marketing Advertising strategies designed to win the loyalty of consumers whose brand preferences are still under development in hopes of gaining their loyalty.

point-of-purchase (P-O-P) advertising Advertising that appears at the point of purchase.

pop-up/pop-under ad An Internet advertisement that appears as a website page is loading or after a page has loaded.

pop-up/pop-under copy Copy to accompany pop-up/pop-under digital/interactive ads.

position A brand's meaning relative to its competitors.

positioning The marketer's attempt to give a brand a certain meaning relative to its competitors.

positioning strategy The key themes or concepts an organization features for communicating the distinctiveness of its product or service to the target segment.

post ads Ads in a social media post that tend to have higher relative response rates because they are within a consumer's post to their network of friends and friends of friends.

pre-decisional distortion A psychological bias in favor of a brand that unconsciously weights incoming information in the direction of the favored brand. It is thought to be due to an emotional response to the brand.

premiums Items that feature the logo of a sponsor and that are offered free, or at a reduced price, with the purchase of another item.

preprinted insert An advertisement delivered to a newspaper fully printed and ready for insertion into the newspaper.

preproduction The stage in the television production process in which the advertiser and advertising agency (or in-house agency staff) carefully work out the precise details of how the creative planning behind an ad can best be brought to life with the opportunities offered by television.

price-off deal A type of sales promotion that offers a consumer cents or even dollars off merchandise at the point of purchase through specially marked packages.

primary demand The demand for an entire product category.

primary demand stimulation Using advertising to create demand for a product category in general.

principle of limited liability An economic principle that allows an investor to risk only his or her shares of a corporation, rather than personal wealth, in business ventures.

principles of design General rules governing the elements within a print advertisement and the arrangement of and relationship between these elements.

privacy seal Logo on certain websites that show the site has been endorsed or is a member of a third-party privacy endorser of privacy.

proactive public relations strategy A public relations strategy that is dictated by marketing objectives, seeks to publicize a company and its brands, and is offensive in spirit rather than defensive.

production facilitator An organization that offers essential services both during and after the production process.

production services A team that takes creative ideas and turns them into advertisements, direct mail pieces, or events materials.

production stage The point at which the storyboard and script for a television ad come to life and are filmed. Also called the *shoot*.

product placement The sales promotion technique of getting a marketer's product featured in movies and television shows.

professionals One of the five types of audiences for advertising, defined as doctors, lawyers, accountants, teachers, or any other professionals who require special training or certification.

program rating The percentage of television households that are in a market and are tuned to a specific program during a specific time period.

projective techniques A type of developmental research designed to allow consumers to project thoughts and feelings (conscious or unconscious) in an indirect and unobtrusive way onto a theoretically neutral stimulus.

promotion agencies Specialized agencies that handle promotional efforts.

proportion The size and tonal relationships between different elements in an advertisement.

psychographics A form of market research that emphasizes the understanding of consumers' activities, interests, and opinions.

publicity Unpaid-for media exposure about a firm's activities or its products and services.

public relations A marketing and management function that focuses on communications that foster goodwill between a firm and its many constituent groups.

public relations audit An internal study that identifies the characteristics of a firm or the aspects of the firm's activities that are positive and newsworthy.

public relations firms Firms that handle the needs of organizations regarding relationships with the local community, competitors, industry associations, and government organizations.

public relations plan A plan that identifies the objectives and activities related to the public relations communications issued by a firm.

puffery The use of absolute superlatives like "Number One" and "Best in the World" in advertisements.

pulsing A media-scheduling strategy that combines elements from continuous and flighting techniques; advertisements are scheduled continuously in media over a period of time, but with periods of much heavier scheduling.

purchase intent A measure of whether or not a consumer intends to buy a product or service in the near future.

Pure Food and Drug Act A 1906 act of Congress requiring manufacturers to list the active ingredients of their products on their labels.

push money A form of trade incentive in which retail salespeople are offered monetary reward for featuring a marketer's brand with shoppers.

push strategy A sales promotion strategy in which marketers devise incentives to encourage purchases by members of the trade to help push a product into the distribution channel.

R

radio networks A type of radio that delivers programming via satellite to affiliate stations across the United States.

radio syndication A type of radio that provides complete programs to stations on a contract basis.

ratings point A measure indicating that 1 percent of all the television households in an area were tuned to the program measured.

reach The number of people or households in a target audience that will be exposed to a media vehicle or schedule at least one time during a given period of time. It is often expressed as a percentage.

reactive public relations strategy A public relations strategy that is dictated by influences outside the control of a company, focuses on problems to be solved rather than opportunities, and requires defensive rather than offensive measures.

rebate A money-back offer requiring a buyer to mail in a form requesting the money back from the manufacturer.

recall tests Tests of how much the viewer of an ad remembers of the message; they are used to measure the cognitive residue of the ad. These are the most commonly employed tests in advertising.

recognition In a test, when the audience members indicate that they have seen an ad before.

recognition tests Tests in which audience members are asked if they recognize an ad or something in an ad. These are the standard cognitive residue test for print ads and promotion.

regional advertising Advertising carried out by producers, wholesalers, distributors, and retailers that concentrate their efforts in a particular geographic region.

repeat purchase A second purchase of a new product after trying it for the first time.

repositioning Returning to the process of segmenting, targeting, and positioning a product or service to arrive at a revised positioning strategy.

resonance test A type of message assessment in which the goal is to determine to what extent the message resonates or rings true with target audience members.

RFM analysis An analysis of how recently and how frequently a customer is buying from an organization and of how much that customer is spending per order and over time.

riding the boards Assessing possible locations for billboard advertising.

rituals Repeated behaviors that affirm, express, and maintain cultural values.

roman The most popular category of type because of its legibility.

rough layout The second stage of the ad layout process, in which the headline is lettered in and the elements of the ad are further refined.

S

sales promotion The use of incentive techniques that create a perception of greater brand value among consumers or distributors.

sampling A sales promotion technique designed to provide a consumer with a trial opportunity.

sans serif A category of type that includes typefaces with no small lines crossing the ends of the main strokes.

satellite and closed-circuit A method of transmitting programming to highly segmented audiences.

script (television) The written version of an ad; it specifies the coordination of the copy elements with the video scenes.

script (typeface) A style of print in which letters connect to one another, resembling handwriting; often used for occasions in which elegance or particularly high quality is appropriate (wedding invitations, etc.).

search engine optimization (SEO) Utilizing a search engine to a company's best advantage.

secondary data Information obtained from existing sources.

segment A portion of the market.

selective attention The processing of only a few advertisements among the many encountered.

selective demand stimulation Using advertising to stimulate demand for a specific brand within a product category.

self-liquidating premium A sales promotion that requires a consumer to pay most of the cost of the item received as a premium.

self-reference criterion (SRC) It is the unconscious reference to one's own cultural values, experiences, and knowledge as a basis for decisions.

self-regulation The advertising industry's attempt to police itself.

serif The small lines that cross the ends of the main strokes in type; also the name for the category of type that has this characteristic.

share of audience A measure of the proportion of households that are using television during a specific time period and are tuned to a particular program.

share of voice Percent of the total advertising in a category (e.g., autos) spent by one brand (e.g., Ford).

shoot The process of recording (shooting) a television advertisement using film or digital recording.

short-copy landing page Digital/interactive copy; a brand offer that may be accessed by a consumer through key word search and has the length and look of a magazine ad.

short-term promotional displays P-O-P materials that are used for six months or less.

single-source data Information provided from individual households about brand purchases, coupon use, and television advertising exposure by combining grocery store scanner data with TV-viewing data from monitoring devices attached to the households' televisions.

single-source tracking services Services that provide data on media exposure, sales, customer demographics, and other related information in one source.

situation analysis In an advertising plan, the section in which the advertiser lays out the most important factors that define the situation and then explains the importance of each factor.

slander Oral defamation that in the context of promotion would occur during television or radio broadcast of an event involving a company and its employees.

slogan A short phrase used in part to help establish an image, identity, or position for a brand or an organization, but mostly used to increase memorability.

slotting fees A type of trade-market sales promotion in which manufacturers make direct cash payments to retailers to ensure shelf space.

social couponing Sites that give or sell price discounts under the condition that a set number of other consumers buy or download the deal.

social meaning What a product or service means in a societal context.

social media Highly accessible Web-based media that allow the sharing of information between individuals and between individuals and groups. Prominent examples are Facebook, Twitter, and LinkedIn.

social media copy Language in social media communications that highlights a brand name or brand features.

social news websites Sites that allow people to discover and share content from anywhere on the Internet by submitting links and stories to a central service.

spam Unsolicited bulk email sent to a large number (often millions) of personal and commercial email addresses.

sponsored stories Ad-like stories (or social media status updates or posts) that can be promoted on social media sites with payment to the social media site.

spot advertising A way of buying television advertising time in which airtime is purchased through local television stations.

square root law The recognition of print ads increases with the square of the illustration.

Starch Readership Services An example of a company that performs recognition tests.

storyboard A frame-by-frame sketch or photo sequence depicting, in sequence, the visual scenes and copy that will be used in an advertisement.

story construction A type of projective technique that asks consumers to tell a story about people depicted in a scene or picture, as a way of gathering information about a brand.

STP marketing Fo segmenting, targeting, positioning. A marketing strategy employed when advertisers focus their efforts on one subgroup of a product's total market.

straight-line copy Advertising copy that explains in straightforward terms why a reader will benefit from use of a product or service.

stratification (social class) A person's relative standing in a social system as produced by systematic inequalities in things such as wealth, income, education, power, and status. Also referred to as *social class*.

subhead In an advertisement, a few words or a short sentence that usually appears above or below the headline and includes important brand information not included in the headline.

subliminal advertising Advertising alleged to work on a subconscious level.

support media Media used to reinforce a message being delivered via some other media vehicle.

sweepstakes A sales promotion in which winners are determined purely by chance.

switchers A market segment made up of consumers who often buy what is on sale or choose brands that offer discount coupons or other price incentives. Also called *variety seekers*.

symbolic value What a product or service means to consumers in a nonliteral way.

system selling Selling a set of interrelated components that fulfills all or a majority of a customer's needs in a particular area.

T

target To focus advertising and promotion effort upon a given segment or segments.

target audience A particular group of consumers singled out for an advertisement or advertising campaign.

taste A generalized set or orientation to consumer preferences.

teaser email Copy written for an email message that is a short message designed to drive readers to a long-copy landing page where they can order the brand directly.

telemarketing A direct marketing medium that involves using the telephone to deliver a spoken appeal.

television syndication Either original programming or programming that first appeared on network TV that is then rebroadcast on either network or cable stations with pending distribution on the Internet.

testimonial An advertisement in which an advocacy position is taken by a spokesperson.

thought listing A type of pretest message research that tries to identify specific thoughts that may be generated by an advertisement.

three-point layout structure A print ad design that establishes three elements in an ad as dominant forces.

thumbnails, or thumbnail sketches The rough first drafts of an ad layout, about one-quarter the size of the finished ad.

top-of-mind The first brand one can remember when asked to name the brands in a category.

top-of-the-mind awareness Keen consumer awareness of a certain brand, indicated by listing that brand first when asked to name a number of brands.

tracking studies Studies that document the apparent effect of advertising over time, assessing attitude change, knowledge, behavioral intent, and self-reported behavior. They are one of the most commonly used advertising and promotion research methods.

trade journals Magazines published specifically for members of a trade that carry highly technical articles.

trade-market sales promotion A type of sales promotion designed to motivate distributors, wholesalers, and retailers to stock and feature a firm's brand in their merchandising programs.

trade reseller Organizations in the marketing channel of distribution that buy products to resell to customers.

trade shows Events where several related products from many manufacturers are displayed and demonstrated to members of the trade.

transit advertising Advertising that appears as both interior and exterior displays on mass transit vehicles and at terminal and station platforms.

trial offers A type of sales promotion in which expensive items are offered on a trial basis to induce consumer trial of a brand.

trial usage An advertising objective to get consumers to use a product new to them on a trial basis.

TV households An estimate of the number of households that are in a market and own a television.

type font A basic set of typeface letters.

U

unfair advertising Defined by Congress as "acts or practices that cause or are likely to cause substantial injury to consumers, which is not reasonably avoidable by consumers themselves and not outweighed by the countervailing benefits to consumers or competition."

unique selling proposition (USP) A promise contained in an advertisement in which the advertised brand offers a specific, unique, and relevant benefit to the consumer.

unity The creation of harmony among the diverse components of an advertisement: headline, subhead, body copy, and illustration.

unmeasured media Media less formally measured for advertising costs and effectiveness (as compared to the measured media): direct mail, catalogs, special events, and other ways to reach business and household consumers.

upfronts A period of media buying in which advertisers purchase time on network television a few months before (May) the new season of shows begin (September). They are thus bought "up-front."

user-generated content (UGC) Consumer created information, such as posted reviews or comments, that adds (or subtracts with a negative post) value to socially embedded websites.

V

value A perception by consumers that a product or service provides satisfaction beyond the cost incurred to acquire the product or service.

value proposition A statement of the functional, emotional, and self-expressive benefits delivered by the brand, which provide value to customers in the target segment.

variety seekers *See* **switchers**.

variety seeking A decision-making mode in which consumers switch their selection among various brands in a given category in a random pattern.

vertical cooperative advertising An advertising technique whereby a manufacturer and dealer (either a wholesaler or retailer) share the expense of advertising.

video on demand (VOD) A cable television service that enables subscribers to select and watch a selection of videos at any time.

video sharing websites Social media sites that have consumers and companies upload videos and watch others' videos for free.

viral marketing The process of consumers marketing to consumers over the Internet through word of mouth transmitted through emails and electronic mailing lists.

virtual identity This is how the consumer or brand uses images and text online to construct or showcase identity.

W

Web 2.0 Describes what people are doing with technology and how they are using it, noting the progression of the Internet to interactive online communication, participation, and engagement.

Web ads Ads online, namely in digital and or/social media, that are intended to drive traffic off of the site where the ad is run.

within-vehicle duplication Exposure to the same advertisement in the same media at different times.

word of mouth In marketing parlance, this is the process of encouraging consumers to talk to each other about a firm's brand or marketing activities.

Z

Zaltman Metaphor Elicitation Technique (ZMET) A research technique to draw out people's buried thoughts and feelings about products and brands by encouraging participants to think in terms of metaphors.

Page references in **bold** print indicate ads or photos. Page references in *italics* indicate tables, charts, or graphs. Page references followed by "n" indicate footnotes.

SUBJECT INDEX

Page references in **bold** print indicate ads or photos. Page references in *italics* indicate tables, charts, or graphs. Page references followed by "n" indicate footnotes.

A

AAAA. *See* American Association of Advertising Agencies (AAAA)
Above-the-line promotion, 247
Abrasion, 192
Accessibility, 113
Accessibility bonus, 113
Accommodation, 11
Account executives (AE), 186
Account planner, 45
Account planning, 45, 158, **158**
Account services, 45
Account team, 190
ACS. *See* American Community Survey (ACS)
ACS data source in, 146
   cable television in, 272, **272**
   internal company sources of, 146
   largest advertisers in, *35*
   race in, 120
ACS source of, 146
   all-in-one single source, 157–158
   computer models and, 256–258
   single source, 157
Action for Children's Television, 69
Activision, 329
Activities, interests and opinions (AIO), 131, 143
Administrative services, 46
Advergames, 295
   and video games, 295–296
Advergaming, 334, 340. *See also* Video game advertising
Advertisements
   audience communication of, 7
   brand meaning through, 143
   comparison, **203,** 203–204
   consumer behavior influenced by, 88
   deceptive elements of, 86, 89
   defined, 9
   direct response, 16, 22, 156, 353, 355–356
   display/banner, 288
   diversity in, **84,** 85–86
   humor in, 149, 207–208
   IBP utilizing, 8–9, **9**
   interstitial, 289
   meanings transmitted by, *123,* 123–124, **124**
   minorities portrayed in, 65–66, 69
   in newspapers, **57**

offensive, 84–85
pop-under, 288
pop-up, 288
principles of design in, 232
with product placement, 212
radio formats of, 225
sales estimations from, 156–157
self-parody in, 72
size/length of, 253
social meaning through, 25, **25**
social media, 288
stereotypes in, 83
target audiences of, 12
television copywriting for, 223–224
transition from idea to, **235**
Advertisers
   agency relationships with, 47
   categories of, 36–39
   commercial data sources to, 146–147
   consumer memory and, 148–149
   consumption and, 67
   focus groups used by, 143
   IBP role of, 39
   largest United States, *35*
   media decisions of, 263
   message placement coordination of, 340
   packaging promotional benefits to, 322–323
   spending, *272*
   top magazine, **269**
   traditional media decisions of, 261–262, 268
   using Internet, **50**
   using media organizations, *49*
Advertising. *See also* Corporate advertising; Developmental advertising; Magazine advertising; Point-of-purchase advertising; Print advertising; Radio advertising; Television advertising
   advocacy, 378
   aerial, 322
   affects happiness and general well-being, 81
   audiences for, 11–14
   and authenticity, 123
   brand, 23
   brief history of, 55–56
   broadcast, 224–225
   as business process, 14–25
   campaign, 9

cause-related, 378–379
to children, 87, 88–89, 90–91
cinema, 322
classified, 267
clutter, 266
communication process, 10–11
competition influenced by, 23–24
consumers aggravated by, 80
consumers educated by, 79–80
controversial products, 88–89
co-op, 266
cooperative, 14, *14,* 266, 315, **316**
corporate image, **376–377,** 378, **379**
corrective, 93
and creativity, 83–85
culture reflected in, 63, **63,** 65
defining, 7
delayed response, 22–23
directory, 322
direct response, 16, 22, 156–157, 353, 355–356
display, 266
economic influence of, 22–25
effect on prices, 24
eras of, 56–72
ethical aspects of, 86–89
and fashion, **123**
FCC regulation of, *92*
focus on, 10
global, 13
IBP and, 4–5
industrialization era of, 56–57
institutional, 23
international, 13, 164
language of, 11–12, 87
local, 13, 14
in marketing mix, 15–21
mass media and, 56, 85–86
mass mediated, 7
media budgets on, 238, *238*
national, 13
organizations, *40*
out-of-home media, 321–322
politics and, 71–72, 86
reaching consumers through, 4
and rebellion, 122–123
regional, 13–14
regulatory agents and, 91–93
regulatory aspects of, 89–97, *92*
remembering and forgetting of, *253*
revenue from, 20–21

sales promotions in, **307**
and self-regulation programs, *94*
social aspects of, 78–86
society and, 57–76
space, **265**
spending, *271*
structure of, 35–36, *36*
subliminal, 64, 85
target audiences of, 50
technology influencing, 29–30
on television, 69
with traditional media, 5
transit, 321–322
truth in, 86–87
types of, 21–23
unfair, 89
in United States, 320, **320**
vertical cooperative, 90
video game, 334
visuals in, 229
Advertising Age, 146
Advertising agencies, 39–42
   advertisers relationships with, 47
   advertising planning role of, 161–162, 164–165, 169, 172, 175–176
   African-Americans and, 68
   agency of record and, 258
   associations and, 95–96
   compensation of, 46–47
   creativity and, 186
   defining, 39
   founding of, 56
   historical context used by, 164–165
   in-house, 42
   Integrated Brand Promotion and, 44
   promotion agencies in, 42–43
   ranking of, *40*
   research methods and, 141
   services of, 43–46, **45**
   structure of, *44*
   types of, 39–42
   of United Kingdom, 70
Advertising campaigns, 9, 9–10, **220**
Advertising clutter, 114
Advertising organizations, *40*
Advertising plans, 161–162
   advertising agencies role in, 161–162, 164–165, 169, 172, 175–176
   advertising planning role of, 175–176